All Propaganda is Lies 1941–1942

Eric Arthur Blair – better known as George Orwell – was born on 25 June 1903 in Bengal. He was educated at Eton and then served with the Indian Imperial Police in Burma. He lived in Paris for two years, and then returned to England where he worked as a private tutor, schoolteacher and bookshop assistant. He fought on the Republican side in the Spanish Civil War and was wounded in the throat. During the Second World War he served as Talks Producer for the Indian Service of the BBC and then joined *Tribune* as its literary editor. He died in London in January 1950.

Dr Peter Davison is Professor of English and Media at De Montfort University, Leicester. He has written and edited fifteen books as well as the Facsimile Edition of the Manuscript of *Nineteen Eighty-Four* and the twenty volumes of Orwell's *Complete Works*. From 1992 to 1994 he was President of the Bibliographical Society, whose journal he edited for twelve years. From 1961 Ian Angus was Deputy Librarian and Keeper of the Orwell Archive at University College, London, and from 1975 Librarian of King's College, London. With Sonia Orwell he co-edited the *Collected Essays, Journalism and Letters of George Orwell* (4 vols., 1986). Since early retirement in 1982 he has divided his time equally between assisting in the editing of this edition and growing olives in Italy.

Sheila Davison was a teacher until she retired, for some time teaching the deaf. She checked and proofread all twenty volumes of the complete edition and assisted with the research and indexing.

Down and Out in Paris and London
Burmese Days
A Clergyman's Daughter
Keep the Aspidistra Flying
The Road to Wigan Pier
Homage to Catalonia
Coming Up for Air
Animal Farm
Nineteen Eighty-Four
A Kind of Compulsion (1903-36)
Facing Unpleasant Facts (1937-39)
A Patriot After All (1940-41)
All Propaganda is Lies (1941-42)
Keeping Our Little Corner Clean (1942-43)
Two Wasted Years (1943)
I Have Tried to Tell the Truth (1943-44)
I Belong to the Left (1945)
Smothered Under Journalism (1946)
It is What I Think (1947-48)
Our Job is to Make Life Worth Living (1949-50)

Also by Peter Davison

Books: *Songs of the British Music Hall: A Critical Study; Popular Appeal in English Drama to 1850; Contemporary Drama and the Popular Dramatic Tradition; Hamlet: Text and Performance; Henry V: Masterguide; Othello: The Critical Debate; Orwell: A Literary Life*

Editions: Anonymous: *The Fair Maid of the Exchange* (with Arthur Brown); Shakespeare: *Richard II*; Shakespeare: *The Merchant of Venice*; Shakespeare: *1 Henry IV*; Shakespeare: *2 Henry IV*; Shakespeare: *The First Quarto of King Richard III*; Marston: *The Dutch Courtesan; Facsimile of the Manuscript of Nineteen Eighty-Four; Sheridan: A Casebook; The Book Encompassed: Studies in Twentieth-Century Bibliography*

Series: *Theatrum Redivivum* 17 Volumes (with James Binns); *Literary Taste, Culture, and Mass Communication* 14 Volumes (with Edward Shils and Rolf Meyersohn)

Academic Journals: *ALTA: University of Birmingham Review*, 1966-70; *The Library: Transactions of the Bibliographical Society*, 1971-82

Publication of *The Complete Works of George Orwell* is a unique
bibliographic event as well as a major step in Orwell
scholarship. Meticulous textual research by
Dr Peter Davison has revealed that all the current editions
of Orwell have been mutilated to a greater or lesser extent.
This authoritative edition incorporates in Volumes 10–20
all Orwell's known essays, poems, plays, letters, journalism,
broadcasts, and diaries, and also letters by his wife, Eileen,
and members of his family. In addition there are very many of
the letters in newspapers and magazines of readers' reactions
to Orwell's articles and reviews. Where the hands of others
have intervened, Orwell's original intentions have been restored.

All Propaganda is Lies

is Lies

1941-1942

GEORGE ORWELL

Edited by Peter Davison
Assisted by Ian Angus and Sheila Davison

SECKER & WARBURG

———

LONDON

Revised and updated edition published by Secker & Warburg 2001

2 4 6 8 10 9 7 5 3 1

First published in Great Britain in 1998 by
Secker & Warburg
Random House, 20 Vauxhall Bridge Road,
London SW1V 2SA

Random House Australia (Pty) Limited
20 Alfred Street, Milsons Point, Sydney,
New South Wales 2061, Australia

Random House New Zealand Limited
18 Poland Road, Glenfield,
Auckland 10, New Zealand

Random House South Africa (Pty) Limited
Endulini, 5A Jubilee Road, Parktown 2193, South Africa

The Random House Group Limited Reg No. 954009
www.randomhouse.co.uk

A CIP catalogue record for this book
is available from the British Library

ISBN 0 436 40405 2

MIX
Paper | Supporting
responsible forestry
FSC® C018179

Typeset in Monophoto Bembo by
Deltatype Limited, Birkenhead, Merseyside

The Random House Group Limited supports The Forest Stewardship
Council® (FSC®), the leading international forest-certification organisation.
Our books carrying the FSC label are printed on FSC®-certified paper.
FSC is the only forest-certification scheme supported by the leading
environmental organisations, including Greenpeace. Our
paper procurement policy can be found at
www.randomhouse.co.uk/environment

Printed and bound in Great Britain by Clays Ltd, St Ives plc

CONTENTS

Titles may be modified and shortened
TBF = BBC Talks Booking Form; dates booked for broadcasts are given in
numerals

Contents

Contents

Contents

Contents

Contents

Contents

INTRODUCTION to VOLUME XIII

18 August 1941 to 31 August 1942: *All Propaganda is Lies*

Orwell joined the staff of the BBC on 18 August 1941 and left on 24 November 1943, although two of the Newsletters he had prepared, one in English for Indonesia and one for translation into Tamil, were broadcast on the two days after he had left. Orwell worked very hard at the BBC as the three volumes devoted to his time there reveal. After his training he joined the Indian section under Zulfaqar Ali Bokhari, who later became Director-General of Radio Pakistan. In addition to Bokhari and Orwell there were, when he joined, three Hindu talks assistants and three secretaries. Between them they had to produce twelve hours of broadcasting a week. In addition there was a Hindustani section at Evesham under Sir Malcolm Darling but Darling's and Bokhari's units were completely separate. A Marathi assistant, Miss Venu Chitale, joined in March 1943 but the transmission time was increased and for many months Bokhari was away in India. (A staff list for the Indian and other sections for 21 August 1943 will be found on pages 17 and 18.) Orwell was responsible for producing three series of commentaries on the news in English, broadcast at first to India, then to Malaya, and finally to Indonesia (the latter two both being occupied by the Japanese), and for further separate series for translation into vernacular languages: Bengali, Marathi, Gujarati, Tamil, and perhaps Hindustani (see *892*). As well as newsletters, there were series of cultural, educational, and political programmes. Political broadcasts did not address specific issues of British, Indian, or Allied politics but rather such general issues as 'Propaganda,', 'The Fifth Column,' 'Living Space,' and 'The New Order' (all given by Mulk Raj Anand); or topics that even today sound contemporary such as 'Moslem Minorities in Europe,' and 'The Status of Women in Europe.' Orwell also ran a series on great books. These, by a variety of speakers from the East discussed, for example, the importance of *The Social Contract*, *Das Kapital*, and even *Mein Kampf.*

Much of the material reproduced in these three volumes is administrative. There are, for example, dozens of Talks Booking Forms (TBF) related to Orwell's programmes which, though they do not make exciting reading, give an essential insight into what was broadcast, by whom, when, and what the speakers were paid. Associated with these forms are dozens of letters which Orwell sent off in connection with the broadcasts, many persuading some of the most distinguished writers and scientists in Britain to spend time for small fees talking to an unknown and uncertain audience thousands of miles away. To supplement this information a thorough search was made of the 'Programmes as Broadcast' reports (for which almost a complete run survives) which note what actually happened at the time, and of the files of *London Calling*, a magazine devoted to the Overseas Service of the BBC (see *2151*).

Perhaps the most remarkable aspect of Orwell's 'propaganda', and very far from being lies, was the attempt at distance teaching, what we should now call 'a university of the air.' Bokhari had initiated talks directed at students studying English literature at Calcutta and Bombay Universities and as soon as Orwell arrived he handed this project over to him. Orwell expanded the range of 'courses' (for such they were) and the thirteen he arranged included series on science, agriculture, and psychology; modern English verse, drama (including Marlowe, Shakespeare, Dryden, Ibsen, Yeats, and Čapek), 'Modern Masterpieces' and American literature. The distinguished speakers included T. S. Eliot (on *Ulysses* and Dryden), E. M. Forster, Cyril Connolly, John Lehmann, V. S. Pritchett, Herbert Read, Stephen Spender, L. A. G. Strong, Harold Laski (on Galsworthy's *Strife*), William Plomer – and Orwell himself (on *Macbeth* and Jack London). Scientists included Joseph Needham, Vere Gordon Childe, Ritchie Calder, C. D. Darlington, J. C. Drummond, and C. H. Waddington; one of Sir Alexander Fleming's team spoke on penicillin; Dr Susan Isaacs, then very influential in the training of teachers, talked about child psychology; in a series devoted to India's problems in AD 2000, Sir John Russell spoke on agriculture and Richard Titmuss on population. In other series unconnected with university syllabuses, the Director of the British Film Institute, Oliver Bell, spoke regularly on film; there was a practical course on drama production, 'Let's Act It Ourselves', run by Norman Marshall with Damyanti and Balraj Sahni, which had long-lasting influence (see introduction to Volume XV); and among programmes on music, talks by Narayana Menon, and also performances by Myra Hess and Moura Lympany.

Many of the speakers were, as a matter of policy, drawn from the expatriate Far Eastern community living in England. Some, such as K. S. Shelvankar, were hardly *persona grata* in India (his Penguin Special, *The Problems of India*, 1940, had been banned in India), and Reginald Reynolds, a Quaker and pacifist, who spoke on prison and whom Orwell wished to speak on Peter Kropotkin, was anything but an Establishment figure. (The Establishment did draw the line at Kropotkin.) Mulk Raj Anand gave many broadcasts in addition to those mentioned above; other speakers included the Turk, K. K. Ardaschir; Hsiao Ch'ien, whose work Orwell reviewed (see *2528*), and who later, as Xiao Qian, made the first translation into Chinese of Joyce's *Ulysses*, published in 1995. Under the innocent-sounding title, 'Today and Yesterday', the Indian speaker, Cedric Dover, discussed a number of subjects still very topical today: 'The Importance of Minorities', 'Race Mixture and World Peace,' 'The Problems of Cultural Expression,' and 'The Federal Idea.' A large number of speakers were women. As well as Venu Chitale, Princess Indira of Kapurthala presented programmes throughout Orwell's time. Speakers and actresses engaged by Orwell included Gladys Calthrop, Clemence Dane, Lilla Erulkar, Lady Grigg (a thorn in Orwell's side), Inez Holden, Vida Hope, Catherine Lacey, Ethel Mannin,

Naomi Mitchison, Eleanor Rathbone, Viscountess Rhondda, Naomi Royde-Smith, Stevie Smith, Zahara Taki, Ellen Wilkinson, Rebecca West, Diana Wong, and many others.

Volume XIII reprints documents used by Orwell in the training course he attended immediately on joining the BBC (see *845*). Although this was described by William Empson, who attended the same course, as 'the Liars' School', it was, in fact, as the documents demonstrate, an intensive introduction to radio and its techniques. There are detailed accounts of the Overseas Service (*846*), and the network and staff of that service (*847*); this includes a document from the papers prepared for Sir Stafford Cripps before he left for India to discuss its independence in 1942 which gives a forthright assessment of those who ran the BBC's service to India.

Orwell was much concerned with establishing a weekly newsletter in English for India and the volume provides an analysis of how this was organised (*892*). This demonstrates that Orwell wrote far more newsletters than had been thought—some 104 or 105 in English and 115 or 116 for translation into vernacular languages—of which only a quarter survive. In his first months Orwell wrote a number of propaganda-like talks such as, 'Paper is Precious' and 'British Rations and the Submarine War'. What this first volume shows is how quickly he moved away from work of that kind to broadcasts that were cultural and educational: propaganda, perhaps, but of a much more worthwhile and sophisticated kind. Not *all* propaganda was lies as he had described it in his War-time Diary on 14 March 1942 (*1025*, p. 229).

Although most of this volume is made up of BBC material, there are a number of reviews and articles and also his advocacy of Mulk Raj Anand's *The Sword and the Sickle*, first in a letter to the *Times Literary Supplement* objecting to its review (by Ranja G. Sahani, then published anonymously; see *1189*) followed by his review of Anand's book (*1257*). Orwell's War-time Diary is also printed, in full, chronologically.

A full General Introduction will be found in the preliminaries to Volume X
See also Introductions to Volumes XIV and XV

ACKNOWLEDGEMENTS and PROVENANCES

specific to Volume XIII

The editor wishes to express his gratitude to the following institutions and libraries, their trustees, curators, and staffs for their co-operation and valuable help, for making copies of Orwell material available, and for allowing it to be reproduced: BBC Written Archives Centre, Caversham; Henry W. and Albert A. Berg Collection, New York Public Library, Astor, Lenox and Tilden Foundations; British Library, Department of Manuscripts (for the Orwell papers, Add. Mss 49384 and 73083); Liddell Hart Centre for Military Archives, King's College London; Sir Stafford Cripps Archive, Nuffield College, Oxford; Routledge Archive, Reading University Library; Harry Ransom Humanities Research Center, University of Texas at Austin; and the Library of University College London for material in the Orwell Archive.

Gratitude is expressed to Routledge for having made their material relating to Orwell available.

I am deeply indebted to the Hon David Astor (Editor of *The Observer*) and Alex Comfort for having given their Orwell letters or made copies of them available to the Orwell Archive.

I would like to thank *The Listener* (by courtesy of the BBC and the Independent Television Association Ltd), *The Observer* and *Partisan Review* for permission to reproduce material which first appeared in their pages.

I would also like to thank the following for allowing me to use material whose copyright they own: Alex Comfort for permission to publish his contribution to 'Pacifism and the War' in *Partisan Review* and a letter he wrote to Orwell; Lady Cripps for permission to publish 'Present Set-up of Indian Broadcasting at the BBC' which is in the Sir Stafford Cripps Archive, Nuffield College, Oxford; Celia Goodman for permission to publish Inez Holden's monologue, 'Poor Relations'; The Trustees of the Liddell Hart Centre for Military Archives for permission to quote from a letter by Captain Basil Liddell Hart; Peter Riley acting on behalf of Peregrine and Juliet Moore for permission to publish Nicholas Moore's letter to *Partisan Review* and his poem, 'That Monstrous Man'; Herbert Read's poem, 'The Contrary Experience,' published by Faber and Faber Ltd and Smith Settle Ltd, is reprinted by permission of the publishers and David Higham Associates; D. S. Savage for permission to publish his contribution to 'Pacifism and the War' in *Partisan Review*; 'After the Funeral' from *The Poems of Dylan Thomas*, published by J. M. Dent and New Directions Publishing Corp. Copyright 1938 by New Directions Publishing Corp. Reprinted by permission of the publishers and David Higham Associates; 'Walking at Night,' 'In the Third Year of the War' and 'Oh come, my joy, my soldier boy . . .' by Henry

Treece. Copyright © The Estate of Henry Treece. Reprinted by permission of John Johnson (Authors' Agent) Ltd, London; A. P. Watt Ltd on behalf of The Literary Executors of the Estate of H. G. Wells for permission to publish H. G. Wells's letter to *The Listener*; and Ingeborg Woodcock for permission to publish George Woodcock's contribution to 'Pacifism and the War' in *Partisan Review*.

For help and invaluable information my thanks are due to Mulk Raj Anand, Laurence Brander, Clive Fleay, Alan Hollinghurst (*The Times Literary Supplement*) and Patricia Methven (Archivist, the Liddell Hart Centre for Military Studies).

A number of individual acknowledgements are made in foot and headnotes to those who have provided information in books or verbally that I have quoted or referred to.

The editor and publishers have made every effort to trace copyright holders of the material published in this volume, but in some cases this has not proved possible. The publishers therefore wish to apologise to the authors or copyright holders of any material which has been reproduced without permission and due acknowledgement.

PROVENANCES

The major part of the documents and letters reproduced in this volume are in the BBC Written Archives Centre, Caversham and it should be taken that any document or letter that does not have its location indicated on the list below is at Caversham. Only documents and letters in other archives have their locations listed below. However, in cases where there are documents or letters at an item that are in different archives, this is indicated, even though one of the archives is the BBC Archive at Caversham, e.g. 1341 Texas, BBC (the top copy of a letter is in the Harry Ransom Humanities Research Center in Texas and the carbon copy is at the BBC Archive at Caversham).

For simplicity's sake, the Orwell papers in the British Library, Department of Manuscripts (Add. Mss 49384 and 73083) are not indicated as such in the location list, but are regarded as being available for consultation in the form of copies in the Orwell Archive.

KEY TO LOCATIONS

BBC   BBC Written Archives Centre, Caversham

Berg   Henry W. and Albert A. Berg Collection, The New York Public Library, Astor, Lenox and Tilden Foundations

LHCMA Liddell Hart Centre for Military Archives, King's College London

Nuffield   Sir Stafford Cripps Archive, Nuffield College Library, Oxford

OA   Orwell Archive, University College London Library

Reading   Routledge Archive, Reading University Library

Texas   Harry Ransom Humanities Research Center, University of Texas at Austin

844 BBC, OA
845 OA
847 BBC, Nuffield
849 OA
853 Berg
854 OA
863 OA
872 Texas
884 OA, Reading
891 OA
892 BBC, OA
972 OA
1025 OA
1027 OA
1043 OA
1046 OA
1064 OA
1075 OA
1080 OA
1083 OA
1098 OA
1100 OA
1106 OA
1108 OA
1119 OA

1124 OA
1130 OA
1141 OA
1149 OA
1155 OA
1172 OA
1182 OA
1187 OA
1193 OA
1195 OA
1209 OA
1211 OA
1216 OA
1218 OA
1221 OA
1224 OA
1231 OA
1246 OA
1253 OA
1258 OA
1261 OA
1262 OA
1282 OA
1309 OA
1319 OA

1322 OA
1331 OA
1336 OA
1341 Texas, BBC
1345 OA
1350 OA
1355 OA
1363 OA
1367 OA
1372 OA
1378 Texas, BBC
1379 OA, LHCMA
1380 OA
1387 OA
1391 OA
1395 OA
1396 LHCMA, OA
1397 LHCMA, OA
1398 LHCMA, OA
1399 OA
1410 OA
1419 OA
1420 OA
1424 OA
1430 OA

Editorial Note

THE CONTENTS are, in the main, arranged in chronological order of Orwell's writing. Letters arising from his articles or reviews are usually grouped immediately after that item and Orwell's replies to those letters follow thereon. If there is a long delay between when it is known an article or essay was completed and its publication, it is printed at the date of completion. If items are printed much earlier in the chronological sequence than their date of publication, a cross-reference is given at the date of publication. All entries, whether written by Orwell or anyone else, including lengthy notes and cross-references, are given an item number. Because the printing of the edition has taken place over seven years, some letters came to light after the initial editing and the numbering of items had been completed. These items (or those that had in consequence to be repositioned) are given a letter after the number: e.g., *335A*. Some items included after printing and page-proofing had been completed are given in a final appendix to Volume XX and two (received by the editor in mid January 1997) in the Introduction to Volume XV. Numbers preceding item titles are in roman; when referred to in notes they are italicised.

The provenance of items is given in the preliminaries to each volume. Every item that requires explanation about its source or date, or about textual problems it may pose, is provided with such an explanation. Some articles and broadcasts exist in more than one version. The basis upon which they have been edited is explained and lists of variant readings provided. No Procrustean bed has been devised into which such items must be constrained; individual circumstances have been taken into account and editorial practice explained.

Although this is not what is called a 'diplomatic edition'—that is, one that represents the original precisely even in all its deformities to the point of reproducing a letter set upside down—the fundamental approach in presenting these texts has been to interfere with them as little as possible consistent with the removal of deformities and typographic errors. Orwell took great pains over the writing of his books: the facsimile edition of *Nineteen Eighty-Four*[1] shows that, but in order to meet the demands of broadcasting and publication schedules he often wrote fast and under great pressure. The speed with which he sometimes wrote meant that what he produced was not always what he would have wished to have published had he had time to revise. And, of course, as with any printing, errors can be introduced by those setting the type. It would be easy in places to surmise what Orwell would have done but I have only made changes where there would otherwise have been confusion. Obvious spelling mistakes, which could well be the compositor's or typist's (and the typist might be Orwell), have been corrected silently, but if there is any doubt, a footnote has drawn attention to the problem.

In brief, therefore, I have tried to present what Orwell wrote in his manuscripts and typescripts, not what I thought he should have written; and what he was represented as having written and not what I think should have been typed or printed on his behalf. This is not a 'warts and all' approach because gross errors are amended, significant changes noted, and textual complexities are discussed in preliminary notes. The aim is to bring Orwell, not the editor's version of Orwell, to the fore. Although textual issues are given due weight, an attempt has been made to produce an attractive, readable text.

The setting of this edition has been directly from xeroxes of original letters (if typed), typed copies of manuscript (prepared by one or other of the editors), surviving scripts for broadcasts, and xeroxes of essays, articles, and reviews as originally published (unless a headnote states otherwise). For *The Collected Essays, Journalism and Letters of George Orwell* a 1968 house style was adopted but for this edition, no attempt has been made to impose a late twentieth-century house style on the very different styles used by journals and editors of fifty to eighty years ago. Texts are therefore reproduced in the style given them in the journals from which they are reprinted. To 'correct' might well cause even more confusion as to what was and was not Orwell's: see below regarding paragraphing. Nevertheless, although it is not possible *to know*, one may sometimes hazard a guess at what underlies a printed text. Thus, I believe that most often when 'address' and 'aggression' are printed, Orwell typed or wrote 'adress' (especially until about the outbreak of World War II) and 'agression.' Although American spellings (such as 'Labor') have been retained in articles published in the United States, on very rare occasions, if I could be certain that a form of a word had been printed that Orwell would not have used—such as the American 'accommodations'—I have changed it to the form he would have used: 'accommodation'. Some variations, especially of proper names, have been accepted even if they look incongruous; so, 'Chiang Kai-Shek' as part of a book title but 'Chiang Kai-shek' throughout the text that follows.

Hyphenation presents tricky problems, especially when the first part of a word appears at the end of a line. Examples can be found in the originals of, for example, 'the middle-class,' 'the middle class', and 'the middleclass.' What should one do when a line ends with 'middle-'? Is it 'fore-deck' or 'foredeck'? If 'fore-' appears at the end of a line of the copy being reproduced, should the word be hyphenated or not? *OED* 1991 still hyphenates; Chambers in 1972 spelt it as one word. Where it would help (and it does not include every problem word), the ninth edition of F. Howard Collins, *Authors' & Printers' Dictionary*, Oxford University Press, 1946 (an edition appropriate to the mature Orwell) has been drawn upon. But Collins does not include fore-deck/foredeck. On a number of occasions Orwell's letters, or the text itself, is either obscure or wrong. In order to avoid the irritating repetition of *sic*, a small degree sign has been placed above the line at the doubtful point (°). It is hoped that this will be clear but inconspicuous. It is not usually repeated to mark a repetition of that characteristic in the same item. Orwell was sparing in his use of the question-mark in his letters; his practice has in the main been followed.

Paragraphing presents intractable problems. Orwell tended to write in long paragraphs. Indeed, it is possible to show from the use of many short paragraphs that News Review scripts so written are not by Orwell. The key example is News Review, 30, 11 July 1942 (1267), for which there is also external evidence that this is not by Orwell. This has twenty-one paragraphs as compared to eight in the script for the following week. It so happens that we know that Orwell was not at the BBC for two weeks before the 11 July nor on that day: he was on holiday, fishing at Callow End, Worcestershire (and on that day caught a single dace). But though paragraph length is helpful in such instances in identifying Orwell's work, that is not always so. It is of no use when considering his articles published in Paris in 1928–29 nor those he wrote for the *Manchester Evening News*. These tend to have extremely short paragraphs—sometimes paragraphs of only a line or two, splitting the sense illogically. A good example is the series of reviews published on 2 November 1944 (2572) where a two-line paragraph about Trollope's *The Small House at Allington* should clearly be part of the preceding four-line paragraph, both relating the books discussed to Barchester; see also *2463, n. 2* and *2608, n. 4*. There is no question but that this is the work of sub-editors. It would often be possible to make a reasonable stab at paragraphing more intelligently, but, as with verbal clarification, the result might be the more confusing as to what really was Orwell's work and what this editor's. It has been thought better to leave the house-styles as they are, even if it is plain that it is not Orwell's style, rather than pass off changes as if the edited concoction represented Orwell's work.

Usually it is fairly certain that titles of essays are Orwell's but it is not always possible to know whether titles of articles are his. Reviews were also frequently given titles. Orwell's own typescript for his review of Harold Laski's *Faith, Reason and Civilisation* (2309), which survived because rejected by the *Manchester Evening News*, has neither heading (other than the name of the author and title of the book being reviewed), nor sub-headings. That would seem to be his style. In nearly every case titles of reviews and groups of letters, and cross-heads inserted by sub-editors, have been cut out. Occasionally such a title is kept if it is an aid to clarity but it is never placed within quotation marks. Other than for his BBC broadcasts (where Orwell's authorship is clear unless stated otherwise), titles are placed within single quotation marks if it is fairly certain that they are Orwell's.

Telegrams and cables are printed in small capitals. Quite often articles and reviews have passages in capitals. These look unsightly and, in the main, they have been reduced to small capitals. The exceptions are where the typography makes a point, as in the sound of an explosion: BOOM! Orwell sometimes abbreviated words. He always wrote an ampersand for 'and' and there are various abbreviated forms for such words as 'about'. It is not always plain just what letters make up abbreviations (and this sometimes applies to his signatures) and these have regularly been spelt out with the exception of the ampersand for 'and'. This serves as a reminder that the original is handwritten. Orwell often shortened some words and abbreviations in his own way, e.g., Gov.t, Sup.ts (Superintendents), NB. and N.W (each with a single stop), and ie.; these forms have been retained. In order that the diaries should readily be apparent for what they are, they have been set in sloped roman (rather than italic, long passages of which can be tiring to the eye), with roman for textual variations. Square and half square brackets are used to differentiate sources for the diaries (see, for example, the headnote to War-Time Diary II, *1025*) and for what was written and actually broadcast (see, for example, Orwell's adaptation of Ignazio Silone's *The Fox*, *2270*). Particular usages are explained in headnotes to broadcasts etc., and before the first entries of diaries and notebooks.

Orwell usually dated his letters but there are exceptions and sometimes he (and Eileen) give only the day of the week. Where a date has to be guessed it is placed within square brackets and a justification for the dating is given. If Orwell simply signs a letter, the name he used is given without comment. If he signs over a typed version of his name, or initials a copy of a letter, what he signed or initialled is given over the typed version. There has been some slight regularisation of his initialling of letters. If he omitted the final stop after 'E. A. B', no stop is added (and, as here, editorial punctuation *follows* the final quotation mark instead of being inside it). Sometimes Orwell placed the stops midway up the letters: 'E·A·B'; this has been regularised to 'E. A. B'.

Wherever changes are made in a text that can be deemed to be even slightly significant the alteration is either placed within square brackets (for example, an obviously missing word) or the alteration is footnoted. Attention should be drawn to one particular category of change. Orwell had a remarkably good memory. He quoted not only poetry but prose from memory. Mulk Raj Anand has said that, at the BBC, Orwell could, and would, quote lengthy passages from the Book of Common Prayer.[2] As so often with people with this gift, the quotation is not always exact. If what Orwell argues depends precisely upon what he is quoting, the quotation is not corrected if it is inaccurate but a footnote gives the correct reading. If his argument does not depend upon the words actually quoted, the quotation is corrected and a footnote records that.

So far as possible, I have endeavoured to footnote everything that might puzzle a reader at the risk of annoying some readers by seeming to annotate too readily and too frequently what is known to them. I have, therefore, tried to identify all references to people, events, books, and institutions. However, I have not been so presumptuous as to attempt to rewrite the history of this century and, in the main, have relied upon a small number of easily accessible histories. Thus, for the Spanish Civil War I have referred in the main to *The Spanish Civil War* by Hugh Thomas; and for the Second World War, to Winston Churchill's and Liddell Hart's histories. The former has useful and conveniently available documents, and the latter was by a historian with whom Orwell corresponded. They were both his contemporaries and he reviewed the work of both men. These have been checked for factual information from more recent sources, one by Continental historians deliberately chosen as an aid to objectivity in an edition that will have world-wide circulation. It is assumed that readers with a particular interest in World War II will draw on their own knowledge and sources and the annotation is relatively light in providing such background information. Similarly, biographical details are, paradoxically, relatively modest for people as well known as T. S. Eliot and E. M. Forster, but far fuller for those who are significant to Orwell but less well known and about whom information is harder to track down, for example, George(s) Kopp, Joseph Czapski, and Victor Serge. It is tricky judging how often biographical and explicatory information should be reproduced. I have assumed most people will not want more than one volume at a time before them and so have repeated myself (often in shortened form with cross-references to fuller notes) more, perhaps, than is strictly necessary. Whilst I would claim that I have made every attempt not to mislead, it is important that historical and biographical information be checked if a detail is significant to a scholar's argument. History, as Orwell was quick to show, is not a matter of simple, indisputable fact. In annotating I have tried not to be contentious nor to direct the reader unfairly, but annotation cannot be wholly impartial.[3]

Each opening is dated. These dates, though drawn from the printed matter, are not necessarily those of the text reproduced on the page on which a date appears. The dates, known or calculated of letters, articles, broadcasts, diaries, etc., will correspond with the running-head date, but, for example, when correspondence (which may have run on for several weeks) springs from an article and follows directly on that article, the date of the article is continued *within square brackets*. Sometimes an item is printed out of chronological order (the reason for which is always given) and the running-head date will again be set within square brackets. Wherever practicable, the running-head date is that of the first item of the opening; if an opening has no date, the last date of a preceding opening is carried forward. Articles published in journals dated by month are considered for the purpose to be published on the first of the month. Inevitably some dates are more specific than is wholly justified, e.g., that for 'British Cookery' (*2954*). However, it is hoped that if readers always treat dates within square brackets with circumspection, the dates will give a clear indication of 'where they are' in Orwell's life.

Great efforts have been made to ensure the accuracy of these volumes. The three editors and Roberta Leighton (in New York) have read and re-read them a total of six times but it is obvious that errors will, as it used to be put so charmingly in the sixteenth century, have 'escaped in the printing.' I offer one plea for understanding. Much of the copy-preparation and proof-reading has been of type set during and after the war when newsprint was in short supply and mere literary articles would be set in microscopic-sized type. Many of the BBC scripts were blown up from microfilm and extremely difficult to puzzle out. When one proof-reads against xeroxes of dim printing on creased paper, the possibilities for error are increased and the eyes so run with tears that vision is impaired. We hope we have corrected most errors, but we know we shall not have caught them all.

P.D.

A slightly fuller version of this note is printed in the preliminaries to Volume X.

1. *George Orwell, Nineteen Eighty-Four: The Facsimile of the Extant Manuscript*, edited by Peter Davison, London, New York, and Weston, Mass., 1984.
2. Information from W. J. West, 22 July 1994.
3. The problems of presenting acceptable history even for the professional historian are well outlined by Norman Davies in *Europe: A History*, Oxford University Press, Oxford and New York, 1996, 2–7. I am obviously attempting nothing so grand, yet even 'simple' historical explication is not always quite so simple.

REFERENCES

References to Orwell's books are to the editions in Vols I to IX of the *Complete Works* (edited P. Davison, published by Secker & Warburg, 1986–87). The pagination is almost always identical with that in the Penguin Twentieth-Century Classics edition, 1989–90. The volumes are numbered in chronological order and references are by volume number (in roman), page, and, if necessary (after a diagonal) line, so: II.37/5 means line five of page 37 of *Burmese Days*. Secker editions have Textual Notes and apparatus. Penguin editions have A Note on the Text; these are not identical with the Secker Textual Notes and Penguin editions do not list variants. There is a 32-page introduction to the Secker *Down and Out in Paris and London*. Items in Volumes X to XX are numbered individually; they (and their notes) are referred to by italicised numerals, e.g. *2736* and *2736 n. 3*.

REFERENCE WORKS: These are the principal reference works frequently consulted:

The Oxford English Dictionary, second edition (Compact Version, Oxford 1991): (OED).
The Dictionary of National Biography (Oxford 1885–1900, with supplements and *The Twentieth-Century*, 1901–): (DNB).
Dictionary of American Biography (New York, 1946, with supplements).
Dictionnaire biographique du mouvement ouvrier français, publié sous la direction de Jean Maitron, 4ᵉ ptie 1914–1939: De la Première à la Seconde Guerre mondiale (t. 16–43, Paris, Les Éditions Ouvrières, 1981–93).
Who's Who; Who Was Who; Who's Who in the Theatre; Who Was Who in Literature 1906–1934 (2 vols., Detroit, 1979); *Who Was Who Among English and European Authors 1931–1949* (3 vols., Detroit 1978); *Contemporary Authors* and its *Cumulative Index* (Detroit, 1993); *Who's Who In Filmland*, edited and compiled by Langford Reed and Hetty Spiers (1928); Roy Busby, *British Music Hall: An Illustrated Who's Who from 1850 to the Present Day* (London and New Hampshire, USA, 1976).
The Feminist Companion to Literature in English, edited by Virginia Blain, Patricia Clements, and Isobel Grundy, Batsford 1990.
The New Cambridge Bibliography of English Literature, edited by George Watson and Ian Willison, 4 vols., Cambridge, 1974–79.
Martin Seymour-Smith, *Guide to Modern World Literature*, 3rd revised edition, Macmillan 1985.
The War Papers, co-ordinating editor, Richard Widdows, 75 Parts, Marshall Cavendish, 1976–78.

The following are referred to by abbreviations:

CEJL: *The Collected Essays, Journalism and Letters of George Orwell*, ed. Sonia Orwell and Ian Angus, 4 volumes, Secker & Warburg 1968; Penguin Books, 1970; references are by volume and page number of the more conveniently available Penguin edition.

Crick: Bernard Crick, *George Orwell: A Life*, 1980; 3rd edition, Penguin Books, Harmondsworth, 1992 edition. References are to the 1992 edition.

Eric & Us: Jacintha Buddicom, *Eric and Us: A Remembrance of George Orwell*, Leslie Frewin, 1974.

Lewis: Peter Lewis, *George Orwell: The Road to 1984*, Heinemann, 1981.

Liddell Hart: B. H. Liddell Hart, *History of the Second World War*, Cassell, 1970; 8th Printing, Pan, 1983.

Orwell Remembered: Audrey Coppard and Bernard Crick, eds., *Orwell Remembered*, Ariel Books, BBC, 1984.

Remembering Orwell: Stephen Wadhams, *Remembering Orwell*, Penguin Books Canada, Markham, Ontario; Penguin Books, Harmondsworth, 1984.

Shelden: Michael Shelden, *Orwell: The Authorised Biography*, Heinemann, London; Harper Collins, New York; 1991. The American pagination differs from that of the English edition; both are given in references, the English first.

Stansky and Abrahams I: Peter Stansky and William Abrahams, *The Unknown Orwell*, Constable 1972; edition referred to here, Granada, St Albans, 1981.

Stansky and Abrahams II: Peter Stansky and William Abrahams, *The Transformation*, Constable 1979; edition referred to here, Granada, St Albans, 1981.

Thomas: Hugh Thomas, *The Spanish Civil War*, 3rd edition; Hamish Hamilton and Penguin Books, Harmondsworth, 1977.

Thompson: John Thompson, *Orwell's London*, Fourth Estate 1984.

West: *Broadcasts*: W. J. West, *Orwell: The War Broadcasts*, Duckworth/BBC 1985.

West: *Commentaries*: W. J. West, *Orwell: The War Commentaries*, Duckworth/BBC, 1985.

Willison: I. R. Willison, 'George Orwell: Some Materials for a Bibliography,' Librarianship Diploma Thesis, University College London, 1953. A copy is held by the Orwell Archive, UCL.

2194 Days of War: *2194 Days of War*, compiled by Cesare Salmaggi and Alfredo Pallavisini, translated by Hugh Young, Arnoldo Mondadori, Milan 1977; rev. edn Galley Press, Leicester 1988.

A Bibliography of works, books, memoirs and essays found helpful in preparing Volumes X to XX of *The Complete Works of George Orwell* will be found in the preliminaries to Volume X.

CHRONOLOGY

THE BBC YEARS

In the main, Orwell's publications, except books, are not listed

25 June 1903 Eric Arthur Blair born in Motihari, Bengal, India.

---

18 Aug 1941–24 Nov 1943 Talks Assistant, later Talks Producer, in the Indian section of the BBC's Eastern Service.

21 November 1941 First of over 200 newsletters written by Orwell for broadcast to India, Malaysia, and Indonesia, in English; and translated for broadcast in Gujarati, Marathi, Bengali, and Tamil.

8 March 1942 First contribution to *The Observer*.

15 May 1942 *Victory or Vested Interest?* published by George Routledge & Sons, containing Orwell's lecture, 'Culture and Democracy'.

Summer 1942 Moves to Maida Vale, London.

11 August 1942 'Voice 1,' first of six literary 'magazines' devised by Orwell for broadcast to India.

19 March 1943 His mother, Ida Blair, dies.

24 August 1943 'I am definitely leaving it [the BBC] probably in about three months' (letter to Rayner Heppenstall).

18 Nov 1943 *Talking to India* published by Allen & Unwin, edited and with an Introduction by Orwell.

23 Nov 1943 Leaves BBC and joins *Tribune* as Literary Editor. Leaves Home Guard on medical grounds.

Nov 1943–Feb 1944 Writes *Animal Farm*.

---

21 January 1950 Orwell dies of pulmonary tuberculosis, aged 46.

THE COMPLETE WORKS OF
GEORGE ORWELL · THIRTEEN

ALL PROPAGANDA IS LIES

844. Orwell's Contract with the BBC

THE BRITISH BROADCASTING CORPORATION

Broadcasting House, London, W. 1

TELEPHONE: WELBECK 4468 TELEGRAMS: BROADCASTS, LONDON

Reference: AS/PO   18th August, 1941

E.A.Blair, Esq.,
Empire Department.

Dear Sir,
      To have pleasure in offering you an engagement as a Talks Assistant in the
Empire Department   on the following terms and conditions:-

      1. You will perform the duties of an assistant in the Empire Service of the
Overseas Division and you will also perform such other duties of any kind (including
the provision of written and spoken contributions to the broadcast programs)
as may reasonably be required by the Corporation..

      2. The Corporation shall be entitled without your further consent or concurrence
(a) to record by any means any performance of any kind which you may, at any time
during this engagement at the request of the Corporation give in any of the
Corporation's programmes (whether broadcast or not) and (b) to reproduce or
authorise others to reproduce by any means a record of any such performance at any
time whether during the subsistence or after the determination of this Agreement.

      3. You agree to devote the whole of your time and attention to the service of the
Corporation and to attend for duty at such hours of the day or night as shall be
from time to time indicated to you at such place or places in the United Kingdom of
Great Britain and Northern Ireland as shall from time to time be decided by the
Corporation.   The Corporation shall at its discretion either pay your reasonable
travelling expenses from London or arrange at the expense of the Corporation for
your transport from London to such place or places.   You further agree not to
undertake work for any other person or firm whatsoever during the continuance of
this engagement without the previous written consent of the Corporation.

      4. You undertake at all times to exercise your talent to the best of your skill
and ability in the interests of the Corporation and to observe all instructions given
to you and to conform to all rules and regulations of the Corporation for the time
being in force.   A copy of the Staff Regulations now in force is enclosed herewith.

      5. You will not, without the previous written consent of the Corporation, publicly
write or speak about the Corporation or its affairs during the continuance of this
engagement.   Furthermore you will not either during or after the determination of
this engagement disclose to any person in any circumstances whatsoever any information, processes or secret matters relative to the business or affairs of the
Corporation, which may have come to your knowledge during the period of this engagement.

                              -1-   Please initial here...........

                                    J65110

3

6. The complete copyright in any work written by you in the course of your
employment under this Agreement shall vest in the Corporation.

7. Your remuneration shall be at the rate of £640. 0. 0d (Six hundred and
forty pounds).................... per annum, payable monthly in arrear.

8. This engagement shall in the first instance be for a trial period of
three months from the 18th August 1941 but the Corporation reserves the right
to terminate it at any time during that period by one month's notice in writing,
and (subject as hereinafter mentioned) if not so determined this engagement will
continue thereafter (subject to satisfactory service) until determined by
two month's notice in writing on either side. Provided that the Corporation
may determine the engagement at any time forthwith by notice in writing (a) if
your references prove unsatisfactory, or (b) if during or within fourteen days
after the expiration of the trial period or any extension thereof, the Corporation
shall not be satisfied with your work or conduct.

9. This engagement does not qualify you for membership of the Corporation's
permanent staff or of the Staff Pension Scheme.

10. In the event of (a) the further performance of the engagement at any time being
prevented by force majeure or any other cause outside your control or the control of the
Corporation, (b) any breach or non-observance on your part of any of the conditions
herein contained, the Corporation may forthwith terminate the engagement without
giving rise to any claim on your part for damages, compensation or otherwise beyond
a claim to remuneration at the appropriate rate down to the date of termination
and without prejudice to any claims outstanding on the part of the Corporation.

We shall be glad if you will kindly confirm your acceptance of this engagement
by signing the declaration at the foot hereof, initialling page one and returning
the letter complete to us, keeping the duplicate which is enclosed for your
information.

Yours faithfully,

for Acting Overseas Establishment Officer

To:
Overseas Establishment Officer,
British Broadcasting Corporation,
Broadcasting House, London, W.1.

Dear Sir,
I accept the engagement offered above upon the terms and conditions
stated.

Yours faithfully,

Date........................

165110

On pages 3 and 4 is Orwell's copy of his contract with the BBC as a talks assistant. He initially signed letters as 'Empire Talks Assistant'; from about 19 January 1942 he signed them as 'Talks Assistant, Indian Section,' and some six months later as 'Talks Producer, Indian Section.' D. Pearson Smith, who signed the contract for the BBC, was one of the assistants to the Overseas Services Establishment Officer. Reproduced by permission of the BBC and the British Library (which holds the original). Reduced to 65% size of original.

845. BBC Induction Course

18–30 August 1941

Orwell was appointed a talks assistant in the Overseas Service of the BBC from Monday, 18 August 1941, at a salary of £640 per annum.[1] On that day he started a short induction course in 'General Broadcasting Technique'—was 'colleged,' in BBC jargon—at Bedford College, University of London, then situated in Regent's Park. According to H. V. L. Swanzy, who came to know Orwell when both attended this course and who later was an assistant in the Overseas News Talks Section, the course had been reduced in length from three months to ten days.[2] William Empson, the poet and scholar,[3] who attended the same course, and who was, like Orwell, a talks assistant, in the Empire Department, recalled the course (referred to by him as 'the Liars' School') as lasting six weeks.[4] Orwell's timetable for that course, a list of participants, and a considerable number of course papers, have survived and are in the Orwell Archive, University College London. Several items are marked to show they were Orwell's copies; one bears Empson's name; others are unmarked.

Twenty-one people are named as being enrolled, but three names are crossed out. Among those attending besides Orwell, Empson, and Swanzy were A. M. Ashraf (one of Orwell's future colleagues); Douglas Cleverdon (Assistant, Features and Drama Department, Bristol, and later the deviser and producer of 'The Brains Trust'); Marius Goring (actor; then, Assistant, German News Talks Unit; Foreign Office, 1941–45); Frank Hardie (Assistant, Overseas Research Unit); Elizabeth Poston (composer; then working as Overseas Music Representative, Bristol); Reginald Pound (Sub-editor, Empire News, Overseas News Department); and Ralph Truman (Announcer, Manchester). Four women provided a staff pool. The Director of Staff Training (DST) was E. A. Harding; the senior instructors were Felix Felton and John Gough; and there were two secretaries for the staff.

The course lasted neither ten days nor six weeks, but ran for two weeks of five and a half days each (then the standard working week), from Monday, 18 August, to Saturday, 30 August. The programme and materials suggest anything but a liars' course. The course consisted of 'instruction in Programme Techniques, accompanied by sketches of the main Engineering and Administrative processes which make practice of them possible in British Broadcasting' (preamble to the training document). There were four lectures, demonstrations, or practical classes on most full days. The terminology is that used in the BBC's course description; for example, 'Play-over' for 'Replay.' In the first week, these, with those conducting them, were:

Chain of Technical Processes between broadcaster and listener (R. T. B. Wynn, Senior Superintendent Engineer). (See 1 below).

Administration of the BBC (G. C. Beadle, Controller—Administration).

Main Kinds of Programmes (DST).

Practical Acoustics and Microphones (Mr. Gough).

Meeting to discuss programme exercises (DST).

Demonstration of studio equipment (Mr. Gough). (These last two sessions were held in Studio 3, Maida Vale. Orwell has written in the margin directions for finding the studio in Delaware Road.)

The BBC in Wartime (Director-General of the BBC).

Feature Programmes (DST).

Planning of Home and Forces Programmes.

Analysis of Empire Service feature script 'Freedom Ferry,' No. 15, 'Missions to Seamen' by Robert Barr (Mr. Felton). (The script survives; see 5 below. Barr should have attended the course.)

Attend rehearsal and live transmission of the above at Monseigneur Cinema, Marble Arch.

Discussion of the programme with the Producer (Francis Dillon) and Mr. Felton.

Radio Transmission and the BBC's Networks (L. Hayes, Head of Overseas Engineering Information Department).

Speech for the Microphone (Mr. Gough).

Recording Systems used by the BBC (M. J. L. Pulling, Superintendent Engineer, Recording).

Demonstration of Recording Equipment (M. J. L. Pulling).

Description of programme uses of film and tape, and demonstration of programme applications of disc recording system (Mr. Gough and representative from Recorded Programmes Department).

Overseas Programme Planning (C. Lawson-Reece, Supervisor of Overseas Planning). (See 6, 7, and 8 below.)

Talks Exercises by Students (DST).

Talks Exercises by Students, followed by analysis and discussion (DST).

Listener Research (R. J. Silvey, Listener Research Director). (See 9, 10, 11 below.)

There were no formal classes on the last day of the first week; that Saturday morning was 'Available for office work.'

Sessions for the second week of the course were:

Programme Routine (S. G. Williams, Assistant Director of Overseas Programme Administration, Supply).

Outside Broadcasts (Michael Standing, Director of Outside Broadcasts).

Magazine Programmes (DST).

Tea party, to meet senior members of the staff.

Read-through, rehearsal, and performance on closed-circuit recording of fifteen-minute feature, produced by DST, with students taking part as cast, programme engineers, junior programme engineers, etc. (This was almost certainly 'The London Policeman, Helper and Friend,' the script of which survives; see 12 below. A full day—four sessions—was devoted to this exercise.)

Play-over and discussion on feature recorded on previous afternoon (DST).

European Intelligence Services (J. S. A. Salt, Director of European Service).

News Talks Production (Donald Boyd, Assistant Senior News Editor, Home Division).

Exercises in making running commentaries and use of recording van (Mr. Gough).

Play-over of running commentaries (Mr. Gough). (This made a fifth, evening, session for this day and lasted one and a quarter hours.)

News Broadcasting.

Radio News Reel (H. P. K. Pooley, Empire News Talks Editor).

Broadcasting to a Dominion (Grenfell Williams, Deputy Director of Empire Service and African Service Director).

Analysis of a feature script (DST). (This script was probably 'Arctic Excursion,' which survives—see 13 below—with annotations in Orwell's hand.)

Play-over of running commentaries recorded on previous day (Mr. Gough). (Again, a fifth, evening, session for this day; on this occasion it was timed to last for two hours.)

Presentation and Continuity (L. Stokes, Overseas Presentation Manager[5]). (Various materials survive from this lecture; see 14, 15, 16 below.)

Use of Music in Productions (Mr. Gough).

Organisation and Problems of the Overseas Division (Sir Stephen Tallents, Controller, Overseas).

The final session on the second Friday was a meeting to discuss the course with the Director of Staff Training and the two senior instructors. Three hours on the last day of the course, Saturday, 30 August, were made available for individual sessions with the staff. The room allocated was the DST's office, so it would seem that all three staff were present at the same time for these discussions.

In addition to Orwell's copy of the course programme, the following documents have survived:

1. 'Chain of Technical Processes between Speaker or Artiste and Listener.'
2. 'Radio Transmission and the BBC's Networks.'
3. Coloured plan showing Red, Green, Yellow, and Blue Network allocations.
4. 'Glossary of Selected Terms Defined in their Relation to Present Practice in British Broadcasting.' This is a twenty-two-page document. One definition is of particular interest in connection with Orwell. 'Actuality' is defined as 'Presentation of real persons and things to give a picture of contemporary life in a particular aspect; documentary.'
5. Script, 'Freedom Ferry' by Robert Barr. First broadcast 20 August 1941.
6. Overseas Programme Schedule for Thursday, 28 August 1941; World Service (Red Network) from London or 10 Abbey Manor; Empire Service (Green Network) from London or Wood Norton.
7. Empire Programme Schedule, Blue and Yellow Networks.
8. Latin American Schedule, Yellow Network.
9. Listener Research Reports.
10. Listener Research Weekly Report No. 32, 2 May 1941.
11. Listener Research, Explanation of System, 29 July 1941.
12. Script, Civilians' War 9, 'The London Policeman, Helper and Friend' by Malcolm Baker-Smith. First broadcast 11 July 1941. Marked, 'slightly changed from the original for Staff Training purposes.' Orwell has written in various light cues and a number of comments. Thus, against the Narrator at one point he has written, 'spoke too soon.' Orwell seems to have played

the Second Policeman. He has written in a few verbal changes, for example, 'No, not by a long stretch' for 'No, not by fifty odd years,' and 'buzzer went' for 'bell went.' At the end of one speech he has written, 'Very slight pause,' and against other speeches indications for a longer pause and 'More voice.' He has also written in details of traffic-noise effects. At the very end he has written, in a space for noting those taking part: 'Members of the 4th Genl. Course in Staff Training Dept.'

13. Script, 'Arctic Excursion' by E. A. F. Harding (presumably, despite the third initial, the Director of Staff Training). This has a number of comments in Orwell's hand drawing attention to matters of technique. These are (with the page numbers): 'Effect before mention of it' (1); 'Throw away clause' (1); 'Start from the home' (1)—that is, indicating the need to relate Lapland to a British audience by referring to steamers leaving Hull for Finland; 'Arrival in Finland gradually led up to' (2); 'Purely time effects' (3); 'Details of journey now less mentioned' (3); 'From now on traveller [one of the characters] begins to take command' (4); 'Keeping rapidly on the move in order to be able to halt presently' (5); 'Commentator introduced here to give the story a restart after halt' (6); 'Speed-up again' (14); 'end on anticlimax' (16); there are also two slight verbal changes.

14. Continuity Script for Eastern Service, 22 August 1941. This has a few pencil markings.

15. Announcer's Report (completed) for 15 August 1941.

16. Empire Presentation Assistant's Report, with extracts from Announcers' Logs for 13 August 1941; signed P. W. Chalmers.

17. Script, 'Dr Johnson Takes It' by Louis MacNeice, broadcast 29 June 1941. This is probably Gladys Young's copy; it is not otherwise marked.

18. Twelve pages from various scripts.

19. 'Research Unit (Overseas): Its Organisation, Work and Personnel.' Among those listed is Tosco Fyvel, with whom Orwell worked on Searchlight Books; see *660, n. 1*.

Filed with these induction course materials are the following documents; 20–22, examples of material regularly circulated; 23, a proposal that might have had particular interest for Orwell:

20. 'Daily Digest of Foreign Broadcasts,' No. 832, Part 1, From Germany and German-occupied territory, 27–28 October 1941. This includes summaries of broadcasts in English for Britain (for example, 'Kick Churchill Out' from the New British Broadcasting Station and reports of broadcasts from Calais); broadcasts in Hindustani for India from Zeesen; German Home broadcasts. It is marked 'W. Empson, Room 206.'

21. 'Daily Digest of Foreign Broadcasts,' No. 832, From other than Germany and German-occupied territory.

22. 'Weekly Analysis of Foreign Broadcasts' for the 112th week of the war, 20–26 October 1941. This is marked with Orwell's name and 'Egton 221' and '246.'

23. 'India of the Future': agenda for a preliminary meeting of the Round Table Discussions Sub-Committee (of which Orwell was a member); Sir Malcolm Darling's proposal; and minutes of meetings of the sub-committee held on 17 December 1942 (when Orwell was present) and 27 January 1943 (when he was not present).

1. Orwell's salary can be put into perspective by comparing it with facts from a questionnaire answered by readers of *Horizon* in January 1941. Shelden records that 16% of the readers earned more than £1,000 a year, putting them in the 'well-off' category, and 10% 'were from the working-class level, which meant they made no more than two hundred pounds a year.' In the spring of 1942 Cyril Connolly was paid £900 a year as literary editor and principal reviewer of *The Observer*, and about £400 a year for editing *Horizon* (*Friends of Promise*, 87, 93). In the light of Orwell's recent straitened circumstances, £640 must have seemed like affluence
2. Henry Swanzy contributed an affectionate and amusing portrait of Orwell at this time to *Remembering Orwell*, 123–25; later memories of Orwell, by Sunday Wilshin, who took over Orwell's work when he resigned in 1943, are on 125–27.
3. William Empson (1906–1984, Kt., 1979), poet and critic, had been Professor of English Literature in Tokyo and Peking before the war Like Orwell, he worked in the Eastern Service of the BBC, broadcasting to China. He was Professor of English Literature at Sheffield University, 1953–71, and achieved scholarly recognition for *Seven Types of Ambiguity* (1930), *Some Versions of Pastoral* (1935), and *The Structure of Complex Words* (1951) *The Times* obituary described him as 'the most famously over-sophisticated man of his time' who 'revolutionized our ways of reading a poem.'
4. See 'Orwell at the BBC' in *The World of George Orwell*, edited by Miriam Gross (1971), 94–99; reprinted in *Orwell Remembered*, 177–83.
5. Probably Leslie Stokes; described by Z. A. Bokhari (see *776, n 1*) as Empire Programme Planner in a letter to Orwell, 23 September 1941. Programme Planning and Presentation were separate departments Bokhari may have mistaken Stokes's role, or Stokes may have been moved. In much of Orwell's time at the BBC, T W Chalmers was Overseas Presentation Director, and Joanna Spicer was the Programme Planner (Staff List, Issue 2, 21 8.43)

846. BBC Overseas Service

Orwell joined his department on the Monday after the induction course concluded. On Thursday, 28 August 1941, R. A. Rendall, the Director of the Empire Service at the time, and shortly after Assistant Controller of the Overseas Service,[1] informed the Empire Talks Director that he had asked Orwell (referred to almost invariably in BBC correspondence as Blair) to report to him on 1 September. Rendall suggested that Orwell be given 'no talks responsibilities before the new schedule but that he spends the intervening time in planning the "Through Eastern Eyes" series with the I.P.O.,[2] and in completing his training by watching some of the more experienced Empire Talks Assistants at work.'

Orwell's first letters organising talks are dated 1 October 1941. If September is considered part of the training period, Empson's 'six weeks' no longer sounds so much at odds with Swanzy's ten days.

Two days after Orwell joined the BBC, the Empire Talks Director[3] sent the following memorandum to Rendall:

I hear that Mr. George Orwell is joining the department in ten days' time. As you know, I have already suggested to Miss Gompertz[4] that she should finally end up in the Eastern Service. She likes this idea, and I think her experience would be most useful in this Service. She will be busy for the next few weeks taking over from Miss Treadgold[5] while Miss Treadgold goes to the School, but she should be free by the end of September.

It seems to me that the arrival of Mr. George Orwell should synchronise with the responsibility being centralised for all talks in English which go out in both the Red and Green networks in the Eastern Service. If you remember, you asked me to arrange with Mr. Bokhari that I should see the scripts for "Through Eastern Eyes", and when I was discussing this project with him he said he would be perfectly happy to work in with this department for all his talks in English.

Anthony Weymouth[6] could still see that all the Talks spaces were filled and could handle such series as "Matters of Moment", but I think it would be an immense advantage if he were working in close cooperation with people who know both the Indian and exile audience intimately.

If you agree to this suggestion I would like to put it into operation immediately, for it seems to me that the new schedule should be planned on this basis. Mr. Bokhari will in any case need help if he is to carry through the very extensive programme he has put up. It would be neat and tidy if we could have this plan in operation from the day Mr. Orwell arrives. Miss Gompertz, although not entirely free for the work in this Service, would be able to attend all meetings in connection with it immediately.

May I have your approval, and then shall you or I get into touch with Mr. Bokhari? I think, incidentally, that Gerald Bullett[7] could probably be of considerable help to him over his literary talks and I would feel much happier about the Service if both Mr. Weymouth and Mr. Bullett, who have no overseas experience, were working in far closer cooperation with people who have that experience.

Orwell started his work for the BBC at 55 Portland Place,[8] first in Room 206 and later in Room 416. Early in June 1942 he moved with his colleagues to 200 Oxford Street, the '200' being associated, according to Eric Robertson, by some of those working there with 'ZOO.'[9] The Summer 1945 issue of the BBC's house journal, *Ariel*, included an interesting, if informal, article, 'A Visit to Overseas H.Q. At 200 Oxford Street' (14–15, 18) that describes the people working there a little after Orwell left.

The Eastern Service was well established by the time Orwell joined, but it was in process of expansion. Programmes for India were in two sections, one under Z. A. Bokhari (see 776, *n. 1*), based in London, and the other under Sir Malcolm Darling, Indian Editor, Hindustani, at Evesham, Worcestershire.[10]

Fairly soon after Orwell's appointment, Bokhari wrote a memorandum to him, dated 23 September 1941, outlining his plans. This was addressed to Orwell at Egton House, Langham Street, London, W1, where he was temporarily located, and where Grenfell Williams, African Service Director, had his office. This memorandum gives a fair picture of the milieu Orwell was entering:

My dear Blair,

These English programmes to India. I am delighted and flattered to have your assistance. I know I shall always enjoy working with you. Let's work out a definite plan. With effect from the 5th October, 1941, this section will be responsible for forty five minutes programme in English every day. The first half-hour falls under our general title "We Speak to India", and the rest is a series of talks entitled "Through Eastern Eyes". Over and above this, this section is responsible for recording and broadcasting Students' Messages twice a week. These messages form part of the Hindustani programmes. So much is definite so far. Perhaps when the Eastern Service Director is appointed, we shall be entrusted with some more work.

Let me first of all discuss the programme "We Speak to India". I presume that with effect from the 5th October, we shall have to change this title because we shall be broadcasting not only on the Green Network, but also on the World Service. I will get in touch with Leslie Stokes (who is the Empire Programme Planner)[11] and see if he can hit upon a new title. This programme comprises cultural programmes—fiction, poetry, drama, music, etc. The rough scheme of the programme is as follows:

On Mondays—We do not originate any programme. It is originated for us by the World Service. In this programme the persons responsible for the World Service and also the Green Network are going to give India on the Green and Red Networks a programme about personalities in the field of drama (film and stage).

On Thursdays—again the programme will be originated for us by the World Service and on every Thursday they propose to broadcast a feature entitled 'Made in England'.

On Sundays—on the Red Network a Religious Service will be broadcast by the World Service people, and we shall originate a programme on the Green Network.

These are our fixtures.

On Tuesdays—I propose to broadcast a programme on literature entitled 'Turning Over A New Leaf'.

On Wednesdays—a programme for women.

On Fridays—'Melody and Harmony'. Scott Goddard and an Indian musician—B. N. Mukerjee—will discuss and demonstrate European and Indian music respectively.

On Saturdays—We shall broadcast, 'Any Questions?' taken from the Forces' Programme on the previous Sunday.

On Sundays—I propose to broadcast 'The History of Mr. Polly', adapted from H. G. Wells's book. It was broadcast in the H. S. and I have pinched it from it.

I have received the syllabuses of various Indian universities and I am negotiating with Herbert Read and trying to get a team of university dons to broadcast talks based on the books prescribed or recommended for various examinations in India. It is all in the melting pot at the moment and as soon as I have some definite plan, I shall let you know and we will get together to thrash it out.[12]

I am also trying to get in touch with Professor Firth[13] and see if we can arrange English lessons for beginners. This, to my mind, is very important.

These plans may seem haphazard to you and I daresay they are. I shall always be delighted to have your suggestions. As soon as we get an Indian on the staff who can be entrusted to announce these programmes, I shall request you to handle these programmes yourself.

'Through Eastern Eyes'—You have the schedule of this series with you. I have written to some of the talkers and the response on the whole has been rather good. As the scripts come in, I shall pass them on to you with my observations. You will kindly go through them with the broadcasters and rehearse them. You will also, in every case, be good enough to write out the announcement for each talk. The announcement should be made in my opinion by an Indian. Do you agree? I think the best plan would be for me, in the first instance, to get in touch with the proposed speakers and as soon as the preliminary details are settled, I should hand over the talker to you and leave him to your tender mercies. In order to get in touch with the various speakers in this series you will have not only my assistance, but also the assistance of

Sarin.[14] For this series he is always at your disposal. He knows Indians in Great Britain rather well—much better than I do—and therefore he is in a position to tell you their interests and their capabilities. In my future invitations to the speakers in the series 'Through Eastern Eyes' I propose to ask them to get in touch with you. If you have any difficulty in dealing with them, you can always requisition my services.

Students' Messages—I propose to hand over the recording and broadcasting of Students' messages (they are in Hindustani) to Sarin as soon as he is familiar with the gadgets.

All this pertains to routine.

We want ideas very badly. Could you kindly put on your thinking-cap. We must start thinking now about our programme for the quarter after next, both under the title "We Speak to India" and "Through Eastern Eyes".

I am sending a copy of this letter to Mr. Rendall and Mr. Grenfell Williams.

When Bokhari wrote, an Eastern Service director had not been appointed. This was to be L. F. Rushbrook Williams.[15] From the surviving correspondence, he seems to have begun work late in October or in early November 1941. He is not included in the distribution list of some forty people for a memorandum of 1 October 1941 from the Supervisor of Overseas Planning (C. Lawson-Reece), but by 15 November 1941 Bokhari could begin a memorandum to him with 'Allow me to point out once again that I am not quite happy about the Bengali Newsletter.'

It was such series that Orwell would participate in and develop. He took a particular interest in the talks—lectures—designed for Indian university students, courses that were modest precursors of the Open University of some thirty years later.

An advance schedule also survives for the Hindustani Service, drawn up for the Eastern Service Committee[16] meeting on 22 October 1941. The Hindustani Service, directed by Sir Malcolm Darling, was based at Wood Norton, Evesham, Worcestershire (now the home of the BBC's Engineering Training Department). Although Orwell was not a member of this section, his work was sometimes included in translation in its broadcasts, especially news commentaries, and he had contact with some of the staff; see, for example, his letter to Balraj Sahni's wife, 3 October 1941, *861*.

In addition to feature programmes, there were various series of news bulletins and of commentaries (or newsletters) in English and in a number of languages spoken in Southeast Asia, China, and Indonesia.

On 20 August 1941, Bokhari gave Rendall a 'rough schedule of progress of the 1345–1400 GMT period on the Green Network, from the 5th October, 1941' for his approval:

Saturday:	Bengali Newsletter
Sunday:	Children's Programme. Anglo-Hindustani
Monday:	Marathi Newsletter
Tuesday:	Gujerati[17] Newsletter
Wednesday:	Pushtu Newsletter
Thursday:	Sindhi Newsletter
Friday:	Punjabi or Parsi. Gujerati Newsletter.

The production of vernacular news commentaries presented recurring difficulties, as Orwell amusingly recalled at the end of his life, because 'apparently, Indians of that race [Marathis] when living in England soon lose their command of their native tongue'; see excerpt from Orwell's last Literary Notebook, *892*.

The schedule for the Eastern Service Committee meeting listed 'Newsletters' as item 3 on the agenda and gave six categories: Tamil, Malay, Thai, Cantonese and Kuoyu, Bengali, and Burmese. Three weeks later, on 15 November, Bokhari expressed doubts about the way the Bengali Newsletter was being prepared, and proposed new arrangements for the Gujarati Newsletter:

BENGALI NEWSLETTERS

Allow me to point out once again that I am not quite happy about the Bengali Newsletter. I have received to-day's script. There is nothing harmful in it, but there is no meat either; it is pudding! And the only thing to do is to write these letters ourselves in English and get translators and announcers to translate and announce them. For such work I don't think we require such highly paid people as Dr. Ghose. I suggest Ajit Mookerjee,[18] 12 Gayton Crescent, N.W. 3. and D. Mojumder, 41 Armitage Road, Golders Green, N.W.11. They are two excellent broadcasters and youngsters who should be employed by us as announcer/ translators for these weekly newsletters. Mr. Mojumder has passed through the 'college'[19] and if you approve of this scheme, will you kindly see Ajit Mookerjee and ask the authorities concerned to put him through the 'college'. In the meantime without committing the B.B.C. to anything, I am having a word with Mookerjee in order to find out how he feels about it.

GUJARATI NEWSLETTERS

I am getting in touch with R. R. Desai. Once or twice he has broadcast messages for us and I found him a good broadcaster. I will find out whether he will be prepared to do the Gujerati° Newsletters for us. I will let you know another Gujerati° name for the newsletter. I am getting in touch with R. R. Desai unofficially and will let you know more about him in a day or two.

The essence of the difficulty Bokhari and his colleagues faced was a demand for a far too rapid increase in the variety of languages to be serviced by understaffed departments. Orwell, with the others, was so severely overworked that there was little time for objective thought.

Orwell was to write news commentaries in English to be broadcast to India and to occupied Malaya and Indonesia in three separate series. He also prepared the English versions of commentaries to be translated into Gujarati, Marathi, Bengali, and Tamil. The commentaries in English for India took over the Saturday slot devoted to 'The Leaders' (what leader-writers were saying in the English newspapers). He himself read the last dozen or so of these commentaries and also read news commentaries in English for listeners in occupied Malaya and Indonesia until he left the BBC.[20] One of the commentaries he wrote was read on his behalf after his departure by John Morris.[21] For a detailed account of Orwell's work on Newsletters, see *892*.

A schedule of Weekly Programme Times drawn up by Bokhari about 8 or 9 January 1942 summarises the programmes in English and Hindustani and shows the developments in broadcasting in Hindustani:

September, October and November, 1941.

English		Weekly programme time
1. We Speak to India	(30 minutes)	150 minutes
2. Through Eastern Eyes	(15 minutes)	105 minutes
3. News from India	(10 minutes)	10 minutes
(Forces Programme)		
Hindustani		
4. Indian Forces in Britain	(30 minutes)	30 minutes
(Forces Programme)		
5. Students' Greetings Programmes	(15 minutes)	30 minutes

December 1941 and January 1942

English		
1. We Speak to India	(30 minutes)	150 minutes
2. Through Eastern Eyes	(15 minutes)	105 minutes
3. News from India (December	(10 minutes)	10 minutes
only) (Forces Programme)		
Hindustani		
4. Indian forces in Britain	(30 minutes)	30 minutes
5. Indian Forces Overseas	(30 minutes)	150 minutes
6. Forces' Greetings Programme	(15 minutes)	30 minutes
7. Students' Greetings Programmes	(15 minutes)	30 minutes
8. Hindustani Feature Programme	(15 minutes)	30 minutes

1. *London Calling*, No. 110 (which gives BBC Overseas Service programmes for 16–22 November 1941, printed 16.10.41), contains a short article about R. A. Rendall (1907–), 'The Man Who Directs the BBC Empire Services' (20). Educated at Winchester and Trinity College, Cambridge, he had joined the BBC as an announcer, something he said he did very badly. He then became involved in an unusually wide range of work for the BBC—in adult education and Group Listening, as a talks executive, and as West of England Regional Programme Director. In 1935 he was seconded as the first programme director of the Palestine Broadcasting Service. Back in England after thirteen months, he was appointed assistant director of television and joined the Overseas Service at the outbreak of war. He was made director of the Empire Service shortly before Orwell joined the BBC and was later Assistant Controller of the Overseas Services. His duties, according to *London Calling*, required him to live day and night at Broadcasting House, taking such sleep as he could in a dormitory bunk. In 1943 he was promoted to Acting Controller of Overseas Services in place of J. Beresford Clark, who later returned to that post, and Rendall's name does not appear in the Staff List for 1945. When Rendall was Assistant Controller, S. J. de Lotbinière was, for a short time, Director of the Empire Service before becoming director of the War Reporting Unit and in 1943 the BBC's Canadian Representative in Toronto. For a jaundiced view of Rendall, see 847, the Cripps' Papers.
2. The Indian Programme Organiser was Zulfaqar Ali Bokhari (see 776, *n. 1*), with whom Orwell was to work closely. See 847, Cripps' Papers, for a favourable independent assessment of his abilities. He became director-general of Pakistan Radio after the war.
3. The reference on this memorandum is MHW/PB implying that 'MHW' was its originator. A search by the records section at Bush House (location of the BBC Overseas Service) has not revealed who 'MHW' was. The Empire Talks Director for much of Orwell's time at the BBC was Norman Collins, and he probably sent this memorandum. Collins (see 236) had been Deputy Chairman of Victor Gollancz Ltd, and some ill-feeling had developed between him and Orwell that continued at the BBC. He later was director of the General Overseas Service and then took over the Light Programme in 1946. In 1947 he was appointed Controller, BBC Television. He resigned in 1950 and later was instrumental in the formation of the independent television service.

4. T. G. M. de L. Gompertz was recorded in the Staff List, Issue 2, 21.8.43, as a talks producer in the Talks Pool of the General Overseas Service, a post she still held at the end of the war.
5. M. Treadgold became a talks producer in the African Service, a post she still held at the end of the war.
6. Anthony Weymouth (Ivo Geikie-Cobb), physician and surgeon, and, as Anthony Weymouth, novelist, was a BBC talks producer for the Overseas Service; see *635, n. 2*.
7. Gerald Bullett (1893–1958), novelist, short-story writer, critic, and poet, had at this time recently published *The Bending Sickle* (1938), *Problems of Religion* (1938), *A Man of Forty* (1940), and *When the Cat's Away* (1940). He was a talks producer and stood in for Orwell when he was ill. He was not included in the Staff List for 21.8.43.
8. 55 Portland Place is now owned by Legal and General Property. In the 1930s it was a block of flats, as it is now. Some plans survive from 1938 and 1955, though most are for conversions made in 1971. It is not possible to locate where the rooms used by Orwell and his colleagues were situated from these.
9. Eric Robertson (1915–1987; OBE), who in 1941–42 worked for the Malay Broadcasting Service, ran the Far Eastern Service of All-India Radio, 1942–45. He had met Orwell at the BBC and for a time worked at 200 Oxford Street.
10. Malcolm Darling (1880–1969; Kt., 1939), tutor of the Raja of Dewas Senior, 1906–09, was made an assistant commissioner in the Indian Civil Service and served in various capacities, 1909–40. He was for a time Registrar to the agricultural co-operative societies of the Punjab, and Vice-Chancellor of Punjab University, 1931, 1937–38. The government of India nominated him to head the BBC's Hindustani Service, from which he retired in 1943. See *Selected Letters of E. M. Forster*, edited by Mary Lago and P. N. Furbank (1983), particularly n. 1 to item 74, Forster's letter to Darling, 14 October 1909. Darling figures prominently in the important study *Anglo-Indians: The Mind of the Indian Civil Service* (1993).
11. See *845, n. 5*. The title was not changed.
12. In a letter of 15 October 1941, Bokhari told Geoffrey Tillotson (1905–1969), of University College London, that BA and MA syllabuses of various Indian universities had been collated and from them 'representative books' had been selected. The 'underlying idea of the series'— and here, in concept and phrasing, Orwell's influence might be detected—was 'to take a single work, sometimes a single poem, and to treat this work as representative of its author. The stylistic qualities of the work might be briefly analysed, and its place in the life and artistic development of the author determined. But the essential point of each talk would be to present a lively appreciation of the personality of the poet as represented in the selected poem, play or novel.' Each talk in the series was to be introduced by Herbert Read (see *522, n. 1*), with whom Orwell was quite closely associated before and after the war. Tillotson was asked to discuss Dryden's poem 'Absalom and Achitophel.' Other distinguished scholars invited included H. S. Bennett, Emmanuel College, Cambridge (on *The Canterbury Tales*, 28 October 1941), and John Butt, also of Cambridge (on *The Way of the World*, the eighth talk in the series, 16 December 1941).
13. John Rupert Firth (1890–1960) took a degree in history at the University of Leeds; joined the Indian Education Service in 1915, saw military service in India, Afghanistan, and Africa, 1916–19; and was Professor of English, University of the Punjab, Lahore, 1919–28. In English universities he specialised in phonetics, the sociology of languages, and linguistics. He undertook research in India in 1937 on the Gujarati and Telugu languages, and in 1940 was Reader in Linguistics and Indian Phonetics, University of London. From 1941 to 1945 his department was almost wholly occupied with Japanese courses for service personnel (*DNB*). In 1944 he was appointed to the first chair of general linguistics in Great Britain by the University of London. His works for a general audience, *Speech* (1930) and *The Tongues of Men* (1937), were successful and reprinted in paperback after his death. He was the only person to serve on the BBC's Eastern Service Committee in a personal capacity; see *n. 16*.
14. I.B. Sarin, an Indian Programme Assistant, was one of Orwell's colleagues. He was later a BBC announcer in Hindustani.
15. Laurence Frederic Rushbrook Williams (1890–1978; CBE, 1923), onetime Fellow of All Souls' College, Oxford; Professor of Modern Indian History, Allahabad University, 1914–19, and Director of the Central Bureau of Information, India, 1920–26, served as adviser in Middle Eastern Affairs to the Ministry of Information, and as Director of the BBC's Eastern

Service, from 1941 to November 1944. He then joined *The Times* (to 1955). His books include *The State of Pakistan* (1962; revised, 1966) and *The East Pakistan Tragedy* (1972). His enlightened attitude to India at this time is expressed in *India* (Oxford Pamphlets on World Affairs, 1940). For comment on his character in the Cripps' Papers, see *847*.

16. The Eastern Service Committee of the BBC was made up of representatives of the India Office, Ministry of Information, Foreign Office, Colonial Office, I[ndian?] E[xecutive?], the Indian Programme Organiser (Z. A. Bokhari), and J. R. Firth (see *n. 13*). It was an advisory body. See also 'Present Set-Up of Indian Broadcasting at the BBC,' Cripps' Papers.

17. Until 2 November 1942, Gujarati was invariably spelt 'Gujerati' in all the Indian Section's correspondence. The incorrect form is retained here in correspondence and memoranda; the correct form is given in headings, summaries of talks booking forms, and editorial references.

18. Ajit Mookerjee (1915–1990) was educated at Calcutta University. In 1937 he published *Folk Art of Bengal*, and then came to London to read for a master's degree in the history of art at London University. He wrote on folk art for *Horizon* and worked for a year in the BBC's Eastern Service. Later he was Director of the Institute of Art, Calcutta, and the head of the National Crafts Museum, New Delhi. He published prolifically, especially on Tantra, influencing many Western writers and academics.

19. Orwell, in his last Literary Notebook, reflects on an experience when working for the BBC. He writes of 'the so-called 'College', the mysterious body (actually I think MI5) which had to O.K. all broadcasters.' This would seem to be a euphemism for Bedford College, the staff training college, which Orwell had recently passed through. See *873, n. 1*, on the urgent necessity of getting an announcer/translator put through the college; and Orwell's War-time Diary, *1573, 15.10.42*, where 'the mysterious bodies which control recruitment for the BBC' are said to be related to MI5 (the British Military Intelligence Security Service).

20. W. J. West states in *Orwell: The War Commentaries* (1985, 219) that after the newsletter to India of 13 March 1943 Orwell had no further part in direct propaganda of this kind. This is at variance with the facts. Orwell's role in this field increased. This volume of the *Complete Works* and West's book vary considerably in substance and content. A brief note on the nature of the differences is given in *892*. Occasionally a note will point to a major discrepancy, but in the main West's readings have been here disregarded. His edition is referred to as West: *Commentaries*. See also *n. 847, n. 6*.

21. For John Morris, later head of the Far Eastern Service, see *1965, n. 1*.

847. BBC Network and Staffs for Overseas Broadcasts

Broadcasts in which Orwell was involved were transmitted via two networks, Green and Red. Networks had been colour-codes from 1936 to facilitate switching, a process now done by computer. The Green Network carried the Empire Service and, during the war, programmes for forces overseas. Although most of the programmes on this network were in English, regular slots were allocated for foreign-language newsletters. Thus, a memorandum from W. M. Goatman (Overseas Information) of 20.2.42, stated that the 1330–1345 Green Network slot would, from 22 February, carry a daily newsletter in Thai. Programmes formerly broadcast at that time would be broadcast a quarter of an hour later.

The Red Network was devoted to 'the three A's'—Asia, Africa, and America. It broadcast in Hindi in 1940; Persian was added in 1941; in 1942 the service was expanded to 8¼ hours a week to include newsletters in Marathi, Sinhala, Hindi, Bengali, Burmese, Gujarati, Malay, and Tamil. The service was further expanded to 11¾ hours per week in 1944, in part for the benefit of the army in Southeast Asia.

At the time of Goatman's memorandum, the wavelengths used for the Green Network broadcasts were GSQ (17.79 Mc/s; 16.86m) and GRV (12.14 Mc/s; 24.92m); Red Network to the Far East, GRO (6.18 Mc/s; 48.54m) from 15.45 GMT.[1]

On 27 November 1941 a member of the BBC's Empire Executive set out the establishment of the Eastern Service of the Empire Department:[2]

Director of Eastern Service (E.S.D.): L. F. Rushbrook Williams
Secretary: Miss P. J. Orr
Assistant E.S.D.: A. F. N. Thavenot
Secretary: Miss K. Walton
Indian Programme Organiser: Z. A. Bokhari
Secretary: Miss Mary Blackburn
5 Indian Programme Assistants: A. A. Ashraf; M. H. Khan; A. L. Bakaya; M. E. Hyder (applied for); B. Sahni
2 Junior Programme Assistants (originally called clerk/typists): I. B. Sarin; one vacancy
Reserve Programme Assistant: Vacant
2 Monitors: Mr. Haq applied for; one vacancy
<u>Talks Assistants</u>
Far East Assistant: William Empson
Secretary: Vacant
Eastern Languages: E. A. Blair
Secretary: Vacant (Miss N. H. Parratt[3] had been assigned to him when the list was typed but her name was crossed out)
Talks Assistant: Miss T. G. M. de L. Gompertz
Secretary: Miss Recacheff
Indian Assistant: Vacant
Secretary: Vacant when the list was typed but Miss Parratt's name written in
(Transcription Assistant: E. Rowan Davies } Seconded from
(Secretary: Miss Gibb   } O.C. Department

The BBC's printed Staff List dated 21 August 1943 shows the position of the section at the time Orwell was completing his service.

EASTERN SERVICE

Eastern Service Director *E.S.D.*	L. F. Rushbrook Williams	Miss P. J. Orr
Eastern Service Organizer *E.S.O.*	C. Lawson-Reece	Miss E. M. Sculthorp
Indian News Editor *I.N.E.*	Sir Malcolm Darling	Miss F. C. M. Page-Turner
Sub-Editor (Indian News)	A. Ellings	
Assistant (Indian News)	M. H. Khan	
Indian Programme Organizer *I.P.O.*	Z. A. Bokhari	Miss A. L. Bateman
Assistant (General)	M. E. Hyder	
Senior Assistant (Programmes)	B. Sahni	
Assistant (Programmes)	I. B. Sarin	Miss J. Light
Talks Producers	E. A. Blair	
	W. Empson	Miss W. M. Bedwell
	Miss E. Sam	
	A. C. Smith	

Assistant (Thai)	A. F. N. Thavenot	Miss F. C. M. Page-Turner
Assistants (Chinese News)	Wang Chang-su Chen Chung-sieu Su Cheng	
Assistant (Marathi)	Miss V. Chitale	
Assistant (Cantonese News)	Ma Yuen-Cheung	
Far East Editor	G. R. Tonkin	
Assistants (Japanese News)	F. Hawley Miss A. Suzuki	
Far East Programme Organizer	C. J. Morris	
Intelligence Officer	L. Brander	Mrs. H. M. Charnley
Assistant	R. B. Bonwit	Mrs. D. A. Christmas

A copy in the BBC Archives is annotated to show that 'E. A. Blair' had left and that C. J. Morris had replaced Rushbrook Williams; G. R. Tonkin (described as Indian News Editor) had replaced Darling.

The kind of staffing difficulties under which the section in general and Bokhari in particular laboured is suggested by a memorandum of 14 November 1941 from Mrs Joanna Spicer[4] of the Empire Executive to the Overseas Service Establishment Officer. Bokhari had outlined three requirements to enable programmes for India operated from London to be sustained:

1. Script writers, since the broadcasts are to include features and dramatic programmes.
2. Copyists for vernacular scripts. There are, of course, no vernacular typewriters and there seems to be no way of obtaining copies of scripts for all the actors in a feature or drama programme, except by making longhand copies and using multigraphing.
3. Mr. Bokhari explained that in the case of Bengali, and other Indian vernacular news letters, there are no Bengalis, etc. who are capable of writing the script. What happens is that the Indian Section writes the script which is translated and delivered by the Bengali, or other, voice. In the circumstances, Mr. Bokhari thinks that it is unsuitable to pay eight or ten guineas a week to this outside contributor and suggests instead that a weekly contract fee of about the same size could be paid to an individual for each of the three vernacular language news letters and that other duties could also be assigned to them.

Almost all Orwell's work for the Indian Section was in the production of new programmes, and this was so, in the main, of the work of his colleagues. However, much that was transmitted to India consisted of recordings of programmes originally heard on the BBC's United Kingdom and Overseas networks. Thus, the popular programme 'The Brains Trust,' originally broadcast in the Home Service, was regularly rebroadcast to India. The Eastern Service schedule for India varied considerably from day to day, and it developed and changed during the time Orwell was at the BBC. Although to offer a day's schedule as 'typical' would be misleading, this schedule, for 13 January 1942, chosen at random, can provide a sense of perspective. It includes only one programme for which Orwell was responsible: the Weekly News Review, read by Z. A. Bokhari. Times are Greenwich Mean Time.

10.45   London Calling
10.50   War Review by Captain Cyril Falls
11.00   News in English
11.15   Weekly News Review read by Z. A. Bokhari
11.30   Gramophone Records 'Songs of England': Commercial disc, Colum-
        bia DB 644   (March selection played by Band of the Grenadier
        Guards)
11.40   Commentary on the Derby
11.55   English Folk Songs and Dances: Commercial disc, Regal MR 3290
12.00   ENSA [Entertainments National Services Association] Overseas
        Half-Hour: 'London Carries On'
12.30   'For Gallantry' No. 8: Sergeant Flavell (Dramatised impressions of
        how British men and women have faced danger)
12.45   'Britain Sings'
13.00   News and News Commentary—Patrick Lacey
13.15   Listening Post No. 533—James Ferguson
13.20   Programme Parade
13.30   A. J. Powell and His Banjo Octet with Maisie Weldon [who gave
        impressions of Marie Lloyd, Evelyn Laye, Harry Weldon, Jessie
        Matthews, and Vera Lynn]
13.55   Wartime Sport—Barrington Dalby
14.00   Irish Half-Hour No. 4 (songs with band)
14.30   Talk by J. B. Priestley
14.45   Masters of the Keyboard: Liszt; played by Louis Kentner and
        presented by Scott Goddard
15.13   Closing Announcements and National Anthem
15.15   Close Down.

A study of all that is reproduced here cannot give a complete picture of what influenced Orwell at this time at the BBC. For example, many of Shridhar Telkar's scripts for the series 'The Debate Continues' and 'Behind the Headlines' are annotated by Orwell 'As b'cast.' What Telkar said would have been toned down to make it appropriate for its context; Telkar had strong views on British relations with India. To appreciate fully the influence of the BBC on Orwell such contacts and the circumstances in which he met those who broadcast must be taken into account. Indeed, Orwell's attitude to broadcasting, and to television in particular, predate this period.

Unless stated otherwise, all Orwell's broadcasts and all the arrangements he made were for the Eastern Service of the BBC.

When Sir Stafford Cripps led a mission to India in March and April 1942 to discuss proposals for Indian independence, he raised with the BBC and the Ministry of Information the alleged ineffectiveness of BBC propaganda as compared with broadcasts made to India by Germany. This prompted an immediate response by the BBC in a memorandum dated 16 March 1942; it is printed in W. J. West, *Orwell: The War Broadcasts* (1985, 33).[5] Among the Cripps Papers at Nuffield College[6] is a sheet dated 16 March 1942 showing the organization of the BBC's Indian Section together with a page of comments, some less than complimentary, on the staff.

[From the Cripps' Papers]
PRESENT SET-UP OF INDIAN BROADCASTING AT THE BBC

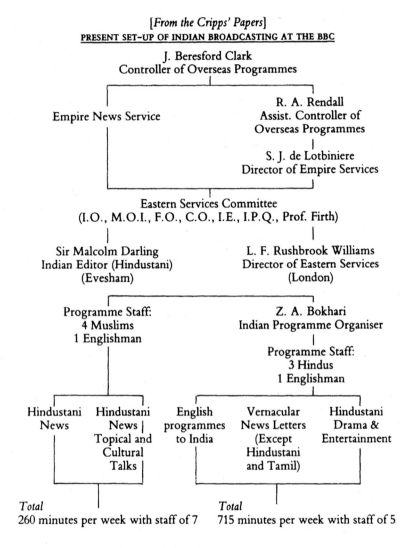

J. Beresford Clark
Controller of Overseas Programmes

Empire News Service

R. A. Rendall
Assist. Controller of
Overseas Programmes

S. J. de Lotbiniere
Director of Empire Services

Eastern Services Committee
(I.O., M.O.I., F.O., C.O., I.E., I.P.Q., Prof. Firth)

Sir Malcolm Darling
Indian Editor (Hindustani)
(Evesham)

L. F. Rushbrook Williams
Director of Eastern Services
(London)

Programme Staff:
4 Muslims
1 Englishman

Z. A. Bokhari
Indian Programme Organiser

Programme Staff:
3 Hindus
1 Englishman

Hindustani News | Hindustani News Topical and Cultural Talks | English programmes to India | Vernacular News Letters (Except Hindustani and Tamil) | Hindustani Drama & Entertainment

Total
260 minutes per week with staff of 7

Total
715 minutes per week with staff of 5

NOTES PREPARED FOR SIR STAFFORD CRIPPS

Sir Malcom° Darling and his staff work at Evesham.

Rushbrook Williams and his staff work in London.

No Indian language is known by Clark, Rendall, Lotbiniere or Rushbrook Williams.

Beresford Clark has been in various administrative positions in the BBC; has never done a programme; is suave, indecisive, conscientious, unimaginative.

Rendall has held administrative positions and is not a programme man: is youngish, well-meaning, discouraged, tired out by routine; never been to India and knows nothing about it.

de Lotbiniere—same as Rendall, but the most hopeful of the bunch.

Rushbrook Williams has spent his life in the service of Indian Princes. He now, apart from the BBC advises Foreign Office (2 days a week), Colonial Office (2 days a week), M.O.I. (2 days a week). Sails with the wind.

Malcolm Darling has had 35 years in India as Revenue Commissioner etc. Never done publicity before. Obstinate, unimaginative, limited and very patronising to Indians. A joke.

Z. A. Bokhari was for 10 years Examiner in Languages in Army Headquarters, India: Afterwards 5 years Station Director, All India Radio, Bombay and Delhi; 2½ years BBC. Excellent speaker and writer.

EXAMPLES. News in Hindustani given from Evesham is direct translation from BBC English bulletins. Result (a) unsuitable for Hindustani-speaking Indians (too understated, too detailed, too long); (b) anglicised, viz. given in a language which is often unattractive to Indians. "Talks" may include anything . . .

SUGGESTIONS. Very little purpose will be served (and no *quick* action achieved) by contacting the high-up machinery. The essential thing is direct contact between a fount of information and Bokhari, who is the one person in this country who combines ideas [of] broadcasting and linguistic ability, experience of the Indian public, and drive. He needs information and guidance. If someone will give him this—and comment on his ideas and proposals—he is perfectly capable of offsetting Axis propaganda. But it is highly desirable that he should control Hindustani talks.

1. Information provided by Bryan Matcham, Head, External Programme Operations, and from BBC Archives.
2. File R13/154/2A. Names and initials have been added here.
3. Miss Parratt's name is clearly typed 'Parrett' on this list, and when written in as Secretary to the Indian Assistant is also clearly spelt with an 'e.' However, when she signed documents, as she quite frequently did on Orwell's behalf, she used 'Parratt.' That spelling has, therefore, been adopted. Nancy H. Parratt (1919–) joined the BBC on 13 June 1941 and left on 15 March 1943 to join the Women's Royal Naval Service (WRNS). She served in the United States, married, and, in May 1946, was demobilized. Efforts to trace her have failed. She wrote to Orwell on 8 December 1949; see *3713*.
4. In the Staff List of 21.8.43, Mrs. Joanna Spicer is shown as Programme Planner for the General Overseas Service. See also *845, n. 5*.
5. This book is referred to hereafter as 'West: *Broadcasts*.' In Appendix C, West prints a very interesting 'Note on development of German broadcasts in Hindustani' and, dated 9 April 1942, a private and confidential memorandum from Rendall on 'Counter-propaganda on Indian themes' (289–93). The *Complete Works* and the text of West: *Commentaries* and West: *Broadcasts* differ considerably in substance and content (contrast, for example, Orwell's imaginary interview with Jonathan Swift, 2 November 1942), but, in the main, these differences are not noted. See also *846, n. 20*.
6. The documents at Nuffield College, Oxford, were found by Clive Fleay, who kindly drew them to the editor's attention. They are located among the Cripps Papers, Box 619–622, BBC File.

848. Film Review

Time and Tide, 23 August 1941

South of Suez; Warner

The opening shots of this film are brilliant photography and make one feel rather sorry that the story has to shift so soon from the African veldt to the mists of London. The plot turns, more or less, on an enormous diamond which is dug out of the clay in a mine where Miles Mander, as a remittance-man with a blackened past, and George Brent, as John Gamble, a tough American adventurer, are working in partnership. The remittance-man is murdered by a rival diamond-miner and John Gamble, falsely suspected of the murder (partly because hell hath no fury like a woman scorned, and he has scorned the wife of the real murderer), has to flee the country. He stows away on a British ship, and five years later turns up in London as a wealthy financier with a comic valet. He still has the famous diamond in his possession and intends to give it to the dead man's daughter, if he can find her. The daughter, meanwhile, has devoted herself to avenging her father and is employing private detectives to find John Gamble, the supposed murderer. The orphaned girl and the wrongly-suspected man meet, and it is hardly necessary to say that they fall in love. This in itself is complicated enough, but there is much more to come. First Gamble comes upon the body of a drowned man and decides to get rid of his identity once and for all by transferring certain papers to the dead man's pocket. He identifies the corpse as "John Gamble," and as a result is put on trial on a charge of murdering himself. In court his real identity is revealed, which is unfortunate, since he is still "wanted" for the original murder. However, he is saved by a highly dramatic incident which it would be unfair to reveal, and the film ends happily for everyone, except the valet, whose wife, from whom he had fled many years earlier, has discovered his whereabouts.

This is a slick and exciting film with no gaps in it. It is not "like real life", but then it is not meant to be. I thought that the best piece of acting in it was that of Eric Blore, as the comic valet, but George Tobias, as the crooked diamond dealer whose machinations are the start of all the trouble, also gave a clever and rather sinister performance.

849. War-time Diary

<u>28.8.41</u>: *I am now definitely an employee of the B.B.C.*
The line on the eastern front, in so far as there is a line, now runs roughly Tallinn, Gomel, Smolensk, Kiev, Dnepropetrovsk, Kherson. The Germans have occupied an area which must be larger than Germany, but have not destroyed the Russian Armies. The British and Russians invaded Iran 3 days ago and the Iranians have already packed up. No rumours that one can take hold of about movements of troops in this country. They have only about a

*month now in which to start something on the continent, and I don't believe
they intend anything of the kind. Beneath the terms of the Churchill-
Roosevelt declaration one can read that American anti-Hitler feeling has
cooled off as a result of the invasion of the U.S.S.R. On the other hand there
is no sign that willingness to endure sacrifices etc. in this country has
increased because of it. There are still popular complaints because we are not
doing enough to help the U.S.S.R. but their whole volume is tiny. I think the
Russian campaign can be taken as settled in the sense that Hitler cannot break
through to the Caucasus and the Middle East this winter, but that he is not
going to collapse and that he has inflicted more damage than he has received.
There is no victory in sight at present. We are in for a long, dreary,
exhausting war, with everyone growing poorer all the time. The new phase
which I foresaw earlier has now started, and the quasi-revolutionary period
which began with Dunkirk is finished. I therefore bring this diary to an end,
as I intended to do when the new phase started.*

This was the last entry in Orwell's War-time Diary until 14 March 1942.

850. 'The Art of Donald McGill'

Horizon, September 1941[1]

Who does not know the "comics" of the cheap stationers' windows, the
penny or twopenny coloured post cards with their endless succession of fat
women in tight bathing-dresses and their crude drawing and unbearable
colours, chiefly hedge-sparrow's egg tint and Post Office red?

This question ought to be rhetorical, but it is a curious fact that many
people seem to be unaware of the existence of these things, or else to have a
vague notion that they are something to be found only at the seaside, like
nigger[2] minstrels or peppermint rock. Actually they are on sale everywhere—they can be bought at nearly any Woolworth's, for example— and
they are evidently produced in enormous numbers, new series constantly
appearing. They are not to be confused with the various other types of comic
illustrated post card, such as the sentimental ones dealing with puppies and
kittens or the Wendyish, sub-pornographic ones which exploit the love-
affairs of children. They are a *genre* of their own, specialising in very "low"
humour, the mother-in-law, baby's nappy, policemen's boots type of joke,
and distinguishable from all the other kinds by having no artistic pretensions.
Some half-dozen publishing houses issue them, though the people who draw
them seem not to be numerous at any one time.

I have associated them especially with the name of Donald McGill because
he is not only the most prolific and by far the best of contemporary post card
artists, but also the most representative, the most perfect[3] in the tradition.
Who Donald McGill is, I do not know.[4] He is apparently a trade name, for at
least one series of post cards is issued simply as "The Donald McGill

Comics", but he is also unquestionably a real person with a style of drawing which is recognisable at a glance. Anyone who examines his post cards in bulk will notice that many of them are not despicable even as drawings, but it would be mere dilettantism to pretend that they have any direct æsthetic value. A comic post card is simply an illustration to a joke, invariably a "low" joke, and it stands or falls by its ability to raise a laugh. Beyond that it has only "ideological" interest. McGill is a clever draughtsman with a real caricaturist's touch in the drawing of faces, but the special value of his post cards is that they are so completely typical. They represent, as it were, the norm of the comic post card. Without being in the least imitative, they are exactly what comic post cards have been any time these last forty years, and from them the meaning and purpose of the whole *genre* can be inferred.

Get hold of a dozen of these things, preferably McGill's—if you pick out from a pile the ones that seem to you funniest, you will probably find that most of them are McGill's—and spread them out on a table. What do you see?

Your first impression is of overpowering vulgarity. This is quite apart from the ever-present obscenity, and apart also from the hideousness of the colours. They have an utter lowness of mental atmosphere which comes out not only in the nature of the jokes but, even more, in the grotesque, staring, blatant quality of the drawings. The designs, like those of a child, are full of heavy lines and empty spaces, and all the figures in them, every gesture and attitude, are deliberately ugly, the faces grinning and vacuous, the women monstrously parodied, with bottoms like Hottentots. Your second impression, however, is of indefinable familiarity. What do these things remind you of? What[5] are they so like? In the first place, of course, they remind you of the barely different post cards which you probably gazed at in your childhood. But more than this, what you are really looking at is something as traditional as Greek tragedy, a sort of sub-world of smacked bottoms and scrawny mothers-in-law which is a part of Western European consciousness. Not that the jokes, taken one by one, are necessarily stale. Not being debarred from smuttiness, comic post cards repeat themselves less often than the joke columns in reputable magazines, but their basic subject-matter, the *kind* of joke they are aiming at, never varies. A few are genuinely witty, in a Max Millerish style. Examples:

"I like seeing experienced girls home."
"But I'm not experienced!"
"You're not home yet!"

"I've been struggling for years to get a fur coat. How did you get yours?"
"I left off struggling."

JUDGE:"You are prevaricating, sir. Did you or did you not sleep with this woman?"
CO-RESPONDENT: "Not a wink, my lord!"

In general, however, they are not witty but humorous, and it must be said for McGill's post cards, in particular, that the drawing is often a good deal funnier than the joke beneath it. Obviously the outstanding characteristic of comic post cards is their obscenity, and I must discuss that more fully later. But I give here a rough analysis of their habitual subject-matter, with such explanatory remarks as seem to be needed:

Sex.—More than half, perhaps three-quarters, of the jokes are sex jokes, ranging from the harmless to the all but unprintable. First favourite is probably the illegitimate baby. Typical captions: "Could you exchange this lucky charm for a baby's feeding-bottle?" "She didn't ask me to the christening, so I'm not going to the wedding." Also newlyweds, old maids, nude statues and women in bathing-dresses. All of these are *ipso facto* funny, mere mention of them being enough to raise a laugh. The cuckoldry joke is very seldom exploited, and there are no references to homosexuality.
Conventions of the sex joke:
(i) Marriage only benefits the women. Every man is plotting seduction and every woman is plotting marriage. No woman ever remains unmarried voluntarily.
(ii) Sex-appeal vanishes at about the age of twenty-five. Well-preserved and good-looking people beyond their first youth are never represented. The amorous honeymooning couple reappear as the grim-visaged wife and shapeless, moustachioed, red-nosed husband, no intermediate stage being allowed for.

Home life.—Next to sex, the henpecked husband is the favourite joke. Typical caption: "Did they get an X-ray of your wife's jaw at the hospital?"—"No, they got a moving picture instead."
Conventions:
(i) There is no such thing as a happy marriage.
(ii) No man ever gets the better of a woman in argument.

Drunkenness.—Both drunkenness and teetotalism are *ipso facto* funny.
Conventions:
(i) All drunken men have optical illusions.
(ii) Drunkenness is something peculiar to middle-aged men. Drunken youths or women are never represented.

W.C. jokes.—There is not a large number of these. Chamberpots are *ipso facto* funny, and so are public lavatories. A typical post card, captioned "A Friend in Need", shows a man's hat blown off his head and disappearing down the steps of a ladies' lavatory.

Inter-working-class snobbery.—Much in these post cards suggests that they are aimed at the better-off working class and poorer middle class. There are many jokes turning on malapropisms, illiteracy, dropped aitches and the rough manners of slum-dwellers. Countless post cards show draggled hags of the stage-charwoman type exchanging "unladylike" abuse. Typical repartee: "I wish you were a statue and I was a pigeon!" A certain number produced since the war treat evacuation from the anti-evacuee angle. There are the usual jokes about tramps, beggars and criminals, and the comic maidservant appears fairly frequently. Also the comic navvy, bargee, etc.; but there are no anti Trade-Union[6] jokes. Broadly speaking, everyone with much over or much under £5 a week is regarded as laughable. The "swell" is almost as automatically a figure of fun as the slum-dweller.

Stock figures.—Foreigners seldom or never appear. The chief locality joke is the Scotsman, who is almost inexhaustible. The lawyer is always a swindler, the clergyman always a nervous idiot who says the wrong thing. The "knut" or "masher" still appears, almost as in Edwardian days, in out-of-date-looking evening-clothes and an opera hat, or even with spats and a knobby cane. Another survival is the Suffragette, one of the big jokes of the pre-1914 period and too valuable to be relinquished. She has reappeared, unchanged in physical appearance, as the Feminist lecturer or Temperance fanatic. A feature of the last few years is the complete absence of anti-Jew post cards. The "Jew joke", always somewhat more ill-natured than the "Scotch joke", disappeared abruptly soon after the rise of Hitler.

Politics.—Any contemporary event, cult or activity which has comic possibilities (for example, "free love", feminism, A.R.P.,[7] nudism) rapidly finds it way into the picture post cards, but their general atmosphere is extremely old-fashioned. The implied political outlook is a Radicalism appropriate to about the year 1900. At normal times they are not only not patriotic, but go in for a mild guying of patriotism, with jokes about "God save the King", the Union Jack, etc. The European situation only began to reflect itself in them at some time in 1939, and first did so through the comic aspects of A.R.P. Even at this date few post cards mention the war except in A.R.P. jokes (fat woman stuck in the mouth of Anderson shelter,[8] Wardens neglecting their duty while young woman undresses at window she has forgotten to black out, etc. etc.). A few express anti-Hitler sentiments of a not very vindictive kind. One, not McGill's, shows Hitler, with the usual hypertrophied backside, bending down to pick a flower. Caption: "What would *you* do, chums?" This is about as high a flight of patriotism as any post card is likely to attain. Unlike the twopenny weekly papers, comic post cards are not the product of any great monopoly company, and eventually they are not regarded as having any importance in forming public opinion. There is no sign in them of any attempt to induce an outlook acceptable to the ruling class.

Here one comes back to the outstanding, all-important feature of comic post cards—their obscenity. It is by this that everyone remembers them, and it is also central to their purpose, though not in a way that is immediately obvious.

A recurrent, almost dominant motif in comic post cards is the woman with the stuck-out behind. In perhaps half of them, or more than half, even when the point of the joke has nothing to do with sex, the same female figure appears, a plump "voluptuous" figure with the dress clinging to it as tightly as another skin and with breasts or buttocks grossly over-emphasised, according to which way it is turned. There can be no doubt that these pictures lift the lid off a very widespread repression, natural enough in a country whose women when young tend to be slim to the point of skimpiness. But at the same time the McGill post card—and this applies to all other post cards in this *genre*—is not intended as pornography but, a subtler thing, as a skit on pornography. The Hottentot figures of the women are caricatures of the Englishman's secret ideal, not portraits of it. When one examines McGill's post cards more closely, one notices that his brand of humour only has meaning in relation to a fairly strict moral code. Whereas in papers like *Esquire*, for instance, or *La Vie Parisienne*, the imaginary background of the jokes is always promiscuity, the utter breakdown of all standards, the background of the McGill post card is marriage. The four leading jokes are nakedness, illegitimate babies, old maids and newly married couples, none of which would seem funny in a really dissolute or even "sophisticated" society. The post cards dealing with honeymoon couples always have the enthusiastic indecency of those village weddings where it is still considered screamingly funny to sew bells to the bridal bed. In one, for example, a young bridegroom is shown getting out of bed the morning after his wedding night. "The first morning in our own little home, darling!" he is saying; "I'll go and get the milk and paper and bring you up a cup of tea." Inset is a picture of the front doorstep; on it are four newspapers and four bottles of milk. This is obscene, if you like, but it is not immoral. Its implication—and this is just the implication [that] *Esquire* or the *New Yorker* would avoid at all costs—is that marriage is something profoundly exciting and important, the biggest event in the average human being's life. So also with jokes about nagging wives and tyrannous mothers-in-law. They do at least imply a stable society in which marriage is indissoluble and family loyalty taken for granted. And bound up with this is something I noted earlier, the fact that there are no pictures, or hardly any, of good-looking people beyond their first youth. There is the "spooning" couple and the middle-aged, cat-and-dog couple, but nothing in between. The liaison, the illicit but more or less decorous love-affair which used to be the stock joke of French comic papers, is not a post card subject. And this reflects, on a comic level, the working-class outlook which takes it as a matter of course that youth and adventure—almost, indeed, individual life—end with marriage. One of the few authentic class-differences, as opposed to class-distinctions, still existing in England is that the working classes age very much earlier. They do not live less long, provided that they survive their childhood, nor do they lose their physical activity earlier, but they do lose very early their youthful appearance. This fact is observable everywhere, but can be most easily verified by watching one of the higher age groups registering for military service; the middle- and upper-class members look, on average, ten years younger than the others. It is usual to attribute this to the harder lives that the working classes have to live, but it is doubtful whether any such difference now exists as would account for it. More probably the truth is that the working classes reach middle age earlier because they accept it earlier. For to look young after, say, thirty is largely a matter of wanting to do so. This generalisation is less true of the better-paid workers, especially those who live in council houses and labour-saving flats, but it is true enough even of them to point to a difference of outlook. And in this, as usual, they are more traditional, more in accord with the Christian past than the well-to-do women who try to stay young at forty by means of physical jerks, cosmetics and avoidance of child-bearing. The impulse to cling to youth at all costs, to attempt to preserve your sexual attraction, to see even in middle age a future for yourself and not merely for your children, is a thing of recent growth and has only precariously established itself. It will probably disappear again when our standard of living drops and our birth-rate rises. "Youth's a stuff will not endure" expresses the normal, traditional attitude. It is this ancient wisdom that McGill and his colleagues are reflecting, no doubt unconsciously, when they allow for no transition stage between the honeymoon couple and those glamourless figures, Mum and Dad.

I have said that at least half McGill's post cards are sex jokes, and a proportion, perhaps ten per cent., are far more obscene than anything else that is now printed in England. Newsagents are occasionally prosecuted for selling them, and there would be many more prosecutions if the broadest jokes were not invariably protected by double meanings. A single example will be enough to show how this is done. In one post card, captioned "They didn't believe her", a young woman is demonstrating, with her hands held apart, something about two feet long to a couple of open-mouthed acquaintances. Behind her on the wall is a stuffed fish in a glass case, and beside that is a photograph of a nearly naked athlete. Obviously it is not the fish that she is referring to, but this could never be proved. Now, it is doubtful whether there is any paper in England that would print a joke of this kind, and certainly there is no paper that does so habitually. There is an immense amount of pornography of a mild sort, countless illustrated papers cashing in on women's legs, but there is no popular literature specialising in the "vulgar", farcical aspect of sex. On the other hand, jokes exactly like McGill's are the ordinary small change of the revue and music-hall stage, and are also to be heard on the radio, at moments when the censor happens to be nodding. In England the gap between what can be said and what can be printed is rather exceptionally wide. Remarks and gestures which hardly anyone objects to on the stage would raise a public outcry if any attempt were made to reproduce them on paper. (Compare Max Miller's stage patter with his weekly column in the *Sunday Dispatch*.) The comic post cards are the only existing exception to this rule, the only medium in which really "low" humour is considered to be printable. Only in post cards and on the variety stage can the stuck-out behind, dog and lamp-post, baby's nappy type of joke be freely exploited. Remembering that, one sees what function these post cards, in their humble way, are performing.

What they are doing is to give expression to the Sancho Panza view of life, the attitude to life that Miss Rebecca West once summed up as "extracting as much fun as possible from smacking behinds in basement kitchens". The Don Quixote–Sancho Panza combination, which of course is simply the ancient dualism of body and soul in fiction form, recurs more frequently in the literature of the last four hundred years than can be explained by mere imitation. It comes up again and again, in endless variations, Bouvard and

Pécuchet, Jeeves and Wooster, Bloom and Dedalus, Holmes and Watson (the Holmes-Watson variant is an exceptionally subtle one, because the usual physical characteristics of two[9] partners have been transposed). Evidently it corresponds to something enduring in our civilisation, not in the sense that either character is to be found in a "pure" state in real life, but in the sense that the two principles, noble folly and base wisdom, exist side by side in nearly every human being. If you look into your own mind, which are you, Don Quixote or Sancho Panza? Almost certainly you are both. There is one part of you that wishes to be a hero or a saint, but another part of you is a little fat man who sees very clearly the advantages of staying alive with a whole skin. He is your unofficial self, the voice of the belly protesting against the soul. His tastes lie towards safety, soft beds, no work, pots of beer and women with "voluptuous" figures. He it is who punctures your fine attitudes and urges you to look after Number One, to be unfaithful to your wife, to bilk your debts, and so on and so forth. Whether you allow yourself to be influenced by him is a different question. But it is simply a lie to say that he is not part of you, just as it is a lie to say that Don Quixote is not part of you either, though most of what is said and written consists of one lie or the other, usually the first.

But though in varying forms he is one of the stock figures of literature, in real life, especially in the way society is ordered, his point of view never gets a fair hearing. There is a constant world-wide conspiracy to pretend that he is not there, or at least that he doesn't matter. Codes of law and morals, or religious systems, never have much room in them for a humorous view of life. Whatever is funny is subversive, every joke is ultimately a custard pie, and the reason why so large a proportion of jokes centre round obscenity is simply that all societies, as the price of survival, have to insist on a fairly high standard of sexual morality. A dirty joke is not, of course, a serious attack upon morality, but it is a sort of mental rebellion, a momentary wish that things were otherwise. So also with all other jokes, which always centre round cowardice, laziness, dishonesty or some other quality which society cannot afford to encourage. Society has always[10] to demand a little more from human beings than it will get in practice. It has to demand faultless discipline and self-sacrifice, it must expect its subjects to work hard, pay their taxes, and be faithful to their wives, it must assume that men think it glorious to die on the battlefield and women want to wear themselves out with child-bearing. The whole of what one may call official literature is founded on such assumptions. I never read the proclamations of generals before battle, the speeches of führers and prime ministers, the solidarity songs of public schools and Left Wing political parties, national anthems, Temperance tracts, papal encyclicals and sermons against gambling and contraception, without seeming to hear in the background a chorus of raspberries from all the millions of common men to whom these high sentiments make no appeal. Nevertheless the high sentiments always win in the end, leaders who offer blood, toil, tears and sweat[11] always get more out of their followers than those who offer safety and a good time. When it comes to the pinch, human beings are heroic. Women face childbed and the scrubbing brush, revolutionaries keep their mouths shut in the torture chamber, battleships go down with their guns still firing when their decks are awash. It is only that the other element in man, the lazy, cowardly, debt-bilking adulterer who is inside all of us, can never be suppressed altogether and needs a hearing occasionally.

The comic post cards are one expression of his point of view, a humble one, less important than the music halls, but still worthy of attention. In a society which is still basically Christian they naturally concentrate on sex jokes; in a totalitarian society, if they had any freedom of expression at all, they would probably concentrate on laziness or cowardice, but at any rate on the unheroic in one form or another. It will not do to condemn them on the ground that they are vulgar and ugly. That is exactly what they are meant to be. Their whole meaning and virtue is in their unredeemed lowness, not only in the sense of obscenity, but lowness of outlook in every direction whatever. The slightest hint of "higher" influences would ruin them utterly. They stand for the worm's-eye view of life, for the music-hall world where marriage is a dirty joke or a comic disaster, where the rent is always behind and the clothes are always up the spout,[12] where the lawyer is always a crook and the Scotsman always a miser, where the newlyweds make fools of themselves on the hideous beds of seaside lodging-houses and the drunken, red-nosed husbands roll home at four in the morning to meet the linen-nightgowned wives who wait for them behind the front door, poker in hand. Their existence, the fact that people want them, is symptomatically important. Like the music halls, they are a sort of saturnalia, a harmless rebellion against virtue. They express only one tendency in the human mind, but a tendency which is always there and will find its own outlet, like water. On the whole, human beings want to be good, but not too good, and not quite all the time. For:

> "there is a just man that perishes in his righteousness, and there is a wicked man that prolongeth his life in his wickedness. Be not righteous over much; neither make thyself over wise; why shouldst thou destroy thyself? Be not overmuch wicked, neither be thou foolish: why shouldst thou die before thy time?"[13]

In the past the mood of the comic post card could enter into the central stream of literature, and jokes barely different from McGill's could casually be[14] uttered between the murders in Shakespeare's tragedies. That is no longer possible, and a whole category of humour, integral to our literature till 1800 or thereabouts, has dwindled down to these ill-drawn post cards, leading a barely legal existence in cheap stationers' windows. The corner of the human heart that they speak for might easily manifest itself in worse forms, and I for one should be sorry to see them vanish.

1. The version given here is that reprinted in *Critical Essays*, second impression (May 1946). The first impression was published in February 1946. This contained a few verbal changes and a number of styling alterations from the version in *Horizon*. Significant variants are listed in the notes below. The consistency in changing word order suggests that the changes are intentional and are probably authorial. The version in the U.S. edition of *Dickens, Dali &*

Others (1946) is almost identical with that in *Critical Essays*. Changes are listed below, identified by *DD&O*. It is fairly evident that a proof or printed text of the version in *Critical Essays* was used to set *DD&O*. The only significant verbal change ('nigger' to 'Negro') was clearly to suit U.S. convention; 'nigger' in its context here was not then as contemptuous in England as it has now become. Typographic devices (such as the long dash after the sub-headings), word division (for example, 'post card' instead of *Horizon*'s one word), one hyphenation in contradistinction to *Horizon*, and the erroneous hyphenation of 'honey-moon,' following end-line hyphenation in *Critical Essays*, all point to the latter providing copy for *DD&O*. This text was reprinted in *A Writer's Reader: Models and Materials for the Essay*, by Philip Webster Souers, John C. Sherwood, and Irma Z. Sherwood (New York, 1950), 124–34. For its specialised readership, paragraphs were numbered and four questions and an assignment topic were set after Orwell's essay. This text (indicated below by *WR*) omits Max Miller's three jokes. Max Miller (1895–1963), one of music hall's great comics, was billed as 'The Cheekie Chappie.' His act underlies Archie Rice's in Osborne's *The Entertainer*. See Orwell's review of *Applesauce, 684*. *Horizon* reproduced two of McGill's cards, but these have not been reprinted since. In one, a soap-box orator advocating temperance is concluding his oration with 'Now I have just one tract left. What shall I do with it?' A wife is depicted with her hand over a fat man's mouth, stopping his answering, and the caption is: 'Don't say it George!' In the other, a vastly overweight man who might be a bookie, accompanied by a shapely young lady, is seen telling a hotel receptionist, 'I and my daughter would like adjoining bedrooms!' A shortened version of the essay was published in *Strand Magazine*, August 1943, see *851*, and a Polish version in *Kultura* (Paris), January 1950.

2. nigger] Negro   *DD&O, WR*
3. perfect] perfectly   *Horizon*
4. Donald McGill (1875–1962) *was* a real person; compare Orwell's doubts about the existence of a Frank Richards in his essay 'Boys' Weeklies.' He began his career in 1904 when he sketched a drawing on the back of a postcard to cheer up a nephew in hospital. By December 1905, *Picture Postcard Magazine* 'picked him out as a designer whose cards would become "widely popular." ' One card, no. 1772, designed in 1916, sold over three million copies It was not of the kind described by Orwell, but showed a little girl in a nightdress at which a puppy was tugging; the caption read: 'Please, Lord, excuse me a minute while I kick Fido!!' He fairly claimed that his cards were not obscene but depicted situations with honest vulgarity, and he was depressed by the way his art-form was allowed to degenerate. See Tonie and Valmai Holt, *Picture Postcards of the Golden Age* (1971), 91–93, Arthur Calder Marshall, *Wish You Were Here* (1966). Orwell, in commenting that McGill was 'a clever draughtsman' could not have known that, from 1897 to 1907, McGill worked as an engineering draughtsman.
5. of? What] of, what   *Horizon*
6. anti Trade-Union] anti-Trade Union   *Horizon*; anti trade union   *DD&O, WR*
7. Air Raid Precautions.
8. An air-raid shelter built in the gardens of individual houses, capable of holding four to six people in modest discomfort. It was designed by Sir William Paterson (1874–1956) at the instigation of Sir John Anderson (see *567, 31.8.39, n. 2*) in 1938. More than three million Andersons were built, and they are credited with saving many lives. A few have survived as makeshift garden sheds.
9. two] the two   *Horizon*
10. has always] always has   *Horizon*
11. Winston Churchill, in addressing the House of Commons, 13 May 1940, said. 'I would say to the House, as I said to those who have joined this Government, "I have nothing to offer but blood, toil, tears, and sweat" ' (*The Second World War*, II, 24; U.S.: *Their Finest Hour*, 25).
12. up the spout] in pawn
13. Ecclesiastes VII: 15–17. The Authorised Version (King James Version) differs slightly: perishes] perisheth; shouldst] shouldest (*twice*); overmuch wicked] over much wicked
14. casually be] be casually   *Horizon*

851. 'Those Seaside Postcards'

Strand Magazine, August 1943

This is a shortened version of 'The Art of Donald McGill' (see *850*), published with the sub-title 'This writer sees virtue in their classic vulgarity.' It is not only shortened but also mildly censored by an oddly squeamish sub-editor (see below). The longest cut is almost four pages of the original, from 'And bound up with this is something I noted earlier . . .' in the second paragraph after '*Politics*' to 'but at any rate on the unheroic in one form or another' in the penultimate paragraph. The quotation from Ecclesiastes was also omitted. Shorter cuts and changes, concentrated in the earlier part, contrast strangely with the nature and tone of the article. Thus, breasts, buttocks, and bottoms are either omitted or replaced by such words as 'figures' or 'behinds.' It is not known whether Orwell was advised in advance that such alterations would be made. One change is of a different order. The phrase 'anti-Jew postcards' was altered to 'anti-Jewish postcards,' the former description being thoughtlessly as well as pejoratively current when Orwell wrote the original article. Orwell received a fee of £8.8s for the version printed in *Strand Magazine*.

The changes recorded below do not include minor variants, nor is the shortening of paragraphs noted. Readings from 'The Art of Donald McGill,' as printed in *Critical Essays*, are given first unless stated otherwise. *SM* = *Strand Magazine*.

they can be bought at nearly any Woolworth's, for example] or were before the war

new series constantly appearing] In an ordinary holiday year millions were sold in Blackpool alone

or the Wendyish, sub-pornographic ones] sub-pornographic *omitted*

Some half-dozen publishing houses issue them, though the people who draw them seem not to be numerous at any one time] *omitted*

I have associated them especially with the name of Donald McGill because he is not only the most prolific] The most prolific

artists, but] artists is Donald McGill. He is

Beyond that it has only "ideological" interest.] *omitted*

This is quite apart from the ever-present obscenity, and apart also from the hideousness of the colours.] *omitted*

bottoms like Hottentots.] figures like Hottentots

sub-world of smacked bottoms] sub-world of smacked behinds

SM *omits the second and third Max Millerish jokes* ('I've been struggling . . .' and 'Judge: "You are prevaricating . . ." ')

beneath] underneath

Obviously the outstanding characteristic of comic post cards is their obscenity . . . as seem to be needed:] *omitted*

SM *omits the sub-headings* Sex, Home life, Drunkenness, W.C. jokes, Inter-working-class snobbery, Stock figures, *and* Politics. *The first sentence of* Stock figures *is changed in SM to read*, 'Among the stock figures, foreigners seldom or never appear.'

The cuckoldry joke is very seldom exploited, and there are no references to homosexuality.] *omitted*

The amorous honeymooning couple . . . no intermediate stage being allowed for.] *omitted*

W.C. jokes.—There is not . . . Chamberpots . . . public lavatories . . . ladies' lavatory.] *omitted*

The implied political outlook is a Radicalism appropriate to about the year 1900.] *omitted*

jokes about "God save the King", the Union Jack] jokes about the Union Jack

Hitler, with the usual hypertrophied backside] Hitler

There is no sign in them of any attempt to induce an outlook acceptable to the ruling class.] *omitted*

Here one comes back to . . . obscenity . . . immediately obvious.] *omitted*
plump "voluptuous" figure with the dress clinging to it as tightly as another skin and with
  breasts or buttocks grossly over-emphasised, according to which way it is turned] plump
  "voluptuous" figure. *This cut contrasts, ironically, with a passage to which the editor of SM
  sniggeringly draws attention in the very next article, 'Spies!' by Parke Cummings: 'The female
  spy's costume consists of a skirt that fits tightly over the torso, and a blouse even more so.
  [Hey, this is not poets' corner! — EDITOR.]'
But at the same time] At the same time
Whereas in papers like *Esquire* . . *La Vie Parisienne* . . . the background of the McGill post card
  is marriage.] *omitted*
those village weddings where it is still considered screamingly funny to sew bells to the bridal
  bed . . . "The first morning in our own little home ". . . four newspapers and four bottles of
  milk.] *omitted*
and this is just the implication [that] *Esquire* or the *New Yorker* would avoid at all costs] *omitted*
And bound up with this is something I noted earlier. . . on the unheroic in one form or another]
  some four pages of the original omitted
Their whole meaning . . . unredeemed lowness . . . obscenity . . ruin them utterly.] *omitted*
marriage is a dirty joke or a comic disaster] marriage is a comic disaster
the newlyweds make fools of themselves on the hideous beds of seaside lodging-houses] *omitted*
For· 'there is a just man that perishes . . . die before thy time?] *omitted*

852. Review of *The Forge* by Arturo Barea; translated and with an introduction by Sir Peter Chalmers Mitchell

Horizon, September 1941[1]

If some Russian writer were at this moment to produce a book of reminiscences of his childhood in 1900, it would be difficult to review it without mentioning the fact that Soviet Russia is now our ally against Germany, and in the same way it is impossible to read *The Forge* without thinking at almost every page of the Spanish Civil War. In fact there is no direct connection, for the book deals only with Señor Barea's early youth and ends in 1914. But the civil war made a deep and painful impression on the English intelligentsia, deeper, I should say, than has yet been made by the war now raging. The man in the street, misled by frivolous newspapers, ignored the whole business, the rich mechanically sided with the enemies of the working class, but to all thinking and decent people the war was a terrible tragedy that has made the word 'Spain' inseparable from the thought of burnt bodies and starving children. One seems to hear the thunder of future battles somewhere behind Señor Barea's pages, and it is as a sort of prologue to the civil war, a picture of the society that made it possible, that his book is most likely to be valued.

He was born into a very poor family, the son actually of a washerwoman, but with uncles and aunts who were slightly richer than his mother. In Catholic countries the clever boy of a peasant family finds his easiest escape from manual labour in the priesthood, but Señor Barea, who had anticlerical relatives and was an early unbeliever himself, after winning a scholarship at a Church school, went to work at thirteen in a draper's shop, and afterwards in a bank. All his good memories are of country places, especially of the forge

33

belonging to his uncle in Mentrida, a magnificent independent peasant of the type now extinct in the industrialized countries. On the other hand his memories of Madrid are low and squalid, a tale of poverty and overwork far more extreme than anything to be found in England. And here, perhaps, in his descriptions of the Madrid slums, of hordes of naked children with their heads full of lice and lecherous priests playing cards for the contents of the poor-boxes, he gives half-consciously the clue to the Spanish Civil War: it is that Spain is a country too poor to have ever known the meaning of decent government. In England we could not have a civil war, not because tyranny and injustice do not exist, but because they are not obvious enough to stir the common people to action. Everything is toned down, padded, as it were, by ancient habits of compromise, by representative institutions, by liberal aristocrats and incorruptible officials, by a 'superstructure' that has existed so long that it is only partly a sham. There are no half-tones in the Spain that Señor Barea is describing. Everything is happening in the open, in the ferocious Spanish sunlight. It is the straightforward corruption of a primitive country, where the capitalist is openly a sweater, the official always a crook, the priest an ignorant bigot or a comic rascal, the brothel a necessary pillar of society. The nature of all problems is obvious, even to a boy of fifteen. Sex, for example:

'My cousin is taking advantage of my being a boy. But she is right. She would be a whore if she were to go to bed with anyone. . . . I'd like to go to bed with the girls, and they would like to come with me, but it is impossible. Men have whores for that; women have to wait until the priest marries them, or they become whores themselves. And, naturally, meantime they get excited. Those who get too excited have to become whores.'

Or politics:

'They were always fighting in Parliament, Maura, Pablo Iglesias, and Lerroux, and they painted on the walls slogans such as "Down with Maura". Sometimes they would write in red, "Maura, up!" The workers were those who wrote "Down with Maura!" Those who wrote "up" were the gentry. . . . At nightfall, when Alcala Street is crowded, a group of young gentlemen will appear shouting "Maura, up!" Then a group of workers and students is formed at once, and begins to shout "Maura, down!" . . . The civil guards charge, but they never attack the gentry.'

When I read that last phrase, 'the civil guards never attack the gentry', there came back to me a memory which is perhaps out of place in a review, but which illustrates the difference of social atmosphere in a country like England and a country like Spain. I am six years old, and I am walking along a street in our little town with my mother and a wealthy local brewer, who is also a magistrate. The tarred fence is covered with chalk drawings, some of which I have made myself. The magistrate stops, points disapprovingly with his stick and says, 'We are going to catch the boys who draw on these walls, and we are going to order them Six Strokes of the Birch Rod'. (It was all in capitals in my mind.) My knees knock together, my tongue cleaves to the roof of my mouth, and at the earliest possible moment I sneak away to spread the dreadful intelligence. In a little while, all the way down the fence, there is a long line of terror-stricken children, all spitting on their handkerchiefs and trying to rub out the drawings. But the interesting thing is that not till many years later, perhaps twenty years, did it occur to me that my fears had been groundless. No magistrate would have condemned me to Six Strokes of the Birch Rod, even if I had been caught drawing on the wall. Such punishments were reserved for the Lower Orders. The Civil Guards charge, but they never attack the gentry. In England it was and still is possible to be unaware of this, but not in the Spain that Señor Barea writes of. There, injustice was unmistakable, politics was a struggle between black and white, every extremist doctrine from Carlism to Anarchism could be held with lunatic clarity. 'Class war' was not merely a phrase, as it has come to be in the Western democracies. But which state of affairs is better is a different question.

This is not primarily a political book, however. It is a fragment of autobiography, and we may hope that others will follow it, for Senor Barea has had a varied and adventurous life. He has travelled widely, he has been both worker and capitalist, he took part in the civil war and he served in the Riff War under General Franco. If the Fascist powers have done no other good, they have at least enriched the English-speaking world by exiling all their best writers. Sir Peter Chalmers Mitchell's translation is vivid and colloquial, but it was a pity to stick all the way through to the 'dramatic present', which seems all right in a Latin language but rapidly becomes tiresome in English.

1. Orwell also reviewed this book in *Time and Tide*, 28 June 1941; see *821*.

853. To Leonard Moore

13 September 1941   Typewritten

111 Langford Court   Abbey Road   London   NW 8

Dear Mr Moore,
I should be obliged if you could put through the enclosed bit of business for me. No doubt we ought to make them pay something, but I should very much like the essay to be in their anthology[1] and it doesn't seem worth haggling over the price. I have told them that they can print it but that I am turning the matter over to you. Perhaps you will accept any reasonable offer. I don't know whether we have to obtain permission from "New Writing" to reprint.

Do you remember a few years back some people in Rangoon asking permission to translate "Burmese Days" into Burmese? Do you happen to know if anything ever came of it?[2] I ask because, as you perhaps know, I am now working in the BBC, and if I ever have to broadcast in English to Burma it might be useful to mention this book, if it was actually translated.

Yours sincerely
Eric A. Blair

1. John Lehmann published 'Shooting an Elephant,' 'Marrakech,' and 'My Country Right or Left' in *New Writing* and *Folios of New Writing* in 1936, 1939, and 1940 respectively. The first was reprinted in *Penguin New Writing* in 1940. Lehmann also anthologised the first and third of these essays, in 1951 and 1952, and 'Marrakech' appeared, with 'Such, Such Were the Joys,' in 1953. What was proposed here is not known.
2. Nothing came of the suggestion; see letter to Moore, 28 June 1938, *458*.

854. Nicholas Moore vs. George Orwell

Partisan Review, January–February 1942

Orwell's London Letter of 15 April 1941 caused the poet Nicholas Moore (1918–1986), editor of the poetry magazine *Seven* (summer 1938–spring 1940) and assistant to Tambimuttu[1] on *Poetry (London)* in the 1940s, to write on 25 August 1941 to the editors of *Partisan Review*. Orwell replied to his letter on 23 September 1941, and both letters were published (Moore's heavily cut) in the January-February issue of *Partisan Review* under the heading 'Nicholas Moore vs. George Orwell.' Moore's letter is given in full below; the passages omitted by *Partisan Review* are in square brackets. One or two oversights in the typing have been corrected silently and titles of journals italicised. The original of Orwell's letter has not been traced. See also *1719* for Moore's letter to *Tribune* in response to Orwell's article 'The End of Henry Miller,' and Orwell's War-time Diary, *1195, 30.5.42,*, where he has pasted in a poem by Moore.

Cambridge, England
August 25, 1941

Dear Sirs,

Apropos of your questionnaire and *Horizon*'s questionnaire and the answer thereto. Firstly I'd like to say that I think the politics of your paper are far superior to *Horizon*'s, and that that undoubtedly accounts in part, as you suggest, for the fact that your articles come out better than *Horizon*'s and your stories and poems less well. The obviously amateurish politics of *Horizon* can scarcely appeal to any of the intellectuals who read it for its literature; for, apart from the fact that no doubt its politics as such are not those of its readers, the political articles compare very poorly in intelligence to those in the *P.R.* [Whether or not the corrollary, that *Horizon*'s stories and poems are better than yours I cannot say, as I'm afraid I haven't seen many copies of *P.R.* recently. But *Horizon*'s being what they are, I should think it unlikely. The standard of both as far as stories are concerned seems high, probably yours the higher. The poetry in both seems not high enough, but perhaps *Horizon* gains by printing more. (But as I say I haven't seen many recent *P.R.*s—I shall remedy that in the future.)]

This letter arises from your July–August issue, which I obtained through *Horizon*, and from the fact that I'm interested in (a) literature (especially poetry) and (b) politics (especially your kind: the partisan nature of your review gives it a value that *Horizon* cannot have.) Considering the partisan nature of your politics I was very surprised to see that you had a London Letter from George Orwell, an omnivorous and omniscient writer whom I greatly suspect. No doubt he writes well. He is extremely plausible, but are not his politics as much at variance with yours as are *Horizon*'s? [The fact that *Horizon* is your counterpart in this country is perhaps symptomatic, and it seems to me that Orwell is nearer politically to them than to you.] The impression that he gives in his London Letter is (though much better expressed) much the impression given by a sequence of *Horizon* editorials. [His description of affairs in this country is indeed very plausible, and perhaps the general impression is true, but he seems to me to be a most glib and superficial writer.] He moves among *Tribune* circles, and the literary left, and you must know how irresponsible that literary left is: that had a pseudo-proletarian admiration for Moscow and social-realism, when it suited it, and, equally under pressure of war lined itself up with Churchill. What I am getting at is, frankly I don't think Orwell is in a position to know what serious writing is being done in this country at the moment: because the literary circle of which he is aware is the circle which grinds out highbrow pseudo-proletarian "kitsch". Once it was communist. Now it is bourgeois pro-Churchill leftist. Nor does Orwell know very much about poetry, or, if he does, show any signs of it. In actual fact there is something of a poetic[2] revival going on: admittedly subjective, (if you like romantic), but not particularly escapist. Its organ, if any, is POETRY (London): its forerunners Dylan Thomas and George Barker. (That is not to say, of course, that it is derivitive in technique or style, for them: but merely that its enthusiasm is). [As for its politics] I would deny utterly Orwell's statement that "a belief in the unity of European civilization, and in international working-class solidarity" doesn't exist any longer. In the particularly Leftist group whose parties Orwell frequents, Fascism has killed it. That particular group happens to have a monopoly of the progressive literary press. *New writing*[3] comes out in sixpenny penguins° and sells like hot cakes. (Hot kitsch fresh from the fake-proletarian oven). *Horizon* is the only extant (subsidized) purveyor of good writing. Politically it again reflects the defeatism of social-democracy and ex-communists. It probably shares Orwell's belief that "to be effectively anti-war in England now one has to be pro-Hitler". Are *P.R.* readers really expected to accept that?

[A further lack of acumen on Orwell's part which is unworthy of *P.R.* political standards, is given away in such chance phrases as that suggesting that "Stalin (is) evidently preparing to go into close partnership with Hitler" (presumably caught by all the baits of the so-called-left government press at the time), and his fear of commenting on the Hess episode. And with regard to the three by-election candidates in Birmingham, what Orwell calls the "Bomb Berlin" candidate, was a man who is an authority on aeroplanes, who was careful to disown that title (given again by the press!), whose platform was a cry for a more intensive preparation for air-war. (A programme now being carried out to some extent by the government.) Such small inaccuracies are, in fact, indicative of quite a lot.

The situation has, of course, changed with the German attack on Russia, in such a way as Orwell least of all could foresee. The papers are full of pro-Russian propaganda, even from those who made a hulla-balloo over Finland: they now praise where they condemned. The Communists support the government in its trip to Russia, and campaign for getting back their daily paper. (No success in that yet: all the other papers print Russian news now!). Superficially this looks very nice. Actually the new supporters of socialism are not likely to understand what it means. Marx takes a back-place in the war-effort, though I suppose the Soviet government's appeals to the German people have some effect on the public here as a contrast to Vansittart's Black Record.[4]]

I hope the *P.R.* continues to provide what America needs and what we here don't get. In my part of the world officers are still saluted in the street (pace George Orwell) and the big cafes have plenty of good food. For food for thought I think I shall have to rely on *P.R.*, *Horizon* being a wet-blanket politically. I think you will be surprised in the "serious writing" that will arise from this England in this war.

Yours sincerely
Nicholas Moore

London, England
September 23, 1941

Sirs:

When I said that the belief in international working class solidarity doesn't exist any longer, I was not thinking of what may or may not be said at the "parties" which Mr. Moore supposes I frequent. I was thinking of the history of Europe during the past ten years and the utter failure of the European working class to stand together in the face of Fascist aggression. The Spanish civil war went on for two and a half years, and during that time there was not one country in which the workers staged even a single strike in aid of their Spanish comrades. So far as I can get at the figures the British working class subscribed to various "aid Spain" funds about one per cent of what they spent during the same period in betting on football and horse-races. Anyone who actually talked to working men at the time knows that it was virtually impossible to get them to see that what happened in Spain concerned them in any way. Ditto with Austria, Manchuria, etc. During the past three months Germany has been at war with Russia and at the time of writing the Germans have overrun the greater part of the Russian industrial areas. If even the shadow of international working class solidarity existed, Stalin would only have to call on the German workers in the name of the Socialist Fatherland for the German war-effort to be sabotaged. Not only does nothing of the kind happen, but the Russians do not even issue any such appeal. They know it is useless. Until Hitler is defeated in the field he can count on the loyalty of his own working class and can even drag Hungarians, Rumanians and what-not after him. At present the world is atomised and no form of internationalism has any power or even much appeal. This may be painful to literary circles in Cambridge, but it is the fact.

"To be effectively anti-war in England now one has to be pro-Hitler." Of course this is so. Ask Stalin whether he wants us to be anti-war in England. Or on the other hand ask Hitler, whose radio praises so warmly the efforts of the PPU and (till recently) the People's Convention. It is a matter of ordinary common sense. If you hinder the war effort of your own side you automatically assist that of the enemy. See Lenin's remarks on the subject.

The rest of Mr. Moore's letter is froth. The attempted buildup of myself as a fashionable "bourgeois leftish" intellectual frequenting "*Tribune* circles" (whatever those may be) and generally saying whatever it pays to say at the moment is based on imagination. Mr. Moore has never seen me, knows nothing about me, who my friends are, what "circles" I frequent, what my income is, or how and where I came by my political opinions. I have no doubt that he did not count on your giving me a chance to reply. His motives for writing the letter are, I should say, tolerably obvious.

Yours,
George Orwell

1. See *867, n. 1*.
2. *Partisan Review* printed this as 'post-poetic,' though 'post-' had been typed over with x's.
3. Moore did not underline titles and tended not to capitalise the second word of a title (so, 'London letter'). He typed this as 'New writing' and it was set so, in roman, in *Partisan Review*. It is presumably the journal edited by John Lehmann to which Orwell occasionally contributed, although here it also makes sense not italicised.
4. *Black Record: Germans Past and Present* (1941). See War-time Diary, *758, 7.2.41, n. 1*.

855. 'No, Not One,'[1]

Review of *No Such Liberty* by Alex Comfort, *The Adelphi*, October 1941

Mr. Murry said years ago that the works of the best modern writers, Joyce, Eliot and the like, simply demonstrated the *impossibility* of great art in a time like the present, and since then we have moved onwards into a period in which any sort of *joy* in writing, any such notion as telling a story for the purpose of pure entertainment, has also become impossible. All writing nowadays is propaganda. If, therefore, I treat Mr. Comfort's novel as a tract, I am only doing what he himself has done already. It is a good novel as novels go at this moment, but the motive for writing it was not what Trollope or Balzac, or even Tolstoy, would have recognised as a novelist's impulse. It was written in order to put forward the "message" of pacifism, and it was to fit that "message" that the main incidents in it were devised. I think I am also justified in assuming that it is autobiographical, not in the sense that the events described in it have actually happened, but in the sense that the author identifies himself with the hero, thinks him worthy of sympathy and agrees with the sentiments that he expresses.

Here is the outline of the story. A young German doctor who has been convalescent for two years in Switzerland returns to Cologne a little before Munich to find that his wife has been helping war-resisters to escape from the country and is in imminent danger of arrest. He and she flee to Holland just in time to escape the massacre which followed on vom Rath's assassination.[2] Partly by accident they reach England, he having been seriously wounded on the way. After his recovery he manages to get a hospital appointment, but at the outbreak of war he is brought before a tribunal and put in the B class of aliens. The reason for this is that he has declared that he will not fight against the Nazis, thinking it better to "overcome Hitler by love". Asked why he did not stay in Germany and overcome Hitler by love there, he admits that there is no answer. In the panic following on the invasion of the Low Countries he is arrested a few minutes after his wife has given birth to a baby and kept for a long time in a concentration camp where he cannot communicate with her and where the conditions of dirt, overcrowding, etc., are as bad as anything in Germany. Finally he is packed on to the "Arandora Star" (it is given another name, of course),[3] sunk at sea, rescued, and put in another somewhat better camp. When he is at last released and makes contact with his wife, it is to find that she has been confined in another camp in which the baby has died of neglect and underfeeding. The book ends with the couple looking forward to sailing for America and hoping that the war fever will not by this time have spread there as well.

Now, before considering the implications of this story, just consider one or two facts which underlie the structure of modern society and which it is necessary to ignore if the pacifist "message" is to be accepted uncritically.

(i) Civilisation rests ultimately on coercion. What holds society together is not the policeman but the good will of common men, and yet that good will is powerless unless the policeman is there to back it up. Any government which refused to use violence in its own defence would cease almost immediately to exist, because it could be overthrown by any body of men, or even any individual, that was less scrupulous. Objectively, whoever is not on the side of the policeman is on the side of the criminal, and vice versa. In so far as it hampers the British war effort, British pacifism is on the side of the Nazis, and German pacifism, if it exists, is on the side of Britain and the U.S.S.R. Since pacifists have more freedom of action in countries where traces of democracy survive, pacifism can act more effectively against democracy than for it. Objectively the pacifist is pro-Nazi.

(ii) Since coercion can never be altogether dispensed with, the only difference is between degrees of violence. During the last twenty years there has been less violence and less militarism inside the English-speaking world than outside it, because there has been more money and more security. The hatred of war which undoubtedly characterises the English-speaking peoples is a reflection of their favoured position. Pacifism is only a considerable force in places where people feel themselves very safe, chiefly maritime states. Even in such places, turn-the-other-cheek pacifism only flourishes among the more prosperous classes, or among workers who have in some way escaped from their own class. The real working class, though they hate war and are immune to jingoism, are never really pacifist, because their life teaches them something different. To abjure violence it is necessary to have no experience of it.

If one keeps the above facts in mind one can, I think, see the events, in Mr. Comfort's novel in truer perspective. It is a question of putting aside subjective feelings and trying to see whither one's actions will lead in practice and where one's motives ultimately spring from. The hero is a research worker—a pathologist. He has not been especially fortunate, he has a defective lung, thanks to the carrying-on of the British blockade into 1919, but in so far as he is a member of the middle class, doing work which he has chosen for himself, he is one of a few million favoured human beings who live ultimately on the degradation of the rest. He wants to get on with his work, wants to be out of reach of Nazi tyranny and regimentation, but he will not *act* against the Nazis in any other way than by running away from them. Arrived in England, he is in terror of being sent back to Germany, but refuses to take part in any physical effort to keep the Nazis out of England. His greatest hope is to get to America, with another three thousand miles of water between himself and the Nazis. He will only get there, you note, if British ships and planes protect him on the way, and having got there he will simply be living under the protection of American ships and planes instead of British ones. If he is lucky he will be able to continue with his work as a pathologist, at the same time keeping up his attitude of moral superiority towards the men who make his work possible. And underlying everything there will still be his position as a research-worker, a favoured person living ultimately on dividends which would cease forthwith if not extorted by the threat of violence.

I do not think this is an unfair summary of Mr. Comfort's book. And I think the relevant fact is that this story of a German doctor is written by an Englishman. The argument which is implied all the way through, and sometimes explicitly stated, that there is next to no difference between Britain and Germany, political persecution is as bad in one as in the other, those who fight against the Nazis always go Nazi themselves, would be more convincing if it came from a German. There are probably sixty thousand German refugees in this country, and there would be hundreds of thousands more if we had not meanly kept them out. Why did they come here if there is virtually no difference between the social atmosphere of the two countries? And how many of them have asked to go back? They have "voted with their feet", as Lenin put it. As I pointed out above, the comparative gentleness of the English-speaking civilisation is due to money and security, but that is not to say that no difference exists. Once let it be admitted, however, that there *is* a certain difference, that it matters quite a lot who wins, and the usual short-term case for pacifism falls to the ground. You can be explicitly pro-Nazi without claiming to be a pacifist—and there is a very strong case for the Nazis, though not many people in this country have the courage to utter it— but you can only pretend that Nazism and capitalist democracy are Tweedledum and Tweedledee if you also pretend that every horror from the June purge onwards has been cancelled by an exactly similar horror in England. In practice this has to be done by means of selection and exaggeration. Mr. Comfort is in effect claiming that a "hard case" is typical. The sufferings of this German doctor in a so-called democratic country are so terrible, he implies, as to wipe out every shred of moral justification for the struggle against Fascism. One must, however, keep a sense of proportion. Before raising a squeal because two thousand internees have only eighteen latrine buckets between them, one might as well remember what has happened these last few years in Poland, in Spain, in Czechoslovakia, etc., etc. If one clings too closely to the "those who fight against Fascism become Fascist themselves" formula, one is simply led into falsification. It is not true, for instance, as Mr. Comfort implies, that there is widespread spy-mania and that the prejudice against foreigners increases as the war gathers in momentum. The feeling against foreigners, which was one of the factors that made the internment of the refugees possible, has greatly died away, and Germans and Italians are now allowed into jobs that they would have been debarred from in peace time. It is not true, as he explicitly says, that the only difference between political persecution in England and in Germany is that in England nobody hears about it. Nor is it true that all the evil in our life is traceable to war or war-preparation. "I knew", he says, "that the English people, like the Germans, had never been happy since they put their trust in rearmament". Were they so conspicuously happy before? Is it not the truth, on the contrary, that rearmament, by reducing unemployment, made the English people somewhat happier, if anything? From my own observation I should say that, by and large, the war itself has made England happier; and this is not an argument in favour of war, but simply tells one something about the nature of so-called peace.

The fact is that the ordinary short-term case for pacifism, the claim that you can best frustrate the Nazis by not resisting them, cannot be sustained. If you don't resist the Nazis you are helping them, and ought to admit it. For then the long-term case for pacifism can be made out. You can say: "Yes, I know I am helping Hitler, and I want to help him. Let him conquer Britain, the U.S.S.R. and America. Let the Nazis rule the world; in the end they will grow into something different". That is at any rate a tenable position. It looks forward into human history, beyond the term of our own lives. What is not tenable is the idea that everything in the garden would be lovely *now* if only we stopped the wicked fighting, and that to fight back is exactly what the Nazis want us to do. Which does Hitler fear more, the P.P.U. or the R.A.F.? Which has he made greater efforts to sabotage? Is he trying to bring America into the war or to keep America out of it? Would he be deeply distressed if the Russians stopped fighting tomorrow? And after all, the history of the last ten years suggests that Hitler has a pretty shrewd idea of his own interests.

The notion that you can somehow defeat violence by submitting to it is simply a flight from fact. As I have said, it is only possible to people who have money and guns between themselves and reality. But why should they want to make this flight, in any case? Because, rightly hating violence, they do not wish to recognise that it is integral to modern society and that their own fine feelings and noble attitudes are all the fruit of injustice backed up by force. They do not want to learn where their incomes come from. Underneath this lies the hard fact, so difficult for many people to face, that individual salvation is not possible, that the choice before human beings is not, as a rule, between good and evil but between two evils. You can let the Nazis rule the world; that is evil; or you can overthrow them by war, which is also evil. There is no other choice before you, and whichever you choose you will not come out with clean hands. It seems to me that the text for our time is not "Woe to him through whom the evil cometh" but the one from which I took the title of this article, "There is not one that is righteous, no, not one".[4] We have all touched pitch, we are all perishing by the sword. We do not have the chance, in a time like this, to say "Tomorrow we can all start being good". That is moonshine. We only have the chance of choosing the lesser evil and of working for the establishment of a new kind of society in which common decency will again be possible. There is no such thing as neutrality in this war. The whole population of the world is involved in it, from the Esquimos to the Andamanese, and since one must inevitably help one side or the other, it is better to know what one is doing and count the cost. Men like Darlan and Laval have at any rate had the courage to make their choice and proclaim it openly. The New Order, they say, must be established at all costs, and "il faut érabouiller l'Angleterre". Mr. Murry appears, at any rate at moments, to think likewise. The Nazis, he says, are "doing the dirty work of the Lord" (they certainly did an exceptionally dirty job when they attacked Russia), and we must be careful "lest in fighting against Hitler we are fighting against God". Those are not pacifist sentiments, since if carried to their logical conclusion they involve not only surrendering to Hitler but helping him in his various forthcoming wars, but they are at least straightforward and courageous. I do not myself see Hitler as the saviour, even the unconscious saviour, of humanity, but there is a strong case for thinking him so, far stronger than most people in England imagine. What there is no case for is to denounce Hitler and at the same time look down your nose at the people who actually keep you out of his clutches. That is simply a highbrow variant of British hypocrisy, a product of capitalism in decay, and the sort of thing for which Europeans, who at any rate understand the nature of a policeman and a dividend, justifiably despise us.

(George Orwell writes cogently and well against a kind of pacifism that was once prevalent but has almost ceased to exist. It has been sweated out of the P.P.U. by keeping up with the dour reality. The number of former pacifist stalwarts who have dropped out is legion. There remain only those who (1) believe it as a matter of religious faith that we should "resist not evil" or (2) hold it as demonstrable to the imagination that Hitlerism is "the scourge of the Lord"—the destructive dynamic of this rotten civilisation: or they hold both together. To label them simply as "helping Hitler" is a simplification to which George Orwell, of all people, should not lend himself, because he must know to what sinister uses such a label can be put. We pacifists claim that we are striving, against tremendous odds, to prepare the only kind of resistance that can ultimately prevail against Hitlerism. We do not look down our noses at the honest men who fight. They are the vanguard, but we—preposterous as it may sound—are the last reserves. We "know what we fight for and love what we know" as surely, and I believe more surely, than George Orwell of the Home Guard does. Anyway, when it comes, as it will, to the last ditch we shall be found in it together: and the streamlined men on the other side will not be all Germans.) Editor[5]

1. Orwell's title.
2. Ernst vom Rath (as 'Vom' in the original) was Third Secretary at the German Embassy in Paris. A Jewish youth, Herschel Grynszpan, shot him there on 7 November 1938, and he died of wounds on 9 November Violent attacks on Jews and Jewish property—'Kristallnacht'—followed.
3. The *Arandora Star* was sunk in the Atlantic by a U-boat on 2 July 1940. It was carrying 1,500 German and Italian internees from Britain to Canada; 613 were drowned.
4. Matthew XVIII:7 and Romans III:10. The Authorized Version has 'offence' for 'evil.' Orwell was probably citing from memory.
5. John Middleton Murry (see *95*) undertook a third stint as editor of *The Adelphi* from July 1941 to 1948.

856. Why Not War Writers?: A Manifesto

Horizon, October 1941

The rôle of writers to-day, when every free nation and every free man and woman is threatened by the Nazi war-machine, is a matter of supreme importance.

Creative writers, poets, novelists and dramatists have a skill, imagination and human understanding which must be utilized as fully as the skill of journalists. They bring home with a depth and vividness impossible to the writer of a newspaper report or feature article, the significance of what is happening all about us, yet seldom to us ourselves or to all of us.

We all live in a very small illuminated circle and our work often loses much of its meaning because we do not see the relation of our every action to the conduct of the war. Books can implant this consciousness. A novel will create a picture which will not be effaced by to-morrow's newspaper. Books can, by reason of their larger scope, include many of the bad things which must be remedied beside the good things which must be made better. Books are less suspect than the newspapers, public estimation of which is very low.

At the beginning of the war, it was assumed that the function of the creative writer was to write a good book about the war . . . after the war.

Experience of two years of war has shown to writers that their function is to write a good book about the war *now*.

When war broke out, many writers were hesitant. They did not see the issues as clearly as they had seen the Spanish Civil War, for example, or the last European war. *The Times* and other papers asked why this war produced no poets. The poets wrote essays on why they couldn't write poetry. The cultural front of writers was broken into dissentient groups of two and three.

With the invasion of Russia, feeling has crystallized. It is no longer possible for anyone to stand back and call the war an imperialist war. For every writer, the war is a war for survival. Without victory our art is doomed.

The Government also is discovering that it is making a mistake in reserving the occupation of journalism but not of creative writing. During the Spanish War writers of international reputation such as Hemingway, Malraux and Silone[1] exerted a deeper influence than journalists. Their propaganda was deeper, more humanly appealing and more imaginative than newspaper men had space or time for.

The Government distinguishes between war artists and war photographers. Both are reserved and the function of each is regarded as distinct. The first has to give a permanent æsthetic significance to the events of the war, the second a news or documentary significance. It would be logical to apply the same principle to writers as to journalists, and give them the same facilities.

As things are, however, writer after writer is called up, or seeing no possibility of using his special talents in the interest of his country, has volunteered for war service.

The demand for books about the lives which other people were leading, for accounts of experiences briefly detailed in the newspapers meant that many newspapermen started to write books. But just as, with the exception of Messrs. Priestley and Wells, novelists make bad journalists, so the journalists make bad novelists. They had the advantage, however, that their journalistic facilities enabled them to collect material.

This was the general picture; the men who could write the books couldn't get the material, and the men who could get the material couldn't write the books. There were, however, some notable exceptions (Leo Walmsley, John Strachey, J. L. Hodgson—Linklater[2] was sent to Iceland).

The first principle, therefore, to be established, is: *Creative writers must receive the same facilities as journalists*.

Journalists are interested in the unusual. For creative writers, the sphere of interest is much wider. The everyday lives of people, the routine jobs, the small sacrifices are often more important because more universal than extraordinary events. For certain writers, however, action, danger and adventure are the greatest source of inspiration; for them the bombs, the submarine, the landing party, the battle front, the bomb-disposal squad. For others, organization, industrial growth, social welfare. Why are there no novels of value about the building of shadow factories, the planning of wartime services, the operation of, shall we say, an evacuation scheme? Why are there no satires on hoarders, or the black market? Why no novels of army life? Because the writers who could write them either have the knowledge but not the time, or the time but not the knowledge to do so.

Before the war, both publishers and writers were constantly on the look-out for book subjects, and all that needed to be done was to find the author or raise the cash to write the book. To-day, subjects abound. But the author cannot get leave from his unit to write the book or, alternatively, cannot get the passes from the M.O.I. to collect the material. The second principle is therefore that—*Creative writers should be used to interpret the war world so that cultural unity is re-established and war effort emotionally co-ordinated.* Though the policy of any creative writer must have a longer term than this, he can meet the national need on the short terms of victory.

Newspaper articles are ephemeral and local. Books have a longer life and a wider circulation. Books can tell Americans, Australians, Canadians, Indians, Russians about the war in Britain, while most newspaper articles would be unintelligible.

Applying our first principle (that the creative writers should be given the same facilities as journalists) we argue that American and Russian poets, dramatists and novelists should be asked to come to Britain and find the material for their writing so that they can interpret to their peoples what is happening here.

Similarly, British writers should be sent to the Americas, the Dominions and Russia so that they can report back, by stories, plays and poems what is happening over there. There is an interchange of material aid; there are political and military alliances; there is a united determination that Nazism and Fascism should be crushed. So there should be a free cultural interchange of creative writers, to establish during war the international understanding that is the chief aim of peace.

In brief, therefore, we propose:

1. The formation of an official group of war writers.

2. Writers to be given the necessary facilities for writing their books.

3. The international exchange of writers to be encouraged and accelerated.

4. A proper proportion of these writers to be of groups most actively engaged in this war.

This statement is prepared by a number of young writers, both in the Forces and in other work of national importance, and is published on their behalf by:

Arthur Calder-Marshall	Arthur Koestler
Cyril Connolly	Alun Lewis
Bonamy Dobrée	George Orwell
Tom Harrisson	Stephen Spender[3]

This Manifesto was discussed by a correspondent who signed himself 'Combatant'[4] in the December 1941 issue of *Horizon*.

WHY NOT WAR WRITERS?

Dear Sir,

You state, admirably, 'an artist must be in the war or out of it', thus explicitly denying the manifesto which bears your name. May I then, without offence, comment on that preposterous document?

What a picture of fun it makes of English writers! First, while Europe was overrun, they were 'hesitant'. Then one enemy fell out, over the division of the spoils, with his larger and wealthier partner. This welcome but not unforeseen diversion 'crystallized' our writers' 'feelings'. They are now for total war. So be it. To the less literary this reasoning seems fatuous, and, in the context, their expression 'the interest of their country' ambiguous, but it is no time to be nice about the terms of revelation. The roads to truth are devious and manifold. We, who have been in the war since the start, suffered a little from the lack of intellectual company; it was comforting to think of the book-reviewers and mass-observers and poets (of a kind) and Left-Book-Club-sub-group-assistant-organizing-secretaries, pouring in, with their crystallized feelings as succulent crystallized plums, to join us in camp. If they want to write about the war, the way is clear for them. Writers whom, in spite of your Word-Controller,[5] you persist in dubbing 'creative' differ from painters and journalists and photographers in[6] that a single pictorial view of their subject is not enough. They must be, or have been, part of it. Whether they write now or later is a question of individual literary digestion. There is plenty of leisure in the armed forces—at any rate for the lower ranks. The atmosphere is uncongenial for writing, but that is all to the good. It has been too easy to write in recent years. Genius overcomes privation and inferiority. If these young men *must* write, they will do it the better for suffering some inconveniences. If they are under no immediate compulsion, let them sit tight and store their minds with material for future use.

But what do your chums propose doing? They will like to form an Official Group; they would go on jaunts to the Americas and Dominions; they would have 'the facilities of journalists' which, as far as I have seen, merely means the privileges of commissioned rank without its obligations—cheap railway tickets, entrance to ward-rooms and officers' messes and investitures; they would 'co-ordinate war-effort emotionally'. Cor, chase my Aunt Nancy round the prickly pear! The General Staff love initials; they would, I am sure, rejoice to put an armlet, D.A.E.C.W.E. on someone's arm and call him Deputy Assistant Emotional Co-ordinator of War Effort. But if anyone ever again feels disposed to raise the old complaint that the English fail to honour their living artists, let him remember their present modest demands.

I am afraid that I do not believe for a moment that these young men want to write; they want to be writers. It is the Trades Union move detecting a slight on their occupational dignity. They have been whimpering for years for a classless society, and now that their own class is threatened with loss of privilege they are aghast. That is the plain meaning of your manifesto.

I notice it is signed by a novelist who, later in the same issue, has a letter on the subject of O.C.T.U.s.[7] Shades of Colonel Bingham![8] That officer made trouble for himself by injudiciously stating what few informed people disputed: that, generally speaking, the proletarian youths who are now being trained as officers have less sense of duty than candidates of gentle birth and humane education. It was injudicious to say this because the demand for officers greatly exceeds the supply of gentlemen, so nothing can be done about it. But the men in charge of O.C.T.U.s. have a difficult job, and Mr. Calder-Marshall is witness to their tolerance. One in three of their candidates are socialist, many of whom are sharp enough in memorizing the facts of their new trade. But duty? Consider a case of Mr. Calder-Marshall; he accepts an eagerly-sought vacancy and takes up three months of his instructors' time. They are trying to make him a leader in battle. But when he gets commissioned rank he makes no effort to serve the regiment who honour him with their badges, but uses his new position as a step to softer employment.

I may not sign my name to a letter dealing with military matters, but if anyone has any curiosity about my identity, please inform him.

Your obedient servant,

Combatant

1. Ernest Hemingway (1899–1961), American novelist, winner of the Nobel Prize for Literature, 1954, wrote and spoke the commentary for the Republican side's propaganda film *The Spanish Earth* (directed by Joris Ivens, 1937). His novel of the Spanish civil war, *For Whom the Bell Tolls* (1940) was made into a popular film. André Malraux, French author (see *3209 n 1*), played an active role on the Republican side in the Spanish civil war, and on the side of the Kuomintang in China, 1925–27. See Orwell's letter of 7 April 1947 to Yvonne Davet regarding the suggestion that Malraux be asked to write an introduction to the French edition of *Homage to Catalonia, 3209*. Ignazio Silone (Secondo Tranquilli) (1900–1978) was an Italian novelist (*Fontamara*, 1933; *Pane e Vino*, 1937, English translation, *Bread and Wine*, 1937) whose anti-Fascism caused him to exile himself from 1931–1944. See also *2870, n. 3*.

2 Leo Walmsley (1892–1966) was a novelist who also wrote *Fishermen at War*, and *British Ports and Harbours* in the 'Britain in Pictures' series (to which Orwell contributed *The English People*). John Strachey (see *304, n. 2*), left-wing politician and later government minister, wrote at this time *A Programme for Progress* (1940), *A Faith to Fight For* (1941), and *Post D· Some Experiences of an Air Raid Warden* (1941). Presumably John Lawrence Hodson (1891–1956; OBE, 1947), journalist, dramatist, novelist, was meant. He was a war correspondent, 1939–42, and worked for the Ministry of Information, 1943–45, on publications and film scripts (including *Desert Victory*). Among his books on the war are *Gentlemen of Dunkirk, being leaves from a war correspondent's diary* (1940), *War in the Sun* (1942), *Home Front . . . 1942–43* (1944), and *British Merchantmen at War, 1939–1944* (1944). His *Before Daybreak* (on World War I) was published in 1941. Orwell may have been particularly interested in Hodson because he had investigated unemployment in nine European countries, 1932–33. Eric Linklater (Robert Russell) (1899–1974), Scottish novelist whose *Juan in America* (1931) was well known, wrote three pamphlets in the series The Army at War: *The Defence of Calais* (1941), *The Northern Garrisons* (1941), and *The Highland Division* (1942). He also wrote, in the War Pamphlets series, *The Cornerstones: A Conversation in Elysium* (1941); *The Campaign in Italy* was published in 1945.

3. Arthur Calder-Marshall (1908–1992), prolific author of novels, short stories, and non-fiction books, worked for the British Petroleum Warfare Department, 1941, and the Ministry of Information Films Division, 1942–45, writing many documentary film scripts. He later took up Orwell's interest in McGill's picture postcards in his *Wish You Were Here: The Art of Donald McGill* (1966). For Cyril Connolly, author and editor, and a longtime friend of Orwell's, see *1, n. 1*. Bonamy Dobrée (1891–1974) was a scholar, academic, and prolific writer on literary subjects. See *1902, n. 1* and Richard Hoggart, 'Dobrée: Teacher and Patron of Young Men' in *Of Books and Humankind· Essays and Poems Presented to Bonamy Dobrée*, edited by John Butt (1964). Tom Harrisson (1911–1976), founder, with Charles Madge, of Mass Observation, 1937 (see *594, n. 1*), organised guerrillas behind Japanese lines in Sarawak, 1944–45. In 1966 he was at the Department of Anthropology, Cornell University. His *Living Through the Blitz* was published in 1976, shortly after he had been killed in a road accident near Bangkok For

Orwell's reviews of the work of Mass Observation, see *1833, 2484, 2742.* For Arthur Koestler, author, journalist, and one-time Communist, see *760, n. 1.* Alun Lewis (1915–1944) was a poet and short-story writer. Among his books were *Raiders' Dawn and Other Poems* (1942), *Ha! Ha! Among the Trumpets* (1945), and *The Last Inspection* (1942). The posthumously collected *In the Green Tree* (1948) includes stories and a number of his letters from India. He killed himself, whether accidentally or deliberately is uncertain, before going into action for the first time on the Arakan front in Burma. Stephen Spender (see *411, n. 2*), critic, novelist, and short-story writer, was, in the 1930s, one of an important group of anti-Fascist writers. He and John Lehmann edited the anthology *Poems for Spain* (1939), and he translated Lorca and Rilke.

4. 'Combatant' was, possibly, Evelyn Waugh (1903–1966), satirical novelist. Although hardly conclusive, he did use descriptions such as 'aghast' and 'injudicious' for an appointment; see his letters to A. D. Peters, 4(?).4.42 and to Laura Waugh, 29.2.44 (*The Letters*, edited by Mark Amory, 1980, 159, 178). 'Combatant' writes of having 'been in the war from the start.' Waugh was commissioned in the Royal Marines in 1939 and later transferred to the Royal Horse Guards.

5. Combatant's use of the expression 'Word Controller' does not derive from the Manifesto but from 'Comment' (the editorial by Cyril Connolly in the same issue of *Horizon*, 229–31). This demanded that dictatorial powers be given to a Word Controller 'to clean up our language': 'War journalism and war oratory have produced an unchecked inflation in our overdriven and exhausted vocabulary.' The Word Controller (George Bernard Shaw was put forward as a good choice) would issue licences: 'Without such a licence it would be a criminal offence to appear in print or on the platform. The licences would be immediately cancelled of all those found using the words "*vital: vitally: virtual: virtually: actual: actually: perhaps: probably.*" ' The more general aim is in the penultimate paragraph: 'In the times in which we live a writer should not be able to put down more than two or three lines without making it obvious whether he has anything to say. The Word Controller, by banning the verbal camouflage of those who doubt, who twist, who are on the make, or who hope for the best, would clarify propaganda and leave literature safely where it belongs, in the hands of the abnormally sane, or the genuinely mad.' The editorial, tinged with irony, should not be taken as wholly unambiguous. Thus, 'The Word Controller, at any rate during the few hours of office before his powers turned his head, would be non-political.' However, its avowed concern that stale rhetoric and false news can bring 'a perfect achievement of civilization into confusion' seems to provide the germ for Orwell's Newspeak, the purpose of which 'was not only to provide a medium of expression for the world-view and mental habits proper to the devotees of Ingsoc, but to make all other modes of thought impossible. . . . Newspeak was designed not to extend but to *diminish* the range of thought, and this purpose was indirectly assisted by cutting the choice of words down to a minimum' (*Nineteen Eighty-Four, CW*, IX, 312–13).

6. in] printed as 'is' in *Horizon*

7. Officer Cadet Training Unit, an army cadet force particularly associated with public schools.

8. *The Times* published a letter 15 January 1941 from Lieutenant-Colonel R. C. Bingham of 168 OCTU on the subject of 'Junior Officers in the New Armies.' He argued that the new armies were being officered by 'classes of society who are new to the job,' that the 'middle, lower middle, and working classes' were receiving the King's commission, and that these, 'unlike the old aristocratic and feudal (almost) classes who led the old Army, have never had "their people" to consider. They have never had anyone to think of but themselves. This aspect of life is completely new to them, and they have very largely fallen down on [the job] in their capacity as Army officers.' Man management was instinctive to 'old school tie men' and could not be taught. This letter caused an outcry, and the Secretary of State for War, David Margesson (see *698, n. 3*) told Parliament that Bingham had committed a breach of King's Regulations, and the Army Council's severe displeasure had been conveyed to him. He was also relieved of his command.

857. To Bhupen Mukerjee[1]

1 October 1941

Dear Dr Mukerjee,[2]

We are running a series of talks entitled THROUGH EASTERN EYES, to which it has been suggested that you might like to contribute. The talks are in the English language but are directed to India, and consist of a series of short chats on British institutions of all kinds, delivered by Indians living in England. We should like it very much if you could do the talk on the Post Office. The date for which this talk is fixed is Tuesday December 16th. The length of the talk would be about 1200 words.

If this idea appeals to you, could you make it convenient to come and see me as soon as possible and talk it over? I could then give you an idea of the sort of thing we want and the general line of approach.

Perhaps you could let me know at the above address whether you feel inclined to undertake this, and if so, what date and time it would be convenient for you to call.

Yours truly
[No name/position][3]

1. Unless otherwise stated, Orwell's letters from the BBC are typewritten carbon copies; the particular BBC address from which he wrote is given in a note only when he changed location.
2. This appears to be Orwell's first letter as a talks assistant He wrote from 55 Portland Place (see *846, n. 8*), where he had room 206 and, later 416. The office of the Director, Rushbrook Williams, was 415. Bokhari (see *776, n. 1*) had written to Mukerjee (or Mookerjee—both spellings occur in the same letter), who worked in the Pay Room at India House (office of the High Commissioner for India), on 27 August 1941. On 16 September, Bokhari proposed Mukerjee give a talk on the shipbuilding industry; three days later he suggested a series of twelve discussions with Scott Goddard on 'Melody and Harmony.' These began on 10 October. On 23 April 1942, Orwell commissioned him to give one of the programmes in the series 'The Music I Like'; see *1112*. Orwell seems to have been assigned to supervise Mukerjee's talk, but Bokhari kept an eye on Orwell's progress. As it turned out, Mukerjee's technique gave rise for concern. Ten days before the talk on the Post Office was due to be given, Bokhari sent Mukerjee a stern warning. This illustrates the kind of problems the BBC's Indian Section staff faced:

    English is not your mother tongue and it isn't my mother tongue. If we want to broadcast in English, we must write out what we have to say and we must stick to it. Your yesterday's broadcast was a great disappointment to me. You did not stick to the script that you submitted to me. You haltered and faltered so much that the whole broadcast was, so to speak, inflicting a physical pain on the listeners, and then you over-ran the allotted time, with the result that we had to cut you abruptly. Even with the best wish in the world it could not have been a judicious cut because your script didn't show what you had to say.

    'Will you be good enough to bear in mind that I want an exact script and I want strict adherance to the script in future. Non-compliance with these requests will compel me to cancel the broadcasts and such a cancellation will hurt me more than you can imagine.'
3. Usually Orwell's name, frequently as Blair, and his position are typed at the foot of letters. If this is not done, '[No name/position]' is noted.

858. To P. H. Chatterjee

2 October 1941   PP/ZAB/MB[1]

Dear Dr. Chatterjee,[2]

I am writing to request you to do a twelve-minute talk for us in English in our series of broadcasts, entitled 'How It Works'. The subject we should like you to take for the fourth talk in this series is 'Rural District Councils', as we understand you have studied this subject and are interested in it. The date of your broadcast is Sunday, 26th October, at 4.0 p.m. at Broadcasting House. The length of your script should be about 1200 words and we shall be obliged if you can let us have a copy of it by Monday, 20th October.

We shall be glad to help you by arranging any necessary interviews, or other facilities, for the preparation of your script.

Should you wish to 'phone me at Broadcasting House, my extension number is: 386.

Yours sincerely,
Eric Blair
Empire Talks Assistant

1. The reference PP = 55 Portland Place. This is usually followed by EB for Eric Blair, though Orwell often wrote over the name George Orwell, sometimes using both names for the same correspondent. Letters were typed for Orwell and surviving drafts indicate that Orwell wrote out many, if not all, of his letters for his typist. The secretary's initials usually follow. Here, ZAB = Bokhari; and MB = Mary Blackburn, Bokhari's secretary in 1940. Orwell's first secretary was Nancy Parratt (NP). Where no initials are given, the style and positioning of the address, salutation, and closing enable the secretary to be identified in most instances. Blemishes customarily found in carbon copies sometimes lead to missing letters, erasure marks, and overtyping; corrections have mostly been made silently. The date is not repeated in reprinting the text of letters and memoranda, and the place of despatch, if a printed letterhead was used for the top copy, must be inferred from the reference. It should be borne in mind that the top copy sent to the addressee might differ—for example, a late postscript might not have been added to the carbon copy. When both top and carbon copies have survived, such discrepancies can be seen.
2. P. H. Chatterjee was confused later with a T. G. Chatterjee. Bokhari wrote to Norman Collins on 29 November 1941 saying, 'We know P.H. He gave us a talk as he says in his letter on English Rural District Councils. He is a dull broadcaster and the subject he suggests for the Home Talks [sic] is, in my opinion, beyond his capabilities.' Nevertheless, he was engaged to give more talks and was commissioned to write Bengali Newsletters; see 1744.

859. BBC Talks Booking Forms, 2.10.41

An essential step in the procedure for booking a speaker was the completion of a booking form. This gave details of the speaker, the series and subject of the talk, recording and broadcasting dates, and contract details (including the fee). Forms initiated by Orwell were often signed by others, particularly Bokhari, and often by one of the secretaries. The essential information from these forms is given here under the date of application.

Dr. P. Chatterjee: 'Through Eastern Eyes,' 'How It Works,' 4, Rural District Councils, their history and how they work; broadcast 26.10.41; fee £7.7s.

P. B. Seal:[1] 'Through Eastern Eyes,' 'The Man in the Street,' 1; broadcast 10.10.41; fee £7.7s.

1. P. B. Seal was suggested as a broadcaster to India by J. P. McGeachy, listed in the August 1943 Staff List as an assistant commentator in the Overseas News Division. His recommendation, 11 August 1941, was passed to Bokhari, who wrote to Seal on 22 September inviting him to submit scripts for talks to be given on 10 and 17 October. Seal had been secretary to three presidents of the Indian National Committee and, according to McGeachy, 'seemed to be one of the leading spirits' at an Indian Nationalist meeting McGeachy had attended. Seal, he said, wanted to broadcast to India 'that now is the time for India to come into an Asiatic anti-Axis front.' He had sent a cable to that effect to Gandhi; this was quoted in a BBC Empire Service bulletin and 'has caused a stir in India.'

860. To Bina Ghosh

3 October 1941

Dear Miss Ghosh,
I have received the script[1] for your broadcast which is booked for October 23rd. There are certain alterations which I think are needed, and we shall have also to rehearse the talk in order to make sure that the timing is correct. It would be well therefore if you could arrange to come and see me here and get this fixed up. I dare say an interview of an hour or two hours would be needed, and it would be better if we could arrange this not later than October 15th. I wonder what day would suit you? Could you be kind enough to write as early as possible, letting me know what day you could call, and at what time?

Yours sincerely
[No name/position]

1. This script, the second in the series 'The Hand that Rocks the Cradle' was commissioned by Bokhari on 15 September 1941. It led to a bitter dispute, which, though only incidentally involving Orwell, is illustrative of the delicate relationships involved in arranging talks to be broadcast to India. The correspondence, which ran from 30 October 1941 to 16 February 1942 and eventually involved J. B. Clark, Controller of Overseas Services (see 846, n. 1), shows that Bokhari was reluctant to commission Dr. Ghosh. They had had 'passages of arms' in the past and he regarded her, rightly or wrongly, as 'rather difficult' and 'anti-Indian,' making 'a habit of running down her own country.' He engaged her only because of the intervention of the Secretary of State for India (L. S. Amery), whose wife knew her. It was, in these circumstances, not surprising that Bokhari asked the new member of staff, Orwell, to supervise this broadcast. Unfortunately, on the day he was to see her, 14 October, he was ill with bronchitis, and did not return until 28 October. Supervision therefore fell, once again, on Bokhari's shoulders. Not satisfied with the script, he asked for it to be rewritten. Dr. Ghosh objected but eventually submitted a new script. Bokhari had informed her that if the script were satisfactory he would not write to her again. That was the usual practice; despatch of the contract would confirm the arrangements. Dr. Ghosh did not turn up to give the broadcast, because, she said, she had not heard the programme 'trailed' in the preceding week. She wrote that she was 'extremely disappointed and disgusted' to hear the talk read by an Englishwoman. The BBC, believing this to be no more than a misunderstanding (a word Dr. Ghosh rejected), offered to pay her in full for the talk, including the fee for reading her script. Apologies and explanations were sent by Joanna Spicer, of the Empire Executive, by L. F. Rushbrook Williams, and eventually by Clark, who pointed out that Dr. Ghosh had made

no effort to contact the BBC when she had doubts as to whether the broadcast was to be made. Given the pressure under which the small staff of the Indian Section worked, their patience in trying to placate Dr. Ghosh was remarkable.

861. To Damyanti Sahni

3 October 1941   PP/EB/MB

Dear Mrs. Sahni,[1]
On Sundays, each week, we are broadcasting a series of twelve-minute talks in English, under the general title 'How it Works' and in this series, I shall be glad if you will give us a talk on 'Theatres'. The date of your broadcast is Sunday, 14th December at 4.0 pm from Broadcasting House. I know this is a long time ahead, but the subject is large and may entail some research on your part, though I understand that you would be interested in this subject and the line of approach can therefore be left to your discretion.

A talk of this kind inevitably entails an exposition of the difference between western and eastern dramatic art, and it is necessary therefore for you to decide how much knowledge of the subject your listeners are likely to have. Apart from talking on the aspect of drama most interesting to you, we suggest that you should give some idea of the difference that the war has made to drama to-day; for instance you might mention the damage that London theatres have suffered in the air raids, the difficulties of dramatic production owing to clothes rationing and the calling-up of young actors and the courageous struggle by which the dramatic profession have carried on, especially in experimental theatres such as the Threshold and the Neighbourhood, and the way the actors to-day are helping to entertain the men in the Services. These are only suggestions. I shall be most interested to read your script.

Yours sincerely,
Eric Blair
Empire Talks Assistant

1. Mr. Balraj Sahni was an Indian Programme assistant stationed at this time at Wood Norton, near Evesham. Orwell's offer of work to the wife of a BBC employee was likely to pose problems. Damyanti Sahni was working at the Shakespeare Memorial Theatre at Stratford-upon-Avon, fourteen miles from Evesham, then under Ben Iden Payne's management. For their drama series with Norman Marshall, 'Let's Act It Ourselves,' see *1639*.

862. To Zahra Taki

4 October 1941   PP/ZAB/MB

Dear Miss Taki,[1]
We are broadcasting a fortnightly series of talks on Thursdays by different Indian women in this country, under the general title 'The Hand that Rocks the Cradle'. I wonder if you will broadcast a talk for us in this series on

Thursday, 4th December, at 4.0 p.m. from Broadcasting House. I do hope you will be able to do this for us. The talk should be of twelve minutes' duration in English.

It is important to avoid overlapping and repetition, so each speaker should concentrate as far as possible on topics interesting to her personally and to women in general, illustrating the talk by her own experiences of life in Britain. The keynotes of every talk should be:

(a) The interests and problems of women are everywhere basically the same.

(b) Women of the West and of the East have much to learn from one another.

So long as this is kept in mind, you should talk about what interests you most—the medical education of women in this country and the opportunities for women doctors in India. The talk should be as vivid and as lively as possible and we suggest that you should recall your own first impressions of English life at close quarters.

Yours sincerely,
Eric Blair
Empire Talks Assistant

1. Zahra Taki was an Indian student at University College Cardiff. Recruited by Bokhari in April 1940, she first spoke in a programme made up of short interviews of Indians living in Britain. She later took part in a broadcast for schools, 'Towards Better Health,' 4 April 1941, and for Darling in a dramatisation, 31 August 1941, and broadcast in English and Hindustani. She submitted her script to Orwell on 16 November 1941. She broadcast again in October 1942, for Princess Indira of Kapurthala, who had asked her on 29 August to give a series of six five-minute talks on why she became a surgeon and her experiences in training and thereafter, especially in overcoming prejudice; such talks would be 'a very real help to Indian womanhood which seems to me to be sadly in need of inspiration.'

863. Hendon Local Labour Party to Orwell

5 October 1941

On 5 October 1941, Mary B. Colebrook, Honorary Secretary of Hendon Garden Suburb Ward, Hendon Local Labour Party, wrote to Orwell on behalf of the Ward's Executive Committee to ask him to allow his name to go forward as their nominee for selection as prospective parliamentary candidate for Hendon. The closing date for nominations was 18 October. Orwell was asked to reply at once. No reply has been traced. It is probable that Orwell declined. The seat was, in any case, a hopeless cause for Labour.

864. To Bina Ghosh

6 October 1941   PP/EB

Dear Miss Ghosh,

Thank you for your letter.[1] I shall expect you here at 11 a.m. on October 14th.

Yours sincerely,
[No name/position]

1. Orwell wrote this at the foot of Dr. Ghosh's letter to him of 5 October, which proposed they meet at this time.

865. To the Chief Clerk, Aylesbury Rural District Council

8 October 1941   EB/BG[1]

Dear Sir,[2]

I rang you up yesterday to ask whether an Indian gentleman, who will shortly be broadcasting to India on the subject of British Local Government, might visit your offices and make certain enquiries. You told me that there was no objection to this.

The bearer of this letter is Dr. P. Chatterjee, the gentleman referred to in my phone call, and I should be greatly obliged if you could give him any facilities that do not inconvenience you.

Yours faithfully,
Eric Blair
Empire Talks Assistant.

1. The initials BG may be those of Miss Gibb, Rowan Davies's secretary. Davies was at this time Transcription Assistant in the Indian Section. He later was School Broadcasting Manager in the Home Service (Staff List, 21.8.43).
2. Probably A. R. Kerrell-Vaughan; see *910*.

866. To H. J. Umrigar

8 October 1941   PP/EB

Dear Mr. Umrigar,

Your name was mentioned to me by Mr. Sarin[1] for a talk in our series "Around the Courts".[2] I wonder if you would care to come along one morning to discuss it with me.

You can ring up my secretary and make an appointment.

Yours truly,
Eric Blair
Empire Talks Assistant

1. I. B. Sarin, Indian Programme Assistant; see *846, n. 14.*

2. The twelve-minute programme 'Around the Courts' was broadcast fortnightly, and was described by Bokhari in some detail in a letter to Chinna Durai, 16 September 1941:

This series will be based on personal visits to the Law Courts by Indian lawyers or law students, but it is important that the talks should not be aimed only at listeners who are professionally interested in the law. There are two main points which I suggest should be emphasised in each talk:

(a) Peculiarities of English Law, its points of difference from or similarity to the Indian Penal Code etc., illustrating the special nature of English civilisation.

(b) The 'human interest' side of the Law Courts.

Wherever possible cases and incidents selected for discussion and illustration should have some bearing on India, even if it is a remote one. Anything which points to some striking difference of social atmosphere between Britain and India, or anything demonstrating that human nature is the same the whole world over, is suitable. Subjects of purely local interest, or involving legal niceties not interesting to the general public, should be avoided. Recall as vividly as possible whatever struck you as unusual or interesting as a newcomer to this country, visiting the Law Courts for the first time and concentrate on that.

The series was inspired by a 'human interest' feature about the law courts that appeared regularly in the London *Evening Standard*.

867. BBC Talks Booking Form, 13.10.41

M. J. Tambimuttu:[1] 'Through Eastern Eyes,' 'The Man in the Street,' his reactions 'to the war situation'; broadcast 17.10.41; fee £7.7s. Signed: Z. A. Bokhari.

1. Tambimuttu (1915–1983), always known by his surname, without initials (given variously here as M. J. and N., the former being correct), or by 'Tambi,' came from Ceylon (Sri Lanka) to Britain in 1937. He was described in an obituary by Hugo Davenport as 'one of the poorest patrons ever to have dispensed largesse to unknown poets.' He brought out fifteen issues of his *Poetry London*, 1939–47, and then, after a dispute with his English business partner, left for New York, where he produced four issues of *Poetry London–New York*. For a time he worked for the Indian delegation to the United Nations. He returned to London in 1968 and, with backing from the Beatles, prepared *Poetry London/Apple*, which took eleven years to gestate (*Sunday Times*, 26 June 1983).

868. Orwell's Vacation and Sick Leave

Orwell's vacation and sick leave are shown in the BBC Left Staff File L1/42 as follows (days of the week have been added):

Dates	Sick	Annual	Bisque[1]	Comments
Tue. 14.10.41—Mon. 27.10.41	14★			
Mon. 1.12.41—Mon. 22.12.41	22★			
Mon. 29.6.42—Mon. 13.7.42		[2 weeks][2]		
Wed. 20.1.43—Thu. 11.2.43	*18* 20 sick★[3]			2 normal off
Fri. 23.4.43—Mon. 26.4.43	[no figures]			1 in lieu Easter &
	given]			2 normally off
Fri. 3.9.43—Mon. 20.9.43		10[4]		
Mon. 11.10.43—Fri. 15.10.43	4			
Mon. 25.10.43—Tue. 26.10.43	1			

★ Sick with certificates for Bronchitis.

Some recorded absences do not, apparently, include the day of return; some probably do (for instance, Orwell dictated and signed a letter on Monday, 22 December 1941). Some seem to include Sundays in the total and some do not. Specific points, noted by superscripts, are:
1. Bisque (derived from 'an extra turn' in a game) meant occasional days of leave over and above annual leave entitlement; for example, for family reasons.
2. No figure is given for the number of days' leave but, the dates apart, Orwell's diary makes it plain that this is annual, not sick, leave.
3. This period includes three Sundays, so 23 days by the calendar (reckoned inclusively) may imply a total of 20; the half-days worked on Saturdays would be considered full days for sick leave. At one stage, 18 days was the total of sick leave (because of '2 normal off'?), but 18 was crossed out.
4. The total number of days, reckoned inclusively, is 18. This period included three Sundays, and the 20th may have been the day of return. When working a 5½-day week, if Friday was taken as leave, the Saturday would count as a full day. Ten days' leave can only be arrived at by calculating that Orwell came in on Friday, 3 September, returned on Monday, the 20th, and the bisque day was taken as two Saturday half-days. However, other evidence shows that a letter Orwell wished sent on 3 September was written 'on his behalf' and John Morris read his Newsletter to Indonesia. What is more, he appears not to have written the English version of the Tamil Newsletter on 2 September 1943, though he wrote letters dated the 2nd.

The dates and categories of leave were abstracted by Mrs. Jacqueline Kavanagh, BBC Written Archives Officer, Caversham.

869. 'From Colliery to Kitchen'

'Through Eastern Eyes,' 21 October 1941

'Programmes as Broadcast' (PasB) for 21 October 1941 lists a talk lasting 14¾ minutes titled 'From Colliery to Kitchen.' It described coal production. The entry states that it was written by 'Eric Blair (Staff)' and read by Bokhari. Orwell was on sick leave at the time the broadcast was transmitted. The script has not been traced. The PasBs are an invaluable (and almost complete) record of what actually was transmitted, rather than what was intended to be broadcast.

870. Room 101

'You asked me once,' said O'Brien, 'what was in Room 101. I told you that you knew the answer already. Everyone knows it. The thing that is in Room 101 is the worst thing in the world.' (*Nineteen Eighty-Four*, 296)

It has often been asked why Orwell chose the number 101 as the setting for Winston Smith's—our—worst experience. Was it any more than an attractive sequence of figures? The answer is possibly to be found in a paper surviving from Orwell's time at the BBC. Although the minutes of Eastern Service meetings do not give the number of the room where they were held, one surviving agenda gives the place of meeting as 'Room 101, 55 Portland Place'—

presumably on the ground floor of the building in which Orwell worked. The agenda is dated Wednesday, October 22, and that day and date make the year 1941. For further details of this committee, see *882*.

871. BBC Talks Booking Form, 24.10.41

Venu Chitale:[1] 'Through Eastern Eyes,' 'The Man in the Street,' fashions are not rationed; broadcast 24.10.41; fee £7.7s. Signed: N. H. Parratt.[2]

1. Miss Venu Chitale (the final 'e' was sometimes written with an acute accent) came from Poona, India, and spoke Marathi. She was introduced to the Indian Section by G. H. Payton, and submitted a trial script 20 September 1940 By the end of October, she was living in London, and by 22 December 1941 had been passed by 'college' to work on Marathi Newsletters. A memorandum from Joanna Spicer (R13/154/2A) authorised her appointment as a junior programme assistant, Grade D, at £363 a year. She was to help in the production of 'Through Eastern Eyes,' be responsible for the Marathi Newsletters (but see *873, n. 1*), and was able to help announce programmes to India in English, 'work which now falls almost entirely on I.P.O.' (Bokhari). She was accommodated in Room 412, 55 Portland Place. In the staff magazine, *Ariel*, Summer 1945, she was described as petite and given to wearing exquisitely embroidered saris (15). See also *914*.
2. Nancy Parratt was Orwell's secretary at this time.

872. Rights to *Down Out in Paris and London* and *Burmese Days*

Letters held by the Harry Ransom Humanities Research Center, University of Texas at Austin, show that on 24 October 1941, Orwell's literary agent, Christy & Moore, wrote to the U.S. publisher of *Down and Out in Paris and London* and *Burmese Days*, Harper & Brothers, in New York, to point out that no royalty account had been submitted since 1938. They asked for an up-to-date statement and any money due. M. Brendel, of Harper's Accounting Department, explained, on 25 November, that both books had been out of print for many years and so no royalty statements had been submitted; it was extremely doubtful if either book would be reprinted. Leonard Moore, acting for Orwell, then asked, on 11 December, if Harper's would object to restoring the rights to their author. On 28 January 1942, Harper's sent cancelled copies of the contracts for *Down and Out* (dated 25 March 1933) and *Burmese Days* (12 March 1934) to P. P. Howe, of Hamish Hamilton's in London, and asked him to organise their exchange with the copies held by Christy & Moore.

More than a year later, on 20 April 1943, Moore wrote again to Harper's, asking for confirmation that the U.S. copyright of *Burmese Days* would be restored to the author. Dorothy Fiske replied on 17 May, stating that Christy & Moore had cancelled the contract on 7 January 1942. Evidently Howe had effected the exchange, and Christy & Moore had forgotten. Moore replied on 29 June giving as an explanation for his firm's oversight the loss of many of their records during the Blitz.

873. To Shridhar Telkar

28 October 1941   PP/EB

Dear Mr. Telkar,[1]

We propose to broadcast a talk under the title "Mind the Doors", about the Tubes and Underground Railways of London, on Tuesday, November 18th, at 4 p.m., from Broadcasting House, and we should be very grateful if you would undertake to do this talk for us. Facilities for any necessary visits, interviews, and so on, can easily be arranged.

You should try to say enough about the London Underground system to give listeners an idea of its extent, the number of passengers it carries daily, etc., and say as much about the technical side of underground electric railways as you think will interest the audience you are addressing. You should also mention the use of the Tube stations during the past year as air raid shelters, and the facilities that now exist there for shelterers. Beyond this, you should simply concentrate on whatever aspect of the subject most interests you. The more graphic and personal you can be, and the more vividly you can convey the sensation of travelling underground to people who know of such things only by hearsay, the better. You should also use your own judgment as to what statistics and technicalities you introduce. I expect you would find it helpful to recall your own first sight of an underground railway, or a moving staircase, and tell your listeners just what struck you as impressive or surprising in that occasion.

I should be glad if you will let me know if you will undertake this. If there are any points you would like to discuss, perhaps you will ring me up and make an appointment to come and see me.

Yours sincerely,
Eric Blair
Empire Talks Assistant

1. Shridhar Madhavrao Telkar, journalist, author (*When East Meets West*, 1931), and editor (*Satire and Burlesque*, 1935), worked as a Marathi translator and announcer for the BBC in 1942 and later ran the Oriental News Agency On 26 January 1942, Bokhari sought approval to hire him for the Marathi Newsletter, and suggested that he be put through the 'college' (see *846, n. 19*). Assurances were given that he would receive only one guinea for making a translation from English into Marathi and two guineas for delivering the broadcast Permission was granted, without vetting by the 'college,' provided Telkar did not write the original newsletter. Orwell does not appear to have been involved in this, and Telkar's work on the Marathi Newsletter did not come under his aegis, although Orwell wrote the English version from which it was translated. On 4 May 1945, *Tribune* published Telkar's long 'Open Letter' to Lord Wavell, the Viceroy of India, then on a visit to London. This rehearsed Britain's imperial record in India and sought to prompt Wavell to take more determined action to end the exploitation. When Wavell had arrived in India in 1943, 'no Viceroy within living memory embarked upon Vice-regal duties with the same prestige'; his task, wrote Telkar, was unenviable, for his 'predecessor had plunged the country into a crisis by an act of provocation: imprisoning the leaders of the Indian people.' Wavell, he said, could have made radical changes. 'No doubt you tried to do your best. You applied a few palliatives You discarded special trains for the Viceroy, made small administrative changes, toured famine areas unconventionally.' But this was all superficial, he wrote. 'Is there today less bitterness, less starvation, less suffering, more civil liberties, more confidence in Britain's intentions towards India?' He reviewed Britain's past record and concluded that Wavell's current mission to

England had failed and that he would return to India to 'storm and fury.' Yet dictators had fallen everywhere, and India would be free.

874. BBC Talks Booking Form, 30.10.41

N.° Tambimuttu: 'Through Eastern Eyes,' 'The Man in the Street'; broadcast 31.10.41; fee £7.7s.

875. Socialists Answer *Left*'s Questions on the War

Left, November 1941

Orwell was one of thirteen people who answered thirty-five questions on the war posed by the journal *Left*. The others were W. Ballantine, H. N. Brailsford, Fenner Brockway, J. R. Campbell, Frank Horrabin, Ethel Mannin, George Padmore, Raymond Postgate, Herbert Read, C. A. Smith (the editor of *Left*), Joseph Southall, and Tom Wintringham. The questions, and Orwell's replies, are preceded by *Left*'s statement of its aim, reprinted from that issue, and the editorial introduction to the first answers received.

AIM

This journal has no policy narrower than the achievement of the classless society and the co-operative commonwealth. It offers itself as a forum for the public discussion of all those differences concerning methods and tactics which create divisions between and within the Parties of the Left. Members of the Labour Party, Co-operative Party, Independent Labour Party, and Communist Party, and socialists belonging to any or no Party, are invited to contribute to its columns. Articles express the views of the author and not necessarily those of the editor.

Editor: C. A. Smith

SOCIALISTS ANSWER OUR QUESTIONS ON THE WAR

Recent issues of LEFT have contained many discussion articles on the nature of the present conflict, the pros and cons of the anti-war attitude, and the policy now to be adopted by Socialists in Britain. The discussion continues on page 249 of this issue. But in order to obtain a wider spread of opinion than our space will allow in articles, and in order to present to our readers this spread of opinion in a form which will make immediately apparent where agreement and disagreement are greatest, we have this month submitted a questionnaire on the war to representatives of every shade of Left-wing opinion—Labour Party, I.L.P., Communist Party, Trade Unionist, Pacifist, Anarchist. In this, LEFT maintains its claim to be a completely open Forum. We publish below the first replies received; further replies may be published next month. In a subsequent issue we propose to attempt an analysis of the views expressed and a detailed summing-up of the discussion to date. Meanwhile, the questionnaire and its replies will doubtless stimulate further discussion. We invite our readers to take part in it—and to give this extremely important issue of Left the widest possible publicity among their friends and co-workers.

		[Orwell]
1	Is the present Anglo-German conflict fundamentally an imperialist war?	No
2	Whether imperialist or not, is it unimportant to British workers whether Britain or German triumphs?	No
3	Is there any important difference, from the worker's standpoint, between British Imperialism and German Nazism?	Yes
4	Is the struggle of China, Norway or Greece imperialistic?	No
5	Does it become so because assisted by Great Britain?	No
6	Should Socialists support the British war effort?	Yes
7	Should Socialists support the present British Government?	Not unreservedly
8	Should Socialists support strikes which have a legitimate industrial objective, even if they retard the war effort?	Yes
9	Is a Peace by Negotiation desirable, at any price?	No
10	Is a Peace by Negotiation possible at present, on terms which would not leave Hitler master of continental Europe and with a free hand to continue the war on one front against the U.S.S.R.?	No
11	Has the German invasion of the U.S.S.R. affected the issue of a negotiated peace now?	No
12	Is the prospect of a negotiated peace likely to stimulate or retard revolutionary opposition to Nazism in the occupied countries?	Retard
13	If the U.S.S.R. is defeated, is the Anglo-American combination likely to achieve victory?	Yes
14	Would victory then be possible by mainly military means?	No
15	If so, is the present British leadership adopting and developing those means with sufficient speed?	No
16	Is the alternative of a psychological offensive a practical one?	?
17	Is it an alternative or a supplementary method? i.e., would revolt be possible throughout the Continent without the continuation of the armed struggle?	No
18	Is the present Government adopting and developing this method adequately?	No

19	If not, is this Government basically incapable of using this method?	Yes
20	Is the present Government, if victorious, likely to establish a durable peace?	Probably
21	Is the U.S.S.R., if its resistance is maintained, likely to dominate the situation at the end of the war and ensure the establishment of Soviet Communism over large areas of Europe?	No
22	Will it be possible to avoid the dominance of either Imperialism or Stalinism at the end of the war?	Yes
23	Is the British Labour Movement the main bulwark against such a situation?	Important, but not the main one
24	Can the British Labour Movement exercise a decisive influence on the course of the war while in a minority position in Parliament?	Yes
25	Is a Socialist, or a predominantly Socialist, Government possible of achievement during the course of the war?	Yes
26	Would it necessarily strengthen or weaken the war effort?	Strengthen
27	Could such a Government be obtained by constitutional means—i.e., by a General Election?	Yes
28	If so, could mass pressure force the present Government to face a General Election?	Yes
29	If not, should the formation of such a Government by revolutionary means be attempted if suitable conditions arose?	Yes
30	Are such conditions likely to arise?	No
31	Would such an attempt fatally weaken the war effort and enable Hitler to strike a decisive blow?	Not if the suitable conditions existed
32	Would it be probable that by that stage Hitler's own internal position would also be extremely insecure?	No
33	Should all Socialists who believe the present Government incapable of defeating Nazism, or who believe that Socialist methods would shorten the war and win the peace, unite in a common front for an intense propaganda drive?	Yes
34	Should this drive be linked with support for "Win the War by Socialism" candidates at present bye-elections?	Yes
35	Could such a drive exert a decisive influence on the course of the war?	Probably

876. BBC Talks Booking Form, 3.11.41

S. Telkar: 'Through Eastern Eyes,' 'Mind the Doors,' talk on the Underground system; broadcast 4.11.41; fee £7.7s.

877. BBC Talks Booking Form, 3.11.41

H. Umrigar: 'Through Eastern Eyes,' 'Around the Courts'; broadcast 27.11.41; fee £7.7s.

878. To S. M. Telkar

10 November 1941   PP/EB

Dear Mr. Telkar,
I am expecting your script on the Parliamentary proceedings this Saturday. I think I have explained to you sufficiently the kind of thing that we want.

I do not wish to make a prolonged contract, as this is against our usual policy, but I would rather have this series done always by the same person, and shall be very glad to carry the arrangement on from week to week so long as your scripts remain satisfactory.

Yours sincerely
Eric Blair
Empire Talks Assistant

879. To Elsie W. D. Boughen, BBC Contracts Department[1]

11 November 1941   Original [No reference]

"THROUGH EASTERN EYES"—Monday 10th November.
The above talk, which was scheduled to be "THE DEBATE CONTINUES" by Sir Hari Singh Gour,[2] had to be cancelled owing to the Prime Minister's speech.[3]

The script was written and Sir Hari Singh Gour was rehearsed, as it was only at the last moment that we heard of the change. This was to be his last talk, and we do not propose to ask him to do another next week instead, as the speaker for the next few talks is already fixed.

[No name/position]

1. Talks booking forms were sent for processing to Elsie Boughen, who (with K. F. Lowe from June 1943) arranged the completion of contracts.
2. Sir Hari Singh Gour (1866–1949; Kt., 1925), barrister, politician, and author, was Vice-Chancellor successively of the universities of Delhi, Nagpur, and Saugor; Leader of the Opposition in the Indian Legislative Assembly, 1921–34; Indian delegate to the Joint Parliamentary Committee on the Government of India Bill, 1936; and President of the Hindu

Association. A memorandum from Bokhari of 3 November 1941 says that Sir Hari was booked to give six talks in this series, the last on 10 November. He was not being asked to broadcast again because he was 'unfortunately not a very good broadcaster' and all his talks 'were written by us.' Shridhar Telkar had been commissioned to continue the series, but Sir Hari was generously willing to give his help. Sir Hari was later reported to have given a talk in this series on 23 November (though the regular broadcast should have been on the 24th), and he certainly contributed a talk on 2 February 1942 (see *944* and *944, n 1*). The Programmes as Broadcast for November 1941 have not survived.

3. In this speech at the annual Guildhall banquet, Churchill said he would 'view with keen sorrow the opening of a conflict between Japan and the English-speaking world.' He hoped that 'the peace of the Pacific will be preserved in accordance with the known wishes of Japan's wisest statesmen. But every preparation to defend British interests in the Far East, and to defend the common cause now at stake, has been and is being made' (*The Second World War*, III, 528–29; U.S.: *The Grand Alliance*, 594). Pearl Harbor was attacked on Sunday, 7 December 1941.

880. To Noel Sircar

12 November 1941   PP/EB

Dear Mr. Sircar,[1]
Many thanks for your letter, with cuttings, which Mr. Bokhari has passed on to me. I am returning them herewith.

If you care to come and see me here, we could perhaps arrange for a talk, but we must fix on a subject. Can you let me know when it would suit you to come. The mornings are my best time.

Yours sincerely,
Eric Blair
For Mr. Bokhari

1. Noel Sircar appears to have broadcast for the first time for the Indian Section on 5 December 1941. He was frequently employed, reading the weekly news reviews on several occasions when Bokhari was away in the autumn of 1942 and broadcasting film criticism.

881. BBC Talks Booking Form, 15.11.41

S. M. Telkar: 'Through Eastern Eyes,' 'The Debate Continues,' 7, 12-minute talk in English on weekly proceedings in the House of Commons; broadcast 17.11.41; fee £7.7s.

882. Eastern Service Meeting

19 November 1941

Orwell, a member of this committee, attended the meeting on 19 November 1941; also present were William Empson and Laurence Brander (the Intelligence Officer for the Eastern Service). Bokhari was absent, as was A. H. Joyce, of the India Office Information Department. By a curious coincidence, one of the two Ministry of Information representatives was also called Blair. Orwell was listed as 'E. A. Blair' but initials were not given for any other name. This can lead to confusion. Thus, Minute 26 (under 'Intelligence'), which referred back to Minute 15 of the previous meeting, 22 October 1941, was a report from 'Mr Blair' on the functions of the Calcutta Committee (made up of businessmen). This must be the Ministry of Information's Blair, because the initials 'E. A.' are not given.[1] This ministry was located in Senate House, University of London, the building that suggested Minitrue, where Winston Smith worked in *Nineteen Eighty-Four*. One of Smith's colleagues at Minitrue was Tillotson (see *Nineteen Eighty-Four*, *CW*, IX, 44), a name possibly suggested by that of Geoffrey Tillotson, who later discussed 'Absalom and Achitophel' in the series of talks for Indian university students. Tillotson's broadcast was scheduled for 23 December 1941.

For the kind of interest A. H. Joyce took in the talks broadcast, see *887*. This was the same Joyce who had given the editor of the Lucknow newspaper the *Pioneer* (who had offered Orwell the post of assistant editor and leader writer at the end of 1937) a report on Orwell based on India Office files; see *426*. This was adverse, though not wholly unfair. Two passages from his report of 18 February 1938 are relevant to Orwell's work at the BBC. 'There is no doubt in my mind as to his ability as a leader writer, though I think you may have to be prepared, in view of what I assess to be not merely a determined Left Wing, but probably an extremist, outlook, plus definite strength of character for difficulties when there is a conflict of views.' He then suggests that the editor, Desmond Young, 'make the arrangements as tentative as possible' until he sees whether Orwell 'fits into the picture,' and he concludes: 'I hope that I have not in any sense been unfair to a man whose intellectual standard is very high, but whose outlook has become soured by circumstances of hardship, though they may have been of his own seeking.' (See Crick, 355–56.)

It should be noted that the Eastern Service is sometimes referred to in BBC documents as the Eastern Services; the former style is always used in this edition. Meetings were held in Room 101, 55 Portland Place; see *870*.

1. It is also possible that this Blair is either A. P. Blair, who wrote the talk 'My Debt to India,' 5, transmitted 14 September 1942, or Charles Blair, whose 'Japan's Threat to Asia,' 1, 'Japan in the Second Half of the Nineteenth Century' was broadcast on 15 September 1942 PasB for 15 September states that the speaker Charles Blair was John Pilcher. This could possibly be Sir John Pilcher (1912–1990), a diplomat who served in Japan, 1936–39, and China, 1939–41 He worked at the Ministry of Information and the Foreign Office, 1941–48, and was Ambassador to Japan, 1967–72. No relative could confirm that he used the pseudonym Charles Blair. Blair and the Calcutta Committee recur at a meeting on 3 February 1943, see *1864*.

883. To L. F. Rushbrook Williams

[19 November 1941]   Handwritten

SUBJECT: SCRIPT FROM MR. CHINNA DURAI[1]

This script as it stands would be no use in "We Speak to India" or "Through Eastern Eyes" but something rather like it might be used in the new schedule of the latter if the series I have suggested are taken up. Meanwhile Mr Chinna Durai has done one broadcast for us and I hope will do more. He is a fairly good broadcaster & has expert knowledge of legal matters & sport (esp. lawn tennis). He is also very pro-British, so all in all I think we ought to make use of him where possible. I am not certain what is his native language (he is a Dravidian) but if suitable in that respect [I] had thought of him as a possibility for one of the newsletters.[2]

[Signed] Eric Blair
for I.P.O.

1. Chinna Durai had been asked by Bokhari on 16 September 1941 to contribute two 12-minute talks to the series 'Around the Courts,' to be transmitted on 30 October and 11 December; see *866, n. 2*. The second talk had to be rewritten because, Bokhari wrote on 8 December, it would be regarded by many listeners 'as a slashing criticism on° the Indian religious law, a matter which is beyond the jurisdiction of the BBC.' Durai was advised to model his revised talk on the feature 'Presented at Court,' run by the *Evening Standard*. The talk was not broadcast on the 11th, but was recorded for transmission later. Durai wrote to Rushbrook Williams on 22 November, sending a copy of this script or a second script, saying: 'My own view is that these are the kind of talks that might tend to create the Commonwealth-Consciousness in India which is so necessary to help India to stay within the Empire. . . . Certain opportunities must be seized for interpreting Britain to India in a favourable light—and the success of the British army in Libya is definitely one such.' He sent further suggestions in December 1941 and February 1942; one proposal was to use only a few broadcasters, but Rushbrook Williams explained that, however talented, such a restricted range of presenters would suggest 'the imposition of a certain brand of taste' and would be undemocratic. Durai continued to be used occasionally as a broadcaster in 1942 and 1943, though not, perhaps, as much as he wished.
2. Orwell was replying to a memorandum from Rushbrook Williams dated 19 November 1941; his reply is written at the foot and on the verso of Williams's memorandum.

884. *Victory or Vested Interest?*

On Saturday, 22 November 1941, Orwell delivered 'Culture and Democracy' (see *885*), the fifth of a series of six lectures organised by the Fabian Society under the general title 'Victory or Vested Interest?' Much was made in the publicity (as was common at this time) of the 'V for Victory' motif, a device Orwell was to use in *Nineteen Eighty-Four*. The first four speakers were G. D. H. Cole (Chairman, Executive of the Fabian Society); Francis Williams (author of *Democracy's Last Battle*); Harold J. Laski (London School of Economics; member of the National Executive of the Labour Party; referred to in the publicity for the lecture series as Secretary of the Labour Party's Reconstruction Committee); and Mary Sutherland (Chief Woman Officer of the Labour Party). Orwell, who was advertised as 'Author of *The Lion and the Unicorn*, etc', was followed by Victor

Gollancz (advertised as Founder of the Left Book Club). The chair for Orwell's lecture was taken by Mrs. Mary Agnes Hamilton; Leonard Woolf was chair for Gollancz. The *Tribune* advertisement, 12 September 1941, had listed Woolf as the final lecturer, with Gollancz taking the chair. The subject was 'Victory in Europe.' The lectures were also announced in *Fabian News*, 52, No. 10, November 1941.

At a Selection Committee meeting of the Labour Book Service on 24 October 1941, it had been agreed that the lectures should be printed and offered to members as the January 1942 choice (Labour Party Archives, LP/LBS 39/2/154 (iii), traced by Clive Fleay). Publication took place on 15 May 1942, with the title *Victory or Vested Interest?* Gollancz's lecture was not included, because he refused permission to reprint it. The lectures were published in two editions, one by George Routledge & Sons and the other by the Labour Book Service. A second impression was issued in July 1942. Orwell's contribution does not differ in any way; indeed, it has the same misprint; see *885, n. 5* below. According to a letter written by T. Murray Ragg on 1 March 1943 to O. Gollancz of the Fabian Society, of the 3,065 copies printed for the Labour Book Service, by that date 2,970 had been sold; and of the 3,246 for Routledge, 3,080 had been sold.

Orwell evidently did not realise publication had taken place until late in July 1942. On the 23rd he wrote in strong terms to Routledge & Sons to complain that they had made 'the most unwarrantable alterations' to his lecture without consulting him (see *1319*). Further, they had not even sent him a copy of the book. Ragg, the Managing Director, replied, putting the blame firmly on the Fabian Society. Routledge, he said, had made no alterations whatsoever and they had supplied copies, as agreed, to the Society: 'it would seem that possibly some official of the Fabian Society made the alterations.'

In some notes Orwell compiled about 1947 listing which of his articles might be collected and published, he said of this reprint, 'This was transcribed from shorthand notes of a lecture, & was grossly altered without my knowledge.' About two years later, in the second half of 1949, when preparing notes for his literary executors, he wrote: 'This was substantially altered and deformed all the way through without my knowledge or consent *after* I had corrected the proofs.' Doubtless for this reason he did not wish it to be reprinted, and it should be read with this caveat in mind.

885. 'Culture and Democracy'

22 November 1941

The word Democracy is habitually used in two meanings which are quite different and are not even complementary to each other, but which are somehow felt to go together. One is the primary sense of the word—a form of society in which power is in the hands of the common people. The other is much vaguer but is more nearly what we mean when we speak of democracy in such a context as this. It means a form of society in which there is considerable respect for the individual, a reasonable amount of freedom of thought, speech and political organization, and what one might call a certain decency in the conduct of the government. It is this rather than any definite political system that we mean by democracy when we contrast it with totalitarianism.

Now in an essay of this sort I don't need to debunk the first definition. I don't need to point out that in England or in any western democracy power is not in fact in the hands of the common people. On the other hand, and particularly in left-wing circles, I think it *is* necessary to say that democracy in the other sense—freedom of speech, respect for the individual and all the rest of it—does have a reality, an importance, which cannot be made away with by mere juggling with words. Nothing is easier, particularly if you have a screen of battleships between you and danger, than to prove in words or on paper that there is no real difference between totalitarianism and "bourgeois" democracy. I haven't the slightest doubt that each of my readers has said that. I have said it frequently. It is the easiest thing in the world to show that all the compulsions which are put upon the individual crudely and openly in a totalitarian state are put upon him in a slightly more subtle way by the money-squeeze in a so-called democratic society. After all, if the Germans are very cruel to the Poles, our own behaviour is not so very nice in India. There are concentration camps in Germany, but didn't we ourselves pen up a lot of innocent people behind barbed wire last year? The S.S. and the Gestapo are horrible things, but if you lived in the slums of Liverpool you probably wouldn't think of the police as angels. Freedom of thought isn't technically restricted in England, but in practice the whole of the Press that matters is in the hands of a small clique of millionaires who can prevent you from saying what you think. Everybody knows that line of thought. It is impossible to go into a left-wing gathering anywhere without hearing it put forward. But I think it is necessary to recognize that it is not only nonsense, but nonsense of a kind which can only be uttered by people who have a screen of money and ships between themselves and reality. For when one has pointed out the essential unfreedom of democratic society, and its similarity with totalitarian society, there does remain the residual difference that in a country like this we are not afraid to stand up and say what we think. Quite probably there is a secret police in England, but the point is that we don't feel afraid of it. I may often have had detectives listening to speeches I have made, but I could safely ignore their presence. The fact is that all demonstrations that totalitarianism and democracy are the same thing—democracy and fascism are twins, in Stalin's words—boil down to saying that a difference of degree is not a difference. This is a fallacy which is as old as history. There is even a Greek name for it which I have forgotten. It is perhaps not particularly important that I can write what I like for a limited public whose influence will extend to a few hundreds more, but it *is* important, symptomatically important at any rate, that after two years of war, during most of which we have been in a very serious jam, I don't feel *more* frightened of doing so than I did two years ago. Even if it could be shown to be true that there is no real difference between democracy and totalitarianism, what at least is never true is that people *feel* them to be the same.

I think what this demonstrates is that not only is there a real difference between old forms of society like our own, which have had the chance to develop a certain decency in their politics, and the newer totalitarian states, but that our type of society is incapable of changing in certain directions unless forcibly altered from the outside. There are certain values which it seems not to lose touch with, even in moments of deadly danger. But notice that I say only that our form of democracy can't of its own accord change in certain directions, not that it can't change at all. It is certain that it *must* change or perish. If there is one thing in the world that is certain, it is that capitalistic democracy in its present form cannot survive. Imagine for a moment that we are not at war and are back in Chamberlain's dear dead days; in those circumstances, if I had to establish that capitalist democracy cannot survive, I think I should do it by pointing out that what are now called democratic nations are not reproducing themselves. Most of the breeding of the world is done in non-democratic countries. As soon as the standard of living rises beyond a certain point and people have a certain power of doing what they want, the birth-rate always falls below replacement level. And that is not due to economic insecurity, which is the fashionable explanation. It is sheer nonsense to say that there is less economic security in Britain and the United States than in the great breeding centres of China and India. On the contrary, it is due to something that goes with capitalist democracy, and that is the principle of hedonism. Our birth-rate is small because people are taught to have a consumer mentality. The chief feature of life in capitalist society during the past twenty years has been an endless struggle to sell goods which there is never enough money to buy; and this has involved teaching ordinary people that things like cars, refrigerators, movies, cigarettes, fur coats and silk stockings are more important than children. However, there is a more immediate argument against the survival of capitalist democracy arising from the fact that we are at war. Once again I don't have to insult left-wing circles by pointing out the weaknesses of a capitalist nation at war. If I were lecturing to readers of the *Daily Telegraph* I should point out that in capitalist society the making of profits is and must be one's main motive, and I should point for example to such things as the fact that in the last week before the outbreak of war people in England were tumbling over one another in their eagerness to sell lead, nickel, copper, rubber, shellac, and so forth, to Germany, in the full knowledge that these things would come back on them in the form of bombs in a few months' time. But when I am writing for a predominantly socialist public, I hardly need to point out the structural weaknesses of capitalist democracy which will force it to change or perish. I prefer to insist on certain weaknesses which are inflicted on us by the hedonistic principle, and by the fact that in a democracy people are called on to vote upon things which in practice they know nothing about.

One of the worst things about democratic society in the last twenty years has been the difficulty of any straight talking or thinking. Let me take one important fact, I might say *the* basic fact about our social structure. That is, that it is founded on cheap coloured labour. As the world is now constituted, we are all standing on the backs of half-starved Asiatic coolies. The standard of living of the British working class has been and is artificially high because it is based on a parasitic economy. The working class is as much involved in the exploitation of coloured labour as anybody else, but so far as I know, nowhere in the British Press in the last twenty years—at any rate in no part of the Press likely to get wide attention—do you find any clear admission of that fact or any straight talking about it. In the last twenty years there were really two policies open to us as a nation living on coloured labour. One was to say frankly: We are the master-race—and remember, that is how Hitler talks to his people, because he is a totalitarian leader and can speak frankly on certain subjects—we are the master-race, we live by exploiting inferior races, let's all get together and squeeze as much out of them as we can. That was one policy; that was what, shall we say, *The Times* ought to have said if it had had the guts. It didn't say it. The other possible policy was to say something like this: We cannot go on exploiting the world for ever, we must do justice to the Indians, the Chinese and all the rest of them, and since our standard of living is artificially high and the process of adjustment is bound to be painful and difficult, we must be ready to lower that standard of living for the time being. Also, since powerful influences will be at work to prevent the underdog from getting his rights, we must arm ourselves against the coming international civil war, instead of simply agitating for higher wages and shorter hours. That is what, for instance, the *Daily Herald* would have said if it had had the guts. Once again, nowhere will you find anything like that in plain words. You simply couldn't say that kind of thing in newspapers which had to live off their circulation and off advertisements for consumption goods. One result of this lack of straight talking was complete inability to prepare for the present war. I don't point to the part played by the Right. That is obvious. But the part played by the Left, which was due to the inherent contradiction in a political party which actually existed to defend wages but which liked to think of itself as having internationalist aims, was almost equally damaging to ourselves. In effect, the policy of the English Left has always been Disarmament and War. It has always stood for a vigorous foreign policy without being willing or able to point out to ordinary people that very heavy sacrifices are necessary in order to pay for the armaments without which a vigorous foreign policy is impossible.

For purposes of demonstration, I have picked out just one fact basic to our situation about which it has been impossible, in the sort of society we have been living in, to tell the truth. No politician in the last twenty years who told the truth about the British Empire could have got himself a political following. And I think one can see from this the inevitable weakness of any democratic society when challenged by other societies which are not democratic, which are ruled by clear-sighted, evil men who know exactly what they want, who don't have to consider things like trade unions or newspapers dependent on advertisements for consumption goods, and who have no difficulty in forcing whole populations to work like slaves and breed like rabbits. In addition, another less noticeable but in the long run equally important factor is the peculiar character of the intelligentsia that grows up in a wealthy capitalist democracy. Our intelligentsia, I mean the left-wing intelligentsia—and please notice that in the last ten years there has been no intelligentsia in England that is not more or less "Left"—is essentially the product of investment capital. It owes its peculiarities partly to that and partly to the exceptional security of our life in England. The thing that always strikes one about the British intelligentsia is its extraordinarily negative outlook, its lack of any firm beliefs or positive aims, and its power of harbouring illusions that would not be possible to people in less sheltered places. In an essay of this length I cannot give an exhaustive list of the illusions of the British intelligentsia. As an example I will take just one obviously silly, obviously fallacious idea which is almost peculiar to Anglo-Saxon civilization, namely Pacifism. Pacifism as put forward by, for instance, the Peace Pledge Union, is such nonsense that no one who has ever been forced into contact with realities would even consider it. Anyone who has any notion at all of the way in which things happen knows that a government which will not use force can always be overthrown by any body of people, even by any one individual, that is less scrupulous. Society as we know it *must* in the last instance be founded on force. A child of six would be able to see that. But in England we have lived for decades past in this extraordinary sheltered state in which you can go your whole life without, for instance, ever seeing a dead man, without ever receiving a blow, without ever spending a night in the open or feeling hungry—without, in consequence, ever needing to look down at the roots on which your own existence is founded. In that kind of atmosphere extraordinary follies are possible and can infect all sorts of people. One can see the result in the attitude of the British intelligentsia towards the present war, which began, in my opinion, about 1935 or 1936, definitely not later than 1936. Between 1935 and 1939 the whole of the left-wing intelligentsia, almost like a flock of sheep, were pro-war. They were in favour of making a firm stand against Germany, although on the whole they were also against arming. Immediately war broke out the left-wing intelligentsia turned anti-war. This was not due to the Russo-German Pact and to the feeling that one must justify Russian policy at all costs. It affected a lot of people who were not particularly pro-Russian in sentiment, and to my knowledge others who were pro-Russian in sentiment did not change their anti-war views on June 22nd. I suggest that this was simply due to the unrealistic attitude which it has been possible to develop in the last twenty years and the mere tendency to discontent which any thinking person has in our kind of society. The best place in which to study the English left-wing mind is the weekly paper, the *New Statesman*, which is a sort of crossing ground for the various intellectual currents of the Left. As a magazine the *New Statesman* seems to me to have only symptomatic value. I have been a regular reader of it for many years and never once have I found in it any coherent policy or any constructive suggestion—anything, in fact, except a general gloom and an automatic discontent with whatever happens to be in progress at the moment. It expresses nothing except the fact that English left-wing intellectuals of all shades do not like the society they are living in but at the same time do not want to face the effort or the responsibility of changing it.

Now notice that all I have said hitherto could have been printed in one of those snooty little minor leading articles in *The Times*. It sounds just like the conventional attack on "highbrows" which A. P. Herbert, etc., are so fond of. But it is very important to realize that there is another side to the question.

Why is it that a wealthy capitalist society seems naturally to breed a discontented intelligentsia like a sort of wart on its surface? The reason is that in such a society as ours the intelligentsia is functionless. In the last twenty years, particularly in Britain and America and almost as much in France, there has been no real job, no place in the structure of society, for the thinking man as such. If he has had a job at all it is only owing to the fact that there is a lot of invested capital knocking about, hence a lot of interest, which goes into the pockets of decadent third-generation rentiers, who spend it in financing picture galleries and literary reviews, which in turn provide an income for artists genuine and spurious. There has been no opportunity for the thinking man, as such, to make himself or feel himself *useful*. This condition persists even when the nation is at war, and even in the most desperate moments of war. I remember early in the war I was talking to the editor of a left-wing weekly paper, and he said to me, "You know Sir Stafford Cripps wrote to the Government on the first day of the war offering his services in any capacity." I said, "So did I." My friend, let's call him X, said, "So did I, but the difference is that Cripps was distinguished enough to get an answer"—the answer being negative, of course. There you have a picture of the humiliating position of the intelligentsia in our type of society. If the Government can use them at all, it uses them not for the talents they actually possess but at best can only turn them into rather inefficient private soldiers or unreliable clerks. And if that is the case in war it is even more so in peace. Look at a map of the world and you will see that nearly a quarter of it is painted red. That is the British Empire—and remember that in spite of all things it is on the whole better to be inside the British Empire than outside it. Well, the whole of that vast empire is administered by people who cannot be called in the narrow sense intellectuals, people who have no contact with the intelligentsia whatever. The intelligentsia during the last twenty years could not take part in that process of administration because the Empire and all its workings were so out of date, so manifestly unjust, that they would necessarily have revolted against it. They lived in a society which automatically deprived them of function and in which the best way to prosper was to be stupid. That is the explanation of their never-failing discontent. In every other way they had opportunities such as the world has never before seen. They had ease, money, security, liberty of thought and even completer moral liberty. Life in Bloomsbury during the last twenty years has been what the moral rebels all through the ages have dreamed about. And yet on the whole the people who were favoured in this way weren't happy, didn't really like the things they ostensibly asked for. They would sooner have had a genuine function in a society which might give them less but took them more seriously.

I have outlined shortly, as examples, just one or two of the inherent weaknesses of capitalist democracy. If you draw a caricature of capitalist democracy you get a picture something like this: at the top a wealthy class living largely on dividends; living on them an enormous army of professional men, servants, tradesmen, psychoanalysts, interior decorators and whatnot; also living on them is a parasitic intelligentsia, earning their keep by pretending to abuse the people who pay them—having the same sort of function in fact as a dog's fleas, which the dog mildly enjoys snapping at; and at the bottom you get a working class with artificially high standards and permanently on strike for the means to buy refrigerators, electric cookers, lipsticks and radiograms. That is an untrue picture, but remember that it is only untrue in the way in which a caricature is untrue. That is how a wealthy country like England appears from the outside. That is how the Italian radio propagandists, for instance, describe us, and though of course they are lying and exaggerating, they do believe a part of what they say.

I claim that a society with these weaknesses, particularly when it is in a desperate predicament, must change or perish. All that I have said of Britain is *a fortiori* true of the U.S.A. I never pick up an American magazine or go to an American film without feeling that if these things are really representative of the American scene, a society of that kind will not stand the shock of war without fundamental change. If our society survives it must survive in a more disciplined, hardened form, with its fat sweated off it and the profit motive abolished. But in saying that, haven't I come near to giving the game away and saying that in order to fight successfully against our enemies we must become exactly like them? The pacifists have a formula, which is easy to repeat and needs no thought, "If you fight against fascism you go fascist yourself." That is a mechanistic form of thought. When a pacifist says to me, "If you fight fascism you become fascist yourself," I always answer, "And if you fight against negroes you turn black." The fact that they usually take several minutes to see the fallacy gives you an idea of the quality of their minds. Actually, to say that by fighting against Nazi Germany we must become exactly like Nazi Germany is to lack any historical sense whatever. The reason why Germany took a particular line of development is contained in the history of Germany, and the reason why England is taking a different line is contained in the history of England. It is important to realize that we *are* taking a different line. Certain things which ought to have happened if the mechanical formula which I mentioned just now were correct, have not happened and show no signs of happening. I come back to the fact that I am not frightened to take my pen and write in this vein—that I am not frightened, if I choose, to say that this is an imperialist war and Churchill is the tool of the capitalist class and that we ought to stop fighting to-morrow. As I said earlier, and it can hardly be repeated too often, the significant thing is not that I can say this, but that I am not *more* frightened of saying it after two years of desperate war in which it is certainly not to the advantage of the Government to have people walking about and saying things of this kind. What that implies is the failure of our society, perhaps its actual lack of power, to develop in a certain direction. There is no sign of any authentically fascist development in Britain at this time. Certain things which could lead to fascism are inevitably going on. Inevitably a centralization of power is taking place, and equally inevitably there is conscription of labour, but the failure beyond a certain point to tamper with freedom of speech indicates that there is no real growth of fascist mentality. The average left-wing intellectual will tell you in his mechanistic way that Churchill is a fascist. Here he is using words in the same manner as Goebbels when he says that Chiang Kai Shek[1] is a Jew. The truth is that the British ruling class are too old-fashioned to develop in a genuinely fascist direction. Let me take one small fact which is symptomatically important—the prohibition in all totalitarian countries of listening in to foreign broadcasts. It is known that the B.B.C. is listened in to all over Europe with passion, though when people are allowed to listen in to the B.B.C. the tendency is rather the opposite. As long as that prohibition exists, the inference must inevitably be drawn that that broadcast which you are forbidden to listen to is probably true. The Germans have an excellent series of broadcasts to England, including a number of spurious stations pretending to be "Freedom" stations inside the British Isles, but nobody listens to them, because it is not forbidden. Now the people directing German propaganda are not fools. You can see from Goebbels's speeches that he is aware that if he could only lift the ban people would stop listening to the B.B.C., but he cannot do so because the notion of giving a free hearing to an enemy is contradictory to the whole fascist outlook. Our own Government is a much more old-fashioned despotism, the kind of pre-fascist despotism which does not care what you think so long as your outward actions are correct. The totalitarian mentality hardly exists here as yet. Hardly anybody lies awake quivering with rage and hatred because somebody a little further down the street is committing "deviations". And I suggest that this failure to develop a totalitarian mental atmosphere, even when the material conditions for it exist, is a sign that provided we can avoid conquest from without, our society will not lose touch with certain habits and values which have been its mark for hundreds of years.

In all this talk about Democracy I have strayed a long way from the other word in the title of this chapter—Culture. As before, the word has at least two meanings. People speak of "culture" in an anthropological sense and in an aesthetic sense. You discover, for instance, an island somewhere in the South Seas where the people practice cannibalism and worship the sun; that is "a culture". Or you buy a copy of the *Oxford Book of English Verse* and learn quotable bits by heart; that is "Culture". But you find a certain connection between the two meanings if you go back to the primary sense of the word. Culture means controlled growth. Any bit of soil will grow plants if it gets enough water, but so long as they grow higgledy-piggledy we call that "Nature". As soon as it is ploughed and things are planted in rows we say that it is "cultivated". But we also speak of soil reaching a high state of culture. If you merely plough up a piece of virgin soil you cannot grow particularly fine products on it; you could not produce the best French wines, or even good peas or asparagus, from a soil of that type. If you till a piece of soil long enough and deep enough, and enrich it in the right way, you can change its whole nature and texture, even its colour. You only do that in order to grow finer plants on it, so that ultimately the value of a soil is judged by its products. So in the long run is a civilization. We say that a civilization has reached a high state of culture when each generation leaves behind a residue of certain things which one can describe roughly as art and wisdom. Almost inevitably a civilization is judged by the art it leaves behind. It is perhaps possible to imagine a high civilization existing as it were in a vacuum, each generation getting a tremendous kick out of life but leaving nothing behind, but, in the nature of things, we have no evidence of any such thing having ever existed. On the other hand, when you dig up some ruined city in the Central American forests and find remarkable sculptures, you say, simply on the evidence of the sculptures, "This was a high civilization, these people had reached a high state of culture." Art is an important symptom. It is a registration, as it were, of man's attitude to the universe at any given moment. A good civilization will produce good works of art, not as its main purpose but as its most important by-product. And in a civilization which is really sound this will apply not only to what we call fine art, but to all the domestic and applied arts—furniture, clothes, houses, pottery, glass, tools and whatnot. They are all, even down to such things as the designs on stamps and coins, symptomatic of the prevailing culture.

Now, when I extend what I am saying to cover such things as clothes and furniture, I may seem to be giving up the cause of culture as lost. For though our age may have produced good major art—I only say "may", you notice—it is unquestionable that in all the minor arts it is an age of unbearable ugliness. You can see more ugly things in Oxford Street in half an hour than you could see among all the savage tribes in the world. What has happened to us, of course, and temporarily thrown our culture off the rails, is the impact of the machine. I am not one of those people who talk as though we could suddenly cut ourselves loose from the machine civilization and return to the Middle Ages. Whatever else history may do, it never travels backwards. But there is no use blinking [at] the fact that when you move into the industrial era you have to pass through an age, perhaps centuries long, of the most horrible ugliness. A primitive person compared with ourselves appears at first sight to have perfect taste. His clothes, for instance, are never ugly. Even if he is dressed only in a bit of cloth no bigger than a handkerchief, he will wear it gracefully. There is a queer little confession of the aesthetic inferiority of Western man in a rule which exists or existed till recently in the British army. A British private soldier is rarely allowed to wear civilian clothes. On the other hand, in the Indian army the sepoys when off duty are always allowed to wear their own clothes, because it is known that, being Indians, they can be trusted to dress themselves becomingly. An Englishman cannot, unless he has had a special kind of training, and even then he is only what is called "well dressed" according to what is no more than an accepted code of ugliness. And yet when one looks deeper one sees that this seeming superiority of taste in the primitive or savage man is an illusion. For the good taste of the primitive collapses with extraordinary promptitude as soon as he comes into contact with machine civilization. Not only does he eagerly seize the most vulgar products of the machine—offer him a five-shilling enamelled German wristwatch and he grabs it with both hands—but his whole aesthetic sense seems to disappear at the first contact. I have seen an Indian dressed only in a loin-cloth and a bowler hat. Even we would not do a thing like that. But so long as he sticks to his original form of dress he has, apparently, perfect taste. The explanation is that throughout long ages he has lived in a culture in which there has been very little change. A certain way of life has been built up, and even the minutest details, even such things as gestures and movements of the body, have been gradually perfected, so that there is not much chance for any one individual to go wrong. We, on the other hand, happen to live at a moment when there is every opportunity to go wrong. We have moved suddenly into the period of machine civilization, which is the most drastic change that has happened in thousands of years. But I think that the idea of a complete and final loss of culture is an illusion. For we made once before an equally drastic change, when we changed from a nomadic to an agricultural way of life, and after all, a new culture was built up. At present we are merely in the process of development, and given a certain continuity one can even prophesy to some small extent what our culture will be like when we possess one again. To say that the present age is cultureless is rather like saying that I am beardless. I have never let my beard grow, but it is potentially there, and up to a point I can tell you what it would be like if it existed. I can tell you that it wouldn't be red, for instance. So also with culture. I can't tell you what our civilization will be like in A.D. 2200, but I think I could prophesy some of its characteristics. I think I can foretell, for instance, that we shall still be using the English language and that it will still have something in common with the English of Shakespeare, always assuming that we have escaped conquest from without.

At the moment that is the crucial point. We are temporarily in the position of having to fight rearguard actions in defence of what is left of civilization, but I don't think there is any reason to be pessimistic about the long-term effects of the arrival of the machine. Ultimately we shall get used to the machine. We do, however, have to defend ourselves against the threat of totalitarianism, which might really bring a swift and final death to civilization. Why is it that everything we mean by culture is menaced by totalitarianism? Because totalitarianism menaces the existence of the individual, and the last four or five hundred years have put the individual so emphatically on the map that it is hard for us to imagine him off it again. To illustrate the impact of totalitarianism on culture I will name only a single art, literature, which in the form in which we know it is incompatible with the totalitarian form of government. At first sight it may seem like begging the question to choose literature rather than any other art, because literature is the one in which the line between fine art and propaganda is hardest to draw, and consequently is the one most immediately affected by political changes. But if the implications are followed up it will be found that in every art, even including such things as pottery or cabinet-making, the interference with the emotions of the individual peculiar to totalitarianism are equally deadening. Why is it that individual literature is incompatible with totalitarianism? We are in the habit of saying that the Nazis are the enemies of literature, but they would prefer not to be its enemies if they knew how to avoid it. If they could suddenly produce a Shakespeare and say, "This is *our* Shakespeare," they would be only too delighted. The reason is that the driving force, the dynamo as you might say, of any artist is his emotions, and his emotions do not necessarily correspond to the political necessity of the moment. The totalitarian state exists for the glorification of the ruling clique, which means that the ruling clique are the prisoners of their own power and are obliged to follow any policy, no matter how self-contradictory, which will keep them in power. And having followed their policy they are obliged to justify it, so that all thought becomes a rationalization of the shifts of power politics. It is not true that an atmosphere of orthodoxy is in itself fatal to literature. To realize that you have only got to think for a moment of the Middle Ages. In the Middle Ages men lived within a framework of thought which was as rigid, I suppose, as the one in which people have to live in Germany to-day. And yet not only could they produce good literature—and in the later Middle Ages it was distinctly *individual* literature—but the thing that always strikes me about the few medieval writers I know is the comparative freedom of their minds. Catholic belief was more or less obligatory, but it didn't cripple them. The difference, of course, is that in the Middle Ages the prevailing orthodoxy *didn't change*, or at least didn't change suddenly. It probably doesn't matter that men should be compelled to live within a certain framework of thought. Everyone's mind is necessarily full of beliefs which he has accepted from the outside and entirely on trust. I couldn't prove, for instance, that the world is round. I could give good reasons for thinking that it is not flat, but to prove that it is round needs pages of mathematics which I should be incapable of understanding. But this unproven belief is something which I have grown up with and never questioned, and which consequently doesn't cause any emotional disturbance in me. On the other hand, if someone suddenly comes to me with a loaded pistol and tells me that I have got to believe that Jews are not human beings, it does something to my emotional life which would necessarily have a damaging effect on any creative work I attempted.

You see there a striking difference between capitalist democracy as it now exists, and totalitarianism. In England, absurdities just as great as any in the totalitarian states are being offered to you all the time, but you are not under any obligation to accept them. Six months ago, for example, Stalin was Bad with a big B. Now he is Good with a big G. A year ago the Finns were Good. Now they are Bad. Mussolini is Bad at this moment, but it would not particularly surprise me to see him Good within a year. But after all, nobody is compelled to swallow this kind of thing. If I write a book I am not forced to say in it that Stalin is Good, I don't have to watch with desperate anxiety lest there should be a political change before the book goes to press, my emotional life is not interfered with. In a totalitarian state it is difficult to imagine any writing above the level of pamphleteering. Here somebody may answer, "But in fact some of the best writers of our time have come to terms with Fascism." This is one of those statements which tend to dissolve when you examine them. It is perfectly true that up to about 1930 the best European writers were on the whole reactionary in tendency, but if they were inclined for a while to be pro-Fascist it was because they made the mistake, which was easy to make before Hitler was in power, of thinking that Fascism was a form of Conservatism. Since then the issue has become clearer, but even so it is possible to make out an impressive list of writers who have accepted Fascism outright. Céline,[2] author of *Voyage au Bout de la Nuit*, is now Exhibit A in

Paris, or at least his books are. Ezra Pound is in Rome doing anti-Semitic broadcasts. Wyndham Lewis for a long time had connections with Mosley's movement, and so had Osbert Sitwell. Roy Campbell[3] fought for Franco in Spain. And there is a long list of French writers who have gone over to the Nazis since the fall of France. All this, however, is somewhat misleading. Roy Campbell and Wyndham Lewis have certainly changed some of their opinions during the last few years, and we don't know much as yet about the motives of the various French writers who have capitulated. Of the writers I mentioned just now, the one whom it is most possible to respect is Céline. There is no question about the venomously anti-left and anti-Jewish tendency of the stuff he has written during the past ten years. But I don't think he can be taken as proof that it is possible for good writers, intelligent, scrupulous men, to make their peace with Fascism. He is simply a good mind gone sour. His writings are essentially an expression of disgust with modern life. I think I described him once as a voice from the cesspool. Rather as Eliot, Maritain[4] and others reacted against the idealistic League of Nations atmosphere of the nineteen-twenties, Céline reacted against the half-baked left-wing orthodoxy of the following decade, and because he was a man in whom disgust and hatred were the chief driving force, he went the whole way, anti-semitism and all. He accepted Nazism as a kind of nihilism. From the Nazi point of view Céline would obviously come under the heading of *kulturbolschewismus*,[5] but as he happens to bear a distinguished name, the Nazis are quite unscrupulous enough to use him against intellectuals elsewhere, as an example of a literary man who has seen the light. But obviously this is no more than a first-generation phenomenon. You can't imagine a literary tradition founded on *Voyage au Bout de la Nuit* and *Mea Culpa*. You can't imagine generation after generation of Célines, all founding their work upon disgust and horror of contemporary life—and certainly that is not the kind of literary tradition that the Nazis want to establish. Céline, or any writer like him, is simply a disgruntled individual who can be temporarily made use of in a moment of chaos.

I think one must conclude that literature as we know it is inseparable from the sanctity of the individual, and therefore is absolutely incompatible with the totalitarian way of life. And what is true of literature is true of nearly everything that we classify under the heading of culture. One must conclude therefore that though our democracy is bound to change—can, in fact, only survive by turning into Socialism—all that we mean by culture is inextricably bound up with democratic values. The destruction of democracy would mean not simply the loss of certain advantages and the acquisition of certain others, but an actual *end* to civilization as we know it. We must defend ourselves against that as we should defend ourselves against an invasion from Mars, because we can hardly imagine an alternative.

But let nothing that I have said be taken as meaning that at this moment we have much in the way of a culture to defend. We are only fighting for the future. We are in the trough of the wave, though we know that presently the wave will go up again. We are not the flowers of a civilization, we only know that, given growth, given continuity, at some time civilization will flower again. In this age we can at best be only the manure of the future. On that perhaps rather depressing note I will conclude.

1. Chiang Kai-shek (1887–1975), Chinese general, took control, in 1926, of the Kuomintang, the National People's Party founded by Sun Yat-sen. He led the fight against the Japanese, who invaded China, 1937–41, and the Communists under Mao Tse-tung; was President of the National Government, 1943–49 and, after fleeing to Taiwan, 1950–75.
2. Céline (Louis-Ferdinand Destouches; 1894–1961), French physician and author, served in the French army in World War I and was severely wounded. From 1928, he worked as a doctor in a poor area of Paris and wrote two significant novels, *Voyage au bout de la nuit* (1932, *Journey to the End of the Night*), a bitter satire on the society of his time, and *Mort à credit* (1936; *Death on the Instalment Plan*), and also the anti-Semitic pamphlets *Bagatelles pour un massacre* (1937; *Mere Trifles for a Massacre*) and *L'Ecole des cadavres* (1938; *School for Corpses*) Rejected when he tried to enlist in 1939, he worked as a ship's doctor, ran a dispensary, and joined the ambulance service. In 1942 he visited Berlin, and in 1944, fearing retribution for his collaboration with the Nazis, tried to flee to Denmark. After being imprisoned in Berlin, he practiced medicine among Vichy expatriates in Germany. In 1945 he escaped to Denmark, where he was imprisoned for fourteen months for collaboration. A French court condemned him in 1950 to a year's imprisonment, a fine of 50,000 francs, and confiscation of half his property. The following year, a military tribunal exonerated him, and he set up a medical practice amongst the poor of Meudon, near Paris. He continued to write; his last work was a trilogy, *Rigodon* (1969).
3. Roy Campbell (1901–1957) was a South African poet, dramatist, and translator; see *2314, n. 1* and *2967, n. 1*.
4. Jacques Maritain (1882–1973), a French Roman Catholic philosopher, wrote more than fifty books. His philosophy was neo-Thomist, and he developed a philosophy of the arts. He taught at Columbia and Princeton universities, 1941–44, was Ambassador to the Vatican, 1945–48, and Professor of Philosophy at Princeton, 1948–60.
5. *kulturbolschewismus*] kulturbolschewsmus   *roman type and lacking medial 'i' in first and second impressions*

886. To M. J. Tambimuttu

25 November 1941   PP/EB

Dear Tambimuttu,
The Facilities Unit have arranged for you to go to see the offices of the Daily Express on December 4th—Thursday—at 9. p. m. I gather that this is a special favour, as they have given up showing people round in the ordinary way.

You should ask for the Commissionaire and tell him what you have come for, and he will know all about it.

Yours sincerely
Eric Blair
Empire Talks Assistant

887. M. Myat Tun: What Trade Unionism Means to the Worker

25 November 1941

Although Orwell was not the author of this broadcast, he was directly involved. Myat Tun had belatedly sent him two different scripts on trade unionism on 20 November; he had found it difficult to compress his source material and asked Orwell to make a selection and edit it. He said he thought 'What Trade Unionism Means to the Worker' was the more interesting of the two treatments.

On 6 December, A. H. Joyce, of the India Office Information Department (see *882*), asked Rushbrook Williams to look at this script. He was amazed, he said, 'that a talk of this nature, especially to a country like Burma, could have been permitted. It must have caused consternation in the minds of the authorities there.' He was surprised that the censor at the BBC, Burton Leach, saw no harm in the talk: 'My own speculation is that this talk was not written by Myat Tun but by some cute trade union propagandist who has, in this instance, succeeded in getting over the air to Burma the kind of broadcast which, I hazard a guess, would never have been permitted in this form, even in our own Home Programme.' Was Joyce hinting at Orwell? He concluded by suggesting that closer supervision of Myat Tun's broadcasts was called for.

Rushbrook Williams replied, on 8 December, that the series 'Through Eastern Eyes' was 'addressed to the English-knowing Indians' and he doubted whether the talk would have any appeal to Burma. He concluded: 'The talk as I saw it in censored form did not seem to me too bad; because its motive was the staunch adherence of the Trade Union movement to the war effort. But I will certainly take your advice and arrange that Myat Tun is very carefully supervised in future.'

Myat Tun gave a talk on Moulmein, Burma, on 6 February 1942, and, on 10 April 1942, Orwell asked him for advice on the pronounciation of Burmese place names.

888. BBC Talks Booking Form, 26.11.41

Dr. P. Chatterjee: 'Through Eastern Eyes,' 'How It Works,' 9; 12-minute talk in English on banks; recorded 28.11.41; broadcast 30.11.41s; fee £7.7s. Signed: N. H. Parratt.

889. To J. Bahadur Singh

26 November 1941   PP/EB

Dear Mr. Singh,[1]
With reference to our conversation yesterday, I am sending you three specimen scripts of our series "The Debate Continues". None of these is altogether satisfactory, but they will give you some idea of what to do, as well as what to avoid, and I have written some comments in red ink in the

margin. If you could let us have a specimen of your own any time within the next three or four weeks, I should be much obliged.

I would also like it very much if you could do us a Christmas Day broadcast of 10 minutes. Christmas in Wartime would be the sort of line, though we will think of some more striking title later. Please let me know as soon as possible whether you can undertake this, as we are now only five weeks from Christmas. The talk can be recorded some days beforehand, so that you will not have to broadcast on Christmas Day.

Yours sincerely
Eric Blair
Empire Talks Assistant.

1. J. Bahadur Singh (1915–), born in Trinidad, was recommended to the BBC by Norman Collins. He read law at Oxford and was President of the Oxford Union, 1940–41 On 27 November 1941, he sent Orwell a script (now in the BBC Archives) he had written for 'students in the American Continent in the "Britain Speaks" series.' On 28 November he wrote agreeing to do the Christmas broadcast. He later was appointed Indian ambassador to Egypt. For his memories of Orwell, see Crick 417.

890. BBC Talks Booking Form, 26.11.41

S. M. Telkar: 'Through Eastern Eyes,' 'The Debate Continues'; broadcast 1.12.41; fee £7.7s. Signed: N. H. Parratt.

891. To David Astor

27 November 1941   Handwritten

111 Langford Court   Abbey Road   NW.8

Dear Mr. Astor,[1]

Many thanks for your letter. I am so overwhelmed with work that I don't know whether I can undertake to write anything at present, but we could meet & discuss it any way. I could meet you some time towards the end of next week.[2] The best place to ring me (I am not on the phone here though the porter's lodge is) is the BBC, Welbeck 4468, Extension 386.

Yours sincerely
George Orwell

1. The Honourable Francis David Langhorne Astor (1912–; CH, 1993) served in the Royal Marines, 1940– 45, and was foreign editor, 1946–48, editor, 1948–75, and Director, 1976–81 of The Observer. As his biographer Richard Cockett has written, 'His principal talent as an editor was his ability to identify and cultivate talent'; he made The Observer 'a paper of ideas.' Its 'golden years' saw it overtaking the circulation of the Sunday Times (September 1946). Orwell contributed significantly to this development, not so much through the articles he wrote, but as a friend and inspirer, as a political guide, and in teaching Astor 'the merits of clear, simple English prose as the best vehicle for communication.' In August 1943 The Observer tried to have Orwell appointed a correspondent in Algiers and Sicily, following the

Allied landings, but there was official obstruction. The paper wanted him to cover the South African election of 1948, when Dr. Malan's Nationalists defeated Smuts's Unionists, but Orwell was by then too ill. Astor regularly circulated Orwell's 'Politics and the English Language' to new staff as a guide to the way in which precise English led to precise thinking (*David Astor and 'The Observer,'* 1991, 141, 135, 131, 126–27.) In *Remembering Orwell*, Astor recalls: 'I'd met Orwell first in 1942; I was introduced to him by Cyril Connolly. I was just beginning at that time to have a say about what went into the *Observer* [which was owned by his father, Viscount Astor]. I was trying to liven it up a bit, to make it more in touch with what was going on. I had asked Cyril for names of writers of politics, and he gave me only one: George Orwell. I'd only read his *Lion and the Unicorn* then, which I thought masterly. I remember our first meeting. It was in a restaurant near the BBC building. I didn't know what he was supposed to look like, but there was this tall, slightly detached person standing there, and as soon as I walked in he came up to me and said, "Are you David Astor?" and began right off like that, as if he'd known you all his life, and you felt he had.' They became good friends, and it was Astor who made arrangements for Orwell to be buried, as he had wished, in a country churchyard according to the rites of the Church of England (218–20). Orwell's first contribution to *The Observer* was 'India Next,' published anonymously, 22 February 1942; see *981*.

2. This would be about Thursday–Saturday, 4–6 December 1941. When shown this letter in April 1985, David Astor could not remember whether this was when they first met or whether it was in 1942, as he says in *Remembering Orwell*.

892. Newsletters, News Reviews, and News Commentaries

One of Orwell's most important duties at the BBC was the writing of weekly newsletters, news reviews, and news commentaries. He did not write news bulletins—'the news' as such; that was reserved to the News Division, upon whose work, together with the newspapers in the library in Broadcasting House, Orwell drew. The dividing lines between letters, reviews, and commentaries are unclear. Although W. J. West's volume of these broadcasts is titled *Orwell: The War Commentaries*, only five scripts of those printed by him and thirty broadcasts not known to him (all to Malaya and Indonesia) out of a total of 219 or 221 are called Commentaries. The most common description is 'Newsletter' or 'News Letter,' used 135 times.

Scripts broadcast in English to India were most frequently titled 'News Review' or 'Weekly News Review'; five were called 'Commentary' and five 'Newsletter' (one of which, for 10.1.42, was altered by hand to 'Weekly News Review'). The PasB ('Programmes as Broadcast': the formal BBC summary of what was transmitted) for 23.7.42 erroneously refers to the 'News in Marathi,' a clerical error. Orwell from time to time referred to his broadcasts as 'weekly commentaries'—as when opening and signing off his broadcast to India of 13.3.43 (see *1952*) and, rather puzzlingly, when advising R. R. Desai in a letter of 19.12.42 (see *1753*) how he should prepare scripts for transmission in Gujarati, saying they should be 'more in the nature of commentaries on the weeks° news and not a Newsletter'—that despite the fact that every one of Orwell's 42 Gujarati broadcasts is described as 'Newsletter' or 'News Letter' in the PasB.

The descriptions given here are those typed or written at the top of the script, or, if scripts are missing (as most are), the description recorded in PasB, with the distinction between News Letter and Newsletter not preserved; 'Newsletter' is used.

Orwell's work in this field was much more extensive than suggested by the 49 newsletters reproduced, rather inaccurately, in West: *Commentaries*. That collection omits texts of three broadcasts (29.11.41, 7.3.42, 21.11.42); prints three scripts which cannot, or can only doubtfully, be attributed to Orwell (2.5.42, 23.5.42, 11.7.42); fails to note that the script for 6.6.42 was not broadcast; and does not record five (or six) occasions on which newsletters were broadcast but for which scripts have not survived (No. 1 in November 1941; 30.5.42; 20.6.42; 5.12.42; 2.1.43; and probably 27.6.42). Orwell seems to have been responsible for 54 or 55 scripts for transmission to India in English, not the 46 (of 49) West attributed to him. There are many errors in and omissions from the texts as reproduced by West, one omission a whole page (for 12.9.42). The texts are not, in fact, 'printed exactly as typed,' as West claims (23). More serious, West fails to note some 175 occasions when Orwell was responsible for preparing scripts in English for translation into Gujarati, Marathi, Bengali, Tamil, or Hindustani or those he wrote, and usually read, to occupied Malaya and Indonesia.

Far from Orwell delivering a 'final message' at the end of his broadcast to India on 13.3.43 (see *1952*), which West claims (219) showed 'his realisation that . . . direct propaganda was not going to be part' of his work for the BBC (a statement that epitomises West's fixation with censorship), Orwell wrote many more newsletters after that date, and broadcast many more. West's assertion has important, and false, implications for the record of Orwell's life and for the charge that he was, as it were, gagged by the BBC. The record shows that he was writing newsletters right up to the moment he left the BBC; the last was broadcast on his behalf two days after his departure.

Orwell seems to have been responsible for the following newsletters:

In English to India (Saturdays)	56 (one not broadcast; one uncertain)
In English to Malaya (Fridays)	30
In English to Indonesia (Fridays)	19 (written by Orwell until he left the BBC)

Of these, Orwell read 12 to India, 28 to Malaya, 16 to Indonesia: 56 in all. He seems to have written English versions for these translations:

Into Gujarati (Mondays)	42 (one less certain; last two recast by Desai, who took over, as exercises)
Into Marathi (Thursdays)	15 (taken over by Venu Chitale)
Into Bengali (Saturdays)	29 (taken over by Dr. P. Chatterjee)
Into Tamil (Wednesdays)	29 (prepared by Orwell until he left the BBC)
Into Hindustani (Saturdays)	1 (possibly more)

Thus it would seem he prepared 104 or 105 newsletters in English and 115 or 116 for translation into vernacular languages: 219 to 221 in all. There may have been others for which records have not been traced.

Of the 55 or 56 scripts in English for India by Orwell, 50 have survived, one only as a printed extract. Of the other scripts, part of one to Malaya, for 28.5.43, and two short extracts from the English versions for the Marathi scripts for 12.3.42 and 19.3.42 have survived. All English originals for vernacular versions and those vernacular scripts were apparently shredded some years ago.

Ascertaining authorship of the scripts is not always simple. Some have 'By George Orwell' written or typed on them; PasBs and talks booking forms often state 'Written by Eric Blair' and sometimes 'Written by George Orwell.' Often what appears to be an ascription to an author is not, and even the facts of transmission cannot always be relied upon. PasBs frequently state that a newsletter is 'by Z. A. Bokhari,' the Indian Programme Organiser, and Bokhari did write scripts, but it seems to mean, for broadcasts in English to India, that Bokhari was the reader. The booking form for Marathi Newsletter 20, for example, states that it was written by E. Blair and translated and read by M. R. Kothari; the equivalent PasB simply says 'read by Mr Kothari.' Just as the PasB does not note that Kothari was the translator, so it is not concerned with authorship. What mattered most for the PasB record was who read the script. That Orwell usually wrote the Weekly News Review for India is indicated, apart from specific ascriptions, by his letters to Princess Indira and others of 10 June 1942 (see *1215*), in which he describes the review as 'a summing-up of the world situation . . . and is written by myself.'

Some scripts of newsletters give precise timing details, on occasion with progress times as well as final timing. PasBs also give timings. These ought to be close to those on the scripts, if not identical. However, for example, the Weekly News Review for 23.5.42, read by Dick Wessel, has a script timing made by Godfrey Kenton[1] of 11 minutes 20 seconds; the PasB gives 13 minutes 30 seconds. This could be a clerical error, or the script may have been further altered just before transmission; or possibly Dick Wessel (whose name appears only this once in the documentation associated with Orwell and the Indian Section) is the South American Service's W. P. Wessel and there has been a confusion of names of speakers and broadcasts. Whatever the reason, 'simple facts' conflict.

A more serious conflict occurs a fortnight later. The script for 6.6.42 bears both censorship stamps (for Security and Policy), signed by Bokhari, and is much amended in Orwell's hand. It is not marked 'As broadcast' (which is not uncommon). However, the PasB, quite exceptionally, shows that in the regular time slot for the newsletter, Princess Indira gave 'The Debate Continues,' which, according to its booking form, was to be transmitted on 8.6.42.

Two more examples of uncertainty: Booking forms for Gujarati Newsletters 18 and 19, for 29.6.42 and 4.7.42, state that they were to be written by Orwell, but he was then on holiday. It is possible he wrote 18 before he left, but it is extremely unlikely that he wrote 19 (and this has not been included in his tally). The Marathi Newsletters are misnumbered from 20 (which is given as 21) to 27. Such a simple mistake, if undetected by a researcher, could lead to all sorts of supposition. Thus, although there is a great deal of information, it is neither complete nor wholly reliable.

Two clues suggest that 'by Bokhari' does not point to his authorship of the weekly news reviews and, indirectly, support Orwell's claim. First, a number of scripts with 'Z. A. Bokhari' written on them also carry, close by, 'Anon.' The script was for, not by, Bokhari. Second, it seems certain from the PasB that the script for 23.5.42 was by Bokhari because a distribution note reads: '1. Empire Presentation / 2. Miss Parratt, 416, 55 P.P.' (Room 416 was Orwell's), whereas the normal destinations were either E.S.D. and Registry or Bokhari and File. The implication is that a copy of the script was being sent to Orwell's secretary so he would know what had been said in a week he was not responsible for the review. One other script has a similar indication, but it is firmly crossed out.

There is one more source of information: the BBC publication for overseas listeners, *London Calling*, which lists programmes to be broadcast, but, because it had to be prepared well in advance, it does not always reflect what happened. Thus, although Orwell read his news reviews from 21 November 1942, he was advertised as doing so only as from 19 December 1942. Illness could also cause a change. Thus, he was listed to read his news reviews on 23 and 30 January and 6 and 13 February 1943, but PasBs show that a talk on Turkey was substituted on 23 January when Orwell became ill on the 20th, and that Anthony Weymouth wrote and read the reviews on the other dates (though Orwell had returned to duty by 12 February). *London Calling* also shows that weekly news reviews were to be broadcast on 6.1.42 and 14.11.42, so that the substitutions, noted in the PasBs, of 'The Debate Continues' and a talk by Sir Ramaswami Mudaliar were last-minute changes.

Did Orwell write different scripts for translation into Indian languages from those he prepared for broadcasting in English to India, Malaya, and Indonesia? Since no vernacular scripts have survived, it is impossible to be sure. News needed updating, of course. Though he was writing commentaries, not news, where the latest information was not necessarily vitally important, commentaries did demand different approaches for different communities, for audiences of different cultures, and for audiences living in territory occupied by the Japanese. Laurence Brander, Eastern Service Intelligence Officer at the time, and the man responsible for recommending that Orwell take over reading his own newsletters, under his pen-name, wrote to the editor, on 6 August 1985, regarding broadcasts for Malaya, that 'my guess would be that the scripts would be different. Orwell was too good a journalist to address a captive people and free listeners in the same way.' There was certainly a practice in the Overseas Service of writing different scripts for different audiences, for example, for the North American and the Pacific & Eastern Services, but practice may have varied in the Indian Section. Since the Bengali Newsletter was broadcast less than three hours after the one to India had been read, it seems likely that it was fairly close to the English-language script. Two scripts for the English-language service to India indicate that they were used also for the Bengali service. That for 26.12.42 has written on it, in the hand of the censor for Security and Policy, S. Ramaam, 'For English & Bengali.' Three weeks later, the script for 16.1.43 has two telling notes: 'Announcer/Tran: S. K. Das Gupta' (the man then presenting the newsletter in Bengali) along with, in the same hand, a broadcast time, 1430-1445 GMT, and the network, Green, for the Bengali transmission. The details for the English-language broadcast are typed on this script: '1115-1130 GMT, Red Network.' There may have been changes in content, but it is probable that the Bengali translation was in the main made from the English-language weekly news review. Orwell's 13 July 1942 letter to M. R. Kothari (see *1276*) certainly suggests that different versions were prepared to suit the audiences aimed at.

The scripts Orwell wrote in English for translation into Tamil and Gujarati, though doubtless using material similar to that in the English-language newsletters for India, Malaya, and Indonesia, may well have been refurbished or even prepared separately. Thus, Orwell wrote his newsletter for Indonesia on 3 September 1943, the day he went on leave; it was read for him by John Morris. The 'equivalent' Tamil Newsletter, for 2 September, was written by M. Phatak instead of by Orwell (even though he had not yet left), suggesting that it was a different script.

Information about the Gujarati service is more plentiful. Orwell is credited with writing the English version from 2 March to 28 December 1942, except for his two weeks of leave. The scripts were translated by R. R. (sometimes with H. L.) Desai. Towards the end of the year, when it was decided that Desai should take over completely, Orwell wrote to him, stressing more than once that he did not wish to dictate the contents, and explaining that he wanted the talks to be 'more in the nature of commentaries on the weeks° news and not a Newsletter' (see *1745, 1753*). He made some suggestions for coverage of the North African campaign and 'the renewed persecution of the Jews in Poland'; both topics were featured in his Weekly News Review for India on 19.12.42. Although Orwell paid considerable attention to Admiral Darlan in that review, however, he did not mention Darlan to Desai until 2 January 1943, by when Darlan had been assassinated. Apart from content, it is evident from such letters to Desai that Orwell was conscious of the need for a different approach, a different tone, for the Gujarati audience. Though anxious that the persecution of the Jews should be given prominence, he knew this could be a delicate matter for Desai: 'you will be best judge of the reactions of your audience.'

It looks from the correspondence as if Orwell wrote different newsletters for translation into Gujarati and Marathi, and variations in timing back that up. Yet the Bengali Newsletter, for which he also provided an English version, went out on the same day as the news review in English for India, and the timings for the pair suggest a close but not complete correspondence of basic text, hardly surprising given the closeness of the times of transmission. See also *995*.

Bokhari, in his letter to Shridhar Telkar of 20 February 1942, stated that the English version of the Marathi Newsletter 'will be prepared by Eric Blair'; see *978*. Exceptionally, two extracts of Marathi Newsletters have survived. That for 12.3.42 was certainly prepared by Orwell, and that for the following week was probably by him. The first extract was reworked in his Weekly News Review of 14.3.42; that in the Marathi Newsletter for 19.3.42 is reproduced exactly in the Weekly News Review two days later. Variations in timing and evidence of reworking and of similarity make it difficult to deduce a general practice, but it looks as if there was some variation and, understandably, some repetition.

Whatever was repeated or freshly drafted for the scripts to be translated into Indian languages, there can be no doubt that Orwell, far from having no part in the BBC's direct propaganda after the conclusion of the series transmitted in English to India, was deeply and continually employed therein, even for a day or two beyond his departure from the service of the BBC.

The introduction of the Weekly News Reviews to India got off to a faltering start. This may have been due to the need to introduce the new programmes into a slot filled by a series gradually being wound down ('The Leaders,' which summarised what English newspaper leader-writers had been saying), but more likely because at a crucial moment Orwell was taken seriously ill with bronchitis and was absent on sick leave 1–22 December 1941. Working out the details is difficult: either one or two early scripts are missing, or there was vagueness in noting the author and/or reader of scripts (not peculiar to these broadcasts); and, quite exceptionally, the PasBs for November 1941 have not survived. The first four weekly news reviews would seem to be:

No. 1: 15 or 22 November

No. 2: 29 November (the extract printed in *Talking to India* can be assigned to this day)

No. 3: 20 December (unnumbered script survives, which refers, probably inaccurately, to a broadcast given the previous week; PasBs has no record of such a broadcast in that week)

No. 4: 3 January (so numbered)

The weekly news reviews then continued regularly, read by Bokhari until he was to return to India on leave in July 1942, when scripts were read by Shridhar

Telkar, Bahadur Singh, Noel Sircar, and Homi Bode. As it happened, because transport was not available, Bokhari did not leave until 29 September, but the arrangements for reading the reviews went ahead. From 21 November 1942, Orwell read his own scripts.

All scripts had to be scrutinised for Security and Policy. Passages of many are crossed out. In this edition, such passages are printed in roman type within square brackets, without comment; additions and substitutions are printed in italic; what was originally written or typed is in the notes at the end. West: *Commentaries* describes all such passages as 'Censored,' which some certainly were. Occasionally the censor's comments are noted, though West ignores these. It is at least possible that some of these cuts were for timing purposes and some for style. In the main, no reference is made here to differences between West: *Commentaries* and this edition; see *846, n. 20, 847, n. 5.* However, some examples will indicate the nature of such differences.

The broadcast for 31.1.42 (see *946*) marks this sentence as censored: 'Brazil is within flying range of West Africa and for at least fifty years the Germans have had designs on it.' It is far from plain why this should have been censored. The Germans presumably knew already the distance their planes would have to and could fly. The next two sentences are also crossed out, down as far as 'much easier to frustrate'; this is not noted in West: *Commentaries* (45–46). It might also be asked why, in the broadcast for 15.8.42, the words 'and the Russians are counter-attacking and in places have forced the enemy on to the defensive' should have attracted the censor's blue pencil. The paragraph beginning 'The operations in Madagascar . . .' in the script for 19.9.42 has a number of cuts but none of these are marked in West: *Commentaries* (152). It is possible these changes were made to improve the style of the text and had nothing to do with censorship. One last example: Orwell's broadcast of 28.11.42 has a passage added in his hand but then crossed through. These five lines are silently omitted from West: *Commentaries* (181).

The reasons for cuts and changes need careful analysis. 'Censored' does not suffice. That cuts were made to ensure correct length is clearly shown from a script not by Orwell, 'The Voice of the Enemy,' broadcast over several networks, 8–10 February 1943 (on the 10th by the Eastern Service). This was censored by Anthony Weymouth, who wrote, 'This is a little too long,' and suggested cuts.

The typescripts reproduced here vary. Some were certainly used in the actual broadcast: that for 14.3.42, in an Indian-language script (Urdu), carries the speaker's (Bokhari's) guide to the pronunciation of a place name. Some are fair copies produced by typists in the General Office; the scripts sometimes have an indication such as 'To G.O.' (for General Office, not George Orwell, who was known at the BBC as Eric Blair). Some scripts have the imprint of the two censors' rubber stamps and occasionally their comments. Some scripts show changes and some do not. Some are absolutely clean scripts, neatly typed, single spaced, with no indication of their having been used in a broadcast. These scripts, and some, but not all, the double-spaced fair copies have typed at the top of their first page the words 'As Broadcast.' Absolutely clean scripts may have been typed after the text had been broadcast as a record of what was said if, perhaps, the original had been greatly altered, making it difficult to follow. Alternatively, fair copies may have been prepared twenty years later on the instructions of R. C. Collison, Head of the BBC Library and Archives. Whatever the explanation, texts which show no changes must not be assumed to represent broadcasts that were unmodified at an earlier stage in their preparation.

A memorandum outlining the development of news commentaries in the Empire Service of the BBC was written by R. A. Rendall, then Assistant Controller of Overseas Programmes, on 9 February 1942 (by which date Weekly News Review 9 had been broadcast to India) for the Controller of Overseas Programmes, J. Beresford Clark. It was marked 'Private and Confidential.' Given the difficulty described in the third paragraph of finding suitable people whose name would carry some weight in the countries addressed, it is remarkable that it was not until 21 November 1942 that Orwell was commissioned to read his own newsletters to India.

NEWS COMMENTARIES IN EMPIRE SERVICES

1. ORIGIN AND DEVELOPMENT.

News commentaries were introduced in Empire Services in the North American transmission during the summer of 1940, as one element in an attempt to adapt our output to the specialised tastes of United States listeners; North American Director had recommended an attempt to attract the enormous audiences known to listen to news analysts on American radio programmes.

"Headline News and Views" consisted of three or four minutes "straight" news summary, followed by a ten-minute talk commenting on and analysing the news from the British point of view. The speakers originally used were Vernon Bartlett, George Slocombe and A. G. Macdonell. Of these, the first two concentrated on direct analysis of international news in the style of a diplomatic correspondent; the third spent much time on counter-propaganda in answer to German radio comment. Difficulties arose when speakers claimed more knowledge both of facts and of official policy than was at that time available to the Corporation through its own contacts; moreover, individual speakers were sometimes disinclined to accept the line recommended by the Corporation on advice from the M.o.I.[2] This suggested that such work could best be done by commentators with staff contracts, who would be (a) more regularly available, (b) in closer touch with Government directives underlying B.B.C. news policy, and (c) under direct control.

An attempt was made to find and build up as personalities men with journalistic experience, preferably men from the Dominions, for by this time the news commentary had been introduced into other transmissions in response to the interest shown. A Canadian, a South African, a Scot on the staff of the European Service and others were all regularly employed, but the search for suitable people for the Pacific transmission was not easy. Criticism received from overseas showed that something more vigorous and more in tune with Australian thought was required. When Sir Keith Murdoch was in London, he reiterated that criticism and was thereafter persuaded to agree (where he had previously refused) to the part-time secondment to the Corporation of Tahu Hole, who now gives Pacific commentaries five times a week.

2. PURPOSE AND VALUE.

The primary purpose of news commentaries is propaganda. They make it possible to "put across" the British view of the news, without sacrificing the reputation that has been carefully built up for veracity and objectivity in news presentation. The commentary can, by its selection of particular events for emphasis and its explanation of tendencies, supply the perspective that is needed, in close proximity to the news bulletins, especially when news as revealed in official communiqués is bad, or fluctuating rapidly. Moreover, it achieves this object in a radio form that is now popular not only in North America but throughout the world. The use of a team of named speakers is consistent with practice in other countries, gives variety and secures the authority and popularity which is associated with the successful "build-up" of a radio personality. The use of Dominion speakers increases the confidence felt by the audience; particularly in times of difficulty or strained relations, there is thought to be great merit in leaving the right type of Dominion speaker free to reflect criticism and in other ways to build up confidence in himself as much as a representative of the Dominion audience as a British spokesman. In this sense the job of the Empire news commentators may sometimes be compared with that of the American broadcasting representatives in this country. A case in point is the recent work of Hole in the Pacific transmission that has been specially praised by the Dominions Office.

3. POLICY SOURCES AND EDITORIAL CONTROL.

Early experience showed that a close policy control was essential for news commentaries, and this could best be obtained by the use of staff commentators speaking under their own names. From the start it was realised that news commentaries must be under the direct control of the News Editor; in practice, the commentator takes his line from the daily "directive" written by the Empire News Editor. The sources of guidance and information on which the Editor bases his directive are various. Confidential "background" information, originally supplied by Foreign Adviser° and now supplied by C.(N.C.) at a daily conference and by C. (Eur.S.)³ at a fortnightly meeting, is added to information and guidance contained in Empax telegrams, Foreign Office guidance supplied through Foreign Adviser's office, guidance cables dispatched daily by the North American Division and weekly by the Empire Division of the M.o.I., and occasional suggestions and requests from the Dominions, Colonial and India Offices. Information, guidance and suggestions from all these sources are discussed daily, before the directive is written, at the Empire Service Directors' conference.

The scripts of news commentaries are vetted by the duty editor in Empire News. Reference of doubtful points through the normal internal and external channels is resorted to when necessary. Shortage of staff in Empire News and dispersal of the Empire Services have handicapped the effectiveness of this machinery; so have the variety of sources of guidance and the inability of the Empire Division of the M.o.I. to supply any long-term policy directive. Direct contact with the three Government offices chiefly concerned is (with the knowledge of the Empire Division of the M.o.I) now improving. The return of Empire News to London will enable Empire News Editor to profit from these improved contacts.

It was thought that the appointment of staff commentators might involve the Corporation in the difficulties of "editorial comment", but in fact this has not proved to be the case. All material broadcast by the Corporation in wartime is regarded overseas as having a certain authority, thus creating a difficult problem of reconciliation between our function as the "voice of Britain" and our function of reflecting fairly in our news reports all types of opinion. The news commentary provides the best answer. The fact that the commentators are in most cases members of the B.B.C. staff does not appear, for the distinction between a "staff contract", a "programme contract" and an ordinary "speaker's contract" has no more than internal significance. The staff contract is simply a convenience, administratively and financially.

Despite the difficulties and risks involved, news commentaries have established themselves as an invaluable element in our propaganda output and one of the most popular features in the programmes.

Germany, Japan, and the USSR, as well as Great Britain, devoted much effort to winning hearts and minds to their respective causes by means of broadcasting. It seems at least likely that those working from Europe had as their inspiration the power of propaganda there and the part radio had played in that. But whether they gave a great deal of thought to the statistical differences between Europe (and later the United States) and India in the spread of this medium remains unknown. Figures do not tell the whole story—relatively more influential people might listen to radio in India than in Europe and audiences for individual radio sets might be much larger – but they are so strikingly different that they are worth noting.[4]

United Kingdom: population 30 June 1939, 47,680,500; radio licences December 1938, 8,856,494, December 1939, 8,893,582

Germany: population 1939 census (excluding Austria and Sudetenland), 69,410,141; radio licenses December 1938, 9,087,000

United States: population 1940, 131,669,275; radio sets estimated, 57,000,000

India: population 1941 census almost 389,000,000; radio licenses 31 December 1940, 100,388

According to these figures, there was, in the given years, one radio for 2.3 people in the USA, for 5.36 people in the UK, for 7.64 people in Germany, but in India, there was one radio for 3,875 people. And to reach the Indian population, the BBC had to broadcast in English, Hindustani, Gujarati, Tamil, Marathi, Bengali, and Sinhalese (mainly for Ceylon). For later figures for India, see *2374* (xv, 343).

Information about newsletters has been derived from correspondence and booking forms filed at the BBC's Written Archives Centre at Caversham, microfilm copies of newsletters in English intended for India, and from the volumes of Programmes as Broadcast at Caversham. The PasBs are almost complete for this period; only those (for the Overseas Service) for November 1941 and for a few days around 18 November 1943 are missing. The absence of PasBs for November 1941 makes it impossible to be certain how and when the first newsletters in English to India in which Orwell was involved were broadcast. In the main, the PasBs provide the best and most accurate record of what actually was broadcast. Yet they are not totally reliable. Thus, on 13 July 1942 this cryptic note appears against the 1300 News for India heading: 'There was no News Commentary as the reader had not arrived.' It is extremely unlikely that complete silence was allowed. Usually there is a note, 'RFU,' if there was a 'Record Fill Up' for even a minute at the end of any item which ran short, with details of what was played (if only for copyright purposes) and of what kind of announcement was made. On another occasion, Saturday, 23 August 1941, it is plain that the entry was made at least a day later. The Announcer trailed (gave advance publicity for) 'The Man Shakespeare,' due to be broadcast to India on 24 August: 'In this trailer I used three poems on Shakespeare by Sir Modh.° Iqbal from "Bang-I-Dara." In spite of this elaborate trailing, the discs of "The Man Shakespeare" were found to be practically unusable on Sunday.' There are other minor inaccuracies. For example, Orwell is 'M. Blair' as author of the English version of the 22.4.43 Tamil Newsletter and 'Eve Blair' as author of this Newsletter on 25.9.43 and 21.10.43. There is also considerable variation in the practice of recording timings; where they are noted, they are reproduced here. Sometimes, PasBs give information found nowhere else; for example, that Charles Blair, who spoke on 'Japan's Threat to Asia' was John Pilcher; see *882, n. 1* and *1485*.

Although out of chronological order, this entry from Orwell's last Literary Notebook is included here because in it he reflects upon his time producing newsletters at the BBC. In the notebook it appears immediately after a 'hospital entry' for 24 March 1949.

In 1943, when I was working for the BBC, one of the weekly "newsletters" that I was responsible for was the Marathi one. These newsletters—actually news commentaries issued once or twice a week in minor languages in which it was impossible to broadcast daily—were composed by someone in the BBC, then translated by a speaker of that language & broadcast by him, under the supervision of a censor who as a rule was also an employee of the BBC.

We always had difficulty with the Marathi newsletter, because, apparently, Indians of that race when living in England soon lose their command of their native tongue. So though there were a number of Marathi students in England, there were not many who were suitable as broadcasters. In 1943 the job was being done by a little man named Kothari, who was almost completely spherical. He had I think been a Communist & certainly been an extreme Nationalist, but was quite reliable because he was genuinely[5] anti-Nazi & pro-Allied. Suddenly the so-called "College", the mysterious body (actually I think M.I.5) which had to O.K. all broadcasters, got onto the fact that Kothari had been in prison—for some political offence while a student, I think. At once Kothari was banned from the air on the ground that no-one who had been in prison could be allowed to broadcast. With some difficulty we got hold of another youth named Jatha, & all went well for some time. Then, after this had been going on for some months, my Marathi assistant, Miss Chitale, came to me & suddenly revealed with great secretiveness that Jatha was not actually writing the broadcasts. He had partly forgotten his own language, & though he could broadcast the newsletter when once written, he could not translate it. Kothari was actually doing the translations & he & Jatha were splitting the fee. I felt it my duty to tell my superior, Dr Rushbrook-Williams,° about this. As it would be very difficult, if possible at all, to find another Marathi broadcaster, he decided that we must wink our eye at what was happening. So the arrangement continued, & we did not officially know anything about it.

It seemed to me that this was a little bit of India transplanted to Britain. But the *perfectly* Indian touch was Miss Chitale holding up her information for several months before disclosing it.

1. Godfrey Kenton (1902–), actor, made his debut in 1922 and joined the BBC in October 1941; he returned to the stage in June 1944. He was not on the staff of the Indian Section.
2. Ministry of Information (Minitrue of *Nineteen Eight-Four*).
3. C.(Eur.S) is Controller European Services. C(N.C.) is not in the long list of official BBC abbreviations. C.(N.) is Controller, News; the second 'C.' may stand for 'Circulation,' for which it is sometimes used.
4. Figures for UK and German radios are from Asa Briggs, *The History of Broadcasting in the United Kingdom*, Vol. 3. *The War of Words*, Appendixes B and C. For his discussion of the BBC's service to India, see 504–12. Other figures are from *Encyclopaedia Britannica Book of the Year, 1942*.
5. Something is crossed out after 'genuinely' and also at the start of the second paragraph.

893. Weekly News Review, [2?]

[29 November 1941]

The text reproduced here is that in *Talking to India*[1] and is dated 'November 1941.' This may have been slightly modified from that broadcast. See the headnote to Newsletter 10 and variants to that text (*970*).

During the past week the Nazi Government has made every attempt to focus the attention of the world on the Anti-Comintern Conference which it has been holding in Berlin.[2] This conference and its pronouncements deserve close attention, because their object is to deceive public opinion in outside countries and to foreshadow the peace plan which Hitler will almost certainly put forward this winter.

From the speeches which Ribbentrop, Hitler's Foreign Minister, and others have made, it is beginning to be clear what sort of picture the Germans intend to put forward in hopes of persuading the world that there is no longer any reason for resisting them. First of all, all those speeches began with the assumption that the Russian resistance is at an end. They say that the whole territory west of Moscow and down to the Caspian Sea has been effectively conquered, and that the Ukraine, with its immense wealth of corn and oil, is now ready to be exploited for the benefit of the German people. They say, therefore, that Germany, or as they call it, Europe, does not need any longer to import goods from across the sea, that it can go on fighting if necessary for thirty years, and consequently that the British air attacks are simply a senseless continuation of a war which is already finished. This, of course, is aimed at the peoples of America who hate war, desire friendly relations with the rest of the world, and might possibly be induced to keep out of the war if they were really convinced that Russia and Britain were defeated, and that Germany intended no further harm.

Together with this picture of a self-sufficient Europe organising itself against Bolshevism and against British air attacks, there goes, of course, a huge flood of lies about the benevolent intentions of Germany towards the conquered peoples. Germany, we are told, does not really wish to rule over subject races, but merely to accept the natural wealth of Europe and Asia for the benefit of everybody. For the time being, the familiar talk about German racial superiority is dropped. Not only are Czechs and other Slavs spoken of as though they were almost the equals of Germans, but the Nazi propagandists even utter high-sounding promises of their intention of liberating the various coloured peoples now under British rule. This comes, it should be noticed, from men who only yesterday were openly describing the coloured races as the natural slaves of the white, and who described negroes, for example, in Hitler's own words as "Semi-apes." And even while the German wireless woos its Indian listeners with promises of independence, it woos the British public by declaring that Germany has no wish to break up the British Empire, and praises the British for the civilising work they have done in India. It thus speaks with many voices at the same moment, caring nothing for inconsistencies, provided that it can sow a little confusion in the ranks of its enemies.

When we turn from the speeches of the Nazi propagandists to the actual facts of the European scene, we see that the whole picture of a rich, happy and united European continent under German rule is built upon lies and delusions. To name first the fact which is most important of all, Russia is not conquered, and the Russian resistance is as strong as ever before. At least twice during the progress of the campaign, the Nazi spokesman—on the second occasion no less a person than Hitler himself—had declared that the Red Army has for all practical purposes ceased to exist. We may wonder then why it is, if no Red Army exists any longer, that the Germans do not simply march into Moscow and down to the oil wells of Baku. The truth is, of course, that the Russian Army is still in being, and that neither Moscow nor Leningrad have° yet fallen. Even if they should fall, the Germans are hardly any nearer to victory, for the Russian Army will still be there, ready to attack them in the spring. When we read these pronouncements which say that Bolshevism has only a few weeks or days of life before it, we should remember the German announcements of a year ago, which stated in just the same way that Great Britain could not possibly continue to resist for more than a few weeks longer. In both cases, the idea was the same, to make the outside world give up all hope of escaping Fascism by spreading the idea that the German Army was invincible.

Hardly less important than the failure to conquer Russia is the failure to win over the peoples of Europe to collaboration in the New Order. The resistance is particularly strong in the Balkan States. All the efforts of the German wireless have failed to conceal the fact that open civil war is now raging in Yugoslavia, where the people have risen against the tyranny of the German and Italian invaders. In France, in Holland and, above all, in

Norway, the traitors whom the Germans have set up as puppet rulers have failed to secure the allegiance of their people, and the people themselves are beginning to see more and more clearly that the Germans come not only as conquerors, but as robbers. France, the Low Countries, Eastern Europe and even Italy, are being systematically stripped of grain, potatoes and other foodstuffs which are sent to Germany, little or nothing being sent in return. In Denmark,[3] once one of the most prosperous countries in Europe, the peasants have had to kill most of their cattle because there is no longer fodder for them. In Spain the population is not far from starvation, and even in Italy—the so-called Ally of Germany—the bread ration has been reduced so low that the ordinary citizen now receives only 7 ounces of bread a day. The Germans are well aware that, though Europe when it is at peace is just capable of feeding itself, it cannot do so while most of its population is working to supply goods for the German war-machine. Therefore, while making speeches about the benefits of the New Order and the wealth of European resources, they also warn their people not to expect any increase in rations because of the conquest of the Ukraine, giving as an excuse the fact that this territory has been too much devastated by the war to produce much food during the next year.

So much for the Anti-Comintern Conference, and the pictures of the New Order which the Germans will try to present when, during the winter months, they begin to talk about peace.

1. For the publication of *Talking to India*, edited by Orwell, see *2359*. This is the first of 'Five Specimens of Propaganda,' after which title 'Extract' is printed in brackets.
2. The conference was held on 25 November 1941.
3. Denmark was not an original, nor a willing, member of the Anti-Comintern Pact, but was forced to accede at this conference, causing the Danish government-in-exile to break off relations with the home government. The Nanking government of occupied China also became a member, introduced by the Japanese.

894. BBC Talks Booking Form, 2.12.41

Noel Sircar: 'Through Eastern Eyes,' 'The Man in the Street,' 9, Street Markets; broadcast 5.12.41; fee £7.7s. Signed: N. H. Parratt.[1]

1. Orwell was on sick leave with bronchitis (recorded as from 1–22 December 1941). He may have returned on Monday, 22 December, because he wrote to Mulk Raj Anand on that day; see also *903, headnote*.

895. BBC Talks Booking Form, 2.12.41

S. M. Telkar: 'Through Eastern Eyes,' 'The Debate Continues,' 10, broadcast 8.12.41; fee £7.7s. Signed: N. H. Parratt.

896. Eastern Service Meeting

10 December 1941

Minute 37: Programmes and Policy

Mr. Bokhari reported telegram from "The Times of India" in response to request for criticism of B.B.C. programmes and their reception, as a result of which programmes had been divided into four categories: (i) in English for English people, (ii) specially designed for Indians who speak English, (iii) news in Hindustani, (iv) features in Hindustani and students' messages: Miss Gompertz was now engaged in improving category (i). In stressing the need for increased specialisation E.S.D. noted the principle of projecting Great Britain to India, as well as the requirements of the exile audience further East. Agreed to work more closely with the Feature Department: features for category (i) to be selected from general output of Empire Service in consultation with D.E.P. and Feature Department, if possible at the commencement of the schedule: D.E.P. to assist Mr. Bokhari with choice of features. Proportions of time allocated to categories (1) and (ii) to be altered as necessary within the service.

Minute 38: Gujerati° and Marathi News Bulletin°

Mr. Bokhari reported weekly news bulletins in Gujerati and Marathi to start shortly.

At the Eastern Service Meeting on 24 December 1941, Rushbrook Williams reported that the start of these 'bulletins' (presumably newsletters are meant, because news bulletins did not come under his aegis) was 'dependent on formal appointment of staff' (Minute 38).

897. BBC Talks Booking Form, 10.12.41

Mrs. S. Lall: 'Through Eastern Eyes,' 'The Hand that Rocks the Cradle,' 'especially for women listeners in India';[1] broadcast 18.12.41; fee £7.7s. Signed: N. H. Parratt.

1. Presumably because Orwell was sick, it was Bokhari who, on 16 October 1941, wrote to Mrs. Lall, wife of the Deputy High Commissioner for India, outlining what was required. His letter was very similar to Orwell's to Zahra Taki; see 862.

898. BBC Talks Booking Form, 10.12.41

S. M. Telkar: 'Through Eastern Eyes,' 'The Debate Continues,' 11; broadcast 13.12.41; fee £7.7s. Signed: N. H. Parratt.

899. BBC Talks Booking Form, 14.12.41

M. Tambimuttu: 'Through Eastern Eyes,' 'How It Works,' 12, on the British press; recorded 19.12.41; broadcast 21.12.41; fee £7.7s. Signed: N. H. Parratt.

900. BBC Talks Booking Form, 17.12.41

Dr. B. N. Mukerjee: 'Through Eastern Eyes,' 'With the Workers,' 11, Post Offices; broadcast 17.12.41; fee £7.7s. Signed: N. H. Parratt.

901. BBC Talks Booking Form, 19.12.41

Bahadur Singh: 'Through Eastern Eyes,' 'England on Christmas Day,' 12-minute talk; recorded 22.12.41; broadcast 25.12.41; fee £7.7s + 11s 8d railway fare [from Oxford]. Signed: N. H. Parratt.

902. BBC Talks Booking Form, 19.12.41

S. Telkar: 'Through Eastern Eyes,' 'The Debate Continues,' 12; broadcast 22.12.41. Signed: N. H. Parratt.

903. War Commentary, 3
20 December 1941

Although Orwell was still on sick leave until Monday, 22 December, it seems probable that he wrote the script for this broadcast, which was read by Bokhari. The fairly long paragraphs are characteristic of Orwell. The typescript seems to be a fair copy of a much amended original or, perhaps, of a manuscript made by Orwell, since it is single-spaced; it could also be a fair copy made in the 1960s. It bears no censors' stamps, nor is it marked 'As broadcast.' PasB has 'War Commentary read by I.P.O.'; timing, 12 minutes.

In making a survey of this week, we have a less resounding period to look back on, than we had last week. But one cannot say that the position is stabilised on any of the fronts. The Germans are still being beaten back in Russia and Libya, and in the Far East the Japanese are still getting further advantages from their first treacherous surprise attack. Penang has been evacuated, and the Japanese have landed on the island of Hongkong. The war is at present one of rapid changes but though the events come quickly their effects will be slow.

People easily forget what they felt about the news, and it may be worth while to look back a bit to another time when there were quick changes. Last winter the British overran Cyrenaica in a rapid campaign of two months or so; we captured Benghazi on the seventh of February. Then the Germans in answer began a drive on Greece, and we were bound in honour to send help to that brave ally. Mr. Churchill and General Wavell had in view a large strategy; they were ready to maintain their obligations everywhere, and keep moving, and take risks. The troops sent to Greece had largely to be taken from Libya. On the seventh of April the British Expeditionary Force entered Greece, and the Axis drive back into Libya began at once. Next day the Italians were already claiming the recapture of Derna. By the eighteenth of April the very rapid Axis advance had been finally held. It had recaptured the whole of Cyrenaica. The Germans succeeded in occupying Greece and Crete, and what we now hear from our brave Greek allies are tragic and horrible stories of starvation. Mr. Churchill, no less than Hitler, had to consider the strategy of the war as a whole. It was on the nineteenth of April that the British troops moved into Iraq, only just in time to prevent the Germans from taking a strong hold there. We thus stopped the German pincer movement, and from then on we had a comparatively stable front, behind which we could pile up in Egypt the supplies of war munitions from America. It was not till last month that we again took the offensive in Libya. By then we had the Russians as our Allies, we had secured Iran against German domination, and we had great supplies of munitions in Egypt. The position had changed entirely. It is in this way that we must consider the periods of rapid change in a vast war of grand strategy. We must use big maps before we can see how things are going at all; and we have been through worse times than this one.

At present the pursuit of the enemy in Libya is still going on. We have captured Derna aerodrome, on the coast, and are driving towards Mekili, on the desert road further south. In these two directions, our columns have covered a hundred miles in two days. Our main attacking force is already west of these two points. The delaying action fought by General Rommel seems now to have exhausted him, but he may make another stand. General Auchinleck, now in command of the Libyan campaign, is a great believer in Indian troops. When serving in India he was anxious to create a corp from the more pacific peoples of the south; "start a tradition now" he said "and in fifty years they will fight as well as the Sikhs." When he was given his army corp it was suggested that its emblem should be the auk, an extinct bird because that is his nick-name, but he said "I learned my soldiering in India; the corp shall bear the emblem of India."

The Russians have recaptured three more towns on the Moscow front. The town of Rusa, 55 miles due west of Moscow, an important junction, was recaptured after desperate German resistance. It is reported that the Russian head-quarters on this front has been moving its base forward twice a day. It was last Wednesday that the Germans first used the word "retreat" about their own army, but they have thought of another word now, and say that they are "rationalising their eastern front". They have admitted a Russian break-through in the south. Hitler in his last speech said that there were one hundred and sixty two thousand German casualties in the whole Russian campaign. It is always interesting to consider how these lies are invented. The campaign had then lasted just one hundred and sixty two days. It looks as if the Germans decided to admit a thousand men lost a day, but not more, and then a patient clerk worked out the sum exactly.[1]

The Japanese successes are still very serious for us. At present the pressure of Japanese troops has died down in Malaya, where heavy casualties have been inflicted on them. Large Indian reinforcements have been landed in Rangoon. The Governor of Hongkong states that heavy fighting is in progress on the island itself. The telegraphic lines to Hongkong have been repaired, but the Japanese claim to have occupied most of the island. They are also making further attacks on the Philippines, where there is heavy fighting. Meanwhile our troops have entered the Portuguese part of Timor island, near Australia, to prevent the Japanese landing which seemed imminent. Dr. Salazar has stated that Portugal will be faithful to her friends and allies.[2]

In all this we must remember that the Japanese power, though great, can only aim at a rapid out-right victory. The three Axis powers together can produce sixty million tons of steel every year, whereas the U.S.A. alone can produce about eighty eight million. This in itself is not a striking difference. But Japan cannot send help to Germany, and Germany cannot send help to Japan. Now the Japanese only produce seven million tons of steel a year. For steel as for many other things they must depend on the stores they have ready.

If the Japanese seem to be making a wild attempt, we must remember that many of them think it their duty to their Emperor, who is their God, to conquer the whole world. This is not a new idea in Japan. Hideyoshi[3] when he died in 1598 was trying to conquer the whole world known to him, and he knew about India and Persia. It was because he failed that Japan closed the country to all foreigners. In January of this year, to take a recent example, a manifesto appeared in the Japanese press signed by Japanese Admirals and Generals stating that it was Japan's mission to set Burma and India free. Japan was of course to do this by conquering them. What it would be like to be free under the heel of Japan the Chinese can tell us, and the Koreans. The Japanese will have to listen to China. In the famous Tamaka Memorial, a secret document presented to the Emperor of Japan in 1927, Baron Tamaka°[4] made one very true remark; "in order to conquer the world", he said, "we must first conquer China". Japan would have been wiser to follow the advice of this militarist leader more exactly. She has let herself [in] for trying to conquer the world, and she has certainly not yet conquered China. The Chinese government, as was stated by the Chinese Ambassador in London has instructed all Chinese everywhere to assist the allied armies, and Chinese in Malaya and the Philippines, for example, are volunteering under the British and American flags. At home China has already 5 million men under arms and her man power is almost inexhaustible.

Meanwhile America is in the long run an inexhaustible arsenal, and the Americans are determined not to have their help limited to the Pacific area.

They have decided to use British Eritrea as the centre at which American experts will receive the great supplies of amunition which America will continue to send to the Near East.

1. In addition to this number of dead, the Germans announced 33,334 men missing and 572,000 wounded (*2194 Days of War*, 30 November 1941). By this time, Leningrad had been invested and the Germans were some twenty-five miles from Moscow.
2. Dr. Antonio de Oliveira Salazar (1889–1970), absolute ruler of Portugal, was, in addition to being premier from 1932 until he suffered a stroke in 1968, Minister of War, 1936–44, and Minister of Foreign Affairs, 1936–47. Portugal remained neutral throughout the war, but did allow Allied facilities in the Azores from 1943. By 'allies' there is probably an implied reference to England, Portugal's oldest ally. They had signed treaties in 1642 and 1654.
3. Hideyoshi Toyotomi (1537–1598), Japanese ruler and general who completed the unification of Japan, attempted the conquest of China, and died after an unsuccessful invasion of Korea in 1597.
4. Tanaka (not Tamaka) Giichi (1863–1929) was created a baron in 1920 and appointed prime minister in 1927. The Tanaka (or Tonaka) Memorial, advocating an expansionist policy in China (1927), is now believed not to be his work although he pursued an aggressive economic policy towards China.

904. Z. A. Bokhari to J. Bahadur Singh

20 December 1941[1]   PP/ZAB

Dear Mr. Bahadur Singh,

I am very grateful to you for sending me the script of your talk on Christmas Day 1941. I am afraid this talk is a bit too impersonal. I would like you, if you would, to go round in the town where you are living[2] and give an eyewitness account of what people are doing. Any personal observations will add to the interest of the programme, and will create more interest than an impersonal talk. For instance, you start with "To-day, as the country celebrates its third Christmas since the outbreak of war, our minds are inevitably carried back to the pre 1939 days." Well, I don't like anything in the nature of a cliché, and I would like you to avoid clichés; on the air they don't sound very nice.

This criticism is in my private and personal capacity, and I hope you will take it as such. Friends can criticise each other, can't they? Can you get in touch with me? Is there [any] possibility of your coming to London for Christmas. If not, would you ring me up. I am sorry that I shall be away on Christmas day, and this talk will be recorded on Monday. Therefore, I must request you to see me before the actual recording session of your talk.

With kind regards
Yours sincerely,
[No name/position]

1. Orwell was away sick until Monday, 22, December, so Bokhari stepped in to complete Orwell's arrangements with Bahadur Singh.
2. Oxford.

905. To Mulk Raj Anand

22 December 1941   PP/EB

Dear Anand,[1]
You will no doubt remember our conversation on the subject of broadcasting. You told me that your time was very full at the moment, but that you might perhaps have time to do some talks after the New Year. We have an idea for a series of talks which I think would just suit you.[2] Do you think you could be kind enough to come and see me some day during the early part of the week beginning December 28th, in my office, at 55, Portland Place, W.1.

You might ring me up in advance and let me know just when you are coming.

Yours sincerely
Eric Blair
Empire Talks Assistant

1. Mulk Raj Anand (1905–), novelist, short-story writer, essayist, and critic, was born in India, fought for the Republicans in the Spanish civil war, though he did not meet Orwell there and taught literature and philosophy to London County Council adult-education classes and wrote scripts and broadcast for the BBC, 1939–45. After the war he lectured in various Indian universities and was made professor of fine arts, University of Punjab, in 1963. He was awarded an International Peace Prize from the World Council of Peace in 1952. Orwell criticised a review of Anand's *The Sword and the Sickle* by Ranjee Shahne in the *Times Literary Supplement*, 23 May 1942, and reviewed the book in *Horizon*, July 1942; see *1189* and *1257*. In a letter of 29 September 1983, Anand wrote this of Orwell: 'In his life his voice was restrained. He talked in furtive whispers. Often he dismissed the ugly realities with cynical good humour. And I seldom saw him show anger on his face, though the two deep lines on his cheeks and the furrowed brow signified permanent despair. He smiled at tea time and he was a good companion in a pub. But he delivered his shafts in a very mellow voice, something peculiarly English deriving from the Cockney sense of humour.' See Abha Sharma Rodrigues, 'George Orwell, the BBC and India: A Critical Study' (Edinburgh University, PhD, 1994); this analyses the relationship between Anand and Orwell.
2. See Orwell's letter of 27 February 1942, *989*, and talks booking form of 5.3.42, *1001*. When Anand was invited to broadcast by Darling on 22 March 1941, he had declined. Orwell was able to overcome his doubts about the propriety of broadcasting for the British.

906. BBC Talks Booking Form, 23.12.41

P. Chatterjee: 'Through Eastern Eyes,' the London County Council in peace and war; broadcast 23.12.41; fee £7.7s. Signed: N. H. Parratt.

907. BBC Talks Booking Form, 23.12.41

Noel Sircar: 'Through Eastern Eyes,' 'The Man in the Street'; broadcast 26.12.41; fee £7.7s. Signed: N. H. Parratt.

908. Review of *Men and Politics* by Louis Fischer

Now and Then, Christmas 1941[1]

The 'political book'—part reportage and part political criticism, usually with a little autobiography thrown in—is a growth of the troubled years from 1933 onwards, and the value of individual books in this genre has depended a good deal upon the orthodoxy of the moment. In periods like that between 1936 and 1939, when fierce controversies were raging and nobody was telling the whole of the truth, it was not easy to write a good political book, even if you knew the facts. Mr. Fischer's book, which is largely about the U.S.S.R., comes at a more fortunate moment. So far as the U.S.S.R. is concerned he evidently *does* know the facts, as far as an outsider can know them, and time itself has done the necessary debunking. After the Russo-German pact the Popular Front orthodoxy of the preceding years became impossible, and on the other hand the German attack on Russia has thrown the whole subject of Russo-German relations into better proportion and wiped out the bitterness caused by the pact itself and by the Finnish episode. Mr. Fischer is left with the conclusion that Stalin is a disgusting tyrant who is nevertheless objectively on our side and must be supported—not a comforting conclusion, perhaps, but more realistic and more likely to produce an interesting book than any that was possible two years ago.

What the majority of readers will probably find most interesting are Mr. Fischer's chapters on the Russian sabotage trials. He saw some of them at close quarters, and in any case in his capacity as newspaper correspondent he had known various of the principal actors in them. The Russian purges are the greatest puzzle of modern times and we can hardly have too many opinions on them. Various explanations are possible, even the explanation that all the charges were true, though this involves accepting certain known contradictions. Mr. Fischer is inclined to think that the confessions of Bukharin, Rakovsky and the rest were obtained by promising them that if they confessed they would not be shot; he even thinks that in some cases the promise may have been kept and the accused men may be still alive. The weakness of this explanation seems to be that the old Bolsheviks, considering the lives they had led, were not the men to care very greatly about being shot or to make incredible confessions which would blacken their names for ever merely for the sake of saving their skins. But it is a fact that any explanation one puts forward can be met by similar objections, and Mr. Fischer's opinion should be treated with respect. One of the great weaknesses of British and American political thought during the past decade has been that people who have lived all their lives in democratic or quasi-democratic countries find it very difficult to imagine the totalitarian atmosphere and tend to translate all that happens abroad into terms of their own experience. This tendency has vitiated most of what has been written about the U.S.S.R., about the Spanish civil war, even about Nazism. Mr. Fischer, who has seen totalitarianism from the inside for many years and still remained a fairly ordinary American with mildly left wing opinions and a profound belief in democracy, makes a valuable corrective to the parlour Bolsheviks on one side and writers like Eugene Lyons[2] on the other.

He has also been everywhere and met everybody. Negrin, Senator Borah, Bernard Shaw, Colonel Lindbergh, Litvinov, Cordell Hull, Bonnet, Bullitt, Churchill and scores of other celebrities, good and evil, move across his pages.[3] The writing of this book has called for considerable intellectual courage, for it has involved admitting that in the past Mr. Fischer held opinions which he now thinks false and also that he engaged in propaganda campaigns which even at the time he could see to be misleading. But that kind of admission is a necessary part of the political reorientation which is now going on. Few journalists of our time can speak from wider knowledge than Mr. Fischer, and no book of political reminiscence written since the outbreak of war is of greater value than this one.

1. *Now and Then* was subtitled *news of books and authors, published occasionally from 30 Bedford Square by Jonathan Cape.* This issue was No. 70, War-time issue No. 7.
2. Eugene Lyons (1898–1985), American journalist and editor born in Russia, wrote many books on the U.S.S.R., including *Assignment in Utopia* (1937), in which the formula $2 + 2 = 5$ appears prominently. Orwell reviewed it, 9 June 1938; see *451.*
3. Dr. Juan Negrín was the Socialist Prime Minister of Spain during the civil war; see *560, 2.8.39, n 3* William E. Borah (1865–1940), U.S. Senator from Idaho, 1907–1940, chairman of the Senate Foreign Relations Committee from 1924, was an opponent of the League of Nations and progressive legislation, but supporter of Roosevelt's New Deal. Charles A. Lindbergh (1902–1974), who became a hero after making the first solo non-stop flight across the Atlantic in 1927, was active in opposing U.S. entanglement in World War II before the Japanese attack on Pearl Harbor, but later helped in the war effort and saw active duty in the Pacific. Maxim Litvinov was the Soviet Union's Commissar of Foreign Affairs, 1930–39, and Ambassador to the United States, 1941–43; see *558, 26.7.39, n. 4.* Cordell Hull (1871–1955), U.S. statesman, judge, 1903–07, member of Congress, 1907–21, 1923–31 and the Senate, 1931–33, Secretary of State, 1933–44, pursued enlightened foreign and economic policies which led to the award of the Nobel Peace Prize in 1945. Georges Bonnet (1889–1973), French Ambassador to the United States, 1937, Foreign Minister, 1938–39, wanted, in 1939, to repudiate the alliance with Poland. William C. Bullitt (1891–1967), U.S. diplomat, was the first U.S. Ambassador to the Soviet Union, 1933–36, Ambassador to France, 1936–41, and special assistant to the Secretary of the Navy, 1942.

909. To J. Chinna Durai

29 December 1941   PP/EB

Dear Mr. Chinna Durai,

I am sending you a copy of your first talk in the series "AROUND THE COURTS", for which you asked the last time you were here.[1]

Yours sincerely,
Eric Blair
Empire Talks Assistant.

1. Bokhari had commissioned Durai in September; for his instructions on what was required, see *866, n. 2*; see also *883.*

910. To A. R. Kerrell-Vaughan

29 December 1941   PP/EB

Dear Sir,
Thank you for your letter of 23rd December 1941. I am sending you a copy of the talk written by Dr. Chatterjee, on Rural District Councils.[1] I hope you will find the talk interesting; we are most grateful to you for helping our speaker.

Yours faithfully,
Eric Blair
Empire Talks Assistant.
Dictated by Mr. Blair and
despatched in his absence by:[2]

1. See *858.*
2. Probably Nancy Parratt, Orwell's secretary.

911. BBC Talks Booking Form, 29.12.41

D. V. Tahmankar:[1] 'Through Eastern Eyes,' 'The News'; broadcast 30.12.41; fee £7.7s.

1. On 23 September 1941, Bokhari signed a talks booking form commissioning J. Tahmankar to give a talk on the House of Commons in the series 'How It Works.' There, as here, the speaker's address is given as The Press Room, Ministry of Information. Despite the different initials, the same person may be intended. D. V. Tahmankar was London editor for United Press of India.

912. BBC Talks Booking Form, 29.12.41

Shridhar Telkar: 'Through Eastern Eyes,' 'The Debate Continues'; broadcast 29.12.41; fee £7.7s.

1942

913. London Letter, 1 January 1942

Partisan Review, March–April 1942

London, England

At this moment nothing is happening politically in England, and since we probably have ahead of us a long exhausting war in which morale will be all-important, I want to use most of this letter in discussing certain currents of thought which are moving to and fro just under the surface. Some of the tendencies I mention may seem to matter very little at present, but they do I think tell one something about possible future developments.

1. Whom Are We Fighting Against?

This question, which obviously had to be answered sooner or later, began to agitate the big public some time in 1941, following on Vansittart's pamphlets and the starting of a German daily paper for the refugees (*Die Zeitung*, mildly Left, circulation about 60,000). Vansittart's thesis is that the Germans are *all* wicked, and not merely the Nazis. I don't need to tell you how gleefully the blimps have seized upon this as a way of escaping from the notion that we are fighting against Fascism. But of late the "only good German is a dead one" line has taken the rather sinister form of a fresh drive against the refugees. The Austrian monarchists have fallen foul of the German leftwingers, whom they accuse of being pan-Germans in disguise, and this delights the blimps, who are always trying to manœuvre their two enemies, Germany and Socialism, into the same place. The point has now been reached where anyone who describes himself as "anti-Fascist" is suspected of being pro-German. But the question is much complicated by the fact that the blimps have a certain amount of right on their side. Vansittart, badly though he writes, is an able man with more background than most of his opponents, and he has insisted on two facts which the pinks have done their best to obscure. One is that much of the Nazi philosophy is not new but is merely a continuation of pan-Germanism, and the other is that Britain cannot have a European policy without having an army. The pinks cannot admit that the German masses are behind Hitler any more than the blimps can admit that their class must be levered out of control if we are to win the war. The controversy has raged for four months or more in the correspondence columns of several papers, and one paper in particular is obviously keeping it going as a way of baiting the refugees and the "reds" generally. No one, however, airs any racial theories about Germany, which is a great advance on the war propaganda of 1914–18.

Ordinary working people do not seem either to hate the Germans or to distinguish between Germans and Nazis. Here and there there was violent anti-German feeling at the time of the bad air-raids, but it has worn off. The term "Hun" has not caught on with the working classes this time. They call the Germans Jerries, which may have a mildly obscene meaning but is not unfriendly. All the blame for everything is placed on Hitler, even more than on the Kaiser during the last war. After an air raid one often used to hear people say "He was over again last night"—"he" being Hitler. The Italians are generally called Eyeties, which is less offensive than Wops, and there is no popular feeling against them whatever, nor against the Japanese as yet. To judge from photos in the newspapers, the land girls are quite ready to get off with Italian prisoners working on the farms. As to the smaller nations who are supposed to be at war with us, no one remembers which is which. The women who a year ago were busy knitting stockings for the Finns are now busy knitting them for the Russians, but there is no ill feeling. The chief impression one derives from all this chaos of opinions is how little the lack of a positive war aim, or even of any definite mental picture of the enemy, matters to people who are at any rate at one in not wanting to be governed by foreigners.

2. Our Allies.

Whatever may be happening among the higher-ups, the effect of the Russian alliance has been a tremendous net increase of pro-Russian senti-ment. It is impossible to discuss the war with ordinary working-class and middle-class people without being struck by this. But the enthusiasm that ordinary people feel for Russia is not coupled with the faintest interest in the Russian political system. All that has happened is that Russia has become respectable. An enormous hammer and sickle flag flies daily over Selfridge's, the biggest shop in London. The Communists have not caused so much friction as I expected. They have been tactful in their posters and public pronouncements, and have gone to unheard-of lengths in supporting Churchill. But though they may have gained in numbers as a result of the Russian alliance, they do not seem to have gained in political influence. To a surprising extent ordinary people fail to grasp that there is any connection between Moscow and the Communist party, or even that Communist policy has changed as a result of Russia's entry into the war. Everyone is delighted that the Germans have failed to take Moscow, but no one sees in this any reason for paying any attention to what Palme Dutt[1] and Co. may say. In practice this attitude is sensible, but at the bottom of it there lies a profound lack of interest in doctrinaire politics. The ban has not been taken off the *Daily Worker*. Immediately after it was suppressed it reappeared as a factory sheet which was illegally printed, but was winked at. Now, under the title of "the *British Worker*," it is sold on the streets without interference. But it has ceased to be a daily and has lost most of its circulation. In the more important parts of the press the Communist influence has not been regained.

There is no corresponding increase in pro-American sentiment—the contrary, if anything. It is true that the entry of Japan and America into the war was expected by everyone, whereas the German invasion of Russia came as a surprise. But our new alliance has simply brought out the immense amount of anti-American feeling that exists in the ordinary low-brow middle class. English cultural feelings towards America are complicated but can be defined fairly accurately. In the middle class, the people who are *not* anti-American are the declassed technician type (people like radio engineers) and the younger intelligentsia. Up till about 1930 nearly all "cultivated" people loathed the U.S.A., which was regarded as the vulgariser of England and Europe. The disappearance of this attitude was probably connected with the fall of Latin and Greek from their dominant position as school subjects. The younger intellectuals have no objection to the American language and tend to have a masochistic attitude towards the U.S.A., which they believe to be richer and more powerful than Britain. Of course it is exactly this that excites the jealousy of the ordinary patriotic middle class. I know people who automatically switch off the radio as soon as any American news comes on, and the most banal English film will always get middle-class support because "it's such a relief of get away from those American voices." Americans are supposed to be boastful, bad-mannered and worshippers of money, and are also suspected of plotting to inherit the British Empire. There is also business jealousy, which is very strong in the trades which have been hit by the Lease-Lend agreement.[2] The working-class attitude is quite different. English working-class people nearly always dislike Americans when in actual contact with them, but they have no preconceived cultural hostility. In the big towns they are being more and more Americanised in speech through the medium of the cinema.

It is uncertain whether English xenophobia is being broken down by the presence in England of large numbers of foreigners. I think it is, but plenty of people disagree with me. There is no doubt that in the summer of 1940 working-class suspicion of foreigners helped to make possible the internment of the refugees. At the time I talked with countless people, and except for Left intellectuals I could find no one who saw anything wrong in it. The blimps were after the refugees because they were largely Socialists, and the working-class line was "what did they want to come here for?" Underlying this, a hangover from an earlier period, was a resentment against these foreigners who were supposedly taking Englishmen's jobs. In the years before the war it was largely Trade Union opposition that prevented a big influx of German Jewish refugees. Of late feelings have grown more friendly, partly because there is no longer a scramble for jobs, but partly also, I think, owing to personal contacts. The foreign troops who are quartered here in large numbers seem to get on unexpectedly well with the population, the Poles in particular being a great success with the girls. On the other hand there is a certain amount of anti-semitism. One is constantly coming on pockets of it, not violent but pronounced enough to be disquieting. The Jews are supposed to dodge military service, to be the worst offenders on the Black Market, etc., etc. I have heard this kind of talk even from country people who had probably never seen a Jew in their lives. But no one wants actually to *do* anything to the Jews, and the idea that the Jews are responsible for the war never seems to have caught on with the big public, in spite of the efforts of the German radio.

3. *Defeatism and German Propaganda.*

Appeasement of the Chamberlain type is not "dead," as the newspapers are constantly assuring us, but is lying very low. But there exists another school of rightwing defeatism which can be conveniently studied in the weekly paper *Truth*. *Truth* has had a curious history and is a distinctly influential paper. At one time it was a non-political factual paper specialising in a genteel form of muckraking (exposure of patent medicine frauds, etc.), and was taken in as a matter of course in every club and regimental mess throughout the Empire. So far as I know it still has the same circulation, but latterly it has taken a definite political and economic line and become a stronghold of the worst kind of rightwing Toryism. Sir Ernest Benn,[3] for instance, writes in it every week. It is not only anti-Labour, but in a discreet way anti-Churchill, anti-Russian and, more markedly, anti-American. It opposed the exchange of naval bases for American destroyers, the only other opposers being the Blackshirts and Communists. The strategy it advocates is to avoid entangling alliances, keep out of Europe and concentrate on self-defence on sea and in the air. The obvious logic of this is to make a compromise peace at the earliest possible moment. The quantity of advertisements for banks and insurance companies which *Truth* contains shows how well it is thought of in those quarters, and recently questions in Parliament brought out the fact that it is partly owned by the Conservative Party machine.

Leftwing defeatism is quite different and much more interesting. One or two of the minor political parties (for instance the British Anarchists, who followed up the German invasion of Russia with a terrific and very able anti-Soviet pamphlet, *The Truth about Russia*) follow a line which by implication is "revolutionary defeatist." The I.L.P. is preaching what amounts to a watered version of the "Ten Propositions" set forth in the *Partisan Review*, but in very indefinite terms, never clearly stating whether or not it "supports" the war. But the really interesting development is the increasing overlap between Fascism and pacifism, both of which overlap to some extent with "left" extremism. The attitude of the very young is more significant than that of the *New Statesman* pinks who war-mongered between 1935 and 1939 and then sulked when the war started. So far as I know, the greater part of the very young intelligentsia are anti-war—this doesn't stop them from serving in the armed forces, of course—don't believe in any "defence of democracy," are inclined to prefer Germany to Britain, and don't feel the horror of Fascism that we who are somewhat older feel. The entry of Russia into the war didn't alter this, though most of these people pay lip-service to Russia. With the out-and-out, turn-the-other-cheek pacifists you come upon the much stranger phenomenon of people who have started by renouncing violence ending by championing Hitler. The antisemitic motif is very strong, though usually soft-pedalled in print. But not many English pacifists have the intellectual courage to think their thoughts down to the roots, and since there is no real answer to the charge that pacifism is objectively pro-Fascist, nearly all pacifist literature is forensic—i.e., specialises in avoiding awkward questions. To take one example, during the earlier period of the war the pacifist monthly the *Adelphi*, edited by Middleton Murry, accepted at its face value the German claim to be a "socialist" state fighting against "plutocratic" Britain, and more or less equated Germany with Russia. Hitler's invasion of Russia made nonsense of this line of thought, and in the five or six issues that have followed the *Adelphi* has performed the surprising feat of not mentioning the Russo-German war. The *Adelphi* has once or twice engaged in Jew-baiting of a mild kind. *Peace News*, now also edited by Middleton Murry, follows its old tradition of opposing war for different and incompatible reasons, at one moment because violence is wicked, at another because peace will "preserve the British Empire," etc.

For some years past there has been a tendency for Fascists and currency reformers to write in the same papers,[4] and it is only recently that they have been joined by the pacifists. I have in front of me a copy of the little anti-war paper *Now* which contains contributions from, among others, the Duke of Bedford, Alexander Comfort, Julian Symons and Hugh Ross Williamson.[5] Alexander Comfort is a "pure" pacifist of the other-cheek school. The Duke of Bedford has for years been one of the main props of the Douglas Credit movement, and is also a devout Anglican, a pacifist or near-pacifist, and a landowner upon an enormous scale. In the early months of the war (then Marquis° of Tavistock[6]) he went to Dublin on his own initiative and obtained or tried to obtain a draft of peace terms from the German Embassy. Recently he has published pamphlets urging the impossibility of winning the war and describing Hitler as a misunderstood man whose good faith has never really been tested.[7] Julian Symons writes in a vaguely Fascist strain but is also given to quoting Lenin. Hugh Ross Williamson has been mixed up in the Fascist movement for some time, but in the split-off section of it to which William Joyce ("Lord Haw Haw") also belongs. Just before the war he and others formed a fresh Fascist party calling itself the People's Party, of which the Duke of Bedford was a member. The People's Party apparently came to nothing, and in the first period of the war Williamson devoted himself to trying to bring about a get-together between the Communists and Mosley's followers. You see here an example of what I mean by the overlap between Fascism and pacifism.

What is interesting is that every section of anti-war opinion has one section of German radio propaganda, as it were, assigned to it. Since the outbreak of war the Germans have done hardly any direct propaganda in England otherwise than by wireless. The best known of their broadcasts, indeed the only ones that can be said to have been listened to to any appreciable extent, are those of William Joyce. No doubt these are often extravagantly untruthful, but they are a more or less responsible type of broadcast, well delivered and giving news rather than straight propaganda. But in addition the Germans maintain four spurious "freedom" stations, actually operating on the continent but pretending to be operating illegally in England. The best known of these is the New British Broadcasting Station, which earlier in the war the Blackshirts used to advertise by means of stickybacks. The general line of these broadcasts is "uncensored news," or "what the Government is hiding from you." They affect a pessimistic, well-informed manner, as of someone who is on the inside of the inside, and go in for enormous figures of shipping losses, etc. They urge the dismissal of Churchill, talk apprehensively about "the Communist danger," and are anti-American. The anti-American strain is even stronger in Joyce's broadcasts. The Americans are swindling us over the Lease-Lend agreement, are gradually absorbing the Empire, etc., etc. More interesting than the New British is the Workers' Challenge Station. This goes in for a line of red-hot revolutionary talks under such titles as "Kick Churchill Out," delivered by an authentic British working man who uses plenty of unprintable words. We are to overthrow the corrupt capitalist government which is selling us to the enemy, and set up a real socialist government which will come to the rescue of our heroic comrades of the Red Army and give us victory over Fascism. (This German station does not hesitate to talk about "the menace of Nazism," "the horrors of the Gestapo," etc.) The Workers' Challenge is not overtly defeatist. The line is always that it is probably too late, the Red Army is done for, but that we *may* be able to save ourselves if only we can "overthrow capitalism," which is to be done by means of strikes, mutinies, sabotage in the armament factories, and so forth. The other two "freedom" stations are the Christian Peace Movement (pacifism) and Radio Caledonia (Scottish nationalism).

You can see how each strain of German propaganda corresponds to one existing, or at any rate potential, defeatist faction. Lord Haw Haw and the New British are aimed at the anti-American middle class, roughly speaking the people who read *Truth*, and the business interests that have suffered from the war. The Workers' Challenge is aimed at the Communists and the Left extremists generally. The Christian Peace Movement is aimed at the P.P.U. I don't want to give the impression, however, that German propaganda has much effect at this moment. There is little doubt that it has been an almost complete flop, especially during the last eighteen months. Various things that have happened have suggested that since the outbreak of war the Germans have not been well informed about internal conditions in England, and much of their propaganda, even if listened to, would fail because of simple psychological errors on which anyone with a real knowledge of England could put them right. But the various strains of defeatist feeling are there, and at some time they may grow. In some of what I have said above I may have seemed to mention people and factions too insignificant to be worth noticing, but in this bloodstained harlequinade in which we are living one never knows what obscure individual or half-lunatic theory may not become important. I do seem to notice a tendency in intellectuals, especially the younger ones, to come to terms with Fascism, and it is a thing to keep one's eye on. The quisling intellectual is a phenomenon of the last two years. Previously we all used to assume that Fascism was so self-evidently horrible that no thinking person would have anything to do with it, and also that the Fascists always wiped out the intelligentsia when they had the opportunity. Neither assumption was true, as we can see from what happened in France. Both Vichy and the Germans have found it quite easy to keep a facade of "French culture" in existence. Plenty of intellectuals were ready to go over, and the Germans were quite ready to make use of them, even when they were "decadent." At this moment Drieu de la Rochelle[8] is editing the *Nouvelle*

Revue Française, Pound is bellowing against the Jews on the Rome radio, and Céline is a valued exhibit in Paris, or at least his books are. All of these would come under the heading of *kulturbolschewismus*, but they are also useful cards to play against the intelligentsia in Britain and the U.S.A. If the Germans got to England, similar things would happen, and I think I could make out at least a preliminary list of the people who would go over.

Not much news here. All is very quiet on the literary front. The paper shortage seems to be favouring the appearance of very short books, which may be all to the good and may possibly bring back the "long-short story," a form which has never had a fair deal in England. I wrongly told you in an earlier letter that Dylan Thomas was in the army. He is physically unfit and is doing jobs for the B.B.C. and the M.O.I. So is nearly everybody that used to be a writer, and most of us rapidly going native.

The food situation is much as before. We had our puddings on Christmas day, but they were a little paler than usual. The tobacco situation has righted itself, but matches are very short. They are watering the beer again, the third time since re-armament. The blackout is gradually relaxing in the absence of air-raids. There are still people sleeping in the Tube stations, but only a handful at each station. The basements of demolished houses have been bricked up and turned into water tanks for use in case of fire. They look just like Roman baths and give the ruins an even more Pompeian look than they had before. The stopping of the air raids has had some queer results. During the worst of the blitz they set in hand huge schemes for levelling waste pieces of ground to make playgrounds, using bomb debris as a subsoil. All these have had to stop in the middle, no more bomb debris being available.

All the best. Yours ever

George Orwell

1. Rajani Palme Dutt (1896–1974), author and journalist, was an executive member of the Communist Party from 1922. He edited the London *Daily Worker*, 1936–38, and wrote a number of political books from the Communist Party standpoint.
2. Lease-Lend, properly Lend-Lease, was an agreement passed by the U.S. Congress, and signed by President Roosevelt 11 March 1941, whereby arms and supplies on a vast scale were given to the Allies—about two-thirds to the British and, under a separate act, nearly a quarter to the U.S.S.R.—to forward the prosecution of the war. Of the $50.6 billion advanced, $7.8 billion was returned in cash and kind (often services for U.S. troops in host countries).
3. Sir Ernest Benn (1875–1954) was founder of Benn's Sixpenny Library and Sixpenny Poets, and publisher of the Blue Guides (travel books). Among his own publications were *Confessions of a Capitalist* (1925), which espoused an 'austere Victorian *laisser-faire*' philosophy (*DNB*) and *Governed to Death* (a pamphlet, 1948). In August 1942 he had a main finger in drafting a manifesto on British liberty and three months later in founding the Society of Individualists.
4. In the September–October issue of *Partisan Review* (445–46), Gorham Munson (1896–1969) took issue with Orwell for seemingly linking Social Creditors and Fascists. Orwell should know, 'through his association with the *New English Weekly* . . . that Social Creditors do not include themselves in the currency reform category; they are revolutionary, not reformist, in their social objective.' Orwell had also omitted to say that the Duke of Bedford had been 'publicly criticized and repudiated by the Social Credit Party of Great Britain on several occasions since the war began. . . . Like the Dean of Canterbury, the Duke of Bedford is a Social Credit renegade.' Orwell's response was printed immediately after Munson's letter:

—I am sorry if I gave the impression that Social Creditors, as such, are pro-

Fascist. Certainly Hargrave and the group now running the *New English Weekly* aren't. I am very glad to hear that they have dropped the Duke of Bedford, and apologise for not having known this, which I ought to have done.—George Orwell.

The pro-Soviet sympathies of the Very Reverend Hewlett Johnson, Dean of Canterbury, 1931–63, led to his being nicknamed 'The Red Dean.' Among the books he wrote were, *The Socialist Sixth of the World*, *Soviet Strength*, and *Christians and Communism*. Despite his left-wing reputation, it was whilst he was Dean that T. S. Eliot's play *Murder in the Cathedral* was given for the first time at Canterbury Cathedral (1935). See also *749, n. 3.*

5. See 'Pacifism and the War: A Controversy,' September–October 1942, *1270*, for responses by George Woodcock, Alex Comfort, and others, with particular reference to the persons named here For the Duke of Bedford, see *ns.* 6 and 7 below. Alexander Comfort (1920–2000), poet, novelist, and medical biologist, was the author of *No Such Liberty* (1941), *France and Other Poems* (1941), *The Almond Tree* (1942), and a miracle play, *Into Egypt* (1942). His *The Joy of Sex* (1972) has sold over ten million copies. He edited *Poetry Folios* 1–10 with Peter Wells, 1942–46. Julian Symons (1912–1994), poet, novelist, and critic, compiled, for Penguin Books, *An Anthology of War Poetry* (1942) Many of his novels are detective stories Hugh Ross Williamson (1901–1978) was a dramatist and critic. In 1946 Orwell contributed to *Now*; see *3104.*

6. The title Marquess of Tavistock is given to the heirs to the Dukes of Bedford. This duke, the twelfth (1888–1953), succeeded to the title in 1940.

7. The Marquess of Tavistock had published in 1940 the account of his negotiations with the German Legation in Dublin, *The Fate of a Peace Effort*. An advertisement at the end of the forty-two-page pamphlet invited readers to buy copies for their friends at six for five shillings and offered leaflets with a summary of the German peace terms at 100 for a shilling. After he became Duke of Bedford, he published more pamphlets, including *Why Blunder On? First Steps in an Emergency Programme to End War, Disease, and Poverty* (February 1942), which argued that the war should be stopped, 'not by surrender, but by a negotiated peace concluded on terms which give the world some prospect of freedom, justice, and economic stability.' Chances of concluding a peace, he wrote, had been rejected 'on the ground that Hitler cannot be trusted—a foolish reason' (14). In another pamphlet, *Propaganda for Proper Geese* (late 1942), he wrote that the 'three chief war propaganda agents in this country are the political speakers, the Press and the B.B.C.,' which 'in war-time are little more than the mouthpiece of the Government and the financiers' (7, 9).

8. Pierre-Eugène Drieu la Rochelle (1893–1945), novelist, short-story writer, journalist, and essayist, oscillated between extreme positions artistically and politically. In his memoir *La Comédie de Charleroi* (1934) he questioned the purpose of war; in an autobiographical novel, *Gilles* (1939), and in other books and stories, he pilloried what he saw as the decline of France, especially its bourgoisie. In the 1930s he joined the French Nazi Party, the Parti Populaire Français. As editor during the Occupation, he turned *Nouvelle Revue Française* into a pro-Nazi journal. He committed suicide at the end of the war. His writing caught the spirit and sense of much that disturbed France and its people between the wars.

914. BBC Talks Booking Form, 1.1.42

Venu Chitale: 'The Hand that Rocks the Cradle,' 'Then and Now'; broadcast 1.1.42 [typed as 1941]; fee £7.7s.[1] Signed: Z. A. Bokhari.

1. A fee was not paid to staff members when they gave such broadcasts, so it would appear that Miss Chitale was not yet on the staff. For Venu Chitale, see *871. n. 1.*

915. Weekly News Review, 4

3 January 1942

This script is the only weekly news review to be numbered. PasB states, '1500 Through Eastern Eyes / Direct talk: News Review written by Eric Blair and read by Z. A. Bokhari.' The typescript is a fair copy, double-spaced, without timings or censors' stamps. It is not marked 'As broadcast.'

During a week in which there has been fighting in almost every quarter of the globe, the two most significant events have not happened upon the battlefield. The first of these events was the signing in Washington of a pact by which no less than 26 nations pledge themselves to put an end to Fascist aggression.[1] The second was the entry of Chinese troops into Burma to take part in the defence of that country. In both these events we can see a demonstration of the solidarity of the free nations of the world, which is ultimately more important than guns and aeroplanes. For if four fifths of humanity stand together, the other fifth cannot defeat them in the long run, however well armed and however cunning they may be.

We have to keep this fact in mind when we assess the news from the Far East and the Pacific. Temporarily the advantage is with the Japanese; it may remain with them for a long time to come. The Americans have been unable to reinforce the heroic garrison of the Philippine Islands, and it is already reported that Manila, the chief town, has fallen into Japanese hands. That does not mean that the fighting in the Philippines is ended, but it does mean that the Japanese are established in another advantageous spot for their attack on Singapore. Simultaneously they have occupied Sarawak in the north of Borneo. This is a strategic rather than an economic gain, for the British forces in Sarawak took care to blow up the oil wells and render them useless before they retreated.

But in order to follow the events of this war, it is more than ever necessary to study the map of the world, and in addition to remember that the world is round. When we hear of those early successes of the Japanese in the Pacific, we may be inclined to think that they offset the defeats which the Germans have received in Russia and Libya. But when we look at the map, we see a different picture, and we see one immense advantage which the democratic powers have over the Fascists. This is that they can communicate with one another. Between the two main axis powers all inter-communication is impossible. It is quite *likely*[2] that within the next few months the Japanese will over-run so much territory in Asia and the Pacific that they will acquire enough tin, rubber, oil and food to keep their own war machine running for several years. But they cannot send one single pound of these materials to the Germans, who will soon be needing them desperately. Similarly, when heavy air warfare develops in the Far East, the enormous aircraft factories of Germany will be of no value to Japan.

Meanwhile, in the other hemisphere the German retreats continue. In Libya the fighting is now at Agedabia, a hundred miles beyond Benghazi. The German and Italian aeroplanes are fiercely attacking Malta, the British island which lies between Italy and Africa, and which has remained impregnable for 18 months.[3] The British and Indian troops have taken thousands of prisoners, who will be sent back to join the Italians who were captured last year and who are now being employed on the making of roads in Africa and the Middle East. Simultaneously a number of American technical experts have arrived in Eritrea, the last African colony of the Italians, which we acquired last year. There they are setting up factories for the manufacture of aeroplanes and other war material, Eritrea being a convenient centre from which to supply both Russia, the Mediterranean and the Far East.

In Russia it is now hardly disguised even by the German propagandists that things are going disastrously for the Germans. Having announced nearly two months ago that Moscow was about to fall, the Germans found themselves compelled instead to retreat, and are now trying to cover up this fact by explaining that they find it convenient to shorten their lines and thus relieve some of the front line troops. But every time that the line is straightened and thus made shorter, another attack from the Russians dents it again, and the Germans are once more forced to retreat. In the centre of the front the chief damage that they are suffering is in the loss of material and also the loss of men, owing to the terrible cold of the Russian winter. In the far north and in the far south the Russians are winning a more definite strategic advantage. Leningrad, which has been almost in a state of siege for five months, is now in all probability about to be relieved. It will be remembered that back in the summer the Germans described the Russian defence of Leningrad as "criminal", declaring that the city could not possibly hold out, and that it was the duty of the Russians to surrender in order to save blood-shed. Now, five months later, the German grip on Leningrad is being forced open. This means not only a loss of prestige for the Germans. If Leningrad is fully relieved it will probably be possible for the Russians to drive Finland out of the war, and once this is done, a way of communication between Britain and Russia easier than any that now exists will have been opened up.

In the Black Sea the Germans are also in great danger. When they first entered the Crimean Peninsula, and captured Odessa, it seemed as though they were going to have everything their own way. From the Crimea, they were expected to cross the narrow strait to the Caucasus and at the worst, the Crimea, which is a comparatively warm climate, would be a valuable place in which to winter a great number of their troops. Nevertheless, they failed to capture the great Russian naval base of Sebastopol, and when the Russians recaptured Rostov the whole picture changed. The Russians are now advancing along the shore of the Black Sea, and at the same time by the use of their navy, they have landed troops on the coast of the Crimea. The German Army in the Crimea is thus in danger of being cut off on the land side and simultaneously attacked from the Sea. It is quite likely that it will be forced to beat a hurried retreat before the Russian armies reach the isthmus that divides the Crimea from the mainland, and in this way another valuable territory in which hundreds of thousands of Germans might have been preserved from the cold of the winter will have been lost.

If we want the most revealing comment on the events in 1941, we can best get it by comparing Hitler's New Year speech with the speech he made just a year ago. At that date he had the victories of 1940 behind him and Britain stood completely alone. Now, the three greatest population blocks of the world, the U.S.A., Soviet Russia and China are on Britain's side, and in return Germany has only gained the assistance of Japan. The German leaders are aware now that they cannot win in the long run, and every word of their speeches reveals this. They say nothing now about a speedy end to the war. At the beginning of 1941, they declared with absolute certainty that there should never be another winter of war. Now they can say only that there is a long war ahead. Admiral Tojo[4] also bids his people prepare for a long war, and the Italian broadcasts also have strangely altered in tone. In the speeches of these men one can read their real determination. They have gambled and lost, and they are determined that since their schemes cannot be carried out, they will at least pull the world down in ruins before they perish. But even the peoples of the Fascist countries who have been so long stupefied by propaganda are not incapable of thought, and it will not be long before they begin to ask themselves how many more years of war and suffering their leaders are going to offer them.

1. On 1 January 1942, twenty-six nations signed the Declaration of the United Nations. This pledged them to continue a joint war effort and not to make a separate peace. The phrase 'United Nations' was coined by President Roosevelt in 1941. The Declaration stemmed from the Atlantic Charter, drafted by Roosevelt and Churchill (with Sumner Welles and Sir Alexander Cadogan) at sea off Newfoundland, and agreed by them on board the U.S. cruiser *Augusta* on 12 August 1941. See Churchill, *The Second World War*, 383–99; U S.: *The Grand Alliance*, 433–50.
2. likely] *underlined in typescript, not an insertion*
3. 18 months] *not* 'ten months' *as in West*
4. Hideki Tojo (1884–1948), lieutenant general (not admiral) and, from 16 October 1941 until the Japanese lost the Mariana Islands in 1944, Prime Minister of Japan. He was hanged as a war criminal in 1948.

916. BBC Talks Booking Form, 5.1.42

Shridhar Telkar: 'Through Eastern Eyes,' 'The Debate Continues'; broadcast 5 and 12.1.42; fee £7.7s each talk.

917. 'Paper Is Precious'

'Through Eastern Eyes,' 8 January 1942

This script, which survives on microfilm, is filed as anonymous in the BBC Archives. It is adjacent to 'Money and Guns' of 20 January 1942, and its style of presentation is the same; that is probably attributable to the General Office, in which it was typed (see *918 headnote*). PasB records that the transmission took 8¾ minutes and was 'by B. Sahni.' It is uncertain whether this means it was simply read by Sahni or read and written by him. Although the evidence is slight, the correction of a spelling with a handwritten 'z' and the written 'for' in the first sentence (the only alterations) look like Orwell's hand. The style, content, and attitude all suggest the Orwell of *Keep the Aspidistra Flying* and *Coming Up for Air*. Note too the reference to the long short-story prospering in France but not in England. West: *Broadcasts* does not include this talk. The broadcast was scheduled to last twelve minutes; a filler was provided by a recording of an 'Indian Song' sung by Pankaj Mulloch.

Before the war, the wood pulp for Great Britain's paper supply came mostly from Sweden, Finland and Soviet Russia. When the Germans invaded Norway the Scandinavian supply was cut off, and though timber could be brought from Russia—indeed, it still is being brought at this moment, for the ships that carry war materials for the Russian front mostly come back laden with wood—the voyage was slow and dangerous. Canada, the other great source of timber, is far away and shipping is precious. So for some months past we have been faced with a shortage of paper—not desperate, but acute enough to make itself felt at almost every moment of the day. Paper is more important than you realise until you are short of it. I want to tell you something about the results of this shortage—and it is a curious fact that though most of them are bad, some of them are good.

Not the biggest, but perhaps the most striking result brought about by the paper shortage is the dwindling of advertisements. England is a country in which, before the war, every available wall was defaced with enormous posters—posters usually advertising food and patent medicines—in brilliant and generally hideous colours. I don't believe that anyone, except perhaps the advertisers themselves, was sorry to see them disappearing, and the bare walls look much nicer without them. As I walked through a Tube station the other night, I noticed that though a few of the big posters urging you to buy beer or chocolate were still there, all of them were old ones, probably dating from before the war. The only new advertisements—and they were very small and modest in comparison—were for theatres, or were government advertisements calling for recruits in the women's services, or were the notices of the London County Council, advertising evening classes. The sight encouraged me, even though it does not particularly please me to think that less beer and less chocolate are being consumed nowadays. It seemed to me a sign that we are passing into a new economic period—a period in which private enterprise will count for less and trade will mean more than an endless struggle to induce people to buy things they do not really want.

But the biggest effect of the paper shortage—and here the results are partly bad, partly good—can be seen in the newspapers and the press generally.

English newspapers are now so small, comparatively speaking, that it is becoming difficult to believe that they were ever really the size they used to be. A few weeks back I happened to turn out from the bottom of a drawer a "Times" of before the war. It seemed so enormous that I found myself wondering not only how anyone could have read through such a bulk of print every day, but even how anyone could hold up a document of such weight in order to read it. Would you credit that nowadays the ordinary English newspaper consists only of four pages—that is, two sheets, of which a certain amount is taken up in photographs? And what is more, we have got so used to newspapers of this size that already we can hardly imagine their being any larger.

Now this result of the paper shortage seems to me on the whole a good one, and I will tell you why. English papers of before the war were terribly commercialised, and their huge bulk was filled up not only with advertisements for useless luxuries, but with imbecilities of every kind—silly news items about burglaries and the private lives of film stars, gossip about lipstick and silk stockings, enormous articles on sport, pages and pages of horse-racing results, even columns of astrology and fortune-telling—any and every kind of cheap sensation calculated to push the real news out of the reader's attention. That was not the case with quite all the English newspapers, but it was the case with most of them. Well, all that kind of thing has gone by the board. The newspapers have very little space to fill up, and Britain is at war, so that there are long official communiques to be printed every day. Naturally, it is the rubbish that gets crowded out first. The papers these days may be a little dull, but at least they are serious. They give the headlines to real news and not to trivialities. Gone also are the newsposters that used to appear in the streets, advertising successive editions of the evening papers. Nowadays the men who sell the papers have little blackboards on which they write their own selection of the news, and these are much more informative and responsible than the printed posters used to be.

But if you turn from the daily papers to what one may call high-brow literature, the effects of the paper shortage have been mostly bad. Supplies of paper to publishers are strictly limited, and no publisher can produce anywhere near the number of books that he was producing before the war. It is very difficult for an unknown writer to get his work published now, for no one wants to risk precious paper on a book that may not sell. Very few books are now appearing by writers who were not previously known to the public, and this would still be the case even if most of the younger men were not already in the army. It is also a very bad time for literary reviews and magazines. Except for one or two sheets so tiny that they ought really to be described as pamphlets, no new periodicals have appeared during the past year. Most of the highbrow magazines, "Scrutiny", "Horizon", the "New Statesman", "Poetry", "Seven" and "Indian Writing", for example, are still in existence, but most of them are greatly reduced in size. Books, also, besides being fewer, tend to be much shorter. The length of books is more affected by merely mechanical considerations than we sometimes realise, and the vogue of very long novels in the ten years preceding the war was probably bound up with the fact that paper is cheap. It is quite likely that the paper famine will bring in a vogue for the very short novel, the so-called long-short story, a form which has always been popular in France, but has seldom prospered in England.[1]

When you go to a shop nowadays it is difficult to get your goods wrapped up. Shopkeepers are not so generous with paper bags as they used to be. Even cigarettes are often sold loose instead of being done up in a packet. During the

Christmas shopping one saw some strange sights, as elderly gentlemen hurried home clutching in their arms unwrapped dolls, teddy bears and toy guns which they had bought for their children. It is said that the nation's biggest wastage is still in wrapping paper, and it is here that there is most room for economy. In addition there is a nation-wide drive to collect wastepaper and send it back to the mills, where it can be repulped and turned into fresh paper again. It comes out rather grey in colour—this is due to the difficulty of getting the printing ink out of it—but still quite usable, and this process can be repeated almost indefinitely. Now and again in a second hand bookshop you will come on an old book printed on very grey paper, and you can tell at a glance that it dates from the final years of the last war, when[2] the paper shortage was as acute as it is now. It is a strange sight to go round one of the great mills where paper is repulped, and to see, apart from the huge bundles of newspaper and wrapping paper, piles of private letters, torn crackers, official documents, posters, bus tickets and streamers from Christmas trees all waiting to go into the vats together.

The shortage of paper is not one of the major privations of the war, and in any case our own shortage is nothing to what the Germans have suffered from the very beginning. But like all the shifts to which one is put in wartime, it is having its effect upon our national life, and like the disappearance of bananas and the shortage of phosforus° for matches, it brings home to one that the world nowadays is a single economic unit and that no part of the world can be separated from any other without suffering hardship in consequence.[3]

1. Compare *913*, second full paragraph from the end: 'The paper shortage seems to be favouring the appearance of very short books . . . and may possibly bring back the "long-short story." '
2. when] *typed as* where
3. As evidence of the need to save paper, the last three lines of the typescript were single-spaced, to avoid the need for a fresh sheet of paper.

918. Weekly News Review, 5

10 January 1942

The title of this script was typed 'NEWSLETTER' but 'LETTER' was crossed through and 'Weekly' written before and 'Review' written after. The numbering from hereon is the editor's. At the head of the script, Bokhari's name is written (as the reader) and 'copied in "GO" ' (for General Office). Towards the top right is written 'To: G.O.' and a little below, 'From LU 6 55PP' (or LH 6); between these two directions is written 'Anon' (for the author—Orwell) and '2 copies.' Orwell's office was then at 55 Portland Place. PasB has 'Weekly News Review, by Z. A. Bokhari.' The mode of x-ing through words and the changes in wording in the course of typing (for example, 'attempts' in line 10 was first typed as 'effort') suggest that Orwell was the typist. The script has cuts and emendations in what appears to be Orwell's hand. The passage crossed through is reproduced in roman type within square brackets; an added passage is in italic; substituted passages are given as notes at the end. These changes should not automatically be regarded as the result of censorship.

The greatest military event of this week has occurred on a battlefield about which we have not lately heard so much, as we have heard about either Russia or Malaya, and that is the battlefield in China. The Japanese invaders have suffered a great defeat at the city of Changsha. If you look at the map, you will see that Changsha is an important railway junction lying on the line between Canton and Hangkow. The Japanese are in possession of Canton, but only precariously, as they won it by means of sea invasion and the Chinese forces are all round them. If they could capture Changsha they might be able to cut off the whole south eastern corner of China. They have now made three determined attempts in three years to capture it, and every time, after proclaiming that it was captured, they have had to fall back with heavy losses. On this occasion it is thought that they have lost 20 or 30 thousand men, and another twenty thousand are surrounded by the Chinese and likely to be destroyed.

This event is not important only for the heroic defenders of China. It cannot be too much emphasised that this is a world war, and every success or failure upon each of the various fronts has its effect upon every other front, from Norway to the Philippine Islands. The more the Japanese are compelled to tie their forces up in China, the less their chances of succeeding in an all-out attack against India and Australia; similarly, the sooner the British and Americans can bring their full power to bear against Japan, the sooner will Chinese soil be cleared of the invader.

It is good news that complete agreement has been reached between General Wavell, the allied commander in chief in the Western Pacific and Marshall Chiang Kai Shek, as to the area of their commands. The entry of Chinese troops into Burma, which we mentioned last week, is a sign that the alliance between Britain and China is not a mere scrap of paper. No one doubts that the war in the Far East will be long and hard. The American forces in the Philippines have been compelled to abandon Manila, the principal town, and the fortress of Corregidor, which guards the entrance of Manila Bay is under constant attack by sea and air. In Malaya the British have fallen back before Japanese forces which greatly outnumber them, and Kuala Lumpur is in danger. The Japanese are now near enough to Singapore for their fighter aeroplanes as well as bombers to fly there; this means that they may now be able to bomb Singapore by day as well as by night. The immediate situation in the Far East turns upon the arrival of British and American reinforcements, especially of aeroplanes, which have to travel enormous distances to get there. The short term outlook in this theatre of war, therefore, is bad. But as to the long term outlook, no one who knows how to estimate the relative forces involved is in doubt about the issue.

President Roosevelt's recent speech announcing the War Budget has cleared up any doubts that might have remained as to America's willingness to prosecute the war to the very end. The figures for tanks, aeroplanes and other armaments which it will be possible for American industry to produce during 1942 and 1943 are so enormous that the Axis propagandists are making every effort to prevent their peoples from even hearing about them. It indicates a great change in American public opinion that the American

Government is now ready to send its forces to fight in no matter what theatre of war. Previously, there were large numbers of Americans who were willing to defend their own country against attack, but who were very hostile to the idea of being involved in war abroad, and specially in Europe. Now this objection has entirely disappeared. Preparations are being made to send American armies not only to the Pacific area, but also to Britain, to take part in the land conquest of Germany which will ultimately be necessary. This was what the Japanese achieved when they made their treacherous attack on December 7th.[1]

On the Russian fronts, the Germans are still retreating, and what is perhaps even more significant, the tone of their official pronouncements has abruptly changed. Until a week or two ago, the German military spokesmen were explaining that the attack on Moscow would have to be postponed until the spring, but that the German armies could quite easily remain on the line they now occupied. Already, however, they are admitting that a further retreat— or, as they prefer to call it, a rectification of the line—will be necessary, and though they do not say so, it seems probable that they will have to retreat a very long way if they are to improve the situation of their troops perceptibly. It has to be remembered that the Germans are fighting both against the Russian cold and against a great Russian army which is far better accustomed to the climate than themselves. Before the end of February, the Germans may well be faced with the alternative of abandoning nearly all their conquests in the northern part of the Russian front, or of seeing hundreds of thousands of soldiers freeze to death.[2]

Mr. Antony° Eden, the British Foreign Secretary, returned only a few days ago from his visit to Moscow. In the speech which he made soon after his arrival, he emphasised the complete agreement that exists between the British and Russian Governments. The Axis broadcasters are now spreading the rumour that Britain and Russia have agreed to carve up the world between them, and that Europe is to be forced at the point of the sword to accept Communism. This is simply a lie. *Great Britain & Soviet Russia have reached complete agreement as to their peace aims, which guarantee*[3] to every nation both access to materials necessary for life, and the right to live under the form of government which it chooses for itself.

In Libya, German and Italian forces are again in retreat. They have managed to make a stand for some days at Jedabla, south west of Benghazi, chiefly because heavy rain prevented the British tanks from attacking. General Rommel, the German commander of the Axis forces, probably also hoped that further reinforcements might reach him from Italy. If so, He° has been disappointed, and the Axis forces are in flight westward, with the British and Indians in pursuit. Rommel's army will probably attempt another stand at Sirte, about halfway between Benghazi and Tripoli. The further west the battle moves, the greater the advantage for the Allied forces, because they have more bases from which their ships and aeroplanes can patrol the middle of the Mediterranean. The Germans are still fiercely attacking Malta in hopes of cutting out one of the most important bases from which our aeroplanes operate. But so far they have made very little impression. Meanwhile, our prisoners in Libya number more than twenty thousand, of whom about a quarter are Germans. [It is significant that though by far the greater number of Axis troops in Africa are Italians, the higher Command is entirely in the hands of the Germans. This is a sign of the relationship between the two nations, Germany and Italy, which is essentially the relationship of master and servant.]

What is perhaps the most interesting and important aspect of the north° African campaign came to light recently, when it was revealed that since the Autumn of 1940 forces of volunteers from the Arab tribe, the Senussi, have been fighting on the side of the British. The Senussi have been treated with peculiar atrocity by the Italians, who evicted[4] them from the more fertile parts of Cyrenaica and penned them up in small areas with the almost openly declared intention of reducing their numbers by starvation. On more than one occasion when there were attempts at revolt, the Italians replied by taking the leading men of the Senussi up in aeroplanes and throwing them from mid air over their native villages, so that they were dashed to pieces before the eyes of their fellow countrymen. Yesterday, Mr. Eden issued on behalf of the British Government a statement that at the end of the war, Britain would in no circumstances allow these ill-treated Arabs to pass once again under Italian rule. Taken together with the liberation of Ethiopia, from which British troops are to be withdrawn as soon as the Italian civil population have gone, this is a better demonstration of Allied war aims than any mere pronouncement unaccompanied by concrete action.

1. This paragraph is marked in the left-hand margin by an elongated square bracket—perhaps as a potential cut if timing required that.
2. It has to be remembered . . . freeze to death.] *square brackets added by hand at beginning and end of this passage; nothing crossed through—possibly a potential cut to save time*
3. *Great Britain & Soviet Russia . . . which guarantee*] *manuscript interlinear substitution for typescript's* which it aimes° at those people in various parts of the world who still have a lingering fear of Bolshevism. The peace aims of Britain and Soviet Russia are defined by the terms of the Atlantic Charter, which the Russian Government has accepted and which guarantees . . .
4. *evicted*] evacuated

919. To Hsiao Ch'ien

14 January 1942   PP/EB

Dear Mr. Hsiao Ch'ien,[1]
Very many thanks for your script, which I like very much. I shall have to make some small alterations but they are only verbal ones. Before we broadcast this one, I should like it if you could do me another to go with this one and to be broadcast before it. The reason is that in this script you deal, as I asked you to, with the more subtle ways in which the Japanese tried to get the Chinese population over to their side. I also want one talk on the ordinary atrocity lines,[2] and I think it better that that one should go first and this one second. I have not bee[n] able yet to meet another Chinese who has been in occupied territory, and from what you said to me and from what you have

said in the script I have no doubt you are able to do it. I want something about the extortions of the Japanese, looting, raping, and the opium traffic etc. Possibly you could make an appointment to come and see me about this. Then perhaps we could broadcast both your scripts next week and the week after.

Yours sincerely,
Eric Blair
Empire Talks Assistant.

1. Hsaio Ch'ien (1909–) was educated at an American mission school in China and then took a BA in journalism at Peking University. In the curriculum vitae he provided the BBC, 7 March 1942, he said, 'I have done some teaching but fiction-writing has been my real job.' He had published nine books in China. In 1942 his *Etching of a Tormented Age* appeared in England; see Orwell's letter to him about this, *1020*. He was literary editor of *Takung Pao*, 1935–39, and came to England in the autumn of 1939. At this time he was on the staff of the School of Oriental and African Studies, University of London. He returned to China in 1949 and for sixteen years experienced persecution and was sent to work as a farm labourer. His autobiography, *Traveller Without a Map*, translated by Jeffrey B. G. Kinkley, was published in 1990. In 1995, as Xiao Qian, his complete translation into Chinese of James Joyce's *Ulysses* was published by the Yilin Press.
2. Contrast this request with the list of atrocities given in Orwell's War-time Diary, *1218*, *11.6.42*. Ch'ien spoke on 'Japan and the New Order' on 26 February 1942 see *1153* for a favourable report from India on this broadcast and on Japanese-occupied China on 5 March 1942; see *943* and *975*.

920. 'Cable to Chunking'

'We Speak to India,' 14 January 1942

PasB notes: 'Cable from Chunking. Read by George Orwell (E. Blair—member of the Indian Section). This was the English version of the talk given in Hindustani in the Hindustani News on the same day.' It was transmitted at 1430. At 15.14½ there was a 9-minute talk, 'Life in Chunking,' also in Hindustani. This had been written in English by Spencer Moore, an Associated Press correspondent, and was translated and read by A. L. Bakaya.

921. 'The Meaning of Scorched Earth'

15 January 1942

PasB notes a transmission in the Eastern Service of this talk, 'written by E. Blair. Read by Balraj Sahni.' The script does not seem to have survived. In his letter to Mulk Raj Anand of 27 February 1942, Orwell wrote: 'I recently wrote myself two talks explaining what is meant by scorched earth and by sabotage'; see *989*. For 'The Meaning of Sabotage,' see *940*.

922. BBC Talks Booking Form, 15.1.42

Shridhar Telkar: 'Through Eastern Eyes,' 'The Debate Continues'; broadcast 19 and 26.1.42; fee £7.7s each talk. Signed: N. H. Parratt.

923. Weekly News Review, 6

17 January 1942

The typescript appears to be a fair copy. There are no censors' stamps. 'As Broadcast' is typed at the top of the first page. PasB has 'by Z. A. Bokhari' (meaning read by him).

During the present week, there has not been any very great change in the strategy of the war. The Japanese advance in Malaya is continuing, and the Japanese are also attacking Celebes and Dutch Borneo, partly with a view to seizing the oil fields, and partly in order to find a jumping off place for fresh attacks against Java, Sumatra and possibly Australia. The little island of Tarakan, off the coast of Borneo, was over run by the Japanese after a few days' fighting. Tarakan is very important because it produces natural oil of such purity that it can be used for aeroplanes without any refinement. The Dutch, however, had made elaborate preparations to wreck the oil wells and the machinery, and it is doubtful whether much of value fell into Japanese hands.

The biggest event of the week has been the Russian advance on Kharkov. They are now within gunshot of the city. Kharkov, besides being a great industrial town, is a road and rail junction of the greatest importance, and it may be said that whoever holds it, holds the way of entry into the Caucasus. The Germans claimed its capture some months back as a great victory, and if they now relinquish it, it will certainly not be willingly. Outside Moscow the German troops at Mojaisk[1] are in a more and more dangerous situation, and will almost certainly have to retreat to avoid encirclement. Outside Leningrad, also, the situation has improved, and railway communications between Moscow and Leningrad have been re-established. The German withdrawal in Russia is "proceeding according to plan", indeed, but it begins to look more and more like a Russian plan.

Meanwhile from Egypt there comes the good news that the Germans and Italians in the fortress of Halfaya have unconditionally surrendered. This means not only that a large number of Axis prisoners have passed into Allied hands, but that there is now no enemy force to contend with between the Egyptian frontier and El Agheila, hundreds of miles to the west.

During a week in which not much has changed in the actual theatres of war, rumour has been busier than ever, and it becomes necessary to consider what steps the Axis powers are likely to take next and to distinguish between probable moves and stories which are put abroad with the idea of misleading public opinion in the democratic countries.

One thing that is almost certain is that the Germans must attack in a new direction within a short time. It is not very much use for Hitler and Mussolini to tell their peoples about the Japanese successes in the Pacific, for the Germans and Italians are well aware that what happens at the other end of the world does not put any food into their bellies.

In what directions could the Germans win quick victories which could be represented as offsetting the failure in Russia? The possibilities are— invasion of Britain; a move through Spain and down the West African coast to seize Dakar and Casablanca; a fresh offensive in the Central Mediterranean; or an invasion of Turkey. We can rule out the first as improbable, though not unthinkable. It is very unlikely that the Germans could succeed in a seaborne invasion of Britain, and if attempting an airborne invasion they are more likely to aim at Ireland, which, even if it succeeded, would be embarrassing for Britain, but not fatal. The move through Spain is likely sooner or later, but it would have certain political disadvantages from the German point of view. The Germans know that they would be bound to lose heavily in attacking Gibraltar, and in crossing the sea to Africa. The move in the Central Mediterranean seems much more likely. The other possible German move, an attack on Turkey, is a likelihood sooner or later, and might form part of the fresh German offensive against Russia in the spring, but the consensus of opinion seems to be that it is not likely to be attempted this year.

Meanwhile, even when there is a lull in the actual fighting, there is one kind of war that never stops for an instant, night or day, and that is the propaganda war. To the Axis powers, propaganda is an actual weapon, like guns or bombs, and to learn how to discount it is as important as taking cover during an air raid.

The Germans, even more than the Japanese, are adepts at propaganda. They cover up every military move by spreading misleading rumours beforehand, they use threats and bribes with equal skill, and they are entirely cynical in promising everything to everybody. To the rich they promise bigger profits, and to the poor they promise higher wages. To the coloured races they promise liberty, and simultaneously they appeal to the white races to combine for the exploitation of the coloured races. The object is always the same to divide and confuse their enemies, so that they can conquer them more easily. The Japanese methods are in essence the same. It is quite impossible to examine and refute every lie that they tell, and much of what they say is extremely persuasive. And yet one can remain quite untouched by Axis propaganda if one follows a simple rule which never fails.

This is, to compare what the Axis powers *say* they will do with what they are actually doing. The Japanese propaganda line at this moment is an extremely clever one. They claim that all they are doing is to set Asia free from European domination. They will drive the British out of India and the Americans out of the Pacific, and as soon as that is done, economic exploitation will be at an end. There will be no more poverty, no more taxation, no more need to be ruled over by foreigners. And in building up the picture of a war of Asia against Europe, they try to rouse as much race hatred as possible by spreading stories of imaginary outrages—rapes, murders and so forth, committed by British and Americans.

It is a very clever line of propaganda and is bound to find some sympathetic hearers. But it is a different matter if one compares these high-sounding promises of the Japanese with their actual behaviour.

For the past 4½ years they have been waging war not against any European power, but against another Asiatic nation, the Chinese. This is their third war of aggression against China in 50 years. On each occasion they have wrenched away a piece of Chinese territory and then exploited it for the benefit of the two or three wealthy families who rule Japan, with absolutely no regard for the native inhabitants. Even in the present war, they are fighting far more against Asiatics than against Europeans. In the Philippine Islands the resistance to Japanese attack is kept up mainly by Filipinos, in Malaya by Indians as much as by the British, in the Dutch East Indies by Javanese and Sumatrans. One of the opening acts of the war was the wanton bombing of Rangoon by the Japanese, in which hundreds of innocent Burmese were killed. Moreover, in those Asiatic territories which the Japanese have ruled over for a long time, we can see what their behaviour actually is towards subject peoples. Not only do they show no sign of setting Korea or Manchuria free, but they do not allow any sort of political liberty to exist. Trade unions are forbidden throughout Japanese territory, including Japan itself. No one in Japan is allowed to listen in to a foreign radio station, on pain of death. In the island of Formosa, where the Japanese found themselves faced with the problem of ruling over a people more primitive than themselves, they dealt with it by simply wiping the aboriginal inhabitants out.

We can see from this what the behaviour of the Japanese, who describe themselves as the deliverers of Asia, is actually like when they have other Asiatic races in their power. Yet it is possible to forget all this if one simply listens to the Japanese promises and forgets about their actions. As the war moves closer to India, Japanese propaganda will become more insistent. At times it may need firm nerves and a clear mind to disregard it. The one safe rule is to remember that acts count far more than words, and that the Japanese must be judged not by what they promise to do to-morrow in India or Burma, but what they did yesterday and are still doing in Korea, Manchuria and China.

1. Mojaisk (also spelled Mozhaisk) fell to the Germans on 18 October 1941.

924. To Sirdar Iqbal 'Ali Shah

17 January 1942   PP/EB

Dear Mr. Shah,[1]
I should like it very much if you could arrange to do a ten minute broadcast talk in English for me. We have a series of talks called "What It Means To

Me", in which the real meaning of the declared war aims of the Allies are discussed. The one I should like you to undertake, if you are willing, is Democracy, and I should like you to discuss as fully as you can what this word means to you from your point of view as an Asiatic who has lived in the west. You can, of course, speak quite freely. If you agree, I should like the talk to be delivered on February 5th, which means that the script should reach my office by January 29th. It should be about 1200 words in length. Could you be kind enough to let me know at once whether you are willing to do this, and if you can manage it by that date?

Yours sincerely,
Eric Blair
Talks Assistant
Indian Section

1. Iqbal 'Ali was recommended, with reservations, by A. E. H. Paxton, Near East Programme Organiser, Wood Norton, to John Pringle of the Home Talks Department. His memorandum of 5 November 1941 gives background information about the proposed broadcaster and some insight into the selection of speakers:

The Sirdar Iqbal 'Ali Shah writes talks for us from time to time. He does not speak Arabic at any rate sufficiently well to deliver his talks himself, and so they are translated and broadcast by our staff. His value to us lies in his name which has a distinguished Muslim sound and the fact that he is known among the intelligentsia in the Arabic-speaking world as the author of several books about Eastern potentates, but I believe his name carries little weight in India where he is regarded as a charlatan. However, I know that he broadcast a talk in the Hindustani service recently, so that it may be that he is not entirely without honour in his own country. He has travelled a great deal in Muslim countries and has recently written talks for us about his experiences in the Caucasus, Turkestan and more recently the Crimea. These annoyed our Axis rivals and stung them to reply.

His English is poor and his statements need careful checking, but if you bear this in mind he could probably do as good a talk for you as Norman Bentwich on Tuesday.

I think that is all I can tell you about the Sirdar, except that he looks like an Indian edition of George Arliss, and acts like the Old Man of the Sea if you come across him in Oxford. Oh! And incidentally, he is neither a Sirdar nor a Shah to the best of my belief.

'Sirdar' (Urdu), as a title, is equivalent to a military commander and 'Shah' (Persian) to king (but compare Mr. King in English). For Iqbal 'Ali's sensitivity on how he was addressed, see *933, n. 1*. George Arliss (1868–1946) was a stage and film actor popular on both sides of the Atlantic who wore a monocle. The American Academy of Motion Picture Arts and Sciences voted him best actor for 1929–30 for his leading role in *Disraeli*. The Sirdar's name was variously spelt in correspondence, and the form reproduced here is that given on each occasion.

925. To Mulk Raj Anand

19 January 1942   PP/EB

Dear Anand,

I don't know how things are progressing about your appointment, but meanwhile would you care to do one or two talks in the ordinary way? You know something, I think, about our new series. Would you like, for instance, to do a talk on H. G. Wells, Bernard Shaw, or some other well-known literary man, on Tuesday 10th February? You know the kind of talk I want. I should also like another of the same type on Tuesday, February 24th. Please let me know about this as soon as possible, as if you decide to do the talks we shall want your first one in about a week before the date of the broadcast.

Yours sincerely,
Eric Blair
Talks Assistant
Indian Section

926. To Cedric Dover

19 January 1942   PP/EB

Dear Mr. Dover,[1]

I have been wondering for some time past whether you would care to do a broadcast for us. Your friend Mr. Hardless told me recently that he thought that you would. I have a vacant date on February 19th for which you might care to do something. We have a series called "What It Means to Me", which are discussions of the abstract ideals for which the Allies are fighting. We have arranged for talks on Democracy and Liberty, but there are a lot of other large questions such as economic security, national sovereignty, emancipation of women and so on. I think it probable that you might like to talk on one of these. You will be able to speak fairly freely. Do you think you could be kind enough to ring me up and make an appointment to see me about this?

Yours sincerely,
Eric Blair
Talks Assistant
Indian Section

1. Cedric Dover (1904–1951) was born in Calcutta and educated there and at the University of Edinburgh. He wrote books and articles, and gave as his special subjects: 'Race, Colour & Social Problems, India, Hybrids & Negro America.' See *633, n. 1.*

927. 'Money and Guns'

'Through Eastern Eyes,' 20 January 1942

The typescript of this broadcast, in the BBC Archives, has written at the top of the first sheet 'Anon.' PasB notes: 'Written by Eric Blair and read by B. Sahni (Members of the Indian Section).' It ran for 11½ minutes.

Very often as you walk down the London streets you see side by side on a newspaper poster the news of a great battle in Russia or the Far East, and the news of a football match or a boxing contest. And maybe on a wall nearby you will see side by side a Government advertisement urging young women to join the A.T.S., and another advertisement, generally rather grimy and tattered-looking, urging the public to buy beer or whisky. And perhaps that makes you stop and ask yourself—how can a people fighting for its life find time for football matches? Isn't there something contradictory in urging people to give up their lives to their country's service, and at the same time urging them to spend their money on luxuries? But this raises the question of recreation in wartime which is not quite so simple as it looks.

A people at war—and that means, as a rule, a people that is working harder and under more trying conditions than usual—cannot get on without rest and amusement. Probably these things are more necessary in wartime than at ordinary times. And yet when you are fighting you cannot afford to waste precious material on luxury goods, because this is primarily a war of machines, and every scrap of metal used up in making gramophones, or every pound of silk used up in making stockings, means less metal for guns and aeroplanes, or less silk for parachutes and barrage balloons. We laughed at Marshal Goering when he said, some years before the war, that Germany had to choose between guns and butter,[1] but he was only wrong in the sense that there was no need for Germany to prepare aggression against her neighbours and thus plunge the whole world into war. Once war has started, every nation has to choose between guns and butter. It is merely a question of proportion. How many guns do you need to defeat the enemy? And how much butter do you need to keep your home population healthy and contented?

Granted that everyone is sufficiently fed and rested, the main problem of war is to divert expenditure from consumption goods to armaments. The working population, including the armed forces when they are on leave or off duty, still need their amusements, [and] as far as possible they must make do with amusements that do not use up much material or labour-time. Also, since England is an island and shipping is very precious, they must make do as far as possible with amusements that do not waste imported materials. Beyond a certain point you cannot lower the spending capacity of the population. As a result of taxation very large incomes have almost ceased to exist, and wages have not kept up with prices, but the spending power of the mass of the people has perhaps actually increased, because there is no longer any unemployment. Boys and girls of eighteen are now earning the wages of adults, and when they have paid for their board and lodging they still have something over every week. The question is, how are they to spend it without diverting much-needed labour to the manufacture of luxury goods? In the answer to this question one can see how the war is altering the habits and even the tastes of the British people.

To make a rough division: the luxuries which have to be discarded in wartime are the more elaborate kinds of food and drink, fashionable clothes, cosmetics and scents—all of which either demand a great deal of labour or use up rare imported materials—personal service, and unnecessary journeys, which use up such precious imported things as rubber and petrol. The amusements which can be encouraged, on the other hand, are games, sports, music, the radio, dancing, literature and the arts generally. Most of these are things in which you create your amusement for yourself, rather than paying other people to create it for you. If you have two hours to spare, and if you spend it in walking, swimming, skating, or playing football, according to the time of year, you have not used up any material or made any call on the nation's labour power. On the other hand, if you use those two hours in sitting in front of the fire and eating chocolates, you are using up coal which has to be dug out of the ground and carried to you by rail, and sugar and cocoa beans which have to be transported half across the world. In the cases of a good many unnecessary luxuries, the government diverted expenditure in the right direction by simply cutting off supplies. For nearly two years no one in Britain has seen a banana, for example, sugar is not too plentiful, oranges are seen only from time to time, matches are cut down to the point at which no one ever wastes a match, travelling is much restricted, clothes are rationed fairly strictly.

At the same time, people who are working all day cannot altogether create their amusements for themselves. It is desirable, therefore, that they should concentrate on the kind of recreation that can be enjoyed communally without much wastage of labour. That brings me back to the thing I mentioned a few minutes ago—the newspaper report of a football match side by side with the report of a battle. Is it not all wrong that ten thousand citizens of a nation at war should spend two hours in watching a football match? Not really, for the only labour they are monopolising is the labour of the twenty-two players. If it is an amateur football match, as it usually is nowadays—a match between the Army and the R.A.F. for instance—those players are not even being paid. And if it is a local match, the ten thousand spectators have not even wasted any coal or petrol in getting there. They have merely had two hours' recreation, which they are probably in need of, almost without any expenditure of labour or material.

You can see from this the way in which the mere necessity of war is bringing about in the English people a more creative attitude towards their amusements. Something symptomatic of this happened during the big air raids. The people who were penned up in the Tube shelters for hours together had nothing to do, and there were no ready-made amusements available. They had to amuse themselves, so they improvised amateur concerts, which were sometimes surprisingly good and successful. But what is perhaps more significant than this is the greatly increased interest in literature that has appeared during the last two years. There has been an enormous increase in reading, partly owing to the great numbers of men who are in the army in lonely camps, where they have little or nothing to do in their spare time. Reading is one of the cheapest and least wasteful recreations in existence. An edition of tens of thousands of copies of a book does not use up as much paper or labour as a single day's issue of one newspaper, and each copy of the book may pass through hundreds of hands before it goes back to the pulping mill. But just because the habit of reading has vastly increased and people cannot read without educating themselves in the process, the average intellectual level of the books published has markedly risen. Great literature, no doubt, is not being produced, but the average book which the ordinary man reads is a better book than it would have been three years ago. One phenomenon of the war has been the enormous sale of Penguin Books, Pelican Books and other cheap editions, most of which would have been regarded by the general public as impossibly highbrow a few years back. And this in turn reacts on the newspapers, making them more serious and less sensational than they were before. It probably reacts also on the radio, and will react in time on the cinema.

Parallel with this is the revival of amateur sport and amateur theatricals in the armed forces, and of recreations, such as gardening, which are not only not wasteful, but actually productive. Though England is not primarily an agricultural country, the English people are fond of gardening, and since the war the government has done everything to encourage this. Allotments are available almost everywhere, even in the big towns, and thousands of men who might otherwise have spent their evenings playing darts in the pub, now spend them in growing vegetables for their families. Similarly, women who in peace time might have been sitting in the cinematograph are now sitting at home knitting socks and helmets for Russian soldiers.

Before the war there was every incentive for the general public to be wasteful, at least so far as their means allowed. Everyone was trying to sell something to everyone else, and the successful man, so it was imagined was the man who sold the most goods and got the most money in return. We have learned now, however, that money is valueless in itself, and only goods count. In learning it we have had to simplify our lives and fall back more and more on the resources of our own minds instead of on synthetic pleasures manufactured for us in Hollywood or by the makers of silk stockings, alcohol and chocolates. And under the pressure of that necessity we are re-discovering the simple pleasures—reading, walking, gardening, swimming, dancing, singing—which we had half forgotten in the wasteful years before the war.

1. Goering, in a broadcast in 1936, said 'Guns will make us powerful; butter will only make us fat,' though he was probably paraphrasing Goebbels's speech of 17 January 1936, in which he said, 'We can do without butter, but . not without arms. One cannot shoot with butter but with guns '

928. To Noel Sircar

20 January 1942   PP/EB

Dear Mr. Sircar,

I understand from my secretary that you would like to do another talk for us. I rang up India House to-day, but was told that you were away with 'flu. Perhaps when you are well again you will send me in your script, and when I have seen it we can fix up a date for you to broadcast, if it is suitable for our series. We should like to have the script as soon as is convenient for you.[1] I hope it will not be long before you are well again.

Yours sincerely,
Eric Blair
Talks Assistant
Indian Section

1. Sircar sent the script for 'Restaurants and Eating Houses' to Orwell on 28 January; Orwell inscribed the covering note, 'Rec[orded]. Fri. 20.2.42   4.45   B.5' (B.5 was Studio B.5) See *982*.

929. Obituary of Maharao of Cutch

20 January 1942

At 1430 in the programme 'We Speak to India,' Orwell (described in PasB as Eric Blair) read an obituary for the Maharao of Cutch (1866–1942) in the Eastern Service. This script, though it has been attributed to Orwell, was taken from the obituary in *The Times*, 20 January 1942.

930. To J. Chinna Durai

21 January 1942   Original   PP/EB

Dear Mr. Chinna Durai,
I am sorry that in error I gave you back the censored copy of your script as well as another copy.[1] Could you send it back to us. We want your original copy, which was corrected and which has the red censorship stamp on it. I am forwarding your contract at the same time.

Yours sincerely,
[Signed] Eric Blair
Eric Blair
Talks Assistant
Indian Section

1. The script was that for 'The Fate of Japan'; see *931*. Durai returned it with Orwell's letter, writing a cheery note at its foot. R. W. Brock, of the India Section of the Ministry of Information, had seen this script in advance and wrote, 15 January, to Rushbrook Williams to urge its use, 'subject to minor revisions necessitated by more recent developments.' He went on, 'Indian Press reactions are strongly adverse to Japan and it is clearly sound policy to sustain and stimulate this trend by every means.' Rushbrook Williams asked Bokhari, 17 January, if anything could be made of this script. 'If so, we shall please M of I as well as C[hinna] D[urai].' The talk was broadcast on 21 January.

931. BBC Talks Booking Form, 21.1.42

J. Chinna Durai: 'Through Eastern Eyes,' 'The Fate of Japan'; broadcast 21.1.42; fee £7.7s. Signed: N. H. Parratt.

932. 'British Rations and the Submarine War'

'Through Eastern Eyes,' 22 January 1942

The typescript for this broadcast states that it was written 'by E. Blair' and read by I. B. Sarin, Programmes Assistant in the Eastern Service. The script carries a rectangular censor's stamp. Unlike the later triangular rubber stamps for Security and for Policy, this one bears only the words 'CENSORED DATE . . . SIGNATURE . . . BBC CENSORSHIP DEPARTMENT.' The censor on this occasion was Norman Collins, then Empire Talks Director. There is a certain irony that the censor, however much a formality his task here, should have been a man Orwell regarded as an adversary from his days with Gollancz, the publishers. At the top of the first page of the script Orwell has written 'As broadcast. 10 mins 10 secs,' the precise timing, for a scheduled 12-minute time-slot. In PasB the title is given as 'Britain's Rations and the Submarine War.'

The second sentence in paragraph five is curious at first sight. Orwell *was* in England during World War I (1914–18) and could speak from his own experience. He has obviously written here bearing in mind that I. B. Sarin, a Hindustani, would be reading his script. The final sentence of the paragraph would seem to be written from Orwell's heart.

As explained in *892*, passages crossed out in the typescript are reproduced in roman type within square brackets. It should not be assumed that such passages were censored. Additions and substitutions are in italic. What was originally written or typed is noted.

Probably you have read in the newspaper or heard on the radio the news that food rations in Britain have been reduced. Everyone was expecting this. The rations of certain foods had been raised in November in order to cover the worst period of the winter, but the public were warned that they would be cut down again later. [when war broke out in the Pacific, because of the increased need for shipping.] The fat ration has been cut down from 10 ounces to 8 ounces a week, and the sugar ration from 12 ounces to 8 ounces. Other foodstuffs are not affected, though naturally there is a shortage in winter of certain unrationed foodstuffs, such as fish *and fruit.*

There is a great deal of evidence that food rationing has not so far done any harm to public health in Britain—rather the contrary, if anything. English people before the war usually ate too much sugar and drank too much tea, and were too inclined to look on meat as their staple food. The war has brought home to a lot of people the value of vegetables, especially raw vegetables. There have been no epidemics of any importance in Britain since the war—not even in the worst period of the air raids, when something of the kind might have been expected—and the figures for all infectious diseases are lower now than they were at this time last year. But to get a true idea of the significance of food rationing in Britain, one has got to make two comparisons. One is with the corresponding rations in Germany, and the other is with the conditions that existed in England in the war of 1914–1918.

If you go through the published lists of British and German rations, you will notice that the only foodstuff in which the German ration is even claimed[1] as being higher is fat. According to the official figures, the German citizen gets a weekly ration of 9 ounces of fat, whereas the British citizen now gets only 8 ounces. But this is misleading, because every British citizen also gets a ration of 4 ounces of bacon; any bacon the German gets is included in his fat ration. In every other rationed foodstuff the British and German allowances are either equal, or the British allowance is higher. Moreover, many substances are rationed in Germany which can be freely bought in any quantity in England. Bread is one example, cocoa is another, and coffee is another. Certain things, tea for example, are literally unobtainable in Germany. An even more important fact is that in Britain you do not have to surrender any of your food coupons if you eat a meal away from home, in a restaurant or a factory canteen, for example. The rationing applies only to foodstuffs which are bought raw and taken home. In Germany this is not the case. And since owing to the conditions of war, in which nearly everyone goes out to work, more and more people eat at least one meal a day away from home, this distinction is a very important one.

To see the significance of this, one has to remember that the Germans are masters of Europe from Norway to the Black Sea. All the food that Europe can supply is at their disposal, and we can be quite sure that they are not sacrificing their own population for the sake of the other Europeans. Indeed, they hardly even pretend to be doing so. It is openly admitted that everywhere in continental Europe food conditions are worse than in Germany, and in some countries, such as Greece, they amount almost to famine. The Germans are looting all Europe to feed themselves, and in spite of that they get less to eat, and less varied food, than we get in Britain.

And now one sees the significance of that other comparison I made—the comparison with conditions in this country in 1914–18. Of course, I was not in England then and I am not pretending to speak out of my own experience. But all English people over 35, or even over 30, have vivid memories of that other war, and I have discussed it with very many people. Without exception they say that food conditions then, at any rate in the second half of 1917 and in 1918, were far worse than they are now. Indeed, people who were children during the other war have told me that their chief memory of the war is a memory of being hungry.

The chief difference, and the reason why we are better off now than people were then, is that the danger of food shortage was foreseen. When the war of 1914 started no one realised that the German submarine warfare would be as successful as it turned out to be, and the food shortage became severe quite suddenly. All of a sudden, it was discovered that there were only a few weeks' food in stock—and you must remember that England is a very small island which probably could not feed itself entirely, even if every inch of it were under cultivation. No arrangements for rationing had been made before-hand, and methods of storing food were nowhere near so efficient as they are now. Nor had the science of food values been studied at that time, as it has during the past twenty years. And meanwhile there was a period about the end of 1917 when the German submarines were sinking twenty or thirty British ships every week. As a result, butter almost ceased to exist in England for about a year, sugar and jam were rarities, and the bread, which in any case was not plentiful, was a dirty grey colour, having been adulterated with potato flour. Meat had to be rationed much more strictly than it is now, for even if you had a meal in a restaurant or a canteen you still had to give up meat coupons. Also, food was not distributed so skilfully as it is now, and one result was enormous queues of women outside the food shops, who sometimes had to wait there for hours before being served. My English friends have often told me that those long queues are one of their principal war memories. I cannot say that you never see food queues now, but at any rate you don't see them very frequently.

This time much has been changed because the Government took the necessary step of rationing essential foodstuffs from the start, and because the submarine menace has been much more effectively dealt with. To realise the difference one has got to remember that in the last war the British navy had the French, Italian and Japanese navies to help it, and towards the end the American as well, whereas during more than a year of this war it had to operate alone, with the Italians as well as the Germans against it. There is no doubt that from the beginning the Germans placed great hopes on the chance of starving Britain into surrender. If you listen in to the German wireless you will hear every week enormous figures of the tonnage of British shipping supposed to have been sunk by German submarines. Some people, who have taken the trouble to keep a note of these figures from the beginning, have found that the Germans claim by now to have sunk far more shipping than Britain ever possessed. [And when Hitler's deputy, Rudolf Hess, fled to England, he disclosed that Hitler's main war-plan was to starve England out.] Even if the German submarines could not cause actual starvation in Britain, they might hope to sink so many ships that the import of war materials would have to stop, and all the available shipping would have to concentrate on carrying food. But nothing of the kind has happened. The flow of goods across the Atlantic—tanks and fighter planes, as well as wheat and beef—has never slackened, and during the last year the number of British ships sunk every month has decreased enormously. And this is in spite of the fact that German submarines can now operate from ports all the way from Norway to Spain, and not only from German and Belgian ports, as in the last war. The methods of detecting and destroying submarines have vastly improved, and with every German submarine that goes to the bottom, Germany's[2] difficulty of finding trained men for this dangerous work becomes harder. In addition, part of Britain's food problem is being solved by the expansion of British agriculture. Two million extra acres were ploughed up during 1940, and another large area was ploughed up during 1941. The more food Britain can grow for herself, the less shipping she need use to import it. The extra labour for the land is being supplied partly by women volunteers, and partly by Italian prisoners. You can see from all this why our food situation in Britain—though I don't want to pretend to you that it is perfect—is far better than what English people had to put up with during the last war, and far better than it is in Germany, even though Germany is systematically robbing all Europe in order to feed herself.

1 'claimed' is heavily underlined in the typescript, perhaps by the speaker.
2. Germany's] the

933. To Sirdar Iqbal 'Ali Shah

22 January 1942   PP/EB

Dear Mr. Shah,[1]
Many thanks for your letter of January 21st. With regard to the points you raise;
1. The time of our broadcasts is 4 p.m. B.S.T. Of course it is necessary to come some time beforehand in order to rehearse. I will let you know the exact time shortly before the broadcast.[2]
2. I am afraid I misled you about this. I now find that this ceremony[3] is already being covered by the B.B.C. and we may be duplicating the fact if we have another talk on it.
3. I do not want to make any definite arrangement yet[4] about reports on the House of Commons, I merely raised that idea in case that job should be vacant later, and in case you should be interested. But in the case of your arranging to do it, it would probably not entail attending the House every day, but only when some evidently important debate is about to take place. These talks are also broadcast at 4 p.m.
I am looking forward to seeing your script on Democracy.

Yours sincerely,
Eric Blair
Talks Assistant
Indian Section

1. On 29 January, the Sirdar wrote in the 'most friendly light' correcting the way Orwell had addressed him. He should, he said, be addressed as 'Dear Sirdar' or as Sirdar Ikbal° 'Ali Shah. When introduced at the microphone, he wished it pointed out that he was an author of almost fifty books published in Britain, and had international experience of matters and men, he was not any Tom, Dick or Harry who had been dragged up to the microphone. He concluded by inviting Orwell to lunch on the day of the broadcast, after which they could drive to Broadcasting House together.
2. This was the broadcast on 'Democracy,' 30 January
3. This was the opening of a zawiah at Cardiff, at which, the Sirdar told A. E. H. Paxton, there would be great juloos (processions), with zikr prayers. The zawiyah (as it is more commonly spelt) was a mosque, which had been destroyed when Cardiff was bombed. Zikr (or dhikr) means, in Arabic, 'reminding oneself' and is applied to Islamic ritual prayer.
4. In his letter, the Sirdar took it as understood that he would begin a series of weekly talks, probably on 10 February, running for six weeks.

934. To Sir Hari Singh Gour

23 January 1942   PP/EB

Dear Sir Hari Singh Gour,
I have been in touch with the Duty Officer of the B.B.C. with reference to your Pass to the House of Commons.[1] It has been arranged that the Pass will be collected by Mr. Sarin on Monday afternoon, and he will send it to you by special messenger on that day. I understand that the House will be sitting on Tuesday, Wednesday and Thursday only, so that the Duty Officer will need

to have the Pass back by Friday morning first thing, at the latest. I shall ask
Mr. Sarin to telephone you to make arrangements about the return of your
Pass.

Yours sincerely,
Eric Blair
Talks Assistant
Indian Section

1. Sir Hari Singh Gour was booked to talk in the series 'The Debate Continues'; see *944* For his
earlier talks, see *879, n. 2.*

935. Weekly News Review, 7

24 January 1942

The typescript for this broadcast is a fair copy, single-spaced, and bears no
censors' stamps. At the top of the first page is typed 'As Broadcast.' PasB gives
the timing as 11 minutes and states, 'read by Z. A. Bokhari.'

On the Far Eastern Front the Japanese advance continues, but somewhat less
rapidly than before, and there are signs that Allied air power in the Pacific is
gradually growing stronger. Meanwhile the Japanese have made two moves
in new directions. One is towards New Guinea, which is a possible jumping
off place for an attack on Australia, and the other westwards from Thailand
into Burma.

The second of these moves is much the more important. An attack on
Australia might be very embarrassing for the Allied powers,[1] but it is not
likely to be decisive because Australia is much too large and too far from
Japan, for the Japanese to be able to over run it in any period of time in which
the war is likely to last. The other move, however, if it is not countered, may
have far-reaching results, both on the war in China and on the war in the
South Pacific.

The Japanese have already captured the town of Tavoy in the far south of
Burma, and they are attacking at the border not far from Moulmein, which is
about 100 miles from Rangoon. Rangoon is immensely important; if you
look at the map you will see that almost all the communications, road, rail
and waterways, in Burma, run north and south,—that is important, north
and south—and that practically there is no route by which goods can travel to
the interior of Burma without passing through the port of Rangoon. This
means that the Burma Road, along which the Chinese armies draw their chief
supplies of war material, depends for its usefulness on Rangoon's remaining
securely in Allied hands. Fortunately, it will be very difficult for the Japanese
to launch a full scale attack in this area, for the reason already given, that
natural communications all run from north to south and not east and west. It
is doubtful whether tanks or heavy artillery can be brought directly from
Thailand into the southern part of Burma, and the attacks the Japanese are
now making seem to be carried out only by infantry and aeroplanes. It should

be possible for British forces to hold them back, especially with the aid of the large number of Chinese reinforcements who are known to have arrived.

If we look further south, the situation is even more critical. It is doubtful whether a fortress as strong as Singapore can be taken by storm, but we have to face the possibility that it may be at least neutralised and rendered almost useless as a base for Allied shipping during a long period. All depends upon the speed with which the Allies can bring reinforcements, especially of fighter aeroplanes, across the immense distances that have to be travelled. But if we look at the Japanese successes, not on a scale of weeks or months, but on a scale of years, then the very fact of these successes gives good ground for hope. All of these successes are due to Japanese naval and air superiority in a given area. Now the combined naval power of the Allied powers, taking the world as a whole, is very much greater than that of the Axis powers, and their combined air power is already about equally great, and is rapidly forging ahead. Germany can still produce aeroplanes and submarines in very large numbers, but a country at the industrial level of Japan cannot compete in what is essentially a war of machines, with the manufacturing capacity of great modern states such as the U.S.A., Britain and the U.S.S.R. In the long run the factor that has been temporarily in Japan's favour, superiority in numbers of ships and aeroplanes, will be reversed, even if it should take several years to do this.

In Russia, the Germans are still retreating and during this week the Russians won a great victory by the capture of Mojaisk, from which the Germans had once hoped to advance for the attack upon Moscow. Seeing that any hope of capturing Moscow this year had obviously been abandoned, the loss of Mojaisk is less important strategically than for its effects on prestige and morale. It is highly significant that up till yesterday the German propagandists had not dared to inform their own people of this disaster, and no doubt they are still searching for some way of presenting the news so that it may seem unimportant. This is very difficult because of the violence with which they had trumpeted the capture of Mojaisk when they took it themselves. The formula of the German military spokesman continues to be that they are not being driven back, but are merely shortening their line with a view to settling into winter quarters, but they have twice announced what their final winter line will be, and have twice been compelled to retreat to positions further back.

The way in which the world picture is gradually changing in favour of the Allies can be seen in the swing of opinion in countries which were recently neutral or in some cases even inclined to favour the Axis. The most important symptom of this has been the outcome of the Pan-American Conference at Rio de Janeiro, an outcome far more favourable to the Allies than would have been possible a year ago.

At this conference all the American republics have come to a substantial agreement and are almost unanimous in their readiness to break off relations with the Axis Powers. Some of the Central American Republics have already done this. Of the larger South American states, the only two which have shown any reluctance are Argentina and Chile. The two Latin American countries which count for most, Mexico and Brazil, have already ranged themselves with the United States.[2]

Parallel with these changes of opinion in South America, there exists almost certainly a widespread stirring of unrest in Europe. The iron censorship imposed by the Nazis makes it very difficult to know for certain what is happening in the conquered countries. But we have a valuable source of information in broadcasts and other propaganda of the Nazis themselves. Both from what they say and from what they do not say it can be inferred with practical certainty that Europe generally is disgusted with the so-called "New Order". Hitler promised the peoples of Europe work, peace and food, and of these he has only been able to give them work in increasing quantities at lower and lower wages. We ought not to assume that the morale of the German people themselves will break down at any time in the near future. But so far as the rest of Europe goes, it is clear that the picture which German propagandists were lately building up of a united Europe all working as one great arsenal for the war against Russia and the Anglo-Saxon powers was simply a mirage.

In Libya the campaign has slowed down after the capture of Halfaya. It is still uncertain whether General Rommel is about to make a fresh attempt to recapture what he has lost,—he has certainly made one big-scale reconnaissance before which our light forces had to withdraw—or whether he is still trying to extricate his forces and retire to Tripoli, but even when events appear to be moving slowly and indecisively, we ought not to lose sight of the North African front, which ties up great quantities of trained men, shipping, and above all, aeroplanes, which the Germans might otherwise be able to use against our Allies in Russia.

1. An attack on Australia was felt at the time to be more than embarrassing. The *Daily Mail*, for example, on 22 January 1942, carried the headline 'Australia Fears War "At Door," ' over a report of a speech by the Australian Prime Minister John Curtin (1885–1945), in which he said: 'Anybody in Australia who fails to perceive the immediate menace which these attacks [on New Guinea] constitute must be lost to all reality. . . . The peril is nearer, clearer, and deadlier than before.' New Guinea was less than 150 miles from Australia, and, the report said, 'it is feared . . . a major onslaught is about to be made on this great sprawling island, possibly as a preliminary to an invasion of Australia.'
2. Brazil broke off diplomatic relations with Japan on 28 January 1942 and declared war on Germany and Italy on 22 August 1942, and on Japan on 6 June 1945. Mexico declared war on the Axis powers on 22 May 1942. Argentina broke off relations with Germany and Japan on 26 January 1944 and declared war on 27 March 1945. Chile declared war on Japan on 14 February 1945. A number of other South American countries had declared war on Japan, Germany, and Italy within a week of the Japanese attack on Pearl Harbor.

936. To Hsiao Ch'ien

24 January 1942   PP/EB

Dear Mr. Hsiao Ch'ien,
Very many thanks for your second talk. I should be very glad to make use of both of these, which are exactly the kind of thing I wanted. I am not quite

certain, however, when to fit them in to my programme and I think the best arrangement will be for you to record them. Do you think you could come here for the recording some day next week. The whole process, rehearsal and recording, will probably take about an hour and a half. The best days for me would be Tuesday, Wednesday or Thursday, but I cannot say in advance what time of day, because it is a question of getting the studio for the recording. Will you ring me up as soon as possible and tell me which day will suit you, and I will then fix things up as rapidly as possible.

Yours sincerely,
Eric Blair
Talks Assistant
Indian Section

937. To Hsiao Ch'ien

27 January 1942   PP/EB

Dear Mr. Hsiao Ch'ien,
I am sending you the typewritten copies of your two talks which you asked for.
    I shall look forward to hearing from you soon.

Yours sincerely,
Eric Blair
Talks Assistant
Indian Section

938. To Cedric Dover

27 January 1942   PP/EB

Dear Dover,
Just to confirm that we agreed yesterday that you should write me two talks, about 1200 words each, on National Sovereignty, and (title to be fixed later) on the changes occurring in Britain owing to increased contacts with foreigners. If convenient to you, the following dates would fit in. Thursday February 19th for the first (National Sovereignty) and Wednesday February 25th for the second. I want the talks to reach me in each case a week beforehand—i.e. the 12th and 18th February. Can you manage this?
    Don't forget to send me a copy of your article for Reynolds's.[1]

Yours
George Orwell.

1. *Reynold's News*, founded 5 May 1850, was a popular, Socialist-inclined Sunday newspaper. It was amalgamated with the *Sunday Citizen* on 20 August 1944 and, under that name, ceased publication on 18 June 1967.

939. To Sirdar Iqbal 'Ali Shah

27 January 1942   PP/EB

Dear Mr. Ali Shah,

Many thanks for your talk,[1] which will do very nicely. The date is <u>Thursday, February 5th</u>. Can you arrange to meet me at 3 p.m. in the reception hall at Broadcasting House on that day. This will give us time to run through the talk a couple of times before the actual broadcast, which is at 4 p.m.

Yours sincerely,
Eric Blair
Talks Assistant
Indian Section

1. On 'Democracy.'

940. 'The Meaning of Sabotage'

'Through Eastern Eyes,' 29 January 1942

The typescript has a few amendments in Orwell's hand and at the head of the first page, also in his hand, is written, 'As broadcast. 10 mins 10 secs.' The talk was censored by R. C. Hardman and read by Balraj Sahni.

Some time back I gave a talk on the scorched earth policy which plays such an important part in this war. The[1] subject of sabotage arises naturally out of this. Sabotage is the tactic of a conquered people, just as scorched earth is the tactic of an army in retreat. But one understands better how it works if one knows something about its origins.

Everyone has heard the word sabotage. It is one of those words that find their way into all languages, but not all of the people who use it know where it comes from. It is really a French word. In parts of Northern France and Flanders the people, at any rate the peasants and working people, wear heavy wooden shoes which are called sabots. Once, many years ago, some working men who had a grievance against their employer threw their sabots into a piece of machinery while it was running, and thus damaged it. This action was nicknamed sabotage, and from then onwards the word came to be used for any action deliberately intended to interfere with industry or destroy valuable property.

The Nazis are now ruling over the greater part of Europe, and one can hardly open a newspaper without reading that in France, or Belgium, or Yugoslavia, or wherever it may be, several more people have been shot for committing sabotage. Now, one did not read these reports, or at any rate one did not read them in *such*[2] numbers, at the beginning of the German occupation. They are a growth of the last year, and they have increased in numbers since Hitler attacked Soviet Russia. The increase of sabotage, and, still more, the seriousness with which the Germans regard it, tell one something about the nature of Nazi rule.

If you listen to German or Japanese propaganda you notice that a great deal of it is taken up with the demand for living space, or "lebensraum" as the Germans call it. The argument is always the same. Germany and Japan are crowded over-populated countries, and they want empty territories which their populations can colonise. These empty territories in the case of Germany are western Russia and the Ukraine, and in the case of Japan they are Manchuria and Australia. If you disregard the propaganda put out by the Fascists, however, and study what they have actually done, you find it is quite a different story. It seems that what the Fascist nations actually want is not empty spaces, but territories already thickly populated. The Japanese did indeed seize part of Manchuria in 1931, but they have not made serious attempts to colonise it, and soon afterwards they followed this aggression up by attacking and over-running the most thickly populated parts of China. At this moment, again, they are attacking and trying to over-run the very thickly populated islands of the Dutch East Indies. The Germans, similarly, have over-run and are holding in subjection the most thickly populated and highly industrialised parts of Europe.

In the sense in which the early settlers colonised America and Australia, it would be quite impossible for the Germans to colonise Belgium and Holland, or for the Japanese to colonise the valley of the Yang-tze-Kiang. There are far too many people there already. But of course, the Fascists have no wish to colonise in that sense. The cry for living-room is only a bluff. What they want is not land but slaves. They want control of large subject populations whom they can force to work for them at very low wages. The German picture of Europe is of two hundred million people all working from morning to night and turning over the products of their work to Germany, and getting in return just as much as will keep them from dying of starvation. The Japanese picture of Asia is similar. To some extent the German aims have already been achieved. But it is just here that the importance of sabotage comes in.

When those Belgium workmen flung their wooden sabots into the machinery, they showed their understanding of something that is not always recognised—the immense power and importance of the ordinary working man. The whole of society rests finally on the manual worker, who always has it in his power to throw it out of gear. It is no use for the Germans to hold the European peoples in subjection unless they can trust them to work. Only a few days of unchecked sabotage, and the whole German war machine would be at a standstill. A few blows from a sledge hammer, in the right place, can stop a power station working. One tug at the wrong signal lever can wreck a train. Quite a small charge of explosive can sink a ship. One box of matches, or one match, can destroy hundreds of tons of cattle fodder. Now, there is no doubt that acts of this kind are being carried out all over Europe, and in greater and *greater* numbers. The constant executions for sabotage, which the Germans themselves announce, show this clearly. All over Europe, from Norway to Greece, there are brave men who have grasped the nature of the German rule and are willing to risk their lives to overthrow it. To some extent this has been going on ever since Hitler came to power. During the Spanish civil war, for instance, it sometimes happened that a shell landed in the Republican lines and failed to explode, and when it was opened, sand or sawdust was found inside it instead of the explosive charge. Some worker in the German or Italian arms factories had risked his life so that at least one shell should not kill his comrades.

But you cannot expect whole populations to risk their lives in this way, especially when they are being watched by the most efficient secret police in the world. The whole European working class, especially in the key industries, lives constantly under the eye of the Gestapo. Here, however, there comes in something which it is almost impossible for the Germans to prevent, and that is what is called passive sabotage. Even if you cannot or dare not wreck the machines, you can at least slow it down and prevent it from working smoothly. This is done by working as slowly and inefficiently as possible, by deliberately wasting time, by shamming illness, and by being as wasteful as possible with material. It is very difficult even for the Gestapo to fix responsibility for this kind of thing, and the effect is a constant friction which holds up the output of materials of war.

This brings out an essential fact: that anyone who consumes more material than he produces is in effect sabotaging the war machine. The worker who deliberately dawdles over his work is not only wasting his own time but other peoples' as well. For he has got to be watched and driven, which means that other potential workers have to be taken away from productive employment. One of the chief features, one[3] might say the distinctive feature, of Fascist rule, is the enormous number of police that it employs. All over Europe, in Germany and in the occupied countries, there are huge armies of police, SS-men, ordinary uniformed police, plain-clothed police and spies and provocateurs of all kinds. They are extremely efficient, and so long as Germany is not defeated in the field they can probably prevent any open revolt, but they represent an enormous diversion of labour, and their mere existence shows the nature of the Germans' difficulties. At this moment, for instance, the Germans profess to be leading a European crusade against Soviet Russia. Yet they dare not raise large armies from the conquered European countries, because they could never trust them not to go over to the enemy. The entire number of the so-called allies of Germany, now fighting in Russia, is pitifully small. In the same way, they cannot really turn over the big business of armaments production to European countries outside Germany, because they are aware that the danger of sabotage exists everywhere. And even the danger can achieve a great deal. Every time a piece of machinery is wrecked or an ammunition dump mysteriously catches fire, precautions have to be redoubled lest the same thing should happen elsewhere. More investigations, more police, more spies are needed, and more people have to be diverted from productive work. If the Germans could really bring about the object they set themselves at the beginning—two hundred and fifty million Europeans, all united and working at full speed—it might perhaps be possible for them to outbuild Great Britain, the United States and Soviet Russia in munitions of war. But they cannot do so, because they cannot trust the conquered peoples and the danger of sabotage confronts them at every turn. When Hitler finally falls, the European workers who idled, shammed sickness, wasted material and damaged machinery in the factories, will have played an important part in his destruction.

1. war. The] war, and the
2. *such*] anywhere near the same
3. *one*] we

941. To Sirdar Iqbal 'Ali Shah

29 January 1942   PP/EB

Dear Mr. Ali Shah,
    The Turkish Ambassador is opening a Turkish Halkevi (I understand that "Halkevi" means "People's House" and is a kind of social and cultural centre) at 14, Fitzhardinge Street, W.1., at 3 p.m. on Thursday February 19th. We want someone to cover the ceremony for the BBC and do a ten minutes' talk on it in English. Would you care to undertake this for us. It might not be possible—in fact it would not—to broadcast the talk on the same day as the ceremony, and I appreciate that it is asking rather a lot to drag up to London twice for this purpose. The BBC would pay your travelling expenses, however. Could you be kind enough to let me know as soon as possible whether you would care to do this?

Yours sincerely,
Eric Blair
Talks Assistant
Indian Section

942. BBC Talks Booking Form, 30.1.42

Mulk Raj Anand: 'Through Eastern Eyes,' 'These Names Will Live,' 1. H. G. Wells; 2. Bernard Shaw; two 12-minute talks; broadcast 10 and 24.2.42; fee £7.7s each talk. Signed: N. H. Parratt.

943. BBC Talks Booking Form, 30.1.42?[1]

Hsiao Chi'en: 'Through Eastern Eyes,' 'What It Means to Me,' 4,[2] Japan and the New Order; recorded 10.2.42; broadcast 26.2.42; fee 'usual' £10.10s. Signed: N. H. Parratt.

1. The question mark was added by hand.
2. Originally this booking form scheduled two talks; the second, 'It Happened in Occupied China,' was booked for transmission on 5.3 42 as No. 5 in the series See *975*

944. BBC Talks Booking Form, 30.1.42

Sir Hari Singh Gour: 'Through Eastern Eyes,' 'The Debate Continues,' 12-minute talk on weekly proceedings in the House of Commons; broadcast 2.2.42; fee £7.7s. Signed: N. H. Parratt.[1]

1. A letter of 4 March 1942 from Rushbrook Williams's secretary to A. H. Joyce, who represented the India Office on the Eastern Service Committee, shows some confusion over the dates of Sir Hari's broadcasts. It omits one, 3 November 1941; gives that for 24 November as 23; and refers to five scripts being sent for the attention of L. S. Amery, Secretary of State for India, although six dates are listed. See also *879, n. 2.*

945. BBC Talks Booking Form, 30.1.42

Sirdar Iqbal 'Ali Shah: 'Through Eastern Eyes,' 'What It Means to Me,' 1, Democracy, 12-minute talk; broadcast 5.2.42; fee £7.7s. Signed: N. H. Parratt. 'Remarks: It is most important that this speaker should be written to as DEAR SIRDAR. On envelope *no Esq.*, Sirdar is a title. He is particular about this.'

946. Newsletter, 8
31 January 1942

All the excisions to this broadcast may be attributed to the censor, but only one is certainly his work. He was A. F. N. Thavenot, listed as 'Assistant (Thai)' in Issue 2 of the BBC Staff List dated 21.8.43 (in which the name E. A. Blair appears as a talks producer). Against the first cut he has written in the margin, 'I do not think it is advisable to say this.' His other comment is that regarding 'vote,' see *n. 2.* The script is marked 'As B'cast' and 'Copied in G[eneral] O[ffice].' PasB has 'Weekly News Review read by Z. A. Bokhari' and gives the timing as 10' 50".

In the Far East the war situation is still serious for the Allies, but there are certain changes in the situation which indicate that British and American reinforcements are reaching the scene of battle. The most important event has been the very heavy losses inflicted on a convoy of Japanese ships in the Straits of Macassar, between Borneo and Celebes. At least ten ships full of Japanese troops have been sunk, and a number of Japanese warships either sunk or damaged.[1] This has been possible because, apart from the powerful Dutch forces on the spot, American ships and aeroplanes have already been able to reach the Dutch East Indies. At present it is still impossible to prevent the Japanese from making landings, but the fate of this convoy points to the difficulties which they will experience in the future. Wherever they have made a landing they have got to supply their troops with arms and usually with food, which have to travel in ships across thousands of miles of sea, with aeroplanes and submarines waiting to attack them. Even now, with all the initial advantages on their side, the Japanese have been losing ships since the outbreak of war at the rate of one a day, and their supply of shipping is very far from inexhaustible.

Simultaneously, in their attacks on Rangoon, the Japanese have lost very heavily in aeroplanes. But further south, in Malaya, they have continued to advance, and it is probable that the British and Indian troops on the mainland of Malaya will have to fall back on the island of Singapore. [If they do so they will blow up the causeway that connects the island with the mainland.] Singapore is a powerful fortress with very heavy guns, with several airfields, and with a population of 600,000, largely composed of Chinese, from which it has been possible to raise a strong defence force to aid the regular forces. [It is unlikely that it can be taken by storm and] It remains to be seen whether the Japanese will risk the enormous losses that are bound to result from any direct attack.

On the Russian front the Russian armies have advanced so deeply into the German lines that they are now threatening both Kharkov, the great industrial city in Southern Russia, and Smolensk, on the road to Poland. Smolensk was, till recently, the headquarters of the German High Command, which has now had to remove itself a hundred miles further back. Perhaps the most significant thing about the Russian campaign is the fact that the Germans barely mention it in their radio announcements. They have still not told their home public about the fall of Mojaisk. To foreign audiences, realising that a piece of news of this kind could not be kept secret outside Germany, they admitted that Mojaisk had fallen, but declared that it was a town of no importance, though they had said just the contrary when they occupied it themselves. People who feel confident about the future do not falsify news in this fashion. [The successes which the Red Army is now having ought not to give us the idea that German resistance is broken. On the contrary, they will certainly stage another big offensive in the spring. But meanwhile they are losing heavily in men and material, and until the end of February, or much later in northern Russia, the snow and ice will be powerful allies on the side of the Russians, who are better equipped for winter warfare. Premier Stalin declared recently that he expected to have destroyed the German armies by the end of 1942, and it is worth remembering that Stalin is not a man who makes boasts lightly.]

In North Africa the battle is still swaying to and fro. After a campaign of two months the Germans are back in Benghazi, which has now changed hands four times. We do not know yet whether the Germans will be able to continue their advance. Probably this will depend upon the amount of material, especially heavy tanks, that they have been able to get across the sea from Italy. But even if they should be able to drive their way back to the position they occupied in November, close to the Egyptian frontier, the balance of advantage will be with the British, for the Germans and Italians have lost heavily in men and in materials of war. [The German army in North Africa was placed there as part of a double-flanking movement intended to converge on the oil wells of Baku and of Irak and Iran. The northern attack was to move *into* the Crimea and the Caucasus, and the southern was to move through Egypt and Palestine. Both moves have so far failed. The Germans have been unable to get beyond the Crimea, or even to establish their position in the Crimea itself, for the great Russian fortress of Sebastopol withstands all attacks. As to the southern flank, the Germans have failed to set foot on Egyptian soil, and indeed are a long way from it at this moment. This is not to deny that the North African campaign has been disappointing to the Allies. It would make a great deal of difference, militarily and politically, if the British could reach Tripoli and thus dominate the central Mediterranean. For as long as the two essential fronts, in the Caucasus and in Egypt, hold firm, the oil which the Germans covet and which they are in ever growing need of, is out of their reach.]

Far-reaching political changes are taking place in Britain and a number of other countries as a result of the new turn that the war took when the Japanese launched their attack. One can see the main happenings in better perspective if one starts by simply listing them. After this the connection between events which at first sight may not seem to have anything to do with one another, becomes clear.

In the first place, American troops have landed in the British Isles. In the second place, a war council which will cover the whole Pacific area is to be set up, probably with headquarters in Washington. Thirdly, it has been arranged that Australia and New Zealand are to have direct representation in the War Cabinet in London. Fourthly, all but two of the Latin-American republics have severed diplomatic relations with the Axis powers. Finally, after a debate on the conduct of the war which lasted for three days, Mr Churchill, the British Prime Minister, has asked the House of Commons for a vote of confidence and has been given it with only one dissentient *vote*.[2]

When taken together, these events, happening in widely separated parts of the earth, all have the same meaning. They mean that the various countries menaced by Axis aggression are coming into closer and closer agreement, both military and political. The United States, Britain and the Dominions are now pooling their troops, their resources and their naval bases, almost as though they were a single nation acting under a common ruler. At the same time, the co-operation of the Anglo-Saxon powers with Soviet Russia and China becomes closer and more friendly. Chinese troops are standing side by side to the British in Burma. Just as British tanks and aeroplanes are fighting on the Russian front. In spite of the danger in the Pacific, the American Government has already declared that it looks on Hitler as the principal enemy, and the sending of American troops to Britain, to play a part in the western theatre of war, is a concrete sign of this. The resolution which eighteen American republics have signed in Rio de Janeiro is of great importance. It is of the highest importance that Brazil, the biggest and most populous country of South America, has ranged itself against the Axis. [Brazil is within flying range of West Africa and for at least fifty years the Germans have had designs on it.[3] The Japanese have similar designs on several South American countries. Now that the whole American continent is forming itself into a common front against the aggressor, these designs—which were to have been carried out in the first place by fifth columns, aided in some cases by local Fascist parties—will be much easier to frustrate.]

Simultaneously the Russian radio has issued a significant warning to the Japanese. In 1938 the Japanese attempted an attack on Vladivostock, and got a lesson which they may forget under the influence of successes elsewhere. The Russians have warned them not to make the same mistake as the Germans— who also imagined that the Red Army was no good – and, in the words of the Russian proverb—"not to sell the bearskin before you have caught the bear".

Finally, one event has happened this week which is not strictly an act of war, but which should be mentioned. The British Government has arranged to relax the blockade and send 8,000 tons of wheat to Greece. They have done this for the quite simple reason that Greece is starving. This is the result of German and Italian rule. The German and Italian Fascists have simply plundered the country for their own benefit, with utter disregard for its Greek inhabitants. The wheat will be sent to Greece through the International Red Cross. There is no guarantee that the Germans will not seize it when it gets there, as they have seized similar supplies sent to France, but the British Government prefers to take this risk, and to send the wheat, rather than stand by and watch a whole innocent population starve. The contrast between the Fascist powers that steal food, and the anti-Fascist powers who bring it to starving people, will not go unnoticed in conquered Europe.

1 On 24 January 1942, four Japanese transports and an escort vessel were sunk; one U S destroyer was damaged (*2194 Days of War*).
2 The censor wrote in the margin here 'This is not strictly accurate Two dissentients were Tellers. If "vote" be added it will be accurate ' The word was added, probably in Orwell's hand. The dissentient voter was James Maxton, leader of the ILP (West· *Commentaries*, 45, n. 51).
3 West· *Commentaries* erroneously marks the conclusion of the cut at this point (46).

947. To Lady Grigg

31 January 1942   PP

Dear Lady Grigg,[1]
Miss Blackburn[2] has been away for a few days with a slight touch of 'flu, but we hope she will be back on Monday.

In the meantime, I am sending you a new pass for the month of February.

I have spoken to the Contracts Department about Lady Woolley and Mrs. de Groot, and they promised to deal with both matters immediately.

Mr. Bokhari has asked me to send you a copy of the letter which he wrote to Miss Royde Smith.

Yours sincerely,
Secretary to Mr. Blair

1 Lady Gertrude Grigg was the wife of the Secretary of State for War, Sir James Grigg (see *1043*, *n 1*) She conducted a weekly programme, 'Women Generally Speaking,' and her influential social position made her difficult to manage. From time to time complaints surfaced in memoranda, and Laurence Brander, the Eastern Service Intelligence Officer, reported scathingly on her competence, but she was able to persuade a number of relatively important

people to speak on her programme. For Orwell's complaint about her and her husband, see *1788*.
2. Mary Blackburn, Programme Assistant.

948. 'Rudyard Kipling'

Horizon, February 1942

This essay took as its starting point the publication of *A Choice of Kipling's Verse*, made and introduced by T. S. Eliot (December 1941). After its publication in *Horizon*, it was included in Secker & Warburg's *Critical Essays* (14 February 1946) and, in the United States, Reynal & Hitchcock's *Dickens, Dali & Others* (29 April 1946). The body of the text is virtually unchanged in these three versions, but Orwell added two footnotes in 1945 and amended a copy of the U.S. edition in three places (and also at one point in the essay 'Raffles and Miss Blandish'). This copy was given by Sonia Orwell to Cyril Connolly about 1961, after he had discovered it in the loft of her flat in Charlotte Street, London. It was given by Deirdre Connolly to A. R. A. Hobson, through whose kindness it has been possible to emend this edition.

The text reproduced here is that of *Critical Essays*, second impression, May 1946, with Orwell's emendations, and amended as indicated in the notes below. There were changes in house-styling in 1945 (mainly in hyphenation and punctuation, double for single quotation marks, and roman for italic type for titles of poems). Typographic similarities show that the text in *Dickens, Dali & Others* was set from that in *Critical Essays*. Its text has one or two variants: one is clearly an aural error ('term' for 'turn'); the U.S. publisher is given for Edmund Wilson's book in the first of Orwell's added notes and the text is slightly cut (see *n. 21*); and there is a variant in recording Murry's use of Kipling in Orwell's footnote (see *n. 26*).

Orwell here, as elsewhere, does not always quote exactly. He doubtless relied on memory, having a good knowledge of what he was quoting. These errors are treated in two ways. The original is corrected if the error does not seem significant, however slightly, to Orwell's argument or to the impression the words might have made upon him. Thus 'Hosts' is given its initial capital, as in Kipling (see *n. 2*). If the form Orwell uses might have been important to him, it is left uncorrected; the proper reading is in the notes. Thus, Orwell substitutes 'thee' for 'you' in his quotation from W. E. Henley (see *n. 14*) and has 'What do they know of England' for 'What should they know of England' (see *n. 24*).

The sources and page references of Kipling's poems quoted by Orwell are from *Rudyard Kipling's Verse: Definitive Edition* (1940; abbreviated to *RKV*). Dates of poems are provided where given in *RKV*. Reference is also made to Kipling's posthumous autobiography, *Something of Myself* (1937), and to Charles Carrington's *Rudyard Kipling: His Life and Work* (1955; Penguin, 1970, to which edition reference is made as 'Carrington').

It was a pity that Mr. Eliot should be so much on the defensive in the long essay with which he prefaces this selection of Kipling's poetry, but it was not to be avoided, because before one can even speak about Kipling one has to clear away a legend that has been created by two sets of people who have not read his works. Kipling is in the peculiar position of having been a by-word for fifty years. During five literary generations every enlightened person has despised him, and at the end of that time nine-tenths of those enlightened persons are forgotten and Kipling is in some sense still there. Mr. Eliot never satisfactorily explains this fact, because in answering the shallow and familiar charge that Kipling is a "Fascist", he falls into the opposite error of defending him where he is not defensible. It is no use pretending that Kipling's view of life, as a whole, can be accepted or even forgiven by any civilised person. It is no use claiming, for instance, that when Kipling describes a British soldier beating a "nigger" with a cleaning rod in order to get money out of him, he is acting merely as a reporter and does not necessarily approve what he describes. There is not the slightest sign anywhere in Kipling's work that he disapproves of that kind of conduct—on the contrary, there is a definite strain of sadism in him, over and above the brutality which a writer of that type has to have. Kipling *is* a jingo imperialist, he *is* morally insensitive and æsthetically disgusting. It is better to start by admitting that, and then to try to find out why it is that he survives while the refined people who have sniggered at him seem to wear so badly.

And yet the "Fascist" charge has to be answered, because the first clue to any understanding of Kipling, morally or politically, is the fact that he was *not* a Fascist. He was further from being one than the most humane or the most "progressive" person is able to be nowadays. An interesting instance of the way in which quotations are parroted to and fro without any attempt to look up their context or discover their meaning is the line from "Recessional", "Lesser breeds without the Law".[1] This line is always good for a snigger in pansy-left circles. It is assumed as a matter of course that the "lesser breeds" are "natives", and a mental picture is called up of some pukka sahib in a pith helmet kicking a coolie. In its context the sense of the line is almost the exact opposite of this. The phrase "lesser breeds" refers almost certainly to the Germans, and especially the pan-German writers, who are "without the Law" in the sense of being lawless, not in the sense of being powerless. The whole poem, conventionally thought of as an orgy of boasting, is a denunciation of power politics, British as well as German. Two stanzas are worth quoting (I am quoting this as politics, not as poetry):

> "If, drunk with sight of power, we loose
> Wild tongues that have not Thee in awe,
> Such boastings as the Gentiles use,
> Or lesser breeds without the Law—
> Lord God of Hosts,[2] be with us yet,
> Lest we forget—lest we forget!

> "For heathen heart that puts her trust
> In reeking tube and iron shard,
> All valiant dust that builds on dust,
> And guarding, calls not Thee to guard,
> For frantic boast and foolish word—
> Thy mercy on Thy People, Lord!"

Much of Kipling's phraseology is taken from the Bible, and no doubt in the second stanza he had in mind the text from Psalm cxxvii.: "Except the Lord build the house, they labour in vain that build it; except the Lord keep the city, the watchman waketh but in vain." It is not a text that makes much impression on the post-Hitler mind. No one, in our time, believes in any sanction greater than military power; no one believes that it is possible to overcome force except by greater force. There is no "law", there is only power. I am not saying that that is a true belief, merely that it is the belief which all modern men do actually hold. Those who pretend otherwise are either intellectual cowards, or power-worshippers under a thin disguise, or have simply not caught up with the age they are living in. Kipling's outlook is pre-Fascist. He still believes that pride comes before a fall and that the gods punish *hubris*. He does not foresee the tank, the bombing plane, the radio and the secret police, or their psychological results.

But in saying this, does not one unsay what I said above about Kipling's jingoism and brutality? No, one is merely saying that the nineteenth-century imperialist outlook and the modern gangster outlook are two different things. Kipling belongs very definitely to the period 1885–1902. The Great War and its aftermath embittered him, but he shows little sign of having learned anything from any event later than the Boer War. He was the prophet of British Imperialism in its expansionist phase (even more than his poems, his solitary novel, *The Light that Failed*,[3] gives you the atmosphere of that time) and also the unofficial historian of the British Army, the old mercenary army which began to change its shape in 1914. All his confidence, his bouncing vulgar vitality, sprang out of limitations which no Fascist or near-Fascist shares.

Kipling spent the later part of his life in sulking, and no doubt it was political disappointment rather than literary vanity that accounted for this. Somehow history had not gone according to plan. After the greatest victory she had ever known, Britain was a lesser world power than before, and Kipling was quite acute enough to see this. The virtue had gone out of the classes he idealised, the young were hedonistic or disaffected, the desire to paint the map red had evaporated. He could not understand what was happening, because he had never had any grasp of the economic forces underlying imperial expansion. It is notable that Kipling does not seem to realise, any more than the average soldier or colonial administrator, that an empire is primarily a money-making concern. Imperialism as he sees it is a sort of forcible evangelising. You turn a Gatling gun[4] on a mob of unarmed "natives", and then you establish, "the Law", which includes roads, railways and a court-house. He could not foresee, therefore, that the same motives which brought the Empire into existence would end by destroying it. It was the same motive, for example, that caused the Malayan jungles to be cleared for rubber estates, and which now causes those estates to be handed over intact to the Japanese.[5] The modern totalitarians know what they are doing, and the nineteenth-century English did not know what they were doing. Both attitudes have their advantages, but Kipling was never able to move forward from one into the other. His outlook, allowing for the fact that after all he was an artist, was that of the salaried bureaucrat who despises the "box-wallah"[6] and often lives a lifetime without realising that the "box-wallah" calls the tune.

But because he identifies himself with the official class, he does possess one thing which "enlightened" people seldom or never possess, and that is a sense of responsibility. The middle-class Left hate him for this quite as much as for his cruelty and vulgarity. All left-wing parties in the highly industrialised countries are at bottom a sham, because they make it their business to fight against something which they do not really wish to destroy. They have internationalist aims, and at the same time they struggle to keep up a standard of life with which those aims are incompatible. We all live by robbing Asiatic coolies, and those of us who are "enlightened" all maintain that those coolies ought to be set free; but our standard of living, and hence our "enlightenment", demands that the robbery shall continue. A humanitarian is always a hypocrite, and Kipling's understanding of this is perhaps the central secret of his power to create telling phrases. It would be difficult to hit off the one-eyed pacifism of the English in fewer words than in the phrase, "making mock of uniforms that guard you while you sleep".[7] It is true that Kipling does not understand the economic aspect of the relationship between the highbrow and the blimp. He does not see that the map is painted red chiefly in order that the coolie may be exploited. Instead of the coolie he sees the Indian Civil Servant; but even on that plane his grasp of function, of who protects whom, is very sound. He sees clearly that men can only be highly civilised while other men, inevitably less civilised, are there to guard and feed them.

How far does Kipling really identify himself with the administrators, soldiers and engineers whose praises he sings? Not so completely as is sometimes assumed. He had travelled very widely while he was still a young man, he had grown up with a brilliant mind in mainly philistine surroundings, and some streak in him that may have been partly neurotic led him to prefer the active man to the sensitive man. The nineteenth-century Anglo-Indians, to name the least sympathetic of his idols, were at any rate people who did things. It may be that all that they did was evil, but they changed the face of the earth (it is instructive to look at a map of Asia and compare the railway system of India with that of the surrounding countries), whereas they could have achieved nothing, could not have maintained themselves in power for a single week, if the normal Anglo-Indian outlook had been that of, say, E. M. Forster. Tawdry and shallow though it is, Kipling's is the only literary picture that we possess of nineteenth-century Anglo-India, and he could only make it because he was just coarse enough to be able to exist and keep his mouth shut in clubs and regimental messes. But he did not greatly resemble the people he admired. I know from several private sources that many of the Anglo-Indians who were Kipling's contemporaries did not like or approve of him. They said, no doubt truly, that he knew nothing about India, and on the other hand, he was from their point of view too much of a highbrow. While in India he tended to mix with "the wrong" people, and because of his dark complexion he was wrongly suspected of having a streak of Asiatic blood. Much in his development is traceable to his having been born in India and having left school early. With a slightly different background he might have been a good novelist or a superlative writer of music-hall songs. But how true is it that he was a vulgar flag-waver, a sort of publicity agent for Cecil Rhodes? It is true, but it is not true that he was a yes-man or a time-server. After his early days, if then, he never courted public opinion. Mr. Eliot says that what is held against him is that he expressed unpopular views in a popular style. This narrows the issue by assuming that "unpopular" means unpopular with the intelligentsia, but it is a fact that Kipling's "message" was one that the big public did not want, and, indeed, has never accepted. The mass of the people, in the 'nineties as now, were anti-militarist, bored by the Empire, and only unconsciously patriotic. Kipling's official admirers are and were the "service" middle class, the people who read *Blackwood's*. In the stupid early years of this century, the blimps, having at last discovered someone who could be called a poet and who was on their side, set Kipling on a pedestal, and some of his more sententious poems, such as "If", were given almost Biblical status. But it is doubtful whether the blimps have ever read him with attention, any more than they have read the Bible. Much of what he says they could not possibly approve. Few people who have criticised England from the inside have said bitterer things about her than this gutter patriot. As a rule it is the British working class that he is attacking, but not always. That phrase about "the flannelled fools at the wicket or the muddied oafs at the goals"[8] sticks like an arrow to this day, and it is aimed at the Eton and Harrow match as well as the Cup-Tie Final. Some of the verses he wrote about the Boer War have a curiously modern ring, so far as their subject-matter goes. "Stellenbosch",[9] which must have been written about 1902, sums up what every intelligent infantry officer was saying in 1918, or is saying now, for that matter.

Kipling's romantic ideas about England and the Empire might not have mattered if he could have held them without having the class-prejudices which at that time went with them. If one examines his best and most representative work, his soldier poems, especially *Barrack-Room Ballads*, one notices that what more than anything else spoils them is an underlying air of patronage. Kipling idealises the army officer, especially the junior officer, and that to an idiotic extent, but the private soldier, though lovable and romantic, has to be a comic. He is always made to speak in a sort of stylised Cockney, not very broad but with all the aitches and final "g's" carefully omitted. Very often the result is as embarrassing as the humorous recitation at a church social. And this accounts for the curious fact that one can often improve Kipling's poems, make them less facetious and less blatant, by simply going through them and translating[10] them from Cockney into standard speech. This is especially true of his refrains, which often have a truly lyrical quality. Two examples will do (one is about a funeral and the other about a wedding):

> "So it's knock out your pipes and follow me!
> And it's finish up your swipes and follow me!
> Oh, hark to the big drum calling,
> Follow me—follow me home!"[11]

and again:

> "Cheer for the Sergeant's wedding—
> Give them one cheer more!
> Grey gun-horses in the lando,
> And a rogue is married to a whore!"[12]

Here I have restored the aitches, etc. Kipling ought to have known better. He ought to have seen that the two closing lines of the first of these stanzas are very beautiful lines, and that ought to have overridden his impulse to make fun of a working-man's accent. In the ancient ballads the lord and the peasant speak the same language. This is impossible to Kipling, who is looking down a distorting class-perspective, and by a piece of poetic justice one of his best lines is spoiled—for "follow me 'ome" is much uglier than "follow me home". But even where it makes no difference musically the facetiousness of his stage Cockney dialect is irritating. However, he is more often quoted aloud than read on the printed page, and most people instinctively make the necessary alterations when they quote him.

Can one imagine any private soldier, in the 'nineties or now, reading *Barrack-Room Ballads* and feeling that here was a writer who spoke for him? It is very hard to do so.[13] Any soldier capable of reading a book of verse would notice at once that Kipling is almost unconscious of the class war that goes on in an army as much as elsewhere. It is not only that he thinks the soldier comic, but that he thinks him patriotic, feudal, a ready admirer of his officers and proud to be a soldier of the Queen. Of course that is partly true, or battles could not be fought, but "What have I done for thee, England, my England?" is essentially a middle-class query.[14] Almost any working man would follow it up immediately with "What has England done for me?" In so far as Kipling grasps this, he simply sets it down to "the intense selfishness of the lower classes" (his own phrase).[15] When he is writing not of British but of "loyal" Indians he carries the "Salaam, sahib" motif to sometimes disgusting lengths. Yet it remains true that he has far more interest in the common soldier, far more anxiety that he shall get a fair deal, than most of the "liberals" of his day or our own. He sees that the soldier is neglected, meanly underpaid and hypocritically despised by the people whose incomes he safeguards. "I came to realise", he says in his posthumous memoirs, "the bare horrors of the private's life, and the unnecessary torments he endured."[16] He is accused of glorifying war, and perhaps he does so, but not in the usual manner, by pretending that war is a sort of football match. Like most people capable of writing battle poetry, Kipling had never been in battle,[17] but his vision of war is realistic. He knows that bullets hurt, that under fire everyone is terrified, that the ordinary soldier never knows what the war is about or what is happening except in his own corner of the battlefield, and that British troops, like other troops, frequently run away:

> "I 'eard the knives be'ind me, but I dursn't face my man,
> Nor I don't know where I went to, 'cause I didn't stop to see,
> Till I 'eard a beggar squealin' out for quarter as 'e ran,
> An' I thought I knew the voice an'—it was me!"[18]

Modernize the style of this, and it might have come out of one of the debunking war books of the nineteen-twenties. Or again:

> "An' now the hugly bullets come peckin' through the dust,
> An' no one wants to face 'em, but every beggar must;
> So, like a man in irons, which isn't glad to go,
> They moves 'em off by companies uncommon stiff an' slow.'[19]

Compare this with:

> "Forward the Light Brigade!
> Was there a man dismayed?
> No! though the soldier knew
> Someone had blundered."[20]

If anything, Kipling overdoes the horrors, for the wars of his youth were hardly wars at all by our standards. Perhaps that is due to the neurotic strain in him, the hunger for cruelty. But at least he knows that men ordered to attack impossible objectives *are* dismayed, and also that fourpence a day is not a generous pension.

How complete or truthful a picture has Kipling left us of the long-service, mercenary army of the late nineteenth century? One must say of this, as of what Kipling wrote about nineteenth-century Anglo-India, that it is not only the best but almost the only literary picture we have. He has put on record an immense amount of stuff that one could otherwise only gather from verbal tradition or from unreadable regimental histories. Perhaps his picture of army life seems fuller and more accurate than it is because any middle-class English person is likely to know enough to fill up the gaps. At any rate, reading the essay on Kipling that Mr. Edmund Wilson has just published or is just about to publish,[21] I was struck by the number of things that are boringly familiar to us and seem to be barely intelligible to an American. But from the body of Kipling's early work there does seem to emerge a vivid and not seriously misleading picture of the old pre-machine-gun army—the sweltering barracks in Gibraltar or Lucknow, the red coats, the pipeclayed belts and the pillbox hats, the beer, the fights, the floggings, hangings and crucifixions, the bugle-calls, the smell of oats and horse-piss, the bellowing sergeants with foot-long moustaches, the bloody skirmishes, invariably mismanaged, the crowded troopships, the cholera-stricken camps, the "native" concubines, the ultimate death in the workhouse. It is a crude, vulgar picture, in which a patriotic music-hall turn[22] seems to have got mixed up with one of Zola's gorier passages, but from it future generations will be able to gather some idea of what a long-term volunteer army was like. On about the same level they will be able to learn something of British India in the days when motorcars and refrigerators were unheard of. It is an error to imagine that we might have had better books on these subjects if, for example, George Moore, or Gissing, or Thomas Hardy, had had Kipling's opportunities. That is the kind of accident that cannot happen. It was not possible that nineteenth-century England should produce a book like *War and Peace*, or like Tolstoy's minor stories of army life, such as *Sebastopol* or *The Cossacks*, not because the talent was necessarily lacking but because no one with sufficient sensitiveness to write such books would ever have made the appropriate contacts. Tolstoy lived in a great military empire in which it seemed natural for almost any young man of family to spend a few years in the army, whereas the British Empire was and still is demilitarised to a degree which continental observers find almost incredible. Civilised men do not readily move away from the centres of civilisation, and in most languages there is a great dearth of what one might call colonial literature. It took a very improbable combination of circumstances to produce Kipling's gaudy tableau, in which Private Ortheris and Mrs. Hauksbee pose against a background of palm trees to the sound of temple bells, and one necessary circumstance was that Kipling himself was only half civilised.

Kipling is the only English writer of our time who has added phrases to the language. The phrases and neologisms which we take over and use without remembering their origin do not always come from writers we admire. It is strange, for instance, to hear the Nazi broadcasters referring to the Russian soldiers as "robots", thus unconsciously borrowing a word from a Czech democrat whom they would have killed if they could have laid hands on him.[23] Here are half a dozen phrases coined by Kipling which one sees quoted in leaderettes in the gutter press or overhears in saloon bars from people who have barely heard his name. It will be seen that they all have a certain characteristic in common:

> "East is East, and West is West.
> The white man's burden.
> What do they know of England who only England know?
> The female of the species is more deadly than the male.
> Somewhere East of Suez.
> Paying the Dane-geld."[24]

There are various others, including some that have outlived their context by many years. The phrase "killing Kruger with your mouth",[25] for instance, was current till very recently. It is also possible that it was Kipling who first let loose the use of the word "Huns" for Germans;[26] at any rate he began using it as soon as the guns opened fire in 1914. But what the phrases I have listed above have in common is that they are all of them phrases which one utters semi-derisively (as it might be "For I'm to be Queen o' the May, mother, I'm to be Queen o' the May"[27]), but which one is bound to make use of sooner or later. Nothing could exceed the contempt of the *New Statesman*, for instance, for Kipling, but how many times during the Munich period did the *New Statesman* find itself quoting that phrase about paying the Dane-geld? The fact is that Kipling, apart from his snack-bar wisdom and his gift for packing much cheap picturesqueness into a few words ("Palm and Pine"— "East of Suez"—"The Road to Mandalay"), is generally talking about things that are of urgent interest. It does not matter, from this point of view, that thinking and decent people generally find themselves on the other side of the fence from him. "White man's burden" instantly conjures up a real problem, even if one feels that it ought to be altered to "black man's burden." One may disagree to the middle of one's bones with the political attitude implied in "The Islanders",[28] but one cannot say that it is a frivolous attitude. Kipling deals in thoughts which are both vulgar and permanent. This raises the question of his special status as a poet, or verse-writer.

Mr. Eliot describes Kipling's metrical work as "verse" and not "poetry", but adds that it is "*great* verse", and further qualifies this by saying that a writer can only be described as a "great verse-writer" if there is some of his work "of which we cannot say whether it is verse or poetry". Apparently Kipling was a versifier who occasionally wrote poems, in which case it was a pity that Mr. Eliot did not specify these poems by name. The trouble is that whenever an æsthetic judgment on Kipling's work seems to be called for, Mr. Eliot is too much on the defensive to be able to speak plainly. What he does not say, and what I think one ought to start by saying in any discussion of Kipling, is that most of Kipling's verse is so horribly vulgar that it gives one the same sensation as one gets from watching a third-rate music-hall performer recite "The Pigtail of Wu Fang Fu" with the purple limelight on his face, *and yet* there is much of it that is capable of giving pleasure to people who know what poetry means. At his worst, and also his most vital, in poems like "Gunga Din" or "Danny Deever",[29] Kipling is almost a shameful pleasure, like the taste for cheap sweets that some people secretly carry into middle life. But even with his best passages one has the same sense of being seduced by something spurious, and yet unquestionably seduced. Unless one is merely a snob and a liar it is impossible to say that no one who cares for poetry could get any pleasure out of such lines as:

> "For the wind is in the palm-trees, and the temple-bells they say,
> 'Come you back, you British soldier; come you back to Mandalay!' "[30]

and yet those lines are not poetry in the same sense as "Felix Randal" or "When icicles hang by the wall" are poetry. One can, perhaps, place Kipling more satisfactorily than by juggling with the words "verse" and "poetry", if one describes him simply as a good bad poet. He is as a poet what Harriet Beecher Stowe was as a novelist.[31] And the mere existence of work of this kind, which is perceived by generation after generation to be vulgar and yet goes on being read, tells one something about the age we live in.

There is a great deal of good bad poetry in English, all of it, I should say, subsequent to 1790. Examples of good bad poems—I am deliberately choosing diverse ones—are "The Bridge of Sighs", "When all the World is Young, Lad", "The Charge of the Light Brigade", Bret Harte's "Dickens in Camp", "The Burial of Sir John Moore", "Jenny Kissed Me", "Keith of Ravelston", "Casabianca".[32] All of these reek of sentimentality, and yet— not these particular poems, perhaps, but poems of this kind, are capable of giving true pleasure to people who can see clearly what is wrong with them. One could fill a fair-sized anthology with good bad poems, if it were not for the significant fact that good bad poetry is usually too well known to be worth reprinting. It is no use pretending that in an age like our own, "good" poetry can have any genuine popularity. It is, and must be, the cult of a very few people, the least tolerated of the arts. Perhaps that statement needs a

certain amount of qualification. True poetry can sometimes be acceptable to
the mass of the people when it disguises itself as something else. One can see
an example of this in the folk-poetry that England still possesses, certain
nursery rhymes and mnemonic rhymes, for instance, and the songs that
soldiers make up, including the words that go to some of the bugle-calls. But
in general ours is a civilisation in which the very word "poetry" evokes a
hostile snigger or, at best, the sort of frozen disgust that most people feel
when they hear the word "God". If you are good at playing the concertina
you could probably go into the nearest public bar and get yourself an
appreciative audience within five minutes. But what would be the attitude of
that same audience if you suggested reading them Shakespeare's sonnets, for
instance? Good bad poetry, however, can get across to the most unpromising
audiences if the right atmosphere has been worked up beforehand. Some
months back Churchill produced a great effect by quoting Clough's
"Endeavour"[33] in one of his broadcast speeches. I listened to this speech
among people who could certainly not be accused of caring for poetry, and I
am convinced that the lapse into verse impressed them and did not embarrass
them. But not even Churchill could have got away with it if he had quoted
anything much better than this.

In so far as a writer of verse can be popular, Kipling has been and probably
still is popular. In his own lifetime some of his poems travelled far beyond the
bounds of the reading public, beyond the world of school prize-days, Boy
Scout singsongs, limp-leather editions, pokerwork and calendars, and out
into the yet vaster world of the music halls. Nevertheless, Mr. Eliot thinks it
worth while to edit him, thus confessing to a taste which others share but are
not always honest enough to mention. The fact that such a thing as good bad
poetry can exist is a sign of the emotional overlap between the intellectual and
the ordinary man. The intellectual *is* different from the ordinary man, but
only in certain sections of his personality, and even then not all the time. But
what is the peculiarity of a good bad poem? A good bad poem is a graceful
monument to the obvious. It records in memorable form—for verse is a
mnemonic device, among other things—some emotion which very nearly
every human being can share. The merit of a poem like "When all the world is
young, lad" is that, however sentimental it may be, its sentiment is "true"
sentiment in the sense that you are bound to find yourself thinking the
thought it expresses sooner or later; and then, if you happen to know the
poem, it will come back into your mind and seem better than it did before.
Such poems are a kind of rhyming proverb, and it is a fact that definitely
popular poetry is usually gnomic or sententious. One example from Kipling
will do:

> "White hands cling to the tightened rein,
> Slipping the spur from the booted heel,
> Tenderest voices cry 'Turn again,'
> Red lips tarnish the scabbarded steel,
> High hopes faint on a warm hearth-stone—
> He travels the fastest who travels alone."[34]

There is a vulgar thought vigorously expressed. It may not be true, but at any rate it is a thought that everyone thinks. Sooner or later you will have occasion to feel that he travels the fastest who travels alone, and there the thought is, ready made and, as it were, waiting for you. So the chances are that, having once heard this line, you will remember it.

One reason for Kipling's power as a good bad poet I have already suggested—his sense of responsibility, which made it possible for him to have a world-view, even though it happened to be a false one. Although he had no direct connection with any political party, Kipling was a Conservative, a thing that does not exist nowadays. Those who now call themselves Conservatives are either Liberals, Fascists or the accomplices of Fascists. He identified himself with the ruling power and not with the opposition. In a gifted writer this seems to us strange and even disgusting, but it did have the advantage of giving Kipling a certain grip on reality. The ruling power is always faced with the question, "In such and such circumstances, what would you *do*?", whereas the opposition is not obliged to take responsibility or make any real decisions. Where it is a permanent and pensioned opposition, as in England, the quality of its thought deteriorates accordingly. Moreover, anyone who starts out with a pessimistic, reactionary view of life tends to be justified by events, for Utopia never arrives and "the gods of the copybook headings", as Kipling himself put it, always return.[35] Kipling sold out to the British governing class, not financially but emotionally. This warped his political judgment, for the British ruling class were not what he imagined, and it led him into abysses of folly and snobbery, but he gained a corresponding advantage from having at least tried to imagine what action and responsibility are like. It is a great thing in his favour that he is not witty, not "daring", has no wish to *épater les bourgeois*. He dealt largely in platitudes, and since we live in a world of platitudes, much of what he said sticks. Even his worst follies seem less shallow and less irritating than the "enlightened" utterances of the same period, such as Wilde's epigrams or the collection of cracker-mottoes at the end of *Man and Superman*.

1. 'Recessional,' *RKV*, 328–29, was written after Queen Victoria's Jubilee and published in *The Times*, 17 July 1897.
2. Hosts] hosts *Horizon, CrE (Critical Essays), DD (Dickens, Dali & Others)*
3. London and Philadelphia, 1891. The U.S. edition has a happy ending. Kipling maintained in his Preface that the English edition is 'as it was originally conceived and written '
4. Patented by R. J. Gatling (1818–1903) in 1862, this was a crank-operated, ten-barrel antecedent of the single-barrel, automatic machine-gun It saw service for fifty years Orwell refers to 'the old pre-machine-gun army' later in his essay.
5. Although Singapore did not surrender until 15 February 1942, most of Malaya had already been over-run.
6 Strictly, a pedlar, but in the context applied derogatively to those working in commerce in India.
7 'Tommy,' *RKV*, 398–99.
8. 'The Islanders' (1902), *RKV*, 301–04; Orwell has 'and' for 'or' and 'goal' for 'goals.'
9 *RKV*, 477–78, which has this note: 'The more notoriously incompetent commanders used to be sent to the town of Stellenbosch, which name presently became a verb.' Kipling tells how the General 'got 'is decorations thick' and 'The Staff 'ad D.S.O.'s till we was sick / An' the soldier—'ad the work to do again!'

10. translating] transplanting   *CrE; emendation by Orwell in DD*
11. ' "Follow Me 'Ome," ' *RKV*, 446–47.
12. 'The Sergeant's Weddin',' *RKV*, 447–49.
13. Contrast Sir George Younghusband (1859–1953), 'one of Kipling's archetypal subalterns,' quoted from his memoirs (1917) by Michael Edwardes in 'Oh to Meet an Army Man: Kipling and the Soldiers' in *Rudyard Kipling, the Man, his Work and his World*, edited by John Gross (1972, 44): 'I myself had served for many years with soldiers, but had never heard the words or expressions that Rudyard Kipling's soldiers used. Many a time did I ask my brother Officers whether they had heard them. No, never. But sure enough, a few years after, the soldiers thought, and talked, and expressed themselves exactly like Rudyard Kipling had taught them in his stories. . . . Rudyard Kipling made the modern soldier.'
14. From 'For England's Sake' by W. E. Henley (1849–1903), who has 'you' for Orwell's 'thee.' Kipling had 'the greatest admiration for Henley's verse and prose' (*Something of Myself—SoM* hereafter—82), and it was Henley who encouraged Kipling by publishing his verse in *The Scots Observer*, beginning with 'Danny Deever,' 22 February 1890.
15. 'Drums of the Fore and Aft' in *Wee Willie Winkie* (Centenary Edition, 1969, 331). It occurs in a story that is a parallel to the poem 'That Day' (see *n. 18* below) and concerns an occasion when, contrary to popular belief, British soldiers fled in terror. Kipling teases out why soldiers don't follow 'their officers into battle' and why they refuse to respond to orders from 'those who had no right to give them' (330). The context of these words, which may be significant, is: 'Armed with imperfect knowledge, cursed with the rudiments of an imagination, hampered by the intense selfishness of the lower classes, and unsupported by any regimental associations. . .' It is not surprising, argues Kipling, that such soldiers falter before a native attack if surrounded only by similarly raw soldiers and if poorly and uncertainly led.
16. *SoM*, 56. Kipling continued by saying he endured 'on account of Christian doctrine which lays down that "the wages of sin is death." '
17. He was, however, a close observer. See *SoM*, chapter VI, 'South Africa,' and his account of the (slightly ironically titled?) 'Battle of Kari Siding' (157–61).
18. 'That Day,' *RKV*, 437–38.
19. 'The 'Eathen,' *RKV*, 451–53. 'They' are the NCOs—'the backbone of the Army is the Non-commissioned Man.'
20. Tennyson, 'The Charge of the Light Brigade.'
21. Orwell's footnote in *CrE*: '1945. Published in a volume of Collected Essays, *The Wound and the Bow*. (Secker & Warburg.)' *DD* gives the U.S. publisher and date: 'Houghton Mifflin, 1941' and omits 'or is just about to publish.' Orwell evidently let this stand.
22. turn] term   *DD*
23. Orwell probably refers to Karel Čapek (1890–1938), novelist and dramatist, whose play *R.U.R.* (1920) features Rossum's Universal Robots and is usually thought to have introduced the word 'robot' into general use. However, according to William Harkins's *Karel Čapek* (1962), it was Karel's brother Josef (1887–1945) who introduced the word, in a story published in 1917. *OED* gives Czech *robota*—statute labour; *robotnik*—serf. Possibly forced labour aptly conveys the sense.
24. 'East is East, and West is West': 'The Ballad of East and West' (1899), *RKV*, 234–38. 'The white man's burden': from the poem of that title (1899), *RKV*, 323–24, significantly subtitled 'The United States and the Philippine Islands.' The poem was first published in the United States, in *McClure's Magazine*. The appeal was initially to Americans, to take responsibility for the less fortunate, to assume a colonial burden. 'What do they know of England who only England know?': 'The English Flag' (1891), *RKV*, 221–24; Kipling has 'What should they know. . . .' 'The female of the species is more deadly than the male': from a poem of that title (1911), *RKV*, 367–69. 'Somewhere East of Suez': 'Mandalay,' *RKV*, 418–20; Kipling has 'somewheres.' 'Paying the Dane-geld': 'Dane-geld,' *RKV*, 712–13.
25. 'The Absent-Minded Beggar,' *RKV*, 459–60. Published 31 October 1899 in the *Daily Mail*; with music composed by Sir Arthur Sullivan, it raised some £250,000 for servicemen and their dependents. Kipling refused to admit the poem to his collected verse for many years. See *SoM*, 150; Carrington, 363–64.
26. Orwell added this note to *CrE*:

'1945. On the first page of his recent book, *Adam and Eve*, Mr. Middleton Murry quoted the well-known lines:

"There are nine and sixty ways
Of constructing tribal lays,
And every single one of them is right."

He attributes these lines to Thackeray. This is probably what is known as a "Freudian error." A civilised person would prefer not to quote Kipling—i.e. would prefer not to feel that it was Kipling who had expressed his thought for him.'

In all editions and reprints this footnote has been keyed to 'Dane-geld,' here, at the end of the second sentence below this note number. In the copy of *DD* Orwell annotated, he marked it to be keyed to 'Germans' (see *headnote*). Page proof of the first impression of *CrE* and *DD* has 'nine and fifty,' as does Murry; Kipling has 'nine and sixty,' ('In the Neolithic Age,' 1895, *RKV*, 342–43). The first two lines should be printed as one; each word of the last line is connected by a long dash. Murry's *Adam and Eve: An Essay towards a New and Better Society* was published in 1944.

'Hun' had been used derogatively for a German in the nineteenth century, but the immediate source of its twentieth-century usage was German: Kaiser Wilhelm II introduced the word when addressing his troops on 27 July 1900, in a much reported speech, just before they sailed for China. Kipling used the word in *The Times*, 22 December 1902: 'the Goth and the shameless Hun' (*OED*, Supplement, II, 1976). See also *1098, n. 2.*

27. Tennyson, 'The May-Queen.'

28. The poem concludes, in italic: '*No doubt but ye are the People . . . / On your own heads, in your own hands, the sin and the saving lies!*' (*RKV*, 304). Kipling records in *SoM* that 'after a few days' newspaper correspondence' these verses 'were dismissed as violent, untimely and untrue' (222).

29. *RKV*, 406–08 and 397–98.

30. 'Mandalay', *RKV*, 418–20, hyphenation and punctuation corrected.

31. Harriet Beecher Stowe (1811–1896), ardent abolitionist, was the author of *Uncle Tom's Cabin* (1852), which brought her fame and aided the anti-slavery cause. She later started another storm, at home and in England, with her article 'The True Story of Lady Byron's Life.'

32. The authors of these poems are: Thomas Hood ('The Bridge of Sighs'); Charles Kingsley ('When all the world is young, lad' from 'Young and Old'); Alfred, Lord Tennyson ('The Charge of the Light Brigade'); Charles Wolfe ('The Burial of Sir John Moore after Corunna'); Leigh Hunt ('Jenny kissed me' from 'Rondeau'); Sidney Dobell ('Keith of Ravelston' from 'A Nuptial Eve'); and Mrs Hemans ('Casabianca,' which includes the line, 'The boy stood on the burning deck').

33. Arthur Hugh Clough (1819–1861) wrote no poem entitled 'Endeavour.' Churchill quoted the last two stanzas of his lyric 'Say not the struggle naught availeth' in his broadcast of 3 May 1941. The last line quoted was obviously directed at the United States, then providing much aid but still seven months away from becoming a combatant: 'But westward, look, the land is bright'; see Churchill, *The Second World War*, III, 209–10; U.S.: *The Grand Alliance*, 237. It is possible that the title 'Endeavour' comes from a reprint of the poem in an anthology.

34. When it was published in 1942 and reprinted in 1946, this verse, the second from 'The Winners' (July 1888), was conflated with the first, so the penultimate line read 'Down to Gehenna or up to the Throne'; in the first line, Orwell mistakenly had 'bridle rein'; and the punctuation at the ends of lines 2, 3, and 4 was, respectively, a semi-colon, an exclamation mark, and a colon. When annotating his copy of *DD*, he changed the text to the form found here, which is as first published, as L'Envoi, to *The Story of the Gadsbys* (Allahabad, 1889). *RKV*, (530) introduced an exclamation mark at the end of line 3 and a full point at the end of line 4. Eliot did not include 'The Winners' in his selection. In the margin of the copy Orwell annotated is written, in black ink, 'Get correct version'; this is crossed out in blue ink—the colour used to make the emendation.

35. 'The God of the Copybook Headings' (1919), *RKV*, 793–95. In the last line Kipling has them 'with terror and slaughter return!'

949. 'The Next Three Months'

'Through Eastern Eyes,' BBC Eastern Service, 1 February 1942
BBC typescript

Today for the first time—and I think it will probably be the only occasion—we are breaking our rule of having only Oriental speakers in this series. The reason is that today we are starting Through Eastern Eyes on its new schedule, and we wanted to give a sort of preliminary talk to let you know what the new schedule will be like and what subjects it will cover. I have been picked out to do this because I have had a good deal to do with arranging the schedule. But I should like to let you know in passing that I am the only European in this Indian section of the B.B.C. All the others are Indians, and the section is presided over by Z. A. Bokhari, whose voice I think you all know.

Well, we are retaining the general idea of Through Eastern Eyes, but we are altering the scope somewhat. Anyone who has listened in to these talks before will know that Through Eastern Eyes is a series of talks in the English language given entirely by Orientals, in most cases Indians. The general idea is to interpret the West, and in particular Great Britain, to India, through the eyes of people who are more or less strangers. An Indian, or a Chinese perhaps, comes to this country, and because everything is more or less new to him he notices a great deal which an Englishman or even an American would take for granted. So we have given you a series of talks on British institutions of every kind, from the Houses of Parliament to the village pub, all of them delivered by Orientals and most of them by people who have been only a few years in this country. We hope that in doing so we have brought the East and the West a little nearer together. This general plan will continue, with the difference that several talks each week are going to have a wider scope and to be more directly connected with the war and the political situation of the world. But I had better start by telling you which series of talks we are *not* altering.

First of all, we are going to continue every Monday with our Parliamentary commentary, which we call The Debate Continues. This gives you a summing-up of the proceedings in the House of Commons during the current week. Tomorrow the speaker in this series will be Sir Hari Singh Gour, whom you have heard giving the talks before. We are also keeping on with our News Commentary every Saturday. This is a weekly discussion of the strategy of the world war, and it is nearly always given by Mr. Z. A. Bokhari. And we are also keeping the series we call The Man in the Street, on Fridays, which tells you about the reactions of ordinary private people to the war. We have had a good many women speakers in this series, and I think we shall continue with that practice. There are some exceptionally talented broadcasters among the Indian women now in this country, and we like to have at least one talk a week with a special appeal to women.

On the next three Sundays following this one you are going to hear the results of the Indian students' competition which was set some time back by the B.B.C. After the results of the competition have been announced the three top entries will be read over the air on three successive Sundays by Indian members of our department. We only wish the winners were here to read them for themselves. But now I want to say something about the three series of talks which are a new departure.

The first of these, on Tuesdays, will be called These Names Will Live. These talks are short sketches—more or less biographical sketches, but giving you an idea of their work and what they stand for—of the outstanding personalities of our time. We aren't sticking only to British personalities—for instance the first talk in the series, which will be given by Mr. Appaswami, the London correspondent of the "Hindu", is on President Roosevelt, and we are having others on Stalin and Chiang-Kai-Shek. Also, we shan't only talk about Politicians and people of that kind—on the contrary, we want to concentrate rather on scientists, artists and literary men. I ask you particularly to listen in two or three weeks' time to Mulk Raj Anand, the Indian novelist—author of "Untouchable", "Two Leaves and a Bud"[1] and so on— who is going to give several talks about some of the best-known English writers.

The next new series, on Wednesdays, is called Today and Yesterday. These talks are discussions of the social changes that are taking place in Britain as a result of the war. There has been considerable and very rapid change in the structure of our life here, often happening in a rather indirect way as the result of measures forced on us by the air raids, by the need for a much bigger mobilisation of labour, and so on. For example, the Excess Profits Tax, food rationing and the fact that there is no longer any unemployment have gone some distance towards equalising the various standards of living in Britain. Again, English agriculture has expanded enormously owing to the need to grow our own food, and as a result of evacuation hundreds of thousands of children who would normally be growing up in big towns are growing up in the country. Or again, the English educational system is being very markedly altered by the redistribution of population, by the fact that fewer people than before can afford to send their children to boarding schools, and by the need to train great numbers of young men as airmen or technicians of one kind and another. Then there are the changes that are occurring in the press and in popular literature, and in the political outlook of the average man. These are the kind of subjects that we shall be discussing in Today and Yesterday.

The third new series is called What it Means to Me. These talks, which will be given every Thursday, are discussions of the abstract ideals for which the anti-Fascist powers are fighting. We constantly hear words and phrases flung to and fro—Democracy, liberty, national sovereignty, economic security, progress, international law. What do they mean in concrete terms? Is democracy simply a matter of dropping your vote into a ballot box? Is liberty any use without economic security? Can any nation in the modern world be really independent? Is progress a reality? These are some of the questions that our speakers are going to discuss.

As to who these speakers will be, they will all be orientals—I mean people whose native land is somewhere East of Suez. Apart from Indians, we have already brought Chinese and Burmese speakers to the microphone in this series, and we shall bring others, as well as Malays, Thais, Turks, and Indonesians, I hope. We are particularly anxious to bring you as many Chinese speakers as possible because of the enormous importance, especially at this moment, of solidarity between India and China. Asia, no less than Europe, is fighting for its life against Fascism, and the more that the two greatest nations of Asia—I mean India and China—know about one another, the better. For that reason we may occasionally interrupt our programme, which is supposed to deal mostly with the West, to give you some specially topical talks by Chinese speakers. I ask you particularly to listen for two talks by Mr. Hsiao Chien,° a Chinese student now in London, who has been in various parts of Japanese-occupied China. He will tell you something of what it means to live under Japanese rule, and of the ways in which the Japanese try to corrupt as well as conquer their victims.

But of course most of our speakers will be Indians. Some of these will be from the regular staff of the B.B.C.—I think you already know the voices of Balraj Sahni, and I. B. Sarin, and Venu Chitale, as well as Z. A. Bokhari himself—but most of them will be independent speakers. There is not a very large number of Indians now in England, but the ones who are here are a very varied and very talented body of people. They include doctors, students, correspondents of Indian papers such as the "Hindu" and the "Amrita Bazar Patrika", writers like Mulk Raj Anand and J. M. Tambimuttu, technical trainees under the Bevin scheme,[2] lawyers, airmen and civil servants. I think I can promise that the subjects on our list will be discussed exhaustively and from many different angles.

This series of talks, Through Eastern Eyes, will be going on for three months, always at the same time of day, that is, 8.30 p.m., Indian Standard Time. We hope anyone who listens and who has any suggestions to make, or any criticisms to offer, will write to us about it, and not be put off by the fact that letters take rather a long time to get here. We are very grateful to the various people in India who have written to us about this series already.

And finally, may I say how happy it makes me to be helping to organise these broadcasts—broadcasts which I believe can be really helpful and constructive at a time like this—to the country in which I was born and with which I have many personal and family ties.

1. *Two Leaves and a Bud* (1937); typescript has 'Bird.'
2. Two schemes named after Ernest Bevin, Minister of Labour in the War Cabinet (see 763, n. 22), were devised during the war. Indian youths were selected for technical training in Britain, and, from December 1943, British youths (called Bevin Boys) were selected by ballot to work in coal mines instead of being conscripted into the armed forces. The Indian Bevin Boys frequently broadcast messages home over the Eastern Service network. On 28 August 1941, for example, three Bevin Boys broadcast messages in the Hindustani Service, and M. M. Beg (a fourth) spoke in Hindustani on 'Working Conditions in England.' On 22 August 1942, a programme was devoted to a fifth batch of Indian Bevin Boys.

950. To T. S. Eliot

2 February 1942   PP/EB

Dear Mr. Eliot,[1]

Bokhari tells me that you have kindly consented to do us a series of six talks on the philosophy of the East and the West. I wonder if you would be able to do these on Mondays, and to start with the first talk on Monday, 16th February (this would mean our having the script some days previously)?

Perhaps you could let me know whether you can manage this. If 16th February is too early we can postpone the date.

Yours sincerely,
Eric Blair
Talks Assistant
Indian Section

1. A biographical note to the BBC pamphlet *Landmarks in American Literature* (see *3101*) says of Eliot that he is 'perhaps the best-known contemporary English poet. An American by birth, he now lives in England. His chief works are *The Waste Land* (1922), *Murder in the Cathedral* (a poetic drama, first performed in 1935), and *Four Quartets* (1945).' The pamphlet, published in October 1946, was one of two that gathered together broadcasts on literature organized by Orwell for the BBC. The other, *Books and Authors*, was published on the same day, both by the Oxford University Press, Bombay. Eliot spoke on Edgar Allan Poe on 12 February 1943; see *1834*.

951. To Sirdar Iqbal 'Ali Shah

2 February 1942   PP/EB

Dear Sirdar,

Very many thanks for your letters dated 29th and 31st January. I will meet you at 3 p.m. at Broadcasting House on Thursday, February 5th, to rehearse your talk, which goes out at 4 p.m. I am very sorry I can't lunch that day, much as I would have liked to, as I have an engagement which was fixed some days back. I have sent in the slip for your contract for the Democracy talk, and I understand they are posting it to you to-day. I will also try to manage to get your contract for the talk on the Turkish Halkevi through before the talk is given. Yes, a ten minute talk is what we want.

Sorry I can't manage lunch.

Yours sincerely,
Eric Blair
Talks Assistant
Indian Section

952. To J. F. Horrabin

3 February 1942   PP/EB

Dear Horrabin,[1]

Very many thanks for the synopses you sent me. I like them very well, my only criticism is that I would like the talks to be a little more definitely about geography, with less direct reference to the war situation. Of course, one must mention the war at every turn, but what I am chiefly after is to try to give people an interest in geography which may lead them to look at an atlas occasionally. I am trying to arrange with one or two Indian papers that at the time of your first talk they shall publish a map of the world and mention your forthcoming talks in connection with it. I should not actually refer to this in anything you say, but I think you can talk with the assumption that some of your hearers will be looking at the map as they listen.

Each of these four talks should take about 12 minutes. I think if you allow 1500 words for each that will be about right. It is very difficult to be sure what audience you are speaking to, but the one I am aiming at is the University students and the better educated Indians generally. I think you can assume, therefore, that you are talking to people who are intelligent and well educated, but have a continental outlook, and very little grasp of world geography. I don't think it would hurt to mention even quite elementary facts, such as the lack of friction in water which makes water communications important.

Could you do these four talks on February 18th, 25th and March 11th and 18th? They will go out at approximately 3.45 p.m. We can arrange about rehearsals and so forth later. If you could manage these dates I want the first talk by February 12th.

Yours sincerely,
Eric Blair
Talks Assistant
Indian Section

1. James Francis Horrabin (1884–1962) was staff artist for the *Star* and *News Chronicle* from 1911 until after World War II, provided graphics for TV, 1946–47, and had been a left-wing Labour Party M.P., 1929–31. He had a particular gift for representing historical processes in the form of maps and was much in demand as an educational illustrator. He also created the children's strip-cartoon series featuring Japhet & Co. For approving comments from India on these talks, see *1154*.

953. BBC Talks Booking Form, 3.2.42

Herbert Read:[1] 'We Speak to India,' 'Masterpieces of English Literature,' 16, 'Sesame & Lilies'° by Ruskin, 20-minute talk; broadcast 3.2.42; fee £10.10s. (= £10.50). Signed: N. H. Parratt.

1. Read (see *522, n. 1*) replaced Lord David Cecil, who was ill. The BBC pamphlet *Landmarks in American Literature* (see *3101*) says that 'Read' is 'a poet and critic of art and letters. His works

include *English Prose Style* (1928), *The Meaning of Art* (1931) and *Art Now* (1933). He is a director of a well-known firm of London publishers [Routledge & Sons].'

954. BBC Talks Booking Form, 5.2.42

J. F. Horrabin: 'We Speak to India,' 'The World Is Round,' four talks on popular geography; broadcast 18 and 25.2.42 and 11 and 25.3.42; fee £10.10s each talk.

955. BBC Talks Booking Form, 5.2.42

Herbert Read: 'We Speak to India,' 'Masterpieces of English Literature,' 16,° 'Abt Vogler' (Browning), script written by Edwin Muir, 'who is unable to broadcast it himself,' about 22 minutes; 'Herbert Read will as usual be giving an introduction about Mr. Edwin Muir'; broadcast 10.2.42; fee £4.4s (= £4.20).

956. BBC Talks Booking Form, 5.2.42

Shridhar Telkar: 'Through Eastern Eyes,' 'The Debate Continues'; broadcast 9, 16, and 23.2.42 and 2.3.42; fee £7.7s each talk. Signed: N. H. Parratt.

957. BBC Talks Booking Form, 5.2.42

Shridhar Telkar: 'Through Eastern Eyes,' 'What It Means to Me,' 2, talk on liberty; broadcast 12.2.42; fee £7.7s. Signed: N. H. Parratt.

958. To P. Chatterjee

6 February 1942   PP/EB

Dear Dr. Chatterjee,
Thank you for your letter of 2nd February.[1] I should like to see your talk when it is finished, but we cannot guarantee to take it, in advance. Also, we are fairly well booked up for the next month or so, and we may not be able to use it immediately. However, if it is suitable, we can record it, if necessary.

Your sincerely,
Eric Blair
Talks Assistant
Indian Section
Dictated by Eric Blair and
despatched in his absence by:

1. Chatterjee had suggested a second talk on the London County Council to show Indians, who were experiencing air-raids for the first time, how the LCC worked during air-raids. On the verso of his letter, Orwell wrote: 'Tell him—yes, will he finish & send the talk but we cannot guarantee in advance to take it and we may not be able to use it immediately We can record it if necessary.' Thus, 'Dictated by Eric Blair' may often mean 'written from notes', Orwell seems frequently to have written out letters he 'dictated ' Nancy Parratt was presumably responsible for typing and despatching this letter

959. To Cedric Dover

6 February 1942   Handwritten draft and typewritten versions   PP/EB

Dear Dover,
Thank you for your letter dated 4th February. Yes, "Nationalism and Beyond" would be a good title. Of course, the approach should be personal, but not *too* personal![1]
We can keep the sense of "Foreign Contacts and Social Change", for the other talk, but perhaps we can think of a catchier title.

Yours sincerely,
Eric Blair
Talks Assistant
Indian Section

1. The manuscript draft written by Orwell on Dover's reply, dated 4 February, gives this sentence as: 'Yes, personal approach but not *too* personal, of course.' The draft is not divided into paragraphs.

960. BBC Talks Booking Form, 6.2.42

M. Myat Tun: 'We Speak to India,' 12-minute talk on Moulmein; broadcast 5.2.42; fee £7.7s. Signed: N. H. Parratt.

961. Weekly News Review, 9

7 February 1942

A neat, single-spaced fair-copy typescript with, typewritten at the top of the first page, 'AS BROADCAST.' There are no censors' stamps. PasB records, 'by Z. A. Bokhari' and a timing of 10½ minutes.

The siege of Singapore has begun. As yet, no major move has been made, and it would be very rash to prophesy the outcome. Looking back over the history of this war, we notice that the siege of fortresses and fortified towns have had such varied results that it is difficult to draw any sure inference from them. Sebastopol and Tobruk held out against all attacks, but in these cases it was possible for the defenders to be supplied by sea. Hongkong, which had only a small garrison, and no water supply of its own, was easily taken. Corregidor, in the Philippine Islands, is still holding out, although the defenders are not being supplied by sea, and have hardly any aeroplanes. Leningrad successfully repulsed all attacks, although its supply route by sea was cut off, or almost cut off. For these varied experiences no definite rule can be deduced, but in forming our conclusions, it is worth keeping these considerations in mind:

The Japanese are bound to be immensely superior in numbers of trained men, and in aeroplanes.

Even if air reinforcements in large quantities arrive, the defence of Singapore will be hampered by lack of airfields, unless it is possible to establish emergency airfields at Sumatra and on the various small islands which lie between Sumatra and the Malayan mainland.

Singapore has a powerful garrison, with very heavy guns, and also a large civilian population, principally Chinese, who are willing and anxious to take part in its defence.

The water supply of Singapore is adequate, and food is not likely to run seriously short, at any rate for several months, even if no supplies can be brought from the outside.

Bearing all these considerations in mind, the one thing we can say with certainty, is that the capture of Singapore cannot be an easy business, and that even if it can be taken by direct assault, this would be impossible without enormous losses, which the Japanese may not be ready to face.

This week, the British Government has granted to the Chinese Republic a loan of fifty million pounds for the purchase of munitions of war. The supply of arms to China is largely dependent on keeping the supply routes open, especially the Burma Road, but even if the Burma Road should be cut, or rendered inaccessible, other routes into China exist, and yet others can be contrived. The Japanese are already uttering threats to India upon the mere rumour of the building of another road from Assam. Meanwhile the loan, which will allow an enormous quantity of materials to be bought and if necessary stored until they can be transported, is the token of the reality of the Alliance between Free Britain and Free China.

Meanwhile, the delaying actions in Burma, in the Dutch East Indies and in the Philippines, continue. The Japanese have lost very heavily in ships and men, in the Straits of Macassar, chiefly owing to the operation of Dutch aircraft, which work from airfields hidden in the jungles. It may ultimately be possible for the Japanese to bring the whole of Borneo under their control, in which case this particular danger will have been eliminated, but their heavy losses in shipping, occurring so early in the war, when all the advantages are on their side, do not augur very well for the future. In their inroads on the Dutch East Indies they are suffering from the "scorched earth" policy as much as from the Dutch and American aircraft and submarines. It is, in fact, not much use to them to over-run territories where they will afterwards have to supply their troops by sea, if those territories have been systematically devastated beforehand. How much the Japanese fear this can be seen from their savage threat to massacre the garrison at Balik Papan,° in Borneo, if the oil refineries there were destroyed.[1] In fact, the oil refineries were destroyed, and the garrison succeeded in fighting its way out, instead of being massacred. The "scorched earth" policy has its limitations, because certain things, for instance, metallic ores, cannot be destroyed, but on the other hand, certain products, such as crude petroleum, are of little value to anyone who captures them if the necessary machinery is lacking. It is comparatively of little use for the Japanese to over-run the various oil-bearing areas, if they have got to take the oil back to Japan to be refined. At the same time, their shipping is needed for transporting food stuffs° and men, and is dwindling, owing to submarine attacks. In spite of the successes which the Japanese have won, it seems probable that their campaign is behind time, and that an Allied counter-attack has been made possible by the delaying battle which is being fought by Chinese, Dutch, British, Indians and Javanese, in the south-west Pacific.

In the Battle of Russia, there is not much to report this week. The Russians are still advancing, but they have not yet captured Kharkov or Smolensk. It now becomes clear that the campaign in Libya should probably be regarded as part of, or at any rate complementary to, the Battle of Russia, and that both this and the Japanese campaign in Asia are part of a single strategic manoeuvre. Almost certainly the plan is for the Germans to break through to the Persian Gulf, capturing the Suez Canal with the southern arm of their attack, and the Caucasian oil-fields with the northern arm, at the same time as the Japanese break through to the Indian Ocean, if possible capturing Rangoon and the naval bases of Ceylon on their way. The two main Axis powers would then be in communication with one another, and Germany's desperate needs for oil, rubber, tin, and other commodities, could be supplied. It can therefore be taken as almost certain that the Germans are making ready for fresh offensives against Southern Russia and against Egypt in the spring, but it is very doubtful whether these offensives can be any more successful than those which have been made during the past Autumn and Winter. The Russians have made good most of their industrial losses by establishing new industrial areas beyond the Ural Mountains, and the British armies in the Middle East are far stronger than they were. They are not even dependent to the same extent as before on sea-borne supplies, because by this time great armament factories have been set up in Eritrea, the province on the Red Sea which was captured from the Italians. There is, unquestionably, hard fighting and perhaps heavy losses ahead of the Allies in the spring, but on a long term view the odds are much more heavily against the Axis than they were at the beginning of 1941.

An extremely important political event has taken place in the Treaty now signed between Abyssinia and Great Britain. The Emperor Haile Selassie, driven out by the cowardly aggression of the Italians six years ago, returns to his throne, Abyssinia takes its place again among the free nations, and the attempted economic domination of the country by foreign interests is at an end. Simultaneously with this, there goes a political change in Egypt, which will be to the advantage of the Allied cause. The Wafdists, the Egyptian nationalist party, who negotiated the Anglo-Egyptian treaty of 1936, have formed a new Government. The Wafdists are a progressive Left Wing party, genuinely representative of the Egyptian people, especially the poorer peasants, and extremely anti-Nazi in sentiment.

Finally, a political event about which it is too early to make exact predictions, but which is almost certain to have good results, is the appointment of Lord Beaverbrook as British Minister of Production. In this position he can co-ordinate the entire output of materials of war in Britain, and any administrative muddles or jealousies between the different services can be eliminated. Lord Beaverbrook is a man of enormous energy, and his efforts as Minister of Aircraft Production probably did as much as any one thing to turn the scale and defeat the German invaders in the summer of 1940. His wide range of personal contacts in the U.S.A. on the one hand, and in Soviet Russia on the other, will be of the greatest value to the Allied cause.

1. Balikpapan had been taken by the Japanese on 24 January 1941. Despite Churchill's statement that 'we had succeeded in demolishing the . . . oil installations' (*The Second World War*, III, 566; U.S.: *The Grand Alliance*, 639), the Japanese were able to use them and it proved necessary for American B-24s to bomb them, 13 August 1943 (*2194 Days of War*). Balikpapan was not recaptured (by the Australians) until July 1945 'in what proved to be the last amphibious operation of the war' (Liddell Hart, *History of the Second World War*, 719; U.S.: 689).

962. Z. A. Bokhari to T. S. Eliot

9 February 1942

Z. A. Bokhari wrote to T. S. Eliot on this date, explaining his and Orwell's absence when Eliot had telephoned: '. . . and I am sorry you couldn't find Blair. He is away ill. Blair is "George Orwell" and he is helping me in my work.' He also asked if Eliot would fix a date in June when he could start his weekly broadcast. There is no entry in the record that Orwell was on sick leave about this time.

963. Annotation to Memorandum re: Sirdar Iqbal 'Ali Shah

9 February 1942

On 13 January 1942, T. F. Lindsay, Assistant Director of the British Council's Press Division, wrote to David Mitchell of the BBC's Turkish Unit to advise him of the forthcoming opening of a Turkish 'Halk Evi' in London. Lindsay sent a copy of his letter to C. Connor at the BBC, and that was eventually passed to Rushbrook Williams, from him to Bokhari, and from Bokhari to Orwell, who was asked to take charge. On one undated memorandum, Orwell wrote this annotation for Bokhari's attention:

I have asked Sirdar Iqbal Ali Shah to undertake this for "Through Eastern Eyes". If he falls through we could perhaps send someone from the staff.

E. A. Blair

On another covering memorandum, dated 9 February 1942, Orwell wrote (presumably for Miss Parratt):

Please send Iqbal Ali Shah a card to remind him.   E. A. B

964. To Empire Talks Manager, Norman Collins
9 February 1942   Original   EB/NP

NEW SERIES OF TALKS BY J. F. HORRABIN

On February 18th we are starting a series of four talks by J. F. Horrabin, cartoonist of The Star and the News Chronicle, and author of several popular geography books.

This series will be called "THE WORLD IS ROUND", and the dates of the talks will be 18th and 25th February, 11th and 25th March. They will be on popular geography.[1]

Dictated by Eric Blair and
signed in his absence by:
[Signed] N. H. Parratt.

1. Collins annotated this memorandum, asking Miss Parratt to arrange for him to see the scripts as early as possible and Mrs. W. Lawton (his secretary?) to inform the Empire Programme Executive and others.

965. To Shridhar Telkar
9 February 1942   PP/EB

Dear Mr. Telkar,
This is to confirm that you will be doing three more talks in our series "The Debate Continues", on February 16th, 23rd, and March 2nd.

I am sorry that there was some misunderstanding about the talk for to-day, and I hope that it has not inconvenienced you too much. It is very kind of you to do it for us at short notice.

Yours sincerely,
Secretary to Mr. Blair.

966. To E. W. D. Boughen, Talks Bookings
10 February 1942   Original   EB/NP

FEE FOR SIRDAR IKBAL° ALI° SHAH.

We have asked Sirdar Ikbal Ali Shah to cover the opening of the Turkish Halkevi (a kind of People's House) on February 19th, in London. He will be coming up to London specially in order to do this, on that day.

There is not yet any particular date fixed for this talk, so that it means he will be obliged to come up from Oxford again specially in order to broadcast his talk, or else to record it. We have already informed him that we will pay his travelling expenses.

The talk will be just over ten minutes' in length, and will be given in English. I imagine that he will be paid a little more than the usual fee for a talk of that length, as he will have the extra bother of going to the opening ceremony, as well as getting the talk written.

I should be glad if you would get in touch with him to tell him that he will receive a fee, as he is very reluctant to do anything until he knows what he will be paid.—Please remember that he should be addressed as—Dear Sirdar—and on the envelope as Sirdar Ikbal Ali Shah—no Esq. is necessary. His address is—4, Turl Street, Oxford.[1]

Dictated by Eric Blair and
signed in his absence by:
[Signed] N. H. Parratt.

1. The memorandum was annotated (by Miss Boughen?), '15gns & £1.6.4 fare,' on 13 February. Miss Boughen made arrangements with Programme Accounts on 17 February for a cash advance to the Sirdar when he made the first visit to London, 19 February, to attend the ceremony: 5 guineas plus fare of 13s 2d = £5.18.2. No date had yet been arranged for the broadcast.

967. Eastern Service Director to Indian Programme Organiser

10 February 1942

Copies of this memorandum were sent to Orwell and E. Rowan Davies.

INDIAN VERNACULAR NEWSLETTERS

When the daily Thai service is instituted, it will occupy the period 1330–1345 GMT. The period 1345–1400 GMT will have to carry Malay, Burmese, Tamil and Bengali. The period 1515–1530 GMT. will be available for Sinhalese, and Marathi, Gujerathi° and Telegu.

968. Meeting with Secretary of State for India

12–16 February 1942

The memoranda that follow outline discussions and problems affecting the Indian Section of the Overseas Service. It is unlikely that Orwell took part in the discussions—not even the Indian Programme Organiser is mentioned in any distribution list. The memorandum of 12 February is marked 'Private & Confidential.' Sir Cecil Graves was Director-General of the BBC; the Secretary of State for India, S.O.S., was L. S. Amery; J. B. Clark was Controller of Overseas Services, C. (O.S.), and R. A. Rendall was his assistant; the Eastern Service Director was L. F. Rushbrook Williams. Laurence Brander was

Intelligence Officer for the Eastern Service. It was Brander who later recommended that Orwell broadcast under that name. Sir Malcolm Darling, the Indian News Editor, was in charge of Hindustani services, operated from Evesham. A.I.R. = All-India Radio.

From Rendall to Rushbrook Williams, 12 February 1942:

There was recently a joint discussion between the Dominions Office, the Ministry of Information and the BBC about broadcasting to Australia held in the Secretary of State's room at the Dominions Office. The valuable guidance and improvement in availability of information in future which resulted from this meeting suggested that similar contact at a high level with other Government Departments would be desirable. Sir Cecil Graves is very anxious that something of the sort should be established with the India Office and has spoken to Mr. Radcliffe of the Ministry of Information about it. It is understood that some meeting at the India Office with Mr. Amery may be arranged in the near future. The BBC representatives would be Sir Cecil Graves, C.(O.S.) or myself, and yourself.

In the meantime, Sir Cecil Graves has asked for a note of possible talking points. Will you prepare one or two points, indicating any difficulties which we have encountered in relation to the policy or the material available for (a) the Hindustani Service, (b) the English Service to Indians? A third question on which a note would be valuable would be rebroadcasting relations with A.I.R.; indeed, it was out of a discussion about this between Sir Cecil Graves and myself that the suggestion for a meeting with Mr. Amery arose. It does seem hardly worth while spending a lot of money on a service from here if it is to be indefinitely limited to the shortwave audience, and it is therefore suggested that we should press for more rebroadcasting facilities.

Another point that should be mentioned is Brander's visit.

It is possible that the Home Division may be represented in order that the question of broadcasts about India in the Home Service can be discussed. If we can let Sir Cecil Graves have some notes before the end of the week, we should be all right. Perhaps we might have a word about this before you start actually drafting the notes?

Rushbrook Williams returned this memorandum to Rendall on 13 February with the following unsigned brief:

POINTS FOR MEETING WITH SECRETARY OF STATE FOR INDIA

1. Liaison between India and Burma Offices over:
   (a) Policy
   (b) Information
is excellent so far as Overseas Services are concerned. From our point of view, the present system by which the India and Burma Offices both volunteer guidance, and provide it at our request, works admirably. Have they any suggestions for improvement on their side? For example, are the channels satisfactory? Is more centralisation desirable? Do they obtain satisfactory action on their requests both from Home and Overseas Divisions?
2. Although the liaison between the B.B.C. Overseas Services and the India and Burma Offices is so satisfactory, the B.B.C. feels that there is still a certain lack of coordination between themselves and All India Radio.° During the three months ending December 1941, there was a small but gratifying

increase in the rebroadcasts by All India Radio° of items in the Eastern Service. During October, the total time occupied by these rebroadcasts was 104 hours 10 minutes. In November, it had risen to 108 hours 15 minutes; in December to 125 hours 5 minutes. In January, largely no doubt on account of the shift of world interest to Singapore and the Dutch East Indies, the figure had dropped to 108 hours 5 minutes. The falling off is no doubt due to the fact that the approach of war to the shores of India has greatly increased domestic pressure upon the transmitting time of All India° Radio; and has given rise to new demands for local items for the improvement of morale, the institution of air raid precautions, and the like. The total figure of rebroadcasts, which varies during the last four months roughly from 104 hours to 125 hours, may at first sight seem large when it is remembered that the total time which the Eastern Services are on the air during any one month is something between 128 and 130 hours. But it should be remembered that the total figure of rebroadcasts by All India Radio is arrived at by adding up the rebroadcasting times of eight separate Indian stations. The average time which each station devotes to rebroadcasting is something like 15 hours per month—and this is the true standard of comparison with the total broadcast of about 130 hours from the B.B.C. Analysis further shows that the great majority of the items rebroadcast are those belonging to the main Empire Talks series which are carried in other Services besides the Eastern. At the present moment, very few items exclusive to the Eastern Service are rebroadcast, despite the fact that these items are chosen with the utmost care, and with expert advice, as being of a kind likely to appeal especially to India. That there is a considerable amount of direct Indian listening on short wave to London is established; but the great number of Indian medium wave listeners are not reached by London items unless these items are rebroadcast by A.I.R. The B.B.C. would be very glad to obtain from A.I.R. more detailed suggestions both as to the kind of items which they would wish to rebroadcast, and as to the reasons why particular items, specially designed for India, are not in fact rebroadcast. Definite criteria, if such there be, employed by A.I.R. as a touchstone of suitability for rebroadcasting, would provide an invaluable guide to the B.B.C.

3.   It has been found that an adequate organisation for listener research is invaluable in broadcasting practice. The India Office and the Government of India have kindly agreed that Mr. Brander, who has recently undergone a course for training in listener research methods in Britain, should visit India in order to report upon the means of organising listener research machinery; and, if the situation requires, to establish such machinery on a tentative basis. The B.B.C. would be very grateful for any facilities which the Government of India could offer to Mr. Brander and for any opportunities with which they could provide him for discussion with officials, whether of the Central or of the Provincial Governments, whose experience would have a bearing upon his work.

Rendall then sent Rushbrook Williams's brief to Clark, writing this slightly elliptical note at the foot of the memorandum:

Here are two copies of E.S.D.'s notes. They cover the main points. A word could be added about our development of service to specialised audiences in vernacular languages. And it might be desirable to say something about the staff problem (previously the Secy of State's main contact with our service to India) but I leave that to you.

[Signed] R. A. Rendall
14.2.42.

On 16 February, Clark sent the brief to the Director-General of the BBC with this memorandum:

As requested, I attach hereto a memorandum of points for this meeting, as prepared by A.C.(OS) and E.S.D. In the interests of having present those most directly concerned with our Eastern Service output, I think it would be best for Rendall (rather than myself) and Rushbrook Williams, to accompany you from this Division. In addition to the points made in the memorandum, the following references might be made:

(a) Advice from the Government of India against the introduction of an early morning news bulletin in Hindustani, owing to the shifting of the centre of war interest in India to the East and Far East from Europe and the Near East. We do not want to press our proposal, but this point supplements paragraph 2, in the memorandum, since it shows the need of better understanding between the G.O.I./A.I.R. and ourselves. (Rendall is fully briefed on this).

(b) A brief word from Rendall about our development of services to specialised audiences in vernacular languages.

(c) The staff problem in which the S.O.S. became involved a few months ago, arising from the recent reorganisation of the Indian Service, over which Darling[1] has proved difficult. There is a supplementary point here about dependence on India for Indian staff, despite which they have given us literally no help for the past year. (I know, of course, that there have been all kinds of personal and other difficulties at the other end).

1. For the difficulty caused by Sir Malcolm Darling, see *984*.

969. To Cyril Connolly

13 February 1942   PP/EB

Dear Cyril,

Confirming our talk yesterday, I want your broadcast to take place on Friday, 13th March, which means that we should have the script not later than 6th March.

The talk should be a half-hour one, i.e. should take not less than 25 minutes and not more than 28. You can do it alone, or in the form of a discussion with somebody else, just as you please, and of course use your discretion about putting in readings from other people's work etc. In a talk of that length it is best to break it up in some way.

You suggested "the thirties" as a subject, and that would do very well. But if you want to choose some other approach, you might let me know fairly soon. I want this series of six talks to more or less cover the literary period 1918–1940.

Yours
Eric Blair
Talks Assistant
Indian Section

970. Newsletter, 10

14 February 1942

This newsletter exists in two forms: a typescript, which may be a fair copy of a much altered original (though it has four words x-ed through, all incorrectly typed and then corrected); and a version of all but the last paragraph reproduced as the second of the five specimens of propaganda in *Talking to India*; see *2359*. The typescript bears no censors' stamps; at its head is typed 'AS BROADCAST'; and written near the top is 'Z. A. Bokhari' and 'Through Eastern Eyes.' The printed text has been slightly modified as well as omitting the final paragraph. PasB describes the broadcast as a News Review by Z. A. Bokhari and times it at 11 minutes. The text reproduced here is that of the typescript; the variant readings of the version in *Talking to India*—presumably Orwell's work in the light of the fall of Singapore, which was surrendered about twenty-four hours after Newsletter 10 was transmitted—are given in the notes. The printed text is dated 'February 1942.'

At this moment of speaking, the struggle for Singapore is still going on, and the vital reservoirs which hold the island's water are still in the hands of the defenders. But we must face the fact that it is unlikely that Singapore can be kept out of Japanese hands much longer.[1] This is a very serious piece of news, and even more serious for Asia than for the West. One American expert has already estimated that the loss of Singapore will lengthen the war by about a year.[2] It is worth, therefore, trying to predict as fully as possible the strategic consequences which this loss entails. Once they are in[3] possession of Singapore, the Japanese surface ships as well as submarines can enter the Indian Ocean. If their forthcoming attacks on the Dutch islands[4] of Sumatra and more particularly Java should also succeed, then they are in entire possession of the main route across the Pacific, leading from America to Africa. If you look at the map, you will see that communications between the United States and India and Africa are not indeed cut off, but that American ships have to travel by a round-about[5] route southward to Australia, or New Zealand, and then north again over immense distances, which confer a great strategical advantage on the Japanese, who are in a more central position, and will, if they can over-run[6] the Dutch East Indies, possess air-fields[7] and naval bases covering the whole of this area.

Supposing that the Japanese can succeed to the extent which we have imagined, what will their next step be? In the first place, they will[8] intensify their attack on Burma, in hopes of capturing Rangoon, the only port through which the Burma Road can be easily supplied. They will[9] make air and naval attacks against the islands in the Indian Ocean, probably beginning with the Andaman Islands, and they will probably[10] attempt an invasion of Ceylon, or of some area in Southern India. Could they get control of Ceylon, they would command the Bay of Bengal sufficiently to prevent any Allied shipping crossing it, and though they would not have complete control of the Western part of the Indian Ocean, they would at least be able to make damaging attacks on British shipping which has passed round the Cape and is on its way to supply the British armies in the Middle East, and our Allies in Russia.

This is not an encouraging picture, and we have deliberately put it at its worst,[11] in order to get a realistic and un-varnished[12] view of the situation. We may even go a step further and consider what the consequences would be if the grandiose Axis offensive of which the Japanese naval offensive is only a part, were totally successful.

It is becoming clearer and clearer, as we have emphasised in earlier news reviews, that the general plan is for the Germans to break through by land, so as to reach the Persian Gulf, while the Japanese gain mastery of the Indian Ocean. In this way,[13] three objects would be achieved at the same time. In the first place, Germany and Japan would be in direct communication with one another, though perhaps only rather precariously so. In the second place, the Burma Road would have ceased to be of much value as a supply route to China, and in the third place, the best supply route to Russia, that is, through the Persian Gulf and Iran, would have been cut. The Germans and Japanese have evidently staked everything on this manœuvre, in the confidence that if they can bring it off, it will have won them the war. The conclusion[14] evidently is that if cut off from Western supplies, China will stop fighting, or at least China's armies will be reduced to guerrilla activity, and the Russian Army will have to retreat behind the Ural mountains. Simultaneously the British Empire will have been cut into two parts,[15] and both Australia and the British dependencies in Africa can be attacked at leisure.

This is the worst that can happen,[16] and during the coming months the Axis powers[17] will make tremendous efforts to bring it about, by renewed offensives in Southern Russia, in North Africa, in Burma, and in the Indian Ocean. It[18] should be emphasised that even should this grandiose plan succeed in its entirety, it would not give the Axis Powers victory, unless the Allied peoples of America, Soviet Russia, Britain and China lost heart. It still remains true that the balance of power, both in men, materials and industrial plant, is heavily against the Axis Powers, and that the main manufacturing centres of the Allied Powers are in places where neither the Germans nor the Japanese can get at them. These main centres where aeroplanes, tanks, ships and guns are being forged, are in North America, which for practical purposes is outside the sphere of war, in equally inaccessible parts of Central Russia and Siberia, and in Britain, which is much nearer the scene of danger, but which the Germans have failed to invade or even to damage seriously by air bombing. The Allied Powers, therefore, are able immensely to outbuild the Axis Powers, and in a year or two years bring together a force which will be all but irresistible. But they have undoubtedly a difficult time ahead, and they may have a period when they are almost in conditions of siege, and when resolution, calmness and faith in final victory, will be at least as important as physical weapons of war.

Meanwhile the immediate effect of events in the Western Pacific is to make the position of India more dangerous, and also immensely more important. With the loss of Singapore,[19] India becomes for the time being the centre of the war, one might say, the centre of the world. With its central position, and its wealth in manpower[20] and raw materials, India will become a more and more important source of supply for China on the one hand and Russia and the Middle East on the other. It should be emphasised that even if Rangoon is lost, with the consequence that the Burma Road ceases to be useable,[21] that does not mean that communication[22] between China and her Allies becomes impossible. There are several other routes into China, both actual and potential. In the first place, there exists the route through Soviet Russia and Sinkiang in Central Asia; secondly, the route already projected, through Assam; thirdly, there is the possibility of a Northern route through Alaska and Manchuria; and fourthly, it may be possible to establish American naval control of the Pacific at some time within the next year. But at the moment, India's position is of vital importance, and Chinese-Indian solidarity will be one of the foremost factors in the war. It is therefore most encouraging news that General Chiang K'ai-Shek,[23] the leader of Republican China, has already visited India, and had an interview both with the Viceroy and with Mr. Nehru. We do not yet know the results of these interviews, but we can at least safely prophesy that if the great peoples of China and India stand together, they cannot be overwhelmed even by the most powerful and ruthless aggressor.

In Britain there have been one of two internal events which have a bearing on the world aspect of the war. Lord Beaverbrook, now in supreme control of production, has made his first speech, and given some important figures about British production during the last year. He revealed that during 1941, Great Britain sent abroad nearly 3,000 tanks, and between nine and ten thousand aeroplanes. Since the bulk of these vast supplies must have gone to Soviet Russia, we can say that the British factories have played an important part in the defeat which the Russians inflicted on the Germans when they kept them out of Moscow and Leningrad. The British factories are now producing at even greater speed than before, but these things are not achieved without sacrifices on the part of the common people, and now that war extends to the Pacific, the calls upon British shipping are even more urgent than before. Soap has just been rationed for the first time during this war. Even now, the British soap ration,[24] like nearly all the other rations, is much bigger than what is received by people living under Axis rule, but the fact that one article of daily use after another has to be rationed, is a sign that British industry is moving more and more from a peace to a war economy. The ordinary people who have to put up with these restrictions do not grumble, and are even heard to say that they would welcome greater sacrifices, if these would set free more shipping for the war effort, since they have a clear understanding of the issue, and set much more store by their liberty than by the comforts they have been accustomed to in peace-time.

1. it is unlikely . . . much longer] the situation in Singapore is precarious
2. One American expert . . . a year] *omitted*
3. entails. Once they are] is likely to entail. If they can get
4. islands] Islands
5. round-about] roundabout
6. over-run] overrun
7. air-fields] airfields
8. will] are likely to
9. will] are also likely to
10. will probably] may
11. This is not . . . at its worst] We have deliberately imagined the situation at its worst
12. un-varnished] unvarnished
13. In this way] If this were successful
14. The conclusion] Their belief
15. Simultaneously the . . . parts] Simultaneously, the eastward sea-routes of the British Empire will have been cut
16. worst that can happen] strategic plan of the Axis powers
17. the Axis powers] they
18. It] But it
19. With the loss of Singapore] If Singapore is lost
20. manpower] man-power
21. useable] usable
22. communication] communications
23. K'ai-Shek] Kai-shek
24. The allowance of soap was one tablet per person a month, with no additional allowance for hard-water areas, such as London. Miners were given additional soap at pit-head baths. Shaving-soap was not rationed but, like razor blades, not always available. See *Nineteen Eighty-Four*: 'Party members were supposed not to go into ordinary shops . . but the rule was not strictly kept, because there were various things such as shoelaces and razor blades which it was impossible to get hold of in any other way' (*CW*, IX, 8).

971. To J. F. Horrabin

[14?] February 1942   Handwritten annotation

J. F. Horrabin sent Orwell a postcard on 13 February 1942 asking how he could hear his broadcasts to India. The card is post-marked 11.15 am 13 February and date-stamped that same day, indicating its receipt at Broadcasting House. Orwell annotated this for his secretary:

Please send him a pc. giving the wavelengths but explain that these broadcasts are hard to pick up in England.

E.A.B

972. To David Astor

Monday, [16 February 1942?¹]   Handwritten

Dear Astor,

Herewith synopsis of the article we spoke of. If satisfactory I can do the article itself within the next few days (I don't know what day the "Observer" goes to press). I can't say *less* than I have indicated, though of course in a leading article one can put these things bluntly or less bluntly. I have shown this draft to Empson who is in agreement with it & would like to follow it up with the China article as before projected.²

You might let me know soon whether to go ahead[.]

Yours
Geo. Orwell

1. The dating of this letter is difficult. It must be related to one of two articles by Orwell published anonymously: 'India Next,' 22 February 1942 (see *981*), or the first 'Mood of the Moment,' 8 March 1942; see *1012*. The word 'synopsis' makes it seem more probable, if not certain, that he refers to the longer piece, 'India Next,' rather than the 300-word 'Mood of the Moment.' India is also suggested by the reference to a companion piece on China by Empson (but see *n. 2*). The reference to when *The Observer* goes to press suggests that the article was to appear soon; therefore this letter has been dated for the Monday immediately before Sunday, 22 February 1942. For Orwell's response to Astor's approach, see *891*. Ivor Brown was editor (see *1480, n. 2*), but Astor recruited new contributors before taking over the editorship in 1948.

2. There are only five brief items on China in *The Observer* from 1 March to 30 June 1942, and no article that could be attributed to either Orwell or Empson. Astor recalled on 14 January 1991 that it was intended that Empson should write on China, but for some reason, now forgotten, he failed to do so.

973. To Sirdar Iqbal 'Ali Shah

16 February 1942   PP/EB

Dear Sirdar,

Thank you for your letter of 14th February. We have been in touch with the British Council, and have arranged that they should send you an invitation for the ceremony on February 19th.

I attach some information about the Halkevi, which we received from the British Council. I hope it covers the points you want to know about.

I think it would be best if we had your talk as soon after the event as possible, and therefore I have arranged for your broadcast to take place on Friday, 20th February, at 4 p.m. B.S.T. This will mean that the script should be in our office on the morning of Friday 20th, so may I suggest that you should come to 55, Portland Place at about 11.30 with your script, and we shall then be able to run through it for timing and so on, at the same time. Perhaps you will kindly let me know if this date is convenient to you.

Yours sincerely
Eric Blair

Evidently the Sirdar failed to confirm the arrangement. A carbon copy of an undated telegram to him from Orwell reads:

SHOULD BE MOST GRATEFUL IF YOU WOULD KINDLY GIVE TALK FRIDAY.

974. To Arthur Calder-Marshall
17 February 1942   PP/EB

Dear Mr. Caulder° Marshall,[1]
I wonder if you would like to do a talk for us in a series of talks on contemporary English literature which we are running for the English-speaking Indian public? These talks are supposed to cover the development of literature from about 1918 onwards, but we are not doing them by periods, but approaching certain aspects of literature separately. I thought that if you liked you might do the last talk in the series, and discuss the economic bases of literature (we can think of a suitable title later). In doing this, one would have to glance at the past, but of course we are chiefly interested in the present and to some extent, the future. With the gradual, or not very gradual, disappearance of unearned incomes and in general of privileged minorities, the economic background of literature is altering, and this is bound to have its effect on technique, subject matter, and so forth. This is the subject I want you to tackle, if it would interest you. Do you think you could let me know about this? It is to be a 28 minute talk, and it would be about 10 weeks from now.

Yours sincerely,
George Orwell
Talks Assistant
Indian Section

1. Arthur Calder-Marshall (see *856, n. 3*) was a prime mover of the manifesto 'Why Not War Writers?' (see *856*), published by *Horizon* in October 1941, so the errors in spelling his surname are probably the typist's. He was at this time working for the Ministry of Information Films Division.

975. BBC Talks Booking Form, 17.2.42

Hsiao Ch'ien: 'Through Eastern Eyes,' 'What It Means to Me,' on Japanese-occupied China; recorded 20.2.42; broadcast 5.3.42; fee £10.10s. Signed: N. H. Parratt. See *919, n. 1*.

976. BBC Talks Booking Form, 17.2.42

Cedric Dover: 'Through Eastern Eyes,' 1. 'What It Means to Me,' on nationalism and beyond; 2. 'Today & Yesterday,' on the importance of minorities; broadcast 19 and 25.2.42; fees £7.7s each talk. Signed: N. H. Parratt.

977. Z. A. Bokhari to Shridhar Telkar

19 February 1942   PP/ZAB/MB

My dear Telkar,[1]
You played truant the other day when you didn't go to the House of Commons to listen to the Debate. That isn't very serious. I do the same, whenever I can! The thing that does matter is that a Pass was kept for you idle at the B.B.C. while many people were straining at the leash to go to the House of Commons. The accommodation given to the B.B.C. at the House of Commons is very limited and therefore it is rather wasteful if nobody makes use of the B.B.C. passes.

We shall be grateful if in future you will ring up the Duty Officer and tell him you are not going to the House. Such a procedure will enable him to make use of the Pass. I hope you will appreciate our point of view.

Yours sincerely,
[Initialled] Z. A. Bokhari
Indian Programme Organiser

1. This letter is indicative of Bokhari's tone in running his section, especially when dealing with those junior to him.

978. Z. A. Bokhari to Shridhar Telkar

20 February 1942   PP/ZAB/MB

My dear Telkar,
Early in March, we hope to start the Marathi News Letter and we are planning to broadcast this News Letter on Thursdays at 4.15 to 4.30 p.m. BST. I want to warn you of this so that you can hold yourself in readiness for the event. The English version[1] will be prepared by Eric Blair and you will be asked to translate it into Marathi and read it over the air.

Yours sincerely,
[Initialled] Z. A. Bokhari
Indian Programme Organiser

1. It is not known how much fresh work Orwell put into writing the English versions for the various vernacular newsletters. Laurence Brander, Intelligence Officer for the Indian Section, informed the editor on 6 August 1985 that his 'guess would be that the scripts would be different.' On 8 September 1985, he wrote: 'The boasting about b'casting in so many Indian languages was propaganda for home consumption, I shd think; did more harm than good. Which Orwell could not know.' See 1276, n. 4.

979. BBC Talks Booking Form, 20.2.42

Sirdar Iqbal 'Ali Shah: 'Through Eastern Eyes,' 'The Man in the Street,' 12-minute talk on the opening of the Turkish Halkevı in London; broadcast 20.2.42; fee £15.15s + £1.6.4 fares (less £5.5s and 13s.2d fare already paid) = £10.10s + 13s 2d.

980. Newsletter, 11

21 February 1942

The typescript is a fair copy, lacking any censors' stamps, with 'AS BROADCAST' typed at the top of the first page. There is an excision and a one-word substitution, probably in Orwell's hand. PasB records 'Weekly News Review by Z. A. Bokhari' and gives the timing as 10′ 45″.

With the fall of Singapore, the war in the Far East enters into its second phase.

It is evident that the Japanese now have two main objectives: one is to cut the Burma Road, in hopes of thus knocking China out of the war, and the other is to widen the sphere of Japanese control in the Western Pacific, to such an extent that the Allies shall have no air or naval bases within attacking distance of Japan. In order to achieve this plan completely, the Japanese would have to control the whole of the East Indies, the whole of Burma, Northern Australia and probably New Zealand and Hawaii. Could they control all these areas, they would have eliminated the danger of British or American counter-attack for the time being, though even then, their safety would depend on keeping Russia out of the war. They are not likely to attain the whole even of these objectives, but they may go some way towards it, and it is clear that their first step must be the conquest of Rangoon and of the big sea-ports of Java. The battle in Burma is already raging, and the attack on Java is obviously imminent.

We cannot say yet how the battle in Burma will end. The Japanese have advanced, but not very rapidly, and the British have been reinforced both with aeroplanes and with Chinese troops. The supply difficulties which decided the issue in Malaya are less acute in the Burma area. If Rangoon should fall, that is an end not actually of the Burma Road, but of the present route by which supplies can reach the Burma Road from India or from Britain. The capture of Rangoon by the Japanese would not end the campaign in Burma because in this case the direction of the Japanese advance must be northward, and there is no question of the Allied army being driven into the sea. But it may be asked: if Rangoon should fall, would it be of any value to continue the campaign in Burma? Yes, because the existing Burma Road is not the only possible route from India into China. Another route is projected and can be brought into use within measurable time, so long as China's resistance can be kept going in the interval.

In this connection, the recent visit of Marshal Chiang K'ai Shek to India is of the highest importance. We know now that Marshal Chiang K'ai Shek had interviews not only with Mr. Nehru, but with Mr. Jinnah and with Mahatma Gandhi. What the political outcome of these interviews was we do not precisely know, but we do know that Marshal Chiang K'ai Shek has affirmed the solidarity of India and China, and has spoken of the projected new route which will enter China far to the north of the present Burma Road. It is clear, therefore, that even if Rangoon is lost, and with it the possibilities of supplying China on any large scale by sea, the retention of Upper Burma will be immensely important to the Allies. Probably the next few months will decide the issue, for during the monsoon which begins in Burma about the end of May, the passage of mechanised troops will be very difficult in Burma, except along the railways and waterways. We must not under-rate the power of the Japanese, who largely possess control of the sea in the Eastern part of the Bay of Bengal, and who will be heavily reinforced now that they can withdraw most of their troops from Malaya.

We must expect also the intensification of the attack on the Americans in the Phillipine° Islands and in the very near future an all-out offensive against Java. It is certain that Java will be a tough nut to crack. The Dutch lack aeroplanes and it has been very difficult to reinforce them to any extent, but they have a large army partly Dutch and partly Javanese, which is well trained and determined to resist fiercely. It is unlikely that there will be much fifth-column activity, for[1] even the Nationalists among the Javanese are aware that they have nothing to hope from a Japanese conquest. They realise that the independence which they wish for is not likely to be gained by passing under Fascist rule. Both the Dutch and the Asiatic inhabitants of the Islands have shown themselves devoted and ruthless in applying the scorched earth policy. They destroyed the oil installations at Palembang on the island of Sumatra so completely that it will be a long time before the Japanese can get any oil out of them, and they are ready to do the same wherever the invaders may advance.

The first bombs have fallen on Australian soil. Darwin, in the northern tip of Queensland, was heavily bombed two days ago.[2] Australia has mobilised the whole of its manpower and is ready to go to extreme lengths in the conscription of property as well in order to put the country completely on a war footing. It is unlikely however that the Japanese will attempt a full-scale invasion of Australia at this stage. The country is too big to be over-run completely, and there are more pressing tasks on hand. Although geographically the Japanese are nearer to Australia, India is in acuter danger, and the solidarity of the Asiatic nations against the common enemy is the most important factor in the war.

In the Western hemisphere, the issue is still in the balance, and will probably remain so until the late spring. The German plan to knock Russia out at one blow has failed, and German prestige has suffered all over Europe, almost as much as the German army has suffered in the cold of the Russian winter. But that winter is drawing to an end, and it is clear that the Germans are making ready to launch another huge offensive towards the Caucasus, as soon as the weather makes this possible, probably about May. In the southern section of this campaign neither side has gained a decisive advantage. The

186

German attempt to invade Egypt has hitherto failed, but so also has the British attempt to drive westwards as far as Tripoli and thus obtain control of the Central Mediterranean. At this date the result of three months' battle has been to leave the British in possession of a portion of Cyrenaica, including the powerful frontier forts of Sollum, Bardia and Halfaya previously held by the Germans. Both sides have supply difficulties to face. The Germans need only bring their supplies across the narrow waist of the Mediterranean, but the British submarines are waiting for them on the way, and have sunk an immense number of ships during the past three months. The British ships supplying the Middle East, on the other hand, have to travel from England, round the Cape of Good Hope, a journey which can only be made three times in a year. Sometimes, however, when supplies of men and materials are urgently needed, the British prefer to send their convoys straight up the Mediterranean, which they are able to do if they choose to escort them heavily enough. Recently a large convoy made the passage through the Mediterranean with the loss of only two ships, and its escorting warships sank or damaged four Italian warships on the way.

The British War Cabinet has been re-constructed. This was in accord with the wishes of the majority of the English people, who wished for the establishment of a smaller War Cabinet, composed of men who are free from departmental duties. The most notable change is the inclusion of Sir Stafford Cripps, recently our Ambassador in Moscow. Sir Stafford Cripps is a man of very varied talents, and is certainly *the*[3] outstanding figure in the British Socialist movement. His inclusion in the Government will probably strengthen the ties between Britain and Soviet Russia, and will make negotiations with the Indian and Chinese political leaders a good deal easier. He enjoys immense prestige in this country because of the uncompromising attitude he has always taken since the German Fascism first became a menace, and because of the success of his recent mission in Moscow. The fact that such a man, without any party machine backing him, can be put into the Government in direct response to the wishes of the common people, is a testimony to the strength of British democracy.

1. *for*] because the Dutch administration in the East Indies has been excellent—and, *crossed through, substitution handwritten*
2. Twelve warships, including USS *Peary*, were sunk.
3. *the*] an, *substitution probably in Orwell's hand*

981. 'India Next'

The Observer, 22 February 1942

On 22 February *The Observer* began a new column, 'The Forum.' This was described as 'a medium for free discussion by various writers' and was published anonymously. It seems probable that the article referred to by Orwell in his undated letter assigned to 16 February (see *972* and *972, ns. 1, 2*) is 'India Next.' David Astor wrote on 23 January 1991 that he was 'sure that "India Next" was

Orwell's first contribution to the "Observer"' because he had no power at that time to commission articles for any part of the paper other than 'The Forum.' Publication of this column lasted only a short time.

In ten of the blackest weeks in our national and imperial history[1] one piece of really good news has passed almost unnoticed by the British public. This is the treaty recently signed between Britain and Abyssinia. Though there are several criticisms that could be levelled against it, the treaty does demonstrate that Britain's claim to be fighting for international decency is justified. The Italians annexed Abyssinia after a cowardly war of aggression, and the British fought to set it free: the inference ought to be obvious enough.

And yet in Asia, given our present policy, the propaganda value of the Abyssinian treaty is doubtful, or worse than doubtful. And meanwhile the Japanese pan-Asiatic propaganda, a thin disguise for an obviously predatory purpose, makes headway all over Asia, even among people who are hardly if at all deceived by it.

So far as southern Asia is concerned, there is probably no real answer to Japanese propaganda except military victories. India, however, is a different matter, and in India it is precisely those forces that have been most hostile to us in our imperial capacity which are our potential allies against Japan and against Fascist aggression generally.

It is easy for even the most ignorant person to grasp that Indian aspirations towards independence are menaced by the Japanese advance, and in addition, nearly all of the most gifted and active among Indian intellectuals are sympathetic towards China and Soviet Russia. Yet it remains true that Japanese propaganda makes headway. What answer can we make to the Japanese cry of "Asia for the Asiatics"? Only that the Japanese claims are lies and that Japanese rule would be worse than our own. It is true, but it is not inspiring. In a positive sense we promise nothing, we hold out no picture of the future. It is hardly to be wondered at if the poorer classes argue that they could not be worse off under the Japanese than they are at present, and sections of the intelligentsia are so blinded by hatred of Britain that they are half ready to betray Russia and China.

Meanwhile India, the second greatest population centre in the world, is not effectively in the war. The number of troops raised hitherto is relatively tiny, and war production is pitiful. This would be a serious matter even if the situation can be stabilised in Asia, but with the Japanese navy in the Indian Ocean and the German armies threatening the Middle East, India becomes the centre of the war—it is hardly an exaggeration to say, the centre of the world. For a long time to come, possibly for years, it may have to act as a supply base from which men and munitions of war can be poured out in two directions, east and west.[2]

How is that huge effort to be made possible? Clearly we have got to win the enthusiasm of the peoples of India; their passive obedience is not enough. And the one sure way of arousing their enthusiasm is to convince them that Indian independence is possible if Britain wins the war, and impossible if Japan wins. We cannot do that by promises, nor by resounding phrases about liberty and democracy; we can only do it by some concrete unmistakable act of generosity, by giving something away that cannot afterwards be taken back. The Abyssinian treaty was a pointer in the right direction. It was a gesture of a kind that our enemies cannot emulate, and it can be repeated on a vaster scale in India.

The general lines of the settlement we should make in India are now clear enough. First, let India be given immediate Dominion status, with the right to secede after the war, if she so desires. Secondly, let the leaders of the principal political parties be invited at once to form a National Government, to remain in office for the duration of the war. Thirdly, let India enter into formal military alliance with Britain and the countries allied to Britain. Fourthly, let a trade agreement be drawn up for the exchange of necessary commodities and the reasonable protection of British interests, terminable some stated number of years after the end of the war.

This plan seems less Utopian now than it would have seemed a year or two ago. There are obvious difficulties in its execution—the Hindu-Moslem rivalry is the most obvious—but the menace of outside attack makes this a propitious moment for getting over them. Both China and U.S.S.R. would welcome a settlement along some such lines as these, and so would at any rate the bulk of American opinion. Our record in India is one of the easiest targets of the Isolationists. Above all, by such a settlement we should take the wind out of the sails of Axis propaganda, once and for all. By helping China and freeing India we should have appropriated "Asia for the Asiatics" to our own use and turned it from a lie into something at least approaching a reality.

We have learned from the events in Malaya—or at least that is the lesson we ought to have learned—that to concede nothing is to lose everything. The implication of the treaties with Abyssinia and Iran is that a generous act performed at the right moment can substitute genuine partnership for the inherently unsatisfactory relationship of master and servant.

1. Orwell probably had in mind the sinking of the battleships *Prince of Wales* and *Repulse* on 10 December 1941; the surrender of Hong Kong, Christmas Day, 1941; and the fall of Singapore, 15 February 1942.
2. The last two sentences of this paragraph are closely related to the second and third sentences of the penultimate paragraph of Newsletter 10, 14 February 1942; see *970*.

982. BBC Talks Booking Form, 23.2.42

Noel Sircar: 'Through Eastern Eyes,' 12-minute talk on restaurants and eating houses; recorded 20.2.42; fee £7.7s. Signed: N. H. Parratt. 'Remarks: To go out in emergency.'[1]

1 This was described on the talks booking form as 'an "ice-box" talk,' that is, a talk that could be slipped in when the scheduled talk could not be transmitted. Sircar had sent Orwell the script on 28 January; Orwell annotated his letter, 'Rec. Fri: 20.2 42. 4.45 B.5' (the studio used).

983. BBC Talks Booking Form, 24.2.42

Lady Grigg: 'We Speak to India,' 'Women Generally Speaking'; '(Present Contract expires after B'cast on Feb: 25th). To arrange and introduce special 13-minute programmes for English-speaking women in India. (Contract to run till the end of March 1942)'; broadcast Wednesdays, 4, 11, 18, 25.3.42; fee £8.8s each talk.

984. Additional Vernacular Newsletters

25–26 February 1942

W. M. Goatman, Overseas Information Officer based at Bedford College, Regent's Park, issued a widely distributed memorandum on 25 February 1942. Z. A. Bokhari, the Indian Programme Organiser, was one of those who received it. Sir Malcolm Darling, head of the Hindustani Service, wrote a sharp memorandum, which drew a rather sarcastic response from Rushbrook Williams addressed to R. A. Rendall, the Assistant Controller. It could well be that this reorganisation underlay the 'difficulty' Darling had been causing his colleagues to which reference is made in the memorandum setting up the meeting with the Secretary of State for India; see 968.

EASTERN SERVICE: (GREEN NETWORK)

From Sunday next, March 1st, (Week 10) the period 15.15–15.30 GMT in the Green Network will be allocated each day as shown below. It will be noted that these arrangements involve the introduction of weekly broadcasts in three additional languages—Gujerati, Sinhalese, and Marathi.

Sundays	Talks in Hindustani (I.P.O.)
Mondays	Gujerati Newsletter (I.P.O.)
Tuesdays	Sinhalese Newsletter (Mr. Rowan Davies)—See Below.
Wednesdays	Indian Soldiers' Messages (already transferred from the period 13.45–14.00 GMT. See my memo of February 20.) (I.P.O.)
Thursdays	Marathi Newsletter (I.P.O.)
Fridays	Indian Soldiers' Messages (already transferred from the period 13.45–14.00 GMT. See my memo of February 20.) (I.P.O.)
Saturdays	Hindustani version of Bengali and English Newsletters (I.P.O.)[1]

It will not be possible for the Sinhalese Newsletter on Tuesdays to begin on March 3rd—the starting date for this new service will be notified as soon as possible.

All the above programmes will be carried on the wavelengths:
GSG   17.79 mc/s   16.86 m. and
GRV   12.04 mc/s   24.92 m.

Darling's response, 26 February 1942, was addressed to Rushbrook Williams, with copies for the Controller, J. B. Clark, and his assistant, Rendall:

I received your memorandum of February 24 yesterday afternoon. It is apparently proposed to extend the Hindustani Service by 15 minutes of

'Talks' on Sundays at 4.15 p.m., and a 15 minute 'Hindustani version of Bengali and English news letters' on Saturdays at the same hour. I am surprised that the Eastern Services Committee has not been given an opportunity of stating its views upon a matter which would seem to fall within its scope. As Editor of the Service, I am still more surprised that I was not consulted or even told of what was impending. Both news and talks are my province and anything done under either head should, I submit, be done under my direction. What is now proposed seems to me a clear breach of the agreement reached on October 6, 1941.

If it is desired to proceed with the two Hindustani items in next week's programme, I am prepared to arrange a talk for Sunday, March 1, at 4.15 p.m., and also a weekly news review on Saturday, March 7. I was already proposing to start one on that date within our half hour, and had taken certain initial steps in this direction. This review would at least have the merit of being original.

Williams wrote this note at the bottom of his copy on the following day and sent it to Rendall:

Please see the above note. Indian Editor has never been concerned with the newsletters arranged from London: nor does the extension fall within the period for which he is responsible. He was, of course, informed of the proposed arrangement as soon as it had been cleared with you and SOPL. I think it is now a little late to cite the "agreement" of October 6 as though he were one High Contracting Party and the Eastern Service another. Can he not be informed soon that he is a part of the Service? And that the 'agreement' did not cover any programme-time except 1400–1430 GMT?

Do you desire me to suspend action until these points are cleared?

Darling's protest did not cause the introduction of the new broadcasts to be suspended. The first Gujarati Newsletter was transmitted on Monday, 2 March, and the first Marathi Newsletter on Thursday, 5 March 1942, as scheduled, according to the PasB. The first Hindustani Newsletter was broadcast on 7 March, but there were no more, and Bokhari's Hindustani broadcasts also stopped in mid-April.

1. For the Hindustani version of Bengali and English Newsletters, see *1011*.

985. Z. A. Bokhari to Shridhar Telkar

25 February 1942   PP/ZAB/MB

My dear Telkar,
This is in continuation of my letter dated the 20th February.

We have now been able to arrange for a weekly News Letter in Marathi.[1] It will start on Thursday, 5th March and the broadcast will go on the air from a Studio at Broadcasting House from 4.15 to 4.30 p.m. BST. Eric Blair will have the English version ready for translation by 10.0 a.m. on Thursday, the 5th March, at 55, Portland Place, W.1., where you will be able to translate it. The Studio will be free for rehearsal before the actual

broadcast, from 3.45 to 4.15 p.m. We are asking the Contract Dept. to get
into touch with you immediately.

Yours sincerely,
[Initialled] Z. A. Bokhari
Indian Programme Organiser

1. For Orwell's comment on the writing of the newsletter in Marathi, see 892.

986. BBC Talks Booking Form, 25.2.42

R. R. Desai: Gujarati News, 1; '(English version written by E. Blair—Indian
Section). Translated and read by R. R. Desai'; broadcast 2.3.42; fee £5.5s + £1.14s
expenses + rail fare from Aberystwyth.¹ Signed: Z. A. Bokhari.

1. R. R. Desai, a postgraduate student at Cambridge whose department had been evacuated to
Aberystwyth, had been approached by Bokhari on 18 November 1941 about doing some
work for the Indian Section. He translated forty-two English versions by Orwell, recast two
more, and travelled down from Aberystwyth each Sunday night to read them. Later he wrote
the newsletters himself. PasB states that the translations were made by R. R. and H. L. Desai
(who lived in London); see 1045, n. 1. On 3 March, Bokhari asked Desai to return the Gujarati
text because it had to be filed with Orwell's English original. For the spelling of Gujarati, see
846, n. 17.

987. BBC Talks Booking Form, 25.2.42

S. M. Telkar: Marathi News Letter, 1; '(Written by E. Blair—Indian Section
Staff). Translated and read by S. M. Telkar'; broadcast 5.3.42; fee £5.5s (to cover
translating and reading). Signed: Z. A. Bokhari.

988. BBC Talks Booking Form, 26.2.42

Cedric Dover: 'Through Eastern Eyes,' 'Today & Yesterday,' on the Federal
Idea; broadcast 4.3.42; fee £7.7s. Signed: N. H. Parratt.

989. To Mulk Raj Anand

27 February 1942   PP/EB

Dear Anand,

I wonder if you would like to do a series of talks on Sundays, which would
mean recording the talks normally on Fridays? I recently wrote myself two
talks explaining what is meant by scorched earth and by sabotage, and it
afterwards occurred to me that as we have about five Sundays vacant, we
might have a series, discussing similar phrases which have passed into general

usage in the last year or two, and are flung to and fro in newspaper articles, broadcasts and so forth, without necessarily being well understood.

I would like you, if you would, to do these talks, starting with one on the phrase Fifth Column, and following up with talks discussing propaganda, living space, new order, pluto-democracy, racialism, and so on. I am sending you as a sort of guidance copies of the first two talks I did. You will see from these that our idea is to make these catch-phrases more intelligible, and at the same time, of course, to do a bit of anti-Fascist propaganda. Could you let me know pretty soon whether this would interest you?

Yours
Eric Blair
Talks Assistant
Indian Section

990. To Arthur Calder-Marshall

[27 February 1942]   Manuscript annotation

Calder-Marshall wrote to Orwell on 26 February 1942 to tell him that the Ministry of Information (for whom he was working) had given permission for him to broadcast to India 'with full fee.' He asked for the date of the broadcast and promised the talk ten days in advance of its delivery.

Orwell annotated this:

Please send him a card informing him of the date. E. A. B

To the left, in pencil, but probably not in Orwell's hand, is the date 'April 14th.'

991. To Cyril Connolly

27 February 1942   PP/EB

Dear Connolly,

I want your talk to be delivered on March 31st, which means that I should have the script *not later than March 21st*. You might let me know if you intend to modify the scope of it in any way, but I think we might as well stick to The Thirties for the title, as it is a good catch title,° and we have already publicised it.

Yours,
Eric Blair
Talks Assistant
Indian Section

992. Newsletter, 12

28 February 1942

The typescript is a fair copy with slight alterations, seemingly in Orwell's hand. There are no censors' stamps and the script has 'AS BROADCAST' typed at its head. PasB has 'Weekly News Review. Written by Eric Blair. Read by Z. A. Bokhari.' The timing is given as 10½ minutes.

During the last week not much has happened in the narrow military sense.

In Burma, the Japanese have advanced somewhat, and Rangoon is definitely in danger. On the other hand, in the air fighting, the British and American pilots defending Rangoon have had the better of it, and the Japanese have lost a large number of planes. The Japanese are now in possession of the whole of the island of Sumatra, and have got a footing on the island of Bali. From these two bases they are in a position to launch a full-scale attack on Java, which is the main stronghold of the Allies[1] in the Far East. As yet, however, they have not been able to attack Java except by air, because the ships in which they hoped to make the invasion have been roughly handled by Dutch and American planes and warships, and a considerable number have been sunk. Probably a Japanese landing on Java cannot be prevented, but from what has happened already it is clear that they are going to lose very heavily, probably more heavily than they can afford.

It cannot be repeated too often that this war turns principally upon the question of supplies, and though the Japanese have won great victories and inflicted great damage on their adversaries, it is doubtful whether they have yet gained much in a material sense. They have certainly gained rubber, tin ore, and territories from which, at least in the future, they may be able to obtain rice; but on the other hand, they have lost a great deal of shipping which they will have difficulty in replacing, and it is doubtful whether they have gained much of their most pressing necessity—oil. In their attack on Palembang in Sumatra, which is by far the richest oilfield in the Far East, the Japanese were so anxious to capture it intact that they tried to do so by means of a surprise attack with parachutists. This failed, however, and though Palembang was ultimately taken, we know now that the Dutch destroyed both the oil wells, and the surface plant, in a most thorough and ruthless manner. The next greatest oilfields of the Far East, those of Burma, are now similarly menaced. If, however, it becomes clear that Rangoon must fall, the oil refineries, which are at Syriam—a few miles from Rangoon—will be blown up, and probably the pipe line which brings oil from Yenangyaung, 400 miles away, will be destroyed as well. If this scorched earth policy is carried out with sufficient thoroughness, their gains will be of no benefit to the Japanese for at least a year, for even where they are able to extract the crude oil from the earth, it is of little value if the refineries have been destroyed. In that case, they can only make use of it by transporting it to their own refineries in Japan, which puts an extra strain on their inadequate shipping, and in any case exposes them to submarine attack on the way home.

We ought not to regard the destruction of the Far Eastern oilfields as pure gain for the Allies, since it means that they, as well as the Japanese, are deprived of the much-needed oil. Both India and China rely on the oil from Burma wells, and the loss of these imposes, or will impose, serious transport difficulties on the Allies. Nevertheless, it remains true that the Allies possess enormous stocks of oil in places, chiefly the United States, which are safe from enemy attack, whereas the Fascist powers cannot solve their oil problem, except by conquest. While we watch the more dramatic events that are happening in Asia, we ought never to forget that the real issue of the war turns upon the German effort to reach the oil wells of the Caucasus. Hitherto, they have failed. If they succeed in their spring offensive the end cannot be foreseen. If they fail again, it is very doubtful whether they will have enough oil to continue the war much longer, and once Germany is defeated, Japan does not present an equally serious problem. Germany, therefore, is the main enemy, and although it may often seem that more is happening in the Far East, it is the struggle on the Russian front and in the Atlantic Ocean that *will in the long run prove serious*.[2]

Although events in a military sense have not moved so rapidly this week as in the preceding weeks, there have been political developments of the highest importance. The British Government has been almost entirely re-fashioned,[3] and though the results of this will not be altogether clear until after the debates which are to take place in Parliament next week, we can already see in general outline the changes which are likely to follow. The chief event has been the entry into the Government of Sir Stafford Cripps, late Ambassador in Moscow. [It can be taken for granted that Sir Stafford would not have accepted office without being certain that large political changes were contemplated, both in Britain's home and foreign policy.][4] In his first speech in his new post, he has already forecast a tightening up of social legislation, which will have the effect of suppressing many useless luxuries, and in general making the way of life of all classes in Great Britain more equal. It is also known that the relationship between Great Britain and India is to be debated in Parliament next week, and it can be taken for granted that that relationship is *the subject of most earnest discussion*.[5] Public opinion in this country is very anxious for a solution of the Indian political deadlock, and equally anxious to see India a willing and active Ally of Britain against the Fascist powers. This popular feeling has crystallised around Sir Stafford Cripps, whose enlightened views on India are well known, and though it is too early to anticipate, it is at least certain that some far-reaching and statesmanlike offer to India will be made in the near future.

Simultaneously with these political changes in Britain, there occurred on March 24th the anniversary of the Red Army, which was the occasion of a speech by Premier Stalin, in which he reviewed the war situation, and also made what amounted to a statement on policy. Considering the atrocious manner in which the Germans have behaved in their invasion of Russia, the speech was notable for its lack of vindictiveness and for the wise and large-minded way in which it distinguished between the German people and their rulers. Stalin ridiculed the lies put about by the German propagandists, to the effect that the Russians aim at exterminating the German race, and at dominating the whole of Europe and imposing Communism upon it by force. He used the memorable phrase—"Hitlers come and Hitlers go, but the German people and the German state remain"—and[6] he made it quite clear that the Russian state would be glad to live in amity with a democratic Germany, which was prepared to leave its neighbours in peace; but he made it equally clear that there was no chance of this happening while the Nazi party and the clique surrounding Hitler remain in power.

The Japanese have made their first attack on the Andaman Islands, in the Indian Ocean south west of Burma, two bombing raids having taken place there recently. This development, which we foretold in our earlier news commentaries, is part of the Japanese attempt to extend their control step by step across the Indian Ocean and thus blockade the main ports of India. No doubt they are also contemplating attacks on Ceylon, on the various small islands in the southern part of the Indian Ocean, and on Madagascar. But they would have to establish naval and air bases in Rangoon and the Andamans before they could venture so far afield as this.

1. The use of the word 'Allies' presented problems. There were doubts in Britain about describing Russia and China as Allies, because there were no treaties of alliance with either. However, 'the Allies' came to be used regularly in Britain in general speech, commentaries, and news bulletins to include both those countries. For the United States there were more serious difficulties in the use of 'Ally.' H. R. Cummings, Editorial Liaison Officer and Deputy Foreign Adviser to the BBC, explained in a memorandum of 25 February 1942, that 'United Nations' must be used when references included the United States: 'There are traditional and constitutional difficulties which prevent the United States Government from regarding themselves as allied to any other Governments, and it was for this reason that President Roosevelt selected the term "United Nations." Therefore the term "Ally" should not be specifically applied to the United States of America.'
2. *will in the long run prove serious*] *handwritten substitution for* really matters
3. Clement Attlee transferred from Lord Privy Seal to Deputy Prime Minister and Secretary of State for Dominion Affairs; Sir Stafford Cripps replaced him as Lord Privy Seal and also became Leader of the House of Commons; Sir John Anderson was now Lord President of the Council; and Oliver Lyttelton was Minister of Production in place of Lord Beaverbrook (who had the title Minister of Supply). For Churchill's account, see *The Second World War*, IV, 65–80; U.S.: *The Hinge of Fate*, 74–91.
4. It can be taken for granted . . . foreign policy] *underlined, not crossed out*
5. *the subject of most earnest discussion*] *handwritten substitution for* about to undergo a great change
6. . . . remain—and] . . . remain. and *in typescript*

993. To C. H. Waddington

28 February 1942   PP/EB

Dear Dr. Waddington,[1]

I wonder whether you would be interested in doing a talk for us in a series which is beginning shortly, and is aimed chiefly at the English-speaking Indian population. These are a series of talks on contemporary literature, and we want the third in the series to be about the influence of science on literature during recent times. You could take very much your own line, and say whatever you thought about it, provided that it is more or less within the scope of the series, i.e. provided that it deals mainly with the English literature of the last twenty years. These are half-hour talks, that is, taking not more than 28 minutes; and with a talk of that length it is better to break it up in some way, either by fairly frequent quotations, or, if you preferred, you could do it in the form of a discussion with somebody else. Do you think you could be kind enough to let me know fairly soon whether this would interest you?

Yours sincerely,
George Orwell
Talks Assistant
Indian Section.

1. Dr. Conrad Hal Waddington (1905–1975; CBE, 1958) was at this time Lecturer in Zoology and Embryology, Strangeways Research Laboratory, Cambridge, and from 1947 Buchanan Professor of Animal Genetics, University of Edinburgh. He undertook operational research for Coastal Command, RAF, 1942–45, and was Scientific Adviser to its C-in-C, 1944–45. His recent publications included *Introduction to Modern Genetics* (1939) and *The Scientific Attitude* (1941). He edited *Science and Ethics*, 1942. For his relationship with Professors J. D. Bernal and Joseph Needham in the Theoretical Biology Club, and for his reaction to Lysenko's genetic theories, see Gary Werskey, *The Visible Collage* (1978), 206–07, 296–98.

994. BBC Talks Booking Form, 28.2.42

Lilla Erulkar: 'Through Eastern Eyes,' 'The Man in the Street,' film acting; broadcast 6.3.42; fee £7.7s. Signed: N. H. Parratt.[1]

1. This talk was booked by Orwell but it may have been initiated by Venu Chitale. On 4 February 1942, she wrote to Erulkar 'to confirm our conversation . . . when you promised to write a talk on the cinema for our series . . . "The Man in the Street."'

995. Gujarati Newsletter, 1

2 March 1942

PasB states: 'First Newsletter in Gujerati:° read live by R. R. Desai of Aberystwyth. Translated by R. R. Desai of Aberystwyth and H. L. Desai of London. 14'00".' No script has been traced.

The talks booking forms for Gujarati Newsletters specify Orwell as the writer of the English versions, though in the minimum information given for those that follow it must be assumed that he did. R. R. Desai (see *986, n. 1*) did most of the translations, assisted initially by H. L. Desai, and read them live. Orwell wrote forty-four newsletters for this service. The last two, for 21 and 28.12.42, were recast by Desai as a training exercise and thereafter he was responsible for writing and transmitting this newsletter. No texts have been traced in either English or Gujarati. For a brief discussion on the possible similarity of or differences between vernacular and English-language newsletters, see *892*.

The time allowed for all newsletters, whether in English or vernacular languages, broadcast in the Eastern Service was fifteen minutes. With allowance for announcements, the maximum time for a newsletter was fourteen minutes. PasB often give timings for the English News Review to India, and the scripts for them often give timings, sometimes in Orwell's hand. The Gujarati, Marathi, and Bengali Newsletters are also often timed (no scripts survive apart from two Marathi extracts in English). Timings are never found for the English-language broadcasts to Malaya and Indonesia, nor for the Tamil Newsletter. Orwell was associated with both groups, so the difference in recording timings may derive from the contrasting approaches of Bokhari, who supervised the first group, and Rowan Davies, who was in charge of the second group.

These timings are of interest in that they can provide clues as to whether Orwell wrote different scripts for different language versions or whether he simply made use, so far as relevance allowed, of a single weekly script. Laurence Brander, then Intelligence Officer, thought Orwell would have written differently for free and occupied countries; (see *892: 1276* indicates he did so). Speed of delivery differs from person to person, and expressing the same thoughts in different languages is even more variable. M. R. Kothari read the three Marathi Newsletters; Desai, the Gujarati Newsletters; Das Gupta, the Bengali; the News Review to India was delivered by Bokhari until the end of July 1942 and by various speakers from then until 21 November 1942, when Orwell took over. A comparison of timings from 14 March 1942 to 13 February 1943, covering English, Gujarati (broadcast two days later), Marathi (two days earlier), and Bengali (same day), sets out the evidence. There is, perhaps, sufficient variation to suggest that although portions of text were probably reused as they stood, and other passages were recast, there was also specific writing for particular audiences, even for the Bengali Newsletters broadcast on the same day as the English. Although it is possible that the vernacular translations did not include all the English text, part of the system Orwell operated involved back-checking the vernacular versions and significant differences over a period would have been spotted. There is nothing to indicate that less than his complete texts were translated.

Date	Weekly News Review in English Timing in minutes	Gujarati Newsletter (two days later) Timing in minutes	Marathi Newsletter (two days earlier) Timing in minutes	Bengali Newsletter (same day) Timing in minutes
14.3.42	10½	12½		
18.4.42	10½	13		
25.4.42	13½	13		
2.5.42	14	11		
9.5.42	13′45″	13		
30 5.42	13½	11		
27 6.42	13½	9′25″		
18 7.42	13½	11		
25.7 42	13½	12′10″	13	
29.8.42	11	9′45″	14	
5 9.42	13′18″	10	12½	13
26.9 42	11	9′40″		11′4″
3 10.42	11′38″	approx. 11		12′20″
24.10.42	13′7″	approx. 12		13′32″

31.10 42	11'20"	10'35"	
7.11.42	9'22"	approx. 10	
28 11 42	12'15"	9	8'30" (?)
12.12.42	13	11'5"	
19 12 42	12'5" (or 12'50")	8'35"	9'20" (+ 1½ mins for women)
26 12 42	13'8" (or 13½)	11'2"	
2.1 43	6¼ (shortened)	10½	7'47"
9.1 43	12'50"		11'4"
16 1 43	13(?)		9
13 2.43	13½		13½

996. To Mulk Raj Anand

2 March 1942   Handwritten draft for postcard

Anand replied to Orwell's letter to him of 27 February (see *989*) on 1 March 1942. He proposed a talk on the phrase 'Fifth Column' and asked how long it took to censor talks. On the verso, Orwell wrote this reply; the date is in another hand:

Draft for pc—
Thanks for yours. So glad you will do the series. Scripts can be censored the day they are broadcast if necessary [bu]t naturally we like them a few days in advance. If you could habitually let me have these talks (which are for Sundays) on Wednesdays it would do.

Yours
E. A. B

997. Z. A. Bokhari to Mrs. Hunt, Empire Executive's Office

3 March 1942

Bokhari wrote to express anxiety that Orwell's secretary was to be assigned for three days a week to William Empson. Orwell had evidently expressed willingness to type his own letters, and Bokhari commented, 'It was extremely gallant of Blair and I know that he could type his letters, provided we don't mind the mistakes!' It was not the typing errors that worried him; it was the weight of work 'entrusted to Blair—Contracts, Studio Bookings and all the other things that are necessary.' If Orwell loses a full-time secretary, Bokhari said, 'I should think twice before I accept the responsibility for the smooth-running of his office.'

This internal memorandum is marked 'Answered by telephone 10.2.42.'

998. Marathi Newsletter, 1

5 March 1942

The English original was written by Orwell and was translated and read by Shridhar Telkar. No script has been traced.

Orwell is credited with fifteen English versions of Marathi Newsletters in this edition; see *892*. One of these, the third, is less certain than the others, which are credited to Orwell on talks booking forms. Extracts from Newsletters 2 and 3 have survived in their English form; see *1019* and *1041*. Newsletter 20 is misnumbered 21, and this error continues to 26 (given as 27). Correct numbering is restored with the second use of 27, 3 September 1942. Venu Chitale seems to have taken over preparing the English versions of this series, but Orwell may have continued to oversee their production. For further information on newsletters, see *892*.

999. To Princess Indira of Kapurthala

5 March 1942   PP/EB/NP

Dear Princess Indira,

I wonder whether you would care to do [us] another talk, as well as "The Debate Continues"? The talk I should very much like you to do, if you have time, is one in our series "Changing Britain", on Clothes. This series deals with the social changes brought about by the war, and a variety of subjects have already been dealt with—from Taxation to Popular Literature.

Perhaps you will let me know, when we meet on Monday, whether you will undertake this talk for me, and if there is anything more that you want to know we can discuss it then. The date of the talk is March 25th, and the script should reach me before March 18th.

Yours sincerely,
Eric Blair
Talks Assistant
Indian Section

1000. To Stephen Spender

5 March 1942   PP/EB

Dear Stephen,

This is to confirm my telephone conversation with you. The talk is to be called "Poetry and Traditionalism", and to take anything up to 28 minutes. It is due to be delivered on March 17th, which means that I want this script by the 14th at the latest. I don't, of course, want to dictate what you will say, but I will just give you a line on the scope of the whole series. These talks are supposed to cover English literature in the period between the two wars, and I want you to discuss the movement which started with Eliot and others about the middle of the last war. I have [given] the talk that title because it seems to me that poetry from Eliot onwards has been actually more in touch with the poetry of the past and with European literature than English poetry from the Romantic Revival up to 1914 had been. Of course, you must say whatever you feel about it. No doubt you will have to mention the younger poets who have come up in the last three or four years, some of whom you were discussing in your last essay in Horizon;[1] but I don't want you to give much space to them because I am getting Herbert Read to do a talk specifically on the literature subsequent to the Auden group, perhaps to be called Surrealism or something like that.

Yours,
Eric Blair
Talks Assistant
Indian Section

1. 'Poetry in 1941,' *Horizon*, February 1942.

1001. BBC Talks Booking Form, 5.3.42

Mulk Raj Anand: 'Through Eastern Eyes,' 'New Weapons of War,' 1–4: 1. Fifth Column, 2. Living Space, 3. Propaganda, 4. New Order; broadcast 15, 22, 29.3.42 and 5.4.42; fee £7.7s each talk. (There was a contract for a fifth later.)

1002. BBC Talks Booking Form, 5.3.42

Princess Indira of Kapurthala: 'Through Eastern Eyes,' 'The Debate Continues'; broadcast 9.3.42; fee £7.7s.

1003. BBC Talks Booking Form, 5.3.42

Mrs. Sujata Khanna: 'Through Eastern Eyes,' 'The Man in the Street,' the Red Cross; broadcast 20.3.42; fee £7.7s.

1004. BBC Talks Booking Form, 5.3.42

S. M. Telkar: 'Through Eastern Eyes,' 'These Names Will Live,' General Sikorski;[1] broadcast 24.3.42; fee £7.7s.

1. After the fall of Poland, General Wladyslaw Sikorski (1881–1943) led the Polish government-in-exile, 1939–43, having been Prime Minister, 1922–23, and Minister of War, 1924–25. He asked the International Red Cross to investigate the massacre of Polish officers at Katyn (April 1940), which caused Stalin to break off Soviet-Polish diplomatic relations in 1943. Sikorski

died in a plane crash near Gibraltar. For Orwell's attempt to reveal the massacre of Polish prisoners, see *2919, n. 1*.

1005. To J. D. Bernal

6 March 1942   PP/EB/NP

Dear Professor Bernal,[1]

I wonder if you would consider doing a series of six half-hour talks for me in [the] Eastern Service? These talks are aimed mainly at the English-speaking Indian population in India. What I had thought of was a sort of history of the rise of modern Science from the end of the Middle Ages onwards, and then followed by a discussion of the future of science and the position of the scientific worker under Capitalism, Fascism and Socialism. I have roughly sketched out the series of talks, but don't, of course, want to tie you down in any way. I would like to know first whether it would interest you to go further in the matter.

Should you agree, the first of the talks would be due about the end of May. If you do not agree to undertake this, or haven't time to do so, I wonder if you could let me know of somebody else who you think would be interested?

Yours sincerely,
George Orwell
Talks Assistant
Indian Section

1. John Desmond Bernal (1901–1971) was Professor of Physics, University of London, 1938–63, and of Crystallography, 1963–68. Among his publications were *The Social Function of Science* (1939; revised, 1967), *Disarmament* (1952), *Marx and Science* (1952), *Science in History* (1954, in 4 vols.; revised, 1969). He was a Marxist. Orwell's Editorial in *Polemic*, No. 3, May 1946 (see *2988*), attacks him, for 'in effect claiming that almost any moral standard can and should be scrapped when political expediency demands it,' but in 1942 Orwell's attitude to Bernal was unformed. Bernal was often referred to as 'Sage,' hence, *Sage: A Life of J. D. Bernal* by Maurice Goldsmith (1980). For those associated with Bernal whom he introduced to Orwell to give talks to India (among them, Needham, Crowther, Farrington), and for his links with Soviet Russia, see Gary Werskey, *The Visible College* (1978, specifically 267). Werskey devotes much attention to Bernal's career, politics, and social thought, and quotes J. G. Crowther's statement that British scientists considered Bernal to be the British scientist who had done most to win the war, a view confirmed by the award by the United States of its Medal of Freedom in 1945 (266).

1006. To Herbert Read

6 March 1942   PP/EB/NP

Dear Read,

I wonder if you would like to do one more literary talk for us, to be delivered on April 7th? Following on the series "Masterpieces of English Literature" which you introduced, I am having one on contemporary English literature, to be called "Literature Between Wars". I want you, if you would, to deal with the new movement which has arisen in the last few years, starting I suppose with Dylan Thomas and George Barker. There is quite a group of young writers centering round the Apocalyptic movement who I think would make material for an interesting talk. I had tentatively named your talk Surrealism, but if you think that this term cannot be strictly applied to literature, we can easily change it. These are half-hour talks as before, i.e. anything up to 28 minutes, and the more you can break up the talk with quotations the better. I wonder if you could let me know about this fairly soon?[1]

Yours sincerely,
Eric Blair
Talks Assistant
Indian Section

1. Read replied on 8 March saying he would gladly do a talk on 'the younger poets.' He also said, 'I thought your Kipling essay excellent—by far the best thing that has been written on him.'

1007. To C. H. Waddington

6 March 1942   Handwritten draft and typewritten versions[1]   PP/EB

Dear Mr.° Waddington,
Thank you very much for your letter of March 5th, I am delighted that you will be able to do this talk for us. We want it to be delivered on March 24th, and it would do if the script reached me by[2] March 22nd. Judging by what you have said about your arrangements, this would give you five or six days in which to write it. Do you think you could manage this? Perhaps you could let me know as soon as possible if this date will be convenient to you.[3]

I shall get in touch with our Contracts Department, who will make the usual arrangements about your fee.[4]

Yours sincerely,
George Orwell
Talks Assistant
Indian Section
Dictated by George Orwell and
dispatched in his absence by:[5]

1. The typed version is reproduced here. The draft omits the first sentence; other variants are given below.
2. by] not later than in draft
3. if this date will be convenient to you] as otherwise I shall have to arrange with someone else in draft
4. I shall get in touch . . . your fee] I am not supposed to make any arrangements about payment, but you can take it that the BBC will pay you at about the usual rate in draft
5. Probably Nancy Parratt.

1008. BBC Talks Booking Form, 6.3.42

R. R. Desai: Gujarati Newsletter, 2; translated and read by R. R. Desai in conjunction with H. L. Desai;[1] broadcast 9.3.42; fee £5.5s. Signed: Z. A. Bokhari.

1. There is no doubt that the English version of this newsletter was written by Orwell, although the first four words of 'English version written by E. Blair' have been crossed out and 'in conjunction with Mr H. L. Desai' written above. This does not make sense; it was probably intended that those words should be added to 'Translated & read by R. R. Desai.'

1009. BBC Talks Booking Form, 6.3.42

S. M. Telkar: Marathi Newsletter, 2; written by E. Blair, 'translated and read by S. M. Telkar—helped by Miss V. Chitale'; broadcast 12.3.42; fee £5.5s. Signed: Z. A. Bokhari.[1]

1. According to PasB, Telkar translated and Chitale read this newsletter. Only a minimum of information from talks booking forms for Marathi and Gujarati Newsletters for which Orwell is believed to have written the English originals is reproduced from here on.

1010. News Review, 13

7 March 1942

PasB states that this News Review was written by Eric Blair and read by Z. A. Bokhari. It gives the timing as 10½ minutes. The typescript is a fair copy with two or three words x-ed through; and 'main' and 'bad' have been added in Orwell's hand. There are no censors' stamps, but one passage has been crossed through and marked off by brackets. At the top of the first page, 'AS BROADCAST' has been typed. This broadcast is omitted silently from West: *Commentaries*. This and later typescripts regularly have 'Macarthur,' corrected in this edition.

During this week, fighting has continued in the same areas as before, but in the Eastern hemisphere the situation has worsened somewhat.

In spite of their heavy losses at sea,[1] the Japanese have succeeded in landing more troops on Java, and the defenders are heavily outnumbered in men—and more important—in aeroplanes. The Japanese are striving to establish themselves across the middle of the island and thus cut the defenders into two separate bodies. They may succeed, and in any case, it is doubtful whether Java can hold out indefinitely in the absence of air reinforcements, which are difficult to send to that area, and which may be more urgently needed elsewhere. But the Dutch, Javanese, and other Allied troops on the island can be counted on to continue fighting bravely, and to cause serious delay in the Japanese time table. From the announcement which has been made by the Dutch Commander-in-Chief, it appears that at need the Allied troops will take up some strong defensive position in the mountainous part of the island, and there keep up a delaying action similar to the heroic stand which is being made by General MacArthur in the Phillipines.° It is now well over two months since the American and Philippine forces were driven out of Manila, and at that time it appeared to the world that the Philippine campaign was as good as over; yet the defence is still going on, and recently General MacArthur has even succeeded in using his tiny air force for offensive operations and sinking a number of Japanese ships. If a similar resistance can be kept up in Java, large numbers of Japanese troops will be tied up, and unable to take part in the invasions which the Japanese are planning further afield.

In Burma, the situation remains as it was a week ago, but the defences are being strengthened in order to inflict the most inconvenient losses to the enemy.

The news from Russia remains good, as it has been for a number of weeks past. Not only are the Russians attacking vigorously everywhere, but in the North not far from Leningrad they appear to have encircled an entire German army, which has little or no chance of escape.[2] At present the Russian winter is just nearing its end, and in the south the snow is beginning to melt. After that, there will be a period of some weeks during which military operations will be almost impossible because of the mud, but in the late spring, probably about May, the Germans will begin the great offensive for which they have been piling up arms the whole winter, and which they hope will be the last. It is uncertain yet whether the *main* German drive will be in Southern Russia towards the Caucasus or through Egypt towards the Middle East, or possibly through Turkey: but in any case their objective remains the same—to reach the shores of the Indian Ocean and the oil fields of Baku, Iran and Iraq. Every move in the Far East must be seen in conjunction with this German campaign, since the main aim of the Fascist nations is to obtain oil, and to join hands with one another. The Japanese objectives are Ceylon, Madagascar, Durban and Aden; the attacks which they may well make against Australia and the mainland of India are subsidiary to this all-important objective of establishing communications with Germany. If the Germans fail again in 1942, as they failed in 1941, to reach the oil fields, it can be taken as certain that they have lost the war, even though their leaders may succeed in disguising this from the German public for some time. It will be seen, therefore, that the Allied Government° have been right to regard the Russian front as the principal one, and to be ready even to suffer great defeats in the Far East, so as to keep our Russian Allies supplied with tanks and aeroplanes. For, dangerous though the Japanese are, the Germans are the main enemy, and Japan can be dealt with once Germany is out of the way.

For the first time British aeroplanes have raided Paris. It was one of the heaviest air-raids of the whole war, and was directed against the big Renault motor car works, which the Germans have taken over for their own use, and in which it is thought that they were turning out 300 aeroplanes a month. These factories have been almost completely wrecked, as is proved by the photographs taken from aeroplanes which returned next day for that purpose. Ever since the Armistice the British have, of course, been raiding the coastal towns which were in the possession of the Germans, but this new decision not to spare Paris probably indicates a hardening of the British and

American attitude towards the puppet Government of Vichy. There is little doubt that most of the leaders of Vichy France, as well as the French Quislings in the Occupied zone, would like to collaborate with Germany and would long ago have put the French Fleet and the French naval bases in North Africa at the disposal of the Germans, if it had not been for one thing: this is the resistance of the French common people, who are almost universally sympathetic to the Allied cause, and hostile to their foreign oppressors. Almost every day the German wireless announces from Paris fresh cases of sabotage, or the assassination of German soldiers by French civilians. The Germans impose the most atrocious penalties—for example, yesterday their wireless announced that they were going to execute 20 hostages for the murder of a single German soldier, and would follow this up by executing 20 more if the culprits were not discovered. And yet the sabotage and the assassinations never seem to grow less. [The French common people have fully grasped by this time what Fascist rule means to them, and they will go on struggling so long as the invader remains in their land. The British raid on Paris killed French civilians, as it was bound to do, but all true Frenchmen will recognize that this was better than to allow the stolen factories to continue manufacturing arms for the enslavement of the world.]

The changes in the British Government have been followed by an unmistakable change in the temper of the country. We do not yet know what proposals will be made when the British relationship with India is debated next week, but we can see already that the inclusion of Sir Stafford Cripps in the Government, and the change in the direction of the War Office are the symptoms of a more vigorous and more democratic policy. The first piece of legislation passed since the new Government, has been a very severe tightening up of the law against those who profiteer in food. These selfish people can now receive as much as 10 years imprisonment, apart from a heavy fine. The call-up is now being extended to women under 20 and to men from 18 to 45. In addition, great changes are being made in the army command, and all officers over 45 are being re-examined to see whether they are physically and mentally active enough to carry out their duties under the strain of modern war. British public opinion, as well as the Government, has been impressed by the successes won by Red Army generals who are often only in their thirties. It is felt that this is a war in which youth is all-important, and in which no kind of consideration of wealth or rank can be allowed to stand in the way of efficiency. The changes now occurring in British national life are all in this direction, and though many of the social effects of war are inevitably *bad* there is no question that the spirit and structure of British life are infinitely more democratic, and wealth is far more evenly distributed than was the case two years ago.

During the last few months, shipping losses have seriously increased. This should not be regarded as a permanent condition however,—it is due to two things: First, to the extension of the war to the Pacific, in the first few weeks of which many British ships were caught unprotected and far from their home ports, and secondly to the appearance of submarines off the coast of the United States, where a convoy system had not yet been completely established. The real object of these German submarine raids is to impress American opinion, and compel the American Government to keep its fleet in home waters, instead of using it against the Japanese. It can be taken for granted that this manoeuvre will fail, though shipping losses in the Western Atlantic may remain heavy for some months to come. Meanwhile, another large detachment of American troops has reached Britain, and many American soldiers are already to be seen in the streets of London. This draft of troops travelled across the Atlantic without any mishap and without even seeing a German submarine. We have only to reflect how nearly impossible it would be for German troops from the East, or Japanese troops from the West, to sail across the ocean and land on the shores of America, to see that effective sea control remains in the hands of the Allied Powers.

1. The losses were mainly Allied. On 27 February, two Dutch cruisers, *Java* and *De Ruyter*, one Dutch destroyer, and two British were sunk and a British and an American cruiser damaged. On 1 March, the Australian cruiser *Perth* and the American cruiser *Houston* were sunk and also one British, two American, and two Dutch destroyers. The Japanese suffered relatively minor losses, and their invasion of Java was virtually unimpeded. See Winston Churchill, *The Second World War*, IV, 129–33; U.S.: *The Hinge of Fate*, 146–50. Weekly News Review 15 (see *1044*) does admit that the Allies lost heavily in the sea battle off Java.
2. On 1 March 1942, the Second Corps of the German 16th Army was encircled southeast of Staraya Russa. After a month-long campaign, the encircled troops were united with the main German army on 21 April 1942. This is not mentioned in a newsletter.

1011. Hindustani Version of Bengali and English Newsletters
7 March 1942

This entry for a Hindustani version of the Bengali and English Newsletters appears in PasB with, immediately below it, 'Newsletter in Marathi read by Venu Chitale (Live: read by member of the staff—no contract—S. Telkar was used as a standby and assisted considerably with the translation, but it was decided that he should not broadcast it — he should receive his fee).'

W. M. Goatman, the Overseas Information Officer, had announced on 25 February 1942 that the Hindustani version would start on 7 March; see *984*. This, however, is the only entry in the PasB for such a newsletter. It might, tenuously, be added to Orwell's tally in that he wrote the original English version, but because it was given at 1515 on the same day that the Weekly News Review in English was transmitted at 1500 and the Bengali Newsletter at 1345, it is unlikely that it entailed extra work for him. That the newsletter was not again transmitted may have been a result of Darling's protests; see *968*. Certainly, the formal arrangement Goatman announced for a 'Hindustani version of Bengali and English Newsletters' ran into the ground; it looks as if Bokhari, who had already been offering a Hindustani Newsletter, changed its title to 'Talk,' if not wholly consistently, but that gradually Darling's claim to control Hindustani broadcasting was upheld.

The reference to the Marathi Newsletter is puzzling. It may simply be designed to set the record straight—that Venu Chitale read the script, mainly translated by Telkar, who had, according to a talks booking form of 25.2.42, been scheduled to translate and read it; see *987*. See also the arrangements for the second Marathi Newsletter, 12 March 1942, *1019*.

1012. 'Mood of the Moment'

The Observer, 8 March 1942

On the seven Sundays 8 March to 19 April 1942, *The Observer* published an anonymous column headed 'Mood of the Moment.' David Astor, who was then recruiting new contributors for *The Observer* (see *972, n. 1*), has identified the first and last of these columns as by Orwell. Looked at without the benefit of Astor's advice, the column for 15 March might appear to be by Orwell but it is probably by someone with a special interest in German affairs, such as Sebastian Haffner, who wrote for Astor and who contributed a book to Orwell and Fyvel's Searchlight Series, *Offensive Against Germany* (1941). It is concerned with the need for greater effort to win the war, and there is a paragraph on the same lines in the preceding day's newsletter to India (omitted from the broadcast). 'Mood of the Moment' for 22 March is about 'muddling through'; that might have appealed to Orwell in the light of his experiences at the BBC at the time, but the column does not read like his work. That for 29 March has a fair amount of detail of the war and mentions the Grantham by-election (which also appears in the relevant newsletter), but there is nothing strikingly like Orwell. The column for 5 April, on birth and death, is distinctly un-Orwellian and that for 12 April, though it picks up a phrase—'winning the peace'—which might have attracted Orwell, would surely be expected to say something about the failure of the Cripps Mission were Orwell its author. Only the columns for 8 March and 19 April are therefore included.

The British people are in a more thoughtful mood than at any time since 1940, and this time there is no bombing and—seemingly—no imminent invasion to turn their discontent outwards.

They have a feeling of frustration because of continued military defeats, they are angry about the Black Market and the muddle over production, and they are interested, for almost the first time within living memory, in the problem of India. They are anxious for Army reform and for a clearer definition of war aims—above all, anxious for the new Government to demonstrate speedily that it represents a change of policy and not merely a change of personnel.

If one had to sum up the prevailing mood in a phrase, the best would probably be, "Make Democracy Real." The concrete demands which are put forward on every side are only the symptoms of an underlying malaise. The general public are not competent to decide on details of policy, and probably they realise that they are not competent. But what they do know, or what they deeply feel, is that Britain is too much tied to the past and to an outworn social system. They feel that there is more waste, more inequality of wealth, more thwarting of intelligence, more nepotism, more privilege, than a nation which has been two years at war can afford.

The changes in the Government, and above all, the inclusion of Sir Stafford Cripps, have raised hopes which may turn out to be extravagant. Even people normally uninterested in politics feel this to be a turning-point. They are ready for the most sweeping changes and the most cruel sacrifices, if need be. Let the Government's next move be visibly in the direction of making

Democracy more real, and the mass of the people will follow without bothering too much about the hardships that lie by the way.

1013. Gujarati Newsletter, 2

9 March 1942

The English original was written by Orwell. No script has been traced.

1014. 'The Re-discovery of Europe'

'Literature Between the Wars,' 1, BBC Eastern Service, 10 March 1942

'The Re-discovery of Europe' has survived in three versions: Orwell's typescript, as broadcast to India, 10 March 1942; a slightly shortened form printed in *The Listener*, 19 March 1942; and, in full, but slightly amended, in *Talking to India*, November 1943, which Orwell prepared and saw through the press. It is this last version that is reproduced here, with an obvious error corrected and two or three of Orwell's preferred forms incorporated. Certain styling changes (such as italic for titles, which Orwell neither underlined nor enclosed within quotation marks) have been accepted silently. Significant differences between the three versions are given in the notes. The typescript is indicated by B, *The Listener* by *TL*, *Talking to India* by *TtI*. Typing errors in the typescript and slight, conventional changes to accidentals are not noted. Orwell's practice in hyphenation is followed.

The version in *The Listener* was slightly shortened, doubtless to enable it to fit the space available, paper then being in short supply. However, space was found for illustrations of Bernard Shaw, H. G. Wells, Arnold Bennett, and John Galsworthy at the head of the left-hand page, and, facing them, illustrations of D. H. Lawrence, James Joyce, T. S. Eliot, and Aldous Huxley. Beneath the first group was the caption, 'About the end of the last war the literary climate had changed—' and beneath the second, '—the typical writer came to be a quite different person.' The principal cuts in this version are given in notes. Correspondence which followed publication in *The Listener* is also given here.

PasB states that this was a talk 'by George Orwell—Eric Blair, member of the Indian Section' and gives this introduction to the series:

> Listeners to our previous series of literary talks, which were compered by Herbert Read, will remember that those talks dealt exclusively with books which have had time to become accepted as classics. In this new series we shall hear about contemporary literature, from the beginning of the last war up to the present day. The first talks will be about English literature and then we shall go on to Russian and Chinese contemporary literature. This evening George Orwell, who is arranging the whole series, is in the studio to give the first talk. He is going to tell you about "The re-discovery° of Europe."

The announcement was probably written by Orwell. No announcer's name is given.

When I was a small boy and was taught history—very badly, of course, as nearly everyone in England is—I used to think of history as a sort of long scroll with thick black lines ruled across it at intervals. Each of these lines marked the end of what was called a "period," and you were given to understand that what came afterwards was completely different from what had gone before. It was almost like a clock striking. For instance, in 1499 you were still in the Middle Ages, with knights in plate armour riding at one another with long lances, and then suddenly the clock struck 1500, and you were in something called the Renaissance, and everyone wore ruffs and doublets and was busy robbing treasure ships on the Spanish Main. There was another very thick black line drawn at the year 1700. After that it was the Eighteenth Century, and people suddenly stopped being Cavaliers and Roundheads and became extraordinarily elegant gentlemen in knee breeches and three-cornered hats. They all powdered their hair, took snuff and talked in exactly balanced sentences, which seemed all the more stilted because for some reason I didn't understand they pronounced most of their S's as F's. The whole of history was like that in my mind—a series of completely different periods changing abruptly at the end of a century, or at any rate at some sharply defined date.

Now in fact these abrupt transitions don't happen, either in politics, manners or literature. Each age lives on into the next—it must do so, because there are innumerable human lives spanning every gap. And yet there are such things as periods. We feel our own age to be deeply different from, for instance, the early Victorian period, and an eighteenth-century sceptic like Gibbon would have felt himself to be among savages if you had suddenly thrust him into the Middle Ages. Every now and again something happens—no doubt it's ultimately traceable to changes in industrial technique, though the connection isn't always obvious—and the whole spirit and tempo of life changes, and people acquire a new outlook which reflects itself in their political behaviour, their manners, their architecture, their literature and everything else. No one could write a poem like Gray's "Elegy in a Country Churchyard" today, for instance, and no one could have written Shakespeare's lyrics in the age of Gray. These things belong in different periods. And though, of course, those black lines across the page of history are an illusion, there are times when the transition is quite rapid, sometimes rapid enough for it to be possible to give it a fairly accurate date. One can say without grossly over-simplifying, "About such and such a year, such-and-such a style of literature began."[1] If I were asked for the starting-point of modern literature—and the fact that we still call it "modern" shows that this particular period isn't finished yet—I should put it at 1917, the year in which T. S. Eliot published his poem "Prufrock." At any rate that date isn't more than five years out. It is certain that about the end of the last war the literary climate changed, the typical writer came to be quite a different person,[2] and the best books of the subsequent period seemed to exist in a different world from the best books of only four or five years before.

To illustrate what I mean, I ask you to compare in your mind two poems which haven't any connection with one another, but which will do for purposes of comparison because each is entirely typical of its period.[3] Compare, for instance, one of Eliot's characteristic earlier poems with a poem of Rupert Brooke, who was, I should say, the most admired English poet in the years before 1914. Perhaps the most representative of Brooke's poems are his patriotic ones, written in the early days of the war. A good one is the sonnet beginning "If I should die, think only this of me: That there's some corner of a foreign field That is for ever England." Now read side by side with this one of Eliot's Sweeney poems; for example, "Sweeney among the Nightingales"—you know,[4] "The circles of the stormy moon Slide westward toward the River Plate." As I say, these poems have no connection in theme or anything else, but it's possible in a way to compare them, because each is representative of its own time and each seemed a good poem when it was written. The second still seems a good poem now.

Not only the technique but the whole spirit, the implied outlook on life, the intellectual paraphernalia of these poems are abysmally different. Between the young Englishman with a public school and university background, going out enthusiastically to die for his country with his head full of English lanes, wild roses and what not, and the rather jaded cosmopolitan American, getting glimpses of eternity in some slightly squalid restaurant in the Latin Quarter of Paris, there is a huge gulf. That might be only an individual difference, but the point is that you come upon rather the same kind of difference, a difference that raises the same comparisons, if you read side by side almost any two characteristic writers of the two periods. It's the same with the novelists as with the poets—Joyce, Lawrence, Huxley and Wyndham Lewis on the one side, and Wells, Bennett and Galsworthy on the other, for instance. The newer writers are immensely less prolific than the older ones, more scrupulous, more interested in technique, less optimistic, and, in general, less confident in their attitude to life. But more than that, you have all the time the feeling that their intellectual and æsthetic background is different, rather as you do when you compare a nineteenth-century French writer such as, say, Flaubert, with a nineteenth-century English writer like Dickens. The Frenchman seems enormously more sophisticated than the Englishman, though he isn't necessarily a better writer because of that. But let me go back a bit and consider what English literature was like in the days before 1914.

The giants of that time were Thomas Hardy—who, however, had stopped writing novels some time earlier—Shaw, Wells, Kipling, Bennett, Galsworthy and, somewhat different from the others—not an Englishman, remember, but a Pole who chose to write in English—Joseph Conrad. There were also A. E. Housman (The Shropshire Lad), and the various Georgian poets, Rupert Brooke and the others. There were also the innumerable comic writers, Sir James Barrie, W. W. Jacobs, Barry Pain and many others. If you read all those writers I've just mentioned, you would get a not misleading picture of the English mind before 1914. There were other literary tendencies at work, there were various Irish writers, for instance, and in a quite different vein, much nearer to our own time, there was the American novelist Henry James, but the main stream was the one I've indicated.[5] But what is the common denominator between writers who are individually as far apart as Bernard Shaw and A. E. Housman, or Thomas Hardy and H. G. Wells? I think the basic fact about nearly all English writers of that time is their complete unawareness of anything outside the contemporary English scene.

Some are better writers than others, some are politically conscious and some aren't, but they are all alike in being untouched by any European influence. This is true even of novelists like Bennett and Galsworthy, who derived in a very superficial sense from French and perhaps Russian models. All of these writers have a background of ordinary, respectable, middle-class English life, and a half-conscious belief that this kind of life will go on for ever, getting more humane and more enlightened all the time. Some of them, like Hardy and Housman, are pessimistic in outlook, but they all at least believe that what is called progress would be desirable if it were possible. Also—a thing that generally goes with lack of æsthetic sensibility—they are all uninterested in the past, at any rate the remote past. It is very rare to find in a writer of that time anything we should now regard as a sense of history. Even Thomas Hardy, when he attempts a huge poetic drama based on the Napoleonic wars—*The Dynasts*, it's called—sees it all from the angle of a patriotic school textbook. Still more, they're all æsthetically uninterested in the past. Arnold Bennett, for instance, wrote a great deal of literary criticism, and it's clear that he is almost unable to see any merit in any book earlier than the nineteenth century, and indeed hasn't much interest in any writer other than his contemporaries. To Bernard Shaw most of the past is simply a mess which ought to be swept away in the name of progress, hygiene, efficiency and what-not. H. G. Wells, though later on he was to write a history of the world, looks at the past with the same sort of surprised disgust as a civilised man contemplating a tribe of cannibals. All of these people, whether they liked their own age or not, at least thought it was better than what had gone before, and took the literary standards of their own time for granted. The basis of all Bernard Shaw's attacks on Shakespeare is really the charge—quite true, of course—that Shakespeare wasn't an enlightened member of the Fabian Society.[6] If any of these writers had been told that the writers immediately subsequent to them would hark back to the English poets of the sixteenth and seventeenth centuries, to the French poets of the mid-nineteenth century and to the philosophers of the Middle Ages, they would have thought it a kind of dilettantism.

But now look at the writers who begin to attract notice—some of them had begun writing rather earlier, of course—immediately after the last war: Joyce, Eliot, Pound, Huxley, Lawrence, Wyndham Lewis. Your first impression of them, compared with the others—this is true even of Lawrence—is that something has been punctured. To begin with, the notion of progress has gone by the board. They don't any longer[7] believe that progress happens or that it ought to happen, they don't any longer believe that men are getting better and better by having lower mortality rates, more effective birth control, better plumbing, more aeroplanes and faster motorcars. Nearly all of them are homesick for the remote past, or some period of the past, from D. H. Lawrence's ancient Etruscans onwards. All of them are politically reactionary, or at best are uninterested in politics. None of them cares twopence about the various hole-and-corner reforms which had seemed important to their predecessors, such as female suffrage, temperance reform, birth control or prevention of cruelty to animals. All of them are more friendly, or at least less hostile, towards the Christian churches than the previous generation had been.

And nearly all of them seem to be æsthetically alive in a way that hardly any English writer since the Romantic Revival had been.

Now, one can best illustrate what I have been saying by means of individual examples, that is, by comparing outstanding books of more or less comparable type in the two periods. As a first example,[8] compare H. G. Wells's short stories—there's a large number of them collected together under the title of *The Country of the Blind*—with D. H. Lawrence's short stories, such as those in *England, my England* and *The Prussian Officer*.

This isn't an unfair comparison, since each of these writers was at his best, or somewhere near his best, in the short story, and each of them was expressing a new vision of life which had a great effect on the young of his generation.[9] The ultimate subject-matter of H. G. Wells's stories is, first of all, scientific discovery, and beyond that the petty snobberies and tragicomedies of contemporary English life, especially lower-middle-class life. His basic "message," to use an expression I don't like, is that Science can solve all the ills that humanity is heir to, but that man is at present too blind to see the possibility of his own powers. The alternation between ambitious Utopian themes, and light comedy, almost in the W. W. Jacobs vein, is very marked in Wells's work. He writes about journeys to the moon and to the bottom of the sea, and also he writes about small shopkeepers dodging bankruptcy and fighting to keep their end up in the frightful snobbery of provincial towns. The connecting link is Wells's belief in Science. He is saying all the time, if only that small shopkeeper could acquire a scientific outlook, his troubles would be ended. And of course he believes that this is going to happen, probably in the quite near future. A few more million pounds for scientific research, a few more generations scientific-ally educated, a few more superstitions shovelled into the dustbin, and the job is done. Now, if you turn to Lawrence's stories, you don't find this belief in Science—rather a hostility towards it, if anything—and you don't find any marked interest in the future, certainly not in a rationalised hedonistic future of the kind that Wells deals in. You don't even find the notion that the small shopkeeper, or any of the other victims of our society, would be better off if he were better educated. What you do find is a persistent implication that man has thrown away his birthright by becoming civilised. The ultimate subject-matter of nearly all Lawrence's books is the failure of contemporary men, especially in the English-speaking countries, to live their lives intensely enough. Naturally he fixes first on their sexual lives, and it is a fact that most of Lawrence's books centre round sex. But he isn't, as is sometimes supposed, demanding more of what people call sexual liberty. He is completely disillusioned about that, and he hates the so-called sophistication of Bohemian intellectuals just as much as he hates the puritanism of the middle class. What he is saying is simply that modern men aren't fully alive, whether they fail through having too narrow standards or through not having any. Granted that they can be fully alive, he doesn't much care what social or political or economic system they live under. He takes the structure of existing society, with its class distinctions and so on, almost for granted in his stories, and doesn't show any very urgent wish to change it. All he asks is that men shall live more simply, nearer to the earth, with more sense of the magic of things like vegetation, fire, water, sex, blood, than they can in a world of celluloid and concrete where the gramophones never stop playing. He imagines—quite likely he is wrong—that savages or primitive peoples live more intensely than civilised men, and he builds up a mythical figure who is not far from being the Noble Savage over again. Finally, he projects these virtues on to the Etruscans, an ancient pre-Roman people who lived in northern Italy and about whom we don't, in fact, know anything. From the point of view of H. G. Wells all this abandonment of Science and Progress, this actual wish to revert to the primitive, is simply heresy and nonsense. And yet one must admit that whether Lawrence's view of life is true or whether it is perverted, it is at least an advance on the Science-worship of H. G. Wells or the shallow Fabian progressivism of writers like Bernard Shaw. It is an advance in the sense that it results from seeing through the other attitude and not from falling short of it. Partly that was the effect of the war of 1914–18, which succeeded in debunking both Science, Progress and civilised man. Progress had finally ended in the biggest massacre in history, Science was something that created bombing planes and poison gas, civilised[10] man, as it turned out, was ready to behave worse than any savage when the pinch came. But Lawrence's discontent with modern machine civilisation would have been the same, no doubt, if the war of 1914–18 had never happened.

Now I want to make another comparison, between James Joyce's great novel *Ulysses*, and John Galsworthy's at any rate very large novel sequence, *The Forsyte Sage*. This time it isn't a fair comparison, in effect it's a comparison between a good book and a bad one, and it also isn't quite correct chronologically, because the later parts of *The Forsyte Saga* were written in the nineteen-twenties. But the parts of it that anyone is likely to remember were written about 1910, and for my purpose the comparison is relevant, because both Joyce and Galsworthy are making efforts to cover an enormous canvas and get the spirit and social history of a whole epoch between the covers of a single book. *The Man of Property* may not seem to us *now* a very profound criticism of society, but it seemed so to its contemporaries, as you can see by what they wrote about it.[11]

Joyce wrote *Ulysses* in the seven years between 1914 and 1921, working away all through the war, to which he probably paid little or no attention, and earning a miserable living as a teacher of languages in Italy and Switzerland. He was quite ready to work seven years in poverty and complete obscurity so as to get his great book[12] onto paper. But what is it that it was so urgently important for him to express? Parts of *Ulysses* aren't very easily intelligible, but from the book as a whole you get two main impressions. The first is that Joyce is interested to the point of obsession with technique. This has been one of the main characteristics of modern literature, though more recently it has been a diminishing one. You get a parallel development in the plastic arts, painters, and even sculptors, being more and more interested in the material they work on, in the brush-marks of a picture, for instance, as against its design, let alone its subject-matter. Joyce is interested in mere words, the sounds and associations of words, even the pattern of words on the paper, in a way that wasn't the case with any of the preceding generation of writers, except to some extent the Polish-English writer, Joseph Conrad. With Joyce you are back to the conception of style, of fine writing, of[13] poetic writing, perhaps even to purple passages. A writer like Bernard Shaw, on the other hand, would have said as a matter of course that the sole use of words is to express exact meanings as shortly as possible. And apart from this technical obsession, the other main theme of *Ulysses* is the squalor, even the meaninglessness of modern life after the triumph of the machine and the collapse of religious belief. Joyce—an Irishman, remember, and it's worth noting that the best English writers during the nineteen- twenties were in many cases not Englishmen—is writing as a Catholic who has lost his faith but has retained the mental framework which he acquired in his Catholic childhood and boyhood.[14] *Ulysses*, which is a very long novel, is a description of the events of a single day, seen mostly through the eyes of an out-at-elbow Jewish commercial traveller. At the time when the book came out there was a great outcry and Joyce was accused of deliberately exploiting the sordid, but as a matter of fact, considering what everyday human life is like when you contemplate it in detail, it doesn't seem that he overdid either the squalor or the silliness of the day's events. What you do feel all through, however, is the conviction from which Joyce can't escape, that the whole of this modern world which he is describing has no meaning in it now that the teachings of the Church are no longer credible. He is yearning after the religious faith which the two or three generations preceding him had had to fight against in the name of religious liberty. But finally the main interest of the book is technical. Quite a considerable proportion of it consists of pastiche or parody— parodies of everything from the Irish legends of the Bronze Age down to contemporary newspaper reports. And one can see there that, like all the characteristic writers of his time, Joyce doesn't derive from the English nineteenth-century writers but from Europe and from the remoter past. Part of his mind is in the Bronze Age, another part in the Middle Ages, another part in the England of Elizabeth. The twentieth century, with its hygiene and its motor-cars, doesn't particularly appeal to him.

Now look again at Galsworthy's book, *The Forsyte Saga*, and you see how comparatively narrow its range is. I have said already that this isn't a fair comparison, and indeed[15] from a strictly literary point of view it's[16] a ridiculous one, but it will do as an illustration, in the sense that both books are intended to give a comprehensive picture of existing society. Well, the thing that strikes one about Galsworthy is that though he's trying to be iconoclastic, he has been utterly unable to move his mind outside the wealthy bourgeois society he is attacking. With only slight modifications he takes all its values for granted. All he conceives to be wrong is that human beings are a little too inhumane, a little too fond of money, and æsthetically not quite sensitive enough. When he sets out to depict what he conceives as the desirable type of human being, it turns out to be simply a cultivated, humanitarian version of the upper-middle-class rentier, the sort of person who in those days used to haunt picture galleries in Italy and subscribe heavily to the Society for the Prevention of Cruelty to Animals. And this fact—the fact that Galsworthy hasn't any really deep aversion to the social types he thinks he is attacking—gives you the clue to his weakness. It is, that he has no contact with anything outside contemporary English society. He may think he doesn't like it, but he is part of it. Its money and security, the ring of battleships that separated it from Europe, have been too much for him.[17] At the bottom of his heart he despises foreigners, just as much as any illiterate business man in Manchester. The feeling you have with Joyce or Eliot, or even Lawrence, that they have got the whole of human history inside their heads and can look outwards from their own place and time towards Europe and the past, isn't to be found in Galsworthy or in any characteristic English writer in the period before 1914.

Finally, one more brief comparison. Compare almost any of H. G. Wells's Utopia books, for instance *A Modern Utopia*,[18] or *The Dream*, or *Men Like Gods*, with Aldous Huxley's *Brave New World*. Again it's rather the same contrast, the contrast between the over-confident and the deflated, between the man who believes innocently in Progress and the man who happens to have been born later and has therefore lived to see that Progress, as it was conceived in the early days of the aeroplane, is just as much of a swindle as reaction.

The obvious explanation of this sharp difference between the dominant writers before and after the war of 1914–18, is the war itself. Some such development would have happened in any case as the insufficiency of modern materialistic civilisation revealed itself, but the war speeded the process, partly by showing how very shallow the veneer of civilisation is, partly by making England less prosperous and therefore less isolated. After 1918 you couldn't live in such a narrow and padded world as you did when Britannia ruled not only the waves but also the markets. One effect of the ghastly history of the last twenty years has been to make a great deal of ancient literature seem much more modern. A lot that has happened in Germany since the rise of Hitler might have come straight out of the later volumes of Gibbon's *Decline and Fall of the Roman Empire*. Recently I saw Shakespeare's *King John* acted[19]—the first time I had seen it, because it is a play which isn't acted very often. When I had read it as a boy it seemed to me archaic, something dug out of a history book and not having anything to do with our own time. Well, when I saw it acted, what with its intrigues and double- crossings, non-aggression pacts, quislings, people changing sides in the middle of a battle, and what-not, it seemed to me extraordinarily up to date. And it was rather the same thing that happened in the literary development between 1910 and 1920. The prevailing temper of the time gave a new reality to all sorts of themes which had seemed out of date and puerile when Bernard Shaw and his Fabians were—so they thought—turning the world into a sort of super garden city.[20] Themes like revenge, patriotism, exile, persecution, race hatred, religious faith, loyalty, leader-worship, suddenly seemed real again. Tamerlane and Genghis Khan seem credible figures now, and Machiavelli seems a serious thinker, as they didn't in 1910. We have got out of a backwater and back into history. I haven't an unqualified admiration for the writers of the early nineteen-twenties, the writers among whom Eliot and Joyce are the[21] chief names. Those who followed them have had to undo a great deal of what they did. Their revulsion from a shallow conception of progress drove them politically in the wrong direction, and it isn't an accident that Ezra Pound, for instance, is now shouting anti-Semitism on the Rome radio. But one must concede that their writings are more grown-up, and have a wider scope, than what went immediately before them. They broke the cultural circle in which

England had existed for something like a century. They re-established contact with Europe, and they brought back the sense of history and the possibility of tragedy. On that basis all subsequent English literature that matters twopence has rested, and the development that Eliot and the others started, back in the closing years of the last war, has not yet run its course.

The Listener published a letter from Robert Nichols[22] on 26 March 1942 about Orwell's broadcast:

May I be suffered to correct some of George Orwell's statements in 'Rediscovery of Europe'? Rupert Brooke wasn't 'the most admired English poet in the years before 1914'. He had published one book of poems. He was chiefly known in Cambridge circles and it wasn't till the publication of *1914 and other Poems* that he achieved a large admiring public. Masefield was far better known and was much admired for his narrative poems.

Mr. Orwell states that the common denominator between Shaw, Housman, Thomas Hardy and Wells is 'the basic fact' of the 'complete unawareness' of nearly all English writers 'of anything outside the contemporary English scene'. 'Complete' is good. Shaw had written two of the most brilliant books in English on Wagner and on Ibsen; he had introduced Brieux to the English, was influenced by Marx, Tolstoy and Nietzsche, was an internationally-known Socialist so little in touch with the Continent that the Belgian Government chose him to state the Belgian case to the Anglo-Saxon world. Housman was an internationally-famous classical scholar in constant touch with world scholarship. Two influences are apparent in his poetry—the poetry of the ancients and of Heine. Hardy was 'almost more frequently to be seen in a London drawing-room or Continental hotel than in the quiet lanes of rural Dorset' (p. 77, Blunden's *Thomas Hardy*). He was somewhat influenced by Schopenhauer, Hartmann and the great Russians, and more profoundly by the Greek tragedians. He was deeply interested in archæology.

It is news to me that Wells was not internationally minded before he wrote his *History, Anticipations, A Modern Utopia, When the Sleeper Wakes* seem to suggest otherwise. Mr. Orwell should read the *Autobiography*. The fact is the awareness of the Continent and of the past in these writers was of different type from the awareness of their successors. Shaw and Wells consider themselves as propagandists rather than artists (though both are capable of creating character and of writing uncommonly good English) and their international interests are social and economic—and in Wells' case scientific— rather than æsthetic, religious, anthropological and cultural.

Arnold Bennett, whom I knew tolerably well, was emphatically not 'unable to see any merit in any book earlier than the nineteenth century': see his *Literary Taste*—his reading list (from Bede onward) is the finest *short* reading list of English literature I know. He was, in point of fact, a very well read man and not only in English literature. He had taught himself Greek, Latin, French and some Italian. He lived for years in Paris, married a French wife and had a wider circle of acquaintances among French writers and painters than any Englishman I've known save Aldous Huxley. The chief influences on his work are Defoe, Balzac, the Goncourts and Zola. Incidentally most that is finest in his finest novel, *The Old Wives' Tale*, takes place in a French background, which has never been better rendered by any Englishman.

No; 'the basic fact' about these writers, as compared with their successors, is not 'their complete unawareness of anything outside the contemporary English scene' but that what they were aware of and interested in differed in kind from what has interested their successors, with whom, I may add, I have no quarrel. To every generation—I belong to Huxley's—its interests, discoveries and sovereign truths. But let us not condescend to Hardy, Bennett, Shaw, Wells—they helped to win us our liberty!—and let us be accurate when we make statements about them.

Robert Nichols

On 9 April 1942, *The Listener* published a letter from H. G. Wells (see also *1064*) and Orwell's reply to Robert Nichols:

Your contributor, George Orwell, has, I gather, been informing your readers that I belong to a despicable generation of parochially-minded writers who believed that the world would be saved from its gathering distresses by 'science'. From my very earliest book to the present time I have been reiterating that unless mankind adapted its social and political institutions to the changes invention and discovery were bringing about, mankind would be destroyed. Modesty prevents my giving you a list of titles, but I find it difficult to believe that anyone who has read *The Time Machine* (1895), *The Island of Dr. Moreau* (1896), *The Land Ironclads* (1903), *The War in the Air* (1908), *The Shape of Things to Come* (1933), *Science and the World Mind* (New Europe Publishing Company, 1942), to give only six examples of a multitude, can be guilty of these foolish generalisations.

H. G. Wells

Mr. Robert Nichols accuses me of misrepresentation because I said that most English writers in the period before 1914 were 'completely unaware' of anything outside the contemporary English scene. He seems to have taken me as meaning that these writers did not know that the continent of Europe or its literature existed. That was certainly not what I meant. I should say that the pigeons in Trafalgar Square are 'completely unaware' of the National Gallery, but I suppose that in some sense they know that the National Gallery exists. What I tried to convey was that none of the dominant English writers of that period ever ridded himself of the most ordinary insular prejudices, founded on money and a large navy, and that none of them shows any sign of being æsthetically influenced by contemporary European writers, as those who came afterwards undoubtedly were. The instances Mr. Nichols uses to refute me simply seem to me to clinch my case. Here are a few footnotes to Mr. Nichols' remarks:

Shaw: it is quite true that Shaw helped to popularise Ibsen. It is also true that he saw in him nothing except a 'great moral teacher' whose plays could be plausibly represented as Socialist tracts. As Mr. Nichols points out, Shaw also championed Brieux, a lifeless tract-writer whose *Les Avariés* (Damaged Goods) was staged in 1917 or thereabouts in hopes of frightening young soldiers about the dangers of venereal disease.[23] Should we say that a French critic who suddenly 'discovered' Upton Sinclair, while ignoring Lawrence and Eliot, showed great awareness of English literature? And what sign is there anywhere in Shaw's critical work (*vide* his attacks on Shakespeare, for example) of any standard of judgment except the politico-moral one?

Arnold Bennett: it is quite true that Arnold Bennett lived long in France and married a French wife. It is also true that he never cured himself of the condescending attitude towards France of a nineteenth-century Englishman, and a north-country Englishman at that. This is obvious all through *An Old Wives' Tale*. I am aware that he drew up lists of 'the best that has been thought and said' which contained the names of many books of the remote past. What I doubt is whether he ever cared deeply about those books. On the other hand (see his voluminous critical writings) he was ready to take the most ephemeral works of his contemporaries seriously.

Thomas Hardy: I said, and I stick to it, that the outlook implied in *The Dynasts* is that of a patriotic school textbook—an English textbook, naturally. Who would guess from Hardy's account of the Peninsular War that Spanish histories of this war do not usually mention the Duke of Wellington?

I could multiply my retorts, but it hardly seems worth while. I am sorry Mr. Nichols thinks I 'condescended' to the writers of the pre-1914 age. I much prefer that age to our own, but it had its limitations, all ultimately traceable to too much money and too much security. The literary generation that followed had been deflated by the war, and if as a result it lost in vigour it gained certain other advantages. Finally, may I remind Mr. Nichols that flattery is no part of the job of a literary critic.

George Orwell

On 16 April 1942, *The Listener* published a second letter from Nichols, to which Orwell did not respond:

Mr. Orwell is a trifle disingenuous. 'What', he asked in his original talk, 'is the common denominator between writers who are individually as far apart as Bernard Shaw and A. E. Housman, or Thomas Hardy and H. G. Wells? I think the basic fact about nearly all English writers of that time is their complete unawareness of anything outside the contemporary English scene. Some are better writers than others, some are politically conscious and some are not, but they are all alike in being untouched by any European influence. This is true even of novelists like Bennett and Galsworthy, who derived in a very superficial sense from French and perhaps Russian models'. I pointed out that some foreign cultural and æsthetic influence was apparent but stressed that 'the international interests' of Shaw and Wells 'are social and economic— and in Wells' case scientific—rather than æsthetic, religious, anthropological and cultural'. Mr. Orwell, unable to deny this fact, now shifts his ground and states *(a)* that I seem to have taken him to mean 'that these writers did not know that the continent of Europe or its literature existed'. (Certainly, that would seem a reasonable interpretation of 'the basic fact is their complete unawareness of anything outside the contemporary English scene'.) Whereas it now appears that what Mr. Orwell meant was *(b)* 'none of the dominant English writers of that period ever ridded himself of the most ordinary insular prejudices, founded on money and a large navy', and *(c)* 'that none of them shows any sign of being æsthetically influenced by contemporary European writers, as those who came afterwards undoubtedly were'.

Let us examine *(b)*. This is mighty vague but if anything is tolerably certain in this world, where black seems to be constantly mistaken for white, it is that Shaw, Wells and Galsworthy spent no small energy as Left Wingers attacking precisely those prejudices that are founded on money and imperialism. (Shaw and Wells were very active Socialists and Galsworthy's *Forsyth Saga* is one long *exposé* of the acquisitive and what-I-have-I-hold attitude. Galsworthy was anti-Imperialist and Wells and Shaw were among the *bêtes noirs*° of the Navy League.[24]) These men were in fact detested and *feared* by 'Society' and the propertied class as no contemporary of Mr. Orwell is by any class.

Now to *(c)*. Mr. Orwell, finding he cannot deny the foreign social and economic influences I referred to, slips in the word 'æsthetic'. It appears Shaw 'saw nothing in Ibsen except a great moral teacher'. Really? Had Ibsen's and Brieux's dramatic form no influence on Shaw? If so, why is that form not the form of Robertson, Sutro, Jones and Pinero?

For Bennett's so-called 'condescending attitude' toward France, I refer Mr. Orwell to the admirable, well-documented *Arnold Bennett, a Study*, by Lafourcade, p. 64. The passage begins 'He could understand, admire and assimilate the essential features of French and Latin civilisation' and continues in a similar vein. If this is 'condescension' my name is Orwell. Mr. Orwell continues, 'I doubt whether he cared deeply about those books'—the English classics listed in *Literary Taste*. Mr. Orwell ignores the rest of that book—an impassioned plea, if my eyes mistake not, for the reading of them. If my eyes deceive me, my memory of Bennett's discourse does not. The fact that 'Spanish historians of the Peninsular War do not usually mention Wellington'— really?—doesn't prove 'the outlook implied in *The Dynasts* is that of a patriotic text-book'. It rather suggests either that these historians are remarkably ill-read or very 'patriotic' in the sense Mr. Orwell deplores.

Robert Nichols

On 14 August 1942, Hsiao Ch'ien (see *919, n. 1*) wrote to Orwell congratulating him on this talk which, he said, 'simply bristles with fresh points covering a wide scope,' and remarking on H. G. Wells's apparent lack of a sense of humour.

1. When I was a small boy . . . such-and-such a style of literature began '] *omitted from TL*
2. quite a different person] a quite different person B; *TL*
3. To illustrate what I mean . . . of its period.] *omitted*
4. you know] *omitted*
5. There were other literary tendencies . . . I've indicated.] *omitted*
6. The basis of all Bernard Shaw's . . . Fabian Society] *omitted*

7. don't any longer] no longer   *TL, and again, later in the sentence*
8. Now, one can best illustrate . . . a first example,] *omitted*
9. This isn't an unfair comparison . . . of his generation.] *omitted*
10. man. Progress had finally ended in the biggest massacre in history, Science was something that created bombing planes and poisoned gas, civilised] *omitted from typescript for broadcast. Without these words the sentence does not make sense. Orwell probably jumped from the first use of 'civilised man' to the second when typing his draft. The passage is included in TL.*
11. This time it isn't a fair comparison . . . what they wrote about it] *omitted*
12. onto] on to   *TL, TtI. The one-word spelling is used in the typescript and was preferred by Orwell in certain contexts.*
13. of] or   *TtI*
14. Joyce—an Irishman . . . childhood and boyhood.] *omitted*
15. I have said already . . . indeed] *omitted*
16. it's] the comparison is   *TL*
17. Its money and security, the ring of battleships that separated it from Europe, have been too much for him.] *omitted*
18. Jacintha Buddicom recalls from her and Orwell's childhood: 'We had in our house a copy of Wells' *Modern Utopia* . . . which was so greatly fancied by Eric that it was eventually given to him' (*Eric and Us*, 39).
19. Orwell reviewed this production of *King John* in 1941 in *Time and Tide*; see *832*.
20. A lot that has happened in Germany since the rise of Hitler . . . a sort of super garden city.] *omitted*
21. the] *omitted from TtI*
22. Probably Robert M. B. Nichols (1893–1944), who was a poet, novelist, and critic. He edited *Anthology of War Poetry, 1914–1918* (1943) and contributed to newspapers and journals, including *The Times*, *The Observer*, *The New Statesman*, and *The Yale Review*.
23. *Les Avariés* by Eugène Brieux (1858–1932) was first performed in 1901. Its translation (with two other plays) was published in England with an introduction by Shaw. The play owes much to Ibsen's *Ghosts*, but it is not without its own dramatic force.
24. The Navy League was an association formed at the end of the nineteenth century to campaign for greater public awareness and support for a strong British Navy as a 'first line of defence.' Its more vociferous supporters were called 'navy-leaguers.'

1015. To Cedric Dover

10 March 1942   PP/EB/NP

Dear Dover,

This is just to confirm with you the talks that we arranged you should do for me, and the dates we fixed on.

The next talk is on 26th March, and the subject is "Race Mixture and World Peace". On the 1st April, in the series "Today & Yesterday" you will be talking on "The Problems of Cultural Expression", and on April 7th, in the series "These Names will live" your talk will be about Paul Robeson

As you know, I should like to have the script of each talk at least a week before the date of broadcast.

Yours sincerely,
Eric Blair
Talks Assistant
Indian Section.
Dictated by Eric Blair and
signed in his absence by:[1]

1. Nancy Parratt.

1016. To Herbert Read

10 March 1942   PP/EB

Dear Read,
Many thanks for your letter of March 8th. As you can't manage April 7th, I wonder whether you would care to record the talk, say on March 31st? If possible, we want to keep these talks in the present order. I hope this arrangement will be convenient for you. Perhaps you will let me know; you might also tell me if you would prefer to do it in the afternoon or the morning, and then[1] I shall make the necessary arrangements.

I agree with you about the title, and I think "The New Romantic Movement" would be much better than the one I suggested in the first place.

Yours sincerely,
Eric Blair
Talks Assistant
Indian Section

1. then] when

1017. BBC Talks Booking Form, 10.3.42

Princess Indira of Kapurthala: 'The Debate Continues'; broadcast 16, 23, 30.3.42[1] and 6.4.42;[2] fee £7.7s each talk. Signed: N. H. Parratt.

1. Owing to 'programme re-arrangements,' Princess Indira did not give the broadcast on the 30th. She had visited the Houses of Parliament and written her script, and so was paid the full fee on the understanding that were the talk to be broadcast at a later date the sum paid would be taken into account 'when fixing a further payment' (letter from Programme Contracts Director, 1 April 1942).
2. Cancelled because the House did not sit (letter from Programme Contracts Director, 10 April 1942).

1018. To C. H. Waddington

11 March 1942   PP/EB

Dear Mr. Waddington,
Thank you for your letter of March 9th. I would prefer it if you could record your talk so that we can put it out on March 24th, as we have already arranged for publicity in India.

I should be very grateful if you could let me know a date that would suit you to come to London to record your talk, perhaps a day or two before the broadcast, and I shall then make all the necessary arrangements.

Yours sincerely,
Eric Blair
Talks Assistant
Indian Section
Dictated by Eric Blair and
despatched in his absence by:[1]

1. Unidentified.

1019. Marathi Newsletter, 2

12 March 1942

The English original was written by Orwell, translated by Shridhar Telkar, and read by Venu Chitale.[1] Although the text in either English or Marathi appears not to have survived, a memorandum from Anthony Weymouth to Rushbrook Williams of 23 March gives a brief extract, with extracts from the newsletter for 19 March and that in English for India of 14 March, giving references to Sir Stafford Cripps. Marathi Newsletter, 2, included the following:

Yesterday came the news that Sir Stafford Cripps is flying to India to consult the Indian political leaders of all parties and to put before them the scheme that has been worked out by the British Government. The Government has not yet announced its plans, except to say that they are aimed at safeguarding the interests of all the parties concerned. At this stage we can say only that the people of Britain are delighted that they should be represented in India by a man of such standing, ability and integrity as Sir Stafford Cripps.

This corresponds more or less to the first three sentences of the English Weekly News Review of 14 March 1942, which Weymouth also reproduced. Since that Review has more to say about Cripps, it is possible the Marathi Newsletter reported more fully than the extract given. For the extract from Marathi Newsletter, 3, in Weymouth's memorandum, see 1041.

1. For the talks booking form for this talk, see 1009.

1020. To Hsiao Ch'ien

13 March 1942   PP/EB

Dear Mr. Hsiao,
I delayed writing to thank you for the copy you sent me of "Etching of a Tormented Age" until I should read it. It interested me very much, it also has brought home to me how complete my ignorance of[1] modern Chinese literature is. I wonder if you would agree to do two talks for us on this subject about the end of April? We are having a series of talks on contemporary

223

literature and we are starting off with six talks on English literature, followed by four on Russian and two on Chinese. I am sure you would be exactly the person to undertake the latter; they are half-hour talks, i.e. not more than about 27 minutes each, and I should want the script in each case about a week before the date of the talk. Could you let me know whether you feel ready to undertake this, and if you do, I can give you further details. In the case of your not being able to broadcast on the actual days, we can easily record the talk beforehand.

Yours sincerely,
Eric Blair
Talks Assistant
Indian Section
Dictated by Eric Blair and
despatched in his absence by:[2]

1. of] is
2. Probably, from the layout of the letter, Nancy Parratt.

1021. BBC Talks Booking Form, 13.3.42

Gujarati Newsletter, 3; English version written by E. Blair, translated and read by R. R. Desai in conjunction with H. L. Desai; broadcast 16.3.42; fee £5.5s + £4.2s.2d expenses. Signed: M. Blackburn.

1022. Weekly News Review, 14

14 March 1942

The fair-copy typescript has two long sections bracketed but not crossed out. The text is headed 'AS BROADCAST' and there is no censor's stamp. The place name Yenangyaung has its pronounciation written above it in Urdu, presumably by the reader, Bokhari. PasB has 'by Z. A. Bokhari' and gives timing as 10½ minutes. The first three sentences, to 'conduct the negotiations,' were included in Weymouth's memorandum of 23 March; see *1019*.

The most important event this week is not military but political. It is the appointment of Sir Stafford Cripps to proceed to India by air and there lay before the leaders of the Indian political parties the scheme which has been worked out by the British Government.

The Government has not yet announced what its plans are and it would be unwise to make a guess at them, but it is at least certain that no one now alive in Britain is more suited to conduct the negotiations. Sir Stafford Cripps has long been recognised as the ablest man in the British Socialist movement, and he is respected for his absolute integrity even by those who are at the opposite pole from him politically. He has had a varied career, and possesses knowledge and experience of a kind not often shared by professional politicians. During the last war he managed an explosives factory on behalf of the Government. After that, for some years he practised as a barrister, and won for himself an enormous reputation for his skill in dealing with intricate civil cases. In spite of this, he has always lived with extreme simplicity and has given away most of his earnings at the Bar to the cause of Socialism and to the support of his weekly Socialist paper, "The Tribune". He is a man of great personal austerity, a vegetarian, a teetotaller and a devout practising Christian. So simple are his manners that he is to be seen every morning having his breakfast in a cheap London eating house, among working men and office employees. In the last few years he has given up practising at the Bar in order to devote himself wholly to politics.

The outstanding thing about Sir Stafford Cripps, however, has always been his utter unwillingness to compromise his political principles. He has sometimes made mistakes, but his worst enemy has never suggested that he cared anything for money, popularity or personal power. About seven years ago, he became dis-satisfied° with the too cautious policy of the Labour Party, and founded the Socialist League, an organisation within the Labour Party, aiming at a more radical Socialist policy, and a firmer front against the Fascist aggression. Its main objectives were to form a Popular Front Government of the same type as then existed in France and Spain, and to bring Great Britain and the other peace-loving nations into closer association with Soviet Russia. This brought him into conflict with the official heads of the Labour Party, who did not at that time grasp the full menace of Fascism. Whereas a lesser man would have given way in order to keep his pre-eminent position within the Labour Party, Cripps preferred to resign, and for several years he was in a very isolated position, only a few members in the House of Commons and a small following in the country at large realising that his policy was the correct one. However, when the Churchill Government was formed in 1940, it was recognised on all sides that no one was so suitable as Sir Stafford Cripps for the British Ambassadorship in Moscow. He discharged his office brilliantly, and undoubtedly did a great deal to make possible a firm alliance between the British and the Russian peoples. Since his return to England, he has followed this up by a series of speeches and broadcasts, by which he has brought home to the ordinary people in Britain the enormous effort which their Russian allies are making, and the necessity of supporting them by every means in our power. Everyone in Britain is delighted to see such an important mission as the one which Cripps is now undertaking, conferred upon a man whom even his critics admit to be gifted, trustworthy and self-sacrificing.

The Japanese are in possession of Rangoon, and probably also of the other main port of Burma, Bassein, which lies westward of Rangoon. The British have blown up the oil refineries at Syriam, near Rangoon, so thoroughly that they will be of no use to the Japanese and they are prepared, if necessary, to destroy the oil wells at Yenangyaung so thoroughly that no one will get any oil from them for the next five years. Whatever else the Japanese may gain from Burma, they will gain nothing to satisfy their most pressing need, which is for oil; nor, so far as we know, have they acquired any worth-while quantity of oil in the Dutch East Indies.

[It is becoming clear that the Japanese are also preparing an attack upon Australia. In the first place presumably against Darwin[1] and the other air fields in the north. The main Japanese aim is to dominate the Indian Ocean, and join hands with the Germans in the Middle East, should the forthcoming German offensive be successful. But as part of this plan, they must also attack Australia, in order to prevent an Allied offensive being launched from there. We know already that huge American re-inforcements are pouring into the Western Pacific, and their destination must be either Australia or New Zealand. The Japanese are also preparing to attack Ceylon and probably the mainland of India, and are also likely to make an attempt upon Madagascar. There are also indications that they are planning a treacherous attack upon Russia of the same kind as they made upon America, to coincide with the German offensive in the west. But the Russians, however, are not likely to be taken unawares.][2]

During this week, full and well-authenticated information has been released about the behaviour of the Japanese army in Hongkong. It has been confirmed by several eye-witnesses who escaped from Hongkong and have now reached Chungking. Among other things, it is known that the Japanese declared a whole quarter of Hongkong to be a military brothel, which means that any woman in it can be raped at will by the Japanese soldiers. In Singapore, according to their own statement on the Tokio[o] radio, the Japanese have taken seventy-three thousand Chinese civilians and subjected them to what they call "severe interrogation", in plainer language, to torture. Exactly similar things happened in Nanking in 1937. We see here the real meaning behind the Japanese slogan "Asia for the Asiatics". It means "Asia for the Japanese, and slavery, impoverishment and torture for all who are unlucky enough to live under their rule."

The Chinese have made it clear that their resistance will continue as before, no matter what happens in Burma. The temporary stoppage of the Burma Road does not vitally matter, since supplies of war material can easily be carried to China in large bombing planes from India. Meanwhile news comes from Chungking that a Free Korean Army has been formed from men who have escaped from Japanese oppression in Korea, and is already fighting side by side with the armies of the Chinese republic.

On the northern sector of the Russian front the German Sixteenth Army, which has been cut off by the Russians, has failed to escape and the Russians have announced that its end is in sight. Even the German wireless now admits that the position of the Sixteenth Army is critical. Recently the Nazi propagandists reviewed their losses during the Russian war and admitted to having had one million five hundred thousand casualties in all—killed, wounded and missing.[3] Even if we believe these figures to be truthful, this means that on average the Germans have had between 5 and 6 thousand casualties *every day*[4] from the moment when the campaign began. Every single day, during the last 8 months, therefore, several thousand German families have had cause to mourn the wanton attack on the Soviet Union which their Nazi rulers have forced upon them. But, since the Germans are not in the habit of overstating their losses, we can assume that the real figures are far higher.

[The British people are disciplining themselves yet harder for the demands of total war. The penalties against those who operate the Black Market in food have been stiffened up, so that offenders can now get as much as 14 years' imprisonment. White flour is to be withdrawn from the market shortly, and only wheatmeal flour allowed. This alone will save half a million tons of shipping space every year. It is probable[5] also that the use of petrol for mere pleasure or convenience will shortly be prohibited. No one complains of these restrictions—on the contrary, the general public are demanding that the restrictions shall be made even stricter, so that the selfish minority who behave as though Britain were not at war can be dealt with once and for all.]

1. Darwin was bombed by the Japanese on 21 March 1942.
2. Not really censored (as West suggests); the body of this paragraph provided the basis for the first paragraph of the next News Review.
3. On 1 March 1942, the German Chief of Staff, General Franz Halder, announced losses of 1,500,626 men: 202,257 killed; 725,642 wounded; 112,617 severely frostbitten; 46,511 missing; and 413,609 taken prisoner (*2194 Days of War*).
4. *every day*] underlined in the typescript (*not an insertion*)
5. probable] probably *in typescript*

1023. To Mulk Raj Anand

[14 March 1942[1]]

MAY WE HAVE YOUR SCRIPT FOR RECORDING TOMORROW IMMEDIATELY.

BLAIR

1. Telegrams were not usually dated. The date given here depends upon its reference to the first of Anand's broadcasts.

1024. To C. H. Waddington

14 March 1942   PP/EB/NP

Dear Mr Waddington,[1]
Thank you for your letter of March 13th. I have arranged with our recorded programmes section for you to record your talk at 10 o'clock on Monday March 23rd, at Levy's Studio, 73, New Bond Street. As you might like to run through the script once for timing purposes, may I suggest that we meet at 9 o'clock at Broadcasting House, in the Entrance hall, and we might then have breakfast together, and run through the script afterwards. Of course, if you are coming up from Cambridge on that day, this would not be possible, so perhaps you will let me know, when you send me the script, whether this arrangement will suit you.
Yes, the talk will require about 4,000 words—the actual timing should be

anything up to 28 minutes—that leaves time for the announcements and so on.

Yours sincerely,
[Initialled] E. A. B
Eric Blair
Talks Assistant
Indian Section
Dictated by Eric Blair and
despatched in his absence by:[2]

1. The source of this letter is a carbon copy; the addressee's name has been overtyped so it is not clear, though that it is Waddington is plain from the name and address typed after the letter with the typist's initials, NP, for Nancy Parratt. The top copy was, presumably, corrected. Similar carbon-copy blemishes are corrected silently elsewhere in this edition. A different typewriter, with a small typeface, which struck 'm' and 'M' very heavily, and 'e' and 'E' far too lightly, produced this letter.
2. By Nancy Parratt Although absent when the letter was despatched, Orwell initialled the copy on his return.

1025. War-time Diary (continued)

Orwell reopened his War-time Diary on 14 March 1942. It exists in two versions: manuscript (without the heading) and typewritten, by Orwell, with the heading 'WAR DIARY (continued).' The versions differ. The manuscript contains words and passages omitted from the typescript (which notes where cuts have been made). Orwell presumably intended the slightly shorter typed version to be used for publication jointly with Inez Holden's diary (see *1326, n. 1* and *1443*). The diary was not published in Orwell's lifetime.

In this edition, sloped roman type is used for all that is common to manuscript and typewritten versions; passages appearing only in the manuscript are set in roman within square half-brackets. Where the typescript has only initials for names, but the name is given in full in the manuscript, that name is incorporated here without brackets, and a note is provided. When typing out the manuscript, Orwell made some verbal changes; in such instances, the typed version is reproduced and manuscript readings are given in the notes. Minor differences of hyphenation and punctuation are not noted; the typescript is followed. Orwell typed 'and' but usually wrote '&'; these two forms are retained. When he typed out his diary, Orwell underlined the dates. The textual notes give the typed version first; the manuscript's reading follows.

14.3.42: *I reopen this diary after an interval of about 6 months, the war being once again in a new phase.*

The actual date of Cripps's departure for India was not given out,[1] *but presumably he has gone by this time. Ordinary public opinion here seems gloomy about his departure. A frequent comment—"They've done it to get him out of the way" (which is also one of the reasons alleged on*[2] *the German wireless). This is very silly and reflects the provincialism of English people who can't grasp that India is of any importance. Better-informed people are* pessimistic because the non-publication of the Government's terms to India indicates almost certainly that they are not good terms. Impossible to discover what powers Cripps has got. Those who may know[3] will disclose nothing and one can draw hints out of them only by indirect means. Eg. I propose in my newsletters,[4] having been instructed to give Cripps a buildup,° to build him up as a political extremist. This draws the warning, "Don't go too far in that direction", which raises the presumption that the higher-ups haven't much hope of full independence being granted[5] to India.

Rumours of all descriptions flying round. Many people appear to suspect that Russia and Germany will conclude a separate peace this year. From studying the German and Russian wireless I have long come to the conclusion that the reports of Russian victories are largely phony,[6] though, of course, the campaign has not gone according to the German plan. ⌈I think the Russians have merely won the kind of victory that we did in the Battle of Britain—ie., staving off defeat for the time being but deciding nothing.⌉ I don't believe in a separate peace unless Russia is definitely knocked out, because I don't see how either Russia or Germany can agree to relinquish the Ukraine. ⌈On the other hand some people think (I had this, eg. from Abrams, a Baltic Russian of strong Stalinist sympathies though probably not a C.P. member) that if the Russians could get the Germans off their soil they would make a sort of undeclared peace and thereafter only keep up a sham fight.⌉

Rumours about Beaverbrook's departure:[7]

a. Cripps insisted on this as a condition of entering the Government.

b. Beaverbrook was got rid of because he is known to be in contact with Goering with a view to a compromise peace.

c. The army insisted on Beaverbrook's removal because he was sending all the aeroplanes etc. to Russia instead of to Libya and the Far East.

I have now been in the BBC about 6 months. Shall remain in it if the political changes I foresee come off, otherwise probably not. Its atmosphere is something half way between a girls' school and a lunatic asylum, and all we are doing at present is useless, or slightly worse than useless. Our radio strategy is even more hopeless than our military strategy. Nevertheless one rapidly becomes propaganda-minded and develops a cunning one did not previously have. Eg. I am regularly alleging in[8] my newsletters that the Japanese are plotting to attack Russia. I don't believe this to be so, but the calculation is:

a. If the Japanese do attack Russia, we can then say "I told you so".

b. If the Russians attack first, we can, having built up the picture of a Japanese plot beforehand, pretend that it was the Japanese who started it.

c. If no war breaks out at[9] all, we can claim that it is because the Japanese are too frightened of Russia.

All propaganda is lies, even when one is telling the truth. I don't think this matters so long as one knows what one is doing, and why.

⌈Current story:

An A.T.[10] stops a Home Guard: "Excuse me, but your front door is open". H.G. "Oh. And did you by any chance see a tall strong sentry guarding the door?"

A.T. "No, all I saw was an old Home Guard lying on a pair of sandbags."
On 11.3.42 I started the rumour that beer is to be rationed, and told it to 3
different people. I shall be interested to see at what date this rumour comes
back to me.¹ [*30.5.42: Never came back. So this casts no light on the
way in which rumours come into being.*]¹¹

Talked for a little while the other day to William Hickey, ¹² *just back from
the USA. He says morale there is appalling. Production is not getting under
way and anti-British feeling of all kinds is rampant, also anti-Russian feeling,
stimulated by the Catholics.*

1. Sir Stafford Cripps flew to India on 22 March, to arrange a compromise settlement with the
   Indian Congress Party, the party of Indian independence. He hoped to obtain Indian
   cooperation during the war and agreement to gradual transition to independence when it was
   over. Nehru and the Congress Party would accept nothing less than complete independence
   and the talks broke down on 10 April.
2. *on*] by
3. *know*] know something
4. See Marathi Newsletter, *1041,* and Weekly News Review, *1044.*
5. *granted*] offered
6. *phony*] phoney
7. Lord Beaverbrook (see *628, n. 11*) had, under Churchill, been Minister of Aircraft
   Production, 1940–41, and Minister of Supply, 1941–42. His contribution was controversial
   but his boundless energy inspired confidence and the supply of planes increased. See
   Newsletter, 12, *992* and *992, n. 3.*
8. *in*] in all
9. *at*] after
10. A member of the (women's) Auxiliary Territorial Serivce, later WRAC—Women's Royal
    Army Corps
11. Orwell's insertion in the manuscript version, which he placed within full square brackets.
12. 'William Hickey' wrote a social-diary column in the *Daily Express* for more than fifty years;
    it was edited by various journalists. At this time, its originator, Tom Driberg (1905–1976), a
    left-wing politician who later became a Labour M.P. (see *1931, n. 1*), was its editor. Orwell
    added a handwritten footnote to the typescript identifying 'William Hickey' as Tom Driberg.

1026. To Cedric Dover

15 March 1942   PP/EB¹

Dear Dover,
I wonder if you would care to give me a talk on Bertrand Russell, in addition
to the other talks you are doing? The date of the broadcast is May 5th, which
gives you plenty of time to get it ready. The talk should be slightly longer
than the others, as it should take about 13½ minutes—our time is being
extended after the middle of April to 15 minutes.

I should be glad if you would let me know about this as soon as possible.

Yours sincerely,
[Initialled] E. A. B
Eric Blair
Talks Assistant
Indian Section

1. Typed on the same machine as *1024*

1027. War-time Diary

15.3.42: *Short air raid alert about 11.30 this morning. No bombs or guns. The first time in 10 months that I had heard this sound. Inwardly rather frightened, and everyone else evidently the same, though studiously taking no notice[1] and indeed not referring to the fact of there being a raid on until the All Clear had sounded.*

1. notice] *followed by* of the sound *in manuscript, but crossed out*

1028. Gujarati Newsletter, 3

16 March 1942

The English original was written by Orwell. No script has been traced. PasB gives timing as 12′30″.

1029. To Cedric Dover

16 March 1942   EB/PP°

Dear Dover,

I understand from Bokhari that you will be recording your discussion with Prof. Joad on Thursday, 26th March, in the afternoon. As you know, I had arranged for your talk on Race Mixture and World Peace to be broadcast on that day, but I think the simplest way of arranging things would be for you to record it on the previous day, Wednesday March 26th,[1] if that will suit you.

I should be grateful if you would ring me up as soon as possible, and let me know about this, and then I can make the necessary arrangements. I think the afternoon would be the best time for you to record, if you have no objections.

Yours sincerely,
Eric Blair
Talks Assistant
Indian Section

On the same day, Bokhari also wrote to Dover:

I am writing on behalf of Mr. Blair. Professor Joad is prepared to discuss the various points raised by you in your script "Utopias and Federations". Subject to your convenience, we have fixed up Thursday March 26th at 3 p.m. at Broadcasting House for an informal discussion between you and Joad, and the recording of the Discussion at 3.30 p.m. at Levy's Studio, 73, New Bond Street. I hope this date and these times will suit you. I wonder if you will be good enough to send a few notes or questions to Joad beforehand. His address is:

4, East Heath Road,
N.W.3.

1. March 25th was intended.

1030. To R. U. Hingorani
16 March 1942   PP/EB

Dear Dr. Hingorani,[1]

Mr. Sahni has spoken to me about you and I have also seen some scripts which you did for the Ministry of Information. I wonder if you could do us a short broadcast talk on the subject of "Thailand"? I am concerned with English language broadcasts to India, aimed mainly at the English-speaking Indian population. I don't suppose most of them know very much about Thailand, and they would probably welcome a talk which gave them some background information, at the same time explaining Thailand's relations with Japan and its reasons for participating in the present war. These talks take about 10½ minutes, which means about 1200 words. There is no immediate hurry, but should you care to do a talk, I would like to have the script within the next few weeks. Perhaps you could be kind enough to let me know about this.

Yours sincerely,
Eric Blair
Talks Assistant
Indian Section

1. R. U. Hingorani submitted a script on 22 March, from his address at 117a Harley Street, London, W.1. The letterhead has 'From Mr. Hingorani,' so he was, presumably, a consultant physician and/or surgeon. See *1068* for Orwell's reply.

1031. To Cedric Dover
16 or 17 March 1942

PLEASE TELEPHONE ABOUT NEXT WEEKS TALKS URGENT.   BLAIR

1032. To C. H. Waddington
17 March 1942   PP/EB

Dear Mr. Waddington,

I have now arranged for you to record your talk on Science and Literature at 2.30 on Monday, March 23rd at Levy's Studio, 73, New Bond Street. I hope this time will suit you.

If you have no other engagement, would you care to have lunch with me at the Barcelona Restaurant,[1] 17, Beak Street, at about 1 p.m.? If you are able to come, I will book a table and we can meet there.

Yours sincerely,
Eric Blair
Talks Assistant
Indian Section

1. Illustrated by W. J. West in *Orwell: The War Broadcasts*, plate 20.

1033. Z. A. Bokhari to Empire Programme Executive

On 17 March 1942, Bokhari wrote to Miss Phillips of the Empire Programme Executive, and Miss E. W. D. Boughen of the Talks Booking Section, to say that no contract would be issued for Shridhar Telkar for a Marathi Newsletter for 19 March. Miss Venu Chitale of the Indian Section staff would translate and read the letter. This, however, 'is not a precedent and we still may have to have two people working on this Newsletter.'

1034. BBC Talks Booking Form, 17.3.42

Cyril Connolly: 'We Speak to India,' 'Literature Between Wars: The 1930's,' 30-minute talk; broadcast 31.3.42; fee £15.15s (= £15.75).

1035. BBC Talks Booking Form, 17.3.42

Gujarati Newsletter, 4, written by E. Blair, translated and read by R. R. Desai; broadcast 23.3.42; fee £5.5s + £4.2.2. expenses. Signed: Z. A. Bokhari.

1036. BBC Talks Booking Form, 17.3.42

Cedric Dover: 'We Speak to India,' 'Discussion on the Federal Idea with Professor Joad (see separate contract)—discussion to last about 20 minutes'; recorded 26.3.42; [not altered—contrast form for Joad]; broadcast date 'not yet fixed'; fee £10.10s.

1037. BBC Talks Booking Form, 17.3.42

C. E. M. Joad: 'We Speak to India,' 'Discussion on the Federal Id[e]a with Cedric Dover (see separate contract)—discussion to last about 20 minutes'; recording date originally 26.3.42 but crossed out and changed in manuscript to 30.3.42; broadcast date 'not yet fixed'; fee £15.15s.

1038. BBC Talks Booking Form, 17.3.42

Herbert Read: 'We Speak to India,' 'Literature Between Wars: The New Romantic Movement,' 30-minute talk; recorded 31.3.42; broadcast 7.4.42; fee £15.15s.

1039. BBC Talks Booking Form, 17.3.42

Stephen Spender: 'We Speak to India,' 'Literature Between Wars, 2: Poetry and Tradition'; broadcast 17.3.42; fee £15.15s. Signed: N. H. Parratt.

1040. BBC Talks Booking Form, 17.3.42

C. H. Waddington: 'We Speak to India,' 'Literature Between Wars: Science and Literature,' 30-minute talk; recorded 23.3.42; broadcast 24.3.42; fee £15.15s. Orwell adds: 'I should be grateful if this contract could be sent as soon as possible. The speaker is anxious to know what fee he will receive.'

1041. Marathi Newsletter, 3
19 March 1942

The English original was written by Orwell; it was translated and read by Venu Chitale. Telkar was not engaged to translate this newsletter, and because Miss Chitale and Orwell were members of the BBC staff it was not necessary to issue a talks booking form. Orwell's authorship of the English version can be deduced from an extract reproduced by Anthony Weymouth in his memorandum of 23 March 1942 giving details of references to Sir Stafford Cripps in Newsletters; see *1019*. The extract given here is almost identical with a passage in Orwell's Weekly News Review in English for 21 March 1942; see *1044*.

News coming in from all parts of the world testifies to the goodwill with which Sir Stafford Cripps's mission to India is regarded. It has been especially warmly welcomed in China. A Government spokesman at a Chungking press conference two days ago remarked: "It is not usual for the spokesman of one government to comment on the internal affairs of an allied country, but in the case of India, I would be failing in my duty if I refrained from expressing the great sympathy and interest with which we follow developments in that country. The appointment of Sir Stafford Cripps has been universally applauded by the Chinese press. It is generally felt here that if any man has the ability and insight to approach India's constitutional problem in the right spirit, that man is Sir Stafford Cripps. The British Cabinet has shown the highest political wisdom in making the appointment. When Sir Stafford meets Mr. Gandhi, Mr. Nehru and other leaders, they may find themselves to be really kindred spirits, working together for the defence of India and for a better world."

1042. To Hsiao Ch'ien

19 March 1942   PP/EB/NP

Dear Mr. Hsiao Ch'ien,

Many thanks for your letter of March 17th. I am afraid it would be very difficult, in fact impossible, to alter the dates of these talks. It might possibly be more convenient for you to do them a little earlier, in which case it will be quite easy for us to have them recorded. The actual dates of the broadcasts are May 19th and 26th, which means I would want the first talk not later than May 15th.

As to the scope of the talks, I want you to cover shortly much the same ground as you did in your book. I don't think it will do to talk on the literature of the last 2,000 years and merely end up with modern literature, because the whole idea of this series is that it should deal with what is contemporary, that is in general, the literature of the last twenty or thirty years. We are having six talks on English literature, four on Russian literature, and are ending up with the two on Chinese literature.

What you said in your book opened up to me a completely new world which I had hitherto known nothing about, and I think it will be the same with our listeners. I want to bring home to them that there is a vigorous modern Chinese literature which is most likely to be accessible to them through English translations. But, of course, you would have to put in just a little background stuff about earlier Chinese literature, in order to show in what way contemporary writing is a new departure.

Yes, I have seen certain Chinese stories in New Writing,[1] and they were what first gave me the idea for these talks. Could you be kind enough to let me know whether you could manage the dates named?

Yours sincerely,
Eric Blair
Talks Assistant
Indian Section

1. John Lehmann (see *312, n. 1*) edited *New Writing*, 1936–39. It became, in turn, *Folios of New Writing*, 1940–41, *Daylight*, 1941, and *New Writing and Daylight*, 1942–46. He also edited *Penguin New Writing*, 1–40, 1940–50. Orwell contributed to *New Writing* and *Folios of New Writing*, and his 'Shooting an Elephant,' published in the former, was reprinted in the first number of *Penguin New Writing*.

1043. To Thomas Jones

c. 20 March 1942

On 26 March, Dr. Thomas Jones (1870–1955; CH), described by Crick as 'Lloyd George's famous Cabinet Secretary,' wrote to Orwell: 'I have done, gladly, what you asked & you can be certain that your memorandum will be read by the S. of S. himself. It seems plain sense—too plain I suppose.' Crick, who discovered Jones's letter in the Orwell Archive, continues: 'No trace of the memorandum or clue to its subject matter survives in either Orwell's or Jones's papers, and as Jones held no official position then and wrote from his private address it is not clear even which Secretary of State it was for, though presumably that for War'[1] (Crick, 425).

However, West notes this must refer to Orwell's diary entry for 27 March 1942 (see *1064*), in which he writes that following the abysmal delay in issuing ammunition to the Home Guard for a surprise call-out, he had sent a memo to Jones, 'who has forwarded it direct to Sir Jas. Grigg.' West is surely right in pointing to the 'Orwellian joke,' for Grigg and especially Lady Grigg were frequent and sometimes troublesome broadcasters. Grigg, West notes, 'usually contrived to speak uncensored, as did many of his wife's guests, to the intense annoyance of Orwell, who was responsible for them (West: *Broadcasts*, 27). West also refers to Orwell's undated complaint about Lady Grigg (see *1788*), which he reproduces (184). Lady Grigg was regarded by Laurence Brander as a singularly amateurish and incompetent broadcaster.

Orwell probably felt that he could not write directly to Grigg and, indeed, that it might be more effective were he to write via a third party of some standing. The explanation for choosing Jones, who no longer held an official position, may lie in Jones's interest in promoting the arts. He had been, in 1939, 'the prime mover in the establishment of the Council for the Encouragement of Music and the Arts (which became the Arts Council of Great Britain) and was its first deputy chairman (1939–42)' (*DNB*). Orwell's part in the manifesto 'Why Not War Writers?' (see *856*) and his contacts with scholars and authors through his BBC work might have brought him into touch with Jones.

1. Sir James Grigg (1890–1964; KCB) was Permanent Under-Secretary of State for War, 1939–42, and Secretary of State for War, 1942–45, replacing Captain the Rt. Hon. H. D. R. Margesson. He was not a member of the War Cabinet, but he had served as Finance Member on the Viceroy of India's Council, and when Churchill set up the India Committee, 25 February 1942, to advise the War Cabinet (chaired by Clement Attlee, Deputy Prime Minister) on Indian affairs, he was included in its membership. Churchill wanted him to accept a peerage but this he declined. Lady Grigg was prominent in the organisation of 'Women Generally Speaking,' broadcast in the BBC's Eastern Service; see *947, n. 1*. See Winston Churchill, *The Second World War*, IV, 71–2; U.S.: *The Hinge of Fate*, 81–82.

1044. Weekly News Review, 15

21 March 1942

This is a fair-copy typescript, with 'AS BROADCAST' typed at its head. There is no censor's stamp, but there are a few textual changes (noted here), probably in Bokhari's hand. The typescript regularly has 'Macarthur,' here corrected to 'MacArthur.' PasB records 'Weekly News Review by Z. A. Bokhari.'

It is now clearer than it was last week that the Japanese are preparing to attack Australia. Their main aim is what it has always been—to join hands with the Germans in the Middle East—but to do this they have got to make sure of their position in both the north and the south Pacific. There have been several indications that they are planning a sudden treacherous attack against Russia, of the same type as they previously made against America. There is no reason to think that the Russians will be taken unawares. The present aim of the Japanese is to capture the main ports in the northern part of Australia so that Australian and American and British troops will have no base nearer than New Zealand from which to make their attack.

At present the Japanese are directing their attacks chiefly against Port Moresby on the island of New Guinea opposite the northern tip of Australia. They are being strongly resisted but *whether*[1] a landing on the Australian mainland *can* be prevented *is not yet clear.*[2] Whether once they have landed the Japanese will find their task an easy one is a different question. Australia is an enormous country which it would take several years to over-run completely, even if there were little or no resistance. It seems probable even though the Japanese may succeed in making their landing and in securing what at first sight appears to be *a firm foothold*,[3] they will end by letting themselves in for rather the same kind of war as they have been waging for four years in China, that is to say, a war in which it is *possible*[4] to conquer empty[5] territory, but next door to impossible to destroy the enemy.

We do not know how strong are the forces which are assembled in Australia to meet the invasion; the Allies lost heavily in ships in the sea battle off Java,[6] and numerically they are not likely to be as strong in the air as the Japanese, because of the enormous distances across which air reinforcements have to be brought. We do know, however, that American reinforcements, both ground troops and aeroplanes, have reached Australia in large quantities, and have been reaching it throughout the last two months, although until now it was considered wiser not to reveal this. Meanwhile General MacArthur, who was commanding the American forces in the Philippines, has been brought to Australia to act as commander in chief of the Allied forces there. General MacArthur's force has now held out in the peninsula south of Manila for three and a half months against an enormously more numerous enemy. The Japanese imagined when they first attacked the Philippines that they had an easy task before them, but they soon found that they were mistaken. This was due primarily to two causes. The first was the fact that General MacArthur, who had foreseen the Japanese invasion many years earlier, had prepared every move in advance. The second was the courage and devotion of the Philippine population, who, instead of going to the Japanese, as the latter had foolishly expected, fought bravely in defence of their country, and thus allowed General MacArthur to possess a far larger army than would have been possible if he had been relying only on American troops. General MacArthur's arrival has been warmly welcomed in Australia, where he is generally recognised to be the best man to conduct the defence. Australia has now mobilised the whole of its man power, which would give it, if necessary, a front line army of about half a million men, besides several millions of war workers of all kinds.

Three days ago news came from Australia of the heavy damage inflicted on the fleet with which the Japanese are attempting their invasion. American aeroplanes raided the base in New Guinea which the Japanese are occupying and either sank or damaged more than twenty Japanese ships. This included two heavy cruisers sunk, and five troop-ships either sunk or set on fire. All this was accomplished with the loss of only one Allied aeroplane. On the following day news came of another successful raid. Nevertheless the Japanese are proceeding with their attacks against Port Moresby, the chief Australian stronghold in New Guinea, and they will no doubt *attempt to invade*[7] the mainland of Australia before long. But they can only do so at the cost of a heavy loss of ships, which they are already short of, and which they will find it harder and harder to replace.

News coming in from all parts of the world testified to the goodwill with which Sir Stafford Cripps's mission to India is regarded. It has been especially warmly welcomed in China. A Government spokesman at a Chungking press conference a few days ago remarked: "It is not usual for the spokesman of one government to comment on the internal affairs of an allied country, but in the case of India, I would be failing in my duty if I refrained from expressing the great sympathy and interest with which we follow developments in that country. The appointment of Sir Stafford Cripps has been universally applauded by the Chinese press. It is generally felt here that if any man has the ability and insight to approach India's constitutional problem in the right spirit, that man is Sir Stafford Cripps. The British Cabinet has shown the highest political wisdom in making the appointment. When Sir Stafford meets the Indian leaders, they may find themselves to be really kindred spirits, working together for the defence of India and for a better world."[8]

Sir Stafford Cripps is expected to arrive in India within the next day or two. How long he will stay is not yet known. *He carries with him the united support and good wishes of the whole Government and people of Britain.*[9]

On the Russian front our allies are now fighting in the suburbs of Kharkov, and it does not seem likely that the Germans can hold on to this town much longer. Kharkov is an important industrial centre, the capture of which several months ago was proclaimed by the Germans as a great victory. They will perhaps give a different account of it when it once again falls into Russian hands. All the recent speeches of the Russian leaders display a confidence about the forthcoming spring campaign, which is in great contrast to the theatrical boasts of the German propagandists. It is clear that apart from the actual fighting and apart from the mobilisation of fresh armies, from Russia's enormous population, the losses which Russia suffered in her war industries when the Germans over-ran the Donetz Basin, have been largely made good. Moreover, the stream of supplies of tanks, aeroplanes and other kinds of war material from Britain and the United States has never ceased all through the winter. We may expect the Germans to make more than one attempt to cut the principal supply route which runs from Britain round the coast of Scandinavia and into the Arctic Sea. The Germans have now at least three powerful warships sheltering somewhere on the Norwegian coast,[10] which have been placed there in order to make several raids on the supply route to Murmansk; only last week, the Tirpitz, Germany's biggest and newest battle-ship, attempted a raid of this type, but was driven back to port by British aeroplanes.

1. *whether*] in all probability
2. *can . . . is not yet clear*] cannot; *the letters* not *crossed out and is not yet clear written in after* prevented
3. *a firm foothold*] important successes
4. *possible*] fairly easy
5. *empty*] *as in transcript, but it could be an error for* enemy *that occurred when the fair copy was made*
6. See note to 'In spite of their heavy losses,' *1010, n. 1.*
7. *attempt to invade*] *handwritten substitution for* succeed in invading
8. Almost the same passage was used in Marathi Newsletter, 3, 19 March 1942; see *1041.*
9. *He carries with him . . . of Britain*] A request has already come from the Burma Government in Mandalay that Sir Stafford shall, if possible, visit Burma in the course of his stay.
10. Orwell probably has in mind the battleships *Scharnhorst* and *Gneisenau* and the heavy cruiser *Prinz Eugen,* which had escaped from Brest to Norway through the English Channel with flotillas of destroyers and motor-torpedo-boats in mid-February 1942, suffering scarcely any damage from British air attacks. This was a serious blow to British esteem and is not mentioned in the newsletters. The *Scharnhorst* was sunk on 26 December 1943 while attacking a convoy to Russia. Little use was made of the other ships except to evacuate German troops at the end of the Russian campaign.

1045. BBC Talks Booking Form, 21.3.42

Gujarati Newsletter, 5; written by E. Blair, translated and read by R. R. Desai 'alone';[1] broadcast 30.3.42; fee £5.5s + £4.2.2 expenses. Signed: Z. A. Bokhari.

1. A note on the form states that 'The other Gujerat,° Mr. H. L. Desai is still ill & will not be able to help.' R. R. Desai continued alone from hereon.

1046. War-time Diary

22.3.42: *Empson tells me that there is a strict ban by the Foreign Office on any suggestion that Japan is going to attack the USSR. So this subject is being studiously avoided in the Far Eastern broadcasts while being pushed all the time in the India broadcasts. They haven't yet got onto the fact that we are saying this, we haven't been warned and don't officially know about the ban, and are making the best of our opportunity while it lasts. The same chaos everywhere on the propaganda front.* [Eg. "Horizon" was nearly stopped from getting its extra paper to print copies for export on the strength of my article on Kipling (all well at the last moment because Harold Nicolson and Duff Cooper[1] intervened), at the same time as the BBC asked me to write a "feature" based on the article.]

German propaganda is inconsistent[2] in quite a different way—ie, deliberately so, with an utter unscrupulousness in offering everything to everybody, freedom to[3] India and a colonial empire to[4] Spain, emancipation to the Kaffirs and stricter race laws to the Boers, etc., etc. All quite sound from a propaganda point of view in my opinion, seeing how politically ignorant the majority of people are, how uninterested in anything outside their immediate affairs, and how little impressed by inconsistency. A few weeks back the NBBS[5] was actually attacking the Workers' Challenge [Station],[6] warning people not to listen to it as it was "financed from Moscow."

The Communists in Mexico are again chasing Victor Serge[7] and other Trotskyist refugees who got there from France, urging their expulsion, etc., etc. Just the same tactics as in Spain. Horribly depressed to see these ancient intrigues coming up again, not so much because they are morally disgusting as from this reflection: for 20 years the Comintern has used these methods and the Comintern has always and everywhere been defeated by the Fascists; therefore we, being tied to them in[8] a species of alliance, shall be defeated with them.

Suspicion that Russia intends making a separate peace now seems widespread. Of the two, it would be easier for Russia to surrender the Ukraine, both on geographical and psychological grounds, but they obviously couldn't give up the Caucasus oilfields without a fight. One possible development is a secret agreement between Hitler and Stalin, Hitler to keep what Russian territory he has overrun, or parts of it, but thereafter to make no further attacks but to direct his offensive southward towards the oilfields of Irak and Iran, Russia and Germany keeping up a sham war meanwhile. It appears to me that a separate peace is distinctly likelier if we do make a continental invasion this year, because if we succeed in embarrassing the Germans and drawing off a large[9] part of their armies,[10] Russia is immediately in a much better position both to win back the occupied territories, and to bargain. I nevertheless think[11] we ought to invade Europe if the shipping will run to it. The one thing that might stop[12] this kind of filthy doublecrossing is a firm alliance between ourselves and the USSR, with war aims declared in detail. Impossible while this government rules us, and probably also while Stalin remains in power[: at least only possible if we could get a different kind of government and then find some way of speaking over Stalin's head to the Russian people].

The same feeling as one had during the Battle of France—that there is no news. This arises principally from endless newspaper-reading. [In connection with my newsletters I now read four or five morning newspapers every day and several editions of the evening ones, besides the daily monitoring report.] The amount of new matter in each piece of print one reads is so small that one gets a general impression that nothing is happening. Besides, when things are going badly one can foresee everything. The only event that has surprised me for weeks past was Cripps's mission to India.

---

1. For Harold Nicolson, critic, biographer, and M.P., see 565, 30.8.39, n. 1. Among his biographies were those of Tennyson, Byron, Swinburne, Lord Curzon, King George V, and

Sainte-Beuve. For Alfred Duff Cooper, diplomat, biographer of Talleyrand and Earl Haig, see *628, n. 6*. He had served briefly as War Cabinet representative in Singapore, and responsibility was partly, if hardly fairly, laid at his door for its fall. He was British representative with the French Committee of National Liberation in North Africa (headed by General de Gaulle), and for three years from September 1944 was British Ambassador in Paris. His autobiography is *Old Men Forget* (1953).

2. Manuscript originally had 'chaotic,' but this was crossed out and replaced by 'inconsistent.'
3. *to*] for
4. *to*] for
5. New British Broadcasting Station broadcast propaganda in English from Germany. For Orwell's description of its policy, see his 'London Letter,' 1 January 1942, *913*. W.J. West devotes a chapter of his *Truth Betrayed* (1987) to the New British Broadcasting Station. He also discusses two other German stations which broadcast to Britain, the Workers Challenge Station and the Christian Peace Movement [station]; he prints three of their broadcasts in an Appendix.
6. This was another station broadcasting propaganda in English from Germany.
7. Victor Serge (Kilbat'chiche; 1890–1947), author and journalist, born in Brussels of exiled Russian intellectuals, was French by adoption. He was associated with the anarchist movement in Paris. After the Russian Revolution, he transferred his activities to Moscow, Leningrad, and Berlin (where he ran a newspaper, the *Communist International*). His close association with Trotsky led to his deportation to Siberia in 1933. After his release, he was Paris correspondent for the POUM during the Spanish civil war. In 1941 he settled in Mexico, where he died, impoverished Among his many books are *From Lenin to Stalin* (1937; translated from French); *Vie et mort de Trotsky* (Paris, 1951), and *Mémoires d'un révolutionnaire 1901–1941* (Paris, 1951; English translation, *Memoirs of a Revolutionary*, 1963). He wrote an introduction to *Révolution et contre-révolution en Espagne* by Joaquín Maurín (1896–1973) co-founder of the POUM (1937). See also *2899, n. 1*.
8. *in*] by
9. *large*] great
10. *armies*] army
11. *think*] think that
12. *stop*] prevent

1047. To Z. A. Bokhari

[23 March 1942?]

On 17 March 1942, Wickham Stead wrote to Sir Malcolm Darling suggesting that Hindustani versions of his talk be broadcast and offering two new talks. One was to be on the impact of mechanisation on the modern world (without reference to Gandhi); the second proposal was for a talk on the 'constructively revolutionary character of creative peace.' On 21 March, Darling sent a memorandum to the Eastern Service Director, L. F. Rushbrook Williams, outlining these proposals. Bokhari and Orwell added handwritten comments to the memorandum. Bokhari wrote, '*Mr Blair* I don't think we shd. What do you think?' Orwell replied:

I.P.O.
I don't think we can fit these talks in, especially as our schedule is rather full already.

E. A. Blair

The memorandum is marked, 'No action.'

1048. Gujarati Newsletter, 4

23 March 1942

The English original was written by Orwell. No script has been traced.

1049. To Amabel Williams-Ellis

23 March 1942   Handwritten draft of postcard

On 20 March 1942, Mrs. Amabel Williams-Ellis[1] wrote to Orwell from her home, Plâs Brondanw, saying that Mulk Raj Anand had suggested she call on Orwell next time she was in London. She asked if she might call on him 'next Thursday' (26 March). Someone has marked her postcard, 'acknowledged by pc. 23/3/ 42.' The draft of that acknowledgment, sent to her London address, is in Orwell's hand.

Can you call here any time on Thursday morning?[2]

Geo. Orwell

1. Mary Amabel Williams-Ellis (1894–1984), author and journalist, was literary editor of *The Spectator*, 1922–23. She wrote stories for children and books on popular science, women in war factories, and biography, among other subjects, and, with her husband, Clough Williams-Ellis, *The Pleasures of Architecture*. Clough Williams-Ellis (1883–1978; Kt., 1972), an architect and founder of Portmeirion, suggested sources of illustrations for *The Road to Wigan Pier*. Orwell probably met him in Victor Gollancz's office to discuss this just a day or two before he left to fight in Spain; see *CW*, V, 228–29.
2. For the result of the meeting with Amabel Williams-Ellis, see Orwell's letter to Lady Grigg, *1062.*

1050. BBC Talks Booking Form, 24.3.42

K. S. Shelvankar: 'Through Eastern Eyes,' 'The Soviet East,' 1: Economic Reconstruction, 2: Cultural Development; 'China,' 1: The Co-operative Movement, 2: Education in Wartime; broadcast 25.3.42, 1, 22, and 29.4.42; fee £8.8s for each talk. Signed: Z. A. Bokhari.[1]

1. Dr. Krishna Shivarao Shelvankar (1906–1996), Indian writer and journalist, was in England during the war as correspondent for Indian newspapers. His book *The Problem of India* (Penguin Special, 1940) was banned in India. This may have prompted Bokhari to write a private note to the Eastern Service Director on 24 March 1942: 'I wish to put on record that I have nothing to do with Shelvankar's talks. He was approached without my consent and his talks were invited without my agreement. Call me a die-hard if you like, but in my opinion the time has not come for us to make such advances towards the truculent damsel—"Miss Nationalism".' See Orwell's War-time Diary, *1064, 27.3.42,* and 1064, n. 1 and his caution to E. M. Forster, *1103.*

1051. To Cedric Dover

25 March 1942   PP/EB

Dear Mr. Dover

In connection with your interview which you are to record with Joad on Monday the 30th, when you are meeting him at Broadcasting House at 2.30 p.m., here is an extract from Joad's letter which we promised to send you:—
"Dear Mr. Bokhari,

Thank you for sending me Mr. Dover's script which I have read with interest. It suffers, I think, from the fact that no very clear thesis is asserted, and no very definite position adopted except in so far as he advocates an Asiatic Federation, including India and China and, conceivably, Russia. For the rest, there are a number of general remarks on Utopias, and a number of general remarks on Federation as a theory or movement in the contemporary world, mainly derogatory. . . . .[1]

I am on the whole favourable to the Utopiasts and warm supporter of Federation in general, but do not want to commit myself on such topics as whether one of the first Federations should or should not be an Indian-Chinese-Malayan Federation. . . . "

Yours sincerely,
Eric Blair
Talks Assistant, Indian Section

1. The ellipses are Orwell's.

1052. To Hsiao Ch'ien

25 March 1942   PP/EB/CEH

Dear Hsiao Chi'en°

(I think we might drop the "Mr.", might we not?), I want your two talks to be on two consecutive weeks, i.e. the second script to be delivered on May 26th and to reach me by about May 22nd (not later than that). I hope you will be able to manage this.

These literary talks seem to go best when they run for about 20 minutes, that is to say, 2500–3000 words. I wouldn't go much over 3000.

I look forward to seeing your article on modern Chinese culture.

Yours sincerely
Geo. Orwell

1053. BBC Talks Booking Form, 25.3.42

Cedric Dover: 'Through Eastern Eyes,' 'What It Means to Me,' Race Mixture and World Peace; recorded 27.3.42; broadcast date not arranged; fee £7.7s. Signed: M Blackburn.

1054. BBC Talks Booking Form, 25.3.42

S. M. Telkar: Marathi Newsletter, 4; 'Written, translated and read (five minutes) by S. M. Telkar. (The rest of the News letter° to be written & read by Staff)'; broadcast 26.3.42; fee £5.5s. Signed: Z. A. Bokhari.

1055. Marathi Newsletters, 4 to 11
26 March–14 May 1942

These newsletters may have come under Orwell's supervision, and it is possible he played some part in drafting the English versions. However, the talks booking forms and the PasBs do not mention him. Some were talks by D. G. Savarkar; one, for 26 March, had a five-minute interview by Shridhar Telkar embedded within the newsletter. On 7 May, Miss Venu Chitale interviewed Mr. Despande as part of the broadcast. On 21 May, D. M. Kanekar read Marathi Newsletter, 12, which according to the talks booking form, Orwell had written; and this transmission also included a five-minute fill-in by Miss Chitale. On 9 July, the script was written by Bokhari. The broadcasts from 16 July to 17 September were certainly based on Orwell's scripts, as the talks booking forms show. It is thus not possible to specify what part Orwell played in the preparation of many of the newsletters in Marathi. Only the fourteen that can be attributed to him with some certainty have been credited to him. See *1054*, for Telkar's writing of Newsletter, 4. An uncertain clue can be found in the carbon copy of a letter from Orwell to Desai, 8 August 1942, in which he refers to making a recording after the Gujarati Newsletter is read; see *1366*. It can be seen in the carbon that 'Marathi' was originally typed for 'Gujarati,' suggesting that Orwell was still associated with the Marathi Newsletter.

1056. To Mulk Raj Anad

26 March 1942   PP/EB/MB

Dear Anand,
Here is an extra carbon copy of your talk—'New Order'—for you to keep. I will bring the top copy with me when I meet you on Friday, 27th March, at 3.45 p.m. at Broadcasting House. You will have time then to rehearse before the actual recording takes place.

Yours sincerely,
[Initialled] E. A. B
Eric Blair
Talks Assistant
Indian Section.

1057. To Gordon Childe[1]
26 March 1942   PP/EB/CEH

Dear Sir

I am arranging some talks on the development of Science for the Eastern Service of the B.B.C., and Professor Bernal, with whom I have discussed the series, suggested that you might care to do the first talk.

I have given as the title "The Birth of Science", intending it to be an account of how what we now mean by Science arose out of magic or in contra-distinction to magic.

These are talks taking about fifteen or twenty minutes, that is to say, something over 2,000 words. The approximate date would be about nine weeks from now.

I will let you have fuller particulars if you are interested in the idea. Perhaps you could be kind enough to let me know fairly soon.[2]

Yours truly,
Eric Blair
Talks Assistant
Indian Section

1. Vere Gordon Childe (1892–1957), Professor of Prehistoric Archaeology, University of Edinburgh, 1927–46; Professor of Prehistoric European Archaeology and Director of the Institute of Archaeology, University of London, 1946–56, was not only an outstanding scholar but a gifted populariser of his subject, notably through *Man Makes Himself* (1936) and *What Happened in History* (1942) though, paradoxically, he was 'not a good teacher, and undergraduate audiences could make little of the mass of recondite learning which was presented to them' (Stuart Piggott, *DNB*). He was a Marxist.
2. The original of this letter has no paragraph indents—perhaps CEH's style (though she indents *1061* and *1062*). Presumably Nancy Parratt was ill or on leave. Her layout and initials reappear on 31 March; see *1067*. Mary Blackburn typed *1056*.

1058. To A. C. G. Egerton, F.R.S.[1]
26 March 1942   PP/EB/CEH

Dear Sir

I am arranging a series of talks on the development of Science for the Eastern Service of the B.B.C. Professor Bernal, with whom I have discussed the series, suggests that you might care to do the third talk, which I have called "Experimental and Applied Science."

These are talks taking fifteen or twenty minutes, which means something over 2,000 words. The approximate date would be about eleven weeks from now.

If you are interested I can give you fuller particulars. Perhaps you could be kind enough to let me know fairly soon whether you would care to undertake this.[2]

Yours truly,
Eric Blair
Talks Assistant
Indian Section

1. Alfred Charles Glyn Egerton (1886–1959; Kt., 1943) was, for seventeen years after World War I, at the Clarendon Laboratory, Oxford, as Reader in Thermodynamics from 1921. He worked especially on fuel flammability for petrol and turbine engines. He became a member of the Advisory Council of the Department of Scientific and Industrial Research. During World War II, he undertook research for the services and was a member of the War Cabinet's scientific advisory committee. In 1942 he reorganised the British Scientific Office in Washington, D.C.
2. The letter is annotated, 'Phoning after Easter,' but not in Orwell's hand.

1059. To Joseph Needham

26 March 1942 PP/EB

The left-hand side of this letter has been torn away; reconstruction is fairly straightforward, but where there is the least possibility of alternative readings, the reconstruction is shown within brackets.

Dear Sir

I am arranging a series of talks on the development of Science for the Eastern Service of the B.B.C. Professor Bernal, with whom I have discussed the series, suggests that you might care to undertake the fourth talk, which I have called provisionally "The Economic Bases of Science". We can think of a better title later.

[Rou]ghly what I want is a discussion of [the] position of Science in different economic systems with particular reference [to] its position in capitalist societies and under Fascism.

I can give you fuller particulars if you are interested in doing the talk. These talks take 15 or 20 minutes, which means something over 2,000 words. The approximate date would be about 12 weeks from now.

Perhaps you could be kind enough to let [me] know whether this interests you.

Yours truly
Eric Blair
Talks Assistant
Indian Section

1. Joseph Needham (1900–1995) was Fellow of Gonville & Caius College, Cambridge, 1924–66; Master, 1966–76; Sir William Dunn Reader in Biochemistry, 1933–66; and Director of the Needham Research Institute (East Asian History of Science Library), Cambridge, from 1976. His many publications and outstanding achievements have been recognised by universities throughout the world. His recent books at the time Orwell wrote to him were *Background to Modern Science* (editor; 1938) and *Biochemistry and Morphogenesis* (1942). Since 1954 he has been publishing *Science and Civilisation in China* (7 volumes in 25 parts). He achieved distinction in widely different fields and is one of a small number of scholars elected a fellow of both the Royal Society (1941) and the British Academy (1971). See Gary Werskey, *The Visible College*, especially for his Marxism and his relationship with J. D. Bernal.

1060. To Reginald Reynolds

26 March 1942   PP/EB/CEH

Dear Reg,[1]

Thanks for your letter dated 25th.

I would like to have a talk on "Prison Literature",[2] but at the moment my schedule is very full up, and I shall have to push it somewhat into the future. I can, however, give you an approximate date. It would be about the middle of July. I haven't actually an empty date before then but what I suggest is that you could do the talk in the fairly near future, and we could have it recorded, and I may be able to push it in earlier if someone else should dry up in the meantime, as sometimes happens. Do you think you could let me have a sort of short synopsis of a page or so telling me approximately what you intend to say? As to the length of the talk, I suggest something of about 20 minutes which generally means 2,000–3,000 words.

I will think over the other subject you suggest.[3] I know how important the subject of soil fertility and conservation of sewage is, but I am doubtful about being able to fit it into any schedule I am responsible for. I should have thought, with a certain amount of tact, you might be able to do something about it for the Home Service.

Hoping to hear from you

Yours
Eric Blair
Talks Assistant
Indian Section

1. Reginald Reynolds (see 560, 2.8.39, n. 4), author of, among other books, *White Sahibs in India: An Examination of British Rule in India* (1937) and *A Prison Anthology*, with A.G. Stock (1938), was a Quaker and much influenced by Gandhi. He became a passionate advocate of freedom for India. In 1937 he supported the non-Communist Republicans in Spain. He was a brilliant speaker for the Independent Labour Party. A pacifist during World War II, he served in Civil Defence as a driver. He was one of those listed by Orwell in his contribution to 'Pacifism and the War' of 12 July 1942 (see 1270) as having been disregarded by George Woodcock in the latter's disapproval of the broadcasts to India. He was joint editor with Orwell of *British Pamphleteers* (Vol. 1, 1948). His excellent autobiography, *My Life and Crimes* (1956) contains one of the best—and usually overlooked—accounts of Orwell, 211–15. He was married to the novelist Ethel Mannin (see 575).
2. Reynolds had experienced a week in Exeter Gaol in 1940 by the device of refusing to pay a fine of 7s 6d plus 9s 0d costs for riding a bicycle without a lamp on a clear moonlit night, incarceration Orwell had been unable to effect for the same purpose: to experience prison (see *My Life and Crimes*, 171ff). Cedric Dover had suggested to Reynolds that Orwell might be interested in a talk for India on prison literature. In his autobiography, Reynolds says he gave two such talks 'in which I was allowed to get away with quotations from the prison writings of Gandhi and Nehru' (214).
3. Reynolds's *Cleanliness and Godliness*—a history of the water closet, written because, as he put it, 'the best part of mankind went down the drain' (*My Life and Crimes*, 186)—was published in 1943 and sold out almost immediately. This talk would include the use of sewage for land fertilisation.

1061. To J. D. Bernal

27 March 1942   PP/EB/CEH

Dear Professor Bernal

I am just writing to confirm the details of the two talks we agreed at our conversation. You are doing the first and sixth talk° in the series. The first "The Birth of Modern Science" will be on 2nd May, and the other "The Future of Science" will be 4 weeks later. These talks should be 15-20 minutes, which means something over 2,000 words.

I wonder if you could let me know the exact title and address of Mr. J. G. Crowther (I am not certain whether these initials are correct) who, you told me, is Scientific Adviser to the British Council.

Yours sincerely
Eric Blair
Talks Assistant
Indian Section

1062. To Lady Grigg

27 March 1942   PP/EB/CEH

Dear Lady Grigg,

I am enclosing herewith your Pass for April.

I wonder how full up your schedule now is. Mrs. Amabel Williams-Ellis was here yesterday, and is anxious to do some talks, not necessarily in the very near future, on popularised Science, Dietetics, Progress of Medicine, and that kind of subject. I think she had in mind a series of two, three or four talks.

I wonder if you could let me know whether you are likely to have any dates open, for instance some time in May or June.

Yours sincerely
Eric Blair
Talks Assistant
Indian Section

1063. BBC Talks Booking Form, 27.3.42

J. Chinna Durai: 'We Speak to India,' Sir Stafford Cripps; broadcast 28.3.42; fee £8.8s. Signed: Z. A. Bokhari.

1064. War-time Diary

<u>27.3.42.</u>   *News of the terms Cripps took to India supposed to be bursting tomorrow. Meanwhile only rumours, all plausible but completely incompatible with one another. The best-supported—that India is to be offered a treaty similar to the Egyptian one. K. S. S.[1] who is our fairly embittered enemy, considers this would be accepted if Indians were given the Ministries of Defence, Finance and Internal Affairs. All the Indians here, after a week or two of gloom, much more optimistic, seeming to have smelt out somehow (perhaps by studying long faces in the India Office) that the terms are not so bad after all.*

[Terrific debate in the House over the affaire Daily Mirror.[2] A. Bevan[3] reading numerous extracts from Morrison's[4] own articles in the D.M., written since war started, to the amusement of Conservatives who are anti-D.M. but can never resist the spectacle of two Socialists slamming one another. Cassandra[5] announces he is resigning to join the army. Prophecy he will be back in journalism within 3 months. But where shall we all be within 3 months any way?]

Government candidate defeated (very small majority) in the Grantham by-election. The first time since the war started that this has happened, I think.

Surprise call-out of our Company of Home Guard a week or two back. It took 4½ hours to assemble the Company and dish out ammunition, and would have taken them[6] another hour to get them into their battle positions. This mainly due to the bottleneck caused by refusing to distribute ammunition but making each man come to HQ to[7] be issued with it there. Sent a memo on this to Dr Tom Jones, who has forwarded it direct to Sir Jas. Grigg.[8] In my own unit I could not get such a memo even as far as the Company Commander—or at least, could not get it attended to.

Crocuses now full out. One seems to catch glimpses of them dimly through a haze of war news.

[Abusive letter from H. G. Wells, who addresses me as "You shit", among other things.[9]

The Vatican is exchanging diplomatic representatives with Tokio. The Vatican now has diplomatic relations[10] with all the Axis powers and—I think—with none of the Allies. A bad sign and yet in a sense a good one, in that this last step means that they have now definitely decided that the Axis and not we stand for the more reactionary policy.]

1. Dr. Krishna S. Shelvankar; see *1050, n. 1*. Despite Orwell's reference to him as 'our fairly embittered enemy,' he broadcast to India under Orwell's aegis.
2. The *Daily Mirror*, a popular leftist daily newspaper, had been called to order by Churchill for taking what he called a defeatist line, that is, critical of the government's handling of the war. After the debate in the House of Commons (see *1065, n. 4*), the affair fizzled out.
3. Aneurin (Nye) Bevan (see *565, 28.8.39, n. 11*), Labour M.P., had been, for most of 1939, in conflict with his party and he was expelled for supporting Sir Stafford's Cripps's Popular Front campaign though his integrity was never in doubt. He edited *Tribune*, 1942–45 (a remarkable achievement for someone who could barely read when he left school at the age of thirteen), and gave Orwell support even when he disagreed with him. His great achievement

was the creation of the National Health Service out of a variety of earlier proposals. His *In Place of Fear* (1952) sets out his philosophy.

4. Herbert Morrison (see *763, n. 28*) was Home Secretary at this time. In the debate Orwell refers to, his subversive writings from World War I, when he was a conscientious objector, were also quoted (Hugh Cudlipp, *Publish and Be Damned*, 195–96).

5. This was the pseudonym of William Connor (1900–1967; Kt., 1966), a well-known radical journalist who wrote this personal column in the *Daily Mirror*. His *English at War* (April 1941) was the most popular of the Searchlight Books edited by T. R. Fyvel and Orwell; it was reprinted three times.

6. *taken them*] taken

7. *to*] &

8. Grigg was then Secretary of State for War. See *1043* for an account of this memorandum and *1043, n. 1* for Grigg.

9. This stemmed initially from Orwell's article 'Wells, Hitler and the World State,' *Horizon*, August 1941 (see *837*) and was further stimulated by his broadcast talk 'The Re-discovery of Europe,' about which Wells wrote to *The Listener*; see *1014*. Inez Holden was present at a 'God-awful row' between Wells and Orwell arising from the *Horizon* article. Orwell thought Wells's belief that the Germans might be defeated quite soon was a disservice to the general public; Wells accused Orwell of being defeatist, though he withdrew that. This outburst passed over reasonably amicably, but was revived when Orwell's broadcast was printed in *The Listener*, leading to the abusive letter mentioned here. Holden wrote to Ian Angus, 21 May 1967, that Orwell very much regretted the *Horizon* article and was sorry he had upset Wells, whom he had always greatly admired. See also Crick, 427–31.

10. relations] *scored through in manuscript and* representatives *substituted*

1065. Weekly News Review, 16

28 March 1942

This very clean typescript bears two rectangular rubber stamps, one indicating as before that the talk has been censored by the BBC Censorship Department; the other, a new stamp, states: 'B.B.C. PASSED FOR POLICY.' Both are signed by Z. A. Bokhari and dated 28 March, the day of the broadcast. The only change is a lengthy cut starting with the second paragraph; here printed within square brackets. This may not be a result of censorship. Apart from the reference to Toungoo, there is nothing new of any moment. The threat to the Burma Road had been frequently discussed by Orwell earlier; the danger of attacks on India and even Ceylon and the blockade of Indian ports had been mentioned; and the danger to India was described as even more acute than to Australia on 21 February. Possibly Orwell or Bokhari thought, on reflection, that there was not much that was novel here and so cut it and substituted the last two paragraphs. The text looks as if it originally ended before the last two paragraphs, at 'fighting for the liberty of France'; half of that page is blank, and the last two paragraphs are typed on a separate sheet. Further, the page number, 5, shows signs of overtyping, as if the typist was unsure of the correct pagination. In the light of what Orwell had been free to say in earlier commentaries, there seems nothing censorable in the passage. The PasB has Weekly News Review by Z. A. Bokhari and gives the timing as approximately 10 minutes.

The Japanese have occupied the Andaman islands,[1] in the Indian Ocean to the south of Burma. They were almost undefended, and the British command decided some time back to abandon them, evacuating a considerable proportion of the civilian population beforehand. The Andamans are 800 miles from Colombo and are about the same from the port of Madras, both of which are now liable to be subjected to air-raids. This is the first step in the Japanese attempt to dominate the Indian Ocean from island bases, which we foretold in earlier newsletters.

[Apart from this, there has been no great change in the situation on the Eastern fronts during the past week. The chief activity has been in Burma where the situation is described as serious. The airfield at Toungoo[2] in Central Burma has been lost to the Japanese. A small Chinese force has been cut off in Toungoo but it is fighting back successfully and this morning news came that it had been reinforced. In Burma the Japanese have several possible objectives, and we do not yet know which they regard as the most important. One objective is the oilfield of Yenangyaung, another is the new road which runs via Burma from India into China. This road is still in process of construction but it could be brought into use quite shortly, and if the Japanese could succeed in cutting it, they would compel supplies from India to China to be sent by a more northerly and more difficult route. The other possible objective of the Japanese is the route leading directly overland from Burma into India by way of Assam. It is quite possible that they are contemplating a land attack upon India, especially Bengal, by this route. Owing to the wild nature of the country, however, they will probably not be able to take a highly mechanised army but will have to rely on infantry and aeroplanes. Against this kind of attack, guerilla forces can be very effective as we have seen in China, and consequently the factor of popular resistance in India will be of the highest importance.

The monsoon begins in Burma about the end of May. After that it is very difficult to move except by water or along the roads and railways. We ought not to assume, however, that this will make the country impassable for the Japanese infantry.] Meanwhile both British and Chinese forces in Burma are fighting back strongly. Two divisions of Chinese troops are serving under the American General Stilwell who is himself under the orders of General-issimo Chiang Kai-Shek.

The Japanese moves against Australia have not made very much progress since last week. Heavy fighting is going on in the interior of the island of New Guinea, but so far the only attacks the Japanese have made against the principal Australian stronghold in the island, Port Moresby, have been air attacks. It will be recalled that last week Australian and American aeroplanes made a very successful attack against the Japanese sea forces, sinking or disabling a number of war-ships and troop transports, and this has probably set the Japanese plan back. General MacArthur, who made such a successful defence in the Philippines, is busy organising the forces in Australia, and has stated already that though he cannot work miracles, he regards himself as being in Australia, not merely to defend, but to attack at the first possible moment. Mr. Curtin, the Premier of Australia, has described Australia as the base from which the Allies can take offensive action against Japan, and has expressed his hope of seeing a speedy settlement of Indian political problems, so that India can take her rightful place at the side of the Allies.

There are signs that the war in the Mediterranean may shortly flare up again. The British Navy have just brought off a brilliant feat by getting a large Convoy of ships to the Island of Malta.[3] One ship in the Convoy was sunk by enemy aircraft, but the Italian Naval force which attempted to attack it was driven off and one of Italy's biggest and newest battleships was hit by a torpedo. The little island of Malta has now had over sixteen hundred air-raids. This is a sign of its strategic importance and of the anxiety of the Axis powers to put it out of action as a base for warships and aeroplanes. As long as Malta, which lies between Italy and Africa, remains in British hands, it is both difficult and dangerous for the Axis to convey their troops to Libya. They have, indeed, lost a vast number of ships containing soldiers or materials of war during the last few months. If you look at the map, you can see that German re-inforcements for Libya only have to travel a few hundred miles across the Mediterranean—whereas most of the British reinforcements have to sail thousands of miles round the Cape of Good Hope and up through the Indian Ocean and the Red Sea to Egypt. In spite of this disadvantage, the British and other Allied forces in Egypt have more than held their own and besides conquering Abyssinia, have made advances into Libya which have twice taken them as far as Benghazi. It can be seen, therefore, that the sea warfare in the Mediterranean is extremely important because, if the Axis could attain control of those waters for only a few weeks, they might be able to pour into Libya an army overwhelmingly greater than the one the British have in Egypt. This army would make the southern arm of the Axis's attack against the Caucasus and the Middle East. As long as the British can hold fast in Egypt therefore, the harder is the task of the Axis forces in the North and the more our Russian Allies are benefited.

The Germans are making great efforts to add to their depleted armies by recruiting fresh troops from Rumania and by bringing Bulgaria more actively into the war. King Boris of Bulgaria, who has always been an Axis sympathiser, is probably in favour of a closer alliance with Germany; but it is doubtful whether the mass of the Bulgarian people, who are very pro-Russian, in their sympathies and indeed almost regard themselves as Russians, can be persuaded into a war against the Soviet Union. There are also signs that Hitler is making renewed efforts to get hold of the remnants of the French Fleet for use against Britain. It remains to be seen whether Marshal Petain, who is at any rate the nominal ruler of unoccupied France, will violate his pledged word by handing the French warships over. Even if he does so, it remains to be seen whether the French sailors will be ready to fire their guns against people who, as they are well aware, are fighting for the liberty of France.

The 'Daily Mirror', one of the most widely read of English newspapers, has been threatened with suppression because of its violent and sometimes irresponsible criticisms of the Government. The question was debated in both Houses of Parliament with the greatest vigour.[4] This may seem waste of time in the middle of a world war, but in fact it is evidence of the extreme regard for freedom of the press which exists in this country. It is very unlikely that the 'Daily Mirror' will actually be suppressed. Even those who are out of sympathy with it politically are against taking so drastic a step, because they know that a free press is one of the strongest supports of national unity and morale, even when it occasionally leads to the publication of undesirable matter. When we look at the newspapers of Germany or Japan, which are simply the mouthpieces of the government, and then at the British newspapers, which are free to criticise or attack the government in any way that does not actually assist the enemy, we see how profound is the difference between totalitarianism and democracy.

Manuel Quezon,[5] President of the Philippine Islands, has arrived in Australia to join General McArthur° and to carry on the business of the Free Filipino Government. It is amusing to record that the Fascist radio has put out no less than three reports that President Quezon had been assassinated by the Americans. They reported this on March 22nd, and later on the same day, they added that Quezon had been assassinated "on the orders of McArthur° because he refused to travel with him to Australia". On March 24th the Rome radio announced yet again that Quezon had been assassinated by British and American agents. And now Quezon has travelled to Australia of his own accord and there affirmed his unconditional loyalty to the Allied cause, and the resolve of the Filipino people to continue the fight against the Japanese invaders. To get to Australia, he had to travel something over a thousand miles, which was a remarkable journey for a man who has been assassinated three times. So much for the truthfulness of Fascist propaganda.

1. The Andaman Islands were occupied by the Japanese on 23 March 1942. The British and Gurkha garrison had been airlifted off by seaplanes almost a fortnight earlier.
2. The town of Toungoo was taken on 30 March, although the area was not abandoned to the Japanese by the Chinese 200th Division until 30 April.
3. Malta was desperate for supplies and suffered incessant air attacks. On 20 March, four merchant ships with 26,000 tons of supplies left Alexandria with an escort of four light cruisers and eleven destroyers in an attempt to reach the island. The Italian Navy, with much heavier ships, made two attacks. Good tactics, rather than firepower, held off the Italians, and little damage was sustained. The British Navy had insufficient fuel and could not refuel at Malta, so the merchant ships had to make the last part of the journey unescorted. One was sunk by air attack some fifty miles from Malta; the other three were sunk in the harbour. Only 5,000 tons of supplies were salvaged, and Malta waited three months before more got through. See Winston Churchill, *The Second World War*, IV, 266–67; U.S.: *The Hinge of Fate*, 297–98; and *2194 Days of War*, 222 (which gives the force as three cruisers, one light cruiser, and seventeen destroyers).
4. The question of the *Daily Mirror*'s alleged irresponsibility centred on a cartoon by Philip Zec which showed a merchant seaman clinging to a life-raft in a rough sea; the caption read:' "The price of petrol has been increased by one penny."—Official.' This seemed to the government and its supporters in and out of Parliament to be unpatriotic, and the *Mirror* was savagely attacked by Herbert Morrison (Labour), Home Secretary, who called the cartoon 'wicked.' To others, the cartoon 'was directed against the wasters of oil' (Wilfrid Roberts, M.P.). The paper was not banned, and Hugh Cudlipp concludes his account of this dispute (*Publish and Be Damned*, 1953, 172–98) by stating that the debate 'caused no loss in circulation, no drop in the price of the newspaper's shares.' It would not be unfair to say that Zec's cartoon summarised Britain's, and the Allies', desperate straits in March 1942 and the frustrated passions they aroused. See also Orwell's War-time Diary for 27.3.42, *1064* and *1064, ns. 2* and *4*.
5. Manuel Luis Quezon (1878–1944), a leader of the movement for independence, had been commissioner for the Philippines in the U.S. Congress, 1909–16, President of the Philippine Senate, 1916–35, and first president of the Philippine Commonwealth, established under the

auspices of the United States, 1935–44. When Japan occupied the Philippines, he was head of the government-in-exile in Australia, March–May 1942, then served on the Pacific War Council in the United States. He died before the date agreed for Philippine independence, 4 July 1946.

1066. Gujarati Newsletter, 5
30 March 1942

The English original was written by Orwell. No script has been traced.

1067. To Hsiao Ch'ien
31 March 1942   PP/EB/NP

PERSONAL

Dear Hsiao Ch'ien,
Many thanks for your letter of March 29th. I am glad you can manage the two dates. As for China's political history, you can say anything you like, because so far as we are concerned there are no complications, and nothing that is likely to cause offence. As to India, it is a more prickly subject, but as you say, there is no particular reason to bring it in here.

Yours,
[No name/position]

1068. To R. U. Hingorani
31 March 1942   Typewritten; handwritten annotation   PP/EB/NP

Dear Dr. Hingorani,
Many thanks for your letter and the script.[1] I hope you will forgive my delay in answering, but my schedule is very full and I have had difficulty in finding a free date for you.

Could you deliver the talk on Friday, April 10th, at 5 p.m., from Broadcasting House? It would do if you come to Broadcasting House about 4 o'clock on that day.

Yours sincerely,
Eric Blair
Talks Assistant
Indian Section

1. Hingorani sent in his script on 22 March He said he had prepared it with the aim of trying to show 'certain circles in India' that Thailand's co-operation with Japan should not be interpreted as 'approval of the latter country.' Orwell annotated the letter, 'I.P.O. For censorship please E.A.B' and 'For 10.4.42'.

1069. To Joseph Needham

31 March 1942   Handwritten draft and typewritten versions
PP/EB/NP

Needham had replied to Orwell's letter of 26 March on the 29th. He said he assumed Bernal had probably had in mind, when suggesting his name to Orwell, his 'recent war pamphlet, "The Nazi Attack on International Science." ' He asked for further details of subjects and speakers proposed.

Dear Professor Needham,
Many thanks for your letter of March 29th. The talks in the series are arranged as follows:

1. The Birth of Science (Prof. Gordon Childe)[1]
2. The Beginnings of Modern Science (Prof. Bernal)
3. Experimental & Applied Science (Prof. A. C. G. Egerton)
4. The Economic Bases of Science (Prof. J. Needham)
5. Science in the USSR (Prof. J. G. Crowther)[2]
6. The Future of Science (Prof. Bernal)

I would have liked to have two talks on the economic bases of science, i.e. two other than the talk on science in a Socialist economy, but we had to compress them into one if we were to have two talks about the origins of science. What I should like you to do[3] is a talk about the effects of capitalism on science, the extent to which it has stimulated its development, and the point at which it becomes a retarding influence, followed by a discussion of the position of "pure" science under Fascism. Fascism evidently doesn't prevent the application of scientific discoveries to practical ends, e.g. war, but it is difficult to see how freedom of research can survive under any totalitarian system.

This roughly is what I want discussed—in something under twenty minutes, if you can manage it.

Yours sincerely,
Eric Blair
Talks Assistant
Indian Section

1. Intentionally or erroneously, the second talk was initially scheduled first. Orwell altered the order in the process of drafting his letter.
2. Crowther is incorrectly titled 'Professor'; see *1117, n. 1*.
3. to do] from you *in draft*

1070. To Amabel Williams-Ellis

31 March 1942   PP/EB

Dear Mrs. Williams-Ellis.
Lady Grigg writes to say that her schedule is full up until about June 10th, and she is rather nervous about arranging talks too far ahead because of possible

changes in the political situation etc. Perhaps you might care to write to her directly suggesting the subjects you wanted to talk about. Lady Grigg arranges the talks for this series more or less independently.

Yours sincerely,
George Orwell
Talks Assistant
Indian Section

1071. BBC Talks Booking Form, 31.3.42

Mulk Raj Anand: 'Through Eastern Eyes,' 'New Weapons of War,' 5 (last in series), 12-minute talk, possible subject, propaganda; recorded 10.4.42; broadcast 12.4.42; fee £7.7s. Signed: Z. A. Bokhari.

1072. BBC Talks Booking Form, 31.3.42

Cedric Dover: 'Through Eastern Eyes,' 'These Names Will Live,' Paul Robeson; broadcast 7.4.42; fee £7.7s. Signed: Z. A. Bokhari.

1073. To V. Gordon Childe
1 April 1942   PP/EB

Dear Professor Childe,

Many thanks for your letter of March 28th. We have made out a schedule of talks as follows:

1. The Birth of Science (Prof. Gordon Childe)
2. The Beginnings of Modern Science (Prof. Bernal)
3. Experimental and Applied Science (Prof. A. C. G. Egerton)
4. The Economic Bases of Science (Prof. J. Needham)
5. Science in the USSR (Prof. J. G. Crowther)
6. The Future of Science (Prof. Bernal)

The idea of having two talks, i.e. yours and Professor Bernal's, on the origins of science was suggested to me by Professor Bernal, who pointed out that there existed a considerable body of scientific knowledge (astronomy and so forth) in ancient times, and that after a period of retrogression science made a new start about the end of the Middle Ages, this time in Europe. We wanted you to cover the earlier period, i.e. the discoveries of the Egyptians, the Caldees,° the Indians, the Greeks and so forth, and Professor Bernal told me that you were much the best person for this purpose. The length of talk we want is 15 to 20 minutes, which means about 2000 words.

You mention that you will be in London from the 15th to the 19th April, and if you care to call then, I can give you any further particulars. The date fixed for your talk is June 2nd, and the time fixed for your talk is 1.15 p.m. If you have to remain in Edinburgh I think it will be possible to have your talk recorded there, but this will have to be done some days before the date of the actual transmission. We are asking the Director of Programmes to get in touch with you.

Yours sincerely,
Eric Blair
Talks Assistant
Indian Section

1074. BBC Talks Booking Form, 1.4.42

Gujarati Newsletter, 6; written by E. Blair, translated and read by R. R. Desai alone; broadcast 6.4.42; fee £5.5s + £2.8.2 + £1.14s fare and expenses. Signed: Z. A. Bokhari.

1075. War-time Diary

<u>1.4.42</u>: *Greatly depressed by the apparent failure of the Cripps mission. Most of the Indians seem down in the mouth about it too. Even the ones who hate England want a solution, I think.* ⌈I believe, however, that in spite of the "take it or leave it" with which our government started off, the terms will actually be modified, perhaps in response to pressure at this end.⌉ *Some think[1] the Russians are behind the Cripps plan[2] and that this accounts for Cripps's confidence in putting forward something so apparently uninviting. Since they are not in the war against Japan the Russians cannot have any official attitude about the Indian affair, but they[3] may serve out a directive to their followers, from whom it will get round to other pro-Russians. But then not many Indians are reliably pro-Russian. No sign yet from the English Communist party, whose behaviour might give a clue to the Russian attitude. It is on this kind of guesswork that we have to frame our propaganda, no clear or useful directive ever being handed out from above.*
Connolly wanted yesterday[4] to quote a passage from "Homage to Catalonia" in his broadcast. I opened the book and came on these sentences:
"One of the most horrible features of war is that all the[5] war-propaganda, all the screaming and lies and hatred, comes invariably from people who are not fighting. . . . It is the same in all wars; the soldiers do the fighting, the journalists do the shouting, and no true patriot ever gets near a front-line trench, except on the briefest of propaganda tours. Sometimes it is a comfort to me to think that the aeroplane is altering the conditions of war. Perhaps when the next great war comes we may see that sight unprecedented in all history, a jingo with a bullet-hole in him."[6]
Here I am in the BBC, less than 5 years after writing that. I suppose sooner or later we all write our own epitaphs.

1. *think*] thınk that
2. *Crıpps plan*] plan
3. *but they*] but
4. *wanted yesterday*] yesterday wanted
5. *all the*] all
6. *Homage to Catalonia, CW,* VI, Appendıx I, 208 and 209.

1076. BBC Talks Booking Form, 2.4.42

E. M. Forster: 'Some Books,' 15-minute talk; broadcast 29.4, 27.5, 24.6.42; £21 each talk. Signed: Z. A. Bokhari.

1077. To Director of Programmes, Edinburgh
3 April 1942   EB/NP

TALK ON SCIENCE—by Prof. V. G. Childe, of Edinburgh University.[1]

We have asked Professor V. G. Childe, of Edinburgh University, to broadcast a talk on "The Birth of Science", the first in a series of 6 scientific talks. The date of the broadcast is June 2nd, at 11.15 GMT, in the Eastern Service. We have suggested to him that he might record in Edinburgh and told him that you will be getting in touch with him, to arrange this. We should be grateful if this could be recorded in disc[2] in Edinburgh, and the discs sent to R.P.D. Library, H.O.

[Signed] Eric Blair
(Eric Blair)

1. Copıes were sent to Mıss Quade, Empire Executıve, Glasgow; Empıre Programmes Executive, London; and Miss Boughen, Talks Bookings, London.
2. This was, of course, before tape-recordıng was available. A system of recordıng on wire—for example, Wırek—shortly became available, though not for general use.

1078. BBC Talks Booking Form, 3.4.42

Dr. Hingorani: 'Through Eastern Eyes,' 10-minute talk on Thailand; broadcast 6.4.42; fee £7.7s. Signed: Z. A. Bokhari.

1079. BBC Talks Booking Form, 3.4.42

Princess Indira of Kapurthala: 'We Speak to India,'' 'I Speak English,' 5 and 6, '30 minute discussion in English and Indian languages between Princess Indira, Professor Firth[2] and Z. A. Bokhari, in which Princess Indira will speak for about 8 to ten minutes in English and Indian languages'; recorded 4.4.42; 5 broadcast

5.4.42, 6 to be broadcast 12.4 (but this is crossed out[3]); fee £8.8s each. Signed: Z. A. Bokhari.

1. As frequently for the series 'Through Eastern Eyes,' the title 'We Speak to India' is preceded by 'in my [Orwell's] programme.' Although here Bokhari participated as well as signed the booking form, this series was under Orwell's direction.
2. Reader and later Professor of Linguistics, University of London, and a member of the BBC's Eastern Service Committee; see *846, n. 13.*
3. The second programme, 6, was not recorded, according to a letter from the Programme Contracts Director, 10 April 1942.

1080. War-time Diary

<u>3.4.42</u>: *Cripps's decision to stay an extra week in India is taken as a good omen. Otherwise not much to be hopeful about. Gandhi is deliberately making trouble* [, sending telegrams of condolence to Bose's[1] family on the report of his death, then telegrams of congratulation when it turned out that the report was untrue. Also urging Indians not to adopt the scorched earth policy if India is invaded]. *Impossible to be quite sure what his game is. Those who are anti-Gandhi allege that he has the worst kind of (Indian) capitalist interests behind him, and it is a fact that he usually seems to be staying at the mansion of some kind of millionaire* [or other. This is not necessarily incompatible with his alleged saintliness. His pacifism may be genuine, however. In the bad period of 1940 he also urged non-resistance in England, should England be invaded]. *I do not know whether Gandhi or Buchman[2] is the nearest equivalent to Rasputin in our time.*

Anand[3] says the morale among the exile Indians here is very low. They are still inclined to think that Japan has no evil designs on India and are all talking of a separate peace with Japan. So much for their declarations of loyalty towards Russia and China. I said to A.[4] that the basic fact about nearly all Indian intellectuals is that they don't expect independence, can't imagine it and at heart don't want it. They want to be permanently in opposition, suffering a painless martyrdom, and are foolish enough to imagine that they could play the same schoolboy games with Japan or Germany as they can with Britain. Somewhat to my surprise he agreed. He says that "opposition mentality" is general among them, especially among the Communists, and that Krishna Menon[5] is "longing for the moment when negotiations will break down". At the same moment as they are coolly talking of betraying China by making a separate peace, they are shouting that the Chinese troops in Burma are not getting proper air support. I remarked that this was childish. A: "You cannot overestimate their childishness, George. It is fathomless". [The question is how far the Indians here reflect the viewpoint of the intellectuals in India. They are further from the danger and have probably, like the rest of us, been infected by the peaceful atmosphere of the last 10 months, but on the other hand nearly all who remain here long become tinged with a western Socialist outlook, so that the Indian intellectuals proper are probably far worse. A. himself has not got these vices. He is genuinely anti-Fascist, and has done violence to his feelings, and probably to his reputation, by backing Britain up because he recognizes that Britain is objectively on the anti-Fascist side.[1]

1. Subhas Chandra Bose (1897–1945) was an Indian nationalist leader and left-wing member of the Indian National Congress. Fiercely anti-British, he organised an Indian National Army to support the Japanese. This he led, unsuccessfully, against the British. He believed that when the INA faced Indian troops led by the British, the latter would not fight but be converted. 'Instead, the revolutionary had reverted to his comfortable mercenary status. INA soldiers took to looting from local tribes' (Mihir Bose, *The Lost Hero* [1982], 236). His followers long believed him to be still alive (despite two Indian government inquiries), but it seems certain he died following a plane crash on 19 August 1945 (*The Lost Hero*, 251–52). See *2359, headnote* for a reference to Orwell's publication of one of Bose's broadcasts from Berlin. See also *1119, n. 5*. Documents released by the War Office in November 1993 show that a substantial number of Indian prisoners of war defected to the Italians, the first 3,000 arriving in Italy in August 1942. A British Intelligence report stated, 'We have by our policy towards India, bred up a new class of officer who may be loyal to India, and perhaps to Congress, but is not necessarily loyal to us' (*Daily Telegraph*, 5 December 1993).
2. Frank Nathan Daniel Buchman (1878–1961), evangelist and propagandist, founded, in 1921, the Moral Re-Armament movement, also known, from its place of foundation, as the Oxford Group Movement, and sometimes as Buchmanism.
3. Mulk Raj Anand; see *905, n. 1*. Typescript has 'A'; manuscript has 'Anand.'
4. A.] him
5. V. K. Krishna Menon (1897–1974), Indian statesman, lawyer, author, and journalist, was then living in England. He was active in British left-wing politics and was spokesman of the Indian Congress Party in England in the struggle for independence. In 1947, when India had become independent, he was High Commissioner for India and he represented India at the United Nations, 1952–61. On 31 January 1943, he was one of six speakers at the 'India Demonstration' at the London Coliseum (*Tribune*, 29 January 1943, 20).

1081. News Review, 17

4 April 1942

The typescript was evidently used for the actual broadcast. It carries two censors' stamps; the censor was Bokhari. There is a cut at the beginning and there are a few verbal changes, some in what looks like Orwell's hand (including the words 'paid Indian'). At the top, the words 'NOT CHECKED WITH BROADCAST' have been amended: 'NOT' is obliterated; 'News Review' is written in. The section from 'Let us imagine that the Japanese' to the end was extracted by Orwell and printed as the third of his five specimens of propaganda in *Talking to India*, and is identical with the typescript used for the broadcast. PasB has Weekly News Review by Z. A. Bokhari and gives the timing as 10½ minutes.

[There is still heavy fighting in Central Burma, but the Allies will probably be forced to retreat a good deal further in the direction of Mandalay.

The day before yesterday, news came that the Japanese had made a landing at Akyab, the port on the Bay of Bengal not very far from Calcutta. This is a serious threat to the British forces at Prome, who might be cut off if they do not retreat and if the Japanese force which has landed is strong enough to cut their communications.][1] The Japanese have several different objectives in their invasion of Burma, and their aims are simultaneously strategic, economic and political. Strategically, they are trying to encircle China so that no further war supplies can be sent there from India, and they are also trying to prepare the way for the invasion of India by sea and land. Over land, they might manage to enter India by the difficult route through Manipur and Assam and simultaneously they might move in the direction of Bengal by successive landing operations along the coast. We cannot be sure that either of these manoeuvres will fail, nor can we assume that the monsoon, which begins in Burma about the end of next month, will slow up the Japanese movement very seriously. We can, however, be fairly sure that either by land or sea, they will not be able to bring a very highly mechanised force, with tanks and heavy guns, to India. They will have to rely chiefly on infantry and aeroplanes, against which *numerous*[2] though ill-armed forces can often put up a successful resistance. A very great deal, therefore, depends on the will of the Indian people to defend themselves and upon their feeling that they have something which is really worth fighting for.

Economically the Japanese aim at plundering Burma of its oil, of its rice, and, insofar as they need it, of its timber. The oil is not of much immediate use to them, even if they get possession of the oil wells, because the refineries near Rangoon have already been destroyed. On the other hand, they have the greatest need of the rice, for their armies and, if they have enough shipping to transport it, for their home population.

Politically the Japanese aim at using Burma as a base for propaganda against India. They are now near enough to India to be able to broadcast on medium wave, and we must expect their propaganda to be enormously intensified during coming weeks. At the moment they are keeping rather quiet, because until the negotiations which Sir Stafford Cripps is conducting have been settled one way or the other, they are not quite certain what attitude to take towards *Pandit* Nehru, *Mahatma*[3] Gandhi and the other Indian political leaders. Should the negotiations end in a satisfactory settlement the Japanese, through their *paid Indian* mouthpieces [Subhas Chandra Bose and Ras Bihari Bose[4]] will open up a campaign of libel against *Pandit* Nehru and the others, whom they will accuse of being the paid agents of British imperialism. Should the negotiations fail, they will praise *Pandit* Nehru to the skies as the man who was not deceived by British promises and who is struggling for the independence of the Indian peoples. Which line they take will depend on the outcome of the negotiations, but one way or another the barrage of propaganda will begin within a week, and it is important for *us in India*[5] to be prepared for it, and not deceived by it.

Simultaneously with this propaganda campaign, the Japanese will point to Burma and Siam as examples of the success of the Japanese New Order, or, as they call it, 'The Co-Prosperity Sphere'. It is clear from the reports coming in that in Lower Burma, especially in the district of Tharrawaddy, the Japanese have managed to induce large numbers of *excitable and adventurous*[6] Burmese to fight on their side in the vain hopes of winning independence for Burma. They will certainly try to repeat this manoeuvre in India. It is important, therefore, to see just how the Japanese Co-Prosperity Sphere works, how it fits in with Japanese and Nazi propaganda, and how both of these compare with the true facts. We can foretell with some certainty what will happen both because of the existing situation and because of the example of what the Germans and Japanese have done in the past.

Let us imagine that the Japanese can gain undisputed possession of the whole of Burma. Let us also suppose that the conquered Burmese are more or less on their side, having believed in the Japanese promise to make Burma independent after the war and having also believed that Japan is going to enrich Burma by gifts of manufactured goods and by stimulating Burmese industries. Now, in these circumstances, what will actually happen? The first *thing* is that the Japanese will take away from the Burmese most of their rice, not only the surplus which they usually export to India, but also a good deal of what they usually eat themselves. The Japanese are bound to do this, because they must have rice for their armies and for their home population. But, it may be said, this does not matter if they pay the Burmese for their rice. The only difficulty is, what are they to pay with? In the first place, they will pay in money which they will print off in exactly such quantities as they think necessary. The Burmese peasant whose rice has been taken from him will get paper notes in return, and it will be two or three months before he will fully grasp that these notes are worthless, because they cannot buy anything. Necessarily they cannot buy anything because, with a great war on their hands, the Japanese cannot manufacture goods for export, even if they had any wish to do so, for the benefit of the people they have conquered. The money which they print will therefore be a painless way of plundering the peoples of Burma, Siam, Malaya and the other territories they have over-run. The Germans have done exactly the same in Europe, using what are called "Occupation Marks," that is to say, money specially printed for the use of the army of occupation. This money has to be accepted by the conquered peoples in return for goods, but in practice it will not buy anything. We may assume, therefore, that should the Japanese get possession of the whole of Burma, it will be only a few months before the Burmese discover that, so far from being liberated and enriched by their Japanese friends, they are being systematically robbed. Probably even the most ignorant Burmese will have grasped this fact by the middle of this winter, when the 1942 rice crop is cut.

If the swindle of the Japanese Co-Prosperity Sphere is so simple as this, why is it that Japanese propaganda should have any success? To answer this question, one should look at Europe, where the same story has been enacted a year or two earlier. There you had the same essential situation. The Germans made promises very similar to the Japanese, they divided and weakened their victims with very similar propaganda, then they invaded and conquered them, and then they proceeded systematically to plunder them by means of worthless money, holding them down with a military occupation and a ruthless police force. When it was too late, the conquered peoples learned the truth about Hitler's New Order. Something very similar has happened in Siam, and is happening, or may be happening, in Burma. We see, therefore, the immense importance of political consciousness and of a sceptical attitude towards tempting propaganda. Just as in Europe, so in Asia, certain peoples have fallen into the clutch of the Fascists because they listened to what the Fascists said, instead of observing what they had actually done. The words which the Japanese are now pouring out towards Burma and will soon be pouring out towards India, are extremely inviting, but their deeds in Korea, in China, in Manchukuo, in Formosa, are less inviting. In all these countries they have held the peoples down with the club and the machine-gun, they have robbed them of their crops and of their raw materials, they have crushed their national movements, interfered with the education of their children, and have failed entirely to develop their resources except in the interests of Japan itself. They have been doing that to Formosa for fifty years, to Korea for forty years, to Manchukuo for ten years, and to the occupied parts of China for five years. To-morrow they hope to do the same to India, to Australia, and possibly even to parts of Africa. Very much, therefore, depends on the steadfastness and common sense of the people to whom the Fascist propaganda is addressed, for it is better to fight back and be free, even though one suffers like the Chinese, than to submit and discover too late that one has been deceived like the people of Siam. To those who say that Japan will set Burma or India free, the best answer is: Why then have they not set free Korea and Formosa, which they have had in their power for so long? To those who say that the Japanese are fighting for the liberation of India, the best answer is: Why then are they fighting against the liberation of China? To those who say that the cause of Japan is the cause of Asia as against the European races, the best answer is: Why then do the Japanese constantly make war against other races who are Asiatics no less than themselves?

1. West: *Broadcasts* does not note the opening cut. This leads to his stating that New Delhi's denial of the report of the Akyab landing broadcast by Tokyo 'cannot have reached London by the time Orwell's talk went out' (72). Evidently news of the denial did become known to Orwell after the text of the broadcast had been typed, hence this deletion. The Japanese were to reach Akyab by land. The British abandoned it a month after this News Review was broadcast.
2. *numerous*] enormous, *handwritten substitution*
3. *Pandit . . . Mahatma*] Mr., *handwritten substitutions (and twice more in the paragraph)*
4. For Subhas Chandra Bose, see *1080, n. 1* and *1119, n. 5*. Ras Bihari Bose (1880?–1945), no relation to Subhas, had worked for India's independence since 1911. Held responsible for organising terrorist movements, he went, in 1915, to Japan. After the failure of Cripps's mission, he was asked by the Japanese to make way for Subhas. He agreed, and on 17 April 1942 the Japanese Cabinet decided to use Subhas 'to present policy' (Mihir Bose, *The Lost Hero*, 191, 197–98, who spells the name Rash Behari Bose).
5. *us in India*] Indian listeners, *handwritten substitution*. This alteration is a neat example of Orwell associating London with his audience in India.
6. *excitable and adventurous*] politically ill-educated, *handwritten substitution*

1082. Gujarati Newsletter, 6

6 April 1942

The English original was written by Orwell. No script has been traced.

1083. War-time Diary

<u>6.4.42</u>: ⌐Yesterday had a look at the bit of the by-pass road which is being built between Uxbridge and Denham. Amazed at the enormous scale of the undertaking. West of Uxbridge is the valley of the Colne, and over this the road runs on a viaduct of brick and concrete pillars, the viaduct being I suppose ¼ mile long. After that it runs on a raised embankment. Each of these pillars is 20 feet high or thereabouts, about 15 by 10 feet thick, and there are two of them every fifteen yards or so. I should say *each pillar* would use 40,000 bricks, exclusive of foundations, and exclusive of the concrete running above, which must use up tons of steel and concrete for every yard of road. Stupendous quantities of steel (for reinforcing) lying about, also huge slabs of granite. Building this viaduct alone must be a job comparable, in the amount of labour it uses up, to building a good-sized warship. And the by-pass is very unlikely to be of any use till after the war, even if finished by that time. Meanwhile there is a labour shortage everywhere. Apparently the people who sell bricks are all-powerful. (Cf. the useless surface-shelters, which even when they were being put up were pronounced to be useless by everyone who knew anything about building, and the unnecessary repairs to un-inhabited private houses which are going on all over London). Evidently when a scandal passes a certain magnitude it becomes invisible.¹

Saw in Denham someone driving a dog-cart, in quite good trim.

1084. To K. K. Ardaschir

7 April 1942   PP/EB

Dear Mr. Ardaschir,¹
I delayed answering your letter because I was trying to find a date to fit in your talk on "The Sick Man Revives";² but I find I cannot use it before roughly the middle of May. There is no reason why we should not record it in the near future, however. Could you let me know a day next week which would be suitable to you for recording, and we will then fix a time. You will, of course, have to come somewhat earlier than the actual hour of recording, in order to rehearse the talk.

The other talk—"Forty Years in England" I cannot use immediately, but would like to keep it by me as an emergency talk, so we could have it recorded at the same time as the other.

Yours sincerely,
Eric Blair
Talks Assistant
Indian Section

1. K. K. Ardaschir (1890–) was born in Bombay, the son of a Persian landowner. He became a journalist on the *Westminster Gazette* in 1910 and worked for several newspapers in Egypt and India; was the author of plays and books; fought in the First Balkan War, 1912–13; and became an officer in the Ottoman Imperial Guard. See Orwell's letter to Mrs. Talbot Rice, *1223*.

2. 'The Sick Man' was the description given by Tsar Nicholas in 1844 to the Ottoman Empire, said to be in decline then for some 250 years Its revival would presumably have been attributed in the talk to the founder of modern Turkey, Kemal Atatürk (1880–1938), a general who abolished the Ottoman caliphate and ruled, and reformed, Turkey as its president, 1923–38.

1085. To V. Gordon Childe

7 April 1942   PP/EB

Dear Professor Childe,
Thank you for your letter of April 4th. I am afraid I did not make it quite clear in my letter of April 1st that the talk could be recorded *in Edinburgh* on discs, and the discs then sent from Edinburgh to London for the broadcast. However, as you will be in London on May 28th, we should prefer to record your talk here, if you will have time for that. I think we should allow about an hour and a quarter, to include rehearsal and timing; so if this arrangement is convenient to you, perhaps you would let me know what time you would prefer to come to Broadcasting House, and I will then make the necessary arrangements at this end.

I am writing again to the Director of Programmes in Edinburgh to tell him that it will not be necessary for him to make arrangements for you to record there now.

I should be grateful if you would kindly let me have a copy of your script at least a week before May 28th, if you agree to record it on that day.

Yours sincerely,
Eric Blair
Talks Assistant
Indian Section

Childe's letter has on its verso a first-draft reply:

Reply: we can arrange to record his talk on May 28th, but will he let us know what time of day will suit him.

E. A. B

1086. BBC Talks Booking Form, 7.4.42

Jack Common:[1] 'We Speak to India,' 'Two 15-minute talks in English, the first on "Peace in Wartime"', title of the second not yet decided'; broadcast 8 and 15.4.42; fee £8.8s each talk + fare 7s 5d. Signed: Z. A. Bokhari.

1 Jack Common was a former Tyneside working-class man whom Orwell had met through *The Adelphi*. His books include *The Freedom of the Streets: Essays on Political Subjects* (1938), *Kiddar's Luck* (1951), and *The Ampersand* (1954); he edited *Seven Shifts* (autobiographical essays by working men) (1938). See *95* and *295, n. 1*. See also *Jack Common's Revolt Against 'An Age of Plenty,'* edited by Huw Beynon and Colin Hutchinson (1980), which contains much of

his fugitive writing. His memoir, 'Orwell at Wallington,' was published after Common's death in *Orwell Remembered*, 139–43.

1087. BBC Talks Booking Form, 9.4.42

Mrs. Bentwich: 'Women Generally Speaking,' 74, introduced by Lady Grigg, title not yet stated for 13-minute talk; broadcast 29.4.42; fee £8.8s. Signed: Z. A. Bokhari.

1088. BBC Talks Booking Form, 9.4.42

Arthur Calder-Marshall: 'Literature Between Wars,' 'Money and the Artist,' 30 minutes; broadcast 14.4.42; fee £15.15s. Signed: Z. A. Bokhari.

1089. BBC Talks Booking Form, 9.4.42

Lady Grigg: 'Women Generally Speaking,' '(Present Contract expires after B'cast on April 29th)'; 'To arrange & introduce special 13-minute programme for women listeners. (Contract to run till end of May 1942)'; broadcast 6, 13, 20, and 27.5.42; fee £8.8s each broadcast. Signed: Z. A. Bokhari.

1090. BBC Talks Booking Form, 9.4.42

Princess Indira of Kapurthala: 'Through Eastern Eyes,' 'The Debate Continues'; broadcast 20 and 27.4.42 and 4.5.42; fee £8.8s each talk. Signed: Z. A. Bokhari.

1091. BBC Talks Booking Form, 9.4.42

K. S. Shelvankar: 'Through Eastern Eyes,' 'These Names Will Live,' Aldous Huxley; broadcast 5.5.42; fee £8.8s. Signed: Z. A. Bokhari.[1]

1. This talk was re-arranged for 12 May 1942 and a new booking form issued; see *1128*.

1092. BBC Talks Booking Form, 9.4.42

S. Telkar: 'Through Eastern Eyes,' 'These Names Will Live,' 1. J. L. Garvin; 2. Frank Owen; broadcast 14 and 21.4.42; fee 1. £7.7s; 2. £8.8s. Signed: Z. A. Bokhari.

1093. BBC Talks Booking Form, 9.4.42

S. Telkar: 'Through Eastern Eyes,' 'Today and Yesterday,' '15 minute talk on Happiness'; broadcast 30.4.42; fee £8.8s. Signed: Z. A. Bokhari.

1094. BBC Talks Booking Form, 9.4.42

Rebecca West: 'Women Generally Speaking,' 73, introduced by Lady Grigg, subject not yet stated for 13-minute talk; broadcast 22.4.42; fee £12.12s.[1] Signed: Z. A. Bokhari.

1. Rebecca West (1892–1983; DBE, 1959), novelist, journalist, and essayist, was invited to read 'from her recent book'—almost certainly *Black Lamb and Grey Falcon: The Record of a Journey through Jugoslavia in 1937* (New York, 1941; London, 1942). She decided to speak instead on 'Nationalism and Internationalism,' according to a memorandum from Bokhari to the Empire Programme Executive and Talks Booking, 16 April 1942. Bokhari took the opportunity presented by the engagement of a distinguished writer to raise the question of the poor fees offered to speakers. It was agreed that the fee of eight guineas (usual for a talk of $12\frac{1}{2}$–15 minutes) should stand, if she read from her book, but if she prepared a talk, she would be offered £12.12s. This led to the explanation that a higher scale had recently been adopted for European Service talks: $6\frac{1}{4}$–$8\frac{1}{2}$ minutes, 6 guineas; $8\frac{3}{4}$–11 minutes, 7gns.; $11\frac{1}{4}$–$13\frac{1}{4}$ minutes, 8gns.; $13\frac{1}{2}$–15 minutes, 9gns. These rates had not been suggested for the Indian/Empire Service because they would seriously affect their budget. Further, many talks to India were fifteen minutes, which would mean another guinea. Since there had been no complaints, it was proposed to stick to the existing scale: $7\frac{1}{2}$–$9\frac{1}{4}$ minutes, 6 guineas; $9\frac{1}{2}$–$12\frac{1}{4}$ minutes, 7gns.; $12\frac{1}{2}$–15 minutes, 8gns. Comments were requested.

1095. To Director of Programmes, Edinburgh
10 April 1942

TALK ON SCIENCE—Professor V. G. Childe.[1]

10th April 1942.

In continuation of my memo dated 3rd April 1942, we have now heard from Professor Childe that he will be in London on May 28th, and he appears to be willing to record the talk on that day down here. This has not yet been definitely arranged yet,[2] but I think that he will agree to this arrangement, so perhaps we may cancel our request for this talk to be recorded in Edinburgh. I hope you have not been put to too much trouble over this.

[Signed] Eric Blair
(Eric Blair)

1. Copies sent to Miss Quade, Empire Executive, Glasgow; and Empire Programmes Executive, London.
2. 'yet' is repeated.

1096. To E. M. Forster

10 April 1942   PP/EB/NP

Dear Mr. Forster,[1]

Mr. Bokhari has asked me to let you know the dates of your next three book talks. We should like you to give them on Wednesdays, 29th April, 27th May, and 24th June. As from April 19th we are changing the times of our programmes, and your talks will now go out at 1.30 p.m., D.B.S.T.[2] I have asked our Contracts Department to get in touch with you.

I understand that you have some books which were sent to you for your last book talk; these were taken out in Mr. Bokhari's name, so that he is responsible for returning them to the BBC Library. They are beginning to ask for some of the books back, so he would be very grateful if you would return them to him, and he will pass them on to the Library.

Yours sincerely,
George Orwell
Talks Assistant
Indian Section

1. Edward Morgan Forster (1879–1970) was described in a biographical note to the BBC pamphlet *Books and Authors*, 29 October 1946: 'E. M. Forster, perhaps the greatest living English novelist, is particularly well known in India on account of his book *A Passage to India* (1924). He revisited India at the end of 1945 to attend the International PEN conference at Jaipur.' See also *600, n. 48.*
2. Double British Summer Time. Clocks were advanced two hours from Greenwich Mean Time during the 'summer' instead of the customary one hour, to make the best use of daylight and aid war production. Farmers were allowed to work to single summer time if they wished. In 1942 DBST ran from 4 April (one month earlier than in 1941) to 8 August (the same as 1941). Single Summer Time ran through the period August to April, that is, including winter.

1097. To M. Myat Tun

10 April 1942   PP/EB

Dear Myat Tun,

I have made out a list of Burmese places which are likely to be in the news shortly, for the use of announcers, so that they may be able to pronounce them more correctly than hitherto. I have writen them down phonetically as best I can, and I would be very glad if you would be kind enough to O.K. this list and also add any other names you can think of which may come into the news and present difficulties to announcers. Of course, I have used here the pronunciations officially in use among Europeans in Burma, but these do not usually differ much from the Burmese pronunciation, except in the case of places like Rangoon, Moulmein, etc.[1]

Yours,
Eric Blair
Talks Assistant
Indian Section

The list follows on a separate sheet:

Akyab	— Ack-yab
Amarpura	— A-ma-ra-poo-rah
Bhamo	— Bah-mo
Katha	— Ka-thah
Kyaukpyu	— Chowk-pyoo (ow as in "now". py as in "keep your head)
Lashio	— La-sho
Magwe	— Ma-gway
Myingyan	— Myin-jarn (my as in "jam your brakes on)
Myitkyina	— Myi-chi-nah (ditto)
Minbu	— Min-boo
Meiktila	— Mek-ti-la
Monywa	— Moan-ywah
Mogok	— Mo-goak[2]
Pakokku	— Pa-ko-koo
Shwebo	— Shway-bo
Shwegu	— Shway-goo
Sagaing	— Sa-gaing (ain as in "mine")
Tengueh	— Ten-gyoo-ay
Yenangyaung	— Yay-nan-noung (own as in "sound")[3]

1. William Empson in *Orwell Remembered* (177–83) states, 'I rather think we each had a brief period as Burmese Editor, but it was I who held that office during the fall of Burma.' The records traced do not indicate that Orwell had any such formal responsibility. This inquiry and the arrangement for Myat Tun to talk about Moulmein (see *960*) seem to be the extent of his involvement with that section of the work.
2. Both words on this line have been written in by Orwell to correct what was originally typed 'Mogoh—Mo-goali.'
3. For Orwell's comments on the continued failure of announcers to pronounce Burmese names correctly, see 'As I Please,' 53, 5 January 1945, *2599*.

1098. War-time Diary

<u>10.4.42</u>:   *British naval losses in the last 3 or 4 days: 2 cruisers and an aircraft carrier sunk, 1 destroyer wrecked.*[1] *Axis losses: 1 cruiser sunk.*
From Nehru's speech today: "Who dies if India live?" How impressed the pinks will be—and how they would snigger at "Who dies if England live?"[2]

1. On 5 April, the heavy cruisers *Dorsetshire* and *Cornwall*, the destroyer *Tenedos*, and the armed merchant-ship *Hector* were sunk by Japanese aircraft operating from carriers in the Indian Ocean. On 9 April (the day 64,000 Filipinos and 12,000 Americans surrendered at Bataan) the aircraft carrier *Hermes* and the destroyer *Vampire* were among a further group of ships sunk by the Japanese in the Indian Ocean, including 135,000 tons of merchant and troop ships.
2. 'Who dies if England live?' comes from Kipling's 'For All We Have and Are' (1914); it also has the line, 'The Hun is at the gate!' (For 'Hun' see *948, n. 26*.) See also *604, n. 5*.

1099. Weekly News Review

11 April 1942

No Weekly News Review in English was broadcast on 11 April 1942. It would have been transmitted at 1500 GMT but the Eastern Service Transmission was closed down at '1439 40 secs,' according to PasB. At 1500 the African Transmission, which, like the Empire Transmission, used the Red Network, carried a speech by Sir Stafford Cripps on his mission to India and its failure. This lasted 25 minutes. Orwell heard Cripps's speech as broadcast from Delhi; see *1100.*

1100. War-time Diary

11.4.42: *It[1] has flopped after all. I don't regard this as final, however.*
Listened-in to Cripps's speech coming from Delhi, which we were re-broadcasting for England etc. These transmissions which we occasionally listen-in to from Delhi are our only clue as to how our own broadcasts sound in India. Always very bad quality and a great deal of background noise which it is impossible to take out in recordings. ⌐The speech good in the earlier part and plain-speaking enough to cause, I should think, a lot of offence. In the later part it rather moved off into the breezy uplands vein.⌐ *It is a curious fact that in the more exalted passages in his speeches Cripps seems to have caught certain inflexions of voice from Churchill. This may point to the fact—which would explain his having undertaken this mission when only having such bad terms to offer—that he is at present much under Churchill's personal influence.*

1. Sir Stafford Cripps's mission to India.

1101. Gujarati Newsletter, 7

13 April 1942

The English original was written by Orwell. No script has been traced. PasB gives timing as $10\frac{1}{2}$ minutes.

1102. Z. A. Bokhari to E. W. D. Boughen, Talks Booking

13 April 1942

This memorandum, which concerned Orwell only indirectly, is indicative of the kinds of everyday problems that occurred in programme management in the Indian Section, faced with too much work and too few people. The 'Indian Editor' referred to (with implied disrespect) was Sir Malcolm Darling: little love was lost between him and Bokhari.

Yesterday, Sunday April 12th, Princess Indira of Kapurthala read a talk for the Hindustani Unit, the duration of which was 10 minutes. For services rendered by her in this connection I presume that the Indian Editor will send a contract slip to you. For the Indian Section in London, she yesterday compered and presented the messages of the Bevin Boys;[1] the duration of the progamme was 15 minutes.

2.° We owe her a special debt of gratitude and a contract in keeping with the quality and quantity of help she gave us when at 5 p.m., without any previous notice, she read a talk, which was to have been given by Mulk Raj Anand. Mulk Raj's talk was recorded, but the records did not arrive in time in the studio, and when they did arrive, instead of Mulk Raj's talk on Propaganda, the brilliant assistant of the R.P.D.[2] brought the records of Dr. Masina's talk on Dietetics.

So the Hindustani Unit, Abbey Manor, owes her the fee for reading a talk in Hindustani, and (2), the Indian Section, London, owes her for compering the Bevin Boys programme, and her heroic performance in reading Mulk Raj Anand's script.

The following day the Contracts Director wrote to Princess Indira[3] thanking her warmly for her help and offering fees totalling 11 guineas.

1. These Bevin Boys were technical trainees from India. The scheme took its name from the Minister of Labour, Ernest Bevin. It is to be distinguished from the later Bevin Boys scheme to conscript young men for the coal mines in Britain; see *949, n. 2.*
2. Recorded Programmes Department.
3. Princess Indira's name was sometimes given as 'Indra,' the Hindu god of the heavens and of rain.

1103. To E. M. Forster

14 April 1942   EB/NP

Dear Mr. Forster,

Many thanks for your letter. As to the questionnaire by the BBC which you mention,[1] I don't think it ever bore much fruit, but I am finding out what replies did come in and will let you have any material which looks as if it might be useful.

I think it would be a good idea to more or less wrap your talk round Anand's novel and the Indian number of "Life & Letters". "Indian Writing" could be mentioned in the same connection, and perhaps also the recent selection of Kipling's poems with Eliot's introduction. A book which is more or less appropos° but unfortunately must *not* be mentioned is K. S. Shelvankar's "The Problem of India".[2] This has been banned in India and if we refer to it the censorship will cut it out. If you could delicately hint that people here are very interested in English-language Indian writers such as Ahmed Ali,[3] etc. it would be a good propaganda point. It might even be worth mentioning that people are becoming more interested in Indian painting, and "Horizon" are shortly publishing an article by an Indian on

Bengali folk painting.[4] One minor cause of trouble with the Indian intelligentsia is that English magazines won't print their stuff.

Yours

George Orwell

1. In Forster's letter of 13 April, responding to Orwell's of the 10th, he said he believed that the BBC had 'instituted an inquiry in India to find out what interested them' and he wondered if this had borne fruit (West: *Broadcasts*, 187).
2. This was a Penguin Special published in 1940. For Bokhari's attitude to Shelvankar, see *1050, n. 1.*
3. Ahmed Ali (b 1906, 1908, or 1910) was a Pakistani writer and Professor of English in Bengal; Listener Research Director for BBC New Delhi, 1942–45; and worked for the government of Pakistan, 1949–60. He was co-editor of *Indian Writing* (London, 1940–45) and *Tomorrow* Bombay (India, 1942–44). Among his publications in English (he also published in Urdu) are the novels *Twilight in Delhi* (1940, 1967; see *623*) and *Ocean of Night* (1964), which reflect on the Muslim heritage in India; and *The Falcon and the Hunted Bird* (1950), translations into English of classical Urdu poetry. A critical work, *Mr Eliot's Penny-World of Dreams*, was published in 1941.
4. Ajit Mookerjee, 'Kalighat Folk Painters,' *Horizon*, June 1942.

1104. BBC Talks Booking Form, 15.4.42

Gujarati Newsletters, 7–13; written by E. Blair; translated and read by R. R. Desai; broadcast 13, 20, and 27.4.42 and 4, 11, 18, and 25.5.42;[1] fee £5.5s + £2.8.2 + £1.14s fare. Signed: Z. A. Bokhari.

1. There are four booking forms to cover these talks. From 20 April the time of day of the broadcast was changed slightly.

1105. News Review, 18

18 April 1942

The words 'News Review' are written at the top of the first page, and the typescript bears both censorship stamps; the censor was Bokhari; the word 'NOT' in 'NOT CHECKED WITH BROADCAST' has not been crossed out. The amendments appear to be in Bokhari's hand. The second sentence originally read: 'We can summarise the news from the battle fronts in a few words before proceeding to discuss the political situation, which is full of possibilities, both hopeful and threatening.' An elongated bracket is drawn in the left-hand margin of the next paragraph and of that beginning 'The British Budget' (both indicated by opening and closing square brackets here); neither is crossed out. These may not have been so marked because they were censored—and there is hardly anything in the first paragraph that would seem to attract a censor's ire—but as alternative cuts in case time were short. Although this script ran for only 10½ minutes, seeming to allow plenty of time for announcements in a 15-minute broadcast, it is noticeable that from 31 January until this date, all timings fell between ten minutes and ten minutes fifty seconds. Only with the next News Review were timings regularly over thirteen minutes for several weeks.

The section 'It is clear from reports that have come in . . .' to '. . . agents of British imperialism' was reprinted as the fourth of the five specimens of propaganda in *Talking to India*. This is verbally identical with the typescript except for the two words noted and a few commas. The typescript has been reproduced here. PasB has Weekly News Review by Z. A. Bokhari and gives the timing as 10½ minutes.

During this week the principal events have been political rather than military. The news from the battle fronts *are° well known & may well be left out. Now let's proceed to discuss* the political situation, which is full of possibilities, both hopeful and threatening.

[In Burma the Japanese have received large reinforcements and have made a further advance. As we foretold in earlier letters, the British have had to abandon the Burmese oil-fields. These had been systematically wrecked beforehand and will be of no direct use to the Japanese. The great oil refinery near Rangoon was in any case destroyed some time ago. Apart from the fortress of Corregidor, fighting is still going on in various parts of the Philippine islands, and American long-range bombers, operating from bases more than a thousand miles away, have made a heavy raid on the Japanese forces. The Japanese plans to invade Australia do not seem to have made any further progress. From the Western theatre of war there is not much to report. The snow in Russia is thawing and for the time being the mud slows down operations, but the heroic Red Army continues to make small advances and the British bombing planes continue their raids on Western Germany.]

Sir Stafford Cripps is expected to reach Britain *shortly*.[1] Now that a week has gone by since the breakdown of negotiations between Sir Stafford Cripps and the Indian political leaders, it is possible to see his mission in clearer perspective and to say something about the reactions to it in various parts of the world.

It is clear from the reports that have come in from many countries that only the supporters of Fascism are pleased by the failure of Sir Stafford Cripps's mission. On the other hand, there is a general feeling that the failure was not complete, in so much that the negotiations have clarified the issue and did not end in such a way as to make further advances impossible. However deep the disagreement, there was no ill-feeling on either side, and no suggestion that either Sir Stafford Cripps or the Indian political leaders were acting other than in good faith. In Britain and the United States Sir Stafford has actually enhanced his already high reputation. He undertook a difficult job in which he risked being personally discredited, and his obvious sincerity has impressed the whole world. The Axis propagandists are attempting to represent the breakdown as a refusal on the part of India to defend herself, and an actual Indian desire to pass under Japanese rule. This is a direct lie, and the Axis broadcasters are only able to support it by deliberately not quoting from the speeches of Mr. Nehru and the other political leaders. Even Mr. Gandhi, though remaining faithful to his programme of non-violence, has not suggested that he wishes to see the Japanese in India, merely that he believes that they should be resisted by spiritual rather than material weapons. Mr. Nehru has not ceased to be anti-British, but he is even more emphatically anti-Japanese. He has asserted in the most vigorous terms possible that Indian resistance will continue and that the Congress party will do nothing to hamper the British war effort, although the failure to alter the political *status quo* will prevent their taking a very direct part in it. He has said, as on many other occasions, that however deep his own objections to the British Government may be, the fact remains that the cause of Britain, of Soviet Russia and China, represents progress, while the cause of Germany and Japan represents re-action, barbarism and oppression. In spite of the difficulty, therefore, of collaborating directly with the British forces, he will do all in his power to raise popular Indian feeling against the aggressor and to make Indians realise that their liberty is inextricably bound up with an Allied victory. For even at the worst, India *may*[2] get its independence from Britain, whereas the idea of India or any other subject nation winning its liberty in a Fascist-ruled[3] world is laughable.

These are not empty words, and the attitude of the mass of the Indian people and also of the leading political parties such as the Congress movement, can undoubtedly make a very great difference to the outcome of the war. Even the fact that it would be difficult for India to equip every Indian with modern weapons does not alter this. Back in 1935 or 1936 when it became clear that a Japanese invasion of China was imminent, many outside observers considered that nothing could be done to stop the Japanese, because the Chinese peasants had little sense of nationality and modern armaments hardly existed on the Chinese side. As it turned out, these predictions were quite false. Ever since 1937, the Japanese have been engaged in an exhausting war in which they have gained very little material benefit, lost great numbers of men, reduced the standard of living of their own working-class and alienated millions of Orientals who might otherwise have been on their side. The reason was that there existed in China a strong popular political movement which could fire the peasants and the town working-class and make them ready to struggle against the invader, pitting[4] their numbers and their courage against superior armaments. Against very heavily mechanised armies, such as the German army, mere popular resistance with rifles and hand grenades may perhaps be ineffective, though the success of the Russian guerrillas makes even this doubtful. But against the sort of army that the Japanese have employed in China, or the sort of army that they are likely to be able to use for the invasion of India—that is, an army mainly of infantry—guerrilla methods can be highly successful and the "scorched earth" policy can immensely hamper the invader. Very much, therefore, turns upon Indian popular enthusiasm and the efforts of Mr. Nehru may turn out to be a thorn in the Japanese side. There is no doubt that the Axis propagandists are well aware that Mr. Nehru, Mr. Azad and the other leading Congress personalities are heart and soul against them, and it will not be very long before they once again begin libelling them as the agents of British imperialism.

[The British Budget was announced 3 days ago, and on the whole has caused satisfaction. Summarising it briefly, its provisions are as follows: It does not add to direct taxation and it actually remits income tax on the lower levels. Roughly speaking the poorer grades of manual workers will be paying less in direct taxation during the current year.

On the other hand, the Budget adds heavily to indirect taxation, almost all of it on luxuries. Tobacco and alcohol are both very heavily taxed, so also are all kinds of luxuries such as fur coats, silk dresses and the like. Certain kinds of very cheap clothes intended to be worn at work will be exempted from taxation. The tax on tobacco will not apply to the armed forces, who will be able to buy each day a certain number of cigarettes at the old price. In general, it is felt to be a democratic Budget, which will hasten the equalisation in the standard of living and the wiping out of class distinctions which is happening in Britain as a result of the war.]

There is very bad news in the fact that Laval has returned to the French Cabinet. Laval is a French millionaire who has been known for many years to be a direct agent of the Nazi Government. He played a leading part in the intrigues which led to the downfall of France and since the Armistice has steadily worked for what is called "collaboration" between France and Germany, meaning that France should throw in its lot with the Axis, send an army to take part in the war against Russia, and use the French Fleet against Britain. For over a year he has been kept out of office, thanks to American pressure, and his return probably means that diplomatic relations between France and the U.S.A. will now come to an end. The American Government is already recalling its ambassador and has advised its nationals to leave France. This is perhaps no bad thing in itself, for there is very little doubt that German submarines operating in the Atlantic have habitually made use of French ports, both in Africa and in the West Indies, and the fact that France and America were theoretically on friendly terms has made these manoeuvres harder to deal with. If relations are broken off, the Americans will at any rate not feel that their hands are tied by the so-called neutrality of France. Nevertheless, there is very great danger that at some critical moment Laval may succeed in throwing the French Fleet into battle against the British Navy, which is already struggling against the combined navies of three nations. That is undoubtedly what he aims at doing, but he may be frustrated by the fact that the common people of France are whole-heartedly anti-Nazi. There is some reason to think that the French sailors would refuse to use their guns against the British, whom they well understand to be fighting for the liberty of France. Disturbances, riots and sabotage continue in Occupied France, and almost every day the German newspapers announce the shooting of fresh batches of hostages. The Germans themselves appear to believe that if a British and American invading force landed in France it would be eagerly helped by the French population. Meanwhile, however, the situation is full of danger, and we can be sure that the Quisling element in France has been assigned some fairly important part in the great spring campaign which the Germans are now preparing.

1. *shortly*] today, *substituted in Bokhari's hand*
2. *may*] *underlined in typescript, not an insertion*
3. Fascist-ruled] *hyphenated in* Talking to India, *not so in typescript*
4. pitting] *as typescript;* Talking to India *has* putting

1106. War-time Diary

<u>18.4.42</u>:   *No question that Cripps's speeches etc. have caused a lot of offence, ie. in India. Outside India I doubt whether many people blame the British government for the breakdown. One trouble at the moment is the tactless utterances of Americans who for years have been blahing about "Indian freedom" and British imperialism, and have suddenly had their eyes opened to the fact that the Indian intelligentsia don't want independence, ie. responsibility. Nehru is making provocative speeches to the effect that all the English are the same, of whatever political party, and*[1] *also trying to make trouble between Britain and the USA by alleging that the USA has done all the real fighting. At the same time he reiterates at intervals that he is not pro-Japanese and Congress will defend India to the last. The BBC thereupon picks out these passages from his speeches and broadcasts them without mentioning the anti-British passages, whereat Nehru complains (quite justly) that he has been misrepresented.* ⌈A recent directive tells us that when one of his speeches contains both anti-British and anti-Japanese passages, we had better ignore it altogether. What a mess it all is.[2] But I think on balance the Cripps mission has done good, because without discrediting Cripps in this country (as it so easily might have done) it has clarified the issue. Whatever is said officially, the inference the whole world will draw is that (*a*) the British ruling class doesn't intend to abdicate and (*b*) India doesn't want independence and therefore won't get it, whatever the outcome of the war.

Talking to Wintringham[3] about the possible Russian attitude towards the Cripps negotiations (of course, not being in the war against Japan, they can't have an official attitude) I said it might make things easier if as many as possible of the military instructors etc. who will later have to be sent to India were Russians. One possible outcome is that India will ultimately be taken over by the USSR, and though I have never believed that the Russians would behave better in India than ourselves, they might behave differently, owing to the different economic set-up. Wintringham said that even in Spain some of the Russian delegates tended to treat the Spaniards as "natives", and would no doubt do likewise[4] in India. It's very hard not to, seeing that in practice the majority of Indians *are* inferior to Europeans and one can't help feeling this and, after a little while, acting accordingly.⌋

American opinion will soon swing back and begin putting all the blame for the Indian situation on the British, as before. It is clear from what American papers one can get hold of that anti-British feeling is in full cry and that all the Isolationists, after a momentary retirement, have re-emerged with the same slogans[5] *as before.* ⌈Father Coughlin's paper,[6] however, has just been excluded from the mails.⌋ *What always horrifies me about American anti-British sentiment is its appalling ignorance. Ditto presumably with anti-American feeling in England.*

1. *political party, and*] party etc., etc
2. *What a mess it all is*] *included in typescript after* misrepresented *and followed by an ellipsis to indicate an omission*
3 Thomas Henry (Tom) Wintringham, writer and soldier, had commanded the British

Battalion of the International Brigade in the Spanish civil war. He later founded Osterley Park Training Centre for the Home Guard. His books include *New Ways of War, Politics of Victory,* and *People's War.* See *721, n. 1.* See David Fernbach, 'Tom Wintringham and Socialist Defense Strategy' *History Workshop,* 14 (1982), 63–91.

4. likewise] *substitution for* so all the more, *which is crossed out*

5. *same slogans*] same programme & slogans

6. Father Charles E. Coughlin (1891–1979), born and educated in Canada, became a Roman Catholic priest and achieved prominence through use of the radio in the United States in the 1930s. As early as 1934, when he founded the National Union for Social Justice, he argued that the United States was being manipulated by Britain into involvement in a new European war; 'I raise my voice,' he said, 'to keep America out of war.' Orwell refers to his magazine, *Social Justice,* in which he expressed near-Fascist views. Its circulation through the mail was forbidden in the United States because it contravened the Espionage Act. It ceased publication in 1942, the year Coughlin was silenced by his ecclesiastical superiors.

1107. 'Mood of the Moment'

The Observer, 19 April 1942   Published anonymously[1]

There is not much grumbling about the Budget. Common ale at tenpence a pint and cigarettes at ten for a shilling, unimaginable a few years ago, now seem hardly worth bothering about. In so far as Sir Kingsley Wood[2] is criticised, it is less for what he has done than for what he has not done. The fact is that this is not a Budget which "soaks the rich." In the matter of direct taxation it benefits the lowest income groups, but it imposes no fresh burdens on the higher groups. It is not much use demonstrating to the common man that, on paper, large incomes don't exist nowadays: they exist, in fact, as he knows by the evidence of his eyes.

It is still not true—and everyone below £500 a year knows it—that we are "all in it together," as we felt ourselves to be for a little while during the big air-raids. That is why discussions of the Budget lead on irrelevantly to remarks about the basic petrol ration or speculations about the price limit in the forthcoming ban on luxury meals. The British people are not envious as peoples go, but they would like to feel, now, with the enemy at several of the gates, that we ARE all in it together, sharing the petty hardships as well as the great ones.

Since 1940 public opinion in this country has generally been a little ahead of the Government. It has demanded—sometimes within the limits of the possible and sometimes not—an invasion of Europe, more aid to Russia, and a tougher attitude towards hostile neutrals. This week the announcement of the Budget swings attention back to home affairs. "Cut us to the bone—but cut us ALL to the bone" would probably express what people are thinking. They want equality of sacrifice at home just as they want effective action abroad, and it is probably a sound instinct which tells them that the two things are interconnected.

1. This was identified by David Astor as Orwell's work. It was the seventh and last of the series 'Mood of the Moment'; see *1012.*

2. Sir Kingsley Wood (1881–1943), Minister of Health, 1935–38, Secretary of State for Air,

1938–40, Lord Privy Seal, 1940, had been Chancellor of the Exchequer since 1940. The tax on beer was increased by two (old) pence; whisky was increased in price by 4s 8d a bottle to £1.2.6; cigarettes were increased from 6½d to 9d (about 3½p) for ten; and the purchase tax on luxuries was doubled.

1108. War-time Diary

19.4.42: *Tokio bombed, or supposed to have been bombed, yesterday.*[1] *Hitherto this comes only from Japanese and German sources. Nowadays one takes it so much for granted that everyone is lying that a report of this kind is never believed until confirmed by both sides. Even an admission by the enemy that his capital had*[2] *been bombed might for some reason or other be a lie.*

[E.[3] says that Anand remarked to her yesterday, as though it were a matter of course, that Britain would make a separate peace this year, and seemed surprised when she demurred. Of course Indians have to say this, and have been saying it ever since 1940, because it furnishes them if necessary with an excuse for being anti-war, and also because if they could allow themselves to think any good of Britain whatever their mental framework would be destroyed. Fyvel told me how in 1940, at the time when Chamberlain was still in the government, he was at a meeting at which Pritt and various Indians were present. The Indians were remarking in their pseudo-Marxist way "Of course the Churchill-Chamberlain government is about to make a compromise peace", whereat Pritt told them that Churchill would never make peace and that the only difference (then) existing in Britain was the difference between Churchill and Chamberlain.]

More and more talk about an invasion of Europe—so much so as to make one think something of the kind must be afoot, otherwise the newspapers would not risk causing disappointment by talking so much about it. Amazed by the unrealism of much of this talk. Nearly everyone seems[4] *still to think that gratitude is*[5] *a factor in power politics. Two assumptions which are habitually made throughout the Left press are a. that opening up a second front is the way to stop Russia making a separate peace, and b. that the more fighting we do the more say we shall have in the final peace settlement. Few people seem to reflect that if an invasion of Europe succeeded to the point of drawing the German armies away from Russia, Stalin would have no strong motive for going on fighting* [, *and that a sell-out of this kind would be quite in line with the Russo-German pact and the agreement which the USSR has evidently entered into with Japan*]. *As to the other assumption, many people talk as though the power to decide policy when a war has been won were a sort of reward for having fought well in it. Of course the people actually able to dominate affairs are those who have the most military power, cf. America at the end of the last war.*

Meanwhile the two steps which could right the situation, a. a clear agreement with the USSR and[6] *a joint (and fairly detailed) declaration of war aims, and b. an invasion of Spain, are politically quite impossible under the present government.*

1. On 18 April 1942, sixteen B-25 bombers, led by Colonel James H. Doolittle, flew from the carrier *Hornet* and bombed Tokyo. The effect was psychological rather than military Because the planes had insufficient fuel to make the return flight, they flew on to China. Bad weather forced several crash-landings; one plane landed near Vladivostok and the crew was interned; two landed in Japanese-held territory and some airmen were executed on 15 October 1942. Of the 80 crew members, 71 survived.
2. *had*] has
3. Eileen Blair.
4. *seems*] appears
5. *is*] is still; still *crossed through in the blue-black ink Orwell used for manuscript emendations*
6. *and*] and with

1109. Gujarati Newsletter, 8

20 April 1942

The English original was written by Orwell. No script has been traced. PasB gives the timing as 13 minutes.

1110. BBC Talks Booking Form, 22.4.42

K. K. Ardaschir: 'The Sick Man Revives,' '43 years in England,' 14-minute talks; recorded 21.4.42; date of broadcast not fixed; fee £8.8s each talk. Signed: Z. A. Bokhari.

1111. BBC Talks Booking Form, 22.4.42

S. Telkar: Marathi Newsletter, 'A Day in the Life of a Factory Worker,' 4-minute talk in Marathi; broadcast 23.4.42; fee £4.4s. Signed: Z. A. Bokhari. (This form was initiated by Miss Venu Chitale.)

1112. BBC Talks Booking Form, 23.4.42

Dr. Bhupen Mukerjee:[1] 'The Music I Like,' 1, 'Folk Songs of Europe,' script of 5 minutes followed by folk songs sung by Miss Maxwell-Lyte; broadcast 25.4.42; fee (for Mukerjee) £4.4s. Signed: Z. A. Bokhari.

1. Bhupen Mukerjee was apparently the first person to whom Orwell wrote after joining the BBC. See *857* and *857, n. 2* for doubts about his technique as a broadcaster.

1113. BBC Talks Booking Form, 23.4.42

Viscountess Rhondda: 'Women Generally Speaking,' '13-minute talk on "Time & Tide"—she is the editor of this well-known paper'; broadcast 6.5.42; fee £10.10s. Signed: Z. A. Bokhari.

1114. BBC Talks Booking Form, 24.4.42

Shridhar Telkar: '4½-minute talk on Sir Stafford Cripps, in a 30-minute programme on Birthdays of the Week'; broadcast 24.4.42; fee £4.4s. Signed: Z. A. Bokhari.

1115. 'Birthdays of the Week': Sir Stafford Cripps, Shakespeare, Hitler

24 April 1942

In this half-hour programme, Shridhar Telkar spoke about Cripps, William Empson about Shakespeare, and Orwell about Hitler. Godfrey Kenton read extracts from Shakespeare's works and Marius Goring[1] read some 550 words, taking five minutes, from James Murphy's translation of *Mein Kampf*. Ten seconds of a BBC recording of Hitler speaking (1933B) were played. Orwell's contribution lasted five minutes. He was introduced, not as Eric Blair, but as 'George Orwell, the well-known author,' according to PasB. Only Telkar's script appears to have survived.

1. Marius Goring (1912–1998), made his acting debut in 1927. He served in the army, 1940–41, then was on the staff of the Foreign Office, 1941–45, supervising BBC broadcasting to Germany in 1941.

1116. News Review, 19

25 April 1942

'News Review' is written at the top of the first page; there are two censorship stamps; Bokhari was the censor. In NOT CHECKED WITH BROADCAST, at the top of the first page, 'NOT' has been crossed out. Some lines of the typescript have been particularly heavily crossed out. West refers to four such lines, but there are about eighteen. These passages are given or described in the notes below; those words that can be made out with reasonable certainty are reproduced and estimates are given of the number of lines or letters and spaces of the obliterated passages. PasB has Weekly News Review by Z. A. Bokhari and the timing as 13 minutes 30 seconds. Amendments appear to be in Bokhari's handwriting. Additions and substitutions are printed in italic; square brackets enclose passages scored through but which can be read in full.

During this week the military situation in Asia has *not greatly changed*.[1] It is known that the Japanese in Burma have been heavily reinforced.[2] The allies have made a further withdrawal since last week.[3] The Japanese efforts to encircle the British forces at Yenangyaung and the Chinese forces at Loikaw have failed. General Wavell's speech of April 21st made it clear that India's air defences have been greatly strengthened, both in planes and in personnel, and this improvement will probably make itself felt on the Burma front, though the lack of airfields in Upper Burma adds to the difficulties of the Allies. The return to Madras of the Provincial Government, which had been temporarily evacuated, is no doubt a result of the improved situation in the air. In their raids on Ceylon and Madras the Japanese are believed to have lost about a hundred planes, and as these planes must have come from air-craft° carriers, they cannot be replaced without some delay. In their Burma campaign the Japanese are racing against time and the weather. They hope to cut not only the Burma road° which runs from Lashio, but also the new roads now under construction between India and China, before the onset of the monsoon, which begins about the middle of May. By the middle of June all low-lying ground in Burma is waterlogged. We ought not to make the mistake of assuming that the coming of the monsoon will completely immobilise the Japanese forces. Even in the most rainy months it is possible to move large bodies of infantry by means of rafts and shallow boats. But the transport of tanks and heavy guns is very difficult and suitable landing grounds for aeroplanes are much fewer. On the whole, therefore, the beginning of the monsoon will be advantageous to the Allies and will *offset*[4] to some extent the advantage in numbers and armaments by which the Japanese have won their successes hitherto.

The Americans and Filipinos° continue their resistance in the fortress of Corregidor and in various other parts of the Philippine islands. On April 18th Tokio was bombed by American aeroplanes, in all probability from aeroplane carriers.[5] The Japanese profess great indignation and make the claim, which is usual with the Axis propagandists, that only non-military objectives were hit. Indeed, to judge from the Axis broadcasts, any bombs that drop from Allied aeroplanes fall so invariably on schools and hospitals that one must assume that Tokio, Berlin, and the other chief cities of the Axis countries contain no other buildings than these. But when we remember that for five years past the Japanese have been bombing totally undefended towns in China, their indignation seems a little ridiculous.

In the Western *struggle*[6] there are three all-important questions which cannot yet be answered with certainty but which we must do our best to answer in order to get a clear picture of the future. These questions are, first, in what direction will the Germans make their main offensive?[7] Secondly, will the British and Americans attempt an invasion of the continent of Europe? Thirdly, what part will France, now under the control of the pro-Nazi millionaire Laval, play in the forthcoming operations?

We have pointed out in earlier newsletters that the Germans are bound to make their greatest effort in the direction of the Caucasus and the Middle East. Their chief needs are to obtain fresh supplies of oil and to join hands with their Japanese allies, and therefore the general direction in which they must move can hardly be questioned. The only doubt hitherto has been as to whether they will make an all-out effort to defeat the Red Army and reach the Caspian Sea, or whether they will attempt to move eastward by a more southerly route. The fact that France is now more closely under German control than before may decide the Germans to make a direct attack on the island of Cyprus and then on Syria. For if they can get control of the French Fleet, they may have enough warships at their disposal to challenge the British control of the Eastern Mediterranean. To capture Cyprus and Syria by air attack alone would be very difficult. It is also quite possible that simultaneously with their main offensive the Germans will make some kind of attack in the west, either against Spain, Gibraltar and West Africa, or against the British Isles. A full-scale invasion of Britain is not likely to succeed, but even an unsuccessful invasion might cause great disorganisation of Industry,° and for this purpose Hitler, who does not care how much blood he sheds, might be ready to risk quite a large force at a critical moment. Britain, however, is well prepared for any such attempt, both on land, on sea and in the air.

We prefer not to make any definite prediction as to whether the Allies will invade Europe this year.[8] It [also] seems clear that the Germans expect some such invasion to be made, and believe that either Norway or France will be the scene of it. They are feverishly at work strengthening their defences in the west, and have probably already withdrawn troops and aeroplanes from the Russian front for this purpose. The British have made another successful commando raid, this time at Boulogne. These commando raids[9] not only do damage to important military objectives but force the Germans to divert a disproportionately large number of men for the defence of their long coast line. Beneath their habitual boasting, the speeches of the German leaders betray great anxiety. They are aware that in the war of 1914–1918 it was the necessity of fighting on two fronts, in Russia and in France, that wore out the German army, and they are afraid of the same thing happening again if the British and the Americans can secure a footing in Europe. In his speech broadcast on April 22nd Hitler once more attempted to frighten the German people into greater efforts by telling them that defeat would mean the utter destruction of Germany. Needless to say this is a lie: a German defeat would mean merely the destruction of the Nazis: but it is a significant change to find the German dictator even discussing the possibility of defeat. It is strange to look back and remember that in the summer of 1940 the Germans were told that the war would be ended in a few weeks, and that at the beginning of 1941 Hitler solemnly promised his people that they would never have to endure another winter of war.

As to developments in France, it seems clear, as we predicted last week, that Laval is bent on *co-operating closely with*[10] the Germans.[11] Indirectly he may be of great use to them *but he will have to go very carefully, for he is hated in France, & popular feeling runs high. Probably he will endeavour to secure his aims little by little: indeed his past record shows that he prefers to work quickly[12] underground & afford his critics little opportunity to find out what he is doing. But his*

282

accession to power has shown how weak is the Vichy régime: & how little it can be relied upon to stand against German demands—whether these include the cession of French possessions overseas or the use of French shipping.[13] South Africa[14] has now severed relations with the Vichy government, and prior to this General Smuts[15] had already announced that any attempt to seize Madagascar on behalf of the Axis would be resisted. There is no further news as yet as to whether Laval will *endeavour to place*[16] the French fleet *at the disposal of the Axis.*[17] It is probably safe to assume that the French sailors, or most of them, would not fight against their former allies *at the bidding of the Germans.*[18] But there remains the danger that during the past year and a half the Germans may have been training crews of their own for this purpose; for though they agreed under the Amistice terms not to make use of the French navy, it is not usual with them to abide by agreements which have become inconvenient. It is clear that anti-Nazi feeling in France is stronger than ever since Laval's accession to power. An attempt has been made on the life of Doriot, the French Fascist and pro-Nazi politician.[19] Statements that fresh batches of French or Belgian hostages have been shot are now almost daily items in the German press.

[Fresh rationing arrangements have been announced in Britain. From June 1st fuel for domestic use is to be rationed, which is expected to save about 10 million tons of coal annually.]

Sir Stafford Cripps arrived in England on April 21st. A survey of the world's press shows that even though his mission has failed for the time being, the world at large, especially in China and the United States, admires him for his integrity and hopes that the negotiations may be re-opened at some time in the future. During this week the Cripps mission will no doubt be debated in the Houses of Parliament, and in our next newsletter we hope to be able to comment more fully upon the reactions in this country.

1. *not greatly changed*] slightly improved
2. reinforced] *originally followed by* but their advance appears to have slowed down and in one section of the front the—*the last eight words are x-ed through and the whole passage crossed out*
3. last week] *originally followed by* but Chinese troops have meanwhile recaptured the oil centre of Yenangyaung and at the *plus 38 letters & spaces, all crossed out. The number of letters and spaces here and elsewhere is an estimate and represents the extent of obliterated words;* centre *is doubtful.*
4. *offset*] *typescript also originally read* offset
5. This was the Allies first air-raid on Japan; see *1108, n. 1.*
6. *struggle*] theatre of war, one thing points to the fact that *plus 31 letters & spaces crossed out*
7. offensive?] *followed by* in the *plus 8 letters & spaces crossed out*
8. this year] *followed by* It may be significant, however, that Lord Beaverbrook, who is in the Cabinet *plus 2 lines crossed out;* Beaverbrook *and* Cabinet *are uncertain. Beaverbrook had been appointed Minister of War Production on 4 February. Since rumours of a second front in Europe were rife, this probably has no firm basis, but on 14 April 1942 the Bolero Plan for the Allied invasion of Europe was accepted by the British government.*
9. raids] *followed by* which *plus 24 letters & spaces crossed out*
10. *co-operating closely with*] delivering the country utterly over to. *On 20 April 1942, Laval broadcast to the French people to the effect that a policy of 'understanding and true reconciliation with Germany must be loyally carried out' (2194 Days of War).*
11. Germans] *followed by two lines crossed out*
12. *quickly*] *perfectly clear in manuscript but* quietly *might have been intended*
13. *but he will have to go . . . French shipping*] *substituted for* 6½ *lines crossed out*

14. South Africa] *followed by 33 letters & spaces crossed out*
15. Jan Christiaan Smuts (1870–1950) was a South African soldier and statesman. Though a Boer, he was, with Louis Botha, instrumental in the creation of the Union of South Africa, 1910. He believed in the co-operation of Boers and British. He signed the Treaty of Versailles, 1918, and was South African Prime Minister, 1919–24 and during World War II. He was highly regarded by Winston Churchill and the British in general.
16. *endeavour to place*] *substituted for 44 letters & spaces crossed out*
17. *at the disposal of the Axis*] *substituted for 86 letters & spaces crossed out*
18. *at the bidding of the Germans*] *substituted for 36 letters & spaces crossed out*
19. Jacques Doriot (1898–1945), originally a Communist, was expelled from the party as a Trotskyist in 1934. He formed the Parti Populaire Français in 1936 and collaborated with the German occupying power during the war. He became intensely hated in France and fled to Germany toward the end of the war. He was killed when his car was strafed by Allied planes. See the review of Jean-Paul Brunet's *Jacques Doriot: Du Communisme au Fascisme* (Paris, 1986) by R. W. Johnson, *London Review of Books*, 9 October 1986.

1117. To J. G. Crowther[1]

25 April 1942   PP/EB/CEH

Dear Sir

I am arranging a series of talks on the Development of Science for the Eastern service of the B.B.C. Professor Bernal, with whom I have discussed the series, suggests that you might care to undertake the fifth talk which I have called "Science in the U.S.S.R." The talk preceding this deals with Science and the Prospects of Science under Fascism and Capitalism, and we want to balance this by another dealing with the position of Science in the only Socialistic country now existing.

I can give you fuller particulars if you are interested in the idea. These are talks of 15 or 20 minutes which means something over 2,000 words. The approximate date would be 13 weeks from now.

Perhaps you could be kind enough to let me know about this fairly soon.

Yours truly
Eric Blair
Talks Assistant
Indian Section

1. James Gerald Crowther (1899–) was *Manchester Guardian* science correspondent, prolific writer on scientific subjects, and an effective populariser of science. His books include *An Outline of the Universe* (1931) and *Science and Life* (1938) and he contributed to the Penguin Special *Science and the World Order* (1942). With R. Whiddington, he wrote an official war history, *Science at War* (1948). See his *Fifty Years with Science* (1970) and Gary Werskey, *The Visible College* (1978), especially 148–53, for his links with the left. The topic offered him was particularly appropriate; his *Industry and Education in Soviet Russia* was published in 1932 and *Soviet Science* in 1936. He became secretary of the World Federation of Scientific Workers (founded in 1946), described by Werskey as 'a progressive "front" organization dedicated to world peace' (277), with which Bernal was closely associated. After the war he was President of the British Peace Committee Executive, described by the Prime Minister, Clement Attlee, as 'bogus,' and Crowther of being, if not a Communist, a fellow-traveller, which Crowther denied. See also *1163, n. 1.*

1118. To V. K. Narayana Menon

25 April 1942   Handwritten draft and typewritten versions   PP/EB

Dear Mr. Menon,[1]
Yes, it will be all right to speak on William Walton instead of your first choice. As to the gramaphone[2] records, that will be all right too, but will you let us know some days before the broadcast what music you will be needing, so that we can be sure of getting hold of the discs. Your whole talk, i.e. including the musical interludes, should take not more than 13½ minutes.

Yours sincerely,
Eric Blair
Talks Assistant
Indian Section

1. Vatakke Kurnpath Narayana Menon (1911–), was the author of *The Development of William Butler Yeats* (1942), reviewed by Orwell in *Horizon* (see *1791*) and *Time and Tide* (see *2017*). He arranged Indian music (with S. Sinha) at the 'India Demonstration' on 31 January 1943 at the London Coliseum.
2. Menon wrote to Orwell (as 'Blaire') on 21 April asking to change the topic of his talk and saying that on 9 June he would speak on the poet Edwin Muir. The letter is date-stamped 22 APR 1942, and Orwell drafted the reply above on the verso. The draft includes the spelling 'gramaphone' and concludes 'any musical interludes, should take 13½ minutes.'

1119. War-time Diary

25.4.42:   *U.S. airmen making a*[1] *forced landing on Russian soil after bombing Tokio have been interned. According to*[2] *the Japanese wireless the Russians are expediting the movement of Japanese agents across Russia from Sweden (and hence from Germany) to Japan.* ⌈If true, this is a new development, this traffic having been stopped at the time when Germany attacked the USSR.⌉

The mystery of Subhas Chandra Bose's whereabouts remains impenetrable. ⌈The leading facts are:—

i. At the time of his disappearance, the British government declared that he had gone to Berlin.

i°A voice, identified as his, broadcasts on the Free India radio (Germany).

iii. The Italian radio has claimed at least once that Bhose° is in Japanese territory.

iv. Indians here seem on the whole to think that he is in Japanese territory.

v. Escape to Japanese territory would have been physically easier than escape in the other direction, though the latter would not be impossible.

vi. The Vichy report of his death in a plane accident between Bangkok and Tokio, though almost certainly mistaken, seemed to suggest that Vichy quarters took it for granted that he was in Japanese territory.

vii. According to engineers it would not be impossible to broadcast his voice scrambled from Tokio to Berlin and there unscramble and rebroadcast it.

There are innumerable other considerations and endless rumours.¹ *The two questions hardest to answer are: If Bose is³ in Japanese territory, why this elaborate effort to make it appear that he is in Berlin, where he is comparatively ineffectual? If Bose is in German territory, how did he get there? Of course it is quite reasonably likely that he got there with Russian connivance. Then the question arises, if the Russians had previously passed Bose⁴ through, did they afterwards tip us off when they came into the war on our side? To know the answer to that would give one a useful clue to their attitude towards ourselves.⁵ Of course one can⁶ get no information about questions of that type here. One has to do one's propaganda in the dark, discreetly sabotaging the policy directives when they seem more than usually silly.*

To judge from their wireless, the Germans believe in a forthcoming invasion, either of France or Norway. What a chance to have a go at Spain! As, however, they have fixed a date for it (May 1st) they may merely be discussing the possibility of invasion in order to jeer when it does not come off. No sign here of any invasion preparations—no rumours about assembly of troops or boats, re-arrangement of railway schedules etc. The most positive sign is Beaverbrook's pro-invasion speech in the USA.

ᴵThere seems to be no news whatever. It must be months since the papers were so empty.ᴵ

Struck by the mediocre physique and poor general appearance of the American soldiers one sees from time to time in the street. The officers usually better than the men, however.

1. *making a*] making
2. *According to*] According *in typescript*
3. *is*] *underlined in manuscript*
4. *Bose*] Bhose
5. Bose escaped from India, with German help, via Afghanistan, in the winter of 1940–41 When he reached Moscow, the Russians 'were extremely hospitable but determinedly evasive about helping him In Berlin the Germans were more receptive' (Mihir Bose, *The Lost Hero*, 162). He was in Germany until 8 February 1943, when he sailed from Kiel in a U-boat (205). See also *1080, n. 1*
6. *can*] *repeated in typescript*

1120. Gujarati Newsletter, 9

27 April 1942

The English original was written by Orwell. No script has been traced. PasB gives timing as 13 minutes.

1121. To J. D. Bernal

27 April 1942   PP/EB

Dear Professor Bernal,
I think that my letter to you of March 27th must have gone astray, but in any case I am sorry that I gave you the wrong date for your first talk. You will be doing the second and sixth talk in the series. The second, "The Birth of Modern Science", will be on Tuesday, 9th June, at 1.15 p.m. DBST from Broadcasting House, and the sixth talk—"The Future of Science" will be on July 7th, at the same time, from Broadcasting House.

I have got Professor Crowther's address, and have written to ask him if he will do the fifth talk, and am waiting for his reply.

I think I told you when we had lunch together that these talks should be between 15 and 20 minutes, which means something over 2,000 words.

Yours sincerely,
Eric Blair
Talks Assistant
Indian Section

1122. To E. M. Forster

27 April 1942   PP/EB

Dear Mr. Forster,
Many thanks for your script. I don't think there is anything in it that needs altering. I don't suppose that Ajit Mukerjee's article[1] is in type yet, as I believe it is going to be published in Horizon for June or July.

It would do very well if you came round to 55 Portland Place at 12 o'clock on Wednesday, as you suggest. You will be going on the air at 1.30, so that will give us time to run through it once and then you can take it away with you.

Yours sincerely,
George Orwell
Talks Assistant
Indian Section

1. On Bengali folk painting; see *1103, n. 4.*

1123. To Reginald Reynolds

27 April 1942   PP/EB

Dear Reg,
Please forgive my long delay in answering: but I couldn't find a vacant date for your talk on Prison Literature.[1] Could you manage June 12th, at 1.15

p.m.? As you collected obviously a large amount of material, it seems to me it might be better to make two talks of it, to be given on two consecutive weeks, that is to say, June 12th and June 19th. You can make it one or two, as you prefer, but please let me know as soon as possible. The broadcast should take 15 to 20 minutes, which means something in the neighbourhood of 2,000 words, and I would like to have each script about a week before the date of the broadcast. Please let me know whether all this will be O.K. If writing on Nehru, Sir Roger Casement,[2] or other notable prisoners, try not to say things that the Censor would cut out!

My wife is working in the Ministry of Food, and is very anxious for Ethel Mannin[3] to broadcast in the Kitchen Front, which you possible° sometimes listen to at 8.15 a.m. [I] wish you would suggest this to her, and ask her, if she is interested, to get in touch either with me or my wife about it.

Yours,
[No name/position]

1. Reynolds had edited *A Prison Anthology* with A. G. Stock (1938); see *1060, n. 1*.
2. Sir Roger Casement (1864–1916) had served as British Consul in Africa and South America and had brought to light evidence of serious malpractice by colonial rulers. Conrad's *Heart of Darkness* owes something to his work. After adopting the Irish nationalist cause, Casement had sought German support during World War I. He was executed as a traitor.
3 Ethel Mannin (see *575*) and Reynolds had been married since 1938.

1124. War-time Diary

<u>27.4.42</u>: [Much speculation about the meaning of Hitler's speech yesterday. In general it gives an impression of pessimism. Beaverbrook's invasion speech is variously interpreted, at its face value, as a pep talk for the Americans, as something to persuade the Russians that we are not leaving them in the lurch, and as the beginning of an attack on Churchill (who may be forced into opposing offensive action). Nowadays, whatever is said or done, one looks instantly for hidden motives and assumes that words mean anything except what they appear to mean.[1]

From the Italian radio, describing life in London:

"Five shillings were given for one egg yesterday, and one pound sterling for a kilogram of potatoes. Rice has disappeared, even from the Black Market, and peas have become the prerogative of millionaires. There is no sugar on the market, although small quantities are still to be found at prohibitive prices".

One would say that this is stupid propaganda, because if such conditions really existed England would stop fighting[1] in a few weeks, and when this fails to happen the listener is bound to see that he has been deceived. But in fact there is no such reaction. You can go on and on telling lies, and the most palpable lies at that, and even if they are not actually believed, there is no strong revulsion either.

We are all drowning in filth. When I talk to anyone or read the writings of *anyone who has any axe to grind, I feel that intellectual honesty and balanced judgement have simply disappeared from the face of the earth. Everyone's thought is forensic, everyone is simply putting a "case" with deliberate suppression of his opponent's point of view, and, what is more, with complete insensitiveness to any sufferings except those of himself and his friends. The Indian nationalist is sunken in self-pity and hatred of Britain and utterly indifferent to the miseries of China, the English pacifist works himself up into frenzies about the²* concentration camps in the Isle of Man and forgets *about those in Germany, etc., etc. One notices this in the case of people one disagrees with, such as Fascists or pacifists³* but in fact everyone is the same, at least everyone who has definite opinions. Everyone is dishonest, and everyone is utterly heartless towards people who are outside the immediate range of his own interests.⁴ What is most striking of all is the way sympathy can be turned on and off like a tap according to political expediency.* ⌐All the pinks, or most of them, who flung themselves to and fro in their rage against Nazi atrocities before the war, forgot all about these atrocities and obviously lost their sympathy with the Jews etc. as soon as the war began to bore them. Ditto with people who hated Russia like poison up to June 22 1941 and then suddenly forgot about the purges, the G.P.U. etc. the moment Russia came into the war. I am not thinking of lying for political ends, but of actual changes in subjective feeling.⌐ *But is there no one who has both firm opinions and a balanced outlook? Actually there are plenty, but they are powerless. All power is in the hands of paranoiacs.*

1. *stop fighting*] be out of the war *originally writen in manuscript, crossed out and* stop fighting *substituted*
2. *about the*] about
3. *such as Fascists or pacifists*] *interlinear insertion in Orwell's hand in typescript. It appears in the manuscript and was evidently omitted when the typescript was prepared.*
4. *interests*] interests & sympathies

1125. To K. K. Ardaschir

28 April 1942   PP/EB/NP

On 23 April 1942, Tamara Talbot Rice,[1] Middle East Section, Ministry of Information, wrote to Bokhari commenting on Ardaschir's talk. She described it as 'a most excellent talk' and requested two small amendments, as given in the letter that follows. Mrs. Talbot Rice's letter is annotated.

Miss Parratt.
Please draft a letter telling Mr A. we shall have to make these minor alterations & therefor° must re-record at a time convenient to him (apologise heavily). E.A.B

Dear Mr. Ardaschir,
After you had recorded your talk—"The Sick Man Revives", I took the opportunity to send the script to the Turkish specialist at the Ministry of

Information. I have just received a reply from them, saying how much they like your talk. They are going to inform the Press Attache in Ankara of the date of the broadcast.

They have, however, suggested that we might make two small amendments in this talk. I hope that you will be agreeable to this, although I am afraid it means that we shall have to ask you to re-record the talk, at your convenience.

On page 1, at the end of the second paragraph, they say—"Though it is true that backsheesh giving still survives in Turkey, the Turks are very sensitive on this point, and I will be grateful if you could have this passage reworded."

On page 3, end of third paragraph. The suggestion that certain of Ataturk's[2] innovations were not all good is likely to be deeply resented in Turkey, and to cause offence there. Turks are discouraged from criticising Ataturk and all foreigners are expected to refrain from doing so, and I believe that this sentence might have unfortunate results in Turkey."

As I expect you know, these broadcasts are heard in Turkey, and I am sure you will agree with me that it would be better to make these emendmeats.° I am very sorry that this means re-recording the last talk, but as they are so enthusiastic about the talk as a whole, I feel personally that it would be well worth while.

If you expect to be in London some time fairly soon, and would find it convenient to come for half an hour to record—I don't think we shall need to rehearse it again—I should be most obliged if you could let me know a day or two in advance, and I will make arrangements to fit in with your plans.

Yours sincerely,
Eric Blair
Talks Assistant
Indian Section

1. Tamara Talbot Rice (1904–1993), writer and art historian, was born Tamara Abelson, daughter of a senior official in the Tsar's Treasury. The family moved to England between 1919 and 1921. In 1927 she married David Talbot Rice, Professor of the History of Fine Art at Edinburgh University from 1934, and spent much time with him abroad on archeological digs. She was a close friend of Evelyn Waugh and one of the 'Brideshead Revisited Circle.' During the war she worked for the Ministry of Information, speaking on Turkish affairs. Her books include *The Seljuks in Asia Minor* (1961) and *Everyday Life in Byzantium* (1967).
2. Kemal Atatürk; see *1084, n. 2.*

1126. BBC Talks Booking Form, 29.4.42

Princess Indira of Kapurthala: 'Through Eastern Eyes,' 'The Debate Continues'; broadcast 11, 18, and 25.5.42 and 1.6.42; fee £8.8s each broadcast. Signed: Z. A. Bokhari.

1127. BBC Talks Booking Form, 29.4.42

Miss Doulat Nanavati:[1] 'The Music I Like,' 4, 5-minute talk, presentation of piano recital by Moura Lympany;[2] broadcast 16.5.42; fee £4.4s. Signed: Z. A. Bokhari. Although initiated by Orwell, the Remarks state, 'This programme is looked after by Dr Clifford.'

1. Doulat Nanavati, a musician, was interviewed by Bokhari and Scott Goddard on 29 August 1941. She wrote to Bokhari on 19 September, thanking him for helping her with her audition and suggesting she give a talk on music because it would be liked by 'people at home.'
2. Moura Lympany (1916–; CBE, 1979), concert pianist, made her debut in 1929 and took second prize in the Ysaye International Pianoforte Competition in Brussels in 1938. She was made a fellow of the Royal Academy of Music in 1948.

1128. BBC Talks Booking Form, 29.4.42

K. S. Shelvankar: 'Through Eastern Eyes,' 'These Names Will Live,' Aldous Huxley; broadcast 12.5.42; fee £8.8s. Signed: Z. A. Bokhari.[1]

1. This talk had been scheduled earlier and postponed; see 1091.

1129. BBC Talks Booking Form, 29.4.42

M. J. Tambimuttu: 'Through Eastern Eyes,' 'These Names Will Live,' T. S. Eliot, 13-minute talk; broadcast 19.5.42; fee £8.8s. Signed: Z. A. Bokhari.

1130. War-time Diary

<u>29.4.42</u>: *Yesterday to the House to hear the India debate. A poor show except for Cripps's speech. They are now sitting in the House of Lords.[1] During Cripps's speech one had the impression that the house was full, but on counting I found only about 200-250 members, which is enough to fill most of the seats. Everything had a somewhat mangy look. Red rexine cushions on the benches—I could swear they used to be red plush at one time. The ushers' shirtfronts were very dingy. When I see this dreary rubbish going on, or when I read about the later days of the League of Nations or the antics of Indian politicians, with their endless changes of front, line-ups, démarches,[2] denunciations, protests and gestures generally, I always remember that the Roman Senate still existed under the later Empire. [This is the twilight of Parliamentary democracy and] these creatures are simply ghosts gibbering in some corner while the real events happen elsewhere.*

1. The chamber of the House of Commons was severely damaged in an air raid on 10 May 1941. The Commons sat in the Lords' chamber, which had been only slightly damaged. The Lords sat in their robing room.

2. The manuscript has the accent; the typescript does not. If either text is so marked, the accent is silently supplied.

1131. [Weekly News Review, 20]

2 May 1942   PP/EB

This newsletter and Number 30, 11.7.42, are almost certainly not by Orwell. Number 23, 23.5.42, is also doubtful, but for different reasons. The style of writing is not Orwell's; both 20 and 30 read as if written by one of the Indian staff members, inclined to a more rhetorical, more florid style. Number 20 has such passages as the following: 'the Axis tyrants feel the chill of their twilight'; 'The meeting of Fuehrer and Duce by the wayside in the mountains of the Salzkammergut was doubtless intended to make the world's flesh creep'; 'the prologue to the smashing repulse'; 'Larger numbers of Italian troops are to be flung into the fire of the Russian front, still stronger forces of the Nazi army admitted to Italy, to pillage at their will'; 'the official report of the conference, jejune as usual [this shows the kind of foreign usage Orwell deplored in 'Politics and the English Language']; 'It is no doubt in Stalin's calculations that grandiose attacks will be delivered'; 'It must . . . be . . . more difficult to concentrate powerful striking forces on the tortuous front [in Russia] than it was in Poland'; 'the sudden impinging of German might on the Russian frontiers.' The last two are far removed from Orwell's style.

There are two typographical features common to 20 and 30 that are not found in typescripts associated with Orwell's newsletters. Both capitalise some proper names, and both, especially 30, make use of shorter paragraphs than does Orwell.

The typescript of 20 is also unusual in being the one of only two newsletters with an annotation in Urdu; this gives the pronunciation of *jejune* (see *1022, headnote*). There are two handwritten manuscript additions—'as they say' and 'in their own words'—and some proper names have been written in block capitals, presumably to aid the reader. The handwriting could be Bokhari's. PasB notes that this broadcast was 'by Z. A. Bokhari' and gives the timing as 14 minutes. The typescript is marked 'As broadcast,' but there are no censors' stamps.

The Japanese have captured Lashio, which is on the main branch of the Burma Road, running eastwards from Mandalay. There is another road further to the north, which runs south-eastward from Bhamo and enters China a good deal to the east of Lashio. This, of course, is still in Allied hands, but it is not a first-class road, and Bhamo is only connected with Mandalay by river. If Mandalay should fall, China is for the time being cut off from the outside world and the Chinese armies will be dependent on airborne supplies until the new roads from India into China are completed. As much as possible of the war materials which had been piled up at Lashio had been removed into China and it is known that the rest were destroyed before the Japanese got there.

At such moments as this it is more than ever necessary to see the whole war, as well as the Burma campaign, in perspective, and to pay no attention either to enemy propaganda or to the rumours brought by refugees from

from Burma, which may often be exaggerated and misleading. The loss of the greater part of Burma is a set-back for the Allied cause, but not an overwhelming one, and cannot be decisive in the major strategy of the war.

There is little to report from either the Philippine Islands or from Australia. The Australian and American aeroplanes continue heavily bombing the Japanese forces in the island of New Guinea and have destroyed much war material and a number of enemy 'planes. Nevertheless, observers on the spot believe that the Japanese intend launching their attack on Australia at some time in the near future.

Comparison of Stalin's Order of the Day with the hysterical speeches which came from Hitler and Mussolini earlier in the week leaves no doubt that the Axis tyrants feel the chill of their twilight while the Russian leader is more confident, and has stronger reasons for confidence, than ever. The meeting of Fuehrer and Duce by the wayside in the mountains of the Salzkammergut was doubtless intended to make the world's flesh creep; but even their own peoples cannot now be completely deceived by the pretence that these conferences produce miracles of victory. Though the two friends met on the eve of Hitler's invasion of Norway and of the ignominy with which Mussolini covered himself and the Fascist army by the invasion of Greece, it will not be forgotten in their two countries that they put their heads together before Hitler plunged into the Russian adventure, and their last meeting was the prologue to the smashing repulse of what the Nazi commanders intended for the final assault on the Russian people.

When the couple meet now, Mussolini must be haunted by bitter memories of the days when he could approach Hitler as an equal. As the most helpless of Quislings he went to Salzburg, and the result of the conference, according to his own mouth-piece, GAYDA, must be to rivet the chains more closely on himself and the Italian people. Larger numbers of Italian troops are to be flung into the fire of the Russian front, still stronger forces of the Nazi army admitted to Italy, to pillage at their will. On this occasion at least we may be sure GAYDA has told the truth. Hitler had with him Marshal KEITEL, the Chief of the Nazi High Command, who has been running round the other slave States of Eastern Europe to collect troops for slaughter and would not let Italy off lightly. The official report of the conference, jejune[1] as usual, nevertheless betrays the nervous confusion of Fuehrer and Duce: they have won *as they say*—"overwhelming victory," but they renew *in their own words*—"stern determination to ensure final victory by all means in their power."

If words were among the means which overwhelm, Russia would have been annihilated several times last summer and last autumn. There is no doubt of the justice of Stalin's estimate that the German army is weaker now than it was ten months ago. The best officers, the best troops and masses of material of the Wehrmacht have been destroyed. Russian resources of man power are incomparably greater than Hitler can scourge to the front from the Reich and all his slave States. Heavy handicaps have been inflicted on Russia's productive power by the loss of the Ukraine, which is not only a rich granary but furnishes over half the normal coal and iron supply of

Russian industry. On the other hand, remarkable success in the movement of factory equipment eastward, in holding the Moscow area and in the expansion of Ural and Siberian production has ensured that the decline of armament manufacture through the overrunning of the Ukraine is far less serious than was feared. More and more munitions and aircraft, Stalin is able to say, are now reaching the front from Russian workshops, while Great Britain and the United States give "ever-greater war assistance".

It is no doubt in Stalin's calculations that grandiose attacks will be delivered. The weight of machinery and men which Nazism can put into such blows is still formidable. Points of the first importance to Russia, such as the Moscow area and the oil-fields of the Caucasus, to say nothing of Leningrad, are much nearer the German lines now than they were last summer. It must, however, be far more difficult to concentrate powerful striking forces on the tortuous front than it was in Poland. Stalin tells his people that the German reserves of men, of oil and of raw materials are at an end. With Hitler in command we must expect that any such approach to exhaustion will produce the fiercest efforts which brutality can extort from a nation trained in a barbarous discipline. The Russian people are assured by their leader that they can make 1942 the year of final defeat for Germany. We may depend on them to do their utmost, convinced that there can be no peace upon earth, no security of freedom or of life worth living, till Nazism is exterpated.° Whatever the course of the struggle, they may count on the maximum strength that we and the other Allied Nations can exert for swift and complete victory.

In their "all-out" war effort, Russian workers have sacrificed the more popular one of their two annual festivals. May Day this year was a working day for the first time since 1918. The occasion was, none the less, observed by the holding of meetings and the display of red streamer banners bearing slogans.

Since the Soviet power was established, the prime significance of May Day for the Russian people has been a patriotic one, and since Stalin told the Stakhanovite workers seven years ago that "life is growing better, life is growing happier," the day has been the occasion of a temporary relaxation from the strain and effort demanded of Soviet workers, and has had something of the quality of the Fourteenth of July in France.

In the celebrations held in past years in the Red Square in Moscow, the Uritsky Square in Leningrad, the Kretchadik in Kiev, and in thousands of towns and villages, there has been more thought for Socialist achievement in the Soviet Union than for the international implications of a day which, as a demonstration of working-class solidarity, had its origin in the Chicago strike of forty-six years ago.[2]

This year more than ever, the patriotic note was dominant, and it was to the events that have happened since last May Day that thoughts were directed—the sudden impinging of German might on the Russian frontiers; the long and bitterly fought withdrawal to the outskirts of the two greatest Russian cities and to the banks of the Volga and Don; the crashing counter-offensive which developed, as winter deepened, into a persistent, dogged advance; and to the allies of Russia, active or potential, the "proletariat of all lands, European patriots, oppressed brother Slavs, and the workers of Germany."

It is the firm belief among Russian workers that it is because their land is a Socialist one that it has withstood Hitler's attempts to disrupt it politically, on the battlefield, and economically. For many years the factory wheels ceased to turn on May 1 as a protest against a system the workers believed exploited them. For twenty-four years they stopped while the Russian workers celebrated[3] their change of system. This year, on the Volga, in the Urals, in Siberia and Central Asia, and in the work- shops near the battle-zone, in besieged Leningrad as in liberated Kalinin, the wheels continued to turn in order to defend that system.

1. So spelt and annotated in Urdu to give its pronounciation—indicative of how strange the word would be for many listeners to this broadcast.
2. May Day was inaugurated at a meeting of the Second Socialist International, Paris, 1889.
3. The words 'twenty-four years . . . celebrated' were first typed after 'and economically. For,' perhaps caused by an eye skipping to the second 'For,' almost certainly indicating the process of copying, in this instance, the production of a fair copy from a (much-amended?) draft

1132. Gujarati Newsletter, 10

4 May 1942

The English original was written by Orwell. No script has been traced. PasB gives timing as 11 minutes.

1133. To Miss E. W. D. Boughen, Talks Bookings

5 May 1942   Original; EB/NP

RE-RECORDING OF TALK BY K. K. ARDASCHIR.
Thursday May 7th 1942, 2.30 – 3.0 p.m.

Mr. K. K. Ardaschir recorded a talk under the title "The Sick Man Revives", on April 21st, to be used at a future date, and I sent in a Booking Slip for this talk. When the Turkish expert at the Ministry of Information saw this script, she requested that two small changes should be made, so that we are obliged to ask Mr. Ardaschir to come up to London again and re-record. I suggest that he should receive a revised fee.[1]

[Signed] Eric Blair
(Eric Blair)

1. An annotation, not in Orwell's hand, notes: 'recording alterations 3 gns.'

1134. To J. D. Bernal

5 May 1942[?]   PP/31

SHOULD BE MOST GRATEFUL FOR SUGGESTIONS FOR SPEAKER TO TAKE YOUR PLACE
IN SCIENCE SERIES.

BLAIR   BROADCASTS.

1135. To J. D. Bernal

5 May 1942   PP/EB

On 27 March 1942, Orwell sent Bernal dates for his two broadcasts: 2 and 30
May. On 27 April, he wrote giving revised dates: 9 June and 7 July. In a letter he
confirmed the arrangements already made and again asked for suggestions; see
1135. On 15 May 1942, he asked C. D. Darlington to take the sixth talk and
gave J. A. Lauwerys as the person doing the talk on 9 June; see *1170*. It is not
known whether Bernal suggested these names.

The reason for the change may have been due to Guy Burgess, then a Home
Service talks producer, who had written to Bernal on 13 April 1942, addressing
him as 'Dear Sage' (a term frequently used by those who knew him well at
Cambridge) and asking him to broadcast, in the Home Service, on science in
the USSR. W. J. West, who reproduces this letter (West: *Broadcasts*, 29–30)
wonders whether 'Burgess warned Bernal about Orwell's hatred of Russian
Communism,' leading to Bernal's belated withdrawal. In the light of Burgess's
traitorous activities, it is revealing to see how he covered himself in
approaching Bernal. He was careful to seek approval, on 9 April, from the
Home Service Talks Director and he hinted at Bernal's lack of 'political
objectivity.' He wrote:

SCIENCE IN THE USSR

This is only meant to be a draft of the letter to Bernal and it is put up for
your comment which I expect will be destructive since I am not clear either,

a) about Science, or

b) about what we really want from Bernal.

I understand that he is doing very important Government work just now.
This may have the effect of muzzling him—it will certainly also produce as a
corollary a difficulty in any attempt on our part to dictate to him what he
should or should not say.

We share, I think, an admiration for his brain though my more recent
meetings with him have done nothing to increase my admiration for his
political objectivity.

Guy Burgess (1911–1963), educated at Eton and Trinity College,
Cambridge, was a good talker and a man of considerable gifts, which he used to
proselytise the cause of Communism. After working for the British security
services and the BBC in liaison with the Foreign Office, he joined the Foreign
Office. His pro-Soviet activities were unsuspected until, in May 1951, he
suddenly left for Moscow with Donald Maclean, where he remained until his
death. Orwell mentions in his diary an evening of conversation with Burgess
and others; see *1211*.

Dear Professor Bernal,
I am very sorry indeed that you will not be able to give the two talks in our series on Science. We made out the schedule of talks as follows:
1. The Birth of Science (Prof. Gordon Childe)
2. The Beginnings of Modern Science (Prof. Bernal)
3. Experimental and Applied Science (Prof. A. C. G. Egerton)
4. The Economic Bases of Science (Prof. Joseph Needham)[1]
5. Science in the USSR (Mr. J. G. Crowther)
6. The Future of Science (Prof. Bernal)
We have now heard from all the other speakers, and they are all willing to give the talks. I shall be most grateful if you can suggest someone to take your place in this series, because I want to be able to have a complete list of speakers cabled to India, as soon as possible, for publicity purposes.

Yours sincerely,
George Orwell
Talks Assistant
Indian Section

1. The name J. G. Crowther was first typed, then Needham's name typed in its place The carbon shows the names one on top of the other, only the top copy presumably having Crowther's name erased.

1136. To Reginald Reynolds

5 May 1942   PP/EB/NP

Dear Reg,
When Dover told me about your talk,[1] I wrote saying that it was the sort of thing we wanted to use later, but could [no]t at this moment. However, after seeing your script, I am not sure it isn't possible from a censorship point of view even now. I am going to get it typed out and then do my best to get it past the censor. This might possibly mean excision of a few phrases, and I could discuss that with you. But we shan't in any case be able to put it on the air till about July, because of my schedule being so full. Of course, by that time the political situation may have altered, and we may be able to speak rather more freely. The line you have taken in your script is one which I am particularly anxious to put across to India in so far as it is possible.

Yours,
[No name/position]

1. This was not, presumably, the talk on prison literature—on which talks were broadcast on 12 and 19 June 1942, see *1204*. Reynolds perhaps discussed the implications of the imprisonment of nationalist leaders in India A Quaker, he was much influenced by Gandhi and was a keen advocate of Indian independence.

1137. To Hsiao Ch'ien

6 May 1942   PP/EB/NP

Dear Hsiao Ch'ien,

May I just remind you about the two talks you promised to do for me on Contemporary Chinese Literature, on May 19th and 26th. I don't know whether you have decided to do the talks direct, or whether you would prefer to record them first, but if you want to record them, I think we ought to make arrangements very soon, so that I can fix up a time to suit you.

I am looking forward very much to seeing your scripts—I hope you will let me have the first one by the beginning of next week at the latest. We can arrange a time to meet for rehearsal later on, if you are going to do the talks direct.

Yours,
George Orwell
Talks Producer
Indian Section
Dictated by George Orwell and
signed in his absence by:
[No name given; presumably Nancy Parratt]

1138. BBC Talks Booking Form, 6.5.42[1]

Mulk Raj Anand: 'Through Eastern Eyes,' 'Meet My Friend'; 'Series of 13 minute discussions & interviews arranged by Mr. Anand, who will get the speakers and broadcast for about 6 to 7 minutes each week. (12 talks in all)'; broadcast 27.5.42, 3, 10, 17, and 24.6.42, 1.7.42; fee £10.10s, 'to cover arrangement of programmes, contacting speakers, preparation & part in programmes.' Signed: Z. A. Bokhari. For Laurence Brander's comment on Anand as a broadcaster, see *1145*.

1. A new series of talks booking forms, dated 24 February 1942, now came into use. They were redesigned, but in practice were precisely equivalent to the earlier forms.

1139. BBC Talks Booking Form, 6.5.42

Hsiao Ch'ien: 'Literature Between Wars,' 11 and 12, Contemporary Chinese Literature; 'these two talks end the series'; broadcast 19 and 26.5.42; fee £12.12s each talk. Signed: Z. A. Bokhari.

1140. BBC Talks Booking Form, 6.5.42

Bahadur Singh: 'Through Eastern Eyes,' Today and Yesterday—Law and Order; recorded 6.5.42; broadcast 2.7.42; fee £8.8s + 13s 2d fare. Signed: Z. A. Bokhari.

1141. War-time Diary

<u>6.5.42</u>: *People do not seem pleased about Madagascar* [1] *as they did about Syria,* [2] *perhaps not grasping equally well its strategical significance, but more, I think, for want of a suitable propaganda buildup beforehand.* ⌈In the case of Syria the obviousness of the danger, the continual stories about German infiltration, and the long uncertainty as to whether the Government would act, gave people the impression that it was public opinion which had forced the decision. For all I know it may even have done so, to some extent. No similar preparation in this case.⌉ *As soon as it became clear that Singapore was in danger I pointed out that we might have to seize Madagascar and had better begin the buildup in our Indian newsletters. I was somewhat choked off even then, and some weeks back a directive came, I suppose from the Foreign Office, that Madagascar was not to be mentioned. Reason given (after the British troops had landed) "So as not to give the show away". Result, the seizure of Madagascar can be represented all over Asia as a piece of imperialist grabbing.*

Saw two women driving in an old-fashioned governess cart today. A week or two back saw two men in a carriage and pair, and one of the men actually wearing a grey bowler hat.

⌈Much speculation as to the authorship of articles in the "Tribune", violently attacking Churchill and signed "Thomas Rainsborough".[3] Considered by some to be Frank Owen,[4] which I do not believe.⌉

1. Allied forces landed at Diégo-Suarez, Madagascar, on 5 May and by September had taken over the island, strategically important in the light of naval losses in the Indian Ocean; see *1098*). It had supported the Vichy government under Pétain.
2. It was rumoured that the Germans would move east from Crete in June 1941. Allied forces therefore invaded Syria, wresting it from Vichy French troops; see *809, 3.6.41* and *ns. 2, 3*.
3. The original Thomas Rainsborough, or Rainborow, was a republican who fought for the Commonwealth in the Civil War. He commanded the warship *Swallow* in 1643 and two years later a regiment in the New Model Army. In 1646 he became an M.P. and led republicans in Parliament but was eventually reconciled with Cromwell. He was fatally wounded in battle in 1648. The name was adopted in *Tribune* to exemplify extreme radical, Leveller-type views; see *1149*. The pseudonym *was* being used by Frank Owen; see *n. 4*.
4. Frank Owen (1905–1979; OBE, military), journalist, author, and broadcaster, was a Liberal M.P., 1929–31; edited the *Daily Express*, 1931–37 and the *Evening Standard*, 1938–41 (both right-wing Beaverbrook newspapers). With Michael Foot (acting editor, *Evening Standard*, 1942; later, Deputy Leader and Leader of the Labour Party, 1976–83) and Peter Howard, he wrote *Guilty Men* (Gollancz 1940), under the pseudonym Cato, which attacked Chamberlain, Halifax, and other Conservative leaders for appeasing Hitler. In *Beaverbrook: A Study in Power and Frustration* (1956), Tom Driberg writes of Owen, 'who had lately been called up but was writing in *Tribune*, under the pseudonym Thomas Rainsborough, articles severely critical of

Churchill and his war strategy' (287). He served in the Royal Armoured Corps and South East Asia Command, 1942–46, and was promoted from trooper to lieutenant colonel by Lord Louis Mountbatten with instructions to produce a daily paper for the command from 1943 despite the strenuous opposition of Sir James Grigg. He reprinted in *SEAC* seven of the occasional pieces Orwell wrote for the *Evening Standard*, 1945–46. He edited the *Daily Mail*, 1947–50, and wrote, among other books, *The Three Dictators* (1940) and *The Fall of Singapore* (1960).

1142. To J. B. S. Haldane
7 May 1942   PP/EB/NP

Dear Mr. Haldane,[1]
We have had sent on to us a script on A.R.P., which you wrote for transmission in Hindustani. It has been suggested that you might like to broadcast it in English as well. If so, I think the best arrangement would be for you to record it at some time in the near future convenient to yourself, and we can keep it for use at a suitable moment. As your script was written in order to be translated, you might care to change certain phrases. I presume you have got a copy by you. Perhaps you could let me know about this.

Yours sincerely,
George Orwell
Talks Producer
Indian Section

1. John Burdon Sanderson Haldane (1892–1964), geneticist and physiologist with a gift for popularising science, was Professor of Genetics, University of London, 1933–37; Professor of Biometry, University College London, 1937–57. He was a Marxist and a regular contributor to the *Daily Worker*. During the Spanish civil war he advised the Spanish government on precautions against air attack; this led to his book *ARP* (1938). In 1925 he had published *Callinicus: A Defence of Chemical Warfare*. His major works include *Animal Biology* (with Julian Huxley) (1927), *Science and Ethics* (1928), *The Causes of Evolution* (1932), *Heredity and Politics* (1938), *The Marxist Philosophy and the Sciences* (1938), *Science in Peace and War* (1940), *New Paths in Genetics* (1941), *A Banned Broadcast and Other Essays* 1946 *Science and Indian Culture* (1965). Following the rise of T. D. Lysenko, the now discredited Soviet biologist, he resigned from the Communist Party, which he had joined in 1942. He spoke at the India Demonstration at the London Coliseum Theatre, 31 January 1943, and in protest at British policy towards India, emigrated to that country in 1957 and took Indian citizenship. He directed India's Genetics and Biometry Laboratory at Orissa, and died in India. For an account of his life, career, political attitudes, and social thought, in particular his relations with J. D. Bernal and Joseph Needham, see Gary Werskey, *The Visible College* (1978). For Orwell's interest in J. R. Baker, Haldane's collaborator on *Biology in Everyday Life* (1933), see *2955*.

1143. To Narayana Menon
7 May 1942   PP/EB

Dear Mr. Menon,
I understand from Miss Chitale that your two talks on Music in her series THE MAN IN THE STREET will not be taking place until about August. I think,

therefore, that it would be better for you to record the two talks for me,—William Walton, for May 26th, and Edwin Muir for June 9th, in Edinburgh. The arrangements for the other two talks will be made by Miss Chitale nearer the time of the broadcasts.

I am therefore writing to our representative in Edinburgh, to ask them to get in touch with you to arrange the recordings. I should be glad if you would kindly let me have the scripts as soon as possible, because I should like to see them before you record them.

Yours sincerely,
Eric Blair
Talks Producer
Indian Section

1144. BBC Talks Booking Form, 7.5.42

Lady Grigg: 'Women Generally Speaking'; broadcast 3, 10, 17, and 24.6.42; fee £8.8s per broadcast. Signed: Z. A. Bokhari. For Laurence Brander's comments on Lady Grigg as a broadcaster about this time, see *1145*.

1145. Laurence Brander's Reports from India on 'Through Eastern Eyes'

12 May and 15 June 1942

On 15 June 1942, J. H. Davenport made a summary of Laurence Brander's first report from India (New Delhi, 12 May 1942); a copy was sent to Rushbrook Williams, Eastern Service Director. Davenport quoted Brander as saying, 'you may take it that 'Through Eastern Eyes' has a definite and large audience in northern India at the present timing, and will have for at least three months more' (5). In Brander's second report from India, 15 June 1942, which Davenport summarised on 2 July, Brander is reported as having made that statement 'on Indian authority, [which] I believed very good.' But Brander continued, 'I very much doubt that. All the people who speak to me about ["Through Eastern Eyes"] say very emphatically that it is poor stuff, and most of them suggest it be dropped. . . . [Indians] listen only to condemn. . . . I think a very fair test we may apply to our programmes is "Would that programme be accepted on the Home Service?"'

Davenport did not know the precise dates of the broadcasts Brander was commenting on, but he thought they had been transmitted in the first fortnight of June 1942. Brander's comments made particular reference to Anand and Lady Grigg: 'Bad voices like Mulk Raj Anand (which does not get over as a voice) and poor material like the Lady Grigg stuff must be rejected always' (5); 'Lady Grigg (probably our most amateurish speaker, I have not found anyone who has ever listened—why not try people who are respected by Indians?) (1).

Rushbrook Williams responded to this summary in a letter to Brander of 14 July. He did not take up the comments on Anand and Grigg, but judged, on the basis of 'the letters which come both to the Corporation and to individuals,' that the earlier report that 'Through Eastern Eyes' had a definite and large audience 'is likely to be more correct. . . .' He went on: 'A great deal of care and ingenuity goes to the formation of these programmes; and although some of the broadcasters themselves may be not of the first rank, there is a definite theme and intention about the entire contents of the period, which to my mind give it considerable value. I must confess I don't see how you can apply to this 'Through Eastern Eyes' period the criterion of acceptability on the Home Service. Actually, it is intended to represent, mutatis mutandum,° much of what the Home Service does in peace-time; but it has to be done by Indians for Indians. Hence its defects. But in criticizing it, I do think you should remember that English as spoken by Indians is often more intelligible to Indians, however quaint the accent may appear to British listeners, than English spoken by Englishmen.'

1. J. H Davenport has not been identified. His name does not appear on the Staff List for 21 August 1943 (Issue 2). A Mr. Davenport (no initials given) attended Eastern Service meetings from September 1942 to January 1943 as a representative of the BBC. He reported under the subject heading 'Publicity.'

1146. London Letter, 8 May 1942

Partisan Review, July–August 1942

The British Crisis[1]

When I last wrote to you things had begun to go wrong in the Far East but nothing was happening politically. Now, I am fairly certain, we are on the edge of the political crisis which I have been expecting for the better part of two years. The situation is very complicated and I dare say that even before this reaches you much will have happened to falsify my predictions, but I will make the best analysis I can.

The basic fact is that people are now as fed up and as ready for a radical policy as they were at the time of Dunkirk, with the difference that they now have, or are inclined to think they have, a potential leader in Stafford Cripps. I don't mean that people in significant numbers are crying out for the introduction of Socialism, merely that the mass of the nation wants certain things that aren't obtainable under a capitalist economy and is willing to pay almost any price to get them. Few people, for instance, seem to me to feel urgently the need for nationalisation of industry, but all except the interested minority would accept nationalisation without a blink if they were told authoritatively that you can't have efficient war-production otherwise. The fact is that "Socialism," called by that name, isn't by itself an effective rallying cry. To the mass of the people "Socialism" just means the discredited Parliamentary Labour Party, and one feature of the time is the widespread disgust with all the old political parties. But what then do people want? I should say that what they articulately want is more social equality, a complete clean-out of the political leadership, an aggressive war strategy and a tighter alliance with the USSR. But one has to consider the background of these desires before trying to predict what political development is now possible.

The war has brought the class nature of their society very sharply home to English people, in two ways. First of all there is the unmistakable fact that all real power depends on class privilege. You can only get certain jobs if you have been to one of the right schools, and if you fail and have to be sacked, then somebody else from one of the right schools takes over, and so it continues. This may go unnoticed when things are prospering, but becomes obvious in moments of disaster. Secondly there are the hardships of war, which are, to put it mildly, tempered for anyone with over £2000 a year. I don't want to bore you with a detailed account of the way in which the food rationing is evaded, but you can take it that whereas ordinary people have to live on an uninteresting diet and do without many luxuries they are accustomed to, the rich go short of absolutely nothing except, perhaps, wines, fruit and sugar. You can be almost unaffected by food rationing without even breaking the law, though there is also a lively Black Market. Then there is bootleg petrol and, quite obviously, widespread evasion of Income Tax. This does not go unnoticed, but nothing happens because the will to crack down on it is not there while money and political power more or less coincide. To give just one example. At long last, and against much opposition in high places, the Ministry of Food is about to cut down "luxury feeding" by limiting the sum of money that can be spent on a meal in a hotel or restaurant. Already, before the law is even passed, ways of evading it have been thought out, and these are discussed almost undisguisedly in the newspapers.

There are other tensions which the war has brought out but which are somewhat less obvious than the jealousy caused by the Black Market or the discontent of soldiers blancoing their gasmasks under the orders of twerps of officers. One is the growing resentment felt by the underpaid armed forces (at any rate the Army) against the high wages of the munition workers. If this were dealt with by raising the soldier's pay to the munition-worker's level the result would be either inflation or the diversion of labour from war-production to consumption goods. The only real remedy is to cut down the civilian worker's wages as well, which could only be made acceptable by the most drastic income cuts all round—briefly, "war communism." And apart from the class struggle in its ordinary sense there are deeper jealousies within the bourgeoisie than foreigners sometimes realise. If you talk with a BBC accent you can get jobs that a proletarian couldn't get, but it is almost impossible to get beyond a certain point unless you belong socially to the Upper Crust. Everywhere able men feel themselves bottled down by incompetent idiots from the county families. Bound up with this is the crushing feeling we have all had in England these last twenty years that if you have brains "they" (the Upper Crust) will see to it that you are kept out of any really important job. During the years of investment capital we produced like a belt of fat the huge blimpocracy which monopolises official and military power and has an instinctive hatred of intelligence. This is probably a more important factor in England than in a "new" country like the USA. It means that our military weakness goes beyond the inherent weakness of a capitalist state. When in England you find a gifted man in a really commanding position it is usually because he happens to have been born into an aristocratic family (examples are Churchill, Cripps, Mountbatten[2]), and even so he only gets there in moments of disaster when others don't want to take responsibility. Aristocrats apart, those who are branded as "clever" can't get their hands on the real levers of power, and they know it. Of course "clever" individuals do occur in the upper strata, but basically it is a class issue, middle class against upper class.

The statement in the March–April PR that "the reins of power are still firmly in the hands of Churchill" is an error. Churchill's position is very shaky. Up to the fall of Singapore it would have been true to say that the mass of the people liked Churchill while disliking the rest of his government, but in recent months his popularity has slumped heavily. In addition he has the rightwing Tories against him (the Tories on the whole have always hated Churchill, though they had to pipe down for a long period), and Beaverbrook is up to some game which I do not fully understand but which must have the object of bringing himself into power. I wouldn't give Churchill many more months of power, but whether he will be replaced by Cripps, Beaverbrook or somebody like Sir John Anderson is still uncertain.

The reason why nearly everyone who was anti-Nazi supported Churchill from the collapse of France onwards was that there was nobody else—i.e., nobody who was already well enough known to be able to step into power and who at the same time could be trusted not to surrender. It is idle to say that in 1940 we ought to have set up a Socialist government; the mass basis for such a thing probably existed, but not the leadership. The Labour party had no guts, the pinks were defeatist, the Communists effectively pro-Nazi, and in any case there did not exist on the Left one single man of really nation-wide reputation. In the months that followed what was wanted was chiefly obstinacy, of which Churchill had plenty. Now, however, the situation has altered. The strategic situation is probably far better than it was in 1940, but the mass of the people don't think so, they are disgusted by defeats some of which they realise were unnecessary, and they have been gradually disillusioned by perceiving that in spite of Churchill's speeches the old gang stays in power and nothing really alters. For the first time since Churchill came to power the government has begun losing by-elections. Of the five most recent it has lost three, and in the two which it didn't lose one opposition candidate was anti-war (I.L.P.[3]) and the other was regarded as a defeatist. In all these elections the polls were extremely low, in one case reaching the depth-record of 24 per cent of the electorate. (Most wartime polls have been low, but one has to write off something for the considerable shift of population.) There is a most obvious loss of the faith in the old parties, and there is a new factor in the presence of Cripps, who enjoys at any rate for the moment a considerable personal reputation. Just at the moment when things were going very badly he came back from Russia in a blaze of undeserved glory. People had by this time forgotten the circumstances in which the Russo-German war broke out and credited Cripps with having "got Russia in on our side." He was, however, cashing in on his earlier political history and on having never sold out his political opinions. There is good reason to think that at that moment, with no party machine under his control, he did not realise how commanding his personal position was. Had he appealed directly to the public, through the channels open to him, he could probably then and there have forced a more radical policy on the government, particularly in the direction of a generous settlement with India. Instead he made the mistake of entering the government and the almost equally bad one of going to India with an offer which was certain to be turned down. I can't put in print the little I know about the inner history of the Cripps-Nehru negotiations, and in any case the story is too complex to be written about in a letter of this length. The important thing is to what extent this failure has discredited Cripps. The people most interested in ditching the negotiations were the pro-Japanese faction in the Indian Congress party, and the British rightwing Tories. Halifax's speech made in New York at the time was interpreted here as an effort to tread on as many Indian toes as possible and thus make a get-together between Cripps and Nehru more difficult. Similar efforts are being made from the opposite end at this moment. The upshot is that Cripps's reputation is damaged in India but not in this country—or, if damaged, then by his entry into the government rather than by the failure in Delhi.

I can't yet give you a worthwhile opinion as to whether Cripps is the man the big public think him, or are half-inclined to think him. He is an enigmatic man who has been politically unstable, and those who know him only agree upon the fact that he is personally honest. His position rests purely upon the popular belief in him, for he has the Labour party machine more or less against him, and the Tories are only temporarily supporting him because they want to use him against Churchill and Beaverbrook and imagine that they can make him into another tame cat like Attlee. Some of the factory workers are inclined to be suspicious of him (one comment reported to me was "Too like Mosley"—meaning too much the man of family who "goes to the people") and the Communists hate him because he is suspected of being anti-Stalin. Beaverbrook already appears to be instituting an attack on Cripps and his newspapers are making use of anti-Stalinist remarks dropped by Cripps in the past. I note that the Germans, to judge from their wireless, would be willing to see Cripps in power if at that price they could get rid of Churchill. They probably calculate that since Cripps has no party machine to rely on he would soon be levered out by the rightwing Tories and make way for Sir John Anderson, Lord Londonderry or someone of that kind. I can't yet say with certainty that Cripps is not merely a secondrate figure to whom the public have tied their hopes, a sort of bubble blown by popular discontent. But at any rate, the way people talked about him when he came back from Moscow was symptomatically important.

There is endless talk about a second front, those who are for and those who are against being divided roughly along political lines. Much that is said is extremely ignorant, but even people with little military knowledge are able

305

to see that in the last few months we have lost by useless defensive actions a force which, if grouped in one place and used offensively, might have achieved something. Public opinion often seems to be ahead of the so-called experts in matters of grand strategy, sometimes even tactics and weapons. I don't myself know whether the opening of a second front is feasible, because I don't know the real facts about the shipping situation; the only clue I have to the latter is that the food situation hasn't altered during the past year. Official policy seems to be to discountenance the idea of a second front, but just possibly that is only military deception. The rightwing papers make much play with our bombing raids on Germany and suggest that we can tie down a million troops along the coast of Europe by continuous commando raids. The latter is nonsense as the commandos can't do much when the nights get short, and after our own experiences few people here believe that bombing can settle anything. In general the big public is offensive-minded and is always pleased when the government shows by violating international law (eg. Oran, Syria, Madagascar) that it is taking the war seriously. Nevertheless the idea of attacking Spain or Spanish Morocco (much the most hopeful area for a second front in my opinion) is seldom raised. It is agreed by all observers that the Army, ie. rank and file and a lot of the junior officers, is exceedingly browned off, but this does not seem to be the case with the Navy and RAF, and it is easy to get recruits for the dangerous corps such as the commandos and parachute troops. An anonymous pamphlet attacking the blimpocracy, button-polishing, etc., recently sold enormously, and this line is also run by the "Daily Mirror," the soldiers' favourite paper, which was nearly suppressed a few weeks back for its criticisms of the higher command. On the other hand the pamphlets which used to appear earlier in the war, complaining about the hardships of army life, seem to have faded out. Perhaps symptomatically important is the story now widely circulated, that the real reason why the higher-ups have stuck out against adopting dive bombers is that these are cheap to manufacture and don't represent much profit. I know nothing as to the truth of this story, but I record the fact that many people believe it. Churchill's speech a few days back in which he referred to possible use of poison gas by the Germans was interpreted as a warning that gas warfare will begin soon. Usual comment: "I hope we start using it first." People seem to me to have got tougher in their attitude, in spite of general discontent and the lack of positive war aims. It is hard to assess how much the man in the street cared about the Singapore disaster. Working-class people seemed to me to be more impressed by the escape of the German warships from Brest.[4] The opinion seems general that Germany is the real enemy, and newspaper efforts to work up a hate over Japanese atrocities failed. My impression is that people will go on fighting indefinitely so long as Germany is in the field, but that if Germany should be knocked out they would not continue the war against Japan unless a real and intelligible war aim were produced.

 I have referred in earlier letters to the great growth of pro-Russian feeling. It is difficult, however, to be sure how deep this goes. A Trotskyist said to me recently that he thought that by their successful resistance the Russians had won back all the credit they lost by the Hitler-Stalin pact and the Finnish war. I don't believe this is so. What has happened is that the USSR has gained a lot of admirers it did not previously have, but many who used to be its uncritical adherents have grown cannier. One notices here a gulf between what is said publicly and privately. In public nobody says a word against the USSR, but in private, apart from the "disillusioned" Stalinists that one is always meeting, I notice a more sceptical attitude among thinking people. One sees this especially in conversations about the second front. The official attitude of the pinks is that if we open up a second front the Russians will be so grateful that they will be our comrades to the last. In reality, to open a second front without a clear agreement beforehand would simply give the Russians the opportunity to make a separate peace; for if we succeeded in drawing the Germans away from their territories, what reason would they have for going on fighting? Another theory favoured in leftwing papers is that the more fighting we do the more say we shall have in the post-war settlement. This again is an illusion; those who dictate the peace treaties are those who have remained strongest, which usually means those who have managed to avoid fighting (eg. the USA in the last war). Considerations of this kind seldom find their way into print but are admitted readily enough in private. I think people have not altogether forgotten the Russo-German pact and that fear of another doublecross partly explains their desire for a closer alliance. But there is also much sentimental boosting of Russia, based on ignorance and played up by all kinds of crooks who are utterly anti-Socialist but see that the Red Army is a popular line. I must take back some of the favourable references I made in earlier letters to the Beaverbrook press. After giving his journalists a free hand for a year or more, during which some of them did good work in enlightening the big public, Beaverbrook has again cracked the whip and is setting his team at work to attack Churchill and, more directly, Cripps. He is simultaneously yapping against fuel-rationing, petrol-rationing and other restrictions on private capitalism, and posing as more Stalinist than the Stalinists. Most of the rightwing press adopts the more cautious line of praising "the great Russian people" (historic parallels with Napoleon, etc.) while keeping silent about the nature of the Russian regime. The "Internationale" is at last being played on the wireless. Molotov's speech on the German atrocities was issued as a White Paper, but in deference to somebody's feelings (I don't know whether Stalin's or the King's) the royal arms were omitted[5] from the cover. People in general want to think well of Russia, though still vaguely hostile to Communism. They would welcome a joint declaration of war aims and a close co-ordination of strategy. I think many people realise that a firm alliance with Russia is difficult while the Munich crew are still more or less in power, but much fewer grasp that the comparative political backwardness of the USA presents another difficulty.

Well, that is the set-up as I see it. It seems to me that we are back to the "revolutionary situation" which existed but was not utilised after Dunkirk. From that time until quite recently one's thoughts necessarily moved in some such progression as this:

We can't win the war with our present social and economic structure.

The structure won't change unless there is a rapid growth in popular consciousness.

The only thing that promotes this growth is military disasters.

One more disaster and we shall lose the war.

In the circumstances all one could do was to "support" the war, which involved supporting Churchill, and hope that in some way it would all come right on the night—ie., that the mere necessities of war, the inevitable drift towards a centralised economy and a more equal standard of living, would force the regime gradually to the left and allow the worst reactionaries to be levered out. No one in his senses supposed that the British ruling classes would legislate themselves out of existence, but they might be manœuvred into a position where their continuance in power was quite obviously in the Nazi interest. In that case the mass of the nation would swing against them and it would be possible to get rid of them with little or no violence. Before writing this off as a hopelessly "reformist" strategy it is worth remembering that England is literally within gunshot of the continent. Revolutionary defeatism, or anything approaching it, is nonsense in our geographical situation. If there were even a week's serious disorganisation in the armed forces the Nazis would be here, after which one might as well stop talking about revolution.

To some small extent things have happened as I foresaw. One can after all discern the outlines of a revolutionary world war. Britain has been forced into alliance with Russia and China and into restoring Abyssinia and making fairly generous treaties with the Middle Eastern countries, and because of, among other things, the need to raise a huge air force a serious breach has been made in the class system. The defeats in the Far East have gone a long way towards killing the old conception of imperialism. But there was a sort of gap in the ladder which we never got over and which it was perhaps impossible to get over while no revolutionary party and no able leftwing leadership existed. This may or may not have been altered by the emergence of Cripps. I think it is certain that a new political party will have to arise if anything is to be changed, and the obvious bankruptcy of the old parties may hasten this. Maybe Cripps will lose his lustre quite quickly if he does not get out of the government. But at present, in his peculiar isolated position, he is the likeliest man for any new movement to crystallise round. If he fails, God save us from the other probable alternatives to Churchill.

I suppose as usual I have written too much. There is not much change in our everyday lives here. The nation went onto brown bread[6] a few weeks back. The basic petrol ration stops next month, which in theory means the end of private motoring. The new luxury taxes are terrific. Cigarettes now cost a shilling for ten and the cheapest beer tenpence a pint (fourpence in 1936). Everyone seems to be working longer and longer hours. Now and again at intervals of weeks one gets one's head above water for a moment and notices with surprise that the earth is still going round the sun. One day I noticed crocuses in the parks, another day pear blossom, another day hawthorn. One seems to catch vague glimpses of these things through a mist of war news.

Yours ever,
George Orwell

1. The article was given this title by the staff of *Partisan Review*, as Orwell notes in his London Letter for March–April 1943; see *1797*. When published, it was given five subheadings, almost certainly by *PR*; they have therefore been omitted.
2. Lord Louis Mountbatten (1900–1979), son of Prince Louis Francis of Battenberg, who relinquished that title in 1917 and assumed the surname Mountbatten, had already achieved fame in command of HMS *Kelly*, in 1939, and later in command of the aircraft carrier *Illustrious*. He was Commodore and then Chief of Combined Operations, 1941–43; Supreme Allied Commander, Southeast Asia, 1943–46, March to August 1947 the last Viceroy of India, Governor-General of India after partition, August 1947–June 1948. He and members of his family were murdered by the Irish Republican Army in August 1979.
3. Independent Labour Party, of which Orwell had been a member from June 1938 until he resigned shortly after the outbreak of war.
4. The battle-cruisers *Scharnhorst* and *Gneisenau*, with the heavy cruiser *Prinz Eugen*, sailed from Brest on 11 February 1942, passed through the Channel, and reached Wilhelmshaven two days later. Despite being warned in advance of their departure by the French Resistance, and notwithstanding individually courageous attempts, the navy and RAF failed to sink them, though *Gneisenau* was damaged. The RAF lost 42 aircraft; the navy, 6 slow Swordfish torpedo-planes. The effect on the public was dismay and anger.
5. omitted] *set as* admitted
6. The 'National Loaf,' for economy and health reasons, was darker than the standard white loaf. It was off-white, and never very popular. No more white bread could be sold after 6 April.

1147. To Mulk Raj Anand

8 May 1942   PP/EB/NP

Dear Mulk,

I have arranged with our Bookings Department that contracts should be sent to you—for the first six talks—and to George Bishop. I should be very grateful if you would let me have the names and addresses of the other speakers as soon as you possibly can, so that we can give you some publicity. When you let me have the names of the speakers I should also like to have a few personal notes about them—their job, anything interesting they have done, and so on. And if there is anything you would like us to say about the series as a whole, do let me know, and we will include it in our publicity notes next week, which is the latest date to send anything in about the first talk, on May 27th.

I think the idea was that you should record the first one, so would you be able to do it on Monday, May 25th? This would mean that I should have a script by May 18th, if you can let me have it by then.

Yours,
[No name/position]

1148. To Diana Wong

8 May 1942   PP/EB/NP

Dear Miss Wong,

I have now been able to fix a date for your broadcast. I should like your talk[1] to be broadcast on Thursday, June 25th, at 1.15 p.m. from Broadcasting House. This would mean that you would have to be there at about 12.30, so that we would have time for rehearsal beforehand. If it is not convenient for you to come then, we could always arrange a recording to suit you beforehand, but I should much prefer it if you could do it direct.

I should be glad if you would let me know as soon as possible which arrangement would suit you best. If you have to record the talk, perhaps you will let me know a day and time that will be convenient for you.

Yours sincerely,\
Eric Blair\
Talks Producer\
Indian Section

1. Diana Wong, actress, spoke on 'My Escape from France.' She later married Roy Plomley (1914–1985), who in 1941 had initiated what proved to be the longest-running series presented by the same broadcaster, 'Desert Island Discs.'

1149. War-time Diary

<u>8.5.42</u>: *According to W.*[1] *a real Anglo-Russian alliance is to be signed up and the Russian delegates are already in London. I don't believe this.*

The Turkish radio (for some time past I think this has been one of the most reliable sources of information) alleges that both Germans and Russians are preparing to use poison gas in the forthcoming battle.

⸢Great naval battle in progress in the Coral Sea.[2] Sinkings claimed by both sides so vast that one does not know what to believe. But from the willingness of the Japanese radio to talk about the battle (they have already named it the Battle of the Coral Sea) the presumption is that they count on making their objective.

My guess as to the identity of 'Thomas Rainsboro': Tom Wintringham. (Right!)

(<u>30.5.42.</u> Wintringham denies authorship of these articles, but I still think he wrote them.)³⸥

1. Fredric Warburg, managing director of Secker & Warburg; see *375, n. 1.*
2. The Battle of the Coral Sea, 4–8 May, was the first naval engagement fought entirely by aircraft, the ships involved never coming into each other's sight. The Americans lost the aircraft carrier *Lexington*, a tanker, a destroyer, 74 planes, and 543 men; the Japanese lost the light carrier *Shoho*, a destroyer, more than 80 planes and more than 1,000 men. (Liddell Hart, *History of the Second World War*, 361–63; U.S.: 346–49.) See also *1150, n. 1.*
3. Entry in parentheses, dated 30 May, was added by Orwell to the manuscript version only

1150. Weekly News Review, 21

9 May 1942

PasB gives this Weekly News Review as by Z. A. Bokhari and the timing as 13′ 45″. The typescript is marked 'As Broadcast' (by alteration of the originally typed line 'NOT CHECKED WITH BROADCAST'); there are no censors' stamps. One passage is set within square brackets but is not crossed through; since it comes towards the end of the broadcast, it might have been an optional cut for timing purposes. There is evidence that the original draft was different. At the top of the fourth page of the typescript, after paragraph five, are two lines crossed out and with a concluding square bracket:

Australia. The Japanese lost seven warships of various sizes and half a dozen aeroplanes, while the Americans lost only three planes.]

The fifth paragraph is clearly complete, ending with 'setback for the Japanese,' so the two lines that follow must once have concluded a paragraph of an earlier draft. The excision may well be a result of censorship but, equally, could simply be because no one was sure what had happened. As Orwell wrote in his diary 8 May: 'Sinkings claimed by both sides so vast that one does not know what to believe'; see *1149*.

On May 5th British forces landed on the island of Madagascar. The Vichy government ordered the garrison to resist, and there was indeed fierce resistance for a short time, but Diego Suarez, the naval base, had surrendered by the evening of May 7th, and almost all the Vichy forces in the island laid down their arms. A certain amount of mopping up may now be necessary, but it can be taken that Madagascar is now under British control. This is an extremely important move in the general strategy of the war against Germany and Japan.

If you look at the map, you can see that this large island dominates the route by which ships coming round the Cape of Good Hope travel either towards Ceylon and India, or towards the Red Sea and the Middle East. In enemy hands, therefore, Madagascar would constitute a most deadly threat to the Allies' war effort; for since it is difficult for British merchant ships to pass through the Mediterranean, the armies in the Middle East and India have to be supplied largely round the Cape. In addition, the supplies that are sent to our Russian Allies, and which are put ashore in the Persian Gulf, go by the same route.

In spite of this danger, the British Government would probably have preferred to take the risk of not occupying Madagascar if a reliable government had been in power in France. However, during the last few weeks effective power in the Vichy government has passed into the hands of Laval, who hardly pretends to be anything more than a tool of the Germans. More than a year ago, while Pétain was still in power, the French handed over Indo-China to the Japanese, to be used as a base for attacks on Siam and Malaya. If even Pétain was willing to do this, it was much more certain that Laval would do the same with Madagascar. Apart from this general probability, it had been known that for months past more and more Japanese in the guise of traders, military attachés, tourists and whatnot, had been pouring into Madagascar in order to prepare the way for a coup d'état. In the circumstances, the British Government had no choice but to forestall the Japanese by entering Madagascar first. It has been made clear that Britain has no intention of annexing Madagascar or of interfering more than is necessary in its internal administration. The British will probably not occupy the whole of the island, but merely the ports, airfields and other places of military importance. Their first task will be to round up the Japanese fifth columnists. Apart from these, the bulk of the inhabitants are probably pro-Ally. The Malagasy population of the island is about four million, and the French population about 25 thousand. It is known that these are divided in sympathies. Earlier in the war, the then Governor of Madagascar was in favour of continuing resistance against the Germans, and in consequence Pétain replaced him by a more pro-Nazi official. Recently a secret radio, supporting General de Gaulle, has been heard broadcasting from Madagascar. We know, therefore, that at least some of the French population are on our side, and the indigenous population, with the threat of German or Japanese tyranny before them, are almost certain to be so. It is regretted that both French and British blood had to be shed in carrying out this operation, but by arriving in over-whelming force the British managed to reduce the bloodshed to a minimum.

Once Madagascar is occupied, it becomes necessary to defend it, and the other islands in the Indian Ocean assume an increased importance. In particular, there are the islands of Mauritius and Reunion, lying somewhat to the east of Madagascar. The Japanese are almost certain at some time to make an attempt upon these islands in order to use them as stepping stones for further attacks. Mauritius is a British possession, but Reunion is under the control of Vichy France and there exists the danger that its rulers may make an attempt to hand it over to the Japanese. However, the British occupation of Madagascar may make a political difference in Reunion, where as elsewhere throughout the French Empire, the Vichy elements are only very insecurely in control.

In Burma, the Japanese have entered Mandalay, and the eastern wing of their army, driving from Lashio, has crossed the China border. On the western flank, British and Chinese forces previously defending Mandalay are retreating northward. By these operations the Japanese have succeeded in temporarily isolating China, which for the time being can only be supplied by air. On the other hand, their other objective of encircling the British and Chinese armies in Upper Burma is not likely to succeed. Some material may have to be abandoned, but the main British and Chinese forces in the eastern part of Upper Burma will probably get away. They may move up the railway to Myitkyina and thence into China, but more likely will have to retreat over the mountains of Manipur into Assam. It is a difficult route, but not impossible, and it is made easier by the fact that great numbers of Indian refugees have passed that way already. Meanwhile the Chinese Republican armies have made a series of daring raids on Shanghai, Nanking, Hangchow and several other cities in the heart of Japanese-occupied China, and two days ago they made another similar raid on Canton. The fact that Chinese armies can thus operate right inside their territory shows how precarious is the Japanese hold even on the parts of China that are marked 'Japanese' on the map. On May 5th the Japanese succeeded in landing on the island of Corregidor, and on May 6th the fortress was forced to surrender, after a resistance of four months. This long delaying action in the Philippines has held up the Japanese attack on Australia, just as the delaying action in Burma has held up the attack on India. Yesterday came news of an air and naval action near the Solomon Islands between the American navy and a Japanese fleet evidently making for Australia. At the moment of speaking the battle is probably still continuing. It is too early to give a detailed account, but it is certain that the Japanese have had very heavy losses, including two aircraft carriers, two or more cruisers, two destroyers and a number of smaller ships, besides transports. The Allies have not yet published figures of their own losses. Until further reports come in a final verdict is not possible, but it can be taken that in all probability this battle has resulted in a serious setback for the Japanese.[1]

With the coming of spring, operations on the Russian front are beginning again. Everything points to the fact that the Caucasus will be the scene of the main German offensive. The Russians are not ceasing from their attacks both there and in the Crimea, their main object being to weaken the Germans beforehand and hamper their concentration. British supplies of war material continue to pour into Russia, through the Arctic Sea, but not without difficulty, for the nights are now very short in the far north, and the Germans have strong fleets of submarines on the Norwegian coast. A few days ago, a sea battle took place in which the British lost a cruiser and the Germans a destroyer, but of 30 merchant ships making up the convoy, 27 got through and delivered their cargoes to our Russian allies. In another broadcast speech, Stalin has again stated confidently that he expects final victory over the Germans during 1942.

The Royal Air Force continues to make heavy bombing raids on the German ports and armament factories. The Germans cannot at present reply by similar raids and are continuing to bomb residential areas in the hope that the suffering which this causes will induce the British Government to stop bombing Germany. In the occupied countries it is clear that the German rule is becoming more and more irksome. On May 4th, the Germans themselves announced that they had just shot seventy-two Dutchmen in one batch for pro-allied activities, and almost every day their newspapers and radio contain similar announcements, that ten, twenty, thirty, Poles, Frenchmen, Belgians, Norwegians or other citizens of the occupied countries have been shot for the same reason. When some piece of sabotage or other pro-allied activity takes place, the German practice is to shoot at once a number of hostages who are usually described as Jews and Communists, and to threaten that if the culprits are not delivered up, further hostages will be shot on a certain date. To an extraordinary extent this method has been a failure, and the people of the occupied countries have refused to collaborate with the invader, even when not to do so means risking their own lives. [Some very interesting eye-witness evidence has just come to light about the British

Commando raid on Saint Nazaire, which took place some weeks ago. It appears now that the local French joined in on the side of the British and that fighting actually continued for three days after the main body of the Commandos had done what it came to do and withdrawn. The Germans took reprisals of the most barbarous kind afterwards and posted notices all along the French coast, saying that hostages would be shot as a matter of routine at any place where British landing-parties appeared.]

In the near future what is known as luxury feeding is going to be prohibited in England. Full details of the law have not been fixed, but it is known that the amount of money anyone can spend on a meal at a hotel or restaurant is to be fixed at a small sum. Taken together with clothes rationing, petrol rationing, universal military service, and the changes which are occurring in the British educational system, this new law is one more step along the path by which Britain, as a result of the war, is becoming more truly a democracy.

1. The Battle of the Coral Sea was the first combined air and naval battle. Winston Churchill, in *The Second World War*, IV, 215–21; U.S.: *The Hinge of Fate*, 245, gives aircraft losses, assessed after the war, as American, 33, Japanese, 43; *2194 Days of War* gives losses as American, 66, Japanese, 'about 70' (237), but see *1149, n. 2*. Despite suffering heavier losses, the Americans succeeded in forcing the Japanese to put off landing at Port Moresby, New Guinea. In the longer term, the Battle of the Coral Sea probably made it impossible for the Japanese to land on the Australian mainland.

1151. Review of *The Wound and the Bow* by Edmund Wilson

The Observer, 10 May 1942

Although in this new book of critical essays Mr. Edmund Wilson ranges from Sophocles to Hemingway via Casanova and Edith Wharton, it is chiefly valuable for two long studies of Dickens and Kipling, both of which incorporate a certain amount of original research, or, at any rate, of little-known information. Writing in 1940 or 1941, after the publication of Miss Gladys Storey's memoir, Mr. Wilson is able to make use of biographical details which earlier critics of Dickens had regarded as either irrelevant or as a disgraceful secret to be hushed up at all costs. The contrast between Dickens's literary personality—his literary emanation, as one might say—and his private life is even more baffling than is usual with creative writers, and if Mr. Wilson reaches no very definite conclusion he does at least throw brilliant flashes of light on some very dark places.

Dickens's last surviving daughter, Mrs. Perugini, wrote a memoir of her father, which she destroyed because it gave "only half the truth," but afterwards conveyed the substance of it verbally to Miss Gladys Storey. It brought out the facts about Ellen Lawless Ternan, who is enigmatically mentioned in Dickens's will and who, in fact, was his mistress during the later years of his life. Mr. Wilson makes the very interesting observation that this girl's name appears in quasi-anagrammatic form in his last three novels (Estella Provis, Bella Wilfer, and Helena Landless). What is remarkable is not that Dickens should have indulged in a mistress but that he evidently behaved with abominable cruelty towards his wife, and at least very tyrannically towards his children.

"I loved my father," said Mrs. Perugini, "better than any man in the world—in a different way, of course. . . . I loved him for his faults." And she added, as she rose and walked to the door: "my father was a wicked man—a very wicked man."

It is a strange epitaph for the author of "Pickwick Papers." If one judges Dickens by his literary personality, the only part of him that now matters, it is clear that he was not a wicked man. The outstanding thing about his work is a certain native goodness, and in the few passages where his moral sense fails him one feels the contrasts immediately. Yet the last person who remembered him remembered him as wicked. One is forced to believe in a sort of split personality, in which David Copperfield rather than Charles Dickens is the real man. Mr. Wilson indeed hints at a definite criminal strain in Dickens, and the essay tails off into a discussion of the meaning of Edwin Drood, about which Mr. Wilson has a new and rather sensational theory.

Dickens was a writer-with-a-purpose, and all serious critics of him have noted this, but they have differed between themselves as to whether his "purpose" was moral or political. At the one extreme there is Chesterton, who very nearly succeeded in turning Dickens into a Catholic medievalist, and at the other there is Mr. T. A. Jackson, who presented Dickens not only as an all-but perfect Marxist but—an even harder feat—as an extreme naturalist. Mr. Wilson is somewhere between the two, but inclines more towards the Jackson school. He is undoubtedly right in pointing out that the themes of Dickens's novels reflect first his belief in and then his disillusionment with the commercial middle-class, and he makes the interesting point that in his last completed novel, "Our Mutual Friend," Dickens shows a sympathy he had not shown before with the petty aristocracy (Wrayburn, Twemlow) and the proletariat (Lizzie Hexam). But he does not add that in "Our Mutual Friend" Dickens's thoughts have come full circle and he has returned to his early notion of individual benevolence as the cure for everything, having apparently despaired of any political solution. Perhaps also he overstresses the element of symbolism in Dickens's work and understresses the mechanical side of commercial story-writing. But this aside this is the best essay[1] on Dickens that has appeared for some time.

If the essay on Kipling is less satisfying it is probably because Kipling is nearer to our own time and therefore more capable of arousing anti-British feeling. I do not know whether Mr. Wilson is one of those Americans who avoid visiting England lest their hatred for it should evaporate, but at times that is the impression he gives. But the Kipling essay contains some very interesting biographical material. Kipling spent several years in the United States, and ended by involving himself in a quarrel in which he behaved in an extremely undignified way, the whole incident probably casting light on his peculiar role as a sedentary apostle of violence. It is a pity that for the rest Mr. Wilson occupies himself principally with Kipling's later stories, those he wrote after 1918. Whatever psychological interest these may possess, something had gone out of Kipling by that time, and the stories are synthetic. Mr. Wilson hardly mentions Kipling's verse, evidently agreeing with the accepted view that Kipling is primarily a prose-writer.

The other essays in the book are slighter, but they include an interesting elucidation of Joyce's "Finnegans Wake." Mr. Wilson at times writes clumsily, even vulgarly, but he is one of the few literary critics of our day who give the impression of being grown up, and of having digested Marx's teachings instead of merely rejecting them or swallowing them whole.

1. The printed text has 'But this side is the best essay'—presumably a compositor's error.

1152. Gujarati Newsletter, 11

11 May 1942

The English original was written by Orwell. No script has been traced. PasB gives timing as 13 minutes with 1-minute filler provided by commercial disc HMV N16472.

1153. To Hsiao Ch'ien

11 May 1942   PP/EB/NP

Dear Hsiao Ch'ien,
We have just received reports from India on our broadcasts during the last half of February. I thought you would be interested in the following, which came from Dacca —

"Talk by Chinese talker on occupied China and Japan's New Order on 26th February very interesting".[1]

We don't receive very many comments from India, so I think this is all the more encouraging! I am very much looking forward to seeing your first talk on Chinese contemporary literature.[2]

Yours sincerely,
George Orwell
Talks Producer
Indian Section

1. For Orwell's instructions to Ch'ien for this talk and a second, on Japanese-occupied China, see *919*.
2. There is no further correspondence between Orwell and Ch'ien and no talks booking form has been traced for this talk.

1154. To J. F. Horrabin

11 May 1942   PP/EB

Dear Horrabin,
We have just received two comments on the talks on Geography you did for me—as the comments only cover the second half of February, they had only heard your first two talks. The report from Delhi says—
"On February 25th J. F. Horrabin's talk on Geography—Sea Lanes—was a very informative comparative study of the strategic importance of the different seas of the present war. The talker had an extremely interesting manner of explaining the background of war in terms of geography."
The report from Trichinopoly says—
"Horrabin's talk "The World is Round" was of outstanding interest".
We don't get very many comments at the moment, but I think these are encouraging, and I hope you will be able to do some more talks for us.[1]

Yours sincerely,
George Orwell
Talks Producer
Indian Section

1. For Orwell's letter to Horrabin about these talks, see *952*. The title for the series of four talks was 'The World Is Round'; see *954*.

1155. War-time Diary

<u>11.5.42</u>: *Another gas warning (in Churchill's speech) last night. I suppose we shall be using it before many weeks are over.*
From a Japanese broadcast: "In order to do justice to the patriotic spirit of the Koreans, the Japanese Government have decided to introduce compulsory military service in Korea".
Rumoured date for the German invasion of Britain: May 25th.

1156. BBC Talks Booking Form, 12.5.42

K. K. Ardaschir: 'The Rebirth of a Nation'; 8-minute talk. 'This talk is completely different from a feature with the same title by Mr. Ardaschir which will go out in Hindustani on the same day'; recorded 12.5.42; broadcast 15.5.42; fee £6.6s (£6.30), altered to £3.3s. Signed: Z. A. Bokhari.

1157. BBC Talks Booking Form, 13.5.42

Cedric Dover: 'Freedom and Cultural Expression'; recorded 5.5.42; broadcast date not fixed; fee £8.8s.

1158. BBC Talks Booking Form, 13.5.42

Cedric Dover: 'These Names Will Live,' Bertrand Russell; broadcast 5.5.42; fee £8.8s.

1159. BBC Talks Booking Form, 13.5.42

From Miss Chitale. Kingsley Martin: 'The Man in the Street,' 'What the Public Wants'; broadcast 15.5.42; fee £8.8s. Signed: Z. A. Bokhari. See *1209, n. 3.*

1160. To Mulk Raj Anand

14 May 1942   EB/PP/NP

Dear Mulk,

Thanks very much for letting me have the list of your first six speakers. We have asked for contracts to be sent to them. There is just one point, and that is, has Sergeant Collett[1] got his Commanding Officer's permission to do the broadcast? If not, would you ask him to get it in writing, or if he can let me have the name and address of his C.O., we can do it from this end. We shall also need the script of that particular discussion in fairly well ahead, because it has to go to our War Office liaison, just as a matter of form.

Yours,
[No name/position]

1. Frederick Collett, of the Army Educational Corps, was the fifth name provided by Anand in a letter of 11 May 1942 (reproduced in West, *Broadcasts,* 193–94). He and the sixth person, Dr. L. Haden Guest, Labour M.P. for Islington, had not confirmed acceptance of the invitation to broadcast. The first four people were George Bishop, actor and civil servant then lecturing on anti-gas decontamination (see *1147*); Albert Edward Manderson, a chimney-sweep and iconoclastic 'Natural philosopher'; Ian Jay Bell, playwright and fire-watcher (for fire-bomb attacks), who had worked on the *Moscow Daily News;* and the writer Inez Holden, a friend of Orwell's, then working in a factory (see *1326*).
   On 22 June 1942, Orwell was sent a letter by Major R. S. P. Mackarness, BBC War Office Liaison Officer, 213 Egton House, regarding Sergeant Collett's contribution to Anand's series 'Meet My Friend,' saying:
   As I explained to you on the telephone, the India Office does not like the underlying tone of this script and believes that the suggestion that Anglo-Indians look upon this country as an alien land in any real sense of the term is untrue. In the second place, the India Office feels that it is most undesirable that a broadcast of this kind should contain what would undoubtedly be interpreted by the Anglo-Indian community in India as propaganda designed to suggest that they have no special place as a minority, and that they should forget that they have English blood in their veins
   This may be putting it strongly, but that the Anglo-Indians have a very special conception of their position in the political and economic life of India is beyond question, and the India Office believes that real offence might be given by this broadcast to listeners among that community.
   The War Office considers that it is most undesirable for a sergeant in His Majesty's Forces to broadcast this kind of thing.

In the circumstances, would you be good enough, if it is not both[er]ing you too much, to let me know what you decide to do with this script?"

This broadcast was to be transmitted on 24.6.42, but PasB does not include any reference to the programme 'Meet My Friend' in the schedules for that day. Mackarness's intervention seems to have been effective.

1161. To Narayana Menon

14 May 1942   EB/NP

Dear Mr. Menon,

Thank you for your letter of May 9th. I am arranging for the music you asked for to be sent to Edinburgh. I am sorry, but the violin Concerto[1] is not allowed to be broadcast, and I am not sending you this.

I shall be glad if you will let me have the script as soon as possible, then I can get it censored down here and pass it on to our Edinburgh office. If you are arranging to record the talk on Edwin Muir at the same time as the talk on Walton, of course I shall need that soon too. In any case, it is best if you can let me have the script of a recorded talk at least 10 days in advance.

I hope that Miss Orr, to whom we have written in connection with your talk, has already got in touch with you.

Yours sincerely,
Eric Blair
Talks Producer
Indian Section

1. By William Walton (1939).

1162. BBC Talks Booking Form, 14.5.42

Professor V. G. Childe: 'Science and Politics,' 1, 'The Birth of Science'; 20-minute talk; recorded 28.5.42; broadcast 2.6.42; 'I have informed the Talks Section in Scotland of this talk'; fee £10.10s + £6.15 fare and £1.14s expenses. Signed: Z. A. Bokhari.

1163. BBC Talks Booking Form, 14.5.42

J. G. Crowther:[1] 'Science and Politics,' 5, 'Science in the USSR'; 20-minute talk; broadcast 7.7.42; fee £10.10s. Signed: Z. A. Bokhari.

1. On 18 May 1942, J G. Crowther, author of many books on the history of science and popular science, provided notes about himself for Orwell: he was born in 1899; had been a scientific correspondent to the *Manchester Guardian*, lecturer on the history of science at Harvard, and adviser to the USSR's Director of Higher Technical Education in 1930. See also *1117, n. 1.*

1164. BBC Talks Booking Form, 14.5.42

Professor A. C. G. Egerton: 'Science and Politics,' 3, 'Experimental & Applied Science'; 20-minute talk; recorded 14.5.42; broadcast 16.6.42; fee £10.10s. Signed: Z. A. Bokhari. Remarks: 'Prof. Egerton is leaving the country shortly, so I should be glad if he could have his contract as soon as possible.'

1165. BBC Talks Booking Form, 14.5.42

Dr. L. Haden Guest, M.C., M.P.:[1] 'Through Eastern Eyes,' 'Meet My Friend,' 6; discussion and interview with M. R. Anand; 13-minute broadcast, Guest to speak 6 or 7 minutes; broadcast 1.7.42; fee £6.6s. Signed: Z. A. Bokhari.

1. Leslie Haden Haden-Guest (1877–1960; 1st Baron Haden-Guest, 1950), author, journalist, physician, and politician, served in the South African and 1914–18 wars. He was a Labour M.P., 1923–27 and 1937–50, and was on the parliamentary committee for the Evacuation of the Civil Population in 1938.

1166. BBC Talks Booking Form, 14.5.42

Inez Holden: 'Through Eastern Eyes,' 'Meet my Friend,' 4; 13-minute broadcast, Holden to speak 6 or 7 minutes; broadcast 17.6.42; fee £6.6s. Signed: Z. A. Bokhari.

1167. BBC Talks Booking Form, 14.5.42

A. E. Manderson:[1] 'Through Eastern Eyes,' 'Meet My Friend,' 2; discussion and interview with Mulk Raj Anand; 13-minute broadcast, Manderson to speak 6 or 7 minutes; broadcast 3.6.42; fee £6.6s. Signed: Z. A. Bokhari.

1. See *1160, n 1*.

1168. BBC Talks Booking Form, 14.5.42

Professor Joseph Needham: 'Science and Politics,' 4, 'The Economic Bases of Science'; broadcast 23.6.42; fee £10.10s + 12s.0d fare. Signed: Z. A. Bokhari.

1169. 'Culture and Democracy'

Orwell's Fabian Society lecture 'Culture and Democracy,' given on 22 November 1941 in the series 'Victory or Vested Interest?' was printed in a pamphlet with the latter title, 15 May 1942 in two editions: by George Routledge & Sons and by The Labour Book Service. See *882*.

1170. To C. D. Darlington
15 May 1942   PP/EB

Dear Dr. Darlington,[1]

I am writing to ask whether you could do a talk for us on July 7th. This is the sixth and last of a series of talks on the history of science which we are broadcasting to India. To give you an idea of the scope of the series, I had better give you a list of the titles of the six talks.

1. "The Birth of Science" by Professor V. G. Childe. (Science among the ancients)

2. "The Beginnings of Modern Science" by Mr. J. A. Lauwerys (From the early Middle Ages to the Industrial Revolution)

3. "Experimental & Applied Science" by Professor Egerton (The subsequent history of science)

4. "The Economic Bases of Science" by Professor Needham (Science under capitalism, Fascism and Socialism)

5. "Science in the USSR" by Mr. J. G. Crowther.

The sixth, which we want you to do, is to be called "The Future of Science.

These talks are supposed to take from 15 to 20 minutes, which means something in the neighbourhood of 2,000 words or perhaps a little over. I should like to have the script by about July 1st. If it is not convenient for you to broadcast on that particular date we can easily record the talk beforehand.

Could you be kind enough to let me know as early as possible whether you can undertake this?

Yours truly,
George Orwell
Talks Producer
Indian Section

1. Cyril Dean Darlington (1903–1981), a specialist on plant breeding, genetics, and chromosomes, was Director of the John Innes Horticultural Institution, 1939–53; Professor of Botany, University of Oxford, and Keeper, Oxford Botanic Garden, 1953–71; President, Rationalist Press Association, 1948 In addition to his specialist studies, he wrote *The Conflict of Science and Society* (a Conway Memorial Lecture, 1948), *The Facts of Life* (1953), and *The Place of Botany in the Life of a University* (1954). Although associated with J. D Bernal (see *1005, n. 1*) and J. G. Crowther (see *1117, n. 1*) in the London-based dining club Tots and Quots, he was an anti-communist, see Gary Werskey, *The Visible College*, 263, 296.

1171. To J. A. Lauwerys

15 May 1942   PP/EB

Dear Mr. Lauwerys,[1]

I am approaching you in hopes that you may agree to do a broadcast talk for us on June 9th, in a series which we are broadcasting to India.

This is a series of six talks on the history of science, and its place in the modern world. The one we hope you will undertake is the second talk, to be called "The Beginnings of Modern Science". The one preceding this, by Professor V. G. Childe, of which I will send you a copy in the course of the next few days, deals with science in ancient times, and we want to follow up with another, roughly speaking covering the period between the early Middle Ages and the Industrial Revolution. Professor Egerton, who is doing the third talk, is dealing with the subsequent history of science, and we are sending you a copy of his talk as well.

These talks are supposed to take between 15 and 20 minutes, which means somewhere about 2,000 words, perhaps a little more. I should like to have the script by about June 2nd, if possible. If the actual date of the broadcast is not convenient to you, it will be quite easy to record it beforehand. It could be recorded in Birmingham instead of London, if you find this more convenient, but other things being equal, we should definitely prefer it if you could deliver the talk here.

Could you let me know as early as possible whether you can undertake this?

Yours truly,
George Orwell
Talks Producer
Indian Section

1 Joseph Albert Lauwerys (1902–1981), a graduate in chemistry and physics, was Lecturer in Methods of Science, University of London, Institute of Education, 1932–41; Reader in Education, 1941–46; Professor of Comparative Education, 1947–70; Director, Atlantic Institute of Education, Nova Scotia, 1970–76, and, among many posts, Chairman of the Basic English Foundation He wrote a number of books on science and also *Film in the School* (1936), *Film and Radio as Educational Media* (1939), *Educational Problems in the Liberated Countries* (1946), and *The Roots of Science in Basic English* (1951).

1172. War-time Diary

<u>15.5.42:</u> *I saw Cripps on Wednesday, the first time I had actually spoken to him. Rather well impressed. He was more approachable and easy-going than I had expected, and quite ready to answer questions. Though aged 53 some of his movements are almost boyish. On the other hand he has decidedly a red nose.* ⌈I saw him in one of the reception rooms, or whatever they are called, off the House of Lords. Some interesting old prints on the walls, coronets on the chairs and on the ashtrays, but everything with the

vaguely decayed look that all Parliamentary institutions now have. A string of non-descript people waiting to see Cripps. As I waited trying to talk to his secretary, a phrase I always remember on these occasions came into my mind—"shivering in ante-rooms". In eighteenth-century biographies you always read about people waiting on their patrons and "shivering in ante-rooms". It is one of those ready made phrases like "leave no stone unturned", and yet how true it is as soon as you get anywhere near politics, or even the more expensive kinds of journalism.[1]

Cripps considers that Bose[1] is definitely[2] in German territory. He says it is known that he got out through Afghanistan. I asked him what he thought of Bose, whom he used to know well, and he described him as "a thoroughly bad egg". I said there seemed little doubt that he is subjectively pro-Fascist. Cripps: "He's pro-Subhas. That is all he really cares about. He will do anything that he thinks will help his[3] career along".

I am not certain, on the evidence of Bose's[4] broadcasts, that this is so. I said I thought very few Indians were reliably anti-Fascist. Cripps disagreed so far as the younger generation go. He said the young Communists and leftwing Socialists are wholeheartedly anti-Fascist and have a western conception of Socialism and internationalism. Let's hope it's so.

1. Subhas Chandra Bose; see *1080, n. 1* and *1119, n. 5.* The manuscript spells the name 'Bhose,' here and later in the paragraph.
2. *is definitely*] is
3. *his*] his own
4. *Bose's*] B's

1173. Weekly News Review, 22

16 May 1942

PasB has this Weekly News Review as by Z. A. Bokhari. The typescript from which this talk is reproduced is marked 'NOT CHECKED WITH BROADCAST.' It carries two censors' stamps; that for Security bears no signature. The text has been considerably shortened, and some words are so obliterated that they cannot be recovered. There is no obvious reason for regarding these cuts as the work of the censor. It is possible that Orwell wrote too much. Thus, on 2 May, the broadcast runs to about 124 lines of typescript (allowing for short lines); that for 9 May, 147 lines of which 11 are cut and two are 'fossils' from an earlier version—so, 134 net; this broadcast has 178 typescript lines, but 39 are cut, leaving 139, almost identical with the length of the preceding week's broadcast; and the final broadcast, May 23, has 135 lines. See *1210 headnote.*

India is now within measurable distance of invasion. At the same time the military situation has not changed greatly during the past week, and for once, instead of my usual commentary, [in which I try to sum up the current news from the battle-fronts[1]] I want to try to give you a more general picture of the war as a whole, which may help to bring the events of the immediate future into better proportion.

War[2] is not an event like a football match, which takes place within a measurable time and between two fixed teams. [In war there is no decision as in a football match, in the sense that there is no such thing as being beaten in a war, unless you decide that you are beaten and voluntarily give up fighting.[3]] When we look at the history of this war, which has now gone on for two and a half years, we see that something which started as a localised struggle has become definitely worldwide, and that a meaning and purpose which were not apparent at the beginning have gradually become clear. More than that, we see that this war is not an isolated event, but part of a worldwide process which began more than ten years ago. It started, properly speaking, in 1931, when the Japanese invaded Manchuria, and the League of Nations failed to take action. From then onwards, we have seen a long series of aggressions, first of all unresisted, then resisted unsuccessfully, then resisted more successfully, until finally the whole picture becomes clear as the struggle of free peoples who see before them the chance of a fuller and happier existence, against comparatively small cliques who are not interested in the general development of humanity but only in advancing their individual power.[4] One country after another is sucked into the struggle, and they are sucked in not purely for reasons of geography, and not purely from economic motives, but primarily for what are called ideological reasons—that is to say, they are practically compelled to take one side or the other, according as their national philosophy is a democratic one or the contrary. Thus it was inevitable that Soviet Russia, however anxious to remain at peace, should, sooner or later, be drawn into the war on the side of the democracies. It was inevitable that Britain and China should ultimately find themselves fighting on the same side, whatever causes of difference there may have been between them in the past. It was inevitable that a progressive state like Mexico should line up with the democracies, in spite of the outstanding disputes between Mexico and the United States. Equally, it was inevitable that Japan should join hands with Germany, even though, if they should be victorious, these two will be fighting one another almost immediately. The Fascist states have a common interest in suppressing liberty everywhere, because if it exists anywhere, it will ultimately spread to their own dominions. In this vast struggle, India finds itself inescapably on the democratic side, and this fact is not really altered by the ancient grievances which India may feel against Britain, nor by the very real desire of Germany and Japan to win India to their side. India is compelled to be with Britain, because a victory of the Germans or the Japanese would postpone Indian independence far longer than the most reactionary British Government would either wish or be able to do. And in fact, in spite of Japanese promises and protestations of friendship, the attack on India has already begun. Bombs have dropped on Indian soil, Japanese troops are advancing dangerously close along the eastern shore of the Bay of Bengal. Willy-nilly, India is already in the struggle; and the outcome of the war—and therefore India's independence—may be determined to a very great extent by the efforts that Indians themselves now make.

In these circumstances, it is useful to look back and consider what has been achieved during the past ten years by those peoples who knew what they wanted and rated liberty above safety. When the Japanese invaded Manchuria in 1931, China was in a state of chaos, and the young Chinese republic was in no condition to resist. Six years later, however, when the invasion of China proper began, order had been restored under the leadership of Marshal Chiang Kai-Shek, and a powerful national spirit had grown up. The Japanese, therefore, were surprised to find that what they regarded as a mere military parade—the 'China incident' was their phrase for it—stretched out indefinitely, causing them endless losses in men and materials and never seeming to come within sight of its end, however many victories they might report in the newspapers. [That war has now been going on for just over five years; all along the Japanese have seemed to have everything in their hands, modern weapons, war materials of every kind, and command of the sea. They have been able to drop bombs by the tens of thousands on Chinese towns where the inhabitants had not even an anti-aircraft gun with which to reply, much less an aeroplane. They have been able to over-run great areas and to seize the important industrial districts of the coastal towns and to kill no one knows how many thousands of Chinese men, women and children and yet somehow, China never seems any nearer to being conquered.] Scores of times the Japanese Government has announced that the 'China incident' is now nearing its end, and yet somehow the 'China incident' never seems to end. What is it that enables the Chinese to fight on, in spite of their enormous physical difficulties? [The reason is partly in their vast manpower and in the industriousness and ingenuity of the Chinese people. But] The main reason is simply that they are fighting for their liberty, and the will to surrender does not exist in them. To such a people, defeats in the field are of little importance. [There are always more of them, and they are always willing to fight.] The campaign in Burma probably had as one of its main objectives the invasion of China from the west, the idea being that if the Chinese were hemmed in on all sides and finally cut off from the outer world, they would be too deeply disheartened to continue fighting. Without doubt, in these circumstances the Chinese would be defeated according to the military text-books. But so they have been many times before, yet their resistance has never slackened. We cannot doubt that it will be so again, and will continue to be so—so long as the Chinese people put the goal of liberty before their eyes.

This is not the only heroic fight against Fascist aggression which has happened during the last ten years. The Spanish people fought for two-and-a-half years against their own Quislings and against the German and Italian invaders, actually fought against odds which—relatively speaking—were greater than those facing China. Their resistance was the resistance of almost unarmed peasants and working men against hoards of trained soldiers with the resources of the German war machine behind them. [At the beginning of the Spanish Civil War, the Republic had practically no army at all, for it was precisely the regular army, under Fascist officers, which had staged the revolt and this army was soon reinforced by great numbers of Italian mercenaries sent by Mussolini, and by German tanks and bombing 'planes. The ordinary working men of the factories, led by their Trade Union Officials, began to organise themselves into Companies and Battalions to make such weapons as they could manage with the rather backward industrial equipment of Spain, and to learn the art of war literally by practice. Men, who in private life were factory workers, or lawyers or orange-growers, found themselves within a few weeks officers, commanding large bodies of men and in many cases commanded them with great competence. Apart from the inequalities of equipment, the Spanish people had great hardships to face. The food situation was none too good even from the first, and the Nazi airmen, serving with General Franco, carried out, wherever they went, the most atrocious raids on open towns, deliberately aiming their bombs on residential working-class districts, with the idea of terrorising the people into surrender.] Yet [in the face of all these difficulties,] they[5] fought for two-and-a-half years, and though at the end, Franco managed to win a kind of victory, his position is now so insecure that it is thought that about a million people—that is about four per cent of the population—are in concentration Camps.°

Britain has now been fighting for two-and-a-half years, and she started almost unarmed against an enemy who had been preparing for six years for just this occasion. In the middle of 1940 France went out of the war, and for exactly a year Britain had to fight alone, with no very sure prospect of help, either from Russia or from America. During that time, the people of London and other towns had to endure the heaviest air raids that the world has yet known. [For about six months, London barely knew a night without a raid and in all, quite fifty-thousand non-combatants, many of them women and children, were killed.] Yet [during that time] the idea of surrender didn't occur to the British people, and the efforts of the German radio to persuade them that they were beaten and had better stop fighting, simply made them laugh. Soviet Russia again has been fighting for nearly a year against the same enemy, and has had to endure great losses of territory, cruel bombing of open towns, and an appalling series of outrages by occupying troops against helpless peasants. Yet not only is the Russian army further than ever from being beaten, but behind the lines, the Russian people are resisting more and more stubbornly, so that the Germans get no benefit from the territories they have occupied. The thing which animates the Russians is the same that animates the Chinese and that animated the people of London under the bombs: the feeling that they are free and that if only they can hold on to their freedom and drive out this foreign invader who is trying to take it away from them, a fuller and happier life lies ahead.

I have said all this because it is quite likely that India has great and unprecedented hardship ahead of her. India has not seen warfare on her own soil for eighty-five years. She[6] may see it, and it may be the cruel modern kind of war which makes no distinction between combatants and non-combatants. There may be hunger and other hardships ahead as well, but India's fate depends ultimately upon the attitude of Indians themselves. India is not only a great country; it is a very big country—as big for instance as Europe without Russia. It cannot be physically over-run, and the Japanese, even if they have the opportunity, will not attempt to occupy the whole of the country. Their efforts will be to paralyse Indian resistance, by terrorism, by lies and by sowing dissentions° among the Indians themselves. They know that if India has the will to resist, India cannot be conquered, whereas if that will fails, the conquest might be comparatively easy. They will approach you therefore by telling you that they have no designs against your liberty or your territory, and simultaneously they will tell you that they are so strong that it is hopeless to resist. They will also libel those among you who are organising national resistance in the hopes of setting one faction against another. Those are the tactics of the Fascists everywhere. The thing that will defeat them is the same thing that has defeated the Japanese assault on China and the German assault on Russia—the resolution and obstinacy of the common people. The German invasion of Russia has been defeated less by weapons than by an act of will, depending on the knowledge of the Russian people that they are fighting for their liberty. If we choose, we can see to-day that this history is repeated in the Japanese invasion of India.

1. Possibly typed as 'battlesfronts'; it is not 'battle-events.'
2. War] The war
3. The first four words of this excised passage are uncertain
4. There is a cut after 'power'; the first twenty letters and spaces are obliterated, followed by 'with the welfare of their own nation.'
5. they] 'the Spanish people'; *the last two words were crossed out and it looks as if (as the sense requires) a* '*y' was added to 'the.'*
6. *She*] It

1174. To E. Rowan-Davies

16 May 1942[1]   Original; probably typed by Orwell

Information Re Burma Campaign

The questions which I think could usefully be asked of the Burma government are: —
i. What number of Burmese voluntarily evacuated themselves along with British troops etc. leaving India, and what proportion of these were officials.
ii. Attitude of Burmese officials when breakdown appeared imminent. Whether there was a marked difference in loyalty between Burmese and Indian officials. To what extent Burmese officials are known to be carrying on under the Japanese occupation.
iii. Behaviour under fire of the Burma regiments and military police. Whether any actual Burmese (not Kachins etc.) were fighting for the British.
iv. What difference appeared between political attitude of the Burmese proper and the Karens, Shans, Chins, Kachins.[2]
v. What number of the Eurasian community, especially in Rangoon, Moulmein, Mandalay evacuated with the British and how many stayed behind under the Japanese occupation. Whether any who remained behind are known to have changed their allegiance.
vi. Behaviour of the Burmese population under bombing raids. Whether these produced resentment against the Japanese, admiration for Japanese air superiority, or mere panic.

vii. The native Christians, especially Karens.[3] Whether interpenetrated to any extent by nationalist movement.

viii. Number of shortwave sets known to have been in Burmese, Indian and Eurasian possession before the invasion.

ix. Detailed information about the Burmese nationalist and leftwing political parties. The main points are:—

a. Numbers and local and social composition of the Thakin party.[4]

b. Extent to which Buddhist priests predominate.

c. What affiliations exist between the Burmese nationalist parties and the Congress and other Indian parties.

d. Burmese Communists, if any, and what affiliations.

e. Extent of Burmese trade union movement and whether it has affiliations with trade unions in India or Europe.

x. Estimated number of Burmese actually fighting on side of Japanese. Whether people of good standing or mainly dacoits etc. Whether they are reported to have fought courageously.

xi. Extent of Japanese infiltration before the invasion. Whether many Japanese are known to speak local languages,[5] especially Burmese, and to what extent they are likely to be dependent on Burmans for monitoring and interpretation generally.

[Signed] Eric Blair 16.5.42

Eric Blair

1. The date at the end looks as if '5' were written, then overwritten by '6.'
2. In addition to Burmese people, the Burmese nation is composed of many ethnic groups, of which these four are among the most important. There were then more than a million Shans, 1.25 million Karens, half a million Chins, and 200,000 Kachens in a total population of approximately 17 million, many of them hill peoples. By 1984 the population had doubled.
3. Most Burmese are Buddhist, as are the Karens, but some 175,000 Karens are Christian.
4. The Thakin movement developed among radicals in the Young Men's Buddhist Association schools (later the National Schools), who resented British rule. Two university students, Aung San and U Nu, who joined the movement after the student strike in 1936, were instrumental in leading Burma to independence. Aung San was among a number of Burmese politicians murdered in July 1947 at the instigation of a former prime minister, U saw. When Burma became an independent republic, on 4 January 1948, U Nu became prime minister. Aung San's daughter, Suu Kyi, born shortly before his murder, led a long fight against the military government of Burma (Myanma). Her National League for Democracy won a landslide victory in 1990 but was not allowed to govern. She was awarded the Nobel Prize for Peace.
5. Orwell, when serving in the Indian Imperial Police in Burma, passed the language examinations in Burmese and in Shaw-Karen.

1175. Gujarati Newsletter, 12

18 May 1942

The English original was written by Orwell. No script has been traced. PasB gives no timing but notes the use of HMV disk N16472 as a music filler.

1176. To J. A. Lauwerys

18 May 1942   EB/NP

Dear Mr. Lauwerys,
Thank you for your letter. Yes, I should like you to say a good deal about the origins of modern scientific methods, the reason why such things as the compass, gunpowder, Arabic numerals and so forth, happened to be discovered about that time. The talk is at 1.15 p.m. DBST.[1] The other suggestion you make is very interesting. We have touched on the fringe of this in so much as we broadcast short biographies of famous living men, in some cases scientists; but the idea of dramatising the important moments in the history of science is very promising, and I will think it over. Unfortunately at this moment we have not the space to undertake anything not already in our schedule. I am sending a copy of Professor Gordon Childe's talk herewith, and look forward to seeing you on June 9th. As the talk is to be at 1.15, I wonder whether you could arrange to be at 200, Oxford Street, at 12.30 p.m.? It is the building beyond Peter Robinson's store, on the corner of Oxford Street and Great Portland Street.

Yours sincerely,
George Orwell
Talks Producer
Indian Section

1. Double British Summer Time As a means of saving power during the war, clocks were advanced two hours in summer, instead of the customary one hour

1177. BBC Talks Booking Form, 18.5.42

Clemence Dane:[1] 'Women Generally Speaking'; 12-minute talk, title not yet fixed; broadcast 3.6.42, time changed from 1145 GMT to 1345; fee £15.15s.[2] Signed: Z. A. Bokhari.

1. Clemence Dane (Winifred Ashton) (1888–1965, CBE, 1953) actress, dramatist, and novelist, made her debut as an actress in 1913, under the name Diana Cortis. Her play *A Bill of Divorcement* was a considerable success in 1921 and can still hold the stage She was regarded as something of a catch by the Indian Section, thus her larger fee See also *1434, n. 1.*
2. The usual fee for such a talk was £8.8s and the talks booking form when first filled in had 'usual' against the fee. Bokhari wrote to the Empire Programme Executive on 18 May to say that for someone of Clemence Dane's eminence even a fee of £15.15s would not be too high Ronald Boswell, the Talks Booking Manager, was authorised to pay £15.15s On 9 June, Boswell issued a memorandum giving the result of negotiations with Dane's agents, Pearn, Pollinger & Higham Ltd, to the effect that a fee of £15.15s would be paid for talks of 10 to 15 minutes and £10.10s for talks of less than ten minutes (including announcement time) Although this talk requisition was initiated by Orwell, Bokhari, seemingly keen to be associated with this programme, wrote to Miss Dane on 27 May 1942 giving details of when and where the broadcast would take place (from the studio at 200 Oxford Street) and asking that the script be sent to him. On 31 May, she telegraphed Bokhari from Cowden, Kent, as the 'post impossible,' to say her script would be delivered on 2 June and that she would prefer its title to be 'English Women as Story Teller.'

1178. BBC Talks Booking Form, 18.5.42

Narayana Menon: 'Through Eastern Eyes,' 'These Names Will Live'; 13-minute talk on 1. William Walton; 2. Edwin Muir; recorded 21.5.42; 1. broadcast 26.5.42; 2. on 9.6.42; fee £5.5s each talk. Signed: Z. A. Bokhari; Remarks: Miss Orr, Talks Section, Edinburgh, is looking after recording arrangements.

1179. BBC Talks Booking Form, 18.5.42

Dr. B. N. Mukerjee: 'The Music I Like'; Dr. Mukerjee to present a programme by the Philharmonic Ensemble; script about 3 minutes in length; broadcast 6.6.42; fee £4.4s. Signed: Z. A. Bokhari. Remarks: note change of address.

1180. To Nancy Parratt

19 May 1942   Handwritten

Please send him[1] pc. about the time etc.

E.A.B

1. Narayana Menon, who had written from Edinburgh on 17 May outlining progress on his talks on William Walton and Edwin Muir and the arrangements he was making to have them recorded in Edinburgh; see 1161 and 1178. He offered to provide a record of Walton's symphony from his own collection to save sending one from London. He also explained that he hadn't made the talk on Walton too technical and had, as far as possible, avoided musical terminology. Orwell's note is written on Menon's letter to him.

1181. To Richard Titmuss

19 May 1942   PP/EB

Dear Mr. Titmuss,[1]

I wonder whether you would consider doing a talk for us in a series which we shall be broadcasting to India during June and July. This is a series dealing with the future of India, and is called A.D. 2000—the idea being that it is an attempt to forecast what is likely to be happening fifty or sixty years hence. We want the second talk in the series, which I have called provisionally "400 Millions", to be on the Indian population problem. You seem to me to be much the most suitable person to do it, and you could approach it from whatever angle you liked; i.e. you could discuss whether the Indian population is likely to go on growing at its present rate, how it will be affected by industrialisation, at what point you think the saturation level of India will be reached, and so on.[2]

These talks are supposed to take between fifteen and 20 minutes, which means something over 2,000 words. I should want the talk to be delivered on July 3rd, at 1.15 p.m., which means that I should like the script by about June

25th. In the case of your not being able actually to broadcast on that day, it is quite easy to record beforehand.

Could you please let me know as soon as possible whether you would like to undertake this?

Yours truly,
[Initialled] E.A.B
George Orwell
Talks Producer
Indian Section

1. Richard Morris Titmuss (1907–1973) is credited by Edward Shils with being one of the three or four people in Britain who had stimulated interest in sociology even though he had no formal academic training ('On the Eve,' *Twentieth Century*, 167, No. 999, 1960, opening of section III). Among his studies which had drawn attention to social problems at this time were *Poverty and Population* (1938) and, with F. Le Gros Clark, *Our Food Problem* (1939). In 1950 he was appointed Professor of Social Administration, London School of Economics.
2. The population of India in 1991 was 843, 930, 861; of Pakistan, 115,524,000 (U.N. estimate), of Bangladesh, 108,000,000. The population of what comprised India in 1942 thus exceeded 1,000 million fifty years later

1182. War-time Diary

<u>19.5.42</u>: *Attlee reminds me of nothing so much as a recently dead fish, before it has had time to stiffen.*

1183. To Mulk Raj Anand

20 May 1942   PP/EB/NP

Dear Mulk,
I have now arranged for your discussion to be recorded on Monday, 25th May, from 12 to 12.45—with rehearsal time from 11.30. I am trying to arrange for a photographer to be there, but as it is Bank Holiday, it may be difficult. We weren't able to contact Bishop on the phone, as he is "travelling" today, but someone in his office said he would not be working on Monday, so I am assuming this time will suit him. I enclose a copy of the script, and I am sending one to Mr. Bishop, together with a note to tell him about the time and place on Monday.

Yours
[Initialled] E.A.B

1184. To Sir John Russell[1]

20 May 1942   PP/EB/NP

Dear Sir,

I am approaching you in hopes that you may care to do a talk in the series which we are broadcasting shortly to India. This series deals with the future of India, and is called A.D. 2000— to indicate that we are trying to predict what is likely to happen about 50 years hence. We particularly want to start off with a talk on the future of Indian Agriculture and we feel that you would be just the person to undertake it, if you care to do so. The talk would be on June 26th at 1.15 p.m. and should take from 15 to 20 minutes, which means something over 2,000 words. I should want the script not later than June 20th. Could you be kind enough to let me know as early as possible whether you would be willing to do this?

If it should be inconvenient for you to broadcast on that date, it would be quite simple to record the talk beforehand.

Yours truly,
Eric Blair
Talks Producer
Indian Section

1. Sir (Edward) John Russell (1872–1970; Kt., 1922) was Director of Rothamsted Experimental Station, 1912–43, and of the Imperial Bureau of Soil Science, 1928–43; Adviser to the Soviet Relations Division, Ministry of Information; Chairman, Agriculture Sub-Committee, UNRRA, 1941–45. One of his many books was *English Farming* (1942).

1185. BBC Talks Booking Form, 20.5.42

Sir Azizul° Huque: 13-minute talk 'on his stay in Egypt on the way to this country'; broadcast 21.5.42; fee £4.4s. Signed: Z. A. Bokhari.

A second form, a BBC/P/81, was initiated and signed by the Indian News Sub-editor, A. Ellings, on 22 May for this same talk but the date of the broadcast was given as 20 May and the fee was £10.10s. This form has the following note: 'The High Commissioner gave a good deal of time to rehearsal for this talk when he was very busy.' The explanation is given in a letter from Miss E. W. D. Boughen of Programme Contracts to the High Commissioner on 27 May. The broadcast on 20 May was in Hindustani and that on the 21st in English.

1186. Marathi Newsletter, 12

21 May 1942

A talks booking form dated 20 May, initiated and signed by Z. A. Bokhari, states that this newsletter was written by E. Blair and translated and read by D. M. Kanekar, for which Kanekar was paid £5.5s. Under 'Remarks' it is explained that the final five minutes of the fifteen allowed for the broadcast 'will be filled in by Miss Chitale (Staff).' According to the PasB (which does not mention Orwell's part in preparing the programme), the broadcast lasted 13′ 25″ and presumably that included Chitale's contribution. No script has been traced. PasB states that Odeon disc SA 3086 was used as a music filler.

1187. War-time Diary

<u>21.5.42:</u>   *Molotov is said to be in London. I don't believe this.*
<u>22.5.42:</u>   *It is said that Molotov is not only in London but that the new Anglo-Russian treaty is already signed.*[1] *This however comes from Warburg,*[2] *who is alternately over-optimistic and over-pessimistic—at any rate, always believes in the imminence of enormous and dramatic changes. If true it would be a godsend for the filling-up of my newsletters. It is getting harder and harder to find anything to put into these, with nothing happening except on the Russian front, and the news from there, whether from Russian or German sources, growing more and more phony. I wish I could spare a week to go through the Russian and German broadcasts of the past year and tot up their various claims. I should say the Germans would have killed 10 million men and the Russians would have advanced to somewhere well out in the Atlantic Ocean.*

1. A twenty-year treaty of collaboration between Russia and Britain was signed in London on 26 May 1942.
2. As in manuscript; 'W.' in typescript.

1188. Weekly News Review, 23

23 May 1942

There are several puzzling aspects about this News Review. The PasB states it is by Z. A. Bokhari; that by itself would, as usual, mean no more than that it was read by him, but here his name is followed by 'Read by Dick Wessel.' This is the only 'Wessel' in Indian Section documents. Possibly he was W. P. Wessel, then working on Spanish programmes for the Latin American Service.

There is evidence that the typescript is a fair copy of a draft, and there are three slight manuscript amendments. One is simply a name in block letters, doubtless to aid the reader; of the other two, one looks to be in Orwell's hand and the other is possibly his; the writing is not Bokhari's. The script bears censors' stamps for Policy and Security, both signed by Bokhari. Unusually, the censorship is dated a day before the broadcast. It has written on it 'As broadcast Godfrey Kenton,' an actor who had joined the BBC in October 1941; see *892, n. 1.* It is strange that he should be involved, and the two amendments might conceivably be in his hand.

The distribution note is also unusual. A copy was sent to Empire Presentation (as usual), and one to 'Miss Parratt, 416, 55PP' (Orwell's office). Perhaps he was being sent a script of a broadcast that he had, exceptionally, not written, so that he would know what had been done. Possibly his involvement in writing Marathi Newsletter, 12, led to Bokhari's filling in for him on this occasion. To complicate matters further, the script shows a timing of 11' 20" but the PasB has 13½ minutes. Despite these uncertainties, the script is most likely Orwell's, but ascription to him should be treated with caution. In paragraph four, 'in hopes' is Orwellian.

The principal events this week have happened on the Russian front. We recorded last week that fighting had broken out again in the Crimean Peninsula. Since then, the Germans have over-run most of the Kerch Peninsula, which is separated from the Caucasus only by a very narrow neck of the Sea of Azov. It is known, however, that fighting is still going on on the westward side of the Strait, and the German claims to have destroyed the Russian army in that sector and to have taken an enormous number of prisoners are just as untrue as their similar reports have been in the past. Meanwhile, further north the Russians have launched an offensive of their own upon a much larger scale. This is directed against the great industrial city of Kharkov, which the Germans took last Autumn. As I speak,[1] the decision is still uncertain. The Russians have advanced on a wide front, destroying great numbers of German tanks, and the communications by which the German forces in Kharkov are supplied are in great danger. The Germans, however, have launched a counter-attack in the south, which may prevent Kharkov from being encircled.

It[2] would be unwise to expect too much from the Russian offensive, which may have been undertaken merely in order to anticipate the Germans and upset their time table. Meanwhile, the Russians have begun another attack in the far north, against the German armies in Finland, and have already made a considerable advance.

The outlines of the spring campaign on the Eastern front are still not clear. Some observers think that the Germans, instead of making another large scale frontal attack against the Russian armies, will strike their main blow against Turkey. If Turkey were over-run they could then make for the oil wells of Iraq and Iran, and at the same time attack Baku by the easier route from the south. It is at any rate certain that for months past the Germans have been doing all in their power to sow distrust between Turkey and Britain, and more especially between Turkey and Soviet Russia, which may be intended to prevent the Turkish Government from taking concerted defence measures beforehand in consultation with the Allies. However, there is no sign that the Turks have been deceived by the German manoeuvres. Turkey is not very well supplied with modern weapons, but imports from Britain and the U.S.A. have to some extent made this good during recent months. The people are resolute and brave fighters, and it is certain that should the Germans make their offensive in this direction they will have to fight hard every inch of the way.

Simultaneously with their attempts to sow distrust between Turkey and Russia, the Germans appear to be making another effort to egg on the Japanese to attack the Russians in Manchuria. They are broadcasting threatening statements about Russia, alleged to have been made by leading

Japanese statesmen. These may or may not be authentic. We have frequently pointed out in these newsletters that the likelihood exists of the Japanese attacking Russia sooner or later, and if they do so, we may be sure that they will do it with the maximum of treachery at a moment when they believe the Russians to be in serious difficulties. The Germans will try to provoke the clash between Russia and Japan as early as possible in hopes that this may prevent further men and materials being brought from Siberia to the Western Front.

In Burma, the greater part of the British forces have reached the Indian frontier in safety. On the eastern sector of this front the Japanese attacks against Yunnan continue. The Japanese are still in possession of Tengueh, but to the south of this the Chinese have recaptured Kanlanchai.[3] It is possible that the Japanese now intend an all out attack against China, one column moving eastward from Burma, another northwards from Siam and another westwards, probably from Fuchow, where they have recently made a fresh landing. China's position at this moment is certainly difficult, and she needs all the help that can possibly be given to her, especially in aeroplanes. It is therefore good news that a large unit of the Royal Air Force has just reached central China. We need not imagine, however, that Chinese resistance is at all likely to be crushed. Marshal Chiang Kai Shek has repeatedly declared that he will go on fighting just as long as is necessary to drive out the invader, and that if need be, he would be ready to withdraw for years into Central Asia and re-organise his armies there. The Japanese are aware that so long as Chinese resistance continues, their gains elsewhere are very precarious. They may have decided that this is the moment to finish with China once and for all, or they may have the intention of capturing all the airfields which are within striking range of Japan itself. Whether they can carry out a full-scale attack against China while also proceeding with their campaigns against Australia and India, and possibly a little while hence with Russia, at the same time, is uncertain.

Bombs have already been dropped on Assam, and the Japanese forces on the eastern coast of the Bay of Bengal are not very far from Chittagong, but this is not the route that they are likely to take in their main attack upon India. The Battle in the Coral Sea, in which the Japanese lost heavily, has no doubt set back their plans for attacking Australia, but those plans still exist, and there are signs of fresh activity in the Japanese controlled islands surrounding New Guinea.[4] Australia is now far more strongly defended than was the case three months ago, and each day that the Japanese attack is delayed gives more time for American reinforcements to arrive.

The disarmament of the French warships lying at Martinique, off the coast of the United States, is proceeding. Before long the United States government will probably have to take similar action against the island of Guadeloupe, also under Vichy control, which has almost certainly been used as a port of call by Axis submarines, and whose wireless station is *used*[5] for pro-Axis propaganda in South America. The accession to power of Laval, who has hardly pretended to be more than a puppet of the Germans, has opened the eyes of the Americans to the danger presented by Vichy France, and we may expect them to take a firmer attitude from now on. Laval's dealings with the Germans have also certainly caused trouble between Germany and the other Axis partner, Italy. The Italians came into the war in the summer of 1940, when they imagined that the fighting was almost over and that they would be able to grab large quantities of loot without having to shed any Italian blood.

Instead of this, they have lost most of their empire and have not received any of the bribes they were promised. In his efforts to get hold of the French fleet, Hitler has evidently made certain concessions to Laval, one of which is the dropping of Italian claims to the island of Corsica and other portions of French territory. It is clear that this causes great resentment among the Italian Fascists, but they are at present quite powerless against their German masters.

The Royal Air Force continue their heavy raids on Germany. On Wednesday they made one of the biggest raids of the war on Mannheim, the centre of the German chemical industry. Two days earlier, they had performed a brilliant feat in torpedoing the German cruiser the Prinz Eugen, which had been in a Norwegian port after being damaged by a British submarine and was making its way back to Germany for repairs. The Prinz Eugen was not sunk, but it is likely to be out of action for the rest of the summer.

Another large draft of American troops, complete with tanks and all other weapons of war, have reached British soil. They crossed the Atlantic without being attacked by the Germans in any way. Public opinion in Britain is more and more anxious for the opening of a second front in Europe, so as to take the pressure off our Russian allies and to make the Germans fight simultaneously on two fronts. We prefer not to express an opinion as to whether this will be done in the near future. In all probability it is mainly a question of shipping, because not only the transporting but still more the supplying of an overseas force uses up an enormous number of ships. The Government has made no definite pronouncement upon the subject, quite naturally, for if they intend to launch an offensive, they cannot be expected to reveal their plans beforehand. In his recent speech, however, Mr. Churchill made the point that after two and a half years of war, so far from being war-weary, the British people are actually demanding offensive action and chiding the Government for being too slow. This, as Mr. Churchill pointed out, is certainly a remarkable advance, when we remember that two years ago Britain stood alone, and was only doubtfully able to defend herself, let alone to contemplate launching attacks on a foreign shore.

1. *I speak*] *handwritten substitution (possibly in Orwell's hand) for* so often
2 *It*] *preceded by a sentence x-ed through·* 'The outlines of the spring campaign on the Eastern front are still not clear'—*the sentence that starts the next paragraph. This indicates that the typist has skipped.to the next paragraph, possibly when typing a manuscript, but, from the clean character of this typescript, it was probably typed from an original typescript.*
3. Kanlanchai is written in capital letters above the typed word, which had been clarified by hand. The capitals do not look like Orwell's, they may have been written by the reader to help him pronounce the name.

4. See *1150, n. 1*.
5. *'used'* corrects a typing error ('sued'); the hand looks very like Orwell's.

1189. To the Editor, *The Times Literary Supplement*
23 May 1942

On 2 May 1942, *The Times Literary Supplement* published (anonymously, as was then the custom) a review of Mulk Raj Anand's *The Sword and the Sickle*. Orwell considered this misleading and wrote to the Editor. The reviewer responded; his comments follow Orwell's letter below.

Orwell may have had a special interest in this book. He reviewed it in *Horizon* in July 1942 (see *1257*), and Anand told W. J. West that Orwell had given the book its title, 'from Blake's poem, during a walk across Primrose Hill in the blackout' (West: *Broadcasts*, 187). 'The poem' is a single verse:

> The sword sung on the barren heath,
> The sickle in the fruitful field:
> The sword he sung a song of death,
> But could not make the sickle yield.

Even the location for giving this title is not without its relation to Blake. The second part of *Jerusalem*, 'To the Jews,' has this for its first stanza:

> The fields from Islington to Marybone,°
> To Primrose Hill and Saint John's Wood,
> Were builded over with pillars of gold,
> And there Jerusalem's pillars stood.

THE SWORD AND THE SICKLE

Sir,—I have just read your reviewer's notice of Mulk Raj Anand's novel "The Sword and the Sickle," and I feel I must protest against what seem to me some very misleading remarks in it. Mr. Anand, says your reviewer, "becomes more and more prejudiced in his outlook. The telescope which he turns on the world has three specks: the anti-bourgeois speck, the anti-rich speck, and the anti-White (which in substance means the anti-British) speck." Later on he adds, "Mr. Anand's references to Europeans betray a lack of insight. What is really disagreeable, however, is the spirit of the novel; it tends to create bad blood between Indians and British, which is a bad thing at any time and a dangerous one at this hour."

The impression given is that this is a propaganda novel concerned chiefly with denouncing the British rule in India, and even with stirring up hatred against the British people. Actually, one thing that is striking about the book is that it hardly contains any European characters at all. Even the few who do flit across its pages are not treated with any very noticeable unfriendliness. It is quite true that in a political sense Mr. Anand is anti-British. But before suggesting that this "limits his horizon" and makes him "more and more prejudiced," one might stop to reflect what sort of treatment the same theme would get from an English writer of similar calibre. Are the portraits of

Anglo-Indians in English novels invariably friendly? (Incidentally, Mr. Anand's book contains a description of one well-known Indian Nationalist which is much more offensive than anything he says about the Europeans). And if Mr. Anand makes it plain that he is anti-imperialist and thinks India ought to be independent, is he not saying something which almost any English intellectual would echo as a matter of course? In novels written by Englishmen a "left" viewpoint is so much taken for granted as to be hardly noticed; yet when your reviewer finds exactly the same thing coming from an Indian, he is annoyed, and does not bother to conceal it. I quite agree that it is undesirable to create bad blood between Indians and British; and one way of doing that is to use words like "Babuism."

Yours truly,
George Orwell.

٭٭ Our Reviewer[1] writes—

Mr. Orwell thinks it "misleading" to call Mr. Anand anti-British and then, to prove his point, he tells us that "in a political sense Mr. Anand is anti-British." Strange logic! No one quarrels with Mr. Anand for being a good Indian, but one does object to his denigration of Europeans by innuendo and oblique reference (one of his characters says that most upper class women in Europe are "semi-prostitutes"). This shows neither art nor humanity. Certainly Mr. Anand's "portrait" of Mr. Gandhi is "offensive," which merely proves that he is also "anti-bourgeois"—for Gandhi despite many of his faults and foibles, is a great man. Mr. Anand simply lampoons him.

There are many Indians who have handled the English tongue with ease and precision. Mr. Anand, on occasion, can be quite good; but there are entire passages in the present novel which are involved, redundant, written in a kind of lofty jargon. All this is "Babuism," a word which might be applied to certain English authors too. The present reviewer is old-fashioned enough to demand breadth of vision and a tolerable texture from a novelist so alert and intelligent as Mr. Anand. It would have been far easier to have damned him with faint praise. But timid patronage or empty laudation is what modern Indian writers dislike most. They wish to be judged like any other artist, English, French, or American.

1. On 12 January 1990, the Deputy Editor of the *TLS*, Alan Hollinghurst, identified the reviewer from the *TLS*'s records as Ranja G. Sahani. The British Library catalogue has no entries under Sahani, and the name looks suspiciously like, and probably was, that of Ranjee G. Shahani. Among Shahani's books listed are *Shakespeare Through Eastern Eyes* (1932), *Indian Pilgrimage* (1939), and *The Amazing English* (1948) He contributed 'The Two Hotels' and 'Paul Valery and India' to *Tribune*, 10 December 1943 and 7 April 1944 respectively when Orwell was Literary Editor. Shahani was born in Hyderabad in 1904 and completed his education at King's College London. He died in 1968. In a letter to Ian Angus, 14 September 1996, Mulk Raj Anand gave his name as Ranjee Shahne.

1190. Gujarati Newsletter, 13

25 May 1942

The English original was written by Orwell. No script has been traced. No timing is given.

1191. BBC Talks Booking Form, 26.5.42

Professor J. B. S. Haldane: 9-minute talk on A.R.P.; 'originally written for translation into Hindustani for Indian Editor. Prof. Haldane read his English version'; recorded 22.5.42; broadcast date not yet arranged; fee £4.4s. Signed: Z. A. Bokhari.

1192. BBC Talks Booking Form, 26.5.42

R. R. Desai: Gujarati Newsletters, 14–18; broadcast 1, 8, 15, 22, and 29.6.42; fee £5.5s + £2.8.2 + 17s 0d each talk. Signed: Z. A. Bokhari.[1]

1. On 26 May 1942, Bokhari wrote to Desai proposing that the BBC obtain Gujarati newspapers for him from India, which would 'be of some help to you in translating,' and asked for suggestions. On 16 June, Miss Chitale sent Desai a reminder, because Bokhari was 'waiting to send the order by cable.' Bokhari had also told Desai that from 1 June 1942 broadcasts would be made from 200 Oxford Street, but a day or two later he sent a telegram asking him to come as usual to 55 Portland Place on 1 June. The talks booking form gives the studio as 200 Oxford Street, as does that of 22 June 1942. The move to 200 Oxford Street was made possibly a day or two after 1 June. It was from this address that Orwell worked for the rest of his time at the BBC. His room number was 310.

1193. War-time Diary

27.5.42.   *Cutting from the D. Express of 26.5.42:*

CAIRO, Monday.—General Auchinleck, in a drive against red tape hindering the war effort in the Middle East,[1] has sent this letter "to all officers and headquarters of this command":—

"An extract from a letter written by Wellington from Spain about 1810 to the Secretary for War, Lord Bradford:

" 'My lord, if I attempted to answer the mass of futile correspondence that surrounds me, I should be debarred from all serious business of campaigning.

" 'So long as I retain an independent position I shall see to it that no officer under my command is debarred, by attending to the futile drivelling of mere quill driving in your lordship's office, from attending to his first duty—which is, as always, to train the private men under his command.' "

General Auchinleck adds: "I know that this does not apply to you; but please see to it that it can never be applied to you or to anyone working under you."—A.P.[2]

This is printed in the papers and even given out over the air, but, after all, the operative fact is that no one does or can talk like that to the War Office nowadays.

More rumours that Molotov is in London. Also cryptic paras in the papers suggesting that this may be so (no mention of names, of course).

1. in a drive . . . Middle East] *omitted from typed version*
2. General . . . A.P.] *omitted from typed version*

1194. News Review, 24

30 May 1942

The script for this broadcast has not been traced. PasB records it as News Review by Z. A. Bokhari and gives its timing as 13½ minutes.

1195. War-time Diary

<u>30.5.42:</u> *Almost every day in the neighbourhood of Upper Regent Street one can see a tiny, elderly, very yellow Japanese, with a face like a suffering monkey's, walking slowly along with an enormous policeman walking beside him. On some days they are holding a solemn conversation. I suppose he is one of the Embassy staff. But whether the policeman is there to prevent him from[1] committing acts of sabotage, or to protect him from the infuriated mob, there is no knowing.*

The Molotov rumour seems to have faded out. Warburg,[2] who accepted the Molotov story without question, has now forgotten it and is full of the inner story of why Garvin[3] was sacked from the "Observer". It was because he refused to attack Churchill. The Astors are determined to get rid of Churchill because he is pro-Russian and the transformation of the "Observer" is part of this manoeuvre. The "Observer" is to lead the attack on Churchill and at the same time canalise the gifted young journalists who are liable to give the war a revolutionary meaning, making them use their energies[4] on futilities until they can be dispensed with. All inherently probable. On the other hand I don't believe that David Astor,[5] who acts as the decoy elephant, is consciously taking part in any such thing.* It is

* *Mentioned this to Tom Harrisson, who has better opportunities of judging than I have He considers it has a base in reality He says the Astors, especially Lady A , are exceedingly intelligent in their way and realise that all they consider worth having will be lost if we do not make a compromise peace They are, of course, anti-Russian, and therefore necessarily anti-Churchill At one time they were actually scheming to make Trenchard Prime Minister The man who would be ideal for their purpose would be Lloyd George, "if he could walk" I agree here, but was somewhat surprised to find Harrisson saying it—would have rather expected him to be pro-Lloyd George He also said he thought it quite possible that Beaverbrook is financing the Communist Party* [Orwell's footnote added to typed version] *amusing to see not only the Beaverbrook press, which is now plus royaliste que le roi so far as Russia is concerned, but the T.U.[6] Weekly "Labour's Northern Voice", suddenly discovering Garvin as a well-known anti-Fascist who has been sacked for his radical opinions. One thing that strikes me about nearly everyone nowadays is the shortness of their memories. Desmond Hawkins[7] told me a little while back that he recently bought some fried fish wrapped up in a sheet of newspaper dating from 1940. On one side was an article proving that the Red Army was no good, and on the other a write-up of that gallant sailor and well-known Anglophile, Admiral Darlan.[8]*

[Pasted into Diary]

THAT MONSTROUS MAN

Denials are no use. War breeds its own
Dark atmosphere. We suffer inconveniences.
We suffer more, we suffer pain at heart,
We suffer with our hands, our feet, our souls.
It is as if you took a charming girl,
This girl, her ears as delicate as shells,
Whose hair blows fluffy in the wind. She is
Your country or yourself, what you alone
Have worshipped.
          Now against the shadowed heart
You hold her, as she once was, beautiful,
But that she might not be by foreign hands
Ravaged and raped she bears more native scars,
With your own rough hands soiled. O Emperor
Of foul confusions, Man, what have you done?
Lest she should walk gay in a foreign sun
You have forgotten she was star of stars,
Have pulled her down to meet the grand demand
Of your own monstrous and indelicate war.
Denials are no use. Now once again
To save her beauty you have caused it pain,
And to yourself have proved that monstrous man.
              Nicholas Moore.[9]

Cf. Alexander Comfort's letter in the last "Horizon"[10]

1. *him from*] him
2. As in manuscript; 'W.' in typescript.
3. J. L. Garvin, right-wing journalist, was the editor of *The Observer*, 1908 to 28 February 1942. At the beginning of the war, he disagreed with Viscount Astor, the proprietor of the paper, who questioned the advisability of Churchill's being Prime Minister and Minister of Defence at the same time. See also *296, n. 8* and *378, n. 1.*
4. *energies*] energy
5. David Astor served in the Royal Marines, 1940–45 (Croix de Guerre, 1944). Viscount Astor had made him, the second son, a minority shareholder in *The Observer*. At this time, David Astor had a voice in the paper's affairs and was later foreign editor, editor, and Director. See *891, n 1*
6. Trades Union.
7. Desmond Hawkins did much free-lance work with the Indian Section of the BBC during the war; see *704* and *739.*
8. Admiral François Darlan, Commander-in-Chief of the French Navy, and Vice-Premier and

Foreign Minister in the Vichy Government from February 1941 to April 1942. When the Allies invaded Morocco and Tunisia (then French territories) in November 1942, a deal, much criticised in Britain and America, was negotiated with him, in order to reduce casualties in completing the occupation of both countries, whereby he became high commissioner and commander-in-chief of naval forces. He was assassinated on 24 December 1942, by Bonnier de la Chapelle. His twenty-year-old assassin was tried by court-martial and executed two days later. As Churchill wrote, this 'relieved the Allies of their embarrassment in working with him' (*The Second World War*, IV, 577–78; U.S.: *The Hinge of Fate*, 644). Churchill accords Darlan a critical but generous obituary: 'Few men have paid more heavily for errors of judgment and failure of character than Admiral Darlan. . . . His life's work had been to recreate the French Navy, and he had raised it to a position it had never held since the days of the French kings. . . . Let him rest in peace, and let us all be thankful we have never had to face the trials under which he broke' (IV, 579–80; U.S.: 645–47).

9. Nicholas Moore (1918–1986) was editor of *Spleen*, 1938–40 (the title also of a book of his verse, 1973), and assistant to Tambimuttu on *Poetry (London)* in the 1940s. He produced nine volumes of poetry before 1949; thereafter, *Spleen* and three posthumously published collections. For his letter to *Partisan Review* about Orwell's 'London Letter' of 15 April 1941 (787), see 854. Orwell gave Moore's poem the reference: *Tribune*, 28 May 1942.

10. For Alexander Comfort, see 913, n. 5 and 1270. *Horizon* printed (May 1942, 358–62) his long letter on the alleged absence of war poetry and the reasons for it. He said three campaigns had been waged against poets. The Rostrevor Hamilton campaign in *The Listener* could be dismissed, because it was, in his opinion, instigated by the Conservative Party. Robert Lynd's articles in *John o' London's Weekly* could also be dismissed, Lynd had not read enough poetry written since 1939 to be able to talk about it. However, Stephen Spender's essay, 'Poetry in 1941' (*Horizon*, February 1942), deserved to be taken seriously. Comfort argued that 'the writers of the last few years see this war as a degenerative, not a conflict process'—something Spender ignored, he wrote. The 'hope of a valid and healthy poetic interpretation of the events of the war is remote at present, though potentially enormous.' His three concluding points were: 1. as the poet, 'like the rest of the nation, is a participant in a common ego-isolation, he cannot write classical interpretative poetry about the war' within Spender's prescription; 2. there was scope for such an interpretation in prose; and 3 there was scope 'for a romantic or fantastic interpretation of the state of mind of humanity rather than of events—an attitude which is gradually appearing in Mr. Spender's own poetry, though he rejects it on principle.' In his contribution to 'Pacifism and War: A Controversy' (see 1270), Orwell quotes several lines from Comfort's letter to *Horizon*.

1196. Gujarati Newsletter, 14

1 June 1942

The English original was written by Orwell. No script has been traced. PasB timing is 11 minutes.

1197. BBC Talks Booking Form, 2.6.42

Princess Indira of Kapurthala: 'The Debate Continues'; broadcast 8, 15, 22, 29.6.42 (from 200 Oxford Street); fee £8.8s each talk. Signed: Z. A. Bokhari.

1198. BBC Talks Booking Form, 3.6.42

From Venu Chitale: Shridhar Telkar: 'The Man in the Street,' 'Popular Novels and the Public Taste'; broadcast 5.6.42; fee £8.8s. Signed: Z. A. Bokhari.

This engagement of one of 'Orwell's' speakers roused a storm and helps explain Bokhari's animosity towards Venu Chitale. It also epitomises his style of management: he sent a copy of his letter to her to Rushbrook Williams, Eastern Service Director. It has the same date as the talks booking form above, and was marked 'URGENT.' It was typed by Mary Blackburn.

BOOKING ARRANGEMENTS FOR SPEAKERS

Tom Harrisson dictated his script on Monday. Arrangements were made to record him yesterday (Tuesday). At the last moment I cancelled the recording for reasons which I have explained to you, but
  (a) no letter exists in the office inviting him to write the talk and no Contract has been issued to him.
Several weeks ago you told me that Mr. Telkar had been asked to give a talk on "Popular Novels and the Public Taste". When I told you that Telkar was not competent to handle such a subject, you said that you could not get out of it because you had commissioned Telkar to write that talk. I regret to note that
  (a) no letter has been issued to him from your office on the subject.
  (b) The Contract was only applied for on the 3rd June, when Telkar is supposed to broadcast on the 5th.
  (c) Till to-day, 3rd June, 3.30 p.m., Telkar's script has not been received.
This is extremely irregular and I would like to know why we should not cancel Telkar's talk. Perhaps you arranged the whole thing with Telkar verbally—a highly irregular practice. Didn't you tell him the date by which his manuscript should arrive? I don't know whether he will send his manuscript tomorrow, but even that, from my point of view, will be too late. We have got to censor the script, edit it, get in touch with the author, obtain his approval and above all, his signed Contract has got to be in the hands of the B.B.C. before he goes on the air. We cannot be too careful about such things. Broadcasters can raise all sorts of difficulties; for instance if Mr. Telkar demands 50 guineas for his talk, we will have to fight his claim in a Court of Law and perhaps lose it. If Mr. Telkar doesn't allow changes in his script, we have no leg to stand on. He hasn't signed his Contract with us. I will be grateful to you for your views on these irregularities which are pregnant with no end of difficulties, if they once start.

Correspondence in the BBC Archives shows that Harrisson's talk was cancelled at the last moment and but two hours after he had broadcast for the Forces programme, because it was 'quite unsuitable for broadcasting.' Harrisson wrote a long letter on 3 June seeking an explanation and pointing out that much of what he had proposed to say had been in his Forces programme talk. He wondered if the BBC's editing of the script had unbalanced his argument, but, he went on, 'knowing Mr Blair, I think that would be highly improbable.' A long correspondence ensued. It is plain that Bokhari, not Orwell, had edited Harrisson's script; on 5 June he wrote, 'In the short time available, it was not possible for me to bring out in 1800 words what you had conveyed in nearly nineteen foolscap pages,' produced when Harrisson dictated his script. The affair was concluded when Harrisson proposed that the matter be forgotten—but he did point out that he had given ninety-six broadcasts between 1933 and 1942—and Bokhari invited Harrisson to lunch with him and Lionel Fielden at their flat. During the course of this dispute, Harrisson wrote Orwell a note on 8 June, marked 'Personal,' asking to meet him for half an hour to discuss the affair 'off the record.' No reply from Orwell has been found, nor any record of whether Harrisson accepted the invitation to lunch.

1199. To the Honourable Mrs. Egerton

4 June 1942   EB/NP

Dear Madam,

Thank you for your letter of May 30th. Professor Egerton's talk will be broadcast on Tuesday, June 16th, at 1.15 p.m. by the clock. It goes out in the Eastern Service, on the short wave—16, 19, 25 and 31 metre bands. But as it is not intended to be heard in this country, reception is very poor, and often it is not possible to pick up anything at all. Professor Egerton's secretary rang me up a little while ago, asking if it would be possible for her to hear the broadcast, and I suggested that she might like to come to my office and listen on a direct line as it goes out, and I wonder whether you would care to do the same. I shall in any case arrange for a listening room for Professor Egerton's secretary, and I believe she will be bringing one or two other people, so if you would like to come, perhaps you will ring me up, and then I can tell you where to come, and at what time.

> Yours faithfully,
> Eric Blair
> Talks Producer
> Indian Section

1200. To Tamara Talbot Rice

4 June 1942   PP/EB

Dear Mrs. Talbot Rice,

We have now been able to arrange a date for the broadcast of Mr. K. K. Ardaschir's talk "The Sick Man Revives", which you censored for us some time ago. It will go out in the Eastern Service on Thursday, 9th July, at 1115 GMT, on the 16, 19, 25 and 31 metre bands.

If you should receive any comments from Ankara we should be most interested to hear about them.

Yours sincerely,
Eric Blair
Talks Producer
Indian Section

1201. Postcard to Richard Titmuss

4 June 1942

Titmuss replied to Orwell's letter of 19 May 1942 (see *1181*) in a letter dated 2 June 1942. Along the top of this was typed [in black] P. C., [in red] Saying script just right; will he let us know when he'd like to record before 3rd July; in pencil in Orwell's hand: Answered 4.6.42.

1202. BBC Talks Booking Form, 4.6.42

Dr. C. D. Darlington: 'Science and Politics,' 6, 'The Future of Science'; 20-minute talk; broadcast 7.7.42; fee £10.10s. Signed: Z. A. Bokhari.

1203. BBC Talks Booking Form, 4.6.42

J. A. Lauwerys: 'Science and Politics,' 2, 'The Beginnings of Modern Science'; broadcast 9.6.42; fee £10.10s + £1.5.9 fare, since 'Lauwerys will be travelling down from Burton Joyce specially to broadcast.' Signed: Z. A. Bokhari.

1204. BBC Talks Booking Form, 4.6.42

Reginald Reynolds: two talks on prison literature; broadcast 12 and 19.6.42; fee £8.8s for each talk. Signed: Z. A. Bokhari.

1205. BBC Talks Booking Form, 4.6.42

Sir John Russell: 'A.D. 2000'; first talk of a series of six on the Future of Indian Agriculture; broadcast 26.6.42; fee £10.10s. Signed: Z. A. Bokhari.

1206. BBC Talks Booking Form, 4.6.42

Shridhar Telkar: 'These Names Will Live,' John Gordon;[1] broadcast 16.6.42; fee £8.8s. Signed: Z. A. Bokhari.

1. John Gordon (1890–1974) was a journalist. He joined the *Daily Express* in 1924; was editor of the *Sunday Express* from 1928; Director of Beaverbrook Newspapers Ltd., from 1931; and President, Institute of Journalists, 1948–49.

1207. BBC Talks Booking Form, 4.6.42

Richard Titmuss: 'A.D. 2000,' 2, 'The Indian Population Problem'; broadcast 3.7.42; fee £10.10s. Signed: Z. A. Bokhari.

1208. BBC Talks Booking Form, 4.6.42

Diana Wong: 'Today and Yesterday,' 'My Escape from France'; broadcast 25.6.42; fee £8.8s. Signed: Z. A. Bokhari.

1209. War-time Diary

4.6.42: *Very hot weather. Struck by the normality of everything—lack of hurry, fewness of uniforms, general unwarlike appearance of the crowds who drift slowly through the streets, pushing prams or loitering in the squares to look at the hawthorn bushes. It is already noticeable that there are much fewer cars, however. Here and there a car with a fuel converter at the back, having slightly the appearance of an old-fashioned milkcart. Evidently there is not so much bootleg petrol about after all.*

6.6.42: *The Molotov rumour still persists. He was here to negotiate the treaty, and has gone back, so it is said. No hint of*[1] *this in any newspaper, however.*

There is said to be much disagreement on the staff of the "New Statesman"[2] *over the question of the Second Front. Having squealed for a year that we must open a second front immediately, Kingsley Martin*[3] *now has cold feet. He says they now say*[4] *that the army cannot be trusted, the soldiers will shoot their officers in the back etc.—this after endeavouring throughout the war to make the soldiers mistrust their officers. Meanwhile I think now that a second front is definitely projected, at any rate if enough shipping can be scraped together.*

1. *of*] about
2. The opening of a second front was almost daily expected. When Dwight D. Eisenhower's arrival in England was reported in the *Daily Express* on 26 June 1942, his photograph was headlined: 'U.S. Second Front general is here.' Although, in response to Stalin's demand that

a Second Front be opened, consideration was given to a cross-Channel landing in August or September 1942, the first new front (not regarded by most people as a Second Front) was not opened until 8 November 1942, and then in North Africa.

3. Kingsley Martin (see *496, n. 4*), left-wing journalist and editor of *The New Statesman* (1931–60), caused the Indian Section considerable trouble, from what he said and from his squabbling about fees. He was regarded as unreliable by the BBC, for not sticking to censored scripts, and was, in effect, barred by the Home Office and Ministry of Information because of his contribution to 'Answering You,' broadcast to North America in December 1941. *West. Broadcasts* prints R. A. Rendall's defence of the BBC's position in 1941 and correspondence in 1943 between C. Lawson-Reece, Eastern Service Organiser; J. B. Clark, Controller, Overseas Service; and L. F. Rushbrook Williams, Eastern Service Director (App. D, 294–99).

4. *they now say*] *Orwell's handwritten insertion on typescript*

1210. Weekly News Review, 25

For 6 June 1942   Not transmitted

This text is reproduced from a typescript bearing both censorship stamps, signed by Z. A. Bokhari, much cut, slightly added to and modified, and not marked as broadcast. The first cut is of no moment; the modification gives more point to what was first written; and the addition introduces an item of late news; both in Orwell's handwriting. The final lengthy cut may have attracted the censor's eye, but could be a matter of programme-fitting. The text as first typed runs to approximately 161 lines; about three were added; and some 34 were cut. The net result is a broadcast of 130 lines, which corresponds with the lengths of those in May (see *1173*). According to *London Calling*, a Weekly News Review was scheduled to be read by Bokhari. 'The Debate Continues' by Princess Indira was substituted for this, according to PasB.

The fighting on the Kharkov front has almost come to a standstill. This does not mean that the German offensive has been abandoned, but it does almost certainly mean that the attack staged by Marshal Timoshenko has disrupted the German time table and put back their plans by several weeks. Many observers now think that the main German attack will begin about the same time as it began last year, that is to say about the middle of June. The Russian summer lasts only four or five months, so that every day by which the Russians can hold up the German time table is a great gain. The main German effort must be in the direction of the Caucasus and the Middle East, but the day before yesterday Hitler made a visit to Finland, which may possibly mean that there will also be important developments on the northern front.

The heavy fighting in Libya, which had just started at the time of our last newsletter, is still going on and the issue is still uncertain. The battle has had two phases, the first of which ended favourably for the British. The German armoured forces, moving eastward, circled right round the British mine-fields with the evident object of destroying the British forces in that area and of attacking the seaport of Tobruk, which has been in British hands for 18 months and lies on the flank of any possible German advance into Egypt. The brunt of the first German attack had to be taken by Indian motorised troops, who behaved with great gallantry. The Germans failed in both of their objects and were driven back, losing about 250 tanks, but instead of retreating the way they had come, they managed to break their way westward through the British minefields, creating a wide gap through which they could bring up further reinforcements. They are now renewing the attack. The British are using a new type of tank which had previously been kept secret, and also two types of planes which had not beforehand been used on the Libyan front and whose presence came as a surprise to the Germans. General Kruewell, second in command of the German forces in Libya, has been taken prisoner. The battle will no doubt have been decided one way or another within a few days. It may end with a tactical victory for the Germans, but after the failure of their first surprise attack, it is very unlikely that they will succeed in reaching Egyptian soil.

On two days of this week, two air raids, far greater in scale than anything yet seen in the history of the world, have been made on Germany. On the night of the 30th of May, over a thousand planes raided Cologne, and on the night of the 1st of June, over a thousand planes raided Essen, in the Ruhr district. These have since been followed up by two further raids, also on a big scale, though not quite so big as the first two. To realise the significance of these figures, one has got to remember the scale of the air raids made hitherto. During the autumn and winter of 1940, Britain suffered a long series of raids which at that time were quite unprecedented. Tremendous havoc was worked[1] on London, Coventry, Bristol and various other English cities. Nevertheless, there is no reason to think that in even the biggest of these raids more than 500 planes took part. In addition, the big bombers now being used by the R.A.F. carry a far heavier load of bombs than anything that could be managed two years ago. In sum, the amount of bombs dropped on either Cologne or Essen would be quite three times as much as the Germans ever dropped in any one of their heaviest raids on Britain. [We in this country know what destruction those raids accomplished and have therefore some picture of what has happened in Germany.] Two days after the Cologne raid, the British reconnaissance planes were sent over as usual to take photographs of the damage which the bombers had done, but even after that period, were unable to get any photographs because of the pall of smoke which still hung over the city. *It should be noticed that these 1000-plane raids were carried out solely by the R.A.F. with planes manufactured in Britain. Later in the year, when the American air force begins to take a hand, it is believed that*[1] it will be possible to carry out raids with as many as two thousand planes at a time. One German city after another will be attacked in this manner. These attacks, however, are not wanton and are not delivered against the civilian population, although non-combatants are inevitably killed in them. Cologne was attacked because it is a great railway junction in which the main German rail-roads cross each other and also an important manufacturing centre. Essen was attacked because it is the centre of the German armaments industry and contains the huge factories of Krupp, supposed to be the largest armaments works in the world. In 1940, when the Germans were bombing Britain, they did not expect retaliation on a very heavy scale, and therefore were not afraid to boast in their propaganda about the slaughter of civilians which they were bringing about and the terror which their raids aroused. Now, when the tables are turned, they are beginning to cry out against the whole business of aerial bombing, which they declare to be both cruel and useless. The people of this country are not revengeful, but they remember what happened to themselves two years ago, and they remember how the Germans talked when they thought themselves safe from retaliation. That they did think themselves safe there can be little doubt. Here, for example, are some extracts from the speeches of Marshal Goering, the Chief of the German Air Force. 'I have personally looked into the air raid defences of the Ruhr. No bombing plane could get there. Not as much as a single bomb could be dropped from an enemy plane'.—August 9th, 1939.

'No hostile aircraft can penetrate the defences of the German air force'.— September 7th, 1939. Many similar statements by the German leaders could be quoted.

These prophecies have been terribly falsified and that fact is no doubt making its impression upon the Germans themselves as well as upon public opinion throughout the world.

During this week there has not been any very great development in the war in the Eastern Hemisphere. The Japanese are now making their main effort against China, and may put off the attempt to invade India for the time being, though they must make it sooner or later. We pointed out last week that the battle of the Coral Sea had not ended, though it had checked, the Japanese advance against Australia, and this has been borne out this week by an attack on Sidney° Harbour made by Japanese submarines. The submarines did no damage worth considering, and it is believed that three of them were sunk.[3] But the fact that they could get there is significant, for Sidney is a very long way to the south of any island in Japanese possession and the submarines must in fact have been launched from surface ships. This suggests the possibility that a Japanese naval force is somewhere off the eastern coast of Australia, and apart from attacks on American convoys, an attempt against the mainland of Australia is always possible. In addition, Japanese aeroplanes have made several small raids on the Aleutian Islands, the chain of islands which run westward from Alaska and almost connect America with Asia. It is too early to determine the object of these raids, which might either be the prelude to a naval attack or be a feint to cover operations elsewhere, but they certainly have some strategic purpose. *An attack on Midway Island, in which a Japanese battleship & a plane-carrier were damaged, has just been reported. It is too early to be sure about the meaning of this action, but it may be the prelude to another Japanese attack on Hawaii.*

The underground struggle in the occupied countries continues. Two days ago there came the news that the editor of the best-known Quisling paper in Occupied France—this paper is the organ of Doriot, the French Fascist leader who is one of the most ardent 'collaborators'—has been assassinated. Just over a week ago there occurred a much more important event of the same kind, when an attempt was made on the life of Heydrich, the chief of the Gestapo in Czechoslovakia. Heydrich was hit by three bullets, and died two days ago, in spite of the efforts of Hitler's own physicians to save him. The Germans are following their usual practice of shooting hostages with the threat that more will be shot unless the real assassins are handed over. According to the special bulletins of their own radio they have already shot well over *two*[4] hundred people for the assassination of Heydrich. This process of intimidation is going on all the time all over Europe. To give just one example, three days ago an official bulletin on the German wireless announced that a French girl, aged only 10, had been sentenced to 25 months' hard labour for assisting escaped prisoners of war. But the very fact that these brutal sentences and shooting of hostages go on and on as they have done now for two years, and seem if anything rather to increase in number, shows how ineffective these methods are to crush the spirit of the common people of Europe.

[The annual conference of the British Labour Party has been held during the past week. The Labour party, as far as present political power goes is the second party in Britain, but numerically it is by far the largest, being as it is the organ of the Trade Unions and the working class generally. Some of the resolutions passed at the conference are therefore of interest for the light they throw on British public opinion. The conference registered its complete confidence in the present Prime Minister, and decided, though only by a very small majority, to continue with the inter-party truce. This is an arrangement by which the main political parties have agreed for the duration of the war not to vote or campaign against one another at by-elections. The conference urged that another effort should be made to resolve the Indian political problem and again by a small majority it voted for the raising of the ban on the Daily Worker. The Daily Worker, which was the Communist daily paper, was suppressed two years ago for what were undoubtedly defeatist activities. Since then the USSR has entered the war and the attitude of the British Communist party has naturally become very different. This, however, is not the issue at stake, as was pointed out by one delegate after another at the Labour party conference. The real issue was freedom of the Press. There is a profound respect for freedom of the Press in this country and even people who detest the politics of the Daily Worker were uneasy at seeing a newspaper suppressed. While passing the resolution that the ban on the Daily Worker should be raised, the Conference also rejected by an overwhelming vote the proposal to co-operate politically with the Communists. The fact that this major political party should be so anxious for the freedom of expression of another party, whose policy it is utterly opposed to, is a sign of the strength of British democracy, even after 3½ years of war.

Besides rationing domestic fuel, the Government has just announced that it is going to take full control of the British coal-mines for the duration of the war. We hope to comment more fully upon this news next week.]

1. worked] *as typescript; perhaps* wrought *or* wreaked *was intended*
2. *It should be noticed . . . it is believed that*] There is no doubt that raids of this magnitude will continue, though not of course every day, and it is thought that by the end of the year, when more American planes are available
3. The depot ship Kuttabull was sunk, with some loss of life. All three submarines were sunk.
4. *two*] a, *handwritten emendation*

1211. War-time Diary

<u>7.6.42</u>: *The Sunday Express has also gone cold on the second front. The official line now appears to be that our air raids are a second front. Obviously there has been some kind of government handout to the papers, telling them to*[1] *pipe down on this subject.* ⌐If the government merely wishes to stop them spreading misleading rumours, the puzzle is why they weren't silenced earlier.⌐ *It is just possible that the invasion has now been definitely decided on and the papers have been told to go anti-second front in order to throw the enemy off the scent. In this labyrinth of lies in which we are living the one explanation one never believes is the obvious one.* ⌐Cf. David Astor's story about the two German Jews meeting in the train:

First Jew. Where are you going to?

Second Jew. Berlin.

First Jew. Liar! You just say that to deceive me. You know that if you say you are going to Berlin I shall think you are going to Leipzig, and all the time, you dirty crook, you really *are* going to Berlin!⌐

Last Tuesday[2] *spent a long evening with Cripps (who had expressed a desire to meet some literary people) together with Empson, Jack Common, David Owen, Norman Cameron, Guy Burgess*[3] *and another man (an official) whose name I didn't get. About 2½ hours of it, with nothing to drink. The usual inconclusive discussion. Cripps, however, very human and willing to listen. The person who stood up to him most successfully was Jack Common. Cripps said several things that amazed and slightly horrified me. One was that many people whose opinion was worth considering believed that the war would be over by October—ie. that Germany would be flat out by that time. When I said that I should look on that as a disaster pure and simple (because if the war were won as easily as that there would have been no real upheaval here and the American millionaires would still be in situ) he appeared not to understand. He said that once the war was won the surviving great powers would in any case have to administer the world as a unit, and seemed not to feel that it made much difference whether the great powers were capitalist or socialist.* ⌐Both David Owen and the man whose name I don't know supported him.⌐ *I saw that I was up against the official mind, which sees everything as a problem in administration and does not grasp that at a certain point, ie. when certain economic interests are menaced,*[4] *public spirit ceases to function.* ⌐The basic assumption of such people is that everyone wants the world to function properly and will do his best to keep the wheels running. They don't realise that most of those who have the power dont° care a damn about the world as a whole and are only intent on feathering their own nests.⌐ *I can't help feeling a strong impression that Cripps has already been got at. Not with money or anything of that kind of course, nor even by flattery and the sense of power, which in all probability he genuinely doesn't care about: but simply by responsibility, which automatically makes a man timid. Besides, as soon as you are in power your*

---

* Very interesting but perhaps rather hard on Cripps to report an impression like this from a private interview [Orwell's handwritten footnote on typescript].

perspectives are foreshortened. Perhaps a bird's eye view is as distorted as a worm's eye view.

⌐Wintringham denies being "Thomas Rainboro' ", I think perhaps with truth. If not Wintringham, it might perhaps be Lord Winster (Commander Fletcher).⌐⁵

1. *handout . . . to*] hand-out telling the papers to, *handwritten*
2. 2 June 1942.
3. William Empson, poet and critic; see *845, n. 3.* For Jack Common, writer and friend of Orwell's, see *95* and *295, n. 1.* David Owen was Sir Stafford Cripps's secretary. The poet Norman Cameron (1905–1953) was a friend and disciple of Robert Graves, with whom he and Alan Hodge edited *Work in Hand* (1942). His *The Winter House and Other Poems* was published in 1935. He also translated from French and German. For Guy Burgess, BBC Talks Producer, and later found to be a traitor, see *1135, n. 1.*
4. *menaced*] threatened
5. Lord Winster (Commander R. T. H. Fletcher, 1885–1961), Liberal M.P., 1923–24; Labour M.P., 1935–42, was Parliamentary Private Secretary to the First Lord of the Admiralty, May 1940–December 1941. 'Rainsborough' was then being used by Frank Owen; see *1141, ns. 3* and *4.*

1212. Gujarati Newsletter, 15

8 June 1942

The English original was written by Orwell. No script has been traced. PasB timing is 12′ 20″.

1213. To K. K. Ardaschir

8 June 1942   PP/EB

On 7 June, Tamara Talbot Rice, the Turkish Specialist at the Ministry of Information, wrote to Orwell to tell him that she had forwarded details of Ardaschir's broadcast 'The Sick Man Revives' to the British Publicity Attaché in Turkey, and asking for details about Ardaschir. She commented that he had 'such real knowledge of Turkey' that she wondered 'whether, if occasion arose, he could at times do a little work for us.' Orwell wrote immediately to Ardaschir; his reply to Mrs. Talbot Rice is dated 15 June 1942 (see *1223*).

Dear Mr. Ardaschir,
I am very sorry, but I am afraid I am simply obliged to send back your script on the Caucasus, because I have no place for it for something like two months, and by that time it might cease to be topical. If I send it back now, you may perhaps be able to place it, or its substance, in the press. I am very sorry about the delay, which was due to our change of office.¹

As to your talk on the Suez Canal, we could fit that in on June 26th. I hope you will be able to let me have the script some days beforehand. It should be the usual length, i.e., 13½ minutes.

Yours sincerely,
Eric Blair
Talks Producer
Indian Section

P.S. We have just had a line from the Ministry of Information about your talk—"The Sick Man Revives"—which is going out on July 9th.[2] They want some information about you for publicity purposes. Do you think you could let me have some particulars of the kind they are likely to want as early as possible?

1. For the move from 55 Portland Place to 200 Oxford Street, see *1192, n. 1.*
2. In the event, as Mrs. Talbot Rice explained to Orwell in a letter dated 14 July 1942, 'atmospherics were so bad on July 9th that Mr. Ardaschir's talk was completely inaudible in Turkey.' It was hoped that the talk would be repeated at a later date, and if it were, she asked for details. See also *1223.*

1214. To E. M. Forster

10 June 1942   PP/EB

Dear Mr. Forster,

I am sending herewith the book on Whitman which you wanted. As to American magazines, the BBC Library seems very poorly provided with them, and I can only tell you of the ones I personally know about—I am referring to the more serious magazines, of course. These are:
Weekly: The Nation; the New Republic; and I think New Masses still exists.
Monthly: The Atlantic Monthly; Harpers; Scribener's;° Decision; Poetry.
Bi-monthly: The Partisan Review.
Quarterly: I don't know, but I think there is a Virginia Quarterly.[1]
  I am sorry to be so unhelpful about this.

Yours,
George Orwell
Talks Producer
Indian Section

1. *The Virginia Quarterly Review* was founded 1925 and is still published.

1215. To Princess Indira of Kapurthala, Bahadur Singh, Noel Sircar, and Shridhar Telkar

10 June 1942   Identical letters; PP/EB/NP

We are considering having a regular rotation of speakers to broadcast our weekly News Review on Saturday afternoons.[1] This is a summing-up of the world situation during the current week, and is written by myself. It goes out at 1.15 p.m. DBST. Would you care to be put on the list, and to do the broadcasting of these reviews either once every four or once every five weeks? It would be possible to arrange the dates a good long time ahead. There will, of course, be a fee for the reading, but as it does not entail any actual composition, it would not be a large one.

Yours sincerely,
[Initialled] E.A.B
Eric Blair
Talks Producer
Indian Section

1. Bokhari, who read the weekly News Commentary in English, written by Orwell, from its inception until 25 July 1942, had been negotiating with the BBC to get some time off to go to India from 22 April 1942. In his absence, readers would be required, and these letters started such arrangements. In the event, Princess Indira did not read, but the others did, joined by Homi Bode. Bokhari's departure was delayed; he left 29 September and got back about 13–14 May 1943. Bahadur Singh (see 889, n. 1) replied on 12 June to say he was only too ready to take part and asked if he could do other work in his vacation Orwell passed Singh's letter to Norman Collins, who, in turn, consulted the Eastern Talks Manager. It was some time before Singh was given regular work.

1216. War-time Diary

<u>10.6.42:</u> *The only time when one hears people singing in the BBC is in the early morning, between 6 and 8. That is the time when the charwomen are at work. A huge army of them arrives all at the same time, they sit in the reception hall waiting for their brooms to be issued to them and making as much noise as a parrot house, and then they have wonderful choruses, all singing together as they sweep the passages. The place has a quite different atmosphere at this time from what it has later in the day.*

1217. To Mulk Raj Anand
11 June 1942   PP/EB

Dear Mulk,
I wonder if you've arranged any more speakers for your series yet? You gave us the name of the first six, ending with Dr. Haden Guest, but now our Publicity Department is beginning to ask for more. I should be glad if you will let me have at least three names,[1] as soon as you can,—that is of course, if you haven't fixed up all six yet.

I will meet you and Inez Holden on Monday at 2 p.m. at 200, Oxford Street.

Yours,
[No name/position]

1. Anand replied on 16 June proposing George Downes, a painter who had also worked as a waiter and run a stall in the Caledonian Market; Dr. Mac Fisher, a zoologist who had worked with Julian Huxley and written for Penguin Books on bird-watching; and was asking André van Gysegham, actor-manager, author of *Theatre in Soviet Russia* (1943). Anand's reply is given in full in West: *Broadcasts*, 199–200.

1218. War-time Diary

<u>11.6.42</u>: 'The Germans announce over the wireless that as the inhabitants of a Czech village called Ladice° (about 1200 inhabitants) were guilty of harbouring the assassins of Heydrich they have shot all the males in the village, sent all the women to concentration camps, sent all the children to be "re-educated", razed the whole village to the ground and changed its name.[1] I am keeping a copy of the announcement, as recorded[2] in the BBC monitoring report.'

From the BBC monitoring report:—
PRAGUE (CZECH HOME STATIONS). IN GERMAN FOR PROTECTORATE. 10.6.42
<u>Heydrich Revenge: Village Wiped Out: All Men Shot</u>: ANNOUNCEMENT

It is officially announced: The search and investigation for the murderers of S.S. Obergruppenfuehrer Gen. Heydrich has established unimpeachable indications (sic) that the population of the locality of Lidice, near Kladno, supported and gave assistance to the circle (sic) of perpetrators in question. In spite of the interrogation of the local inhabitants, the pertinent means of evidence were secured without the help of the population. The attitude of the inhabitants to the outrage thus manifested, is manifested also by other acts hostile to the Reich, by the discoveries of printed matter hostile to the Reich, of dumps of arms and ammunition, of an illegal wireless transmitter, of huge quantities of controlled goods, as well as by the fact that inhabitants of the locality are in active enemy service abroad. Since the inhabitants of this village (sic) have flagrantly violated the laws which have been issued, by their activity and by the support given to the murderers of S.S. Obergruppen-fuehrer Heydrich, the male adults have been shot, the women have been sent to a concentration camp and the children have been handed over to the appropriate educational authorities. The buildings of the locality have been levelled to the ground, and the name of the community has been obliterated.
(Note: This is an identical repetition, in German, of an announcement made in Czech, from Prague at 19.00, when reception was very bad).

It does not particularly surprise me that people do this kind of thing, nor even that they announce that they are doing them. What does impress me, however, is that other people's reaction to such happenings is governed solely by the political fashion of the moment. Thus before the war the pinks believed any and every horror story that came out of Germany or China. Now the pinks no longer believe in German or Japanese atrocities and automatically write off all horror stories as "propaganda". In a little while you will be jeered at if you suggest that the story of Lidice could possibly be true.[3] *And yet there the facts are, announced by the Germans themselves and recorded on gramaphone° discs*[4] *which no doubt will still be available. Cf. the long list of atrocities from 1914 onwards* [, German atrocities in Belgium, Bolshevik atrocities, Turkish atrocities, British atrocities in India, American atrocities in Nicaragua, Nazi atrocities, Italian atrocities in Abyssinia and Cyrenaica, red and white atrocities in Spain, Japanese atrocities in China[5]—] *in every case believed in or disbelieved in according to political predilection, with utter non-interest in the facts and with complete willingness to alter one's beliefs as soon as the political scene alters.*[6]

Atrocities (post 1918)

Date	Believed in by the Right	Believed in by the Left
1920	Turkish atrocities (Smyrna) [7]	Turkish atrocities (Smyrna) [7]
1920	Sinn Fein atrocities	Black and Tan atrocities
(circa)	Bolshevik atrocities	British atrocities in India (Amritsar)
1923		French atrocities (the Ruhr)
1928		American atrocities (Nicaragua) [8]
1933	Bolshevik atrocities (White Sea canal etc.) [9]	
1934–9[10]		German[11] atrocities
1935		Italian atrocities (Abyssinia) [12]
1936–9	Red atrocities in Spain	Fascist atrocities in Spain
1937	Bolshevik atrocities (the purges)	Japanese atrocities[13]
1939 et seq.	German atrocities	British atrocities (Isle of Man etc.) [14]
1941 et seq.[15]	Japanese atrocities	

1. Reinhard Heydrich (1904–1942), head of the Reich Main Security Office (the Gestapo, criminal police, and SS Security Service), deputy to Heinrich Himmler, leading organizer of the Nazi 'final solution,' was appointed 'Protector of Bohemia and Moravia' in September 1941. On 27 May 1942, he was wounded by Czech patriots trained in England and died on 4 June. In reprisal, the village of Lidice was 'exterminated.' The population had been about 2,000, and very few survived. Humphrey Jennings made a deeply moving film of the incident, as if it had occurred in the Welsh village of Ystradgynlais (*The Silent Village*, 1943), as part of the British government's propaganda to further support for the defeat of Nazism. A copy of the pamphlet describing the film is in Orwell's pamphlet collection; see *3733*. Throughout his manuscript, Orwell spells the village 'Ladice.'

2. *recorded*] reported, *crossed through in manuscript*. The version given here was typed by Orwell; for the copy of the BBC's monitoring report, see *1224*.

3. *be true*] true

4. *discs*] records, *crossed through in manuscript*

5. Orwell had written to Hsiao Ch'ien on 14 January 1942 asking for 'one talk on the ordinary atrocity lines' in connection with the Japanese invasion of China; see *919*. This was broadcast on 26 February 1942.

6. In the manuscript the table of atrocities is on the verso page facing the end of this diary entry. It forms a separate leaf in the typescript, and Orwell typed a footnote, 'See table of atrocities.' The tables differ slightly; see following notes.

7. Both entries were omitted from typed version.
8. *(Nicaragua)*] (Nicaragua) (?)
9. *(White Sea canal etc.)*] (Ukraine famine)
10. Typed version has only '1934.'
11. *German*] Nazi
12. *(Abyssinia)*] (Abyssinia & Cyrenaica)
13. *Japanese atrocities*] Japanese atrocities (Nanking)
14. *(Isle of Man etc.)*] (the ss. Dunera etc.). Under the Government Regulation 18B, because of exaggerated fears that amongst those who had come to Britain as refugees, especially from Nazi Germany, there were concealed spies and saboteurs, thousands of innocent people were interned on the Isle of Man. Although bitterly ironic, this hardly amounted to an atrocity in the grim scale of such horrors. The deporting of Jews on the S.S *Dunera* to Australia on similar grounds was also misconceived, and led to treatment that was cruel as well as stupid.
15. Typescript has 'seq.' only once, between '1939' and '1941.'

1219. Weekly News Review, 26

13 June 1942

The fairly extensive changes made to this commentary were designed to update the news and make it more accurate. The modifications were crammed in and most appear to be in Orwell's hand, but the smallness and faintness of the writing makes identification difficult. Although the typescript carries two censorship stamps, signed by Bokhari, it is not marked 'As broadcast'; it is likely that a fair copy would have been made, in order that Bokhari could read fluently. The pronounciation and spelling of Lidice are as given in the typescript. PasB has Weekly News Review by Z. A. Bokhari.

By far the most important event during this week is the Anglo-Russian Treaty, the terms of which were published last night.

It would be almost impossible to over-estimate the significance of this event, which may well have a beneficial effect on world history for decades to come. Before the declaration of the new Treaty Britain and Russia were of course in alliance, but it was the rather loose and unsatisfactory alliance of people who are forced to fight on the same side because they are attacked by the same enemy, but who are liable to develop new disagreements as soon as the danger is over. The relationship between Soviet Russia and the United States was even more indefinite. Now, however, there is a close formal agreement between Britain and Russia for clearly stated ends, and the United States, though not as yet a signatory of the agreement, is in complete sympathy.

In this short news review we cannot give the terms of the Treaty in complete detail, but we can summarise them sufficiently. In the first place, the British and Russian governments undertake not only to give each other all military assistance against Germany and the other European Fascist states, but undertake not to make any separate peace either with Hitlerite Germany or with any German Government which still retains aggressive intentions.

This qualification is extremely important. There is no doubt that the Germans have long hoped to buy either Russia or Britain out of the war, so as to follow their usual practice of dealing with their enemies one at a time. And one way they might possibly have done this was by a pretended change of policy, which would make it appear that the clique responsible for German aggressions had now been got rid of, and Germany had no further war-like aims. It has always been a possibility that there might be some kind of coup d'etat, either by the German Army Commanders, or the so-called moderates of the Nazi Party, who would get rid of Hitler and then declare that the cause of the trouble had been removed, and there was no sense in continuing the war. This pretence would have been aimed at either Russia, Britain or the United States, whichever power seemed most war-weary at a given moment. The new Anglo-Russian Treaty practically removes this possibility. It means that the war is being fought not merely for the destruction of Hitler and the figure-heads of the Nazi Party, but for all those forces in Germany who are interested in aggressive foreign wars. Reduced to simple words, this part of the Anglo-Russian Treaty means that Russia and Britain will not stop fighting while Germany has an army.

Secondly, Russia and Britain pledge themselves to post-war collaboration. In the first place, each promises to go to the help of the other, should either be attacked after the present war is over. Even more important than this, the two countries pledge themselves to collaborate in re-establishing the prosperity of Europe. They agree to give one another economic assistance after the war and to pool their efforts in order to restore peace, order, and a decent standard of living to the war-scarred countries of Europe. They agree also to do this without attempting any territorial acquisitions for themselves, and without attempting any interference in the internal affairs of other states. This implies, incidentally, that Russia and Britain will not interfere in the internal affairs of one another, which means that the two regimes are now in far greater political and economic agreement than would have been possible or even thinkable five years ago. It means, in fact, that the ancient ghost of Bolshevism and "bloody revolution" has been laid for ever. The Treaty will be ratified at once, and it is to operate for a period of 20 years, before coming up for renewal.

Two very significant remarks were made by Mr. Eden, the British Foreign Secretary, when he announced the terms of the Treaty in the House of Commons. In the first place, he announced that it has no secret clauses. In the second place, he announced that Russia, Britain and the United States had reached full agreement about the *momentous tasks of* opening of a second front in Europe during 1942. Just what they have agreed is, needless to say, a secret.

After visiting London first, M. Molotov also visited Washington. The terms of the Treaty between Russia and the United States will no doubt be published shortly. The Treaty was actually signed in London on May 26th. M. Molotov's arrival and departure were very well guarded secrets; although known to a certain number of people in London, they got no further. In particular the Germans were completely in the dark about the whole visit. Although their wireless now claims to have known all about the impending Treaty, it in fact made absolutely no reference to it or to Molotov's visit until the news was made public in Britain.

As we have had to devote some minutes to the Anglo-Russian Treaty, we must comment on the rest of the news more briefly than usual this week. The situation in Libya is less favourable than it was a week ago. After holding out for sixteen days, the Free French and Indian garrison at Bir Hakeim has had to be evacuated, which has allowed the Germans to clear their right flank and thus attack our main positions in greater force. The battle will probably continue with intensity for some time. The Germans may make further advances, and it is possible that they are planning to synchronise their tank attack with an attack by air-borne troops from Crete. But[1] on the whole, the chances are against their capturing the strong-hold of Tobruk, and still more heavily against their succeeding in breaking into Egypt.

A great naval battle has taken place in the Pacific [, the full outcome of which is not yet clear]. A week ago we reported that the Japanese fleet had made an unsuccessful attack on Midway Island, and since then fuller figures of their losses have come in. It is now known that they lost 4[2] plane-carriers and a *number of other ships. Full figures for the Battle of the Coral Sea have now also been released, and it appears from those that in the two battles the Japanese lost 37 ships of various classes sunk or damaged, including a battleship and 5 cruisers sunk.*[3] Almost simultaneously with *the action of Midway island*[°4] the Japanese made some kind of attack upon the Aleutian Islands, the chain of islands which almost connect America with Asia in the far north. It is not certain yet what has happened *but it does not appear from American reports that the Japanese have landed on any island which is inhabited. They may be planning an attack on*[5] the main American base, Dutch Harbour, *or they may merely be making a demonstration*[6] in the Aleutian Islands in order to cover up their defeat *at*[7] Midway Island. We shall be able to report on this more fully next week.

Heavy fighting is going on in Eastern China, in the neighbourhood of Nanchang. The Japanese also claim to have made in-roads into Inner Mongolia, through which one of the routes between China and Soviet Russia runs. Although they now say that they are about to bring the so-called China incident to an end once and for all, they no doubt remember that they have been saying this for five years, and the China incident is still continuing. Probably, therefore, what the Japanese are aiming at at the moment is not so much the final conquest of China, as to capture the air-fields not far from the Eastern coast, from which Japan itself might be bombed. Meanwhile, the Chinese government has announced that fresh British and American air force units have arrived in China.

Mr. Oliver Lyttelton,[8] British Minister of Production, has just announced the truly staggering figures of Britain's current war production. He announces, among other things, that Britain is now producing vehicles for war purposes—this of course includes tanks—at the rate of two hundred and fifty thousand a year; big guns at forty thousand a year, and ammunition for those guns at the rate of twenty-five million rounds. He announces also that Britain's aircraft production has made a hundred per-cent increase, that is to say, the rate has doubled since the last quarter of 1940, while the production of merchant shipping has increased by fifty seven per cent. Some of the effects of this large-scale war production can be seen in the continued air-raids on

359

Germany, which at the moment are not quite as terrible as the thousand plane raid we reported last week, but are still very big raids by any normal standard.

We will end our review with a comparatively small item of news, which is nevertheless worth reporting, because it shows more clearly than whole books could do, what Fascism means. Following on the assassination of Heydrich, the Gestapo chief in Czechoslovakia, the Germans, up till three days ago, had already shot over two hundred hostages. These figures are from their own official wireless statements. Then, two days ago, they followed up these announcements of shooting by announcing over the air the action they had taken against a Czech village whose inhabitants were accused of having assisted Heydrich's assassins.

"Since the inhabitants of this village", states the German wireless, "have frequently violated the laws which have been issued, by their activity and by the support given to the murderers of Heydrich, the male adults have been shot, the women have been sent to a concentration camp, and the children have been handed over to appropriate educational authorities. The buildings of the locality have been levelled to the ground, and the name of the community has been obliterated."

Notice that these are the words of the Germans themselves, broadcast to the whole world in at least two languages. The Czech village, named Ladice° (pronounced *Lideetia*)° was a village of about twelve hundred inhabitants. We may assume, therefore, that the Germans have killed about three hundred men, sent about three hundred women to the concentration camp, and about six hundred children to what they call "appropriate educational authorities", which in practice means to labour camps, and all this upon the mere suspicion of having helped the assassins of a man who is himself known all over Europe as a blood-stained murderer. But more significant than the act, is the impudence with which it is broadcast to the world, almost as though it was something to be proud of. And most significant of all is the fact that more than three years after their seizure of Czechoslovakia, the Germans are compelled to commit these barbarities in order to hold down a people whom they pretend to be benefitting by their wise and disinterested rule.[9]

1. Crete. But] Crete, but
2. 4] two
3. *number of other ships . . . and 5 cruisers sunk*] destroyer, and suffered damage to a number of other ships, including three battleships. *Only the first three words are crossed out; the intention must have been to cancel the remainder. Also, Orwell originally wrote* 'destroyed' *for* 'damaged.' At the Battle of Midway, the Japanese lost four aircraft carriers, a cruiser, 332 aircraft, and 3,500 men, amongst whom were some of their best pilots. The Americans achieved this important victory with the loss of one aircraft carrier, 1 destroyer, 150 aircraft, and 307 men. The battle marked the turning-point in the Pacific war (see *2194 Days of War*, 253).
4. *the action of Midway island*°] this
5. *but it does not appear . . . planning an attack on*] The Japanese claim to have made landings, but it is probable that if they *had* done so, they have only landed on uninhabited islets, with the object of attacking
6. *or they may . . . demonstration*] later. It is also possible that they have merely claimed landings
7. *at*] on; *change not clearly made*
8. Oliver Lyttelton (1893–1974; Lord Chandos, 1954), appointed President of the Board of

Trade in 1940 by Churchill and later was Minister of State in the Middle East. When the War Cabinet was reconstructed in February 1942, he was appointed Minister of Production, a post he held until Churchill resigned, 23 May 1945. He was Secretary of State for the Colonies, 1951–54.
9. Later figures showed that 173 males were shot and 296 women and children were sent to Ravensbrück concentration camp, from which very few returned. In September, 252 people were condemned to death for sheltering those who had killed Heydrich, and relatives of two of the families involved were sent to Mauthausen concentration camp.

1220. To C. D. Darlington

13 June 1942   PP/EB/NP

Dear Dr. Darlington,

You are already doing a talk for us in the series "Science and Politics", and I am wondering whether you would like to do another, of approximately the same length, in a series called "A.D. 2000". The idea of this series is to give some kind of picture of what will probably be happening in 50 or 60 years time. The one I would like you to undertake is the third in the series, to be called "India in the Steel Age", and to deal with the industrialisation of India. You could have an entirely free hand, and could talk about how far India is likely to become industrialised, whether you think it ought to do so, how the industrialisation is to be brought about, or whatever other aspect of the subject you prefer. To give you an idea of the general scope of these talks, here are the subjects dealt with in the other five—

1. Agriculture
2. The population problem
4. Education
5. Religion
6. India's Cultural Future.

The date of the talk would be on July 10th, which would mean that I should want the script by about the beginning of July. Perhaps you would be kind enough to let me know whether you would like to undertake this. As this is in the same week as your other talk, if it is inconvenient to you to make two visits, you could record the second talk on the same day as you deliver the first.

Yours sincerely,
George Orwell
Talks Producer
Indian Section

1221. War-time Diary

<u>13.6.42</u>: *The most impressive fact about the Molotov visit is that the Germans knew nothing about it. Not a word on the radio about Molotov's presence in London till the signature of the treaty was officially announced,*

*although all the while the German radio was shouting about the bolshevisa-
tion of Britain. Obviously they would have spilt the beans if they had[1]
known. Taken in conjunction with certain other things (eg. the capture last
year of two very amateurish spies dropped by parachute, with portable
wireless transmitters and actually with chunks of German sausage in their
suitcases) this suggests that the German spy system in this country cannot be
up to much*

A sequence of four newspaper cuttings is pasted into the manuscript Diary at this
point:

*From editorial of the "Tribune" of 12.6.42, on the death of Wm. Mellor.
Their idea of "Vigorous style".[2]*

His death will be particularly mourned by old readers of "Tribune". He
was Editor of the paper when it was launched in January, 1937. The
concluding paragraphs of the Editorial of the first number might well be
quoted here. They are a worthy summary of his Socialist outlook and a fair
example of his vigorous style as a writer:—
  "The situation is a *dynamic* one. Either we *go forward* now to socialism or
there will be a widespread *retrogression* to that *Fascist barbarism* into which
the larger part of Europe has been *plunged*. For the Hitlers and Mussolinis
cannot afford to wait: their grim gamble demands conquest or disaster.
Our Baldwins and Edens cannot long shuffle and *evade the issues* they pose.
The Labour movement must choose. It has come now to the *turning point*
of its history.
  "To *go forward* is to conquer. To stay still is to choose defeat. Another
1931, even another 1935, is an invitation to the enemy. Our weakness is his
strength; in our divisions and doubts he *lives and moves and has his being*. We
do not proclaim the class war; it is here amongst us every day. We do not
ask for civil conflict; it is those who weaken our forces by disunity who
invite its onset. We ask for the socialism that has been the living principle of
our movement. We ask for the unity that has been the *broad basis* of its
strength."

(From Hitler's speeches, quoted in Reynolds's[2] of 21.6.42)

  Nov. 3: This enemy's (Russia's) backbone is already broken and he will
never rise again.
  Nov. 10: We are now at the beginning of the last great battle of the year
which will smash the enemy and, with him, Britain.
  Feb. 24: Now that the worst of the cold is over . . . it is impossible for
me to leave my headquarters, where preparations have been made for the
final struggle.
  Feb. 28: I will not set foot in the Reich until the last Russian army has
been annihilated.
  March 15: Only to-day do we realise the full extent of the preparations
made by our enemies. The German Army has attacked and annihilated
again and again the ever-renewed Russian forces, only to meet with fresh

masses of men. The Russians will be annihilatingly defeated by us in the coming summer.

"Tribune" of 12.6.42. (article by Wilfred Macartney). Cf. prewar references to Axis censorship, radio hypnosis etc. Cf. also German official statements in the Cologne raid. (Cf. above)[4]

Hitler appears to have much more confidence in his people than our leaders have in the British people. "Victory at any price" is not a cry of despair—it is a bugle call to a nation prepared to sacrifice everything for victory. The Germans cannot be charged with withholding information from their people of disaster; the simple reason is that only in Russia have they encountered disaster in the loss of the first campaign; and it is extremely doubtful—at least one cannot discover it in Hitler's speeches—that the German people are unaware of the colossal nature of the job undertaken in attempting to destroy the only Socialist Commonwealth on earth. It is equally doubtful whether the British people who have been jollied along from the beginning of this war on sunshine stories, are actually conscious of the power of the Axis.

How we live in 1942 (cutting from "E. Standard")

Illustration of five women, captioned 'Russia's Tommy-Gun Girls are Ready to Fight.'

1. *had*] had really
2. The words italicized were underlined in the newspaper cutting by Orwell. "Tribune" was italicized in the original but has been reproduced as here to avoid confusion with words marked by Orwell. William Mellor (1888–1942), left-wing journalist and author, edited the *Daily Herald*, which he had joined in 1903, from 1926 to 1930. He was then Assistant Managing Editor of Odhams Press until he became editor of *Tribune*, 1 January 1937. He wrote *Direct Action* (1920) and, with G. D. H. Cole, *The Meaning of Industrial Freedom* (1918). He was a member of the National Council of the Socialist League.
3. *Reynolds's*] Reynold's News. See *938, n. 1.*
4. *above*] opposite. *The cutting was pasted on the facing page.*

1222. Gujarati Newsletter, 16

15 June 1942

The English original was written by Orwell. No script has been traced.

1223. To Tamara Talbot Rice

15 June 1942   PP/EB/NP

Dear Mrs. Talbot Rice,
In reply to your letter of June 7th, here are some details about Mr. Ardaschir.[1]
Born in Bombay, March 28, 1890.
Son of a Persian landowner.

Became a journalist in 1910 under Mr. J. A. Spender, "Westminster Gazette", subsequently serving on newspapers in Egypt and India.
Author of various plays and books.
Fought in the first Balkan war and became an officer in the Ottoman Imperial Guard
Lived a long while in Turkey and other countries of the Middle East.

He has done several talks for me, and also for the Hindustani Section, but he does not work full time here. I am sure he would be delighted to help you at any time, if occasion arose.

Thank you for letting me know about the title of the talk on Turkey; we shall call it "Turkey Past and Present" as you suggested.

Yours sincerely,
Eric Blair
Talks Producer
Indian Section

1. On receiving Mrs. Talbot Rice's letter of 7 June (see *1213*), Orwell wrote to Ardaschir for details. This letter is based on his reply; its phrasing is, in part, identical with Orwell's annotations to Ardaschir's letter. Ardaschir also mentioned that he had come to England when he was eight years old and had been educated at Blundell's School. See *1084, n. 1* and also Orwell's reference for him, *1995.*

1224. War-time Diary

<u>15.6.42:</u> *No question now that the second front has been decided on. All the papers talk of it as a certainty and Moscow is publicising it widely. Whether it is really feasible remains to be seen, of course.*

Pasted sideways in the manuscript is the following BBC monitoring report, with Orwell's manuscript caption beneath it. He also pasted in his own typed report of the liquidation of Lidice, in the entry for 11 June (see 1218). The texts are verbally the same.

In a broadcast preceding the announcement of further executions, the Prague wireless said last night that "the threat of execution by shooting does not apply to anyone giving information which may help to discover the assailant against S.S. Obergrueppenfuerhrer Heydrich, if this information is supplied at the latest at 20.00 on the 18th June, 1942, to any office of the Gestapo or of any other police office. Anybody who hears of any information that could be helpful in discovering the culprits of the attack must give this information within 24 hours to one of the offices mentioned above. Everybody fulfilling this order will be given an adequate reward. Anybody who does not act in accordance with this order will be shot, together with his family" (Prague in Czech 19.00).

<u>15.6.42:</u> *Cutting from BBC monitoring report. Typical of many similar German announcements.*

1225. To Joseph Needham
17 June 1942   PP/EB

Dear Mr. Needham,
Thank you very much for your script, which reached me just after my secretary rang you up. I am sending you copies of the scripts that we have had in this series up to date.[1] Your talk is just the kind of thing I wanted.

Can you come to my office at 200, Oxford Street, at about 12.30 on Tuesday? We want you to broadcast the talk direct, at 1.15 p.m., and that will give you time to run through it once for timing. 200, Oxford Street, is on the corner of Great Portland Street and Oxford Street, and the entrance is opposite Studio One Cinema. Thank you for correcting me about your description, I will see that it is given correctly in the announcements preceding your talk. I shall look forward to seeing you on Tuesday.

Yours sincerely,
Eric Blair
Talks Producer
Indian Section

1. On 16 June 1942, Professor Needham had written to ask if he could see some other scripts.

1226. Z. A. Bokhari to Shridhar Telkar
18 June 1942

There seems to be no record of Telkar having been asked to prepare a broadcast on Timoshenko, the Soviet general who was much concerned with the training of the Russian army; see *1267, n. 2.* It may have been requested by Orwell for his series 'These Names Will Live'—Telkar had been commissioned to write on John Gordon (see *1206*)—but it may have been initiated by Telkar. The style of Bokhari's comments on Czarist and Communist rule, and his abrupt opening, reveal something of his attitude and approach.

My dear Telkar,
Your very interesting script on "Timoshenko".

It will be out of place for me to express my views on Communism in this letter, but I feel there is no need to drag in propaganda for a communist state in this programme. It is out of place. I also feel that there it is a waste of time at the present juncture to rake up the black spots of Czarist rule. Here and there we find references in your programme which have no bearing on Timoshenko's life. From a purely literary angle the repeated comments on social injustice and foreign intervention troops and the like merely hold up the story and are therefore in my opinion harmful to the script.

I want you to take these comments in the spirit in which they are given. I will be only too glad to discuss the script with you if you so desire. I do hope you will see my point of view. This is a private letter. I am returning your script with this note.

1227. To Tambimuttu

18–19(?) June 1942

YOUR TALK ON AUGUSTUS JOHN[1] BROADCAST TUESDAY NEXT PLEASE BRING SCRIPT TWO HUNDRED OXFORD STREET IMMEDIATELY

BLAIR BROADCASTS

1. Augustus John (1878–1961), a distinguished British painter. In his youth he roamed England with gypsies and made many paintings of them, but it is for his portraits that he will probably be remembered, among them those of the cellist Guilhermina Suggia, Thomas Hardy, Shaw, T. E. Lawrence, Yeats, and Dylan Thomas. He was elected to the Royal Academy in 1928; resigned following a fierce disagreement in 1938; and was re-elected in 1946

1228. Weekly News Review, 27

20 June 1942

PasB has Weekly News Review by Z. A. Bokhari, as usual, but no script has been traced. Orwell did not go on leave until the weekend of 27 June, returning to work on Monday, 13 July, so he would have been available to write this script.

1229. BBC Talks Booking Form, 20.6.42

Lady Grigg: 'Women Generally Speaking'; broadcast 1, 8, 15, and 29.7.42; fee £8.8s each talk. Signed: Z. A. Bokhari.

1230. BBC Talks Booking Form, 20.6.42

Princess Indira of Kapurthala: 'The Debate Continues'; broadcast 6, 13, 20, and 27.7.42; fee £8.8s each talk. Signed: Z. A. Bokhari.

1231. War-time Diary

21.6.42: *The thing that strikes one in the BBC—and it is evidently the same in various of the other departments—is not so much the moral squalor and the ultimate futility of what we are doing, as the feeling of frustration, the impossibility of getting anything done, even any successful piece of scoundrelism. Our policy is so ill-defined, the disorganisation is so great* ⌊, there are so many changes of plan⌋ *and the fear and hatred of intelligence are so all-pervading, that one cannot plan any sort of wireless campaign whatever.* ⌊When one plans some series of talks, with some more or less definite propaganda line behind it, one is first told to go ahead, then choked off on the ground that this or that is "injudicious" or "premature", then told again to go ahead, then told to water everything down and cut out any plain statements that may have crept in here and there, then told to "modify" the series in some way that removes its original meaning; and then at the last moment the whole thing is suddenly cancelled by some mysterious edict from above and one is told to improvise some different series which one feels no interest in and which in any case has no definite idea behind it.[1] *One is constantly putting sheer rubbish on the air because of having talks which sounded[1] too intelligent cancelled at the last moment. In addition the organisation is so overstaffed that numbers of people have almost literally nothing to do. But even when one manages to get something fairly good on the air one is weighed down by the knowledge that hardly anybody is listening. Except, I suppose, in Europe the BBC simply isn't listened to overseas, a fact known to everyone concerned with overseas broadcasting.* ⌈Some listener research has been done in America and it is known that in the whole of the USA about 300,000 people listen to the BBC. In India or Australia the number would not be anywhere near that.⌉ *It has come out recently that (two years after the Empire service was started) plenty of Indians with shortwave sets don't even know that the BBC broadcasts to India.*

It is the same with the only other public activity I take part in, the Home Guard. After two years no real training has been done, no specialised tactics worked out, no battle positions fixed upon, no fortifications built—all this owing to endless changes of plan and complete vagueness as to what we are supposed to be aiming at. Details of organisation, battle positions etc. have been changed so frequently that hardly anyone knows at any given moment what the current arrangements are supposed to be. To give just one example, for well over a year our company has been trying to dig a system of trenches in Regents Park, in case airborne troops land[2] there. Though dug over and over again these trenches have never once been in a completed state, because when they are half done there is always a change of plan and fresh orders. Ditto with everything. Whatever one undertakes, one starts[3] with the knowledge that presently there will come a sudden change of orders, and then another change, and so on indefinitely. Nothing ever happens except continuous dithering, resulting in progressive disillusionment all round. The best one can hope is that it is much the same on the other side.

1. *sounded*] sound
2. *land*] should land
3. *starts*] starts out

1232. Gujarati Newsletter, 17

22 June 1942

The English original was written by Orwell. No script has been traced. The PasB gives timing as 11½ minutes.

1233. BBC Talks Booking Form, 22.6.42

R. R. Desai: Gujarati Newsletters 19–22; broadcast 6, 13, 20, and 27.7.42; fee £5.5s + £2.8.2 + £1.1.4 expenses. Signed: Z. A. Bokhari.

1234. BBC Talks Booking Form, 22.6.42

M. J. Tambimuttu: 'These Names Will Live'; 13-minute talk on Augustus John; broadcast 23.6.42; fee £8.8s. Signed: Z. A. Bokhari.

1235. BBC Talks Booking Form, 22.6.42

S. Telkar: 'A Year Ago Today,' anniversary of Russia's entry into the war; 5-minute talk; broadcast 22.6.42; fee £4.4s. Signed: Z. A. Bokhari.

1236. To Mulk Raj Anand

23 June 1942   PP/EB

Dear Mulk,

I am writing to ask whether you would care to do us another talk in a forthcoming series. This series is called "Open Letters"; the idea is to discuss the origins and political meaning of the war and to put this in a simple popular form we are going to do it in the form of open letters to imaginary people representing the most important trends of modern thought. The one I would like you to do is the Letter to a Chinese Guerilla. The date of this will be July 30th, at 1.15 p.m. DBST. No doubt you will understand that though I want the talks to be of a popular intelligible type, I also hope they will provide a serious discussion of modern political problems. As far as possible your talk should have a direct bearing on India. Could you please let me know as early as possible whether you would like to undertake this. If you are able to do it, I should want the script not later than July 23rd.

Yours,
[Initialled] E.A.B
George Orwell
Talks Producer
Indian Section

Similar letters were sent on the same day to at least four other people. They, and the variations in their letters, were: R. R. Desai (Letter to a Nazi; August 13; script due by August 6; 'We can discuss it further if you like when I get back from my holiday, on July 13th'); Cedric Dover (Letter to a Liberal; August 20; script due by August 13; signed Eric Blair; Dover telephoned on 29 June, agreeing but wanting to know how long the talk was to be); K. S. Shelvankar (Letter to a Pacifist; August 6; we can arrange to meet and discuss the matter further; script due by July 30; carbon copy of letter is marked with a large 'NO'; see *1311*); M. J. Tambimuttu (Letter to a Marxist; September 10; script due '*not later than September 3rd*'; signed Eric Blair. Tambimuttu replied on 29 June, sending a wealth of suggestions. He described them as 'vague ideas,' but they were quite precise and often imaginative, ranging from the literature, posters, and type-face of the London Transport Board to the little-magazine phenomenon. He also commented, 'The Indian Section [of the BBC] as a friend wrote to me seem to be doing all the good things.'

1237. To Sir Frank Brown[1]

23 June 1942   PP/EB

Dear Sir,
I am writing to you because it has been suggested to me that you might be able to advise us about selecting a speaker for a forthcoming talk.

We are looking for a speaker on the Future of Education in India. We have a series of talks called 'A.D. 2000', which deal with the probable condition of India about 50 or 60 years from now. We want one on education and we naturally are looking for a speaker with some experience of India, though not necessarily very prolonged experience. The date of the talk is July 17th, which means that we want to make sure of engaging our speaker within the next week or so. Could you be kind enough to give me your advice? If you could reply by telephone, it might save time. My telephone number is Euston 3400, and the extension 180.

I am sorry to trouble you, but I am anxious to have the advice of somebody with expert knowledge of this matter.

Yours truly
Eric Blair
Talks Producer
Indian Section

1. Sir Frank Herbert Brown, CIE (1868–1959), was a journalist who had worked in India on the *Bombay Gazette* and the *Indian Daily Telegraph*, and was on the staff of the London *Times* from 1902 to 1954.

1238. To J. G. Crowther

23 June 1942   PP/EB

Dear Mr. Crowther,

I am extremely sorry for all the inconvenience which must have been caused by the wrong date having been put on your contract.[1] I am afraid that the fault lay in my office, and I hope you will accept my apologies. I understand from my secretary that you have very kindly agreed to do the talk on Tuesday next, June 30th, and that you will be able to let us have the script on Monday some time.

I will arrange for someone in the Indian Section to meet you at about 12.30 p.m. on the 30th. The address is 200, Oxford Street, on the corner of Oxford Street and Great Portland Street, and the entrance is opposite Studio One Cinema. I am sorry that I shall be away on leave[2] and therefore unable to meet you.

I think you may be interested to know that we have asked Dr. Darlington to do another talk for us in the Eastern Service, this time on the Industrialisation of India, in a series called "A.D. 2000."

Yours sincerely,
Eric Blair
Talks Producer
Indian Section

1. The talks booking form (see *1163*) gave the date as 7 July 1942, but it is not known if that was the date on the contract.
2. Orwell was to be on leave from Saturday, 27 June 1942 (possibly from about noon) to Sunday, 12 July 1942—hence the flood of letters written on 23 June.

1239. To C. R. Fay

23 June 1942   PP/EB

Dear Professor Fay,[1]

I am writing to ask whether it would interest you to do a talk in one of our forthcoming series in the Eastern Service. These talks are in the form of short discussions between people with special knowledge of subjects of current interest. The one I hope you will undertake is on the Co-operative Movement, and the speaker with whom I suggest you should hold your discussion is Miss Digby.[2] These broadcasts take about 13½ minutes, which means probably that your contribution would be in the neighbourhood of 750 words. The date of this broadcast would be August 28th, at 12.45 p.m. BST. This means that I should like to have the script by August 21st if possible. If you agree, I will make all the arrangements for the necessary meeting and discussion. Could you be kind enough to let me know as soon as possible whether this interests you?

Yours sincerely,
[Initialled] E.A.B
George Orwell
Talks Producer
Indian Section

1. Charles Ryle Fay (1884–1961) was Professor of Economic History, University of Toronto, 1921–30; Reader in Economic History, University of Cambridge from 1930. He wrote several books on the co-operative movement and on co-partnership in industry.
2. Fay replied on 29 June asking how one discussed something with one's secretary; Miss Digby was, he said, secretary to the Horace Plunkett Foundation, of which he was Chairman. Further, Miss Digby had never been to India. He suggested, instead, E. V. Lucette (Ceylon), a Trustee of the Horace Plunkett Foundation, or A. Cavendish (Malaya). The foundation (now Plunkett Foundation for Cooperative Studies) was named after Sir Horace Curzon Plunkett (1854–1932), a pioneer of the agricultural co-operative movement, who in 1919 endowed a trust to undertake research and disseminate information in this field. Orwell explains in his next letter to Fay (see *1296*) that 'Miss Digby' *was* the name given to him. Margaret Digby was the author of *Producers and Consumers* (1928, rev. 1938), *The Digest of Co-operative Law at Home and Abroad* (1933), *The World Cooperative Movement* (1948), and *Horace Plunkett: An Anglo-American Irishman* (1949). It must have been obvious to Fay which Miss Digby Orwell meant; her first two books were published by the Horace Plunkett Foundation.

1240. To Noel Sircar

23 June 1942   PP/EB

Dear Sircar,
This is to confirm that you are going to undertake the monthly Film Commentary in our new schedule, starting on July 28th, at 1.45 p.m. DBST.
Your next date will be August 25th, and the time will then be 12.45 p.m. BST.

Yours sincerely,
[Initialled] E.A.B
Eric Blair
Talks Producer
Indian Section

1241. To L. F. Easterbrook

23 June 1942

Orwell wrote to a number of pairs of speakers on the same date suggesting discussions on subjects of current interest. These were to constitute a series entitled 'I'd Like It Explained.' The letter to L. F. Easterbrook is given in full and followed by a list of the known pairings with significant variations from this letter.

Dear Mr. Easterbrook,[1]
I am writing to ask whether it would interest you to do a talk in one of our

forthcoming series in the Eastern Service. These talks are in the form of short discussions between people with special knowledge of subjects of current interest. The one I hope you will undertake is on Agriculture, and the speaker with whom I suggest you should hold your discussion is Sir John Russell. These broadcasts take about 13½ minutes, which means probably that your contribution would be in the neighbourhood of 750 words. The date of this broadcast would be August 14th, at 12.45 p.m. BST. This means that I should like to have the script by August 7th if possible. If you agree, I will make all the arrangements for the necessary meeting and discussion. Could you be kind enough to let me know as soon as possible whether this interests you?

Yours sincerely,
[Initialled] E.A.B
George Orwell
Talks Producer
Indian Section

Easterbrook replied on 28 June agreeing to participate. He was to be partnered by Sir John Russell (see *1184, n. 1*), the letter to whom began with a paragraph about Russell's contribution to the 'A.D. 2000' series; see *1205*.

Many thanks for your script, which is just what I wanted. Can we meet at 12.30 at 200, Oxford Street, which is on the corner of Oxford Street and Great Portland Street—the entrance is opposite Studio One Cinema?

The other pairs were:

2. Michael Foot and J. L. Garvin[2] on the Press; scheduled for 7 August, script due by 31 July.
3. J. B. S. Haldane and Dr C. H. Waddington[3] on Scientific Research; scheduled for 21 August, script due by 14 August.
4. Professor Harold Laski and Lord Winterton[4] on the future of Parliament; scheduled for 4 September, script due by 28 August.
5. Peter Masefield and Oliver Stewart[5] on aviation; scheduled for 31 July, script due by 24 July. (Oliver Stewart wrote on 29 June declining because he would be away; his place was taken by E. C. Bowyer; see *1305, n. 1*.
6. T. C. Worsley[6] with someone not yet selected, on education.

Before despatching his letter to Haldane, Orwell sent a draft to Rushbrook Williams, with this memorandum:

Subject: TALK BY J.B.S. HALDANE.

I attach a letter which I have drafted to Professor Haldane, asking him if he would care to do a talk for us in a new series to start shortly called "I'd Like it Explained". I should be most grateful if you would obtain permission for me to approach him. I think the attached letter gives all the information you will need.

[Signed] Eric Blair
(Eric Blair)

This is annotated, first by Rushbrook Williams and then by S. J. de Lotbinière,[7] at the time his superior. Both annotations are dated 24 June 1942:

'Is there any objection here? We have asked him before to do ARP and his script was useful, "inoffensive", and excellent value.'

'This is all right. I hope he'll say nothing which will make us frightened of using him again.'

The original of the letter to Haldane has survived (Haldane Papers, University College London) and on its verso Haldane drafted a reply, explaining that he had to undertake research as well as talk about it. The Navy had a fairly urgent problem for him and he could not give up a whole day, though he might manage an evening. Bokhari replied on 2 July explaining that Orwell was on leave and asking Haldane to suggest a date and time, with an alternative; every effort would then be made to arrange an evening recording with C. H. Waddington. That letter has been annotated 'Wed or Thurs 7 pm'—presumably 15 and 16 July. Orwell sent Haldane a telegram, probably on 13 July, suggesting 15 July at 7.00 P.M.

1. Laurence Frank Easterbrook (1893–1965; OBE), journalist and founder and editor of the British-American News Service, was agricultural correspondent, *Daily Telegraph*, 1933–36, and *News Chronicle*, from 1936; Public Relations Officer to the Ministry of Agriculture, 1939–41; and government agricultural representative to the United States in 1940. He wrote, for the British Council, *British Agriculture* (1943), *Machines on the Farm* (1943), and *Youth and the Land* (1944). His *New Hope for the Countryside* (1943) was published by the Industrial Christian Fellowship. He also contributed to *The New Statesman, Fortnightly Review*, and other magazines.
2. Michael Foot (1913–), politician, journalist, and author, entered Parliament in 1945 and was Leader of the Labour Party, 1980–83; assistant editor of *Tribune*, 1937–38, Editor, 1948–52, 1955–60, Managing Director, 1945–74. He had also been acting editor, *London Evening Standard*, 1942, and political columnist for the *Daily Herald*, 1944–64. He wrote *Guilty Men* (with Frank Owen and Peter Howard) and *Armistice 1918–39*, both published in 1940. For J L. Garvin, see *296, n. 8*.
3. For J. B. S. Haldane, see *1142, n. 1;* for C. H. Waddington, *993, n. 1*.
4. Harold Joseph Laski (1893–1950), political scientist at the London School of Economics, a Marxist, a leading member of the Labour Party, and popular lecturer, was assistant to Attlee, the Deputy Prime Minister. He endeavoured to establish a popular front against fascism during the Spanish civil war, believing socialism was the only effective alternative to the menace of fascism. Among his many books were: *Authority in the Modern State* (1919), *Grammar of Politics* (1925), *The State in Theory and Practice* (1935), *The Rise of European Liberalism* (1936), *The American Presidency: An Interpretation* (1940), *Reflections on the Revolution of Our Time* (1943), *Faith, Reason, and Civilization* (1944), and *The American Democracy: A Commentary and Interpretation* (1948). Earl Winterton (1883–1962) entered Parliament in 1904, representing Horsham until his retirement in 1951. He served in World War I, was Under-Secretary of State for India, 1922–24 and 1924–29, and was later Paymaster-General.
5. Peter Masefield (1914–; Kt., 1972) was war correspondent with the RAF and the U.S. Eighth Air Force, 1939–43; air correspondent for the *Sunday Times*, 1940–43; personal secretary to Lord Beaverbrook, Lord Privy Seal, on post-war civil air transport, 1943–45; Air Attaché, British Embassy, Washington, 1945–46; Chief Executive of British European Airways, 1949–55; and Chairman, British Airports Authority, 1965–71. Oliver Stewart (1895–1976; MC), writer and broadcaster, was editor of *Aeronautics*, 1939–62, and air correspondent for the *Manchester Guardian*, 1941–58.
6. Thomas Cuthbert Worsley (1907–1977), author, critic, and, for a time, schoolmaster at Wellington (where Orwell spent a term in 1917), was literary editor of *The New Statesman* (which he joined in 1939) after the war, during which he served in the RAF. He wrote *Education Today—and Tomorrow* (with W. H. Auden) (1939), *Behind the Battle*, about the

Spanish civil war (1939), *Barbarians and Philistines: Democracy and the Public Schools* (1940), *The End of the 'Old School Tie,'* a Searchlight Book, the series Orwell edited with Tosco Fyvel (1941), and *The Fellow Travellers: A Memoir of the Thirties* (1971). Valentine Cunningham described him as one of the group that included Auden, Spender, and Isherwood, which 'flaunted public admiration and adulation' of one another in the thirties (*British Writers of the Thirties*, 136–37).

7. S. J. de Lotbinière was Director of Empire Services in the schedule prepared for Sir Stafford Cripps in March 1942. He was later Director of the War Reporting Unit (Staff List, 21.8.43), and an annotation to that list shows his appointment as BBC representative in Canada.

1242. To S. M. Telkar

23 June 1942   PP/EB

Dear Telkar,

This is to confirm that you are going to undertake TOPICS OF THE WEEK, in the new schedule. The first will be on July 29th, at 1.15 p.m. DBST, and I should want the script by Monday of that week, that is, July 27th.

As you know, after August 8th, we revert to ordinary Summer Time, so that on and from August 12th, your talk will go out at 12.15 p.m. BST.

Yours sincerely,
[Initialled] E.A.B
Eric Blair
Talks Producer
Indian Section

1243. To T. C. Worsley

23 June 1942   PP/EB

Dear Mr. Worsley,

I am writing to ask whether it would interest you to do a talk in one of our forthcoming series in the Eastern Service. These talks are in the form of short discussions between people with special knowledge of subjects of current interest. The one I hope you will undertake is on Education. I haven't yet selected the other speaker, but obviously we shall choose someone who is more disposed to defend the current educational system than you are. These broadcasts take about 13½ minutes, which means probably that your contribution would be in the neighbourhood of 750 words. The date of this broadcast would be September 11th, at 12.45 p.m. BST. This means that I should like to have the script by September 4th if possible. [If] you agree, I will make all the arrangements for the necessary meeting and discussion. Could you be kind enough to let me know as soon as possible whether this interests you?

Yours sincerely,
[Initialled] E.A.B
George Orwell
Talks Producer
Indian Section

1244. BBC Talks Booking Form, 24.6.42

K. K. Ardaschir: 'The Marriage of the Seas'; a talk on the Suez Canal; 13 minutes; recorded 23.6.42; broadcast 26.6.42; special fee, £10.10s to cover research work and all expenses. Signed: Z. A. Bokhari.

1245. BBC Talks Booking Form, 24.6.42

E. M. Forster: 'Some Books'; monthly talks on books; 13 minutes; broadcast 22.7.42, 19.8.42, 16.9.42, and 14.10.42; fee £21 each talk. Signed: Z. A. Bokhari.

1246. War-time Diary

<u>24.6.42</u>: *Listened-in last night to Lord Haw Haw—not Joyce,[1] who apparently has been off the air for some time, but a man who sounded to me like a South African, followed by another with more of a cockney voice. There was a good deal about the Congress of the Free India movement in Bangkok. Was amazed to notice that all the Indian names were mispronounced, and grossly mispronounced—eg. Ras Behari Bose[2] rendered as Rash Beery Bose. Yet after all the Indians who are broadcasting from Germany are available for advice on these points. They probably go in and out of the same building as Lord Haw Haw every day. It is rather encouraging to see this kind of slovenliness happening on the other side as well.*

1. For William Joyce, who broadcast from Berlin as 'Lord Haw Haw,' see *662, n. 1.*
2. For Ras Behari Bose, see *1081, n. 4.*

1247. To Mulk Raj Anand

25 June 1942   PP/EB

Dear Mulk,

I'm afraid I didn't tell you when you were here the other day that the last date for the Meet My Friend talks will be 22nd July, which means, I am afraid, that the talk by Andre van Gysegham°[1] will have to be the last in the series.[2]

I am getting in touch with the Contracts Department about the last three speakers, and they will receive their contracts in due course.

Yours sincerely,
George Orwell
Talks Producer
Indian Section

P.S. I find now that you haven't given me the addresses of any of these people, so I can't issue the contract slips. If you will let me know before I go away, or else tell Mr. Bokhari's secretary, then we can get on with the contracts.

1. André van Gyseghem (1906–), actor and producer, made his debut in 1927. He toured Scandinavia and the Baltic States, 1938, and took a special interest in the Russian theatre, writing *Theatre in Soviet Russia* (1943). He directed the India Demonstration at the London Coliseum, 31 January 1943, in which Narayana Menon, Krishna Menon, and J. B. S. Haldane participated.
2. The series was designed to consist of twelve talks; after the first six, three more names were put forward by Anand on 16 June 1942. Possibly the complaint about Sergeant Collett's script (see *1160, n. 1*), the left-wing political attitudes of some of those selected by Anand, and the rather idiosyncratic nature of his choices combined to make the series less than appealing to authority.

1248. To C. H. Waddington

25–26 (?) June 1942   PP/31

SHOULD BE GRATEFUL FOR FULLEST INFORMATION REGARDING ALL TITLES OF WORKS FROM WHICH YOU QUOTED IN YOUR RECORDING ON TWENTY-FOURTH° STOP SUGGEST YOU TELEPHONE REVERSED CHARGE

BLAIR BROADCASTS

1249. BBC Talks Booking Form, 26.6.42

Mulk Raj Anand: 'Meet My Friend,' 7–9; 'Last three in series of 13-minute discussions & interviews arranged by Mr. Anand, who will get the speakers and broadcast for about 6–7 minutes each week. (Last 3 talks)'; recorded 6, 13,[1] and 20.7.42; broadcast 8, 15, and 22.7.42; fee £10.10s each programme 'to cover contacting of speakers & preparation and broadcasting of part in discussion.' Signed: Z. A. Bokhari. Remarks: 'This series, originally intended to cover 12 talks, has been cut down to *9 only.*'

1. On 7 July, whilst Orwell was on holiday, Bokhari wrote to Dr. James Fisher, c/o Dr. Julian Huxley at the London Zoo, to make arrangements for recording and transmitting this discussion with Anand.

1250. BBC Talks Booking Form, 26.6.42

Clemence Dane: 'Women Generally Speaking'; two 12-minute talks, 1. Reading; 2. Reading (books recommended); broadcast 1 and 8.7.42; fee £15.15s each (altered from £8.8s; see *1177, n. 2*). Signed: Z. A. Bokhari.

1251. BBC Talks Booking Form, 26.6.42

André van Gyseghem:[1] 'Meet My Friend,' 8; recorded 13.7.42; broadcast 15.7.42; fee £6.6s. Signed: Z. A. Bokhari. This form is crossed through and marked 'Cancelled.'

1. Although the booking was cancelled, Orwell asked him to talk on *The Cherry Orchard*, 20.10.43.

1252. BBC Talks Booking Form, 26.6.42

Dr. Bhupen Mukerjee: 'The Music I Like'; the Luton Band in conjunction with Dr. Dennis Wright; script about 3 minutes; broadcast 27.6.42; fee £3.3s. Signed: Z. A. Bokhari.

1253. War-time Diary

<u>26.6.42</u>: *Everyone very defeatist after the Libya business.* [1] *Some of the papers going cold on the Second Front again. Tom Driberg* [2] *("William Hickey") wins the Malden by-election, scoring twice as many votes as the Conservative candidate. That makes 4 out of the last 6 elections that the Government has lost.*

1. The sudden fall of Tobruk to Rommel's forces on 21 June 1942, despite its having held out for eight months in 1941 before being relieved in December of that year. The loss was a blow to morale second only to the fall of Singapore. Twenty-five thousand troops were taken prisoner. For a brief account of what led to the splitting of the Eighth Army in a vain attempt to keep Tobruk, and Churchill's part in this, see Liddell Hart, *History of the Second World War*, 287; U.S.: 276; and for the retreat to El Alamein, fifty-five miles from Alexandria, see 287–303; U.S.: 276–91. Much blame fell on General Sir Claude Auchinleck (1884–1981), who was relieved of his command after Churchill visited Cairo, 4 August, though he was held in high esteem by Rommel, who thought he had handled his forces with considerable skill (Liddell Hart, 301–02; U.S.: 289). After the war he was given the thankless task of dividing the Indian Army between newly independent India and Pakistan. He did this so well that he was appointed commander of each army by the newly independent governments.
2. See *1025, n. 12.*

1254. Weekly News Review, 28

27 June 1942

Orwell began his annual leave after duty on this day—he is recorded as being away from Monday 29 June—and returned to work on Monday, 13 July. It is likely that he prepared this script, which has not been traced, before departing. PasB records, as usual, Weekly News Review read by Z. A. Bokhari and gives the timing as 13½ minutes. However, 'by Z. A. Bokhari' is the description given in PasB for the transmission on 4 and 11 July, when Orwell was fishing at

Callow End, Worcestershire. The probability is that Orwell wrote the script for 27 June but not those for 4 July (which have not survived) or 11 July (see *1267*, *headnote*). This illustrates again the problem posed by the phrase 'by Z. A. Bokhari.' It is taken to mean 'read by' when applied in the PasBs to the Weekly News Reviews; this can be demonstrated by occasional statements that a script was written by Orwell. See also *1268*. There is a degree of uncertainty here that cannot satisfactorily be resolved.

1255. Gujarati Newsletter, 18

29 June 1942

Orwell officially began his two weeks' leave on Monday, 29 June, though he would be free from about noon on the preceding Saturday at the latest. No script has been traced, but he is credited with writing the English version of this newsletter according to the talks booking form and also those for 6 and 13 July (the latter being the day he returned to duty). It is very unlikely that he wrote the two July newsletters, but he may have prepared that for 29 June before he left. According to the PasB, this is a little shorter than most Gujarati Newsletters. Its timing is given as 9' 25", whereas these newsletters usually ran (according to surviving timings) from 10 to 13 minutes. He may have hurriedly put it together based on what was available to him about Friday, 26 June. Though there can be no certainty, this newsletter is credited to Orwell; those for 6 and 13 July are not. See also Bengali Newsletter for 11 July 1942 (*1268*), for which Orwell was scheduled to write the English version.

1256. Z. A. Bokhari to L. F. Easterbrook and to Sir John Russell

30 June 1942

Whilst Orwell was on leave, Bokhari filled in for him, and these letters on Orwell's behalf are included in order to maintain the continuity of the arrangements Orwell initiated.

Dear Mr. Easterbrook
Thank you very much for your letter to Orwell dated the 28th June. He is on leave and I am looking after his office during his absence.

Sir John Russell cannot manage to broadcast on the 14th August. I have therefore written to him to suggest a date before the 14th August, when you could both record the talk, if the suggested date is convenient to you also. I have mentioned to him that Tuesdays and Thursdays are your best days. This means that the script will have to be prepared earlier than the 7th August. I hope it will not be too inconvenient for you to send us your script before that date. I shall let you know the exact date for the recording, when I hear from Sir John Russell. We are very grateful to you for your co-operation.

29 June 1942

Dear Sir John,
I am writing to you after five years. We met in India and then we travelled together on the good old Tuscania. I hope we shall meet again. George Orwell is on leave and during his absence, I am looking after his office.

I have received your letter of the 27th June, addressed to him. It will not be advisable to interrupt your leave. I wonder if you would care to record your talk before you go on leave. I will get in touch with Mr. Easterbrook and find out if the date which is convenient to you is also convenient to him. Easterbrook in a letter to us says that he is in London two or three times a week and Tuesdays and Thursdays are his best days. Perhaps you will kindly suggest a Tuesday or Thursday which will suit you for recording this talk, before you go on leave.

1257. Review of *The Sword and the Sickle* by Mulk Raj Anand

Horizon, July 1942

In this war we have one weapon which our enemies cannot use against us, and that is the English language. Several other languages are spoken by larger numbers of people, but there is no other that has any claim to be a world-wide *lingua franca*. The Japanese administrators in the Philippines, the Chinese delegates in India, the Indian nationalists in Berlin, are all obliged to do their business in English. Therefore, although Mr. Anand's novel would still be interesting on its own merits if it had been written by an Englishman, it is impossible to read it without remembering every few pages that it is also a cultural curiosity. The growth, especially during the last few years, of an English-language Indian literature is a strange phenomenon, and it will have its effect on the post-war world, if not on the outcome of the war itself.

This novel is a sequel to *The Village* and *Across the Black Waters*. The Sikh sepoy who has fought in France and spent years as a prisoner in Germany comes home to find himself—partly because he is suspected of disaffection and partly because that is the normal fate of all soldiers in all wars—cheated out of the reward that he had imagined that he was fighting for. The rest of the story deals mostly with the peasant movement and the beginnings of the Indian Communist Party. Now, any book about India written by an Indian must at this date almost unavoidably be the story of a grievance, and I notice that Mr. Anand has already got himself into trouble by what is wrongly described as his bitterness. In reality, the book's comparative lack of bitterness is a roundabout demonstration of the English 'bad conscience' towards India. In a novel on the same subject by an English intellectual, what would you expect to find? An endless masochistic denunciation of his own race, and a series of traditional caricatures of Anglo-Indian society, with its unbearable club life, its chota pegs,[1] etc., etc. In the scene as the Indian sees it, however, the English hardly enter. They are merely a permanent evil, something taken almost for granted, like the climate, and though the ultimate objective is to get rid of British rule, it is almost forgotten among the

379

weaknesses and internecine struggles of the revolutionaries themselves. European characters barely appear in the story—a reminder that in India only about one person in a thousand is technically white—and of the few that do it cannot be said that they are treated worse than the other characters. They are not treated sympathetically either, for on the whole the characterization is harsh and derisive (to give just one example, Mr. Gandhi's head is described as resembling 'a raw purple turnip'), and the whole book is full of the Indian melancholy and of the horribly ugly, degrading scenes which offend one's eyes all the time in the starved countries of the East. Although it ends on a comparatively hopeful note this novel does not break the rule that books about India are depressing. Probably they must be so, quite apart from the question-mark they raise in the English conscience, because while the world remains in anything like its present shape the central problem of India, its poverty, is not soluble. How much of the special atmosphere of English-language Indian literature is due to its subject-matter is uncertain, but in reading Mr. Anand's work, or that of Ahmed Ali[2] and several others, it is difficult not to feel that by this time another dialect, comparable perhaps to Irish-English, has grown up. One quotation will do to illustrate this:

'Conscious of his responsibility for the misadventures into which he had led them, Lalu bent down and strained to lever the dead bodies with trembling hands. A sharp odour of decomposing flesh shot up to his nostrils from Chandra's body, while his hands were smeared with blood from Nandu's neck. He sat up imagining the smell to be a whiff of the foul virulence of bacterial decay, ensuing from the vegetation of the forest through which they had come. But, as he bent down again, there was no disguising the stink of the corpse. And, in a flash, he realized that though Nandu's blood was hot now, it would soon be cold and the body would stink if it was carried all the way to Allahabad.'

There is a vaguely unEnglish flavour about this ('shot up to his nostrils', for instance, is not quite an English idiom), and yet it is obviously the work of a man who is not only at ease with the English language but thinks in it and would probably write in it by preference. This raises the question of the future, if any, of English-language Indian literature. At present English is to a great extent the official and business language of India: five million Indians are literate in it and millions more speak a debased version of it; there is a huge English-language Indian Press, and the only English magazine devoted wholly to poetry is edited by Indians. On average, too, Indians write and even pronounce English far better than any European race. Will this state of affairs continue? It is inconceivable that the present relationship between the two countries will last much longer, and when it vanishes the economic inducements for learning English will also tend to disappear. Presumably, therefore, the fate of the English language in Asia is either to fade out or to survive as a pidgin language useful for business and technical purposes. It might survive, in dialect form, as the mother-tongue of the small Eurasian community, but it is difficult to believe that it has a literary future. Mr. Anand and Ahmed Ali are much better writers than the average run of English novelists, but they are not likely to have many successors. Why, then, is it that their books have at this moment an importance that goes beyond their literary merit? Partly because they are interpreting Asia to the West, but more, I think, because they act as a Westernizing influence among their own countrymen. And at present there are reasons why the second function is more important than the first.

Anyone who has to deal in propaganda knows that a sudden change came over the Indian scene as soon as Japan entered the war. Many, perhaps most, Indian intellectuals are emotionally pro-Japanese. From their point of view Britain is the enemy, China means nothing to them, Russia is an object of lip-service only. But is it the case that the Indian anti-British intelligentsia actually wishes to see China permanently enslaved, the Soviet Union destroyed, Europe a Nazi concentration camp? No, that is not fair either: it is merely that the nationalism of defeated peoples is necessarily revengeful and short-sighted. If you discuss this question with an Indian you get an answer something like this: 'Half of me is a Socialist but the other half is a Nationalist. I know what Fascism means, I know very well that I ought to be on your side, but I hate your people so much that if we can get rid of them I hardly care what happens afterwards. I tell you that there are moments when all I want is to see China, Japan and India get together and destroy Western civilization, not only in Asia, but in Europe.' This outlook is widespread among the coloured peoples. Its emotional roots are obvious enough, the various disguises in which it is wrapped are easily seen through, but it is there, and it contains a great danger, to us and to the world. The only answer to the self-pity and race-hatred common among Indians is to point out that others besides Indians are oppressed. The only answer to nationalism is international Socialism, and the contact of Indians—to a lesser extent, of all Asiatics— with Socialist literature and Socialist thought generally is through the English language. As a general rule, Indians are reliably anti-Fascist in proportion as they are Westernized. That is why at the beginning of this review I described the English language as a weapon of war. It is a funnel for ideas deadly to the Fascist view of life. Mr. Anand does not like us very much, and some of his colleagues hate us very bitterly; but so long as they voice their hatred in English they are in a species of alliance with us, and an ultimate decent settlement with the Indians whom we have wronged but also helped to awaken remains possible.[3]

1. Whisky or brandy with soda; 'chota' is Hindi for 'small'; 'peg' is English for 'measure.'
2. For Ahmed Ali, see *1103, n. 3*.
3. In a letter to Ian Angus (14.9.96) Anand said Orwell 'took it upon himself' to review this book 'and almost forced it on Cyril Connolly.' See *1189*.

1258. War-time Diary

<u>1.7.42</u>: *At Callow End, Worcs. (staying on a farm). No noise except aero-planes, birds and the mowers cutting the hay. No mention of the war except with reference to the* [1] *Italian prisoners, who are working on some of the farms. They seem to be considered good workers and for fruit-picking are*

preferred to the town people who come out from Worcester and are described as "artful". In spite of the feeding difficulties, plenty of pigs, poultry, geese and turkeys about. Cream for every meal at this place.[2]

ᶦHuge bombers flying overhead all day. Also aeroplanes doing extraordinary things, eg. towing other planes by a wire (perhaps gliders?) or carrying smaller planes perched on their backs.ᶦ

1. *to the*] to
2. Although some cream-making was permitted for sale locally, production on the normal scale and general distribution were stopped to conserve resources.

1259. BBC Talks Booking Form, 3.7.42

C. D. Darlington: 'A.D. 2000,' 3, 'India in the Steel Age'; industrialisation of India; 20-minute talk; recorded 7.7.42; broadcast 10.7.42; fee £10.10s. Signed: Z. A. Bokhari.[1]

1. Although this was said to emanate from Orwell, it was prepared after he had gone on leave. On 1 July, Bokhari wrote to Darlington, explaining that he was 'looking after his [Orwell's] office,' and suggesting that whilst Darlington was at the studio on 7 July to broadcast live his talk on 'The Future of Science' it might be convenient to record his 'A.D. 2000' talk—but see *1220.*

1260. BBC Talks Booking Form, 3.7.42

Bahadur Singh: 'These Names Will Live'; Lindsay, Master of Balliol; broadcast 14.7.42; fee £8.8s + 13s 2d fare. Signed: Z. A. Bokhari.[1]

1. This also was said to have been initiated by Orwell. On 4 July, Bokhari wrote to Singh reminding him of the arrangements.

1261. War-time Diary

3.7.42:   *Vote of censure defeated 475–25. This figure means that there were very few abstentions. The same trick as usual—the debate twisted into a demand for a vote of confidence in Churchill himself, which has to be given, since there is no one to take Churchill's place. Things are made much easier for the government by the obvious bad motives of some of its chief attackers, eg. Hore-Belisha.*[1] *I don't know how much longer this comedy can go on, but not much longer.*

No reference to the second front in Churchill's speech.

The Japanese are evidently going to attack Russia fairly soon. They appear to be firmly lodged in the outer Aleutians, which can't have any meaning except as a move to cut communications between Russia and the USA.

The pinks are panicking to an extent they haven't equalled since Dunkirk. The New Statesman's leading article is headed "Facing the Spectre". They take the loss of Egypt for granted. Heaven knows whether this will actually happen, but these people have prophecied° the loss of Egypt so often before that their doing so again is almost enough to persuade one that it won't happen. It is curious how they always do what the Germans want them to do—eg., for some time past, demanding that we stop the raids on Germany and send our bombers to Egypt. A little earlier we were to send our bombers to India. In each case the same move as was being demanded by the German "freedom" stations. A thing that strikes one also is the airy disdain with which all the pinks talk of our air raids on Germany—air raids make very little impression, etc., etc. And these are the people who squealed loudest during the blitz on London.

4.7.42: *Everyone seems stupefied by Wardlaw-Milne's[2] suggestion* ⌈in the speech moving the vote of censure,⌉ *that the Duke of Gloucester should be made Commander-in-Chief. The most likely explanation is that Gloucester was intended to act as dummy for somebody else* ⌈(Possibly Mountbatten?)⌉ *Even so one could hardly imagine a worse figurehead than this fat mental defective.*

Pubs in this village shut quite a lot of the time for lack of beer. Possibly only due to the recent spell of hot weather. This is a hop area and I find the farmers have been asked not to cut down their acreage of hops,[3] indeed some have increased it. All these hops go for beer, at least all the high-grade ones.

10.7.42: *A day or two ago a couple of lorries belonging to the Navy arrived with a party of Wrens[4] and sailors who put in several hours work weeding out the turnips in Mr. Phillips's[5] field. All the village women delighted by the appearance of the sailors in their blue trousers and white singlets. "Don't they look clean, like! I like sailors. They always look so clean".* ⌈The sailors and Wrens also seemed to enjoy their outing and drinks in the pub afterwards. It appeared that they belonged to some volunteer organisation which sends workers out as they are needed.⌉ *Mrs Phillips explains it: "It's the voluntary organisation from Malvern.[6] Sometimes it's A.Ts[7] they send and sometimes[8] sailors. Of course we like having them. Well, it makes you a bit independent of your own work-people, you see. The work-people, they're awful nowadays. Just do so much and no more.* ⌈They know you can't do without them, you see. And you can't get a woman to do a bit indoors nowadays. The girls won't stay here, with no picture-house in the village. I do have a woman who comes in, but I can't get any work out of her.⌉ *It helps a bit when you get a few voluntary workers. Makes you more independent, like".*

How right and proper it all is ⌈when you consider how necessary it is that agricultural work should not be neglected, and how right and proper also that town people should get a bit of contact with the soil.⌉ *Yet these voluntary organisations, plus the work done by soldiers in the[9] hay-making etc., and the[10] Italian prisoners, are simply blackleg labour.*

The Government wins at Salisbury. Hipwell, the editor of "Reveille",[11] was the Independent candidate. Wherever this mountebank stands the Government wins automatically. How grateful they must be to him, if indeed they aren't actually paying him to do it.

The "Blue Bell" again shut for lack of beer. Quite serious boozing for 4 or

5 days of the week, then drought. [Sometimes, however, when they are shut the local officers are to be seen drinking in a private room, the common soldiers as well as the labourers being shut out. The "Red Lion" in the next village, goes on a different system which the proprietor explains to me: "I don't hold with giving it all to the summer visitors. If beer's short, let the locals come first, I say. A lot of days I keep the pub door shut, and then only the locals know the way in at the back. A man that's working in the fields needs his beer, 'specially with the food they got to eat nowadays. But I rations 'em. I says to 'em, 'Now look here, you want your beer regular, don't you? Wouldn't you rather have a pint with your dinner every day than four pints one day and three the next?' Same with the soldiers. I don't like to refuse beer to a soldier, but I only lets 'em have a pint their first drink. After that it's 'Half pints only, boys'. Like that it gets shared out a bit."[1]

1. Leslie Hore-Belisha was Secretary of State for War, 1937–40; an Independent M.P., 1942–45. Chamberlain appointed him Secretary for War in 1937, but dismissed him in 1940. Churchill did not give him a place in his government, and he remained out of office throughout the war. For his earlier career, see *556, 19.7.39, n. 1.*
2. Sir John Wardlaw-Milne (1879–1967) was Unionist M.P. for Kidderminster, 1922–45; Chairman of House of Commons Select Committee on National Expenditure, and author of pamphlets on financial matters. He was strongly opposed to Churchill and moved the vote of censure in which he made this proposal. As Churchill put it, 'This proved injurious to his case.' See *The Second World War*, IV, 356–66; U.S.: *The Hinge of Fate*, 397, for the debate and Wardlaw-Milne's proposal in particular.
3. Orwell mistakenly typed 'hope.'
4. Women's Royal Naval Service.
5. Presumably the farmer at whose farm Orwell was staying. There is no indication as to whether Eileen was able to get leave at the same time as her husband.
6. Malvern, far inland, might seem an unlikely setting for a naval establishment, but a radar research base and an initial training unit were sited there.
7. Auxiliary Territorial Service, the women's army service, now the WRAC, Women's Royal Army Corps.
8. *sometimes*] sometimes it's
9. *in the*] in
10. *and the*] and
11. W. R. Hipwell.

1262. Fishing

On the verso of the penultimate page of Volume III of the War-time Diary, facing 11 and 15 October 1942, is a list of what Orwell had caught when fishing on a farm at Callow End, Worcestershire, during his leave from the BBC. Days of the week have been added.

Sunday	28.6.42	2 dace
	29.6.42	1 dace
	30.6.42	1 dace, 2 eels
Wednesday	1.7.42	—
	2.7.42	4 dace (roach?)

	3.7.42	1 dace
	4.7.42	2 dace
Sunday	5.7.42	—
	6.7.42	—
	7.7.42	1 dace
Wednesday	8.7.42	—
	9.7.42	5 dace, 1 perch
	10.7.42	—
Saturday	11.7.42	1 dace

1263. News Review, 29

4 July 1942

No script has been traced. PasB has 'News Review by Z. A. Bokhari.' Since Orwell was away in Worcestershire on holiday, it is extremely unlikely he wrote this script, and it is not credited to him. See *1256* and *1268*.

1264. Z. A. Bokhari to L. F. Easterbrook and to Sir John Russell

4 July 1942

Dear Mr. Easterbrook
We have had a message from Sir John Russell to the effect that he will be in London on Tuesday next, 7th July and he would very much like to have a preliminary discussion with you if you can conveniently manage it. I suggest that you should meet in my office (Room 322 at 200 Oxford Street, W.1.—not far from Oxford Circus) at 2.45 p.m. on that day, when you will be able to discuss your joint talk on "Agriculture" in our series "I'd Like It Explained". I do hope this appointment will be convenient to you.

Sir John Russell also suggests recording your discussion together on the following Tuesday, 14th July, sometime during the morning, but I think we shall be able to arrange that more easily after the preliminary discussion and while you are at 200 Oxford Street.

Dear Sir John,
Thank you very much for your telephone message. We have written to Mr. Easterbrook, suggesting that you and he should meet in my office (Room 322, at 200 Oxford Street, W.1.) on Tuesday, 7th July, at 2.45 p.m. We have informed your Secretary at the Ministry of Information of this appointment, and as far as she knows, the time is convenient to you.

With regard to your suggestion for recording your discussion with Mr. F. Easterbrook on Tuesday, 14th July, I think we might leave the arrangements for this recording till we meet together on Tuesday next, 7th July.

1265. Gujarati Newsletter, 19

6 July 1942

No script has been traced. PasB gives the timing as 13′ 20″. Since Orwell was on holiday in Worcestershire, it is extremely improbable that he wrote the English version, and it is not credited to him here despite the statement made on the relevant talks booking form; see *1256*.

1266. Z. A. Bokhari to Princess Indira of Kapurthala, J. Bahadur Singh, Noel Sircar, Shridhar Telkar

9 July 1942

Except for the booking dates, the same letter was sent to each news reader. Princess Indira was booked for 22 August, Singh for 8 August and 5 September, Sircar for 15 August and 12 September, Telkar for 1 and 29 August. Talks booking forms were issued for each person on 9 July; these included the statement (varied as appropriate): 'Mr B. Singh is one of the 4 Indians we have asked to *read* this weekly News Review, in turn. (It is written by E. Blair).' A fee of £3. 3s was offered for each broadcast.

In the event, Princess Indira did not read on 22 August, nor, so far as can be ascertained, on any other occasion; her place was taken by Homi Bode. The letter reproduced is that to Bahadur Singh:

I understand that Mr. Blair has already approached you about our idea of having a different speaker to present our weekly News Review in English in our programme "Through Eastern Eyes", and I understand that you are willing to help us in this matter.

The News Review is written by Eric Blair and is usually ready (except for last minute alterations) on Fridays during the afternoon. The time of the broadcast is 1115–1130 GMT on Saturdays. We shall be grateful if you can undertake to present this News Review for us on these Saturdays, 8th August and 5th September at 1115 GMT. No doubt it will be possible for you to see Mr. Blair sometime during the morning on Saturday to discuss and rehearse.

1267. News Review, 30

11 July 1942

A script for this broadcast survives. There are very slight manuscript changes; it bears both censorship stamps, the censor being Bokhari; it is marked 'As B'cast,' but the hand in which this is written is not Orwell's. Two things suggest that this broadcast, like News Review 20, for 2.5.42 (see *1131*), was not written by Orwell: his whereabouts at the time and characteristics of its presentation.

On 11 July, Orwell was staying on a farm at Callow End in Worcestershire, where he had been since 1 July. He recorded when he went fishing—every day from 28 June to 11 July inclusive—and on the 11th he caught a dace; see *1262*.

The typescript shows characteristics not found in scripts associated with Orwell. Until the last page, all personal and place names are typed in capitals (here, in capitals and small capitals)—even such obvious ones as Egypt and Don; the paragraphs are much shorter on average than those in commentaries that can definitely be shown to be Orwell's: there are twenty-one as compared with eight in the broadcast for the following Saturday. The typing is that of a competent amateur—presumably the scriptwriter and the style is certainly not Orwell's. This newsletter is not, therefore, included among those credited to Orwell. It is reproduced for comparison. PasB has 'Weekly News Review by Z. A. Bokhari' and gives the timing as 13′ 30″. See also *1254*.

During this week the two great German offensives in RUSSIA and AFRICA have continued. As you know, the long-term strategical aim of the Germans is to drive through, by a vast pincer movement, to the Oil of Iraq and the Caucasus, and from there to join forces with the Japanese. The essential thing for us is that this drive should be held, and if we do that we need not grudge temporary losses of territory, and may look with confidence to the future.

For the last four days, there has been a lull in the fighting in EGYPT. It is now over. The battle has flared up again at the northern end of our defence line, about seventy miles west of ALEXANDRIA. The new flare-up follows an intensified day and night offensive by the Royal Air Force. Only two nights ago, our heavy bombers started an assault on great masses of Axis transport on the road to the front. The attacks went on all day, and British front-line soldiers said that the ground in front of them was sometimes obscured by bomb explosions.

After the first rush of the German tank columns had been halted, there was ground for hope that we might launch a powerful counter-offensive immediately. The German forces were extremely exhausted and their lengthened supply lines were not working smoothly. However, our own losses had also been great, and the four days had to elapse; it may be that the Germans have had time for recuperation and reinforcement. Meanwhile, though we have great stores of arms in EGYPT and the Middle East, the reinforcements of those stores is necessarily a slow process. In that sense the German supply-lines there in EGYPT are shorter than ours.

One very encouraging feature of the war in EGYPT has been the firm behaviour of the Egyptian people and their leaders. There has been no panic; the country is united under its natural leader[1] and the people are said to be treating the German propaganda, especially the leaflets which are scattered from aeroplanes, with contempt; and meanwhile strong measures have been taken against war profiteers. The struggle for EGYPT will be carried on with determination by the Egyptian people as well as by the Allied Armies.

In Russia the Germans have launched two new offensives, well to the north of the tremendous battle still raging along the middle reaches of the DON. One is about a hundred-and-forty miles south-east of KHARKOV, where the Germans have advanced sixty miles to the east since they captured IZYUM last month. The other is forty-five miles south of ROSS-OSH,° on the

387

main MOSCOW–CAUCASUS railway, from which the Russians have already had to withdraw. Meanwhile, the heavy German offensive against VORONEZH, over one hundred miles to the north, is still going on. Moscow radio says the fighting there is becoming even more intense, and that on Friday morning an important position held by the Germans was recaptured. London papers emphasize the threat of this heavy German offensive and the need to send further supplies to Russia; the British as a whole feel the greatest admiration for the courageous resistance of the Russians. The most serious strategical effect of the drive is the Russian loss of their main railway from the Caucasus to Moscow.

The attack on the DON can no longer be viewed in isolation from the rest of the Soviet front. The immediate objective is undoubtedly the cutting-off of the Southern Army. Already the situation in which TIMOSHENKO[2] find[s] himself in relation to the rest of the front is serious. The Germans are trying to rupture his direct communication with the north, and they seem determined to leave him no alternative route.

The Soviet announcement of the evacuation of ROSSOSH is significant. This town lies one hundred miles to the south of VORONEZH. A week ago the German forces were still at VOLCHANSK, a hundred miles to the west. The rapidity of the Nazi advance indicates a general Soviet withdrawal along this stretch of the DON. The strategic sacrifice of this territory is serious because from ROSSOSH ran a lateral railway line to the east and connected with the Moscow railway.

This was one of the many strategic lines built in recent years and is not marked on most maps. But now it, too, has passed under German control. The fact that the mass of the German armies is still on the western bank of the DON is not an insuperable difficulty, for von BOCK;[3] the river in these regions is not very wide,[4] and at this time of the year is shallow and easily crossed.

The real problem for the Soviet Supreme Command is to anticipate the direction of the German attack. The general opinion, of course, is the CAUCASUS, oil and the Middle East. But there are equally strong indications that what Hitler needs as much as oil is a quick political as well as military victory over the Soviet Union.

It would be dangerous to overlook the sudden switching northward of von BOCK's armies in a great enveloping movement to the rear of Moscow, while the frontal attack which is already under way is pressed from the KALININ-RZEV district.

Midway between VORONEZH and ROSSOSH the railway from KHARKOV and KUPYANSK crosses the DON and runs first east, and then north-east. Just over a hundred miles from the DON it cuts the first important Moscow line and about seventy miles further, the second running south-east.

These are not the immediate possibilities but the undoubted possible developments of the war. TIMOSHENKO's forces are fighting back here and maintaining their positions there. But this is modern fluid war and once a point of the Soviet defence is penetrated, we must be prepared to see the Nazis using every possible means to widen the gap.

Further information has been coming in about the behaviour of the

Japanese in territories they have over-run. The Japanese in JAVA are trying to blame the Dutch for the famine which they are expecting because of Japanese robbery and maladministration. In fact the Dutch never destroyed any stocks of food destined for internal consumption in the islands. The island of AMBOYNA, for example, is not self-supporting and had large stocks of rice; these were confiscated by the Japanese. TOKYO radio has made an urgent appeal for 30,000 Japanese to go to the Dutch East Indies for administration; the Dutch had only about half as many Europeans in their Civil Service. All small businesses in Japan, the Berlin radio said, are to be liquidated, and their owners employed in industries in the newly-acquired territories. These are clearly to put the Javanese traders out of business. Furthermore, Japanese peasants and fishermen are being slipped[5] over in large numbers. All JAVANESE fishing boats have been requisitioned by the JAPANESE, who have re-started fishing under strict government control. The population of JAVA is nearly eight hundred to the square mile. It is obvious that the JAVANESE must expect fearful hardships if the JAPANESE occupation continues. Meanwhile all INDONESIAN political organisations in JAVA have been abolished by JAPANESE decree; all must collaborate with the military authorities.

In NEW GUINEA, a Japanese proclamation demands that "all and everyone must bow their heads whenever they see Japanese soldiers." They must learn JAPANESE. All property has been "frozen". They must not write letters or listen to the wireless.

The JAPANESE are behaving fairly well in BURMA, because they expect soon to have to fight for BURMA and are anxious not to be much hated there. They are chiefly concerned to make the BURMANS hate and suspect the Indians and the Chinese, the Shan tribes[6] in the north hate and suspect the Chinese and the Burmans, the Thailanders hate and suspect the Burmans and the Chinese. Such is the JAPANESE plan for speedy peace and freedom in Asia.

You can now get news of the campaign as it develops direct from RUSSIA, as the Russians are broadcasting to India themselves.

Let us turn to the fighting in China.

Chungking reports that in Kiangsi the Japanese thrusts from the capital have been thrown back. The Chinese claim to have encircled 30,000 Japanese troops. Further east, in Chekiang, reinforced Japanese troops are advancing towards the port of Wenchow. Far to the north west of this fighting, in the mountains between Shanshi and Honan provinces, the Japanese are said to be withdrawing towards the bases from which they launched their offensive last month. The Chinese say that the battle is in its closing stages, and has been a defeat for the Japanese.

Thus heavy fighting is still going on in China, mainly in the Eastern provinces where the Japanese are afraid that airfields might be used to bomb Japan. The Japanese may also still hope to exhaust the Chinese by keeping up a considerable strain; it is known that most of the Japanese armies are still in China.

In this week, as you know, occurred the anniversary of the start of the Sino Japanese war. China has now entered her sixth year of determined and successful resistance to aggression, and she calls the anniversary Reconstruction Day. There were great celebrations in England; not only the official meetings for speeches by the Chinese Ambassador and other distinguished speakers; all over the country the mayors of urban and district councils have called meetings to honour the Chinese resistance and collect gifts for the China Fund. The determination of CHINA has excited great admiration in England.

Today all the 42-year-old women of Britain are registering for National Service. Many of them are married women with children and many will only be asked to undertake part-time war work near their homes. Over eight million women have now been registered for service in England and from 15,000 to 20,000 a week are being transferred to Women's Services or to war work. Britain is determined to resist the aggression to the end.

1. Farouk I (1920–1965), King of Egypt, 1936–52. His reign was marked by corruption, and opposition to him increased sharply after Egypt's defeat by Israel, 1948–49. This led to his overthrow by Gamal Abdul Nasser in July 1952; he was forced to abdicate in favour of his infant son. Egypt was declared a republic in June 1953.
2. Semën Konstantinovich Timoshenko (1895–1970) was born a peasant, served in the ranks of the Tsar's army in World War I, commanded a Red Army cavalry division against White Russian forces in Poland and southern Russia, and commanded an army group in the war against Finland, 1939–40. Later he had the task of stopping the Germans before Moscow, and then replaced Marshal Budënny on the South-Western Front, where he was unable to prevent the German advance into the Crimea. On 12 July 1942 the Soviets established the 'Stalingrad Front' under his command. He was a stern disciplinarian and the only pre-war marshal to retain authority throughout the war. See also 1226.
3. Fedor von Bock (1880–1945), German Field-Marshal, had served with outstanding bravery in World War I and commanded German forces invading Poland, Holland, Belgium, and France, 1939–40, and Army Group Centre in the attack on Russia in 1941. He was removed from command in December 1941 when affected by physical and mental exhaustion, but succeeded Field-Marshal Rundstedt as commander of Army Group South from January to July 1942. He was killed during an Allied air raid in Schleswig-Holstein in the closing stages of the war.
4. not very wide] not much wider than the Thames in London; *handwritten alteration (not by Orwell)*
5. Possibly 'shipped' was intended.
6. tribes] tubes *in typescript*

1268. Bengali Newsletter

11 July 1942

A talks booking form survives for 27 June 1942, initiated by Bokhari, which states that S. K. Das Gupta was commissioned to translate and read the Bengali Newsletter for Saturday, 11 July at 4.30 DBST, and that this would be written by 'Eric Blair, Indian Section.' Blair's name has been crossed through, however, and Z. A. Bokhari written over it (by Bokhari). Orwell was on holiday; see 1254.

Two letters from Bokhari to Das Gupta, 27 June and 8 July 1942, fill in some minor details. The English version was to be ready at 200 Oxford Street at any time after 10:30 A.M. on the Saturday of the broadcast, 'but I dare say you will not want to come here quite as early as that.' The translation should be begun at once, but 'You can always go away between finishing the translation, timing it—and actually broadcasting it at 3.45 DBST.' On 8 July, Bokhari gives a time three-quarters of an hour in advance of that given earlier. The transmission was from 200 Oxford Street.

What is unclear is the extent to which Orwell was involved in preparing English versions for translation into Bengali before this date. He certainly prepared such versions from 18 July 1942 to at least 16 January 1943.

1269. To *Picture Post*

11 July 1942

On 27 June 1942, *Picture Post* published 'the first article in an important new series,' 'Britain's Silent Revolution' by J. B. Priestley. The series asked 'What is happening in Britain? What kind of a country is being shaped by the war?' At the head of Priestley's article was this statement in bold type: 'We are threatened with decay—but the war has saved us. Some of the old are uprooted; some of the new blessings are steadily growing. Here is our great chance to fashion a really healthy society.' On 4 July, Vernon Bartlett, M.P., wrote on 'The Revolt Against Party Politics' and on 11 July, a column was run, 'What They Say About Bartlett and Priestley.' Two letters were printed in response to Priestley's article, one from the Bishop of Bradford and one from George Orwell:

I am in agreement with Mr. Priestley as to the general direction in which our society is moving, but do not share his apparent belief that things will *inevitably* happen fast enough to prevent the old gang getting their claws into us again. Two years ago I would have echoed his optimistic utterances more confidently than I would now. At that time an appalling disaster had brought this country to what looked like the first stage of revolution, and one could be excused for believing that class privilege and economic inequality would quite rapidly disappear under the pressure of danger. Obviously this has failed to happen. But I do agree with Mr. Priestley that the sort of society we knew before 1939 is not likely to return. I don't share the belief which some people still seem to hold, that "this is a capitalist war," and that if we win it we shall simply see the British ruling class in power again. What I should like to hear about in Mr. Priestley's next article is not "What?" but "How?"—just *how* we are to set about getting the truly democratic society we want.

George Orwell, Abbey Road, NW 8.

1270. Pacifism and the War: A Controversy. By D. S. Savage, George Woodcock, Alex Comfort, George Orwell

Partisan Review, September–October 1942. Orwell's contribution is dated 12 July 1942

D. S. Savage:[1]

A few brief comments on George Orwell's March–April *London Letter*. [See *913*.]

It is fashionable nowadays to equate Fascism with Germany. We must fight Fascism, therefore we must fight Germany. Thus Mr. Orwell, "the greater part of the very young intelligentsia . . . don't feel the horror of Fascism that we who are somewhat older feel," also, "there is no real answer to the charge that pacifism is objectively pro-Fascist." *Answer:* Fascism is not a force confined to any one nation. We can just as soon get it here as anywhere else. The characteristic markings of Fascism are, curtailment of individual and minority liberties; abolition of private life and private values and substitution of State life and public values (patriotism); external imposition of discipline (militarism); prevalence of mass-values and mass-mentality; falsification of intellectual activity under State pressure. These are all tendencies of present-day Britain. The pacifist opposes every one of these, and might therefore be called the *only genuine* opponent of Fascism.

Don't let us be misled by *names*. Fascism is quite capable of calling itself Democracy or even Socialism. It's the reality under the name that matters. War demands totalitarian organization of society. Germany organized herself on that basis prior to embarking on war. Britain now finds herself compelled to take the same measures after involvement in war. Germans call it National Socialism. We call it Democracy. The result is the same.

Let us assume that Mr. Orwell means "objectively pro-German." (If so, his loose terminology is surely indicative of very loose thinking.) Who is "objective"?—Mr. Orwell, a partisan of one particular side in the struggle? According to this type of reasoning, a German or Japanese pacifist would be "objectively pro-British." This is puerile. Mr. Orwell is assuming that the pacifist shares his chauvinistic predilections. On the contrary, we regard the war as a disaster to humanity. Who is to say that a British victory will be less disastrous than a German one? The last British victory was pretty meaningless.

Mr. Orwell, in all his recent writings on the subject, shows a total inability to grasp the real nature of pacifism. Let me try, in a few words, to enlighten him.

Mr. Orwell is himself a "politician," with a politician's outlook on things. He consequently sees pacifism primarily as a political phenomenon. That is just what it isn't. Primarily it is a moral phenomenon. Political movements are based on programme and organization. With pacifism, programme and organization are quite subsidiary. Pacifism springs from conscience—i.e., from within the individual human being. "*Peace News*," says Orwell, "follows its old tradition of opposing war for different and incompatible reasons." There are certainly innumerable reasons why war should be opposed, but the chief reason is the diabolical nature of modern warfare, with its diabolical repercussions upon human personality and values. I am not referring only to the act of warfare itself, but the whole complex of events which is war. The corruption and hollowness revealed in the prosecution of this war are too contemptible for words. Certainly I will accept my share of responsibility for them, but I won't fight in a war to *extend* that corruption and hollowness.

Perhaps I ought to try and give expression to what many of us pacifists feel about Germany in relation to ourselves, since Mr. Orwell brings up this point. Needless to say, we have no love for Fascism, and our entire attitude is one of personal resistance to all forms of Fascism, as they impinge upon us in concrete form. (Whereas Orwell swallows the concrete encroachments and waves his arms at a distant bogey.) Not only will we not fight, nor lend a hand with the war, but the "intellectuals" among us would scorn to mentally compromise themselves with the Government. Orwell dislikes the French intellectuals licking up Hitler's crumbs, but what's the difference between them and our intellectuals who are licking up Churchill's? However: we [who] "don't believe in any 'defence of democracy,' are inclined to prefer Germany to Britain, and don't feel the horror of Fascism that we who are somewhat older feel." I can only speak for myself, of course, but surely the 'defence of democracy' is best served by defending one's own concrete liberties, not by equating democracy with Britain, and allowing all democracy to be destroyed in order that we may fight better—for "Britain"; and Orwell should not need to be told what, or who, "Britain" now is.

I am not greatly taken in by Britain's "democracy," particularly as it is gradually vanishing under the pressure of the war. Certainly I would never fight and kill for such a phantasm. I do not greatly admire the part "my country" has played in world events. I consider that spiritually Britain has lost all meaning; she once stood for something, perhaps, but who can pretend that the *idea* of "Britain" now counts for anything in the world? This is not cynicism. I feel identified with my country in a deep sense, and want her to regain her meaning, her soul, if that be possible: but the unloading of a billion tons of bombs on Germany won't help this forward an inch. The pretence exists in some quarters that, although Britain has been a sick nation, now, engaged in war, she has "found her soul," and by this one gathers that the sickness was exemplified by Chamberlain and the soul-finding by Churchill. Unfortunately, deep changes do not occur so easily as that. England does not even know what she is fighting for, only what she is fighting against. The pacifists' "championing" of Hitler referred to by Orwell is simply a recognition by us that Hitler and Germany contain a real historical dynamic, whereas we do not. Whereas the rest of the nation is content with calling down obloquy on Hitler's head, we regard this as superficial. Hitler requires, not condemnation, but understanding. This does not mean that we like, or defend him. Personally I do not care for Hitler. He is, however, "realler" than Chamberlain,

Churchill, Cripps, etc., in that he is the vehicle of raw historical forces, whereas they are stuffed dummies, waxwork figures, living in unreality. We do not desire a German "victory"; we would not lift a finger to help either Britain or Germany to "win"; but there would be a profound justice, I feel, however terrible, in a German victory. (In actuality, any ruler would find us rather awkward customers, one no less than another.)

Now, how about Mr. Orwell's own position, and the position of people like him? I would ask him to consider, first, the company he keeps. Who are his leaders? What is the actual social system which he is fighting to defend? What hopes has he of diverting the stream of history the way *he* wants it to go? Brave words and muddled thinking cannot disguise the fact that Mr. Orwell, like all the other supporters of the war, shipping magnates, coal owners, proletarians, university professors, Sunday journalists, Trade Union leaders, Church dignitaries, scoundrels and honest men, is being swept along by history, not directing it. Like them, he will be deposited, along with other detritus, where history decides, not where he thinks. Mr. Orwell is, I believe, a man of integrity, an honest man. But that does not make up for his superficiality. And can we afford superficiality, at any time, still less times like these?

May 11, 1942
Dry Drayton, England

George Woodcock:[2]

I hope you will allow me to comment in your columns on certain references in George Orwell's London Letter to the review *Now*, of which I am editor.

Orwell suggests that this paper has a Fascist tendency, and names two of its contributors, Hugh Ross Williamson and the Duke of Bedford,[3] to prove his case. In fact, *Now* was established early in the war as a review for publishing literary matter and also as a forum for controversial writing which could not readily find publication under wartime conditions. Not all the writers were opposed to the war, and of the fifty odd contributors to the seven numbers only two, those named by Orwell, were even reputed to have Fascist tendencies. Neither of these men contributed more than one article to the review. The remaining writers included anarchists, Stalinists, Trotskyists, pacifists and New Statesman moderates. Julian Huxley and Herbert Read, two of its best-known contributors, can hardly be accused of Fascism!

The reference to the article by Julian Symons is, in my opinion, unjust. Orwell gives no idea of its subject and does not quote a single sentence to prove his assertion that it is "vaguely Fascist"! No one in England, except Orwell and possibly the Stalinists, would think of suggesting that Julian Symons has any Fascist tendencies. On the contrary, he has been consistently anti-Fascist, and the article mentioned, which attacks *Now's* former lack of a definite political line, is Marxist in tendency.

I do not propose to defend Hugh Ross Williamson or the Duke of Bedford—although I would mention that neither of them belonged to the B.U.F. and that the People's Party, although it may have contained former

Fascists, was not a Fascist party and contained many honest pacifists and socialists, like Ben Green, whose wrongful imprisonment and maltreatment in gaol caused a major scandal. I would also point out that if we are to expose antecedents, Orwell himself does not come off very well. Comrade Orwell, the former police official of British Imperialism (from which the Fascists learnt all they know) in those regions of the Far East where the sun at last sets for ever on the bedraggled Union Jack! Comrade Orwell, former fellow traveller of the pacifists and regular contributor to the pacifist *Adelphi*—which he now attacks! Comrade Orwell, former extreme Left-Winger, I.L.P. partisan and defender of anarchists (see *Homage to Catalonia*)! And now Comrade Orwell who returns to his old imperialist allegiances and works at the B.B.C., conducting British propaganda to fox the Indian masses! It would seem that Orwell himself shows to a surprising degree the overlapping of left-wing, pacifist and reactionary tendencies of which he accuses others!

Adverting to *Now*, I would mention that this review has abandoned its position as an independent forum, and has now become the cultural review of the British anarchist movement. Perhaps Mr. Orwell will regard this as another proof of his mystic and blimpish trinity.

Finally, I would point out two inaccuracies in Orwell's letter. The anarchist pamphlet to which he refers is entitled "The Russian Myth," and the editor of the *Adelphi* during the earlier part of the war was not John Middleton Murry, but the late Max Plowman.

May 19, 1942
Richmond, England

Alex Comfort:[4]

I see that Mr. Orwell is intellectual-hunting again, in your pages this time, and that he has made the discovery that almost every writer under thirty in this country has his feet already on the slippery slope to Fascism, or at least to compromise. It seems I am a "pure pacifist of the other-cheek" variety, a piece of horticultural eulogy I'm glad I did not miss, and that I deserve a spanking for associating with such disreputables as the Duke of Bedford and the—perfectly harmless—Ross Williamson. The trouble is that some of your American readers may not realise Mr. Orwell's status in this country and take his commentary seriously. We all like him here, though the standard of his pamphleteering is going down of late, and we know him as the preacher of a doctrine of Physical Courage as an Asset to the left wing intellectual, and so forth. I think we all agree that he is pretty thoroughly out of touch with any writing under thirty years of age, and his last two public performances—a reproof in sorrow to my book "No Such Liberty," and this "London Letter" of his—suggest that he still has not grasped why most of the post-Thirties poets are pacifists, or what their pacifism would entail if Hitler arrived here.

Mr. Orwell calls us "objectively pro-fascist." I suppose he means that we are letting anti-fascism go by default. If we suggest to him that we, who have the single intention of salvaging English artistic culture when the crash comes, are the only people likely to continue to hold genuinely anti-fascist values, he will not be convinced. But perhaps he will grant that Hitler's greatest and irretrievable victory over here was when he persuaded the English people that the only way to lick Fascism was to imitate it. He puts us in a dilemma which cannot be practically rebutted, only broken away from—"If I win, you have political fascism victorious: if you want to beat me, you must assimilate as much of its philosophy as you can, so that I am bound to win either way." Accordingly we began feverishly jamming into our national life all the minor pieces of Fascist practise which did not include socialist methods, sitting on the Press "because this is Total War," making our soldiers jab blood bladders while loudspeakers howl propaganda at them, because the German army consisted of efficient yahoos. The only people who said that to defeat Fascism one must (a) try to understand it and (b) refuse to accept its tenets oneself were the pacifists. It looks as if Mr. Orwell and his warlike friends were being not objectively but constructively supporters of the entire philosophical apparatus which they quite genuinely detest.

What, again, does Mr. Orwell imagine the role of the artist should be in occupied territory? He should protest with all his force, where and when he can, against such evils as he sees—but can he do this more usefully by temporarily accepting the status quo, or by skirmishing in Epping Forest with a pocket full of hand grenades? I think that English writers honour, and will follow when the opportunity comes, the example of integrity which Gide has set. We are going to be entrusted with the job of saving what remains of the structure of civilized values from Hitler or alternatively from Churchill and his bladder-prickers. The men who, like Orwell, could have helped, are calling us Fascists and presumably dancing round the ruins of Munster Cathedral. We prefer not to join them, and if, in the pursuit of our task we find ourselves obliged to publish in the same paper as the Devil himself, the others having politely refused us as unorthodox, we shall have very few qualms.

May 18, 1942
Brentwood, England

George Orwell:

Since I don't suppose you want to fill an entire number of PR with squalid controversies imported from across the Atlantic, I will lump together the various letters you have sent on to me (from Messrs. Savage, Woodcock and Comfort), as the central issue in all of them is the same. But I must afterwards deal separately with some points of fact raised in various of the letters.

Pacifism. Pacifism is objectively pro-Fascist. This is elementary common sense. If you hamper the war-effort of one side you automatically help that of the other. Nor is there any real way of remaining outside such a war as the present one. In practice, "he that is not with me is against me." The idea that you can somehow remain aloof from and superior to the struggle, while living on food which British sailors have to risk their lives to bring you, is a bourgeois illusion bred of money and security. Mr. Savage remarks that "according to this type of reasoning, a German or Japanese pacifist would be 'objectively pro-British'." But of course he would be! That is why pacifist activities are not permitted in those countries (in both of them the penalty is, or can be, beheading) while both the Germans and the Japanese do all they can to encourage the spread of pacifism in British and American territories. The Germans even run a spurious "freedom" station which serves out pacifist propaganda indistinguishable from that of the PPU. They would stimulate pacifism in Russia as well if they could, but in that case they have tougher babies to deal with. In so far as it takes effect at all, pacifist propaganda can only be effective *against* those countries where a certain amount of freedom of speech is still permitted; in other words it is helpful to totalitarianism.

I am not interested in pacifism as a "moral phenomenon." If Mr. Savage and others imagine that one can somehow "overcome" the German army by lying on one's back, let them go on imagining it, but let them also wonder occasionally whether this is not an illusion due to security, too much money and a simple ignorance of the way in which things actually happen. As an ex-Indian civil servant, it always makes me shout with laughter to hear, for instance, Gandhi named as an example of the success of non-violence. As long as twenty years ago it was cynically admitted in Anglo-Indian circles that Gandhi was very useful to the British government. So he will be to the Japanese if they get there. Despotic governments can stand "moral force" till the cows come home; what they fear is physical force. But though not much interested in the "theory" of pacifism, I *am* interested in the psychological processes by which pacifists who have started out with an alleged horror of violence end up with a marked tendency to be fascinated by the success and power of Nazism. Even pacifists who wouldn't own to any such fascination are beginning to claim that a Nazi victory is desirable in itself. In the letter you sent on to me, Mr. Comfort considers that an artist in occupied territory ought to "protest against such evils as he sees," but considers that this is best done by "temporarily accepting the status quo" (like Déat[5] or Bergery,[6] for instance?) A few weeks back he was hoping for a Nazi victory because of the stimulating effect it would have upon the Arts:

"As far as I can see, no therapy short of complete military defeat has any chance of re-establishing the common stability of literature and of the man in the street. One can imagine the greater the adversity the greater the sudden realization of a stream of imaginative work, and the greater the sudden katharsis of poetry, from the isolated interpretation of war as calamity to the realization of the imaginative and actual tragedy of Man. When we have access again to the literature of the war years in France, Poland and Czechoslovakia, I am confident that that is what we shall find." (From a letter to *Horizon*.)[7]

I pass over the money-sheltered ignorance capable of believing that literary life is still going on in, for instance, Poland, and remark merely that statements like this justify me in saying that our English pacifists are tending towards active pro-Fascism. But I don't particularly object to that. What I object to is the intellectual cowardice of people who are objectively and to some extent emotionally pro-Fascist, but who don't care to say so and take refuge behind the formula "I am just as anti-Fascist as anyone, but—." The result of this is that so-called peace propaganda is just as dishonest and intellectually disgusting as war propaganda. Like war propaganda, it concentrates on putting forward a "case," obscuring the opponent's point of view and avoiding awkward questions. The line normally followed is "Those who fight against Fascism go Fascist themselves." In order to evade the quite obvious objections that can be raised to this, the following propaganda-tricks are used:

1. The Fascising processes occurring in Britain as a result of war are systematically exaggerated.

2. The actual record of Fascism, especially its pre-war history, is ignored or pooh-poohed as "propaganda." Discussion of what the world would actually be like if the Axis dominated it is evaded.

3. Those who want to struggle against Fascism are accused of being wholehearted defenders of capitalist "democracy." The fact that the rich everywhere tend to be pro-Fascist and the working class are nearly always anti-Fascist is hushed-up.

4. It is tacitly pretended that the war is only between Britain and Germany. Mention of Russia and China, and their fate if Fascism is permitted to win, is avoided. (You won't find one word about Russia or China in the three letters you sent to me.)

Now as to one or two points of fact which I must deal with if your correspondents' letters are to be printed in full.

My past and present. Mr. Woodcock tries to discredit me by saying that (a) I once served in the Indian Imperial Police, (b) I have written articles for the *Adelphi* and was mixed up with the Trotskyists in Spain, and (c) that I am at the BBC "conducting British propaganda to fox the Indian masses." With regard to (a), it is quite true that I served five years in the Indian Police. It is also true that I gave up that job, partly because it didn't suit me but mainly because I would not any longer be a servant of imperialism. I am against imperialism because I know something about it from the inside. The whole history of this is to be found in my writings, including a novel[8] which I think I can claim was a kind of prophecy of what happened this year in Burma. (b) Of course I have written for the *Adelphi*. Why not? I once wrote an article for a vegetarian paper. Does that make me a vegetarian? I was associated with the Trotskyists in Spain. It was chance that I was serving in the POUM militia and not another, and I largely disagreed with the POUM "line" and told its leaders so freely, but when they were afterwards accused of pro-Fascist activities I defended them as best I could. How does this contradict my present anti-Hitler attitude? It is news to me that Trotskyists are either pacifists or pro-Fascists. (c) Does Mr. Woodcock really know what kind of stuff I put out in the Indian broadcasts? He does not—though I would be quite glad to tell him about it. He is careful not to mention what other people are associated with these Indian broadcasts. One for instance is Herbert Read, whom he mentions with approval. Others are T. S. Eliot, E. M. Forster, Reginald Reynolds,[9] Stephen Spender, J. B. S. Haldane, Tom Wintringham. Most of our broadcasters are Indian leftwing intellectuals, from Liberals to

Trotskyists, some of them bitterly anti-British. They don't do it to "fox the Indian masses" but because they know what a Fascist victory would mean to the chances of India's independence. Why not try to find out what I am doing before accusing my good faith?

"*Mr. Orwell is intellectual-hunting again*" (Mr. Comfort). I have never attacked "the intellectuals" or "the intelligentsia" en bloc. I have used a lot of ink and done myself a lot of harm by attacking the successive literary cliques which have infested this country, not because they were intellectuals but precisely because they were *not* what I mean by true intellectuals. The life of a clique is about five years and I have been writing long enough to see three of them come and two go—the Catholic gang, the Stalinist gang, and the present Pacifist or, as they are sometimes nicknamed, Fascifist gang. My case against all of them is that they write mentally dishonest propaganda and degrade literary criticism to mutual arse-licking. But even within these various schools I would differentiate between individuals. I would never think of coupling Christopher Dawson with Arnold Lunn, or Malraux with Palme Dutt, or Max Plowman with the Duke of Bedford. And even the work of one individual can exist at very different levels. For instance Mr. Comfort himself wrote one poem I value greatly ("The Atoll in the Mind"), and I wish he would write more of them instead of lifeless propaganda tracts dressed up as novels. But this letter he has chosen to send you is a different matter. Instead of answering what I have said he tries to prejudice an audience to whom I am little known by a misrepresentation of my general line and sneers about my "status" in England. (A writer isn't judged by his "status," he is judged by his work.) That is on a par with "peace" propaganda which has to avoid mention of Hitler's invasion of Russia, and it is not what I mean by intellectual honesty. It is just because I do take the function of the intelligentsia seriously that I don't like the sneers, libels, parrot phrases and financially profitable back-scratching which flourish in our English literary world, and perhaps in yours also.

July 12, 1942
London, England

1. Derek Stanley Savage (1917–) is a poet, critic, and contributor to *Now, Focus, Horizon, Politics*. His books include *The Autumn World* (poems), (1939), *The Personal Principle: Studies in Modern Poetry* (1944), *Hamlet and the Pirates* (1950) and *The Cottagers' Companion*. He has worked for the Transport and General Workers Union, Christian Aid, and the Anglican Pacifist Fellowship. He contributed a rather hostile chapter on Orwell to *The New Pelican Guide to English Literature*, edited by Boris Ford (1983).

2. George Woodcock (1912–1995) born in Canada of Anglo-Welsh parents who took him to England soon after his birth, returned to Canada in 1949 with his German-born wife. Anarchist, critic, writer, editor, he was university lecturer, 1954–1967, at the University of Washington until excluded from the United States in 1956 as an anarchist, then in British Columbia. He edited *Now*, 1940–47, and *Canadian Literature*, 1958–77. His many books include *New Life to the Land (Anarchist Proposals for Agriculture)* (1942), *William Godwin* (1946), *The Writer and Politics* (1948), *The Crystal Spirit: A Study of George Orwell* (1967, 1984), and *Orwell's Message: 1984 and the Present* (1984). After this controversy, he and Orwell corresponded and became friends. His 'Recollections of George Orwell,' *Northern Review*, August-September 1953, is reprinted in *Orwell Remembered* (199–210); he wrote the introduction to *Remembering Orwell*. Orwell later contributed to *Now* (see *3104*).

3. For the reference to 'Fascist tendency,' the Duke of Bedford, Hugh Ross Williamson, and Julian Symons, see *913, ns. 5, 6, 7.*
4. For Alexander Comfort, poet, critic, and medical biologist, see *913, n. 5.* George Woodcock wrote on 'The Poetry of Comfort' in *Poetry Quarterly,* 9, 1947.
5 Marcel Déat (1894–1955) was a French Socialist Deputy, 1926–36, who then gave active support to Hitler; in his article 'Mourir pour Dantzig?' April 1939, he argued that France should not defend Poland if it were attacked. He was Minister of Work and Social Affairs in the Vichy Government, 1944–45. Condemned to death in his absence after the war, he was permitted to live out his life in Italy.
6. Gaston Bergery (1892–1974), Secretary of the 1918 Committee of War Reparations, and editor of the weekly *La Flèche,* 1934–39, he was a pacifist and supported the Munich Agreement. He became a member of the Vichy National Council, and ambassador in Moscow, 1941, and Ankara, 1942–44 In 1949 he was acquitted of charges of collaboration while in Ankara.
7. See *1195, n. 10.*
8. *Burmese Days.*
9. Reginald Reynolds was a Quaker and during World War II a pacifist. Despite that, he and Orwell became friends and colleagues. See also *1060, n. 1.*

1271. A. M. Ashraf's Broadcasts

On 12 July 1942, Tamara Talbot Rice, Turkish Specialist, Middle East Section of the Ministry of Information, wrote to Orwell and the News & Talks Editor of the Hindustani Service about two programmes which Ashraf (one of Orwell's colleagues in the Indian Section) was to give. That on 20 July was to be a report on his interview with the Turkish Ambassador to Britain; that on the 19th was a talk for children. Both were to be transmitted in Hindustani. Mrs. Talbot Rice wanted to see the script for the interview before the broadcast and also the programme for children if Turkey was mentioned. She explained that she was anxious that nothing should be broadcast that might cause offence or difficulty in Turkey.

Rushbrook Williams took it upon himself to answer her and did so with his tongue firmly in his cheek. Of course she could see the script for 20 July, he wrote, though he couldn't imagine that the Turkish Ambassador would say anything to offend his own people, and he thought it likely that the number of Turks who could understand Hindustani was bound to be limited. In any case, the programme was not beamed for reception in Turkey. However, a script—in Hindustani—would be sent to her to check. As for the children's programme, it would not mention Turkey.

Although this inquiry was neatly deflected, and doubtless gave members of the Indian Section some amusement, it is a fair example of how delicately they had to balance conflicting interests.

1272. Gujarati Newsletter, 20
13 July 1942

No script has been traced. PasB gives the timing as 12 minutes. Although Orwell returned from holiday on the day this Newsletter was broadcast, it is hardly likely that he prepared the script and it is not credited to him here despite the statement made on the relevant talks booking form. See *1255*.

1273. To Cyril Connolly
13 July 1942   EB/NP

Dear Cyril,
Did Anand ask you about reading a poem in our forthcoming magazine programme "Voice?"

You might let me know as we want to get the programme all sewn up as soon as possible.

Yours,
[Initialled] E.A.B
Eric Blair
Talks Producer
Indian Section

1274. To Cedric Dover
13 July 1942   Handwritten draft and typewritten versions   PP/EB/NP

Dear Dover,
Thanks for yours of 11.7.42. I'd like to see Miss Wingfield's "Open Letter"[1] but my schedule is full to the[2] end of August, so I can't actually broadcast it *before* then. Could I just see it (not worth doing[3] alterations in advance), and then perhaps we can decide what to do with it.

Yours,
[Initialled] E.A.B
Eric Blair
Talks Producer
Indian Section

1. Dover had written to Orwell regarding the Open Letter Orwell had commissioned on 23 June 1942; see *1236* and *1236, n. 1*. This was to be 'to a Liberal.' Dover modified it slightly to 'Open Letter to a Liberal Man,' but he had first written 'Coloured' Man, anticipating Susan Wingfield's 'Letter to a Coloured Man.' He mentioned that Wingfield's Letter concluded his new book. It pointed to 'the responsibility of the coloured peoples and what they should do.' Dover thought it could be reshaped to make an excellent talk.
2. The draft (written on Dover's letter) omits 'the.'
3. Draft has 'worth doing'; Parratt misread this and typed 'with any.'

1275. To J. B. S. Haldane

13 July 1942?[1]

REFERENCE BROADCAST CAN YOU MANAGE FIFTEENTH JULY SEVEN P.M. SHARP AT 200 OXFORD STREET STOP   WILL TAKE ABOUT TWO HOURS STOP   IMPORTANT TO LET ME KNOW IF UNABLE TO COME

ORWELL BROADCASTS

1. Since Orwell returned from leave on 13 July and the broadcast was to be recorded on 21 August (see *1241*), this telegram must have been sent on either the 13th or 14th. The programme was 'I'd Like It Explained,' a dialogue with C. H. Waddington (to whom a telegram was also sent) on 'Scientific Research.' Recording in the evening was owing to Haldane's inability to give up a day of his research.

1276. To M. R. Kothari

13 July 1942   PP/EB/NP

Dear Mr. Kothari,

I understand that you are willing to do the next Marathi Newsletter for us.[1] Could you be kind enough to come here and pick it up from Miss Chitale on Wednesday evening? I can't send it, as it won't be done until the evening and if posted might not reach you till late on Thursday. You can then perhaps get on with it on Wednesday night and come and finish off the translation here on Thursday morning.[2]

When you are translating these letters,[3] I particularly want you to consult me about any point which in your view is unsuitable propaganda, or the expression of any opinion that you do not feel inclined to sponsor. We particularly aim at making these newsletters as truthful as possible, while also suiting them to the special community they are aimed at.[4] I will have a talk with you about that on Wednesday or Thursday.

Yours sincerely,
Eric Blair
Talks Producer
Indian Section

1. Orwell's authorship of the English originals of Marathi, Bengali, and Gujarati Newsletters is attested by the talks booking forms for those who translated them into the vernacular languages. Thus, together with the Weekly News Review in English, he was for at least three months responsible for four newsletters each week.
2. Orwell wrote to Kothari on the Monday he returned from leave; Wednesday evening was the 15th, and the broadcast was transmitted on Thursday, 16 July.
3. When you are translating these letters] *handwritten (by Miss Parratt?) above the line typed:* 'If you continue doing these letters.' *Miss Parratt probably rubbed out the line she had typed on the top copy sent to Kothari.*
4. This shows conclusively that the different vernacular versions were tailored to suit their audiences, as Laurence Brander suspected; see *892* and *995*.

1277. BBC Talks Booking Form, 13.7.42

S. K. Das Gupta[1] to translate and read the Bengali Newsletter, written by E. Blair (Staff) in English; broadcast 18 and 25.7.42, 1, 8, 15, 22, and 29.8.42, 5, 12, 19, and 26.9.42, 3.10.42; fee £4.4s to cover translation and reading. Signed: Z. A. Bokhari.[2]

1. Das Gupta, a translator and sub-editor for the journal *Haftawar Akhbar*, had been suggested by Bokhari as a suitable person to serve as a switch censor for Bengali in Bokhari's absence in India. Evidence that he was translating from Orwell's English-language Newsletter for India is to be found on the script for Weekly News Review, 53, 16 January 1943; see *1825, headnote*.
2. The newsletter for 25 July was modified so that most of what Das Gupta translated was not broadcast in order that the High Commissioner could give a talk in Bengali (see *1325*). Bokhari had suggested that it would be more economical to arrange a three-month contract for Das Gupta instead of paying by the week. He was therefore informed on 15 July that, because he was being offered a long-term contract, the fee would be reduced from five guineas to four, in line with BBC practice.

1278. To L. F. Easterbrook

14 July 1942   PP/EB

Dear Mr. Easterbrook,
I am sending herewith Sir John Russell's draft for his part in the forthcoming dialogue with you. His suggestion was that you should write what you wanted to say, after which we will work it up into a proper discussion. You will notice, however, that Sir John Russell has talked almost entirely about Indian agriculture. It is not altogether suitable for us from this end to talk to Indians exclusively about conditions in their country, and I really wanted the talk to deal with modern developments in agriculture generally. Do you think, therefore, that you could cast your talk in a more general vein, but particularly with reference to agricultural development in temperate countries. If we have something of that sort from you, I think we can work the two up into a balanced discussion.

Could you let me have the script within four or five days from now;[1] we have arranged the recording for July 22nd, and I should be glad if you could come to 200, Oxford Street at 10.15 a.m. on that day. The recording will finish at about 11.45 a.m.

Yours sincerely,
George Orwell
Talks Producer
Indian Section

1. Easterbrook wrote on 18 July sending modifications to his script.

1279. To J. F. Horrabin

14 July 1942   PP/EB

Dear Horrabin,

Would you be willing to undertake some more talks for us, rather after the style of the ones you did before? I should think a series of four would be about the right thing. I don't quite know what line to suggest. Your last ones were very well received and I don't know whether you couldn't simply sketch in in greater detail the outline which you did in a rather general way last time. Naturally what we are concerned with in these talks is primarily the strategy of the war and secondarily the raw materials situation, both during the war and in the re-construction afterwards. Could you think of something along these lines which you would like to do?

I want a reply quickly, because I have got to get this thing settled quite soon.

Yours sincerely,
George Orwell
Talks Producer
Indian Section

1280. To Peter Masefield

14 July 1942   PP/EB

Dear Mr. Masefield,

I enclose a copy of the letter which should have reached you some time ago.

I shall look forward to hearing from you about the other speaker to take part in the discussion, as soon as possible, so that I can arrange about the publicity for this talk.

Yours sincerely,
George Orwell
Talks Producer
Indian Section

1281. To Sir John Russell

14 July 1942   PP/EB

Dear Sir John,

Thank you very much for the first draft of your contribution to the discussion on Agriculture, which Mr. Bokhari has passed on to me. I have sent a copy to Mr. Easterbrook, and as soon as I receive his contribution I will get it [int]o its final form and send you a copy.

We have arranged for your recording on July 22nd. The studio is booked for rehearsal from 10.15 a.m., and the recording will finish about 11.45 a.m. I hope this time will be convenient to you. I shall look forward to seeing you at 200, Oxford Street on the 22nd.

Yours sincerely,
George Orwell
Talks Producer
Indian Section

1282. To Alex Comfort

15 July 1942   Typewritten

10a Mortimer Crescent   NW 6

Dear Mr Comfort,
The Partisan Review sent me a copy of the letter you had written them, along with some others. I believe they are going to print all the letters, or extracts from them, and my reply. But there was one point I didn't care to answer in print. You queried my reference to "antisemitism" (by the way I didn't say antisemitism but Jew-baiting, a very different thing) in the Adelphi. Of course I was thinking of Max Plowman, who hated Jews, and though he was aware of this tendency in himself and struggled against it, sometimes let it influence his editorship. I had two particular instances in mind. The first was when Macmurray's book "The Clue to History" was published in 1938. This was a rather unbalanced book and extremely pro-Jew in tendency. Max was infuriated by this and had the book reviewed by five separate people, including himself and myself, in one issue of the Adelphi. His own review (you could look it up—round about December 1938) was definitely provocative in tone. Later on he got the Adelphi involved in a controversy with some Jew whose name I don't remember, Cohen I think, about the alleged warmongering activities of the Jews. Having got the Jew hopping mad and said his own say in a very snooty manner, Max suddenly declared the controversy closed, not allowing the Jew to reply. This would be some time in 1939. Since the war Murry has at least once referred with apparent approval to Hitler's "elimination" of the Jews.

The reason why I don't care to print anything about this is because Max was a very old friend of mine and was very good to me, and his wife might hear about [it] and feel hurt if I actually name names. In my reply in the Partisan Review I put in a note to the effect that I was answering this privately, but I daresay they'll omit both this and your query,[1] as I have explained the circumstances to Dwight Macdonald.

Yours truly
George Orwell

Alex Comfort replied on 16 July 1942:

Dear Mr. Orwell
Thank you very much for writing to me. I didn't know about Max in this

connection, and you were entirely right. I shouldn't really have replied to you where the Adelphi was concerned, as I have only known it since the war: I rather took it that you meant that Jew baiting in it was a recent thing—a feature which had cropped up during the period you were reporting on. (I suppose Max's foible was of pretty long standing)[2]

I thought some of the things you said should have been far more fully answered, but doubted if P.R. would have room for more than a squib-retort. I honestly don't think that the last lot of us are any more constructively pro-Fascist than our predecessors, but from the people I encounter, I would say they were nearer to Russian nihilism than any contemporary line of thought.

However, I often want to remonstrate with Peace News, not for being Fascist, but for trying, as you say, to get away with both ends of the same argument. I have written a commination to J.M.M.[3] but he did not print it. He needs another beginning "cursed is the man who imagines one can assume opposite viewpoints and say that whichever turns out to be true, his main contention is right."

I'd like an opportunity of congratulating you over that Horizon article on Donald M'Gill°. It was the best example of an analysis I think I ever read.

I'll be writing to the editor of P.R. and explain that I entirely agree with you, on seeing the references. I didn't want to put you on the spot over a personal question like that, and I apologize for my ignorance

All good wishes and many thanks
Alex Comfort

I'd like to have started an argument over that review of yours,[4] but the Adelphi hadn't room to unleash me. Anyhow, thank you for doing it. It made me revise several ideas.

1. *Partisan Review* omitted all reference to this topic.
2. The sentence in parentheses and the postscript are manuscript additions to a typewritten letter.
3. John Middleton Murry.
4. Orwell's review of Comfort's novel *No Such Liberty, The Adelphi*, October 1941; see *855*.

1283. BBC Talks Booking Form, 15.7.42

Mulk Raj Anand: 'Open Letter to a Chinese Guerilla'; 13½-minute talk; broadcast 30.7.42; fee £9.9s. Signed: Z. A. Bokhari.

1284. BBC Talks Booking Form, 15.7.42

R. R. Desai: 'Open Letter,' 3, 'Open Letter to a Nazi'; broadcast 13.8.42; fee £9.9s + £2.8.2 + £1.14.0 expenses. Signed: Z. A. Bokhari.

1285. BBC Talks Booking Form, 15.7.42

R. R. Desai: Gujarati Newsletters 23–31; broadcast 3, 10, 17, 24, and 31.8.42, 7, 14, 21, and 28.9.42; fee £5.5s + £2.8.2 + £1.14.0 expenses. Signed: Z. A. Bokhari.

1286. BBC Talks Booking Form, 15.7.42

L. F. Easterbrook: 'I'd Like It Explained,' 3; Agriculture; '13½ minute discussion with Sir John Russell on AGRICULTURE—each speaker will talk for about 6½ minutes' [quoted words were crossed through]; recorded 22.7.42; broadcast 14.8.42; fee £8.8s + 12s 7d rail fare. Signed: Z. A. Bokhari.

A similar form (with crossing through but without rail fare) was prepared for Sir John Russell.

On the same day, forms were prepared for Number 4 in the series for J. B. S. Haldane and Dr. C. H. Waddington, also with the crossed-through passage. This was on Scientific Research and was recorded on 15 July 1942, broadcast on 21 August 1942. The fees were the same; Haldane received 17s 0d expenses and Waddington 12s 0d for fares. The expense allowance was because the recording finished so late (10:0 P.M.).

1287. BBC Talks Booking Form, 15.7.42

Lady Grigg: 'Women Generally Speaking'; broadcast 5, 12, 19, and 26.8.42; fee £8.8s each talk. Signed: Z. A. Bokhari.

1288. BBC Talks Booking Form, 15.7.42

Sir Aziz-ul-Huque, CIE, D.Litt, High Commissioner for India: translation and reading of Bengali Newsletter, written by E. Blair; broadcast 25.7.42; fee 'usual'—£10.10s.[1] Signed: Z. A. Bokhari.

1. The usualness of this fee depended upon the recipient. For a high commissioner it was £10.10s; for Das Gupta, the agreed fee of £5.5s was reduced to £4.4s, see 1277, n. 2 and 1325.

1289. BBC Talks Booking Form, 15.7.42

Princess Indira of Kapurthala: 'The Debate Continues'; broadcast 3, 10, 17, 24 and 31.8.42; fee £9.9s each talk. Signed: Z. A. Bokhari.

1290. BBC Talks Booking Form, 15.7.42

Noel Sircar: film commentary; 13½ minutes on current films in India; broadcast 28.7.42 and 25.8.42; fee £9.9s for each programme. Signed: Z. A. Bokhari.

1291. BBC Talks Booking Form, 15.7.42

S. Telkar: 'Topic of the Week'; 13½-minute talk on the outstanding topic of the week; broadcast 29.7.42, 5, 12, and 19.8.42; fee £9.9s for each programme. Signed: Z. A. Bokhari.

1292. Marathi Newsletter, 20
16 July 1942

The talks booking form misnumbers this newsletter as 21. It is described as 'Written by E. Blair, Indian Section. Translated & read by M. R. Kothari.' Kothari's fee was £5.5s and the form was signed by Bokhari. Similar details are given on booking forms up to and including Newsletter 29, 17 September 1942. The incorrect numbering continued up to and including Newsletter 26 (given as 27). Correct numbering was then restored; so there are two successive 27s. No script has survived, and PasB does not give the timing.

1293. To H. N. Brailsford and to G. M. Young
16 July 1942   PP/EB

Dear Mr. Brailsford,[1]
I am writing to ask whether it would interest you to do a talk in one of our forthcoming series in the Eastern Service. These talks are in the form of short discussions between people with special knowledge of subjects of current interest. The one I hope you will undertake is on the Press, and the speaker with whom I suggest you should hold your discussion is G. M. Young. These broadcasts take about 13½ minutes, which means probably that your contribution would be in the neighbourhood of 750 words. The date of this broadcast would be August 7th, at 1.45 p.m. DBST. This means that I should like to have the script by July 31st if possible. If you agree, I will make all the arrangements for the necessary meeting and discussion. Could you be kind enough to let me know as soon as possible whether this interests you?

Yours sincerely,
George Orwell
Talks Producer
Indian Section

An identical letter was sent to G. M. Young.[2]

1. Henry Noel Brailsford (see *424, n. 3*) was a socialist intellectual, author, political journalist and leader writer for the *Manchester Guardian, Tribune, Daily News*, and *Nation*. He joined the ILP in 1907 and edited its journal, the *New Leader*, 1922–26. His publications include *The War of Steel and Gold* (1914), *Shelley, Godwin and their Circle* (1913), *Voltaire* (1935), and *Subject India* (1943), which last Orwell reviewed in *The Nation*, 20 November 1943; see *2365*. Fredric Warburg recalls a conversation in which Brailsford said that, if forced to choose between the Nazi and Communist totalitarian systems, the choice must fall on Communism: 'It is at least progressive and rational, while Nazism is the apotheosis of lunacy, anti-semitism and brutality' (*An Occupation for Gentlemen*, 205). The BBC expressed doubts as to his 'reliability' because his views were too leftist and he advocated independence for India. In November 1941, permission was sought to allow him to broadcast, and this was passed up the administrative hierarchy from the Controller of the BBC Home Division to its Director General. It was decided he could speak only on subjects to which he could lay special claim 'so long as the B.B.C. (i.e. not only Home Talks) selection of speeches shows a less definite inclination towards the left than it does at present.' This arcane ruling seems not to have filtered downwards, though it shows how attempts were made to exert political control of choice of speakers in Orwell's time at the B.B.C. Between December 1941 and March 1942 Brailsford gave at least six talks to listeners overseas and several more thereafter, though not always without controversy. On this occasion, according to an annotation on the carbon copy of the letter, Brailsford 'declined by 'phone.' For Orwell, Brailsford, and the Spanish Civil War, see *424*.

2. George Malcolm Young (1882–1959), after teaching at Oxford for two or three years, became a civil servant in 1908, joining the Board of Education. In 1911 he became the first secretary to what was to become known as the University Grants Committee. He accompanied a member of the War Cabinet, Arthur Henderson, to Russia in 1917, but after the war, in a spirit of disillusionment, resigned from the civil service and devoted himself to writing and editing. His books include *Early Victorian England* (1934), *Charles I and Cromwell* (1935), *Stanley Baldwin* (1952), several collections of essays and editions of Hardy, Meredith, Macaulay, and historical documents.

1294. To J. Chinna Durai

16 July 1942   PP/EB

Dear Mr. Chinna Durai,

I am very glad that you are willing to do another talk for us. The series is called OPEN LETTERS; the idea is to discuss the origins and political meaning of the war and to put this in a simple popular form we are going to do it in the form of open letters to imaginary people representing the most important trends of modern thought. The one I should like you to do is the Letter to a Pacifist. This should, of course, have some reference to India and to the special Indian situation of this moment, but you will of course understand that we are not anxious to tread on any toes, and particularly it would be undesirable to make anything in the nature of an attack on Mr. Gandhi at this moment.[1] Therefore while you can speak quite vigorously on the subject of Pacifism anything which might raise the idea of Gandhi's particular view point should be couched in rather general terms. But please write freely, as if there is anything which seems indiscreet we can easily tone it down at the time of rehearsal. I have arranged for the talk to be recorded on July 24th, and should like you to come to Broadcasting House at 2.30 p.m. on that day. Can you let me have the script a day or two before that?[2]

Yours sincerely,
Eric Blair
Talks Producer

1. For official direction regarding Gandhi and Pacifism, see 3 (a) of the secret memorandum 'Guidance on India,' *1295*.
2. Durai despatched the script on 22 July 1942. Orwell sent it to Bokhari for censorship; see *1311*.

1295. From Michael Barkway, Chief (News) Editor, Empire Services

16 July 1942

On 16 July 1942, Michael Barkway issued a memorandum headed 'Guidance on India,' for the 'interim period' to 7 August 1942. It was marked 'Secret.' It was one of the first fruits of the reorganisation of the Empire News Department (which did not include Orwell's section) announced in an internal memorandum from J. B. Clark, Controller, Overseas Services, on 6 July 1942, which stated that Michael Barkway was to assist R. A. Rendall, A.C. (O.S.), 'in the political direction of the Empire Service as a whole, with a view to securing the closer integration of the service that the move to Oxford Street makes possible.'

Barkway's memorandum is marked for distribution to the Eastern Service, and although it is likely that Orwell saw it, his name does not appear on the copy reproduced here. It is dated, coincidentally, on the same day that Orwell wrote to Chinna Durai (see *1294*) and his letter is in accord with this directive.

Barkway had been Empire News Editor, and was replaced by his assistant, B. Moore, who also continued as Deputy to the head of the department. In the Staff List for 21 August 1943, Barkway is shown as holding a temporary appointment as correspondent in the United States for the Foreign News Section; Moore is listed as Editor, Overseas News Broadcasts.

The following note on India is on lines agreed with E.S.D., and is intended to cover the interim period until the All India Congress Party meets on August 7th.

We want to keep up a persistent propaganda about India, in order to focus the weight of world opinion so far as we can on those Indians who have not yet finally committed themselves to Gandhi's policy.

In the Eastern Service, and the 1800 bulletin, all available world comment in an anti-Congress sense should be reflected.

In other Services discussion about India should be kept going, both to explain the British Government's attitude and to win over any wavering people who may be influenced by Congress propaganda, and to stimulate public and press opinion which will be reported back to India.

The most important lines to get across are these:—

(1) The sincerity of the British pledge of Indian independence after the war. We must go on stressing that this principle is firmly established once and for all. It isn't only a pledge to India. Britain's honour and good faith before the eyes of the world are involved, and there can be no going back.

(2) The importance of the defence of India to the United Nations. The defence of India is much more than a British interest. It is essential to the whole cause of the United Nations—to China as much as to Russia, to Egypt as much as to Australia. It is a responsibility that we must fulfil.

(3) The impossibility of assuring the defence of India by yielding to the Congress demands.

(a) Congress is dominated by Gandhi who is utterly and completely committed to Pacifism. He assumes that the Indian Army would be disbanded under a National Government and he proposes to send emissaries to the Axis to persuade them of the futility of war.

(b) If a National Government were formed it would have to take over control of the railways, the public utilities and every kind of public service without which the defence forces could not operate;

(c) The Provisional Government which Congress wants, as they made clear during the conversations with Cripps (which should frequently be recalled), is a Government dominated by Congress and responsible to nobody. The Muslims, the Sikhs, the Depressed classes and many others would be bitterly opposed to it, and the Muslims if not the others, would be ready to press their opposition to the point of civil war.

(4) The unrepresentative nature of Congress. We must keep on giving reminders of the achievements of the Indian Army, of the great weight of Ind[ian] public support for the war effort and of the very large extent to which the Government of India is already Indianised. The issue is not between India and Britain, but between Congress on the one hand, and non-Congress India and the United Nat[ions] on the other.

1296. To C. R. Fay

16 July 1942   PP/EB

Dear Professor Fay,

Many thanks for your letter. I am sorry for the delay in replying, but I have been on leave. I am afraid I did not explain very well in my first letter what I wanted. There ⌊is⌋ no particular importance in the speakers [who] take part in these discussions having been or not been to India, as what is chiefly intended is to interpret western affairs for the benefit of Indian listeners. We cast these talks in the form of discussions because in that way we find that we often get a more lively and conversational account than when there is only one speaker. When I enquired the names of suitable speakers to discuss the Co-operative movement your name and Miss Digby's were given to me.[1] Miss Digby has already answered agreeing to take part in the discussion, but if you feel that this discussion would not be a real one, we can perhaps arrange with one or two of the other speakers whom you name to take part, such as Mr. Lucette from Ceylon. There will in any case be an Indian speaker present to ask a few questions and get the discussion going.

Yours sincerely,
George Orwell
Talks Producer
Indian Section

1. See *1239*, *n. 2*.

1297. BBC Talks Booking Form, 17.7.42

Cedric Dover: 'Open Letter,' 4, to a Liberal; broadcast 20.8.42; fee £8.8s. Signed: Z. A. Bokhari.

1298. BBC Talks Booking Form, 17.7.42

J. Chinna Durai: 'Open Letter,' 2, to a Pacifist; recorded 24.7.42 at Broadcasting House; broadcast 6.8.42 from 200 Oxford Street; fee £8.8s. Signed: Z. A. Bokhari.

1299. Weekly News Review, 31

18 July 1942

The typescript for this broadcast has the two additions shown; it bears two censorship stamps; the censor was Bokhari. The indication 'NOT CHECKED WITH BROADCAST' has not been amended. The insertion in the first paragraph, which is very small and hard to read, could be in Orwell's hand. PasB has 'News Review by Z. A. Bokhari' and an almost indecipherable timing, which is probably 13½ minutes.

The German offensive against our Russian allies is now at its height, and it would be stupid to disguise the fact that the situation is very serious. The main German drive, as we foretold in earlier newsletters, is south eastward towards the region of the Caucasus. The Germans have now crossed the upper reaches of the River Don, and fighting is now going on around and inside the important town of Voronezh. & *their advance here seems to have been halted but* they are also making fierce attacks further south in the direction of Rostov, the important city near the mouth of the Don and the Donets, which the Russians recaptured from the Germans last year, and in the direction of Stalingrad on the Volga. Both Rostov and Stalingrad are in danger.

In these attacks the Germans' aim is evidently two-fold. The final aim is, of course, to capture the oil fields of the Caucasus and the Middle East, but the more immediate aim is to cut communications between this area and the more northerly parts of Russia. By crossing the Don near Voronezh, they have already cut one important route northward, since this move has put them across the railway between Voronezh and Rostov. A further advance might leave only one railway line from this area open to the Russians, while if the Germans could get as far as Stalingrad all direct railway communication between the Caucasus region and the northern fronts of Moscow and Leningrad would be cut. This does not, of course, mean that the Russian oil could not any longer be transported, but it would mean that it would have to be transported by round about routes and largely by river, putting an enormous extra strain on the Russian transport system.

This phase of the war is essentially a struggle for oil. The Germans are trying to win for themselves the fresh supplies of oil that would allow them to continue their campaign of aggression, and at the same time trying to strangle the Russian people by cutting their supplies of oil and thus starving both their war industries and their agriculture. Taking the long view, we may say that either the Germans must reach the Caspian Sea this year or they have lost the war, though they might be able to go on fighting for a considerable time. If they do reach the Caspian Sea and get possession of the oil areas, that *doesn't mean that they have won the war, but it* does mean that their capacity to fight is greatly prolonged, and the task of the allies becomes very much heavier. The Germans are throwing all they can into this battle in a desperate effort to finish with Russia before the growing strength of Britain and America can be brought against them in the west. The objective with which they actually started the Russian campaign a year ago, that of destroying the Russian armies, has not been achieved, and as they now probably realise, never will be achieved. The Russian losses have been enormous, but so have those of the Germans who are less able to bear them. The Soviet Government has just issued a casualty list giving the German losses in the last two months as nine hundred thousand and their own at three hundred and fifty thousand. On the whole, in spite of the gravity of the crisis at this moment, we may look forward with some confidence, remembering that last year the Germans started their offensive a month or more earlier than they started it this year, and still failed to reach a decision before winter over-came° them.

In Egypt, the German attack which looked so threatening ten days ago appears to have been halted. The two armies are still almost where they were a week ago, near El Alamein on the Egyptian coast. The Germans have made and at this moment are still making strong attacks, but so far without succeeding in dislodging the British from their positions. On the other hand the British have succeeded in making small advances and taking between two and three thousand prisoners. We ought not to imagine that the danger to Egypt has been removed, but at any rate the German plan of reaching Alexandria and perhaps Cairo in one swift rush has vanished. It is more easy for the German armies in Africa to receive fresh supplies than it is for the British, because their supplies are only making the short trip from Italy while ours are travelling round the Cape of Good Hope. But in the present battle the supply situation favours the British, who are nearer to their bases, and during the last ten days have been bringing up reinforcements from Egypt and probably from the Middle East. It seems likely that while the Germans have numerical superiority in tanks and possibly in men, the command of the air lies more with the British. We must expect the Germans to make further attacks, because it would not only be valuable to them to capture our naval base at Alexandria, but also because this is the southern prong of the offensive against the oil regions in which the Russian attack is the northern prong. On the other hand, if the Germans do not succeed in advancing further into Egypt in the near future, they have not much to gain by staying where they are. Probably, therefore, they will make one more all out effort to break through and if that fails, will fall back into Italian Libya.

Political developments in the Middle East following on the German success in Libya have probably been very disappointing to the Axis. The German and Italian promises to liberate Egypt have not made any impression. It is indeed difficult to see how they could do so, when on one side of Egypt lies Libya, which is under the very oppressive rule of the Italians, and on the other side lies Abyssinia, which was wantonly attacked and oppressed by the Italians until the British and Abyssinian armies set it free last year. The Egyptian answer to German and Italian promises is, not unnaturally, 'If you are so anxious to set others free, why don't you start by setting free the Arabs of Libya?' We reported last week that the Turkish Premier, Dr Refik Saydam, had died, and the Germans probably hoped that he would be succeeded by some statesman less friendly to the Allies. He has been succeeded, however, by Mr Sarajoglu,[1] who is also known as a firm friend of Britain, and was one of those who drew up the Turkish-British Alliance. The American Government has notified the Vichy Government that in the case of the Germans advancing further into Egypt, they will support any move the British may make to deal with the Vichy warships now interned at Alexandria. One object of the German offensive was probably to get hold of these ships, which include a battle-ship and some cruisers; now this design is foiled, for if Alexandria should prove to be in danger, the British will either sink these ships or remove them via the Suez Canal.

The German battleship the *Tirpitz* has been torpedoed and damaged, by a Russian submarine. This is the only heavy warship left to the Germans, and though it is a new ship of enormous power it has not yet been employed very successfully. Last time it emerged in an attempt to harry the convoys going to Murmansk, it was driven back into harbour by British torpedo carrying planes and this time it has received damage which will probably keep it out of action for several months. The struggle to keep supplies flowing into Russia through the port of Murmansk continues ceaselessly, and is not achieved without losses to the Allies. Another big convoy has got there within the last week. The Germans have made fantastic claims about the number of ships sunk by their aeroplanes and submarines. Those can be disregarded,[2] but it is known that some of the ships in the convoy were lost, a thing which cannot be avoided at this time of year when in the far north there is no night, and the sun shines continuously for about six weeks.

The island of La Mayotte, near Madagascar has been taken over by the British from Vichy France. This was achieved without blood-shed. Though a small operation, this was an important one, since German submarines were probably operating from the island and now that it is in British hands, the journey round Africa will be safer for our ships.

Four days ago, July 14th, was one of the great national anniversaries of France, the anniversary of the fall of the Bastille more than 150 years ago. The Bastille was the prison in which the French kings locked up their political opponents and its capture by the people of Paris was the first step in the French Revolution and the downfall of the French monarchy.[3] That day has been celebrated in France every year until now. This year Marshal Pétain, the puppet ruler of the Germans, forbade the usual celebrations and ordered July 14th to be observed as a day of mourning. It was extensively celebrated, however, in Britain and in all the other territories where the Free French Forces are serving, and British aeroplanes marked the day by scattering over France five million (5,000,000) leaflets promising that before very long July 14th should again be celebrated as the birthday of the Republic and the day of France's liberation from tyranny.

1. Şükrü Saracoğlu (1887–1953) was Turkish Foreign Minister, 1938–42, and in 1939 was responsible for concluding a treaty of alliance with France and the United Kingdom However, as Prime Minister (1942–46), he continued Turkey's policy of neutrality until February 1945, when Turkey declared war on the Axis powers. For Churchill's discussions with Saracoğlu on 31 January 1943, see *The Second World War*, IV, 630–36; U.S.: *The Hinge of Fate*, 705–10.
2. Convoy PQ-17 suffered a disastrous fate. Of 39 ships, 23 merchant ships and one rescue ship were lost. The Royal Naval escort was ordered to abandon the merchant ships. The Russian claim to have damaged *Tirpitz* proved unfounded.
3. Though symbolically the end of the *ancien régime*, the Bastille held only seven prisoners when it was stormed in 1789, one of whom was the Marquis de Sade.

1300. Bengali Newsletter, 1

18 July 1942

The English original was written by Orwell, and translated and read by S. K. Das Gupta.[1] No script has been traced.

1. Das Gupta (see *1277, n. 1*) was the regular translator and reader of this newsletter and is not hereafter listed except when a talks booking form is prepared for him. In December 1942 Mrs. Renu Ghosh joined him in adding news of special interest to Bengali women; see *1681* and *1720*.

1301. Vida Hope

18 July 1942   PP/EB

Dear Miss Hope,[1]

I am writing to ask you whether you would be interested in taking part in a somewhat experimental programme which we are producing for the first time on 11th August. This programme is called "Voice", and is a kind of spoken magazine, with poems, short stories and so forth. We have for the first number a monologue by Inez Holden,[2] which could make a very good item, if read by a suitable actress. It was written for print, and therefore will need a certain amount of alteration, but we can manage that. It would take about 6 minutes, possibly even less. I think it would probably be a case of two rehearsals, besides the actual recording of the programme.

As this programme is something in the nature of an experiment, the fees involved will not be very large—I don't want to be handicapped in advance by incurring great expenses. Would you be interested to hear more of this? If so, could you be kind enough to let me know as early as possible?

Yours truly,
George Orwell
Talks Producer
Indian Section

1. Vida Hope (1918–1963) was an actress and director currently in *Whitehall Follies* at the Ambassadors in London. She had appeared in Herbert Farjeon's *Diversion 2*; Orwell had reviewed this 'mixture,' as it was called, in *Time & Tide*, 11 January 1941, and described her performance as 'delightful' (see *744*).
2. 'Poor Relation.' For Inez Holden, see *1326, n. 1*. Hope was paid £6.6s for reading this monologue.

1302. To J. F. Horrabin

18 July 1942   Handwritten draft and typewritten version   PP/EB

Dear Horrabin,
Many thanks for yours of 17th July. I think of the two "The War of the Three Oceans" would be the best title. Could you let me have your synopsis fairly soon (for 13½ minute talks as before)?

Yours,
George Orwell
Talks Producer
Indian Section
Dictated by George Orwell and
dispatched in his absence by:[1]

1. Although said to be dictated, Horrabin's letter to Orwell of 17 July has the complete text of this letter in Orwell's hand on its verso. The letter was probably sent by Nancy Parratt.

1303. To J. A. Lauwerys
18 July 1942   PP/EB/NP

Dear Mr. Lauwerys,
I am sorry for having rather long delayed in sending back these copies of your script. I was much interested in them, but I am afraid we cannot do anything of that kind just at present, owing to the pressure of other material. I am, however, keeping in mind your idea of dramatising lives of great individual figures, in the scientific world, as I think it is something we could profitably do when the programme is a bit emptier.

Yours sincerely,
George Orwell
Talks Producer
Indian Section

1304. Gujarati Newsletter, 21
20 July 1942

The English original was written by Orwell. No script has been traced. PasB gives timing as 11 minutes.

1305. To E. C. Bowyer
21 July 1942   PP/EB/NP

Dear Mr. Bowyer,
Mr. Peter Masefield tells me that you have very kindly agreed to do a discussion with him in the Eastern Service, on Aviation. These broadcasts take about 13½ minutes, which [mea]ns probably that your contribution would be in the neighbourhood of 750 words. The date of this broadcast would be July 31st, at 1.45 p.m. DBST. This means that I should like the script by the end of this week if possible.

I should be glad if you could let me have as soon as possible a few details about yourself, for our advance publicity. If you care to ring up my office, my secretary can take down the details. My telephone number is Euston 3400, Extension 195.[1]

Yours sincerely,
George Orwell
Talks Producer
Indian Section

1. E. C. Bowyer was on the staff of the Information Department of the Society of British Aircraft Constructors. He wrote to Orwell on 23 July; he was at a loss to know what sort of details to supply, and wondered what a human story about oneself was. See last section of Orwell's letter to Horrabin, *1317*.

1306. To Henry Wickham Steed

21 July 1942   PP/EB

Dear Mr. Wickham Steed,[1]

Following on our telephone conversation, the discussion we wanted for the 7th August is to deal with the Press, and more particularly with the freedom of the Press. The [way] we usually do it is to ask each speaker to write out more or less what he wants to say, after which we work the two statements up into a dialogue which is then rehearsed and recorded. I haven't yet arranged for a speaker to debate with you, but we are trying to get Mr. Hamilton Fyfe.[2] As these broadcasts take about 13½ minutes, your contribution should be about 750 words. I wonder if you could be kind enough to let me have it by the end of July. This will give us time to arrange a recording about August 5th.

Yours sincerely,
George Orwell
Talks Producer
Indian Section

1. Henry Wickham Steed (1871–1956) joined the *Times* in 1896 and was its editor, 1919–22. He then bought the *Review of Reviews*, which he edited, 1923–30. He lectured at King's College London on Central European history, 1925–38, and broadcast on world affairs in the BBC Overseas Service, 1937–47.
2 Henry Hamilton Fyfe (1869–1951), a journalist who first worked on the *Morning Advertiser* in 1902, edited the *Daily Mirror*, 1903–07, and was special correspondent to the *Daily Mail*, 1907–18 His most famous journalistic achievement was his telegram concerning the retreat from Mons in 1914, which laid bare the full measure of the disaster facing Britain. From 1922 he edited or worked in various capacities for the *Daily Herald*, the *Daily Chronicle*, and *Reynold's News*.

1307. BBC Talks Booking Form, 21.7.42

E. C. Bowyer: 'I'd Like It Explained,' 1, Aviation (with Peter Masefield); broadcast 31.7.42; fee £8.8s. Signed: Z. A. Bokhari.

1308. BBC Talks Booking Form, 21.7.42

Peter Masefield: 'I'd Like It Explained,' 1, Aviation (with E. C. Bowyer); broadcast 31.7.42; fee £8.8s. Signed: Z. A. Bokhari.

1309. War-time Diary

<u>22.7.42</u>: *From Ahmed Ali's[1] last letter from India:*
 "Here is a little bit of old Delhi which might interest you.
 "In a busy street a newsboy was shouting[2] in Urdu: 'Pandit Jawaharlal[3] saying his rosary the other way round'. What he meant was that he had changed his attitude towards the Government. Questioned he said: 'You can never be sure of him, today he says side with the Government and help in the war effort, tomorrow just the opposite'. He turned away from me and began shouting his cry, adding: 'Jawaharlal has given a challenge to the Government'. I could not find this 'challenge' in the papers.
 "Other newsboys selling Urdu papers: 'Germany has smashed Russia in the very first attack'. Needless to say I read just the opposite in my English papers the next morning. Obviously the Urdu papers had repeated what Berlin had said. No one stops the newsboys shouting what they like.
 "One day going in a tonga I heard the driver shout to his horse as he shied: 'Why do you get back like our Sarkar! Go forward like Hitler!' and he swore".
 ["Its rather fun going out to the bazars and markets and listening to the loud gossip—provided, of course, it is not unbearably hot. I shall tell you more from time to time, if you are interested."]

1. Listener Research Director, BBC New Delhi Office; see *1103, n. 3.*
2. *shouting*] from shouting
3. Pandit Jawaharlal Nehru (1889–1964), General Secretary and then President of the Indian National Congress, was educated at Harrow and Cambridge. After the massacre at Amritsar in 1919, he joined the fight for independence and was particularly associated with Gandhi, although at times they opposed one another's policies. Frequently imprisoned by the British, he became India's first prime minister when independence was achieved in 1947.

1310. Marathi Newsletter, 21

23 July 1942

Misnumbered as 22 on the talks booking form; no script has been traced. It was written by Orwell, and translated and read by M. R. Kothari. PasB gives the timing as 13 minutes.

1311. To Z. A. Bokhari

23 July 1942   Handwritten

I.P.O.
For censorship please (6.8.42.)
The tone of this is pretty tough but I think O.K. I have marked one or two passages which I feel are a bit doubtful.[1]

E. A. Blair   23.7.42

1. This memorandum is written at the foot of a letter from Chinna Durai of 22 July 1942, sent with his script. In a hand other than Orwell's (Bokhari's?) are the title, 'Open Letter to a Pacifist,' and 'Recording to-morrow, Friday 24th July.' Boldly written on Durai's letter is 'URGENT,' presumably referring to the need for censorship. See *1294*.

1312. To Cyril Connolly
23 July 1942   PP/EB

Dear Cyril,
As you lost our last letter,[1] I will explain again about the magazine "Voice". The lay-out of the first number is to be more or less as follows. First a sort of editorial by myself, then a poem by somebody (we are going to have people reading their own poems as much as possible), then a monologue by Inez Holden and probably read by Vida Hope; then a poem by Herbert Read, and then one by Henry Treece, in order to represent the newest school of poetry. We shall then have a discussion of this poem by the four or five people present. And then, in order to round off, I want you to read a poem of a different type, to make a contrast, and I suggested your reading that one of Auden's first because I heard you read it very successfully before, and secondly because it has a sort of serene quality which would tone in rather well with the signature tune we always put at the end of these programmes. With the audience that we are aiming at, one need not bother about a poem of this sort being rather stale.

The date of the first issue of "Voice" is August 11th. I think this programme will need at the least one rehearsal and then on a later day the recording of the whole programme. In each case, we shall if possible, have to get all the contributors together at one time, as we must if possible, tie the thing together neatly. But I don't suppose it means more than a couple of hours at each session. I will let you know exact dates later.

Yours,
(George Orwell)

1. 13 July; see *1273*.

1313. To T. S. Eliot
23 July 1942   PP/EB

Dear Eliot,
Very many thanks for your kind letter. I believe Bokhari is arranging with you to read your three latest long poems during the latter part of October. I wonder if I can also interest you in a rather experimental programme which we are starting shortly? This is a spoken magazine, which we are calling "Voice", and it will be devoted mainly to poetry, and as far as possible we are getting people to read their own poems. We are bringing out the first number

on August 11th, and if it is not a failure we are likely to continue with at any rate three more numbers, at monthly intervals. I will tell you how the first one goes off, and you might find it interesting to take part in a later number.

Your sincerely,
George Orwell
Talks Producer
Indian Section

1314. To Cyril Falls

23 July 1942   PP/EB/NP

Dear Captain Falls,[1]
Following on our telephone conversation, you may like to hear more exactly what we want from you in your broadcast. The idea of this broadcast is to give Indian listeners some information about recent progress in Mechanised Warfare, and so far as possible about future developments. If you can compress what you think about this into about seven or eight hundred words and send it to me not later than September 10th, I will then combine it with General Fuller's[2] statement, so as to make a dialogue, and you and General Fuller can come here at a date we will arrange to suit you round about September 15th, and you can make any alterations you like in the script before we rehearse and record the broadcast. I think, as this is for the Indian audience, you ought [no]t to assume so much knowledge of the subject as you could with a British audience.

Yours sincerely,
George Orwell
Talks Producer
Indian Section

1. Captain Cyril Bentham Falls (1888–1971), author, journalist, and military commentator, broadcast regularly for the BBC on the progress of the war. In addition to several official military histories, he wrote a critical study of Rudyard Kipling and some fiction.
2. Major-General J. F. C. Fuller; see *1316, n. 1*.

1315. To C. R. Fay

23 July 1942   PP/EB/NP

Dear Professor Fay,
Many thanks for your letter dated July 18th. We will communicate with Mr. Lucette or someone similar as you suggest, as we have no wish to take up your valuable time unnecessarily.[1]

I am sorry you have been troubled for nothing.

Yours truly,
George Orwell
Talks Producer
Indian Section

1. For Fay, see *1239* and *1296*; for Lucette, see *1239, n. 2.*

1316. To J. F. C. Fuller

23 July 1942   PP/EB/NP

Dear General Fuller,

I am writing to ask whether you would care to take part in a forthcoming broadcast in the Eastern Service. We have a series addressed to the Indian public, called "I'd Like it Explained", in which subjects of current interest are discussed by experts, in response to questions by an Indian interviewer. We would like it very much if you would discuss the subject of Mechanised Warfare with Captain Cyril Falls, who has already said that he is willing to take part if you are. These talks take 13½ minutes, which means that each of the two people taking part in the discussion has about 750 to 800 words to say. The way we usually do it is to ask each speaker to write out at about that length what he thinks on the subject, after which I work the two statements up into a discussion. The speakers then meet, make any alterations they think fit in their speeches, and then rehearse and record the discussion.

This talk is fixed for September 18th, which means that I should want your script not later than September 10th. Could you please let me know whether you are willing to undertake this?[1] My telephone number is Euston 3400, Extension 195.

I may say that apart from considerations of security censorship, you have almost complete freedom of speech in these transmissions.

Yours truly,
Eric Blair
Talks Producer
Indian Section

1. Major-General J. F. C. Fuller (1878–1966; CB, DSO), soldier and author, served with distinction in the South African war and World War I. From 1920 he published many books on military history and current and future warfare, among them *Decisive Battles* (1939–40; enlarged, 1954–56); *Machine Warfare* (1941), and *Armoured Warfare* (1943). He declined Orwell's invitation by telephone and also wrote on 28 July regretting that he had too much work on hand to enable him to take part. See also *1379, headnote.* In January 1993 Fuller's name appeared in a list of eighty-two suspected collaborators released by the Public Record Office under the system which belatedly makes available for public scrutiny documents previously sealed as confidential. Fuller's name headed the list of those to be arrested immediately if Hitler's forces landed in Britain. He had been identified by the security services 'as the military strongman willing to take part in, if not preside over, a British Vichy.' Field-Marshal Lord Carver, in his entry on Fuller in the *Dictionary of National Biography*, described Fuller as believing in 'an idealised form of fascism' in the 1930s (*Sunday Telegraph*, 10 January 1993).

Orwell's pamphlet collection includes Fuller's *March to Sanity. What the British Union* [of Fascists] *has to Offer Britain* (n.d.; prewar).

1317. To J. F. Horrabin
23 July 1942   PP/EB

Dear Horrabin,

Very many thanks for the synopsis,[1] which sounds most stimulating. As you know, [we] got same good responses to your last lot of talks, and I will again make efforts to do some advance publicity for this lot. The first talk will be on August 7th, at 1.15 p.m. DBST, so I hope to receive your first talk about the end of this month. The following talks will be on August 14th, 21st and 28th, at *12.15 p.m. BST*. Could you let us have a few facts about your career and so forth for purposes of publicity. I know that you are connected with Plebs,[2] the News Chronicle and Star and the Tribune, but any other such details would be of interest. Our publicity people are very anxious for what they call "human interest stories" about speakers. Have you anything of this kind to communicate?

Yours
(George Orwell)

1. Of the series of four programmes, 'War of the Three Oceans,' broadcast 7, 14, 21, and 28 August 1942. Sidney Horniblow followed this with a series of six programmes, starting 4 September 1942; see *1438*.
2. *The PLEBS: Organ of the National Council of Labour Colleges* Founded in Oxford in 1909, it adopted its subtitle when it moved to London in 1919. It advertised itself as 'Labour's liveliest monthly.' The editor from 1936 to 1950 was J. P. M Millar (1893–1989), General Secretary of the National Council of Labour Colleges, 1921–64. Horrabin wrote to the journal in April 1940 saying he had read every issue since the first.

1318. To Reginald Reynolds
23 July 1942   PP/EB

Dear Reg,

Very many thanks for your letter. The idea you suggest is very interesting, and I will do my best to get it across for some future date, but I think frankly the chances[1] are against its being accepted, because it will tread on rather a lot of toes. However, we will see. As to the questions you ask about our audience, the talks in this particular transmission are aimed entirely at the English-speaking Indian audience. Of course, there is nothing to prevent Europeans in India from listening, but these talks are not meant for them, and they reach India at a time of day—5 p.m.—when Europeans are not likely to be listening except perhaps the women. The audience we are particularly after are the school and University students, and we really go on the principle of the more highbrow the better, except of course that we try to avoid using difficult language and purely local allusions, which might confuse people who are listening to something in a language which is foreign to them. I will let you know how I get on about the synopsis you sent me, and meanwhile I am always anxious to hear new ideas although actually the schedule is pretty full up at present.

Yours,
[No name/position]

1. chances] changes *in typescript*

1319. To Routledge & Sons Ltd.

23 July 1942   NP

The British Broadcasting Corporation,
Broadcasting House,
London, W.I. [letterhead]

Dear Sir,
My attention has just been drawn to a book published by you entitled "Victory or Vested Interests", in which you have included a lecture of mine delivered last year for the Fabian Society. I submitted this lecture to you in type-written form, and, I believe, corrected the proofs. I now find that you have been through it and made the most unwarrantable alterations about which I was not even consulted—a fact which I should never even have discovered if I had not bought a copy of the book, as you did not even send me one. I am communicating with my literary agents to see what remedy I have against this treatment, but meanwhile, I should be glad to have an explanation from you. I shall be obliged by an early answer.[1]

Yours truly,
[Signed] Geo. Orwell
(George Orwell)

1. T. Murray Ragg, the Managing Director, replied on 24 July explaining that they had made no alterations and had delivered copies as instructed by the Fabian Society. He suggested that someone at the Society had made the alterations. See *884, headnote* for a full account.

1320. To G. M. Young

23 July 1942   PP/EB/NP

Dear Mr. Young,
I am sorry you do not feel equal to broadcasting on the Press, but I quite see your objection. How would you like to take part in a similar discussion on the subject of Education? This talk is fixed for September 11th, and we have already fixed on T. C. Worsley, whose work you probably know, as one speaker. We should like it very much if you could be the other, and you may

perhaps find this subject more congenial. Worsley will doubtless attack the current educational system very violently, and you may feel more inclined to defend[1] it, so the basis of a real discussion is probably there.

Could you let me know as soon as possible whether you are interested, and in that case I will give you a more detailed directive. I may say, however, that by the method we usually adopt in these discussion[s], it is possible to get the whole thing over with only one visit to London.

As to copies of the Gem and Magnet,[2] I am sorry to say I have been unable to procure you any. My surviving copies are all in the country where I cannot get at them, and as they discontinued publishing them more than a year ago, I cannot procure any copies here. But I will see that[3] you get some sooner or later.

Yours sincerely,
George Orwell
Talks Producer
Indian Section

1. defend] defence, *typed in error*
2. Two of the magazines for boys discussed by Orwell in his article 'Boys' Weeklies,' *Horizon*, March 1940; see *598*.
3. that] what, *typed in error*

1321. BBC Talks Booking Form, 23.7.42

Narayana Menon: 'A.D. 2000,' 6; last in series; 15-minute talk on 'East or West? India's Cultural Future'; broadcast 31.7.42; fee £9.9s. Signed: Z. A. Bokhari.[1]

1. On 9 July, Bokhari had written to Menon saying 'Mr. Blair, who deals with talks in English to India' had Menon's name down for this topic. It was, he wrote, a subject very near to his heart and he hoped Menon would do it. He misleadingly gave the length as 18–20 minutes, and he listed other talks in the series: Darlington on 'India in the Steel Age' (see *1220*), Titmuss on India's population problem (see *1181*), Russell on 'The Future of Indian Agriculture' (see *1184*), and 'The Future of Education in India,' by Sir Henry Sharp, presumably suggested by Sir Frank Brown (see *1237*); no correspondence with Sharp has been traced. Bokhari went on: 'These talks have all been given by experts and though they might come under the heading "Speculation", they have all been based on facts.'

1322. War-time Diary

23.7.42: *I now make entries in this diary much more seldom than I used to, for the reason that I literally have not any spare time. And yet I am doing nothing that is not futility and have less and less to show for the time I waste. It seems to be the same with everyone—the most fearful feeling of frustration, of just footling round doing imbecile things, not imbecile because they are a part of the war and war is inherently foolish, but things which in fact don't help or in any way affect the war effort, but are considered necessary by the huge bureaucratic machine in which we are all caught up. Much of the stuff that goes out from the BBC is just shot into the stratosphere, not listened to by anybody and known by those responsible for it to be not listened to by anybody. And round this futile stuff hundreds of skilled workers are grouped* [*, costing the country tens of thousands per annum,*] *and tagging onto them are thousands of others who in effect have no real job but have found themselves a quiet niche and are sitting in it pretending to work. The same everywhere, especially in the Ministries.*

[However, the bread one casts on the waters sometimes fetches up in strange places. We did a series of 6 talks on modern English literature, very highbrow and, I believe, completely un-listened to in India. Hsiao Chi'en, the Chinese student, reads the talks in the "Listener" and is so impressed that he begins writing a book in Chinese on modern Western literature, drawing largely on our talks. So the propaganda aimed at India misses India and accidentally hits China. Perhaps the best way to influence India would be by broadcasting to China.]

The Indian Communist party, and its press, legalised again. I should say after this they will have to take the ban off the "Daily Worker", [1] *otherwise the position is too absurd.*

This reminds me of the story David Owen *[2] told me and which I believe I didn't enter in this diary. Cripps on his arrival in India asked the Viceroy to release the interned Communists. The Viceroy consented (I believe most of them have been released since), but at the last moment got cold feet and said nervously: "But how can you be sure they're really Communists?"*

We are going to have to increase our consumption of potatoes by 20 percent, so it is said. Partly to save bread, and partly to dispose of this year's potato crop, which is enormous. [3]

* *Then secretary to Stafford Cripps* [Orwell's handwritten footnote in typescript].

1. "Daily Worker",] "Daily Worker";
2 Arthur David Kemp Owen (1904–1970) was personal assistant to Cripps, the Lord Privy Seal, 19 February–21 November 1942.
3. The Ministry of Food (where Eileen worked) promoted a cartoon character, Potato Pete, in a campaign to persuade people to eat a pound of potatoes a day.

1323. To P. Chatterjee

24 July 1942   PP/EB/NP

Dear Dr. Chatterjee,
Thank you for your script and your letter of July 23rd. [1] I found the script very interesting, but I am afraid that our series "The Man in the Street" came [to] an end this week, and I shall not be able to fit it into any of the new series.

I am therefore returning your script. I am sorry we are unable to use it, but I hope you will understand my difficulty. This, of course, reflects in no way on the literary merit of your work.

Yours sincerely,
Eric Blair
Talks Producer
Indian Section

1. On 23 July, Chatterjee had sent Orwell a script on the 'LCC [London County Council] in War.' He apologised in a covering letter for the long delay; see *958*.

1324. Weekly News Review, 32

25 July 1942

The typescript has no title; 'Weekly News Review' is the description in the PasB, which gives the timing as 13' 30", and the usual 'by Z. A. Bokhari.' The typescript shows no changes; it bears both censorship stamps, and the censor was Bokhari. The talk was the last to be read by him before his departure for India for eight months. The script is not marked as having been checked with the broadcast. The section from 'If we look at the Axis propaganda . . .' to the end of the penultimate paragraph was the fifth and last specimen of propaganda reprinted by Orwell in *Talking to India*. This extract was preceded by the line, 'Here are a few notes on the nature of current Axis propaganda' adapted from a little earlier in the broadcast script.

This week, although very important events are happening, the situation has not altered radically since our last news letter. We are going, therefore, to summarize the events of the week more shortly than usual, and then, as we do from time to time, to discuss the current trends of Axis propaganda addressed to India. We do this because this propaganda has no other purpose than to deceive, and by viewing it objectively, it is often possible to infer the real intentions which it conceals.

Here is a short summary of the week's events. On the southern part of the Russian front, the situation has deteriorated, and Rostov is at the least in very great danger. The Germans are already claiming that Rostov has fallen. This claim should be treated with scepticism until confirmed from Russian sources, but it is unquestionable that the rapid advance of the Germans into the bend of the Don river puts this important town in great danger. The vital strategic point is not so much Rostov itself as Stalingrad on the Volga, and beyond that Astrakhan on the Caspian Sea. These are undoubtedly the German objectives, and if they have not reached Astrakhan before winter, it may be said with fair certainty that they have lost the war. Further north, at Voronezh, the Russian counter attacks have been successful. The Red Army has recrossed the Don and the Germans appear to have lost heavily in men and materials.

In Egypt, the situation has greatly improved. The British have made successful counter attacks, pushing the Germans back some miles and

427

capturing six thousand prisoners in the last ten days. The Indian troops have greatly distinguished themselves in these actions, several Baluchistan regiments being specially picked out for honourable mention. At the moment the Germans are probably short of aircraft, owing to the demands of the Russian front, but they are well provided with tanks, and in particular with anti-tank artillery. We must expect them to make one more large-scale attempt to break into Egypt, but their chances of doing so have grown less in the last fortnight. Should they fail in this final attempt, they will probably retreat at least to the frontiers of Libya.

There is heavy fighting in Eastern China, and the town of Wenchow has twice changed hands. It is in Japanese hands at present. The Mexican Government has taken over the oil wells in that country previously owned and operated by Japan. Reports which came from usually reliable sources suggest that the Japanese are contemplating an unannounced attack on Russia, about the end of this month. Naturally, they will choose the best moment and will probably wait till they believe that the Russians are in serious difficulties in the West. But we may be sure that the Soviet Government is well acquainted with their plans and has made suitable preparations.

We will now add a few notes on the nature of current Axis propaganda. We said current, because it is important to notice that this propaganda changes completely according to circumstances, not being concerned with revealing the truth in any way, but simply with influencing public opinion in a direction favourable to the Axis. The biggest example of such a change was when the Germans invaded Russia. Up to this moment, they exploited their pretended friendship with Russia for all it was worth, and described themselves as the Allies of a Socialist country fighting against plutocracy. They had no sooner invaded Russia than they began to describe themselves as the defenders of European civilisation against Bolshevism, appealing to the propertied classes in their second line of propaganda, just as they had appealed to the property-less classes in the first. This sudden reversal in Axis propaganda—and we choose it merely as the most outstanding example from many similar ones—should be enough to save anyone who happens to listen to it, from taking Axis propaganda at its face value.

If we look at the Axis propaganda specially directed towards India at this moment, we find that it all boils down to the pretence to be fighting against Imperialism. The Japanese slogan is "Asia for the Asiatics," and very similar phrases are a daily occurrence in German and Italian propaganda. The world picture presented by Axis propagandists is something like this. Britain and America are in possession of nearly the whole world, and are using their power in order to exploit the greater part of humanity and make hundred[s] of millions of human beings live lives of toil and misery in order to pour money into the pockets of the few hundred millionaires in London and New York. Germany, Italy and Japan are fighting against this unjust oppression, not in any way for their own interests, but simply in order to set the enslaved peoples free. When they have achieved their object, they will retire from any countries they may have had to occupy, freely granting the previously subject peoples full independence. Thus the Japanese assure the Indians that if they invaded India, it would be with no intention of settling there, but merely in order to drive the British out, after which they will retire again. Simultaneously, the Germans and Italians are assuring the Egyptians that they have no designs whatever upon Egyptian territory, but are merely invading Egypt in order to expel the British, after which they too will retire to their own territories. Similar promises are made all over the world, to any inhabitants of Allied countries who may be supposed to be dis-contented° with their present lot.

Needless to say, these promises are, on the face of it, absurd. It is clear that if the Germans, Italians and Japanese were really the enemies of Imperialism, they would start by liberating their own subject peoples. The Japanese would liberate Korea, Manchuria and Formosa, and would retire from the parts of China which they have overrun since 1937. The Italians, instead of making promises to the Egyptians, would set free the Arabs of Libya, and in any case would never have committed the aggression against the Abyssinians, which was justly avenged last year. As for the Germans, in order to make good their promises, they would have to liberate the whole of Europe.

These facts are self-evident. For Germany to call Britain Imperialistic is at best the pot calling the kettle black. Nevertheless, the Axis propagandists are not so silly as this may seem to imply. They go upon two principles, both of them sound in the short run, though probably not in the long run. The first principle is that if you promise people what they want, they will always believe you. The second is that very few people either know or are interested in knowing what is being done or said in other parts of the world than their own. The Axis propagandists know, therefore, that in their propaganda to various countries they can contradict themselves grossly without much danger of being detected. Here, for example, is one instance of such self-contradiction. At the same moment that the Axis broadcasts are assuring India that they are the friends of the coloured peoples, as against the British, they are assuring the Dutch of South Africa that they are the friends of the white race as against the black. Indeed, this conviction is inherent in the whole of Axis propaganda, since the central thesis of Nazi theory is the superiority of the white races over the Asiatic and African races and the Jews. The Germans go even further than their Italian colleagues by claiming that all that is worth while in human history has been achieved by people with blue eyes. Naturally this doctrine is left out when Berlin is broadcasting to India or Africa. The Japanese might seem to be debarred from holding any such theory, but in fact they have, and for centuries have had, a racial theory even more extreme than that of the Germans. They believe the Japanese race to be divine, all other races being hereditarily inferior; and they have incidentally a contemptuous nickname ("KORUMBA") for the negroes and other darker-skinned races. Both of these peoples, the Germans and the Japanese, and perhaps also the Italians, commit their aggressions[1] upon the theory firmly believed in by many of them that since they are superior races, they have a divine right to govern the earth. These ideas are mentioned quite freely in their home press and broadcasts, and even for outside consumption when they consider it suitable. A good many German broadcasts addressed to Britain, for example, have suggested fairly openly that the German and Anglo-Saxon peoples, as the principal[2] members of the white race, have a common interest, and ought to get together for the combined exploitation of the world. Needless to say, neither India nor Africa are supposed to hear anything of this, and since, in fact, those people have not access to the Press or Radio outside their own countries, these flagrant contradictions do generally go unnoticed.

We have made this the subject of our talk this week, because we are well aware of the nature of the Axis propaganda now being addressed to India, and we think it wise to answer it from time to time, not for the sake of exposing individual falsehoods, which would take too long, and is not worth while, but merely to issue a general warning which may help our listeners to see the world situation in perspective. Next time, therefore, that you come across a piece of plausible Axis propaganda, it is worth asking yourself this question—"If they say this to me, what are they likely to be saying to Europe, to America, to Africa, to Britain, or to China?"

A little thought along these lines will often help to counteract that other tendency which Axis broadcasters play upon, the tendency to believe any story which tells us what we want to hear.

1 The typescript has 'agressions,' the spelling commonly used by Orwell and found in the draft manuscript of *Nineteen Eighty-Four*.
2 principal] principle *in typescript*

1325. Bengali Newsletter, 2

25 July 1942

S. K. Das Gupta was booked to translate and read this newsletter, the original of which was written by Orwell, but only four minutes was transmitted; the bulk of the broadcast was a talk in Bengali by the High Commissioner for India, Sir Aziz-ul-Huque, lasting nine minutes (see *1277*). Bokhari wrote to the High Commissioner on 8 July to make arrangements for a preliminary rehearsal and he thanked him for 'consenting to give us a talk on Indians in England' as soon as he had completed a tour he was to make. In a confidential memorandum of 15 July to Miss E. W. D. Boughen attached to the booking form Sir Aziz, Bokhari said:

> I am sending a Booking Slip asking for a Contract to be issued to Sir Aziz-ul-Huque C.I.E., D.Litt. for translating and reading the Bengali Newsletter on Saturday, 25th July. (Please note, though this is confidential, that Mr. S. K. Das Gupta will be helping with the Translation).
> I understand that the previous High Commissioner[s]—Sir Firoz Khan Noon and Mr. S. Lall—were paid 10 guineas for each broadcast. It is very strongly recommended that at least the same fee should be offered to the present High Commissioner.

The matter of Das Gupta's fee of £4.4s for translating and, in effect, not reading all the script which Orwell had written, then arose. A memorandum from Bokhari to Miss Boughen of about 26 July suggested that he should receive an *extra* payment for reading part of the newsletter, even though that was what he had originally been commissioned to do. Then, thinking better of this, he added a P.S.: 'Or shall we leave all this, until Das Gupta approaches us?' Possibly Bokhari was confused because, on 16 July, Miss Boughen, for the Programme Contracts Director, had written to Das Gupta to say he would not be reading the Newsletter, only translating it, and she would get into touch with him later about the fee he would be paid.

1326. To Inez Holden

25 July 1942   PP/EB/NP

Dear Inez,[1]
We still have not contacted the actress we want to do your monologue, and therefore I have not yet attempted the changes which are needed to put it into spoken form. We were trying to get Vida Hope, but she has not yet replied to my letter. So I am now trying to get Joan Sterndale-Bennett.[2] Can you by any chance come in here (200 Oxford Street) on Friday afternoon, July 31st, at about 2.30 p.m.? I am trying to get all the contributors together then. It may not be possible to do the re-arrangement of your monologue before that time. Please let me know as soon as possible whether you can manage this.

Yours,
George Orwell
Talks Producer
Indian Section

1. Inez Holden (1906–1974), novelist, short-story writer, journalist, and broadcaster, was a cousin of Celia Kirwan (later Celia Goodman; see *3590A*), twin sister of Arthur Koestler's wife, Mamaine. She proved a good friend to the Orwells, offering them her flat at 106 George Street, Portman Square, in the summer of 1944 when the Orwells were bombed out of theirs. She and Orwell talked of jointly publishing their war diaries; see *1443*. She identified a number of those represented only by initials in Orwell's War-time Diary and was a prime source of information about Orwell's argument with H G. Wells. For her work at the Information Research Department in 1949 and Orwell, see *3590A* and *B*.
2. Joan Sterndale-Bennett had performed with Vida Hope in *Diversion 2*, which Orwell reviewed for *Time and Tide*; see *744*. He had warmly praised her work.

1327. To Herbert Read

25 July 1942   PP/EB

Dear Read,
About our magazine programme "Voice", in which we hope you are going to take part. Can you by any chance come in here next Friday afternoon about 2.30 p.m.? Even if you can't manage that particular time, it would no doubt do if you could come at some time in the afternoon. I am making efforts on that day to get hold of Henry Treece,[1] who presents the biggest difficulty as

he lives out of London. It will probably be easy enough to get hold of the others. Please let me know as soon as possible.

It may interest you to know that I am having a row with your publishers,[2] who, however, tell me that it is not their fault, but that of the Fabian Society. I will let you know developments later.

Yours,
George Orwell
Talks Producer
Indian Section

1. Henry Treece (1911–1966) was a poet, novelist, and writer for children, currently serving in the RAF. Most of his poetry was published in Orwell's lifetime; he concentrated thereafter on fiction. His books then included *Towards a Personal Armageddon* (1941), and *Invitation and Warning* (1942). His *Collected Poems* was published in New York in 1946. He edited a number of anthologies (several with S. Schimanski) and also *Herbert Read: An Introduction to His Work by Various Hands* (1944). He was one of the New Apocalyptics, a poetic movement of the early 1940s. Orwell reviewed his *The New Apocalypse* in *Life and Letters*, June 1940; see *630*.
2. Routledge & Kegan Paul, for whom Read worked; see *1319*.

1328. To Henry Wickham Steed

25 July 1942   PP/EB/NP

Dear Mr. Wickham Steed,
Many thanks for your letter. I am sorry that I am unable to arrange a recording for August 5th, as I originally suggested.

I understand that 5.30 p.m. will suit you on Thursday, August 6th, and I have accordingly arranged for the recording to take place at Broadcasting House, at 5.30 p.m. Allowing time for rehearsal, you should be free by 6.45 p.m. I hope this will be convenient to you.

Yours sincerely,
George Orwell
Talks Producer
Indian Section

1329. To Henry Treece

25 July 1942   PP/EB

Dear Mr. Treece,
Very many thanks for sending along a selection of poems, which Mulk Raj Anand has brought to me. I have been through them and provisionally picked out three, which I think suitable for broadcasting. We have to consider two things, the first is that we can only broadcast something fairly short, and secondly we have to broadcast what is fairly easily intelligible because, although we are aiming at making this programme highbrow, we are speaking to people whose English is not necessarily perfect, and also because

something which is merely h[e]ard and not read needs to be comparatively simple. However, we may change the selection when you come here. I wonder whether you could come to London next Friday afternoon, about 2.30. (July 31st), and I will try to get as many of the other people taking part in the programme as possible together, so that we can do something towards [ty]ing the whole programme together. I should be very glad to put you up for the night so that you don't need to be troubled about times for getting back. Could you please let me know as soon as possible whether you can manage this?

Yours sincerely,
George Orwell
Talks Producer
Indian Section

1330. BBC Talks Booking Form, 25.7.42

Wickham Steed: 'I'd Like It Explained,' 2, 'The Press'; 13½ minute discussion with Mr. Hamilton Fyfe, in which Mr. Steed will speak for 6½ minutes'; recorded 6.8.42; broadcast 7.8.42; fee £8.8s. Signed: Z. A. Bokhari.

1331. War-time Diary

<u>26.7.42</u>: *Yesterday and today, on the Home Guard manoeuvres, passing various small camps of soldiers in the woods, radiolocation*[1] *stations etc. Struck by the appearance of the soldiers, their magnificent health and the brutalised look in their faces. All young and fresh, with round fat limbs and rosy faces with beautiful clear skins. But sullen brutish expressions—not fierce or wicked in any way, but simply stupefied by boredom, loneliness, discontent, endless tiredness and mere physical health.*

1. Radar.

1332. Gujarati Newsletter, 22

27 July 1942

The English original was written by Orwell. No script has been traced. PasB gives timing as 12' 10".

1333. To E. C. Bowyer

27 July 1942   PP/EB

Dear Mr. Bowyer,

Many thanks for your letter. The publicity people were very please° with what you gave us. I found the script very interesting, and I don't think there will have to be many alterations; there will be one minor one, however. This series is supposed to be conducted entirely by Indians and the majority of the talks are so. Where we are obliged to have a talk done by Europeans, we always have one Indian taking part, more or less in the capacity of an interviewer. I am arranging this in your case. The Indian speaker will put in a remark or two of his own, and possibly we might transfer to him one or two of the questions which you and Mr. Masefield ask of one another. No doubt it will be quite easy to arrange this during the rehearsal. I think it will be necessary to have one rehearsal of the talk. I wonder whether you could manage 4.30 p.m. on Thursday, July 30th? I am writing to Mr. Masefield to ask him the same. Failing that, it might be better to come about an hour before the talk is held on Friday. Could you please let me know about this at once?

Yours sincerely,
George Orwell
Talks Producer
Indian Section

1334. To Peter Masefield

27 July 1942   PP/EB

Dear Mr. Masefield,

Very many thanks for your script and [for] the trouble you have taken in working it up into a dialogue yourself. There will not be any serious alterations to make, but there will have to be one minor one. This series is supposed to be conducted entirely by Indians, and the majority of the talks are so. Where we are obliged to have a talk done by Europeans, we always have one Indian taking part, more or less in the capacity of an interviewer. I am arranging this in your case. The Indian speaker will put in a remark or two of his own, and possibly we might transfer to him one or two of the questions which you and Mr. Bowyer ask of one another. No doubt it will be quite easy to arrange this during the rehearsal. I think it will be necessary to have one rehearsal on the talk. [I] wonder whether you could manage 4.30 p.m. on Thursday, July 30th? I am writing to Mr. Bowyer to ask him the same. Failing that, it might be better to come about an hour before the talk is held on Friday. Could you please let me know about this at once?

Yours sincerely,
George Orwell
Talks Producer
Indian Section

1335. To T. C. Worsley

27 July 1942   PP/EB

Dear Worsley,

About the discussion on Education that you are doing for us. I am sorry for the delay, but we hesitated some time about the other speaker before fixing on G. M. Young, who I think will do very well. The procedure I suggest is as follows: you let me have your piece, about 750 words, saying what you think about the subject, I send it on to Young to criticise and then, having received his remarks, work it up into a dialogue which can be emended and rehearsed by both of you before being recorded. I think that method should work out reasonably well.

As to the manner of treatment. We are dealing with the Indian (student) public which can't be depended on to know all about conditions here. Therefore, although the Public Schools and what they stand for ought to be mentioned, they should not be the exclusive subject. The real point at issue (and here is where Young is likely to disagree, making a real discussion) is whether education should aim at fostering aristocratic or democratic values; and incidentally whether current English educational methods are suited to the modern world. I fancy you will not find it very difficult to produce something along these lines.

I hope things are going well with you. Looking forward to seeing you.

Yours,
George Orwell
Talks Producer
Indian Section

1336. War-time Diary

27.7.42: Talking today with Sultana, one of the Maltese broadcasters. He says he is able to keep in fairly good touch with Malta and conditions are very bad there. "The last letter I get this morning was like a—how you say? (much gesticulation)—like a sieve. All the pieces what the censor cut out, you understand. But I make something out of it, all the same." He went on to tell me, among other things, that 5 lb[1] of potatoes now cost the equivalent of 8 shillings. ⌐He considers that of the two convoys which recently endeavoured to reach Malta the one from England, which succeeded in getting there, carried munitions, and the one from Egypt, which failed to get there, carried food.⌐ *I said, "Why can't they send dehydrated food by plane?" He shrugged his shoulders, seeming to feel instinctively that the British government would never go to that much trouble over Malta. Yet it seems that the Maltese are solidly pro-British, thanks to Mussolini, no doubt.*

⌐The German broadcasts are claiming that Voroshilov[2] is in London, which is not very likely and has not been rumoured here. Probably a shot in the dark to offset their recent failure over Molotov,[3] and made on the calculation that *some* high-up Russian military delegate is likely to be here at this moment. If the story should turn out to be true, I shall have to revise my ideas about the German secret service in this country.[1]

The crowd at the Second Front meeting in Trafalgar Square[4] *estimated at 40,000 in the rightwing papers and 60,000 in the leftwing. Perhaps 50,000 in reality. My spy reports that in spite of the present Communist line of "all power to Churchill", the Communist speakers in fact attacked the Government very bitterly.*[5]

28.7.42: *Today I have read less newspapers than usual, but the ones I have seen have gone cold on the Second Front, except for the "News-Chronicle".* [The "Evening News" published an anti-Second Front article (by General Brownrigg[6]) on its front page.] *I remarked on this to Herbert Read who said gloomily "The Government has told them to shut up about it".* [It is true of course that if they are intending to start something they must still seem to deny it.] *Read said he thought the position in Russia was desperate and seemed very upset about it, though in the past he has been even more anti-Stalin than I. I said to him, "Don't you feel quite differently towards the Russians now they are in a jam?" and he agreed. For that matter I felt quite differently towards England when I saw that England was in a jam. Looking back I see that I was anti-Russian (or more exactly anti-Stalin) during the years when Russia appeared to be powerful, militarily and politically, ie. 1933 to 1941. Before and after those dates I was pro-Russian. One could interpret this in several different ways.*

A small raid on the outskirts of London last night. The new rocket guns,[7] *some of which are*[8] *manned by Home Guards, were in action* [and are said to have brought down some planes (8 planes down altogether).]

This is the first time the Home Guard can properly be said to have been in action, a little over 2[9] *years after its formation.*

The Germans never admit damage to military objectives, but they acknowledge civilian casualties after our bigger raids. After the Hamburg raid of 2 nights ago they described the casualties as heavy. The papers here reproduce this with pride. Two years ago we would all have been aghast at the idea of killing civilians. I remember saying to someone during the blitz, when the RAF were hitting back as best they could, "In a year's time you'll see headlines in the Daily Express: 'Successful Raid on Berlin Orphanage. Babies Set on Fire' ". It hasn't come to that yet, but that is the direction we are going in.

---

1 5 *lb*] 5 lbs
2. For General Kliment Voroshilov, see *567, 31.8 39, n. 1.* Churchill was to meet him, on 12 August 1942, but in Moscow (see Winston Churchill, *The Second World War*, IV 429; U.S.: *The Hinge of Fate*, 494).
3. For Vyacheslav Molotov, see *565, 28.8.39, 4.* Churchill gives an account of a private talk with him at this time in *The Second World War* (IV, 436–37; U.S.: *The Hinge of Fate*, 484). A principal issue at stake was the opening of a Second Front.
4. *Square*] Square yesterday
5. *bitterly*] violently
6. Lieutenant-General Sir W. Douglas S. Brownrigg (1886–1946) was Adjutant-General to the

British Expeditionary Force, 1939–40. He retired in 1940 but was appointed Zone and Sector Commander of the Home Guard, 1941.
7. The anti-aircraft branch of the Home Guard, under General Sir Frederick Pile (1884–1976, Bt.), was equipped with rocket launchers. These were each capable of firing two one-hundredweight rockets and were massed in batteries of sixty-four. Not all the rockets would necessarily be fired at once. The rockets were not particularly accurate, but they created a 'box' of shrapnel capable of damaging and bringing down planes. They were less use against low-flying planes in built-up areas because they were liable to take the roofs off houses surrounding the battery. Orwell probably dropped 'now' from the typescript (see *n. 8*) because these guns, though to a small extent manned by full-time servicemen, were, like the spigot mortar, chiefly Home Guard weapons.
8. *are*] are now
9. *2*] two

1337. To Mr. Baddeley[1]

29 July 1942   PP/EB

Dear Mr. Baddeley,
I enclose a copy of a script written [by] Peter Masefield (Air correspondent of the Sunday Times) and E. C. Bowyer (Information Department of the Society of British Aircraft Constructors) for censorship.

The discussion will be broadcast at 1.15 p.m. on Friday, July 31st, in the Eastern Service of the BBC. I should be glad if I could have the script back by Friday morning. My address is—Room 310, 200, Oxford Street, W.1.

Yours sincerely,
Eric Blair
Talks Producer
Indian Section

1. Unidentified. The letter is addressed to Room 117, ICI House, Milbank. Censorship of Bowyer's later scripts was done at the Admiralty and, for the RAF, at Queen Anne's Gate (see *1856* and *1876*). This may have been an earlier Air Ministry censorship address.

1338. To Peter Masefield and to E. C. Bowyer

29 July 1942   PP/EB/NP

Dear Mr. Masefield,
I enclose a copy of the script of your discussion with Mr. Bowyer, in which I have inserted one or two questions for the Indian interviewer to ask you.

I shall expect you on Friday, July 31st, at about 12 o'clock, at my office at 200, Oxford Street—this is on the corner of Great Portland Street and Oxford Street.[1]

Yours sincerely,
George Orwell
Talks Producer
Indian Section

1. Identical letters were sent to the two men, with only the names transposed.

1339. Marathi Newsletter, 22

30 July 1942

This was misnumbered as 23. PasB gives Bokhari as announcer and Miss Chitale as switch censor. The script was written by Orwell and read by M. R. Kothari. The timing is given as 13′ 5″. The talks booking form has Orwell as author of the script and Kothari as reader crossed through in ink, but the evidence of the PasB that Kothari read the script suggests that this was an error. No script has been traced.

1340. To Herbert Read

30 July 1942   PP/EB

Dear Read,
In furtherance to our conversation, we more or less got started on our radio magazine "Voice" to-day, and we are very anxious that you should take part. This would mean two sessions, one the sort of final dress rehearsal, and the other the actual recording. I doubt whether it is feasible to telescope them into one, though it might be. If you can't make two visits to London for this, you could just record the two poems I want you to read; but I would like you, if possible, to be there to take part in the discussion. The poems I want you to read are your own poem, "The Contrary Experience", which should come at the beginning of the programme, and at the end Wordsworth's sonnet "The World is too much with us". You could choose another if you like, but I think this will fit in well. Treece unfortunately cannot come, because he has an exam, or something, but his poems are being read by John Atkins,[1] who does them quite well. I will send you a copy of the script as soon as it is more or less in shape. Please let me know about this as soon as possible.

Yours,
George Orwell
Talks Producer
Indian Section

1. John Atkins (1916–), author, critic, and university teacher, interviewer for Mass Observation, 1939–41 was literary editor of *Tribune* from 1942 until Orwell took over in November 1943 when Atkins was called up for war service. From 1944 to 1947, he edited *Albion*. His books include studies of Hemingway (1952), Koestler (1954), Aldous Huxley (1955), Graham Greene (1963), and J. B. Priestley (1981), general critical works, and novels. In 1953 he published *George Orwell: A Literary and Biographical Study*.

1341. To Henry Treece

30 July 1942   Top and carbon copies   PP/EB/NP

Dear Mr. Treece,
Many thanks for your letter. I am so sorry you can't come this time, but I

think I shall still use some of your poems. I selected three provisionally and will let you know which we actually do use, and get someone else to read them.[1] Perhaps another time, when you are actually in London, you could come in and record a poem which we could stick into a later programme. That particular operation does not take long, perhaps half an hour, but we have to arrange the recording beforehand which means about a day's notice.

Hoping to meet you some time.

Yours sincerely,
[Signed] Geo. Orwell
George Orwell
Talks Producer
Indian Section

1. They were read by John Atkins, see *1340*

1342. BBC Talks Booking Form, 31.7.42

Narayana Menon: 'Presenting a programme of gramophone records for 12 minutes—Mr Menon chose the records & spoke for about 2 minutes'; broadcast 31.7.42; fee £3.13.6. Signed: Z. A. Bokhari. Remarks: 'This followed Mr. Menon's talk in the series 'A.D. 2000,' for which he has already received a contract,' see *1321*.

1343. [Weekly News Review], 33

1 August 1942

It had been expected that Bokhari would by this time have been on his way to India, but he did not sail until 29 September, and returned on 13–14 May 1943. However, though Bokhari censored this script, it was read by Shridhar Telkar as planned (see *1266*). Neither the typescript nor PasB has a title; the former simply says; 'Read by Shridhar Telkar of the Oriental News Agency.' The script carries both censorship stamps and has been checked with the broadcast. Apart from some mistypings and a false start or two, the only emendations are a few words probably obliterated for stylistic reasons, for example, in the first paragraph, 'very' before 'roundabout' and an adjective before 'train.' These have not been noted here.

On the Russian front the news continues to be extremely grave. The Germans have now crossed the Don river, and are moving south into the Caucasus area. The important city of Rostov fell several days back, and it is south of Rostov that the German advance has been most rapid. It is uncertain how far they have yet got. They have at any rate entered Bataisk, about 50 miles south of Rostov, where there are a few oil wells. We can assume that the Russians blocked these or otherwise put them out of action when it became clear that they might fall into German hands. Simultaneously with this southward movement another body of German troops has been moving eastward into the angle of the Don, in the direction of the important town of Stalingrad. Here, however, they have been stopped, and all their efforts to cross the Don, as also further north near Voronezh, have failed. In general the position is such that the entire body of Russian troops in the Caucasus area is in danger of being cut off from the more northern parts of Russia. Even should the Germans reach Stalingrad, communications between Moscow and Leningrad on the one hand, and the Caucasus region on the other, do indeed exist, but by roundabout routes which put a strain on transport. Of course, even if the Germans should succeed in separating the northern and southern Russian armies, that does not mean that they have reached the oil, which is their chief objective. They have still got to meet the Russian armies in the Caucasus, and the British Ninth Army in the Middle East. But they might, by severing the communication between this all-important oil area and the rest of Russia, starve the northern Russian armies of oil for their vehicles, and at the same time strike a very severe blow at the economic life of the whole of the Soviet Union. Russian agriculture is done mainly with tractor ploughs, which need constant supplies of oil. There are natural sources of oil in Russia in several areas apart from the Caucasus, including considerable supplies beyond the Ural mountains, in places where it is impossible for the Germans to get at them. It is also probable that the Soviet Government has placed large dumps of oil all over the country, in preparation for just such an emergency as this. Meanwhile, however, the productive capacity of the Russian armaments factories must be adversely affected, both by the loss of territory and by the extra strain on communications. The war is now at its climax, and it is no use denying that the situation is very bad—as bad as, or perhaps worse, than it was in the autumn of last year. Nevertheless, the campaign has not gone according to the German plan. The destruction of the Red Army, which was the primary aim of the Germans, has not been accomplished, and the German commentators are beginning to admit that it cannot be accomplished. Politically, the German attempt to subjugate Soviet Russia has been an utter failure. There has been no kind of Quisling activity whatever in the occupied areas[1] and the Germans do not even pretend that the inhabitants are anything but hostile to them. It is significant that recently they have enormously increased the number of their armed police force—a silent confession that the so-called New Order can only be maintained by naked force. Although the Germans have now over-run large and very rich territories, these are not of much direct use to them, since they have not the labour to exploit them, they cannot successfully force the inhabitants to work, and they have to contend everywhere with the results of a scorched earth policy carried out with extreme thoroughness. In a positive sense, therefore, the Germans have not gained much by their conquests, and probably will not gain much. In a negative sense however, they have gained by reducing the offensive power of our Russian Allies, and this will remain so until the territories at least as far west as Kharkov have been won back.

In Egypt, there is little to report since last week. The British have made several successful attacks, but all the activities have been on a comparatively small scale. It is evident that the hope of swiftly reaching the Suez Canal, about which the Axis broadcasters were talking so unguardedly a fortnight ago, has now faded. The present stage of the Egyptian campaign is being fought largely by Indian troops, who have won themselves very high praise from the Commander in Chief.

On Sunday, July 26th, a huge meeting was held in London, to demand the opening of a Second Front in Western Europe. It was attended by people of all kinds, and the crowd numbered not less than fifty thousand people. We do not care to express any opinion as to whether the British and American Governments will or will not open a second front° this year. It is obvious that whatever the Government's intentions may be, it cannot disclose them prematurely, but it is important to realise that the mere idea of the opening of a Second Front deeply affects the strategy of the war. On their own statement, the Germans are feverishly at work fortifying the whole Western coast of Europe against a possible attack, and the danger on their flank probably prevents them from using their full air strength on the Russian front. The British air attacks on Germany continue relentlessly and the Germans are only able to retaliate against Britain on a very small scale. There have been several small air raids on London and other British cities during the last week, but the anti-aircraft defences are now so good that in each case the raiding force lost 10 per cent of its strength. On July 27th, there was another large scale British raid on Hamburg, carried out by about five hundred bombing planes, which even on the German admission, caused extensive damage. It was followed two days later by another raid on about the same scale. There is little doubt that these raids are going to become greater and greater both in numbers and volume. The American as well as the British air force is now beginning to take part in them, and American planes are arriving in Britain in ever greater numbers. The Chief of the Bomber Command broadcast some[2] nights ago to the German people, warning them of the heavier and heavier raids that are to come. The Germans cry out against these raids, declaring the whole policy of bombing to be wicked and inhumane, having apparently forgotten that only a year or two ago, they themselves were bombing London and other residential cities and openly boasting of the slaughter they were achieving among the civilian population. At that time Britain was not able to retaliate on a big scale, and the Germans probably imagined that this state of affairs would continue. Now that the tables are turned, they talk in a different vein. This, however, will make no difference, and the raids will increase in volume, so that before long a raid carried out by a thousand bombers will seem almost a commonplace. We do not express any opinion as to whether this air activity is or is not a prelude to an Allied invasion of Europe, but we can at least say that should such an invasion be made, the raids will have weakened the German power to resist, and helped to secure air superiority over the coast, which is indispensable if any landing is to be attempted. The British people, though recognising that the decision must rest with the Government, which alone possesses the necessary information, are extremely eager for the invasion to be made, and would be willing even to risk a great disaster if this helped our Russian allies by drawing off the German armies from the Eastern front.

Fighting has flared up again in New Guinea, where the Japanese have made a fresh landing on the northern coast.[3] The Japanese forces made another attempt to advance on Port Moresby, the possession of which is indispensable to them if they are to invade Australia, but they have been successfully beaten back.

British subjects living abroad are to be made liable for National Service.

The harvest in the British Isles is estimated to be by far the largest that has ever been known. This applies both to wheat and other cereals and even more to potatoes. Since the outbreak of war an extra six million acres have been brought under cultivation in the British Isles, and Britain is now producing about two thirds of its own food. This is a marked change from the conditions of peace time when almost all food was imported from abroad. At the same time, so far as can be discovered from reports and observations, the German harvest this year is a very poor one.

1 This was not correct, though Orwell probably did not realise this. The forced return of Soviet citizens, especially Cossacks and Ukrainians, at the end of the war, and their fate, tells a different story. German propaganda made much of those in occupied countries who chose to fight alongside or as part of German armies. The English-language edition of *Signal*, the fortnightly published by the Wehrmacht, April 1940–March 1945, under the authority of the Ministry of Propaganda, and intended for occupied and neutral countries, publicized many of them. An article, 'For Europe . . .' by Hanns Hubmann, featured the French Volunteer Legion (with a picture of Lieutenant Jacques Doriot; see *1116, n. 19*), the Spanish 'Blue Division,' and 'Germanic volunteers' from Belgium, Holland, Denmark, and Norway serving in the SS. There was a large picture of General Andrei Vlasov (1900–1946) and two Cossacks who had allied themselves to the Germans. The caption under the first picture stated: 'General Vlassov° stands out among the leaders of the various nationalities fighting as volunteers. In the world press his name has frequently been bracketed with Moscow which he defended as a Soviet general. When he realized the gulf between the Soviet programme and the real interests of his nation were not to be bridged, he resolutely faced the consequences'; he switched allegiance (see *Hitler's Wartime Picture Magazine—Signal*, edited by S. L. Mayer, 1978, unnumbered pages). The English-language edition, one of twenty different language versions, was sent in small quantities to the United States before Pearl Harbor, but was mainly intended for Ireland and the occupied Channel Islands (Mayer's Introduction).
2. The original had 'two'; this was obliterated and in the margin is a faint scrawl, interpreted as 'some.'
3. About two lines that follow have been x-ed out (lower-case 'x,' not the capitals Orwell usually used) during the typing. There appears to be a reference to Port Moresby, so this passage may be a false start for the sentence that follows. This is a change made during composition; it is not a result of censorship.

1344. Bengali Newsletter, 3

1 August 1942

The English original was written by Orwell. No script has been traced.

1345. War-time Diary

1.8.42: *If the figures given are correct, the Germans have lost about 10 per cent of their strength in each of the last raids. According to Peter Masefield this isn't anything to do with the new guns but has all been done by the night fighters. He also told me*[1] *that the new FW 190 fighter is much better than any fighter we now have in actual service.* ⌈An aircraft construction man named Bowyer who was broadcasting together with him agreed with this.⌉ *Oliver Stewart considers that the recent German raids are reconnaissance raids and that they intend starting the big blitz again soon, at any rate if they can get their hands free in Russia.*

Not much to do over the bank holiday week end. Busy at every odd moment making a hen-house.[2] *This kind of thing now needs great ingenuity owing to the extreme difficulty of getting hold of timber. No sense of guilt or time-wasting when I do anything of this type—on the contrary, a vague feeling that any* sane *occupation must be useful, or at any rate justifiable.*

1. *told me*] told me off the record
2. See letter to K. K. Ardaschır, 4 November 1942, *1631*, ın whıch Orwell asks to buy 'another pullet' from hım. The weekend would have been spent at the Orwells' cottage at Wallıngton.

1346. Review of *Charles de Gaulle* by Philippe Barrès[1]

The Observer, 2 August 1942

Mr. Philippe Barrès's book may be taken as the "official" biography of General de Gaulle, and it probably gives as full and frank an account of the Free French movement as was possible at the time when it was written—that is, some time during the summer of 1941. Necessarily silent on certain points, such as the Syrian campaign and the unsuccessful Dakar expedition, it gives much valuable detail about the circumstances of the French collapse, and it has the merit of quoting most of the relevant documents in full.

As is now widely known, General de Gaulle's views on mechanised warfare, ignored by his own countrymen, were taken up and acted upon by the Germans, who seem actually to have built up their armoured divisions for the Polish campaign on the specifications set forth in de Gaulle's book, published five years earlier. In the years between Hitler's rise to power and the outbreak of war de Gaulle had agitated as best he could, chiefly through Paul Reynaud, for a more modern conception of war than was implied in the Maginot line and a five-million conscript army, and Chapter V. of Mr. Barrès's book gives the text of the memorandum which he submitted to the High Command in January of 1940, after five months of "phony" war. In general terms this document foretold exactly what did happen a few months later.

Needless to say, his warnings went unheeded. De Gaulle languished in obscurity till the Battle of France, when for a brief period he held an important command and won some minor successes with the inadequate forces at his disposal. It was fortunate that in these few weeks he earned sufficient renown to make him the natural rallying-point of those Frenchmen who wanted to go on fighting. But why had no one, outside Germany, listened to his teachings earlier? If one thinks simply in technical terms, this is easy enough to understand. The two wars were only twenty-one years apart, and the generals who had won the war of 1914, or thought they had, were still in command. It was their instinct to see that nothing was changed, just as the Duke of Wellington struggled to keep the British Army the same in the eighteen-fifties as it had been at Waterloo. There was also the pacifism of public opinion, disillusioned by victory and only too ready for an inert defensive policy, as in England. But Mr. Barrès barely touches on the deeper political and economic causes of the French collapse. A book of this kind, written while events are still in the making, is bound to avoid certain issues. The delicacy of the situation lies in the fact that whereas in France the "collaborators" are the politicians of the Right, the Free French are of literally all political colours. General de Gaulle himself, denounced daily over the radio as a Jewish Marxist and freemason, is a Catholic of the provincial aristocracy and perhaps of royalist antecedents. Mr. Barrès is naturally rather anxious to avoid tying a political programme on to the Free French movement, though since the book was written some steps in that direction have been taken. In his pages de Gaulle appears simply as the personification of "la patrie," of the simple instinct which makes decent men of all shades of opinion unite against a foreign conqueror. On that level this book is a worthy tribute. The American translation could be improved upon.[2]

1. 'Barrès' is spelt 'Barrês' in The *Observer*.
2. See Orwell's letters to Liddell Hart, 12 and 19 August, 1942, *1379, 1396*, and *1379 headnote* regarding this review.

1347. Gujarati Newsletter, 23

3 August 1942

The English original was written by Orwell. No script has been traced. PasB gives timing as 11 minutes and an uncertain number of seconds.

1348. To Henry Wickham Steed

3 August 1942   PP/EB/NP

Dear Mr. Wickham Steed,
Many thanks for the revised draft of your discussion with Hamilton Fyfe. I am enclosing a carbon copy for you to glance through. You will notice that I have made one or two small alterations, in order to make room for an Indian interviewer. I have also cut out one or two passages, as it seemed to me to be a little on the long side.

I shall look forward to seeing you on Thursday, August 6th. As the recording and rehearsal are to be at Broadcasting House, I shall meet you in the entrance hall there.

Yours sincerely
[Initialled] E.A.B
George Orwell
Talks Producer
Indian Section

1349. BBC Talks Booking Form, 3.8.42

J. F. Horrabin: 'War of the Three Oceans'; 'on the geography of the war'; broadcast 7, 14, 21, and 28.8.42; fee £9.9s each talk. Signed: Z. A. Bokhari.

Norman Collins, the Empire Talks Manager, was greatly impressed by these broadcasts and on 31 August 1942 suggested that the Pacific, Eastern, and African Services consider using them, but they found the material too intractable. Ormond Wilson, Empire News Talks Editor, wrote to Horrabin on 5 September to say that Orwell had passed on his scripts and that the BBC would like to broadcast the talks in the North American and Pacific Services, but that lack of time would mean cutting the four fifteen-minute talks to three, each of ten minutes. For Orwell's response to the broadcast, see *1387*.

1350. War-time Diary

_3.8.42:_   _D. A._ [1]_says Churchill is in Moscow._ [2]_He also says_[3]_there isn't going to be any second front. However, if a second front is intended, the Government must do all it can to spread the contrary impression beforehand,_ [and D. A. might be one of the people used to plant the rumour.

D. A. says that when the commandos land the Germans never fight but always clear out immediately. No doubt they have orders to do so. This fact is not allowed to be published—presumable reason, to prevent the public from becoming over-confident.[1]

According to D. A., Cripps does intend to resign from the Government[4] _and has his alternative policy ready. He can't, of course, speak of this in public but will do so in private. However, I hear that Macmurray_[5] _when staying with Cripps recently could get nothing whatever out of him as to his political intentions._

1. David Astor.
2. Churchill arrived in Cairo on this day, then, via Teheran, reached Moscow on 12 August. He and Stalin did discuss the opening of a second front (see *The Second World War*, IV, 411, 430–33; U.S: *The Hinge of Fate*, 477–83, 486.)
3. *says*] says that
4. Cripps (see *554, n. 7*) came near to resignation but did not leave the War Cabinet until 22 November 1942, the day he was appointed Minister of Aircraft Production, a post he held until the end of the war in Europe.
5. John Macmurray (1891–1876) was Grote Professor of the Philosophy of Mind and Logic, University of London; see *2071, n. 1*.

1351. Programmes Preview by Venu Chitale with amendments by Orwell

4 August 1942

Venu Chitale's monthly programme preview was evidently written as well as delivered by her: her style is chatty and quite different from Orwell's. This particular script, however, has extensive passages revised by Orwell, whose hand is easily distinguished from hers. In the following extract from the full preview, sections in Orwell's hand are printed in italic. The heavy punctuation has mainly been added in ink and is doubtless to aid delivery. For an extract from a later Programme Preview, in which Miss Chitale describes Orwell's wife, Eileen Blair, see *1759.*

. . . Tomorrow, in our programme "Through Eastern Eyes", Shridhar Telkar will again present his *weekly talk* "Topic of the Week". Mr. Telkar, as is well-known, is the Editor of the Oriental News Agency. During his long stay in this country, as a journalist, he has had many opportunities, to observe and study politics, and social opinions. Last week, he spoke about the demand of the British Public, for a Second Front in Europe. He brings a keen and analytical mind to bear on his subjects. I know what he's going to tell you tomorrow, but I must not say! Because I shall be giving away his [underlined] show. Anyway listen in on Wednesdays to Shridhar Telkar's "Topic of the Week".
. . .

On Thursdays will be broadcast to you the "Open Letters", *which explain the origins of the war in a simple popular way.* Among the writers of these letters are Cedric Dover, Jaya Deva, Raja Ratnam, and others. The series was started last Thursday, by Mulk Raj Anand, with a letter, to the widow [underlined], of a Chinese guerrilla, Madame Shelley Wong. Cedric Dover, whose voice is familiar to many listeners in India, will address his letter to a Liberal. Jaya Deva, author of the sensational book "Japan's Kampf", will write to a Conservative, wheras° Raja Ratnam, who is well known among the new Indian writers in Great Britain, will address his letter to a Quisling [underlined]. (Pause)
Some months back, you may have listened to some talks by J. F. Horrabin on world geography. Well, we are lucky enough to have been able to fix up another four talks by him. J. F. Horrabin, former M. P., is well known as a cartoonist. His work has been appearing in the "News Chronicle" and "The Star" for the last 20 years. Mr. Horrabin, is also famous, for his books of war-maps. It was he who drew the maps for H. G. Wells's "Outline of History", and also *for* Jawaharlal Nehru's "Glimpses of World History". *The title of his talks is "The War of the Three Oceans", & they will take place on Fridays from 5 to 5.15 Indian Standard Time. The first will be on Friday the 7th. Anyone who enjoyed his previous series, "The World is Round", will find these, even more stimulating.*
Last Friday, you probably heard, the first of our new series, "I'd Like it Explained" [underlined]. In this series, as we have already pointed out,

experts on various subjects of current interest, will hold discussions, and they will answer questions put to them, by Indian interviewers, interested in the subject. Wickham Steed, the well-known broadcaster, Hamilton Fyfe, Sir John Russell, L. F. Easterbrook, C. H. Waddington, Professor *J.B.S.* Haldane, & Professor Laski, are only, a few, of the eminent, and brilliant men, who will hold these radio discussions. Wickham Steed, will speak on the Press, Sir John Russell on Agriculture, Professor Haldane on Scientific Research; while Laski [underlined in ink] will speak on the Future [underlined] of Parliament [underlined]. *So* Listen in, on Fridays to hear many questions answered.

Our listeners in India must have missed Z. A. Bokhari's voice last Saturday, in the News Review period. Mr. Bokhari is very pressed for time, and he has consequently, had to pass this task, of reviewing the events of the war, onto° others.[1] Shridar° Telkar, Noel Sircar, Bahadur Singh, and Homi Bode are the competent men, who will share the responsibility, of presenting you, with the News Review of the week.

The Parliamentary debate which continues from week to week . . .

[There is finally, a trail for Sir Aziz-ul-Huque's 'Indians in Great Britain' and the Programme Preview concludes:]

We hope all of you who know English will listen to this programme which is arranged especially.[2] We bring you every week news, reviews, talks, discussions, music [last five words underlined]—things that are of interest and entertainment to you. *Please remember the times. Every day* we broadcast from London to listeners in India between 4.45 and 5.30 Indian Standard Time, on 16, 19, 25 and 31 metre bands. Good bye everybody.

1. Orwell evidently acquiesced in the impression being given that someone else was involved in the production of the News Review. It is most unlikely that listeners would appreciate knowing that those presenting the reviews had not also written them.
2. 'of you who know English' is probably not in Orwell's hand; the words 'your benefit' after 'especially' ('for' having been crossed out) have been allowed to stand and possibly 'for your benefit' was read out.

1352. BBC Talks Booking Form, 4.8.42

Mulk Raj Anand: 'Voice,' 1: A Magazine Programme; 'Helping with production of the programme and taking part in discussion of about 10 minutes' duration'; recorded 8.8.42; broadcast 11.8.42; fee £5.5s, 'to cover part in discussion & assistance with production of prog.' Signed: Z. A. Bokhari. Remarks: 'Please note that Mr. Anand will be required for rehearsal on 6.8.42 from 2.30–4 p.m.'

1353. BBC Talks Booking Form, 4.8.42

Inez Holden: 'Voice,' 1; 'Helping with the production of the programme and taking part in discussion of about 10 minutes' duration'; recorded 8.8.42; broadcast 11.8.42; fee £5.5s. Signed: Z. A. Bokhari. Remarks: Miss Holden 'has written a monologue for this programme, to be read by Vida Hope. This is being covered by Miss Alexander.'[1]

1. Miss B. H. Alexander dealt with copyright and permissions.

1354. BBC Talks Booking Form, 4.8.42

Herbert Read: 'Voice,' 1; 'Reading two poems—1. The Contrary Experience by Herbert Read, and 2. The world is too much with us by Wordsworth. About 5 minutes' duration'; recorded 4.8.42; broadcast 11.8.42; fee £2.2s (£2.10). Signed: Z. A. Bokhari. Remarks: 'The copyright of Mr. Read's poems will be covered by Miss Alexander.'

1355. War-time Diary

<u>4.8.42</u>: *The Turkish radio (among others) also says Churchill is in Moscow.*
<u>5.8.42</u>: *General dismay over the Government of India's rash act in publishing the documents seized in the[1] police raid on Congress headquarters.[2]* ⌈As usual the crucial document is capable of more than one interpretation and the resulting squabble will simply turn wavering elements in Congress more anti-British.⌉ *The anti-Indian feeling which the publication has aroused in America, and perhaps Russia and China, is not in the long run any good to us.*

The Russian government announces discovery of a Tsarist plot, quite in the old style. I can't help a vague feeling that this is somehow linked up with the simultaneous discovery of Gandhi's plot with the Japanese.

1. *the*] their
2. After the failure of Cripps's mission to India, Congress had become increasingly intransigent. At the beginning of August Gandhi inaugurated a campaign of civil disobedience. In attempting to ensure order, the government of India raided Congress headquarters and seized the text of the original draft of the Resolution on Indian Independence submitted to the Congress Working Committee and published it.

1356. To Miss E. W. D. Boughen, Talks Bookings

5 August 1942   Original   EB/NP

TOPIC OF THE WEEK—Talk by S. Telkar

Mr. Telkar was asked to do a series of talks on TOPIC OF THE WEEK. The second talk in this series should have been broadcast to-day (August 5th) at 1115 GMT in the Eastern Transmission. Mr. Telkar prepared a script and came to this office prepared to broadcast it, but it had been decided at a policy meeting at the last moment that the subject about which he had written should not be mentioned in our broadcasts at present. We were therefore obliged not to use this talk, and used an ice-box talk[1] instead. In view of these circumstances, I think that Mr. Telkar should be paid the full fee for his talk, as he was fully prepared to broadcast it, and actually arrived at the appointed time to rehearse the talk. I should be grateful if this could be arranged for me.[2]

[Signed] Eric Blair
(Eric Blair)

1. Talks held in reserve. Such talks were broadcast when scheduled programmes could not be transmitted.
2. On 7 August, the Programme Contracts Director wrote to Telkar saying that he would be paid the full contract fee of nine guineas.

1357. Marathi Newsletter, 23

6 August 1942

This was misnumbered as 24. The English original was written by Orwell. No script has been traced.

1358. To Cedric Dover

6 August 1942   PP/EB

Dear Dover,
This is to confirm that you are doing two talks for us in the series BOOKS THAT CHANGED THE WORLD, which is starting shortly. The date of the talk on The Descent of Man is October 1st, and Uncle Tom's Cabin on October 8th. The talks are of 13½ minutes' duration, and go on the air at 12.15 p.m. BST. I should like to have the scripts in each case one week before the date of broadcast.

Yours sincerely,
Eric Blair
Talks Producer
Indian Section

1359. To Cyril Falls

6 August 1942   PP/EB

Dear Captain Falls,

Major Fuller has written refusing to broadcast, on the grounds that he is too busy. Can you suggest somebody else? I should be grateful if you would let me know fairly soon what suggestions you have to make, if any.[1]

Yours sincerely,
[Signed] Geo. Orwell
George Orwell
Talks Producer
Indian Section

1. The carbon is annotated 'declined to do talk by phone.'

1360. To Narayana Menon

6 August 1942   PP/EB

Dear Mr. Menon,

We are shortly starting a new series of talks called BOOKS THAT CHANGED THE WORLD, and are wondering if you would like [to] take part in it.

This series is supposed to deal with outstanding books in the European literature of the last 200 years which have a direct effect on public opinion and caused people to see some major problem in a new light. The one we should like you to undertake is Gulliver's Travels, on September 17th, at 12.15 p.m. I think you should start with the assumption that your audience has heard of the book but is not necessarily well acquainted with it. The talk should not therefore be a mere critique of the book but should give a clear account of what it is about and show just how, why and to what extent it influenced public opinion. You should give the date of the book's publication and say at any rate a few words about the Social background of the time. It may also be of interest to say a word or two about the author, but the main emphasis should be on the book itself. The talk will be of 13½ minutes duration. Could you be kind enough to let me know whether you can undertake this?

Yours sincerely,
[Signed] Eric Blair
Eric Blair

1361. To Naomi Mitchison

6 August 1942   [PP/EB]

Dear Mrs. Mitchison,[1]
We would like it very much if you would broadcast in one of the series of talks we do for India. These talks are intended for the English-speaking Indians, and not the Europeans. We have a series in which various subjects are discussed by two experts, in response to questions by an Indian interviewer. We would like you to take part in one discussing the emancipation of women, present and future. We have had to give this the rather vulgar title of "The Cradle and the Desk", just to make it sound more interesting than the mere phrase "Female Emancipation". Of course this subject is a very important one for India, and one cannot assume that opinion there has moved nearly as far as in Britain. Have you any suggestions as to whom you would like to debate with? We would prefer it to be another woman, and it makes a more real debate if it is someone with whom you are to some extent in disagreement. The date fixed for the broadcast is September 25th, at 12.45 p.m. Could you be kind enough to let me know about this as early as possible?

Yours sincerely,
[Signed] Geo. Orwell
George Orwell
Talks Producer
Indian Section

1. Naomi Mitchison (see *454, n. 1*), a prolific author, advocated many progressive social and political causes. Since 1963 she has been Tribal Adviser to Bakgatla, Botswana, and for many years served on the Scottish Highlands Development Board.

1362. To K. S. Shelvankar

6 August 1942   PP/EB

Dear Shelvankar,
I am writing to ask whether you would c[ar]e to do two more broadcasts for us. I was very sorry the last one fell through, [bu]t the present ones that I have in mind are less likely to cause any awkwardness. We are planning a series called BOOKS THAT CHANGED THE WORLD, dealing with books which can be said to have actually influenced events directly by their impact on [the big][1] public. I should like you to undertake two, namely, Rousseau's Social Contract, and Marx's Kapital. Of course, you will realise that the first book was meant to represent the rise of the idea of liberalism, just as the second represents the rise of the idea of socialism. Marx, of course, we must deal with, but you might possibly think that some other book should be used instead of the Social Contract,—for example, perhaps something of Voltaire's or Tom Paine. I think, however, that Rousseau's book was one

that did actually have the effect. I think this series may be quite interesting. Please let me know as soon as possible whether you are interested in doing this, and I can let you have further details. The dates of the broadcasts are September 24th and October 22nd. In case you are away or anything of that kind we could always arrange recordings.

Yours sincerely,
[Initialled] E. A. B
George Orwell
Indian Section

1. These two words have been erased, and the carbon copy, from which this letter is reproduced, is badly smeared. There is no question that both words were typed, first without a space between them and then spaced, but just possibly 'big' was erased from the top copy.

1363. War-time Diary

7.8.42: ⌈Hugh Slater is very despondent about the war. He says that at the rate at which the Russians have been retreating it is not possible that Timoshenko has really got his army away intact, as reported. He also says that the tone of the Moscow press and wireless shows that morale in Russia must be very bad.⌉ *Like almost everyone I know, except Warburg, Hugh Slater[1] considers that there isn't going to be any Second Front. This is the inference everyone draws from Churchill's visit to Moscow.[2] People say, "Why should he go to Moscow to tell them we're going to[3] open a second front? He must have gone there to tell them we can't do it". Everyone agrees with my suggestion that it would be a good job if Churchill were sunk on the way back,[4] like Kitchener.[5]* ⌈Of course the possibility remains that Churchill isn't in Moscow.⌉

Last night for the first time took a Sten gun to pieces.[6] There is almost nothing to learn in it. ⌈No spare parts. If the gun goes seriously wrong you simply chuck it away and get another.⌉ *Weight of the gun with-out magazine is 5½ pounds[7]*—⌈weight of the Tommy gun would be 12–15 lb. Estimated price is not 50/- as I had imagined, but 18/-.⌉ *I can see a million or two million of these things, each with 500 cartridges and a book of instructions, floating down all over Europe on little parachutes. If the Government had the guts to do that they would really have burned their boats.*

1. *Hugh Slater*] he
2. The following passage is crossed through in the manuscript: 'The question asked on every side is, "If the Second Front is going to be opened, what point is there in Churchill going to Moscow? He must have gone there to tell them we can't do it." '
3. The manuscript originally had 'we can't,' but this is crossed through and altered to read as in typescript.
4. *the way back*] his way home
5. Field Marshal Horatio Herbert Kitchener, 1st Earl Kitchener, who had reconquered the Sudan (1896–98) and was successful against the Boers in the South African War (1900–02), was regarded as a hero by the British populace. At the outbreak of World War I he was appointed Secretary of State for War. He was drowned when HMS *Hampshire*, taking him on a mission

to Russia, struck a mine. He realized earlier than most the need to raise a large army and rapidly increased the strength of 'Kitchener's Army,' as it was called, from twenty to seventy divisions. He found co-operative work difficult and was less popular with Cabinet colleagues than with the general public. Orwell's second published work, 21 July 1916, was a poem on the subject of this loss; see 24.

6. In 1940 the only sub-machine-gun available to the British was the American Thompson, but at least 100,000 were lost at sea on their way from the United States, causing an urgent need for a cheap home-produced automatic. The Sten, named from its designers, Major R. Vernon Sheppard and Harold J. Turpin, and the place of its manufacture, Enfield, cost only £2.10s, did not rely on machined parts, and had no wooden stock. The magazine, based on the German 9mm MP 40, had a tendency to jam or fire single shots unexpectedly. But the Sten proved highly successful and was much favoured by resistance fighters.

7. *pounds*] lb

1364. News Review, 34

8 August 1942

The typescript is headed 'News Review. J Bahadur Singh Student of Law Oxford University.' Singh was the reader. It bears two censorship stamps; the censor was Bokhari. It is marked 'As broadcast' by adapting the 'NOT CHECKED WITH BROADCAST' statement, the handwritten 'As' looking much as if written by Orwell. There is a short cut, which is reproduced here in square brackets, but the words are not scored through in the typescript; and three words have been obliterated but can be recovered with reasonable certainty.

On the Russian front the general movement continues to be the same as we reported last week. The Germans are still advancing southward, though somewhat less rapidly than before, and it may be taken that they have definitely cut the railway connecting Stalingrad with the Black Sea and the Caucasus area. They claim to have reached the Kuban river, which runs into the Black Sea near Novorossisk; but it is doubtful whether they have actually done it as yet. Further north, they have failed to make any progress towards Stalingrad. Probably they have not, in the present campaign, captured anything that is of much direct use to them, but they have succeeded in almost separating the northern and southern parts of the Russian front, and thus making it much harder for the northern Russian armies to get their supplies of oil. Much depends on the quantity of oil and other war materials which the Soviet Government had stored beforehand at strategic points. In spite of the striking German successes of the last month, the Soviet Government's pronouncements are as firm and confident as ever and we may assume that from their knowledge of the situation they know that though the campaign has reached its climax, that campaign is far from desperate. The aim of the Germans is first to destroy the Russian Armies as a fighting force, and secondly to win themselves an unlimited supply of oil. The aim of the Allied nations is to gather strength as quickly as possible and see to it that the German armies are forced to spend another winter in the Russian snow. The Germans' aims do not now look as though they can be fully achieved this year, and in spite of all the confident predictions of victory on the Nazi wireless, the prospect of another winter like the last one, with Anglo-American strength mounting up, and the German soldiers dying of cold by tens of thousands, is probably a nightmare to the leaders who have brought Germany to its present pass.

It is important, however, to see each campaign in perspective and to realise that however little they may like one another, the two major powers of the Axis are for the time being acting in concert. During recent weeks, we have not said very much in our newsletters about the far° Eastern end of the war. Except for some rather indecisive actions in China, the Japanese were not attacking, but were building up their strength for two, or possibly three, offensives which they will probably undertake in the near future. We reported last week that there has been fresh activity in New Guinea and during the last week it has become clearer that the Japanese are going to launch another attack against Port Moresby, perhaps on a bigger scale than hitherto. Air reconnaissance also shows that they have occupied some small uninhabited islands about 200 miles north of Australia. These moves cannot have any meaning except as a prelude to an attack against the mainland of Australia and we must write this down as one of the campaigns which the Japanese are likely to undertake shortly. They will probably attack Australia, not merely because they have always coveted the possession of it, but because it is there that British and American strength is most greatly increasing, and it is from there that a counter-attack against the Southern Asian Archipelago can be undertaken. Simultaneously, however, the Japanese seem to be also preparing attacks on both Russia and India. It is known that they have greatly increased their forces on the borders of Manchuria and also that they have been bringing reinforcements into Burma. The RAF has been bombing the port of Akyab, which probably indicates the presence there of Japanese transports. It is not certain that the Japanese will attack India, but as in the case of Australia, they must do so if they wish to prevent a counter-attack against themselves being prepared. It may be asked why they have not attacked India already, since they probably had a good opportunity to do so three or four months ago, when the British were being driven out of Burma and British naval strength in the Indian Ocean had been much weakened by the loss of the two battleships at Singapore. The reasons for the Japanese not attacking India are two, or possibly three. The first is the monsoon, which makes landing operations difficult, and slows down the movement of troops in low-lying country. The second reason developed a little later in the heavy Japanese naval losses in their two unsuccessful battles against the Americans. So far as we know, the Japanese lost at least five aircraft carriers—which would also mean the loss of several hundred aeroplanes and several thousand trained men—in these two encounters; and without a sufficient force of aircraft carriers they probably do not feel equal to attacking the coast of India against land based aircraft. The lost aircraft carriers can be replaced, but this would mean several months' work. The third possible reason was that the Japanese were hoping for political strife in India to reach such a pitch that if they made the invasion they would be greeted as friends by at least a large section of the population. In thus holding back they showed caution, but they also allowed the Allied forces in India to be immensely strengthened. It is not our place to comment on India's internal politics, but we may say that the recent pronouncements of the Working Committee of the Congress Party at least do not favour the theory that the Japanese would be welcomed as friends if they came.

[As to the attack on Russia, it is simply a matter of choosing an opportune moment. Whereas the Japanese might possibly hold on to their conquests while leaving India and Australia alone, their aims and those of Soviet Russia are absolutely incompatible. The conquest of Siberia has, in fact, been a Japanese objective for the last forty or fifty years.] We reported in earlier newsletters that the Japanese had established themselves in the Aleutian Islands. They are only in two uninhabited islands at the top of the Archipelago, but from air reconnaissance it is estimated that there are about ten thousand of them there. It may not be easy to get them out again, since the whole of this area is constantly enveloped in storms and mist, which makes movements by ships and aeroplanes difficult. The Japanese seizure of these two islands cannot have any purpose but to establish themselves across the route between Russia and America and thus to cut off the supplies of war materials which would flow across the northern Pacific if war should break out in Manchuria.

We may take it [as absolutely certain] that an attack against Vladivostok— no doubt a treacherous and unannounced attack—comes high on the Japanese programme. If it does not take place, that will only be because the Japanese fear the strength of the Red Army. We do not profess to say which of these three possible moves, an offensive against India, against Australia, or against Russia, will come first, but we do say with certainty that all three are highly probable, and that so far as India is concerned, the situation depends quite largely on the courage, foresight and hard work of the peoples of India themselves.

There is little to report from Egypt. We merely mention this front in order to remind our listeners that the lack of activity there does not mean that the campaign is at an end. The fact that the Germans did not retreat again after being stopped at El Alamein must mean that they intend another attack. Otherwise, they would have had no reason for staying in so inconvenient a position. Both the Axis and the Allied Forces are building up their strength in tanks and aeroplanes as quickly as possible. It must not be forgotten, as we have pointed out in earlier newsletters, that the supply problem in this area is easier for the Germans than for ourselves. Probably, therefore, another major battle is to be expected in Egypt within the next week or two.

The British have made two more heavy air raids, on Dusseldorf and on Duisburg. These recent raids have not been carried out by a thousand planes, like the earlier ones, but in most cases by five or six hundred. The actual weight of bombs dropped, however, is hardly less than in the thousand bomber raids. Exact figures cannot be given, but it appears that in the recent raids on Dusseldorf and on Hamburg the RAF each time dropped three or four hundred tons of bombs on its objective. This is a greater weight of bombs than has ever been dropped on Britain, even including the terrible raid which almost wiped out the city of Coventry. From our experience in this country, we can get some impression of what is now happening to various German industrial towns. The Germans have continued to make raids on London and other cities, but only on a very small scale, and in several of these raids, the attacking force has lost about ten per cent of its strength. It is probable, however, that these raids are made largely for reconnaissance, and to test the new anti-aircraft defences which have been developed in Britain during the past year. Large scale raids on Britain may be resumed this autumn, at any rate, if the Germans are able to disengage a sufficient part of their air force from Russia.

From Palestine comes the very good news that a Palestinian regiment is being raised, in which both Jews and Arabs are serving. Thus the obvious, unmistakable menace of Fascist aggression is helping to solve one of the most difficult political problems the world contains, and people who only yesterday were political enemies find that they have a common interest in defending their country against the invader.

1365. Bengali Newsletter, 4

8 August 1942

The English original was written by Orwell. No script has been traced. PasB gives the timing as 11′ 45″.

1366. To R. R. Desai

8 August 1942   PP/EB

Dear Desai,

I had been hoping to receive the script of your Open Letter to a Nazi, but it still has not arrived. I hope it has not got lost in the post. I am afraid that I must see the script before you record it, so I have had to cancel the arrangements for you to record tomorrow—Sunday. I have instead arranged for a recording at 5 p.m. on Monday, after the Gujarati[1] newsletter. I should be glad if you will kindly leave the script with reception for me to see on Monday morning.

I am sorry about these changes in our arrangements, but I'm afraid it can't be helped.

Yours sincerely,
Eric Blair
Talks Producer
Indian Section

1. Gujarati] Marathi *originally typed*

1367. War-time Diary

<u>9.8.42</u>: *Fired the Sten gun for the first time today. No kick, no vibration, very little noise, and reasonable accuracy. Out of about 2500 rounds fired, 2 stoppages, in each case due to a dud cartridge—treatment, simply to work the bolt by hand.*

1368. Gujarati Newsletter, 24
10 August 1942

The English original was written by Orwell. No script has been traced.

1369. To E. M. Forster
10 August 1942   PP/EB/NP

Dear Mr. Forster,
Owing to the change in the hour, your talk on Some Books, on August 19th will be at 12.30 p.m. BST,[1] instead of 1.30 p.m.

I am also looking after your introductory talk in the series "My Debt to India", on Friday next. This goes on the air at 12.15 p.m. BST. I think the best thing would be for you to come in at about 11.30 a.m., and we can run through it once for timing. Sir Malcolm Darling has passed the script on to me, and it will be ready for you to broadcast from on Friday.

Yours sincerely,
George Orwell
Talks Producer
Indian Section

1. The time had been put back one hour from Double British Summer Time on the night of 8–9 August 1942.

1370. To Harold Laski
10 August 1942   PP/EB/NP

Dear Professor Laski,
I hope you haven't forgotten the discussion on the future of Parliament you are doing for us with Lord Winterton. I think Gerald Bullett reminded you of it on Friday over the telephone. I think the best way of doing this particular one is for you to write out at approximately the right length, that is to say, about 750 words, your ideas about the future of Parliament, and we will then send it on to Lord Winterton for his criticisms; then on the basis of the two statements we can work up a discussion. I don't of course want to dictate

what you should say, but I think what your talk should discuss is first of all, whether representative Government as we know it is likely to continue and ought to continue, and if so, what reforms are needed in the British Parliamentary system. The date of the talk is September 4th. I wonder if you could let [me] have your preliminary draft not later than August 20th?

Yours sincerely,
George Orwell
Talks Producer
Indian Section

1371. To Lord Winterton

10 August 1942   PP/EB/NP

Dear Lord Winterton,
Many thanks for your letter of 6th August. I think perhaps the best way of doing this particular discussion will be to let Professor Laski write what he thinks about the future of Parliament, and then send his draft on to you to criticise, and on the basis of the two statements we can work up a discussion. I am communicating with him to this effect, and will send you on his stuff as soon as I can get hold of it.

Yours sincerely,
George Orwell
Talks Producer
Indian Section

1372. War-time Diary

_10.8.42:_   _Nehru, Gandhi, Azad_ [1] _and many others in jail. Rioting over most of India, a number of deaths, countless arrests. Ghastly speech by Amery,_ [2] _speaking of Nehru and Co. as "wicked men", "saboteurs" etc. This of course broadcast on the Empire service and rebroadcast by AIR._ [3] _The best joke of all was that the Germans did their best to jam it, unfortunately without success._

Terrible feeling of depression among the Indians and everyone sympathetic to India. [Even Bokhari, a Moslem League[4] man, almost in tears and talking about resigning from the BBC.] _It is strange, but quite truly the way the British Government is now behaving_ [5] _upsets me more than a military defeat._

1. Abdul Kalam Azad (1888–1958), Indian Nationalist Moslem leader, was spokesman for the Indian National Congress in the 1945 independence negotiations. His _India Wins Freedom_ was published in 1959.
2. Leo Amery, Conservative M.P., was Secretary of State for India, 1940–45; see _554, n. 5._
3. All-India Radio.
4. The Moslem League was founded as a religious organisation to protect the interests of Moslems in British India. It supported the Indian National Congress until 1935, when Hindu

interests dominated the Congress Party and the League was developed into a political organisation. It was led by Mohammed Ali Jinnah and demanded the partition of India. When Pakistan was set up in 1947, the League secured control of its first Constituent Assembly.
5. *behaving*] behaving in India

1373. 'Voice,' 1: A Magazine Programme
11 August 1942

The text is taken from the prompter's copy, probably typed by Orwell. It carries both Security and Policy censorship stamps, signed by Bokhari on 8 August 1942. The script is annotated 'As recorded,' and timed at 27½ minutes. Some slight amendments are in Orwell's hand. The readings of the original typescript are given in notes. All passages quoted in this and later editions of Voice are reproduced as in the script unless noted; slight errors of typing or in punctuation are corrected silently.

Cast: Vida Hope; Herbert Read; William Empson; John Atkins; Inez Holden; Mulk Raj Anand; George Orwell.

EDITORIAL—by George Orwell

This is the worst possible moment to be starting a magazine. While we sit here talking in a more or less highbrow manner—talking about art and literature and whatnot—tens of thousands of tanks are racing across the steppes of the Don and battleships upside down[1] are searching for one another in the wastes of the Pacific. I suppose during every second that we sit here at least one human being will be dying a violent death. It may seem a little dilettante to be starting a magazine concerned primarily with poetry at a moment when, quite literally, the fate of the world is being decided by bombs and bullets. However our[2] magazine—"Voice" we are calling it— isn't quite an ordinary magazine. To begin with it doesn't use up any paper or the labour of any printers or booksellers. All it needs is a little electrical power and half a dozen voices. It doesn't have to be delivered at your door, and you don't have to pay for it. It can't be described as a wasteful form of entertainment. Moreover there are some of us who feel[3] that it is exactly at times[4] like the present that literature ought not to be[5] forgotten. As a matter of fact this business of pumping words into the ether, its potentialities and the actual uses it is put to, has its solemn side.[6] According to some authorities wireless waves, or some wireless waves, don't merely circle our planet, but travel on endlessly through space at the speed of light, in which case what we are saying this afternoon should be audible in the great nebula in Orion nearly a million years hence. If there are intelligent beings there, as there well may be, though Sir James Jeans[7] doesn't think it likely,[8] it won't hurt them to pick up a few specimens of twentieth century verse[9] along with the swing music and the latest wad of lies from Berlin. But I'm not apologising for our magazine, merely introducing it. I ask you to note therefore that it will appear once monthly on a Tuesday, that it will contain prose but will make a speciality of[10] contemporary poetry, and that it will make particular efforts

459

to publish the work of the younger poets who have been handicapped by the paper shortage and whose work isn't so well known as it ought to be.

"Voice" has now been in existence nearly[11] three minutes. I hope it already has a few readers, or I should say listeners. I hope as you sit there you are imagining the magazine in front of you. It's only a small volume, about twenty pages. One advantage of a magazine of this kind is that you can choose your own cover design. I should favour something in light blue or a nice light grey, but you can take your choice. Now turn to the first page. It's good quality paper, you notice, prewar paper—you don't see paper like that in other magazines[12] nowadays—and[13] nice wide margins. Fortunately we have no advertisements, so on page one is the Table of Contents. Here is the table of contents:—

Page 2.   This editorial that you are listening to.

Page 4.   A poem by Herbert Read, "The Contrary Experience", read by himself.

Page 6.   "Poor Relation", a monologue by Inez Holden, recited by Vida Hope.

Page 10. A poem by Dylan Thomas "In Memory of Ann Jones", read by William Empson.

Page 11. A short commentary on Dylan Thomas by several voices.

Page 12. Three poems by Henry Treece, read by John Atkins.

Page 15. Open Forum, a discussion of Henry Treece's poems by George Orwell, John Atkins, Mulk Raj Anand, William Empson, and others.

Page 18. A sonnet by William Wordsworth, read by Herbert Read.

Also on page one, underneath the Table of Contents, are the Notes on Contributors. It is usual to put this at the end of a magazine, but we choose to put it at the beginning. It tells you about this month's contributors in the order in which they appear. Herbert Read hardly needs introducing to listeners in India, but he is the poet and critic, author of *In Retreat*, and *English Prose Style*. Inez Holden is a novelist, best known as the author of "*Night Shift*". Vida Hope is the well known character actress who has appeared at the Unity Theatre[14] and had some brilliant successes in some of Herbert Farjeon's[15] revues. Dylan Thomas, author of "*The Map of Love*", *Portrait of the Author of a Young Dog*, and other books, is probably the best-known of the younger English poets. At this moment he is at work making documentary films.[16] William Empson, also a poet, is author of *Seven Types of Ambiguity*. Henry Treece is one of the leading representatives of the Apocalyptic School, the most recent movement in English poetry, indeed the only new movement that can be said to have appeared since the war. He is serving in the RAF, which is why he is not here today, but his poems are being read by his personal friend John Atkins, who is on the staff of the "Tribune", the Socialist weekly paper. George Orwell—who is speaking to you now—[17] is the novelist and journalist, best known as the author of "The Road to Wigan Pier". Mulk Raj Anand is an Indian novelist, who writes in English. His most recent book is "*The Sword and the Sickle*", just published, but he is also the author of "*Untouchable*", *Two Leaves and a Bud*, and various others. He too ought not to need much introduction to the listeners on this service.

That brings us to the end of Page three. Now please turn to page four. Here is Herbert Read, reading his poem "*The Contrary Experience*":

READ: I   (RECORDING: DOX. 3226)[18]

You cry like a gull cries
dipping low where the tide has ebbed
over the vapid reaches: your impulse
died in the second summer of the war.

The years dip their boughs
brokenly, over the uncovered springs.
Hands wasted for love and poetry
finger the hostile gunmetal.

Called to meaningless action
you hesitate
meditating faith to a conscience
more patently noble.

II

But even as you wait
like Arjune in his chariot
the ancient wisdom whispers:
Live in action!

I do not forget my oath
taken in the frosty dawn
when the shadows stretched
from horizon to horizon:

Not to repeat the false act
not to inflict pain
to suffer, to hope, to build
to analyse the indulgent heart.

Three tribulations compelled that faith:
a brother left at Beaurevoir
the broken eyes of brothers everywhere
the unavailing courage of the killed.

Wounds dried like sealing-wax
upon this bond.
But time has broken
the proud mind.

No resolve can defeat suffering
no desire establish joy.
Beyond joy and suffering
is the equable heart

not indifferent to glory
if it lead to death
seeking death
if it lead to the only life.

III

Libya, Egypt, Hellas
the same tide ebbing, the same gull crying
desolate shores and rocky deserts
hunger, thirst, death

The storm threatening and the air still
but other wings
vibrating in the ominous hush
and the ethereal voice

thrilling and clear

Rise as the lark rises
over the grey dried grasses
buffeted against the storm's sullen breath
rising sing!

ORWELL: Now please turn to page 6. This is called "Poor Relation". It's a monologue of Inez Holden, recited by Vida Hope:[19]

VIDA HOPE: (Recorded: DOX 3146)

POOR RELATION, by Inez Holden

Oh Cousin Nina. I had no idea it was your at home today, oh I see it isn't today and it isn't your at home, just a few friends. You are so popular, only the other day Mr. Sweeting said to me "Your cousin Lady Crane has a whole host of friends". Yes indeed I did change your library books for you. No they're not at all too heavy for me to carry, I managed to have a little rest and a read on the way. Of course I can keep them for you till I go. Oh, and there's my darling little Mr. Wellington! Who's a dear little doggie, then, wagging his little tail like an angel and those great big soulful eyes.

No thank you Mrs. Gregson I never take intoxicating beverages, oh well then if it's very mild just a little. You've filled the glass up to the brim but I can always leave some for Mr. Manners can't I—No I didn't mean you Mr. Manners (laughs nervously). It's just a saying you know. Oh Cousin Nina what a lovely necklace. It's rather like mine. But of course mine are only paste. You always have such beautiful bijouterie and you set it off so well too.

No thank you Cousin Nina I don't need to sit down, you see I was sitting down for such a long time on the way coming here. Two whole twopenny bus rides. You live right in London's heart you know. London's heart and heart of London. That's rather an apt little phrase. I seem to have killed two birds with one stone. Not that I mean you are a bird Cousin Nina (sound of drinking). Little did I think when I left home this morning that I should find myself at this grand gathering of people. I've been to several cocktail parties before but only on the films you know. It was such a good thing I put on my best hat, wasn't it? Oh I'm so glad you like it. I remember how Cousin Nina wore it last year when it was new, right on one side, with such an air, and the very next month she gave it to me. But I think its rather better straight on me, don't you? Oh, it will last me a long time yet, Cousin Nina always was ahead of the fashion—but poor little me just lags behind—at least my hats do. I wonder, Mrs. Gregson, if you have ever read Mab's Ladies' Journal of Mode, it's full of little hints, I always read it and listen to the wireless every Friday evening at seven thirty. I never have a dull moment. Oh I beg your pardon. There I go—all over your beautiful dress! Do let me dry it for you before it stains the cloth. No, no, please let me do it. A stitch in time saves nine you know. (Sound of Glasses breaking). Oh dear, if I go on like this it will be nine.

I always remember when I was a little girl I was taken on Sunday afternoons to Castle Beverley, Cousin Nina's family seat you know. She was known as the dainty one but I am afraid they called me a terrible tomboy. In fact they used to call me Madcap Madge if you'll believe it. Do you know when I took Mr. Wellington out for a walk the other day I tripped over his lead right in the centre of the High Street, poor Wellington, he doesn't like such contretemps at all, just look at him now sitting on his velvet cushion—a dear little doggie then. As Cousin Nina says you can always tell a well bred pekinese. In China they used to walk at the head of processions, that's what we want now isn't it, leadership for the masses. Oh I've just remembered I got his powders for him, they're here in the blue shopping bag Cousin Nina, the one you gave me yourself the last Christmas but two, yes of course I'll give them to him later. Oh do look at these lovely little sausages on sticks! Fancy all these delicious things just to eat in the afternoon, doesn't Cousin Nina do us well? I shan't need any supper this evening. Oh there now, I've laddered Cousin Nina, that's what I call my stockings you know because they were given to me by my cousin.

Oh no Cousin Nina it's quite all right I can easily get home in good time, there's no hurry at all, the buses are all lighted nowadays, and I manage the whole journey in under an hour. No you mustn't tire yourself with getting me ginger beer. I'll just drink this again, it's quite good enough for me. (Sound of drinking, genteel but rather noisy). Oh are you all going? Goodby Mr. Mannering, I have enjoyed our conversation, goodbye Mrs. Gregson, don't forget Mab's Weekly.

Of course I quite understand you have to go and dress for dinner now Cousin Nina, you're so much in demand, you're always saying that you hardly get a moment to yourself, so I won't take up any more of your valuable time but just sit here quietly keeping Mr. Wellington company—he on his chair and me on my velvet cushion. Now what am I saying? Of course I mean the other way round, don't I? I'll read the book I got from the library for you today "How Green was the Wind"—I mean "Gone with the Bengal Lancer"—such a romantic title. I'm sure I shan't nearly have finished when it's time for me to catch the bus home. Come along, Mr. Wellington, we're all alone aren't we? And who got his little powders for him today? And who's going to stuff them down his throat? Just like your disgusting horrible mistress you beastly little pekinese! (Yelping of dog).

(6 mins. 10 secs.)

ORWELL: Now please turn to page 10. This is a poem by Dylan Thomas. It's called "In memory of Ann Jones":—[20]

EMPSON:

IN MEMORY OF ANN JONES

By Dylan Thomas.

But I, Ann's bard on a raised hearth, call all
The seas to service that her wood-tongued virtue
Babble like a bellbuoy over the hymning heads,
Bow down the walls of the ferned and foxy woods
That her love sing and swing through a brown chapel,
Bless her bent spirit with four, crossing birds.
Her flesh was meek[21] as milk, but this skyward statue
With the wild breast and blessed and giant skull
Is carved from her in a room with a wet window

In a fiercely mourning house in a crooked year.
I know her scrubbed and sour humble hands
Lie with religion in their cramp, her threadbare
Whisper in a damp word, her wits drilled hollow.
Her fist of a face died clenched on a round pain;
And sculptured Ann is seventy years of stone.
These cloud-sopped, marble hands, this monumental
Argument of the hewn voice, gesture and psalm
Storm me forever over her grave until
The stuffed lung of the fox twitch and cry Love
And the strutting fern lay seed[22] on the black sill.

(Discussion on Dylan Thomas's Poem).

ORWELL: Has anybody any opinions on that? I suppose the obvious criticism is that it doesn't mean anything. But I also doubt whether it's meant to. After all, a bird's song doesn't mean anything except that the bird is happy.

EMPSON: Lazy people, when they are confronted with good poetry like Dylan Thomas's, which they can see is good, or have been told is good, but which they won't work at, are always saying it is Just Noise, or Purely Musical. This is nonsense, and it's very unfair to Dylan Thomas. That poem is full of exact meanings, and the sound would have no effect if it wasn't. I don't know any poet more packed with meaning than Dylan Thomas, and the use of the technique with sound is wholly to bring out and clarify the meaning.

ANAND: But its° also true that his poetry has become a good deal less obscure in an ordinary prose sense lately. This poem, for instance, is much more intelligible than most of his later work. Listen:

Her fist of a face died clenched on a round pain:
And sculptured Ann is seventy years of stone.

That has a meaning that you can grasp at first hearing, hasn't it?

ORWELL: Yes, I admit you grasp at a glance that this is a poem about an old woman, but just listen again to the last five lines:

These cloud-sopped, marble hands, this monumental
Argument of the hewn voice, gesture and psalm
Storm me forever over her grave until
The stuffed lung of the fox twitch and cry Love
And the strutting fern lay seed on the black sill.

The last two lines in particular defy interpretation and even the syntax is a bit funny. But as sound, that seems to me very fine.

EMPSON: I think he takes for granted that she had a fern in a pot and a stuffed fox in her cottage parlour. The comparisons of woods and seas and so on are of course meant to tell you about the breadth of her own nature and it's strength and kindness. It may be obscure, but it is obviously not meaningless.

ATKINS: There is one poet today who uses a lot of Dylan Thomas's methods, and has been influenced by him to a great extent, but consciously controls his material more than Dylan—I mean Henry Treece.

ORWELL: All right—will you read us something by Treece?

ATKINS: I'd like to read three of his poems. The first is called "Walking at Night". . . .

WALKING AT NIGHT—by Henry Treece
Thus I would walk abroad when gentle night
Puts on her friend's cool cloak and bids me come,
Walk among beds of lightly sleeping flowers,
Budded in silver dreams of friendliness.

And I would lie among the dainty herbs,
Like catmint, parsley or exquisite thyme,
To hear the late bird, crying, hurry home
Across the moon's great watchful eye, to love . . .

These things, like dreams of princesses and pearls,
Come to me more as iron days groan on;
The brush of blood paints not a ruined world,
But thyme and parsley underneath the moon.

———————

ATKINS: Oh come, my joy, my soldier boy,
With your golden buttons, your scarlet coat,
Oh let me play with your twinkling sword
And sail away in your wonderful boat!

The soldier came and took the boy.
Together they marched the dusty roads.
Instead of war, they sang at Fairs,
And mended old chairs with river reeds.

The boy put on a little black patch
And learned to sing on a tearful note;
The soldier sold his twinkling sword
To buy a crutch and a jet-black flute.

And when the summer sun rode high
They laughed the length of the shining day;
But when the robin stood in the hedge
The little lad's courage drained away.

Oh soldier, my soldier, take me home
To the nut-brown cottage under the hill.
My mother is waiting, I'm certain sure;
She's far too old to draw at the well!

As snowflakes fell the boy spoke so,
For twenty years, ah twenty years;
But a look in the soldier's eyes said no,
And the roads of England were wet with tears.

One morning, waking on the moors,
The lad laughed loud at the corpse at his side.
He buried the soldier under a stone,
But kept the flute to soothe his pride.

The days dragged on and he came to a town,
Where he got a red jacket for chopping wood;
And meeting a madman by the way,
He bartered the flute for a twinkling sword.

And so he walked the width of the land
With a warlike word and a jaunty air,
Looking out for a likely lad
With the head of a fool and the heart of a bard.

ATKINS: IN THE THIRD YEAR OF THE WAR by Henry Treece

I dream now of green places,
And the gentle kine
Wading knee-deep in rushes;

I dream of singing birds,
And Summer rain
And gracious, homely words.

But I wake to bitter winds,
And blown sand's whine
Across forgotten lands;

And empty skies at night,
And cold star-shine
Where lonely spirits meet.

I feel all this, my dear,
Alone, my love, alone
With all the old fear.

I dream now there is no ending,
No golden, breathless dawn
Only seeking, seeking without finding.

ORWELL: My criticism of the first of these three poems you read—Walking
At Night—is that there are too many adjectives in it, and what adjectives!
"Gentle" night, "dainty" herbs, "exquisite" Thyme, it's almost like
something out of Georgian poetry in 1913. I thought that when I first
read the poem, but when I heard you read it aloud just now, another
analogy struck me. It reminded me of bits out of A Midsummer Night's
Dream—you know, that stuff about "When you and I Upon faint
primrose beds were wont to lie". It's too sugary altogether.

ATKINS: That's only a criticism of the first poem, isn't it? You don't mean it
to apply to the other two?

OREWLL: No. The second poem is in quite a different category. It's more
like a ballad.

EMPSON: Actually it's a savage attack on militaristic sentiment.

ORWELL: Possibly, but as I was saying, I should say the last one—In the
Third Year of [the] War could be compared with the first, and it
doesn't have the same faults. I'm only suggesting that by this very
undisciplined manner of writing, you get a very uneven effect,
sometimes to the point of absurdity.

EMPSON: Merely in passing, I should like to say that the first poem is very much better than the third.

HOLDEN: I rather like that uneven effect. Even the first poem isn't what you call sugary all the way through. "The brush of blood paints not a ruined world" isn't a Georgian line. It's quite a different kind of imagery—a sort of surrealism.

ANAND: I should be inclined to say that the word which most exactly describes these poems is "romantic".

ATKINS: Yes, the poets of the Apocalyptic school—and I should say most of the younger poets writing now—definitely label themselves romantic. They are in revolt against the classical attitude. They are even more in revolt against the school which went immediately before them—the Auden-MacNeice school, which is classical by implication. It isn't the classical form they object to, so much as the content and purpose of the Auden-MacNeice school. According to MacNeice's book on Modern Poetry, the emphasis of all his school is on "information and statement" in other words, they are didactic poets. At the back of their own minds is the idea of the poet as a citizen or even a member of a political party. That means discipline from the outside, which is the essence of classicism.

HOLDEN: The question is, what do you mean by classical and romantic?

EMPSON: These distinctions seem to me all nonsense. Treece is a perfectly good poet, and that means he is using the whole instrument, mind and passions and senses. These poems are no more all Romance than Dylan Thomas's poems are all Noise. Whether Treece has been irritated by a prose book by MacNeice is quite another thing; if he was, I daresay he was quite right. But his writing has plenty of intellectual toughness under it to carry it. And it's absurd for anybo[d]y to think that they're somehow praising him by saying that he hasn't.

ANAND: Well, no one said so.

ATKINS: I don't suggest that Treece or anyone like that is less intellectual, which was what you seem to imply, but that they are less influenced by certain departments of the modern world, the political department—and are more open to other influences, such as nature—in fact, a definite return to the Georgian attitude. Their criticism of Auden and Co. would be that they are working only on one cylinder.

ORWELL: I think this is quite largely a sterile quarrel between generations. I think your choice of what is called classical and romantic is quite largely made for you by the time you live in. In a time like ours, you can't really remain unaffected by politics, and if there is a difference in this particular matter between the Auden school and the Treece school, I should say it was simply a difference between two kinds of politics.

ANAND: I should say that periods of classicism have alternated with periods of romanticism, and the distinction has lasted so long that there must be something in it.

ORWELL: Well, just for a change, lets go back to a period when the distinction between classical and romantic was probably clearer than it is now. Read, what about reading one of Wordsworth's sonnets. Read the one about the World is Too Much with Us. It won't spoil by repetition . . .

(DISC OF READ)
WORDSWORTH SONNET
Read by Herbert Read

The world is too much with us: late and soon,
Getting and spending, we lay waste our powers:
Little we see in Nature that is ours;
We have given our hearts away, a sordid boon!
This sea that bares her bosom to the moon;
The winds that will be howling at all hours,
And are up-gathered now like sleeping flowers;
For this, for everything, we are out of tune;
It moves us not. – Great God! I'd rather be
A Pagan suckled in a creed outworn;
So might I, standing on this pleasant lea,
Have glimpses that would make me less forlorn;
Have sight of Proteus rising from the sea;
Or hear old Triton blow his wreathèd horn.

1. This curious expression seems to mean battleships 'down under'—in the Antipodes.
2. However our] however *originally concluded the sentence*
3. Moreover there are some of us who feel] Moreover some of us—those of us who are collaborating in the production of this magazine—feel
4. times] a time
5. that literature ought not to be] that it is most important that poetry should not be
6. has its solemn side] is rather a solemn thought
7. Sir James H. Jeans (1877–1946), physicist and mathematician, wrote a number of books aimed at the general reader, including *The Universe Around Us* (1929) and *Through Space and Time* (1934), as well as scholarly studies. Orwell may have had in mind his proposition that matter is in a continuous process of creation.
8. doesn't think it likely] thinks it unlikely, we feel that
9. verse] poetry
10. it will contain prose but will make a speciality of] it will specialise in
11. nearly] about
12. other magazines] any other magazine. *The 's' of 'magazines' is simply a blot.*
13. 'and' is cropped.
14. The Unity Theatre was a left-wing theatre which began life in St. Jude's church hall near King's Cross Station, North London. After some success, it converted a Methodist church hall near Mornington Crescent into a 300-seat theatre, opened on 27 November 1937. Among early successes were Clifford Odets's *Waiting for Lefty*, *Busmen* (1938, which adapted Living Newspaper techniques to dramatise the London bus strike of 1937 from a leftist point of view), and a 'pantomime,' *Babes in the Wood* (1938–39). The theatre burned down in 1975.
15. Herbert Farjeon (1887–1945) was a drama critic and, often with his sister, Eleanor Farjeon (1881–1965), a witty librettist. They wrote *The Two Bouquets* (1936–38), *The Little Review* (1939), *Diversion* (1940), and *Diversion 2*, in which Vida Hope appeared; for Orwell's review in *Time and Tide*, see 744.
16. Welsh poet Dylan Thomas (see *608, n. 9*) wrote a number of documentary film scripts and worked on films including *New Towns for Old* (1942), *Our Country*, (1944), *When We Build Again* (1945). His radio writing was collected in *Quite Early One Morning* (1954). The second title given by Orwell should be *Portrait of the Artist as a Young Dog* (1940).

17. —who is speaking to you now—] *interlinear insertion*
18. A BBC record reference number, not a commercial record company's number. Columbia at this time used these same letters.
19. ORWELL: Now please . . . recited by Vida Hope] *added*
20. ORWELL: Now please . . . of Ann Jones':—] *added*
21. meek] neat *in broadcast text*
22. The incorrect singular (for 'seeds') has been allowed to stand because Orwell later says the last two lines defy interpretation; 'seeds' enables the line to be explained.

1374. Anniversary of the Month

11 August 1942

PasB records that immediately after Voice, 1, Anniversary of the Month was broadcast in the series 'Through Eastern Eyes.' The programme had been recorded (BBC number, SOX 3422). Those taking part were: M. M. Haque, Una Marson, Geoffrey Kenton, George Orwell, A. L. Bakaya, and Arthur Lewis. All but the last were noted as members of the staff. Commercial records used were Decca F 6908; HMV 4218; Decca F 6912 (each for less than one minute) and HMV DB 5067 (for 1½ minutes). No script has been traced.

1375. To K. K. Ardaschir

11 August 1942   PP/EB/NP

Dear Ardaschir,
I am sending back the script on Turkey, Great Britain and the Axis, because, though it is a very good talk, I can't possibly use it at the time, and [it] will date. As to the other four talks, I can't commission all four, but I would like it very much if you would do the one on Byron, which we will then have recorded for use at a suitable moment. Don't put in anything that would date, will you, because I shall not be quite certain when I shall use it. The sooner you can send the script and we can arrange the recording the better.

Yours
Eric Blair
Talks Producer
Indian Section

1376. To Vida Hope

11 August 1942   PP/EB

Dear Miss Hope,
I am sorry about this morning, and hope [I][1] did not make some kind of fresh mistake. [I] had arranged to meet you at the Barcelona Restaurant in order to listen to our programme at 1.15, having forgotten that by that time the clocks

would be back,[2] so that the programme actually went out at 12.15. My secretary rang up both the theatre and your private address, and explained the change of time to your friend, asking you to come here at about ten past 12, in time for the programme. When you did not appear we were afraid you must be waiting at the Barcelona Restaurant, so we rang up there, but you were not there either, so we left a message. I hope very much that you have not been inconvenienced in any way. You did not, I may say, lose much by missing the programme, as it was spoilt in transmission, but your particular contribution went out quite satisfactorily.

Yours sincerely,
George Orwell
Talks Producer
Indian Section

1. The 'I' is almost certain, but the punchhole has cut away all but an upper serif, and this is followed by an 'o,' which looks as if it may have been erased from the top copy.
2. See *1369, n. 1*.

1377. To Naomi Mitchison

11 August 1942   PP/EB

Dear Mrs. Mitchison,
Many thanks for your letter. I think, as you feel rather uncertain in your mind about the broadcast, it might be better to write it off. As a matter of fact, when I picked on your name for this discussion, I did not realise that you were living so far away. It is a very long way[1] to come for one broadcast, and a discussion, of course, has to be done on the spot. I am sorry that you have been troubled even with thinking about this, but I hope perhaps you will do something for us at some later date.

Yours sincerely,
George Orwell
Talks Producer
Indian Section

1. Naomi Mitchison lived at Campbeltown, Argyll (about forty miles southeast of where Orwell would later live on Jura).

1378. To Henry Treece

11 August 1942   Top and carbon copies   PP/EB/NP

Dear Treece,
I delayed answering your letter of August 6th until the programme in which your poems appear should have gone out. I am very sorry to say it was a complete muck-up, owing to some technical hitch, and consisting largely of

scratching noises and so forth. However, you will be glad to hear that your poems went out quite O.K., read by John Atkins, who I think delivered them reasonably well. I trust that this kind of thing won't happen again. Next time we have the programme we may think it safer to broadcast it live, in which case this sort of accident does not happen. But still, if you are in town some time, you might ring me up and arrange about recording one or two of your poems, which I can always use somewhere or other, if not in the Voice programme. I am sending back the manuscripts which you kindly sent. The three poems which were used were "Walking at Night", "In the Third Year of [the] War", and the one beginning "Oh come my joy, my soldier boy".

Yours sincerely,
[Signed] Geo. Orwell
George Orwell
Talks Producer
Indian section

1379. To B. H. Liddell Hart

12 August 1942   Typewritten

On 8 August 1942, Captain Basil Liddell Hart[1] wrote to Orwell expressing surprise that someone of his penetration had been misled by Philippe Barrès's *Charles de Gaulle*, which Orwell had reviewed in *The Observer* on 2 August (see *1346*), in so far as it discussed the evolution of mechanized warfare and the use of armoured divisions. He sent Orwell six pages of notes to show that it was not de Gaulle who had devised modern methods of tank warfare, which the Germans, rather than the French or British, had adopted, but a British officer, Colonel J. F. C. Fuller (see *1316, n. 1*) in 1927. Two years later, the British War Office had issued 'the first official manual on mechanized warfare . . . embodying the new conception.' This included the organisation and methods that were to become the foundation of Panzer attacks. General de Gaulle's book, *Vers L'Armée de Métier* (1934), had only ten of its 122 pages devoted to tactics, in the English translation. This, said Liddell Hart, was hardly surprising, since de Gaulle's 'first personal experience with tanks was not until three years later, in 1937.'

10a Mortimer Crescent   London NW 6

Dear Captain Liddell Hart,

Many thanks for your letter. I am sorry I accepted too readily the legend of the Germans having taken their tank theories from de Gaulle. The "Observer" had to compress my review of Barres's book by cutting out a passage from de Gaulle's memorandum of early in 1940. I hadn't seen this memorandum till seeing it in Barres's book, and it certainly did seem to me to foretell what happened a few months later with considerable prescience. The story of "the man the Germans learned from" had already been built up elsewhere, and I had already more or less accepted it, not, of course, being much versed in military literature. I had read many of your own writings but didn't realise that the Germans had drawn on them to that extent. And I was more ready to accept de Gaulle as a revolutionary innovator because of the obviously old-fashioned nature of the French army as a whole. I was in French Morocco from the autumn of 1938 to the spring of 1939, and with war obviously imminent I naturally observed the French colonial army as closely as I could, even to the point of getting hold of some of their infantry textbooks. I was struck by the antiquated nature of everything, though I know very little of military matters. I could if you wish write to the "Observer" and say that I was mistaken and had transferred some of your thunder to de Gaulle, but from a political point of view I don't like writing de Gaulle down. It was a misfortune that we didn't succeed in getting a leftwing politician of standing out of France, but since de Gaulle is the only figure we have at present to represent the Free French we must make the best of him.

No, I didn't write "Bless 'Em All".[2] I am not in the army because I am not physically fit (Class IV!) but I have been in the Home Guard from the beginning and could write a rather similar booklet about that. I don't know who the author is except that he is an Australian. The book has had a fairly large sale, 15–20,000 copies, and has probably done a lot of good.

I should like to meet you some time when you are in London. I never get out of London as I am working in the BBC. I expect Humphrey Slater is a mutual friend of ours.

Yours sincerely
Geo. Orwell

1. For Sir Basil Liddell Hart, author of books on military subjects, see 556, 16.7.39, n. 1.
2. Liddell Hart asked Orwell whether he had written *Bless 'Em All* because he so admired the book that he had 'distributed quite a number of copies . . . in quarters where I thought it might do some good.' The full title of the book, published pseudonymously by Boomerang, is *Bless 'Em All: An Analysis of the British Army, Its Morale, Efficiency and Leadership, Written from Inside Knowledge* (1942). 'Boomerang' was Alan W. Wood, an Australian who had worked on Beaverbrook newspapers before the war and who, according to Fredric Warburg, 'died far too young'; see *All Authors Are Equal* (1973), 17. This sixty-four page pamphlet, published by Secker & Warburg in 1942, had an initial print run of 5,000 copies, but its lively critique of the British army, and particularly its leaders, preponderantly Old Etonians, resulted in the sale of 37,625 copies in the first fifteen months. See *All Authors Are Equal*, 17–19).

1380. War-time Diary

<u>12.8.42</u>: *Appalling policy handout this morning about affairs in India. The riots are of no significance—situation is well in hand—after all the number of deaths is not large, etc., etc. As to the participation of students in the riots, this is explained along "boys will be boys" lines. "We all know that students everywhere are only too glad to join in any kind of rag", etc., etc. Almost everyone utterly disgusted. Some of the Indians when they hear this kind of stuff turn quite pale, a strange sight.*

Most of the press taking a tough line, the Rothermere press disgustingly so. If these repressive measures in India are seemingly successful for the time being, the effects in this country will be very bad. All seems set for a big come-back of the reactionaries, and it almost begins to appear as though leaving Russia in the lurch were part of the manoeuvre. ⌐This afternoon shown in strict confidence by David Owen[1] Amery's statement [on] postwar policy towards Burma, based on Dorman-Smith's[2] report. It envisages a return to "direct rule" for a period of 5–7 years, Burma's reconstruction to be financed by Britain and the big British firms to be re-established on much the same terms as before. Please God no document of this kind gets into enemy hands. I did however get from Owen and from the confidential document one useful piece of information—that, so far as is known, the scorched earth policy was really carried out with extreme thoroughness.⌐

1. For David Owen, see *1322, n. 2*.
2. Sir Reginald Hugh Dorman-Smith (1899–1977) was Governor of Burma in 1941 and during the British withdrawal in 1942.

1381. Marathi Newsletter, 24

13 August 1942

This was misnumbered as 25. The English original was written by Orwell. No script has been traced. PasB gives switch censor as B. Sahni.

1382. To R. R. Desai

13 August 1942   PP/EB/NP

Dear Mr. Desai,
Thank you for your letter. I am sorry, but on enquiry I find it is not possible to sell copies of discs to speakers. I suppose you realise that these discs cannot be played on an ordinary gramophone, or at least, cannot be played often. There is some process of making a matrix from which ordinary discs can be struck off, but it appears that the BBC either never did this, or has discontinued doing it. I'm sorry about this.

Yours sincerely,
Eric Blair
Talks Producer
Indian Section

1383. To Ethel Mannin

13 August 1942   PP/EB/NP

Dear Ethel Mannin,[1]
I am wondering if you would like to take part in one of our broadcasts on September 25th. In this series we have discussions on matters of current

interest by two Europeans who start off by answering questions put to them by an Indian interviewer. The subject we should like you to debate is female emancipation. This, of course, is a subject of great interest to India, and roughly what we want discussed is how far women benefit by escaping from home and whether in the long run it is desirable for them to undertake the same work as men. We thought you might like to debate with Mrs. Eugenie Fordham,[2] of the British Association for International Understanding, who has expressed herself willing to take part. We think you would probably take a more strongly feminist standpoint than she would, which will give the basis for a real discussion. If you are interested, can you let me know, and then we will arrange details.

Yours,
George Orwell
Talks Producer
Indian Section

1. Ethel Mannin (see 575) was a writer and wife of Reginald Reynolds, one of Orwell's broadcasters; see 1060, n. 1.
2. In 'Speakers for Week 51,' 7 December 1942, Orwell described Mrs. Fordham as Assistant Director of British Survey at the British Association for International Understanding. She had, he said, read law at Cambridge and in that week would give a talk, 'Tessa—a Polish Baby.' She later prepared the second, revised, edition of Florence A. George's King Edward's Cookery Book (1950).

1384. BBC Talks Booking Form, 13.8.42

M. R. Kothari: Marathi Newsletters 24, 25, 26 (incorrectly numbered for 23, 24, 25); 'Written by Eric Blair, translated & read by Mr. Kothari'; broadcast 6, 13, and 20.8.42; fee £5.5s each date for translating and reading. Signed: Z. A. Bokhari.

1385. To M. R. Kothari

14 August 1942   PP/EB/NP

Dear Mr. Kothari,
I have been through your memorandum on the Marathi newsletters with Mr. Bokhari. He is a little doubtful about changing the form of them along the lines you suggest at present, but is willing to hear more of it. What he suggests is that you should write a specimen newsletter of the kind that you think suitable. You could either write an imaginary one, or if you like, take one of our past newsletters as the basis for the facts. For me to study it, you will have to write it in English, but you will understand that what matters is not the quality of the English, but the manner of approach and method of

arranging the material. I should be glad to see this any time you are able to prepare it.

Yours sincerely,
Eric Blair
Talks Producer
Indian Section

1386. To M. R. Kothari

14 August 1942   PP/EB

Dear Mr. Kothari,
I should be grateful if you will kindly fill in the enclosed form, which we need for our records.

In answer to the question "Application for employment as . . .", you should write Announcer/Translator. I should like to point out that this is a mere formality, and all the regular Announcer/Translators are asked to fill in one of these forms.

Yours sincerely,
Eric Blair
Talks Producer
Indian Section

1387. War-time Diary

14.8.42: *Horrabin was broadcasting today, and as always we introduced him as the man who drew the maps for Wells's Outline of History and Nehru's Glimpses of World History.[1] This had been extensively trailed and advertised beforehand, Horrabin's connection with Nehru being naturally a draw for India.[2] Today the reference to Nehru was cut out from the announcement— N. being in prison and therefore having become Bad.*

1. Properly, *Glimpses of World History: Being Further Letters to His Daughter, written in Prison, and containing a Rambling Account of History for Young People* (Allahabad, 1934); revised edition printed, with fifty maps by J. F. Horrabin (see *497, n. 4*) in 1939 by Lindsay Drummond. According to Inez Holden (see *1326, n. 1*), in a private communication, Orwell thought of asking Drummond to publish his and her war diaries.
2. Manuscript has 'Nehru naturally being a draw with Indian listeners.'

1388. Weekly News Review, 35

15 August 1942

The typescript has not been marked as checked with the broadcast but it bears two censorship stamps; the censor was Bokhari. There are a few changes and short cuts in the early part of the script. These appear to be in Orwell's hand. The anticipation towards the end of the script (see *n.* 7) suggests that this typescript is a copy. The script was read by Noel Sircar.

The Russian front still continues to be the most important one, but during the past week there have also been new and significant developments in the South Pacific. We will deal with the Russian front first.

During the past week, until a few days ago, the main German drive was still southward in the direction of the Caucasus. During the last two days, however, the Germans have made fresh attacks eastward, in the direction of Stalingrad—*an important industrial town, situated on the River Volga which is itself a very important line of supply between the Caucasus and the rest of Russia.*[1] So far these eastward attacks have not had much success. The Germans have gained little if any ground[, and the Russians are counter-attacking and in places have forced the enemy on the defensive]. Stalingrad, however, may be menaced from a new direction if the Germans gain much more ground to the south, as this might enable them to attack this very important objective from two sides. In the south, the German advance during the past week, though not very rapid, has been almost continuous. In places they are now actually in the foot-hills of the Caucasus mountains. It is uncertain whether the [important] oil town of Maikop is actually in German hands. All that is certain is that fierce fighting is taking place in that area, and Maikop itself has been heavily bombed and largely destroyed. Besides their advance southward and south-westward, the Germans have also advanced westward along the foot of the Caucasus mountains and claim to be only about 200 miles west of the Caspian Sea. The whole of this movement is full of the greatest danger for our Russian allies. By advancing so swiftly to the south, the Germans have *endangered the position of*[2] the Russian armies on the shores of the Sea of Azov, & *also endangered Novorossisk as a naval base. If it should be lost,* the only *harbour*[3] on the Black Sea left to the Russians *would*[4] be Batum, near the Turkish border. This may not be sufficient for their purposes, since a fleet needs not only harbours, but stores and workshops of every kind. The whole situation, therefore, is full of the greatest danger, and indeed, is as menacing as it was in the autumn of last year.

However, that is not to say that even if they can clean up the whole of the area which they are now attacking, the Germans would find this victory a decisive one. No gains in the area *North of the Caucasus mountains*[5] can really solve the German's oil problem. If you look at the map, you will note that the great chain of the Caucasus mountains runs straight across from the Black Sea to the Caspian Sea. [, the mountains at either end rising almost straight out of the water.] South of the mountains, on the east side, is the great oil town of Baku. This is the main source of Russian oil, and is one of the most important, if not <u>the</u> most important, oil area in the world. That is the German objective and they have got to cross the mountains to reach it. They are already somewhere near Pyatigorsk, which is at the beginning of one of the military roads across the Caucasus, but it is unlikely that they will succeed in fighting their way across the mountains this year, and it is doubtful whether they will try. These mountains are the highest in Europe and intense cold sets in any time from October onwards, so that the risks of beginning a campaign in this area in mid-August are very great. It is more probable that the Germans will try to move down to the Baku area along the coast of the Caspian Sea. This means moving through very narrow passes, which we may count on the Russians to defend with the utmost determination. And in weighing their chances, one has also to take into consideration the possibility of the Germans being faced by an unexpected attack in Western Europe. Whether this will happen, we still cannot predict, but it is at least certain from the tone of their newspapers and wireless that the Germans *consider it possible.*[6]

Last week, we reported that the Japanese were showing fresh activity in New Guinea, obviously as a prelude to another attack on Port Moresby. However, between now and then, the American and Australian forces forestalled them by an attack of their own. About four days ago, news came that the Americans were attacking Tulagi, in the Solomon Islands. The first reports were only of an air and sea action, but we now know that the Americans have also landed ground troops on three of the islands, and though the reports that have come in are very meagre, it is known that these troops have established themselves on shore, and are holding their ground. We shall probably be able to give a full account of this action, which is almost certainly a very important one, next week. In the meantime, we can only give a bare outline of the facts, and at the same time explain their strategic meaning. All we know is that the Americans have landed troops, that in doing so they have lost a cruiser, and had other vessels damaged, and that they are expecting fairly heavy casualties. It is probable, though not yet officially confirmed, that two important airfields hitherto held by the Japanese have been captured by the Allied Forces. No information can be obtained from the Japanese reports, as these constantly contradict one another, and are obviously only put out for propaganda purposes. It is evident, however, that things are not going altogether well from the Japanese point of view. As to the meaning of this move, it is best understood by looking at the map. The Solomon Islands lie eastward of New Guinea and north-eastward of Australia. From bases here, the Japanese submarines and aeroplanes can attack American ships, bringing supplies to Australia. If the Americans can obtain possession of the Solomon Islands, their supply route to Australia is not only made much safer, but can be shortened, as their ships will not have to make such a wide detour to avoid Japanese submarines. But the purpose of the move is also an offensive one. If the Solomons were in Allied hands, the position of the Japanese in New Guinea would be made much more difficult, and they could probably be forced to withdraw from there. This action, therefore, is probably the first step in an Allied offensive in the South Pacific. We do not predict yet whether it will be successful; it must be remembered that actions of this kind are difficult to carry out, and that it was in attempting something similar that the Japanese lost so heavily at Midway Island. The tone of the American communiqués, however, is confident. While the main operation takes place against the Solomon Islands, Allied aeroplanes from Australia are heavily bombing the Japanese in New

Guinea, and have forced them to retreat from the positions which they occupied recently. The object of this move no doubt is to tie down Japanese forces in New Guinea, and prevent them from reinforcing the Solomons. Simultaneously with the attack on the Solomons, the American navy has made another attack on the Japanese in the Aleutian Islands. It is known that damage has been inflicted[7] and several ships sunk. This, however, is a comparatively unimportant action, and it does not appear that any attempt has been made to land troops.

There is little news from Egypt. Both sides are being reinforced, and it is known that American troops have now arrived and are ready to take part side by side with the British in any forthcoming action. In the central Mediterranean there has been an important air and sea battle which has resulted in the island of Malta receiving a large consignment of fresh supplies, including fighter aeroplanes. A British convoy fought its way along the 1000 miles between Gibraltar and Malta against continuous attacks by Axis aeroplanes and submarines, and got through to its objective, though with the loss of a cruiser and an old aircraft carrier. We have not yet received full reports of Axis losses, but it is known that they lost 2 submarines sunk and had two cruisers damaged by torpedoes. The geographical position makes it impossible to reinforce Malta without suffering losses on the way, but these are justified since Malta lies midway between Italy and Africa, and its aeroplanes make constant attacks on Axis supplies crossing to Tripoli. The desperate effort the Axis have made to overwhelm Malta by bombing show how important it is for the Allies to hold on to it.[8]

There have been a number of German air raids on Britain, all of them on a very small scale. It is uncertain whether these raids are made in order to give the German people the impression that their air force is avenging the British raids on Germany, or whether they are undertaken for reconnaissance, in preparation for heavier attacks to be made later. The RAF continues with its attacks and during this week has made a very heavy raid on Duisburg, and two others on Mainz. In the latter attack, apart from hundreds of tons of explosive bombs, 50 thousand incendiary bombs were dropped. The Air Ministry has recently issued exact figures about our bombing of Germany. They show, in the first place, that in June and July 1942 the RAF dropped on Germany more than 4 times the weight of bombs dropped during the same period of 1940; and also that there have now been about a dozen raids in which the RAF have dropped a far greater load of bombs than the Germans ever dropped in their heaviest raids on Britain. Although raids on this scale cannot be undertaken every day, because the weather is not always suitable, there is no doubt that their number will constantly increase as the American as well as the British air force comes into play.

The news of riots, shootings, guerilla warfare [and][9] arrests, reprisals and threats against the civilian population comes in almost continuously from all over Europe. It is clear that not only in the Balkans, but even in parts of Western Europe, a state not far removed from civil war has been reached. For example a few[10] days ago the German wireless laconically announced that 93 persons, described as terrorists, had been shot that day, in the single city of

Paris. In all areas along the Atlantic coast, the Germans have issued decrees threatening the most savage penalties against anyone who should assist an invading Allied force, and more or less openly admit that the people in the occupied territories are heart and soul for the Allies. When we look back two years, and remember how confidently the Germans boasted that they would make the New Order a success, and eliminate every trace of British and American influence on the Continent, we realise how completely the Germans have lost the political side of the war, even though in a military sense they are still undefeated.

1. —*an important . . . rest of Russia.*], the possession of which is indispensable to them if they are to reach the Caspian Sea area. West, *Commentaries* reads 'town' as 'base,' but, though unclear, 'town' is more likely.
2. *endangered the position of*] already cut off
3. *, & also endangered . . . harbour*] . If they should be forced to retreat by sea the naval base of Novorossisk might be lost. This means that the only important base
4. *would*] will
5. *North of the Caucasus mountains*] in which they are now in
6. *consider it possible*] greatly fear it
7. *It is known . . . inflicted*] *first typed after* reinforcing the Solomons, *then x-ed through*
8. See *1403, n. 3.*
9. A comma should have been added after 'warfare' when 'and' was crossed out.
10. 'two' was typed, but x-ed through and 'a few' typed as interlinear insertion

1389. Bengali Newsletter, 5

15 August 1942

The English original was written by Orwell. No script has been traced.

1390. Gujarati Newsletter, 25

17 August 1942

The English original was written by Orwell. No script has been traced. PasB gives switch censor as I. B. Sarin.

1391. To Tom Wintringham

17 August 1942   PP/EB

Dear Wintringham,
I am in general agreement with the document you sent me,[1] and so are most of the people I know, but I think that from the point of view of propaganda approach it is all wrong. In effect, it demands two separate things which the average reader will get mixed up, first, the setting up of a committee, and secondly, the programme which that committee is to use as a basis for

discussion. I should start by putting forward boldly and above all with an eye to intelligibility a programme for India coupled with the statement that this is what the Indian political leaders would accept. I would *not* start with any talk about setting up committees; in the first place because it depresses people merely to hear about committees, and in any case because the procedure you suggest would take months to carry through, and would probably lead to an inconclusive announcement. I should head my leaflet or whatever it is RELEASE NEHRU—REOPEN NEGOTIATIONS and then set forth the plan for India in six simple clauses, viz:

1). India to be declared independent immediately.
2). An interim national government from the leading political parties on a proportional basis.
3). India to enter into full alliance with the United Nations.
4). The leading political parties to co-operate in the war effort to their utmost capacity.
5). The existing administration to be disturbed as little as possible during the war period.
6). Some kind of trade agreement allowing for a reasonable safe-guarding of British interests.

Those are the six points. They should be accompanied by an authoritative statement from the Congress Party that they are willing to accept those terms—as they would be—and that if granted these terms they would co-operate in crushing the pro-Japanese faction. Point 6 should carry with it a rider to the effect that the British and Indian Governments will jointly guarantee the pensions of British officials in India. In this way at small cost one could neutralise a not unimportant source of opposition in this country.

All I have said could be got on to a leaflet of a page or two pages, and I think might get a hearing. It is most important to make this matter simple and arresting as it has been so horribly misrepresented in the press and the big public is thoroughly bored by India and only half aware of its strategic significance. Ditto with America.

Yours,
[No name/position]

1. Tom Wintringham sent Orwell a copy of the press release issued by the Common Wealth National Committee on 15 August 1942. This was issued over the names of J. B. Priestley (Chairman), Richard Acland (Vice-Chairman), and Tom Wintringham (Vice-Chairman). For Common Wealth and Richard Acland, see *609, n. 2*; *1429, n. 1*. For Wintringham, see *721, n. 1*; *1106, n. 3*. The stature of the novelist, playwright, and commentator J. B. Priestley (1894–1984) was considerable at this time and was further enhanced by his inspiring broadcasts, especially after Dunkirk. He was seen by many as akin to Churchill in his dogged determination; even in the darkest days he was sure the war would end in Britain's favour. He also argued forcefully for a better Britain when peace came. See also *698, n. 2* and *1429, n. 1*.

1392. To Peggotty Freeman

18 August 1942   PP/EB

Dear Miss Freeman,
Your letter has been passed on to me by Balraj Sahni. We would like to have a short obituary notice of Ram Mahum[1] in the Indian Service, if we can arrange someone to do it. It seems hardly worth while anyone coming up from Cambridge to do a five minute broadcast, but meanwhile I am communicating with Narayana Menon to see whether he can either do the broadcast for us, or tell us somebody else who is now in London who can do it. In the case of our being able to arrange this, I will send you a copy of the script.

Yours sincerely,
Eric Blair
Talks Producer
Indian Section

1. Narayana Menon (see *1118, n. 1*) broadcast a five-minute obituary to India on 25 August 1942. Effraim Nahum (not Mahum), born in 1919, was killed when a lone German raider dropped a stick of bombs on Cambridge. Menon described him as one of the outstanding members of the student scientific community. His parents, originally from Syria and Palestine, had settled in Manchester. As a boy he was associated with a left-wing paper, *Out of Bounds*, produced by schoolboys. He went to Cambridge in 1937 and plunged into political activities in connexion with the Spanish civil war, yet he gained a double first in physics. In 1940 he became chairman of the Cambridge University Labour Federation (from whose address Miss Freeman wrote) and started work 'of great national importance' at the Cavendish Laboratory. A mobile x-ray unit named after him was being sponsored, Menon said. In his talk, Menon also said that such was the esteem felt for Ram Nahum that the place he lived, Ram's Yard, was named after him. However, that name had existed earlier.

1393. To Leonora Lockhart

18 August 1942   Copy (so marked)

Dear Miss Lockhart,
I am approaching you in the hope that you will do a talk on Basic English in the Indian Service of the BBC, on October 2nd.[1] This series of talks, in which I want you to take part, is called "I'd Like it Explained", and the talks usually take the form of a dialogue between two experts, who are questioned by an Indian interviewer. In the case of Basic English, I think it would be better not to have a discussion, but simply an interview in which the method is explained from the ground upwards, because it is here a case of putting on the map something which many of our listeners will not have heard of, and others will have heard a distorted version of. In trying to put over the idea of Basic English to India, we are liable to encounter a certain amount of opposition from Indians who already speak standard English, but what I am chiefly concerned with is to popularise the idea that Basic English will be particularly useful as between Indians, Chinese and other Orientals who don't know one another's languages, and that we have as an initial advantage

the fact that between five and ten million Indians know a certain amount of standard English. We would therefore frame the interview along these lines. I hope you will undertake this, as I am particularly anxious to have this subject put on the map, with a view to dealing with it more elaborately later.

Yours truly,
George Orwell
Talks Producer
Indian Section

1. The letter is annotated: 'Oct 2   12.15 English   5.15 Indian.' The script is in the BBC Archives. It is titled 'Basic English' and was programme No. 10 in the series 'I'd Like It Explained.' It was broadcast in the Eastern Service on 2 October 1942. Basic English was developed in the 1920s by C. K. Ogden; see Orwell's letters to him of 16 December 1942, *1746* and 1 March 1944, *2427*.

1394. To Ethel Mannin

18 August 1942   PP/EB/NP

Dear Ethel Mannin,
Thanks for your letter. I suggest that you go ahead and produce a draft of about 750 words, showing roughly what you feel about the present and future position of women, and the conflicting claims of work and home life. I will then sent° it on to Mrs. Fordham, who will make what comments she thinks fit, and from that, we will work up a proper dialogue. I should like your draft by the end of this month. We have ascertained that your fee will be 10 guineas.

Yours
[Initialled] E. A. B
George Orwell
Talks Producer
Indian Section

1395. War-time Diary

<u>18.8.42:</u>   *From Georges Kopp's[1] last letter from Marseilles (after some rigmarole about the engineering work he has been doing):[2] ". . . I am about to start production on an industrial scale. But I am not at all certain that I shall actually do so,[3] because I have definite contracts with my firm, which has, I am afraid, developed lately connections which reduce considerably its independence and it is possible that another firm would eventually profit by my work, which I should hate since I have no arrangements at all with the latter and will not, for the time being, be prepared to sign any. If I am compelled to stop, I really don't know what I am going to do; I wish some of my very dear friends to whom I have written repeatedly would not be as slow*

and as passive as they seem to be. If no prospects open in this field, I contemplate to make use of another process of mine, related to bridge-building [, which, you may remember, I have put into successful operation at San Mateo before the war."]

Translated: "I am afraid France is going into full alliance with Germany. If the Second Front is not opened soon I shall do my best to escape to England".

1. Georges Kopp (1902–1951), Russian-born Belgian who was Orwell's commander in Spain, see *359, n. 2; 535, n. 1.*
2. *'(after some rigmarole . . . doing)'* is an interlinear insertion in the manuscript replacing 'I have been* asked by the boss I had in North Africa in 1940 to establish here a certain industrial process of mine, which might help a lot° French industry & transportation.' '*ie. I was' [Orwell's handwritten footnote in manuscript].
3. *do so*] go on

1396. To B. H. Liddell Hart

19 August 1942   Typewritten

10a Mortimer Crescent   NW 6

Dear Captain Lidell° Hart,
Many thanks for your letter and the two enclosed pamphlets. I have written some notes on them, rather garrulous I fear, which it may interest you to see.[1]

Any time you are in London I should like very much to meet you. Of the above telephone numbers, the Maida Vale one is best before 9 am or after 7 pm the other in the middle of the day.

Yours sincerely
Geo. Orwell

1. For Orwell's notes, see *1397* and *1398.*

1397. Notes on SOME POINTS ABOUT THE HOME GUARD

This paper deals chiefly with recruitment, organisation and training and I am in substantial agreement with it, but suggest it does not tackle boldly enough the central weakness of the Home Guard, its officers and the method of their recruitment. Anyone acquainted with the Home Guard knows that its officers are (a) chosen almost entirely on a class basis and with no sort of qualifying examination, (b) usually old, ignorant and unimaginative, (c) in many cases politically frightened of their command and anxious to prevent it from turning into a People's Army, and (d) frequently sceptical about the very possibility of a German invasion and merely members of the Home Guard because they enjoy standing men in a row and barking at them, and in some cases because they have a half-conscious intention of raising a sort of auxiliary police force for use against the working class after the war.

I am surprised that this paper does not mention the fact that there is no recognized channel of promotion in the Home Guard, such as exists at least in theory in the Army. A private who wishes to try for a commission has no way of setting about it except by personal intrigue. The existing officers now have, in theory, full military powers over their men, but they themselves are self-selected, or have been picked out on personal grounds by earlier officers who were self-selected. When the Home Guard (then LDV) was first formed the local bourgeoisie and blimpocracy appointed themselves officers, afterwards assuming regular military titles, and since then have selected the men who shall serve under them, not unnaturally picking out those who were of their own class and seemed to them politically O.K. Later the various regulations were passed bringing members of the Home Guard under the Army Act and forbidding them to resign, so that you have the position of officers who have never passed any kind of examination or had to show any kind of qualification except those of social position, enjoying (theoretically) full powers as military commanders. There are safeguards in the facts that in practice these powers cannot be applied tyrannically, and that since the Home Guard is unpaid and officership entails a lot of work those who become officers are usually of good character. But there is no guarantee whatever that they will be militarily efficient or politically reliable. At the same time while the Home Guard is unpaid it is inevitable that most of the officers will come from the higher income groups, as an officer has to spend quite a lot of money besides needing a telephone etc., etc. The net result is that having started out as a sort of anti-fascist militia the Home Guard has ended by being more sharply stratified on class lines than the regular army.

To some extent this could be rectified. I suggest that anyone writing on the organisation of the Home Guard should agitate for (a) officers to be appointed by examination only, existing officers to be examined as well as new ones, (b) any man serving in the ranks to have the right to apply for a commission, (c) officers from platoon commander upwards to be full-time and paid at army rates, (d) no officer over 55 to hold other than administrative posts, and (e) political instruction on the origins of the war to form part of Home Guard training (say once a month) and those applying for commissions to be examined in this subject along with the strictly military ones.

1398. Notes on THE ROLE OF THE HOME GUARD

This paper is concerned more with the strategical and tactical use of the Home Guard. Much of it I am not qualified to pass judgment on, but I suggest that the central issue is the probable nature of a German invasion. The paper seems to take for granted that the Germans could invade England with a large army, but that their parachutists or airborne troops would probably be landed in country districts where only a few men could be concentrated against them. From this it is inferred that so far as possible the Home Guard should be made mobile, so as to economise its forces and allow larger numbers of the regular forces to be withdrawn from Britain. Clearly one has only guesswork to go on, but I feel that more attention ought to be paid to the possibility of large-scale "nuisance raids" not aimed at actually conquering Britain but at paralysing industry etc. It is difficult to believe that the Germans could land, say, ½ a million men with heavy equipment on our shores without having complete command of the sea as well as the air for several weeks, in which case we should have lost the war already. On the other hand if they were willing to throw away a few scores of thousands of highly trained men they might achieve a devastating effect by parachutists and airborne troops whose orders would be to destroy as much as possible before being rounded up. To get the best results these would have to be landed in big towns, in which, eg. in London, there are plenty of spaces where parachutes can be dropped and carrier planes can be at least crash-landed. It is possible also that the war will see the development of "air commandos" in which airborne troops temporarily overrun an area of some square miles, do their work of destruction and then take off again with at least the greater part of their original strength. The dispersal of industry resulting from air-raids would make this easier to achieve. But putting aside this possibility, it is calculated that in a single morning round about dawn the Germans could land 30,000 parachutists and airborne troops in London. Even if they were all disposed of by the same evening they could work tremendous havoc in the mean time, and in practice they would probably be able to go on fighting and thus dislocating work and communications for several days. Little attention has been paid anywhere to this possibility, which seems to me a very strong one. On the other hand, with regard to making the Home Guard mobile, training has been distorted to a certain extent by an attempt, not actually to make the Home Guard mobile but to treat it as though it were so. There is less and less emphasis on local defence and more train[ing] in fairly large units, while the men are repeatedly told that they "may have to fight anywhere". London units are being taught more and more about fighting in open country while training in street fighting has been almost abandoned since 1941. I suggest we ought to face the fact that the Home Guard cannot be made mobile because, apart from transport difficulties, most of the men are working and even in an invasion the economic life of the country will have to go on in areas where there is no fighting at the moment. If special mobile platoons or other units were formed they would have to be full-time, in which case they would consist either of people not working (ie too old), or in effect would be regular soldiers, in which case they might as well be recruited into the army in the ordinary way. I suggest therefore that the whole emphasis ought to be on *local* defence, and that the first care of a commander should be to see that his men know every inch of their particular area and can be mobilised in the minimum of time. They should never, of course, be told that their responsibility stops at the edges of their own area, but they should be taught to identify with this area and feel ready to defend it to the death. In this way the only advantages the Home Guard is likely to have over well-trained invaders, ie. local knowledge and the consciousness of fighting for their own homes, would be best exploited.

The above are only my own opinions and open to contradiction. What is certain however is that the training and dispositions of the Home Guard have suffered from those in command having *no* picture in their minds of the kind of invasion they may have to meet, and in many cases not believing invasion to be a possibility at all. When one sees the way in which men are trained, or not trained, and the frivolous aimless way in which one plan after another is taken up, vaguely talked about for a while and then dropped, one sees at a glance that those at the top are simply playing at soldiers and would behave quite differently if they believed in a German invasion and wanted to counter it. In my own unit, for example, during two years not one single parade has been employed in teaching the men the details of their locality; the lower ranks are even discouraged from buying large-scale maps of the district. Nor is there any properly arranged scheme of mobilisation, nor any prearranged battle positions, nor any real defensive posts. In addition private property considerations are allowed to hamper training at every step. All this would change swiftly if those in command believed themselves to be preparing for a real eventuality of a kind they could more or less foresee. This leads back to my remarks in the other set of notes on the provision of proper officers. But even as things are at present, there are two measures which would make the Home Guard much more efficient against a sudden unexpected invasion. These are (a) distribution of ammunition. At present, at least in London, weapons are in the men's own possession, but ammunition is only to be issued after mobilisation. This means a bottleneck of several hours, even supposing the ammunition finally gets distributed, which it might not in some cases, as the ammunition dumps are centralised and liable to capture. Also (b) subject to reasonable safeguards the Home Guard should be empowered to take over such premises as they think necessary for constructing fortified positions. At present private property is sacrosanct, with the result that strongpoints have to be constructed, if at all, in usually unsuitable positions.

1399. War-time Diary

<u>19.8.42:</u> *Big Commando raid on Dieppe today. Raid was still continuing this evening. Just conceivably the first step in an invasion, or a try-out for the first step, though I don't think so. The warning that was broadcast to the French people that this was only a raid and they were not to join in would in that case be a bluff.*

1400. Marathi Newsletter, 25

20 August 1942

This was misnumbered as 26. The English original was written by Orwell. No script has been traced. PasB gives timing as 13′ 49″.

1401. To Edmund Blunden

20 August 1942   PP/EB/NP

Dear Mr. Blunden,[1]

I wonder if you would like to take part in a magazine programme which we do once a month on the Indian Service. This programme is chiefly devoted to poetry, [and] where possible we try to get writers to read their own verse. We should like it very much if you could read one poem for us. There are two or three I have in mind, but we shall have to wait a little before making a definite choice. This broadcast takes place on Tuesday, September 8th at 12.15 p.m., and I think we are going to broadcast it live, owing to the difficulty of recording a long programme successfully, but if you could not arrange to be there on that particular day, you could perhaps record your poem on some earlier date, and we could use that in the middle of the live programme. Could you be kind enough to let me know as early as possible whether you would like to do this, as I have all the details of the programme to arrange.

Yours sincerely,
George Orwell
Talks Producer
Indian section

1. Edmund Charles Blunden (1896–1974), poet and scholar. A biographical note to the BBC pamphlet *Books and Authors* (see *3101*) states: 'Edmund Blunden is the author of *Undertones of War, Shelley, Cricket Country*, and many volumes of poetry and criticism. He was awarded the Hawthornden Prize in 1922 for his volume of poems *The Shepherd*, and the Benson Medal of the Royal Society of Literature in 1931. In 1924–27 he was Professor of English Literature at Tokyo University. For some years after 1931 he was Fellow and Tutor in English Literature at Merton College, Oxford. He is now on the staff of the *Times Literary Supplement*.' Blunden served in World War I and was awarded the Military Cross. His experiences are memorably recalled in *Undertones of War* (1928). As well as the appointments mentioned above, he was assistant editor of *The Athenaeum* for a time after that war and after World War II was Professor of English, University of Hong Kong and then Professor of Poetry, University of Oxford, 1966–68; he resigned owing to ill health. In addition to publishing much poetry, he edited the work of others, including John Clare, Bret Harte, Christopher Smart, Leigh Hunt, William Collins, and Wilfred Owen, and wrote biographies of Leigh Hunt, Lamb, Shelley, and Keats. *Cricket Country* (1944) was published in the same series as Orwell's *The English People* (1947) and was reviewed by Orwell in the *Manchester Evening News*, 20 April 1944; see *2455*.

1402. To Lord Winterton

21 August 1942   PP/EB/NP

Dear Lord Winterton,

I am sending you herewith the draft of Professor Laski's remarks. I am very sorry that it was not possible to get them through before you left for the country, but we only received them from Professor Laski about mid-day today. I trust that they will reach you some time to-morrow, Saturday.

Meanwhile, I am expecting to see you at about 5.30 p.m. on Thursday next, at 200, Oxford Street.

Yours sincerely,
George Orwell
Talks Assistant
Indian Section

1403. News Review, 36

22 August 1942

The typescript bears both censorship stamps, censored by Bokhari, two slight manuscript alterations in Orwell's hand, and the note 'As broadcast 11 mins E.A.B'. Five lines were typed and then x-ed through (see *n. 2*); a few words x-ed through elsewhere have not been noted. Princess Indira was scheduled to read this News Review but her place was taken by Homi Bode.[1]

On Tuesday of this week, the news was released that the British Prime Minister, Mr. Churchill, has been in Moscow, to confer with Premier Stalin and other leading representatives of the United Nations. No pronouncement has been made yet as to the conclusions reached, but it is known that these were satisfactory, and it can be taken as certain that some important move was decided upon. This is the fourth occasion on which Mr. Churchill has travelled halfway round the world to confer with the leader of an Allied nation. Grave though the situation is for the Allies, the comparative ease with which the Allied Nations can confer with one another is an index of the real strategic situation, for whereas it is a comparatively simple matter for Mr. Churchill to go to Moscow or to Washington, it would be utterly impossible for Hitler to visit Tokyo, unless he travelled by submarine and took perhaps six months over the journey. The United Nations are in full communication with one another, while the Fascist powers control only two separate areas at opposite ends of the world

Mr. Churchill arrived at a critical moment for our Russian Allies. During the past week the general direction of the fighting in Southern Russia was much as before. The Germans have made further advances on the Caucasus front, and have definitely over-run the important oil centre of Maikop. Before evacuating the town, the Russians removed or destroyed all the machinery and the existing stocks of oil, so that the capture of this area is no direct gain to the Germans, although it is a severe loss to the Russians. At the same time the German attack in this area has fanned out to east and to west, the easterly attack moving towards the other important oil area of Grosney, while the westward one endangers the port of Novorossisk, the most important Russian naval base on the Black Sea. One column of German troops appears to be trying to cross the Caucasus mountains, but there has been no news of this movement for some days past. Further north, Stalingrad, the strategic key to the whole of this campaign, is firmly in

Russian hands, though it is menaced by a German attack from the south, as well as from the west. The Germans claim to have over-run the whole territory within the elbow of the Don, at the angle of which lies Stalingrad, but they have not succeeded in crossing the river anywhere in this area. Further north, at Voronezh and in the areas of Moscow and Leningrad, the Russians have made attacks which have had some success and which are no doubt designed chiefly to draw off the German forces from other fronts. Seeing the whole of this campaign in perspective as well as we can, we may say that though the Germans have had great successes, they are not within sight of securing the decisive victory which they hoped to complete before the onset of winter.

The fighting in the Solomon Islands which we reported last week has resulted in a brilliant success for the Allies, after nearly a fortnight of hard fighting. The American and Australian forces are now in control of three of the islands, including Tulagi, which possesses the most important harbour in this area. Yesterday's official report described the Allied forces as "mopping up"—that is, crushing sporadic resistance after defeating the enemy's main force. Guerilla fighting will probably continue for a long time to come, but so long as the Allies hold the landing grounds and the main anchorages they can prevent the Solomon Islands from being used as a base for attacks on shipping coming from America to Australia. The Japanese continue to put out extravagant reports of losses inflicted on the Allies, but they have contradicted themselves over and over again and in the last two days have significantly changed their tune. After several times announcing that they were about to issue a report on the fighting in the Solomon Islands, they have suddenly stated that no report will be issued as yet—a tacit admission of failure. The Allied success, however, was not achieved without losses. It is known that an American cruiser was sunk, and the Australian cruiser the Canberra was also sunk a few days ago.[2]

A few days back, American troops also landed in the Gilbert Islands, 900 miles north east of the Solomons, and destroyed air-field installations. This, however, was only a raid, and the troops re-embarked again afterwards.

We are now able to give fuller figures of the naval battle in the Mediterranean, as the result of which a British convoy reached Malta with much-needed supplies. The British naval losses were a cruiser, a light cruiser, a destroyer and an old aircraft carrier. The Axis losses were 2 submarines, between 60 and 70 aeroplanes, and two cruisers damaged.[3] It is impossible for the Allies to reinforce Malta without losing ships in the process, because after leaving Gibraltar any convoy has to pass through 1,000 miles of sea over which land-based Axis aeroplanes can operate. But such losses are well justified, since Malta is an ideal base for bombing Italy and for raiding Axis supplies on their way to Libya. The people of Malta throughout the past two years have gone through a most terrible experience of endless bombing, and fairly severe food shortage, and have behaved with unexampled courage. They are well aware of what would happen to their liberty if the Axis won the war, and Malta passed under Fascist rule, and consequently have suffered their long ordeal without even a murmur, at moments when food was very short and the island barely possessed any fighter aeroplanes with which to hit back at its attackers. The arrival of the recent convoy will ease Malta's position considerably.

German submarines have recently sunk several Brazilian passenger ships in the most wanton way, drowning a large number of people. This has caused great popular indignation in Brazil, where there have been large demonstrations in favour of the Allies, and the offices of German-subsidised newspapers have been wrecked by the crowd. The President of Brazil has promised that in compensation for the sinking, German ships interned in Brazilian ports will be seized, and the property of Axis nationals in Brazil confiscated. In addition a hundred Germans have been arrested as hostages. The unprovoked sinking of Brazilian ships will have its effect in other South American countries besides Brazil.[4]

More and more the peoples of the South American Republics are coming to realise how important it is that all free nations should stand together against the aggressor states, who are the natural enemies of their independence and their national institutions.

On Wednesday of this week there took place the largest combined operations raid of the war, on Dieppe on the French coast, about 60 miles from the coast of Britain. British, Canadian, Free French and American troops took part, the whole force evidently numbering 5,000 or[5] 10,000 men. They remained on shore about 10 hours, and successfully destroyed batteries of artillery and other military objectives, before re-embarking. Tanks were successfully landed, and took part in the operations.[6] This is probably the first time in this war that tanks have been landed from small boats on to an open beach. It is known that there were heavy casualties on both sides and very heavy losses of aeroplanes. The Germans are known to have lost about 90 planes destroyed for certain and a large number were reported as probably destroyed, so that 130 would be a conservative figure for their total loss. The British lost nearly 100 planes. These losses are much more serious for the Germans than for the British, as the great part of the German air force is now on the Russian front, and any *large*[7] loss of planes means that others have to be brought across Europe to replace them.

When the raid began, the BBC repeatedly broadcast to the French people, warning them that this was only a raid and not an invasion of Europe, and that they had better remain in their houses and not join in the fighting. There was good reason for doing this. On a previous occasion, in the raid on Saint Nazaire, the French population, seeing their chance of striking a blow against the Germans who have been oppressing them for two years, rose and fought on the side of the British. Afterwards, when the raid was over and the British troops had re-embarked, the Germans committed fearful atrocities against the local population, and the British Government had no wish that such a thing as this should be repeated, and therefore carefully warned the French population to remain aloof. The broadcasters added, however, "We shall warn you when the real invasion comes, and then will be your opportunity to get weapons in to your hands and regain your liberty." Whether or not this raid was a try-out for a full-scale invasion, it has at least demonstrated that the

Allies are able to land troops in large numbers on the most strongly-defended points of the French shore—a thing which only a few weeks ago the Germans were boastfully declaring to be impossible.

1. Homi Bode was later to be one of six advertised speakers at a public meeting held at Conway Hall to demand the unconditional release of Mahatma Gandhi and other political prisoners arrested by the British in India on 9 August 1942 for supporting a 'Quit India' resolution passed by the All-India Congress. The meeting was advertised in *Tribune* on 19 February 1943 and held that same night. On 10 February Gandhi had begun a fast; this led to fears for his life. He ended the fast on 1 March 1943.
2. Five lines were typed after 'a few days ago' and then x-ed through. They appear to be a false start for the news about the landing on the Gilbert Islands that follows. On 23 August Churchill proposed that a British cruiser be given to the Australian navy as a replacement for the *Canberra*, and *Shropshire* was presented to the Australians (*The Second World War*, IV, 462; U.S.: *The Hinge of Fate*, 514).
3. In order to escort thirteen merchant ships and three tankers, a force of four aircraft carriers, two battleships, seven cruisers, thirty-four destroyers, eight submarines, and some twenty smaller craft was assembled. The convoy sailed from Gibraltar on 10 August and was attacked from the 11th, when the *Eagle*—the old aircraft carrier, formerly of the Chilean navy—was sunk. Its planes had to land on *Victorious*, which jettisoned some of its planes to make room for them. The cruisers *Manchester* and *Cairo* and the destroyer *Foresight* were also sunk. Several more British ships were damaged. Of the merchant ships, five arrived at Malta and landed some 30,000 tons of materials. The Axis forces had fortunately broken off the action at a critical moment, and the submarine *Safari* later damaged two Italian cruisers, *Bolzano* and *Attendolo* (*2194 Days of War*, 278).
4. Brazil declared war on Germany and Italy the day this news review was broadcast.
5. *5000 or*] about
6. Churchill wrote in *The Second World War*, 'Dieppe occupies a place of its own in the story of the war, and the grim casualty figures must not class it as a failure. . . . Tactically it was a mine of experience. It shed revealing light on many shortcomings in our outlook' (IV, 459; U.S.: *The Hinge of Fate*, 511). For further details, see Orwell's War-time Diary, *1410*, 22.8.42, especially *ns. 2* and *6*.
7. *large*] serious

1404. Bengali Newsletter, 6

22 August 1942

The English original was written by Orwell. No script has been traced. PasB gives timing as 11′ 5″.

1405. BBC Talks Booking Form, 22.8.42

Princess Indira of Kapurthala: 'The Debate Continues'; broadcast 7, 14, 21, and 28.9.42; fee £9.9s each talk. Signed: Z. A. Bokhari.

1406. BBC Talks Booking Form, 22.8.42

Professor Harold Laski: 'I'd Like It Explained,' 6, 'The Future of Parliament' (with Lord Winterton); broadcast 4.9.42; fee £8.8s. Signed: Z. A. Bokhari. The booking form is marked 'Duplicate.' [An identical form survives for Earl Winterton, but is not marked 'Duplicate.']

1407. BBC Talks Booking Form, 22.8.42

J. M. Tambimuttu: 'Open Letter,' 7, To a Marxist; broadcast 10.9.42; fee £9.9s. Signed: Z. A. Bokhari.

1408. BBC Talks Booking Form, 22.8.42

Shridhar Telkar: 'Topic of the Week,' 5–10; broadcast 2, 9, 16, 23, and 30.9.42; fee £9.9s each talk. Signed: Z. A. Bokhari.

1409. BBC Talks Booking Form, 22.8.42

T. C. Worsley: 'I'd Like It Explained,' 'Education' (with G. M. Young); broadcast 11.9.42; fee £8.8s + £2.0.5 + 17s 0d fare and expenses. Signed: Z. A. Bokhari. [The form is marked 'see separate contract' for G. M. Young, but his form seems not to have survived.]

1410. War-time Diary

<u>22.8.42:</u> David Astor[1] *very damping about the Dieppe raid, which he saw at more or less close quarters and which he says was an almost complete failure except for the very heavy destruction of German fighter planes, which was not part of the plan. He says that the affair was definitely misrepresented in the press[2] and is now being misrepresented in the reports to the P.M., and that the main facts were:—Something over 5000 men were engaged, of whom at least 2000 were killed or prisoners. It was not intended to stay longer on shore[3] than was actually done (ie. till[4] about 4 pm), but the idea was to destroy all the defences of Dieppe, and the attempt to do this was an utter failure. In fact only comparatively trivial damage was done, a few batteries of guns knocked out etc., and only one of the three main parties really made its objective. The others did not get far and many were massacred on the beach by artillery fire. The defences were formidable and would have been difficult to deal with even if there had been artillery support, as the guns were sunk in the face of the cliffs or under enormous concrete coverings. More tank-*

landing craft were sunk than got ashore. About 20 or 30 tanks were landed but none got off again. The newspaper photos which showed tanks apparently being brought back to England[5] were intentionally misleading. The general impression was that the Germans knew of the raid beforehand.[6] Almost as soon as it was begun they had a man broadcasting a spurious "eye-witness" account[7] from somewhere further up the coast, and another man broadcasting false orders in English. On the other hand the Germans were evidently surprised by the strength of the air support. Whereas normally they have kept their fighters on the ground so as to conserve their strength, they sent them into the air as soon as they heard that tanks were landing, and lost a number of planes variously estimated, but considered by some RAF officers to be[8] as high as 270. Owing to the British strength in the air the destroyers were able to lie outside Dieppe all day. One was sunk, but this was by a shore battery. When a request came to attack some objective on shore, the destroyers formed in line and raced inshore firing their guns[9] while the fighter planes supported them overhead.

David Astor considers that this definitely proves that an invasion of Europe is impossible. ⌈Of course we can't feel sure that he hasn't been planted to say this, considering who his parents are.⌉[10] I can't help feeling that to get ashore at all at such a strongly defended spot, without either bomber support, artillery support except for the guns of the destroyers (4.9 guns I suppose) or airborne troops, was a considerable achievement.

1. David Astor] D.A. *on typescript here and in last paragraph. Astor was then serving in the Royal Marines.*
2. The Dieppe raid proved, at least in the short term, a sad waste except in so far as it brought home to senior servicemen the lessons to be learned for future landings. More than 6,000 men, mainly Canadian, were involved and well over half were killed, wounded, or captured. Churchill states that of 5,000 Canadians, 18% were killed and nearly 2,000 were captured (*The Second World War*, IV, 459; U.S.: *The Hinge of Fate*, 511. See also *1403, n. 6*). All 27 tanks landed were almost immediately destroyed; the RAF lost 70 planes, and 34 ships were sunk. The Germans admitted losing 297 killed and 294 wounded or captured, and 48 planes. The newspapers claimed in headlines at the time, 'Big Hun Losses' (*Daily Mirror*, 20 August 1942), but as *The War Papers*, 22 (1977) put it, 'they might have added, "Even Bigger Allied Losses." '
3. *longer on shore*] on shore longer *in manuscript*
4. *ie. till*] ie. dawn till
5. *being brought back to England*] returning *in manuscript*
6. It was alleged that the Germans had cracked British codes and so had advance notice of the raid, but it seems that the first warning was given by German trawlers just as the Allied flotilla approached the coast. The failure of the raid was publicly put down to 'careless talk' or even to an advertisement for soap flakes which showed a woman pruning a tree dressed in what was headlined as 'BEACH COAT from DIEPPE.' A newspaper cutting of this advertisement, which appeared in the *Daily Telegraph*, 15.8.42, was annotated by Orwell, 'Advert. popularly believed to have given the Germans advance warning of the Dieppe raid.' (The cutting is in Box 39 of Orwell's pamphlet collection in the British Library; see *3733*.) The film *Next of Kin* (1942), made to drive home the lesson that careless talk could endanger such enterprises, began its life as a shorter services training film. Churchill maintains, 'Our post-war examination of their records shows that the Germans did not receive, through leakages of information, any special warning of our attention to attack' (*The Second World War*, IV, 458; U.S.: *The Hinge of Fate*, 510, reads slightly differently).
7. *account*] account of the raid *in manuscript*, 'of the raid' *crossed out*

8. *to be*] to have been
9. *their guns*] their forward guns
10. The passage within half brackets appears in the manuscript, was typed, and the typed version then heavily crossed out.

1411. To G. M. Young

[23 August 1942?]

CAN YOU MANAGE RECORDING TUESDAY AFTERNOON FIRST SEPTEMBER LETTER FOLLOWS.

ORWELL BROADCASTS

Reply Paid. Please.

1412. Gujarati Newsletter, 26

24 August 1942

The English original was written by Orwell. No script has been traced. PasB gives timing as 11′ 22″.

1413. To Peggotty Freeman

24 August 1942   Handwritten draft and typewritten[1]   PP/EB/NP

Dear Miss Freeman,
Enclosed is a copy of the talk Narayana Menon is doing on Ram Nahum.[2] As you see it is only a short thing, about five minutes, which is all we had space for. It will go out about 12.30 p.m. BST to-morrow—Tuesday 25th—on wavelengths 16, 19, 25, and 13 metres.
I am afraid it is too late to inform anyone abroad, but I did not receive your letter asking about this till this morning.

Yours sincerely,
Eric Blair
Talks Producer
Indian Section

1. Orwell's handwritten draft of this letter survives on the verso of Miss Freeman's letter to him of 22 August. Both letters are filed with Narayana Menon's letters. Orwell did not include the wavelengths in his draft: Nancy Parratt presumably added these.
2. For details of Menon's talk, see *1392, n. 1.*

1414. To G. M. Young

24 August 1942   PP/EB/NP

Dear Mr. Young,

I am sending herewith a copy of Worsley's remarks. He apologises for its coming so late, but his time has been rather full in the R. A. F. He says that [he] will be in London from August 26th to September 2nd. I suggest therefore that if you could let me have *your* criticisms of Worsley (about 750 words) by Friday of this week (28th) or Saturday morning (29th) at latest, we could all meet on Tuesday afternoon (September 1st) and have the discussion recorded. I am sorry to give such short notice. Please let me know at once if you can do Tuesday afternoon.

Yours sincerely,
George Orwell
Talks Producer
Indian Section

1415. To G. M. Young

[25 August 1942?]

TITCHENER ONLY WANTS YOU THURSDAY ABSOLUTELY NECESSARY RECORD YOUR TALK TUESDAY AS WORSLEYS LEAVE EXPIRES WEDNESDAY STOP WISH YOU LUNCH WITH ME AND WORSLEY ONE P. M. BARCELONA RESTAURANT TUESDAY

ORWELL BROADCASTS

Reply Paid please.[1]

1. Young did not take part and almost a year later used this experience as part of his basis for an attack on the BBC in the *Sunday Times*, 'Some Questions for the BBC,' 27 June 1943. He wrote of the BBC's 'most reckless vilification of English institutions, the most grotesque distortions of English history, and the most ignorant adulation of foreign achievements.' R. W. Foot, Director General of the BBC, took up these charges with him, and Young sent a long reply, 3 July, which was typed and circulated within the BBC. He referred, among other things, to a discussion on English education in which he had been invited to participate but which, in September 1942, he had described as 'Abstract, declamatory and quite unsuitable for India.' He suggested they get the script from Orwell. This programme was, he said, 'a reckless vilification of an institution.' He had therefore withdrawn from the programme (which also included T. C. Worsley) and was replaced by N. G. Fisher. The script was found, and a report on it said, 'There does not seem to be anything in the script to justify G. M. Young's description.' Young later complained that he had not received a reply to his letter of 3 July. After making several drafts, the Director General eventually sent a short note to say that the evidence provided by Young was 'so extremely thin' as not to call for an answer (28 October 1943). Norman George Fisher (1910–1972), Assistant to Education Secretary, Cambridgeshire, 1938–46, served during the war in the Royal Army Service Corps and the Royal Army Education Corps, becoming commandant of the Army School of Education in 1943. Among his post-war posts were Chief Education Officer, Manchester, 1949–55; Principal of the Staff College of the National Coal Board, 1955–61; Chairman, North Regional Advisory Council of the BBC, 1953–55, and, from 1968, Chairman of Butterworth's, publishers.

1416. BBC Talks Booking Form, 25.8.42

Lady Grigg: 'Women Generally Speaking'; broadcast 2, 9, 16, 23, and 30.9.42; fee £8.8s each broadcast. Signed: Z. A. Bokhari.

1417. BBC Talks Booking Form, 25.8.42

M. R. Kothari: Marathi Newsletter, 27 [misnumbered for 26]; '(Written by E. Blair Indian Section) Translated & read by M. R. Kothari'; broadcast 27.8.42; fee £5.5s. Signed: Z. A. Bokhari.

1418. BBC Talks Booking Form, 25.8.42

Narayana Menon: 5-minute talk on Ram Nahum, an Egyptian undergraduate;[1] broadcast 25.8.42; fee £4.4s. Signed: Z. A. Bokhari.

1. He had, in fact, graduated; see *1392, n. 1*.

1419. War-time Diary

25.8.42: One of the many rumours circulating among Indians here is that Nehru, Gandhi and others have been deported to South Africa. This is the kind of thing that results from press censorship and suppressing newspapers.

1420. To Alex Comfort

26 August 1942   Typewritten

10a Mortimer Crescent   London   NW 6

Dear Comfort

I have delayed answering your letter because I lost it and couldn't remember the address, but I have now obtained this from "Horizon". Yes, I'd like to write something for the new magazine[1] when it appears. You didn't say when you expected to start, though. I am frightfully busy with one thing and another, but I can find some time provided it isn't in the too near future. I don't know if people are too absolutely fed up with the Spanish civil war to want to hear more about it, but I have an idea for an article I have been wanting to write for some time, saying various things one couldn't say while the war was still on. Otherwise something in the critical line, perhaps. You might let me know about dates, also length.

Yours
Geo. Orwell

1. *New Road: New Directions in English Art and Letters*, 5 vols. (1943–49). Vols. I and II (1943–44) only were edited by Alex Comfort (with) John Bayliss. Orwell wrote 'Looking Back on the Spanish War' for the first volume; see *1421*. For Comfort, see *913, n. 5*.

1421. 'Looking Back on the Spanish War'

[1942?]

It has not proved possible to date this essay, nor even to find out exactly when it was published. It has therefore been placed immediately after Alex Comfort's request for something for the journal he was bringing out. When it appeared in *New Road* (probably June 1943; see letter to Forster, 2 July 1943, *2171*), sections IV, V, and VI were ommitted—to Orwell's annoyance (see *2518*, XVI/298). The complete essay was published in *Such, Such Were the Joys* (New York, 1953) and *England Your England* (London, 1953). No typescript has been traced. Sections I, II, III, and VII are almost identical in *New Road* and the 1953 volumes. Differences in wording are noted here; stylistic changes are not. An editorial note in *New Road* dates the essay 1942:

"As a representative of the NEW WRITING school in English literature during 1942, we print excerpts from an essay on the Spanish Civil War, by George Orwell. The sections omitted from this essay dealt with the danger that, by the falsification of history, political leaders might obtain control of the past as well as of the future, and with the political attitude of the Great Powers during the Civil War. Political writing as a literary form is becoming a neglected art. Mr. Orwell is probably its most talented contemporary exponent."

i

First of all the physical memories, the sounds, the smells and the surfaces of things.

It is curious that more vividly than anything that came afterwards in the Spanish War I remember the week of so-called training that we received before being sent to the front—the huge cavalry barracks in Barcelona with its draughty stables and cobbled yards, the icy cold of the pump where one washed, the filthy meals made tolerable by pannikins of wine, the trousered militiawomen chopping firewood, and the roll-call in the early mornings where my prosaic English name made a sort of comic interlude among the resounding Spanish ones, Manuel Gonzalez, Pedro Aguilar, Ramon Fenellosa, Roque Ballaster, Jaime Domenech, Sebastian Viltron, Ramon Nuvo Bosch. I name those particular men because I remember the faces of all of them. Except for two who were mere riff-raff and have doubtless become good Falangists by this time, it is probable that all of them are dead. Two of them I know to be dead. The eldest would have been about twenty-five, the youngest sixteen.

One of the essential experiences of war is never to be[1] able to escape from disgusting smells of human origin. Latrines are an overworked subject in war literature, and I would not mention them if it were not that the latrine in our barracks did its necessary bit towards puncturing my own illusions about the Spanish Civil War. The Latin type of latrine, at which you have to squat, is bad enough at its best, but these were made of some kind of polished stone so slippery that it was all you could do to keep on your feet. In addition they were always blocked. Now I have plenty of other disgusting things in my memory, but I believe it was these latrines that first brought home to me the thought, so often to recur: "Here we are, soldiers of a revolutionary army, defending Democracy against Fascism, fighting a war which is *about* something, and the detail of our lives is just as sordid and degrading as it could be in prison, let alone in a bourgeois army." Many other things reinforced this impression later; for instance, the boredom and animal hunger of trench life, the squalid intrigues over scraps of food, the mean, nagging quarrels which people exhausted by lack of sleep indulge in.

The essential horror of army life (whoever has been a soldier will know what I mean by the essential horror of army life) is barely affected by the nature of the war you happen to be fighting in. Discipline, for instance, is ultimately the same in all armies. Orders have to be obeyed and enforced by punishment if necessary, the relationship of officer and man has to be the relationship of superior and inferior. The picture of war set forth in books like *All Quiet on the Western Front* is substantially true. Bullets hurt, corpses stink, men under fire are often so frightened that they wet their trousers. It is true that the social background from which an army springs will colour its training, tactics and general efficiency, and also that the consciousness of being in the right can bolster up morale, though this affects the civilian population more than the troops. (People forget that a soldier anywhere near the front line is usually too hungry, or frightened, or cold, or, above all, too tired to bother about the political origins of the war.) But the laws of nature are not suspended for a "red" army any more than for a "white" one. A louse is a louse and a bomb is a bomb, even though the cause you are fighting for happens to be just.

Why is it worth while to point out anything so obvious? Because the bulk of the British and American intelligentsia were manifestly unaware of it then, and are now. Our memories are short nowadays, but look back a bit, dig out the files of *New Masses* or the *Daily Worker*, and just have a look at the romantic warmongering muck that our left-wingers were spilling at that time. All the stale old phrases! And the unimaginative callousness of it! The sang-froid with which London faced the bombing of Madrid! Here I am not bothering about the counter-propagandists of the Right, the Lunns, Garvins *et hoc genus*; they go without saying. But here were the very people who for twenty years had hooted and jeered at the "glory" of war, at atrocity stories, at patriotism, even at physical courage, coming out with stuff that with the alteration of a few names would have fitted into the *Daily Mail* of 1918. If there was one thing that the British intelligentsia were committed to, it was the debunking version of war, the theory that war is all corpses and latrines and never leads to any good result. Well, the same people who in 1933 sniggered pityingly if you said that in certain circumstances you would fight for your country, in 1937 were denouncing you as a Trotsky-Fascist if you suggested that the stories in *New Masses* about freshly wounded men clamouring to get back into the fighting might be exaggerated. And the Left intelligentsia made their swing-over from "War is hell" to "War is glorious" not only with no sense of incongruity but almost without any intervening stage. Later the bulk of them were to make other transitions equally violent. There must be a quite large number of people, a sort of central core of the intelligentsia, who approved the "King and Country" declaration in 1935, shouted for a "firm line" against Germany in 1937, supported the People's Convention in 1940, and are demanding a Second Front now.[2]

As far as the mass of the people go, the extraordinary swings of opinion which occur nowadays, the emotions which can be turned on and off like a tap, are the result of newspaper and radio hypnosis. In the intelligentsia I should say they result rather from money and mere physical safety. At a given moment they may be "pro-war" or "anti-war", but in either case they have no realistic picture of war in their minds. When they enthused over the Spanish War they knew, of course, that people were being killed and that to be killed is unpleasant, but they did feel that for a soldier in the Spanish Republican Army the experience of war was somehow not degrading. Somehow the latrines stank less, discipline was less irksome. You have only to glance at the *New Statesman* to see that they believed that; exactly similar blah is being written about the Red army at this moment. We have become too civilised to grasp the obvious. For the truth is very simple. To survive you often have to fight, and to fight you have to dirty yourself. War is evil, and it is often the lesser evil. Those who take the sword perish by the sword, and those who don't take the sword perish by smelly diseases. The fact that such a platitude is worth writing down shows what the years of *rentier* capitalism have done to us.

ii

In connection with what I have just said, a footnote on atrocities.

I have little direct evidence about the atrocities in the Spanish Civil War. I know that some were committed by the Republicans, and far more (they are still continuing) by the Fascists. But what impressed me then, and has impressed me ever since, is that atrocities are believed in or disbelieved in solely on grounds of political predilection. Everyone believes in the atrocities of the enemy and disbelieves in those of his own side, without ever bothering to examine the evidence. Recently I drew up a table of atrocities during the period between 1918 and the present,[3] there was never a year when atrocities were not occurring somewhere or other, and there was hardly a single case when the Left and the Right believed in the same stories simultaneously. And stranger yet, at any moment the situation can suddenly reverse itself and yesterday's proved-to-the-hilt atrocity story can become a ridiculous lie, merely because the political landscape has changed.

In the present war we are in the curious situation that our "atrocity campaign" was done largely before the war started, and done mostly by the Left, the people who normally pride themselves on their incredulity. In the same period the Right, the atrocity-mongers of 1914–18, were gazing at Nazi Germany and flatly refusing to see any evil in it. Then as soon as war broke out it was the pro-Nazis of yesterday who were repeating horror-stories, while the anti-Nazis suddenly found themselves doubting whether the Gestapo really existed. Nor was this solely the result of the Russo-German Pact. It was partly because before the war the Left had wrongly believed that Britain and Germany would never fight and were therefore able to be anti-German and anti-British simultaneously; partly also because official war-propaganda, with its disgusting hypocrisy and self-righteousness, always tends to make thinking people sympathise with the enemy. Part of the price we paid for the systematic lying of 1914–18 was the exaggerated pro-German reaction which followed. During the years 1918–33 you were hooted at in left-wing circles if you suggested that Germany bore even a fraction of responsibility for the war. In all the denunciations of Versailles I listened to during those years I don't think I ever once heard the question, "What would have happened if Germany had won?" even mentioned, let alone discussed. So also with atrocities. The truth, it is felt, becomes untruth when your enemy utters it. Recently I noticed that the very people who swallowed any and every horror story about the Japanese in Nanking in 1937 refused to believe exactly the same stories about Hong Kong in 1942. There was even a tendency to feel that the Nanking atrocities had become, as it were, retrospectively untrue because the British Government now drew attention to them.

But unfortunately the truth about atrocities is far worse than that they are lied about and made into propaganda. The truth is that they happen. The fact often adduced as a reason for scepticism—that the same horror stories come up in war after war—merely makes it rather more likely that these stories are true. Evidently they are widespread fantasies, and war provides an opportunity of putting them into practice. Also, although it has ceased to be fashionable to say so, there is little question that what one may roughly call the "whites" commit far more and worse atrocities than the "reds". There is not the slightest doubt, for instance, about the behaviour of the Japanese in China. Nor is there much doubt about the long tale of Fascist outrages during the last ten years in Europe. The volume of testimony is enormous, and a respectable proportion of it comes from the German press and radio. These things really happened, that is the thing to keep one's eye on. They happened even though Lord Halifax said they happened. The raping and butchering in Chinese cities, the tortures in the cellars of the Gestapo, the elderly Jewish professors flung into cesspools, the machine-gunning of refugees along the Spanish roads—they all happened, and they did not happen any the less because the *Daily Telegraph* has suddenly found out about them when it is five years too late.

iii

Two memories, the first not proving anything in particular, the second, I think, giving one a certain insight into the atmosphere of a revolutionary period.

Early one morning another man and I had gone out to snipe at the Fascists in the trenches outside Huesca. Their line and ours here lay three hundred yards apart, at which range our aged rifles would not shoot accurately, but by sneaking out to a spot about a hundred yards from the Fascist trench you might, if you were lucky, get a shot at someone through a gap in the parapet. Unfortunately the ground between was a flat beetfield with no cover except a few ditches, and it was necessary to go out while it was still dark and return soon after dawn, before the light became too good. This time no Fascists appeared, and we stayed too long and were caught by the dawn. We were in a ditch, but behind us were two hundred yards of flat ground with hardly enough cover for a rabbit. We were still trying to nerve ourselves to make a dash for it when there was an uproar and a blowing of whistles in the Fascist trench. Some of our aeroplanes were coming over. At this moment a man, presumably carrying a message to an officer, jumped out of the trench and ran along the top of the parapet in full view. He was half-dressed and was holding up his trousers with both hands as he ran. I refrained from shooting at him. It is true that I am a poor shot and unlikely to hit a running man at a hundred yards, and also that I was thinking chiefly about getting back to our trench while the Fascists had their attention fixed on the aeroplanes. Still, I did not shoot partly because of that detail about the trousers. I had come here to shoot at "Fascists"; but a man who is holding up his trousers isn't a "Fascist", he is visibly a fellow creature, similar to yourself, and you don't feel like shooting at him.

What does this incident demonstrate? Nothing very much, because it is the kind of thing that happens all the time in all wars. The other is different. I don't suppose that in telling it I can make it moving to you who read it, but I ask you to believe that it is moving to me, as an incident characteristic of the moral atmosphere of a particular moment in time.

One of the recruits who joined us while I was at the barracks was a wild-looking boy from the back streets of Barcelona. He was ragged and barefooted. He was also extremely dark (Arab blood, I dare say), and made gestures you do not usually see a European make; one in particular—the arm outstretched, the palm vertical—was a gesture characteristic of Indians. One day a bundle of cigars, which you could still buy dirt cheap at that time, was stolen out of my bunk. Rather foolishly I reported this to the officer, and one of the scallywags I have already mentioned promptly came forward and said quite untruly that twenty-five pesetas had been stolen from his bunk. For some reason the officer instantly decided that the brown-faced boy must be the thief. They were very hard on stealing in the militia, and in theory people could be shot for it. The wretched boy allowed himself to be led off to the guardroom to be searched. What most struck me was that he barely attempted to protest his innocence. In the fatalism of his attitude you could see the desperate poverty in which he had been bred. The officer ordered him to take his clothes off. With a humility which was horrible to me he stripped himself naked, and his clothes were searched. Of course neither the cigars nor the money were there; in fact he had not stolen them. What was most painful of all was that he seemed no less ashamed after his innocence had been established. That night I took him to the pictures and gave him brandy and chocolate. But that too was horrible—I mean the attempt to wipe out an injury with money. For a few minutes I had half believed him to be a thief, and that could not be wiped out.

Well, a few weeks later, at the front, I had trouble with one of the men in my section. By this time I was a "*cabo*", or corporal, in command of twelve men. It was static warfare, horribly cold, and the chief job was getting sentries to stay awake and at their posts. One day a man suddenly refused to go to a certain post, which he said, quite truly, was exposed to enemy fire. He was a feeble creature, and I seized hold of him and began to drag him towards his post. This roused the feelings of the others against me, for Spaniards, I think, resent being touched more than we do. Instantly I was surrounded by a ring of shouting men: "Fascist! Fascist! Let that man go! This isn't a bourgeois army. Fascist!" etc., etc. As best I could in my bad Spanish I shouted back that orders had got to be obeyed, and the row developed into one of those enormous arguments by means of which discipline is gradually hammered out in revolutionary armies. Some said I was right, others said I was wrong. But the point is that the one who took my side the most warmly of all was the brown-faced boy. As soon as he saw what was happening he sprang into the ring and began passionately defending me. With his strange, wild, Indian gesture he kept exclaiming, "He's the best corporal we've got!" (*!No hay cabo como el!*) Later on he applied for leave to exchange into my section.

Why is this incident touching to me? Because in any normal circumstances it would have been impossible for good feelings ever to be re-established between this boy and myself. The implied accusation of theft would not have been made any better, probably somewhat worse, by my efforts to make amends. One of the effects of safe and civilised life is an immense over-sensitiveness which makes all the primary emotions seem somewhat disgusting. Generosity is as painful as meanness, gratitude as hateful as ingratitude. But in Spain in 1936 we were not living in a normal time. It was a time when generous feelings and gestures were easier than they ordinarily are. I could relate a dozen similar incidents, not really communicable but bound up in my own mind with the special atmosphere of the time, the shabby clothes and the gay-coloured revolutionary posters, the universal use of the word "comrade", the anti-Fascist ballads printed on flimsy paper and sold for a penny, the phrases like "international proletarian solidarity", pathetically repeated by ignorant men who believed them to mean something. Could you feel friendly towards somebody, and stick up for him in a quarrel, after you had been ignominiously searched in his presence for property you were supposed to have stolen from him? No, you couldn't; but you might if you had both been through some emotionally widening experience. That is one of the by-products of revolution, though in this case it was only the beginnings of a revolution, and obviously foredoomed to failure.

iv

The struggle for power between the Spanish Republican parties is an unhappy, far-off thing which I have no wish to revive at this date. I only mention it in order to say: believe nothing, or next to nothing, of what you read about internal affairs on the Government side. It is all, from whatever source, party propaganda—that is to say, lies. The broad truth about the war is simple enough. The Spanish bourgeoisie saw their chance of crushing the labour movement, and took it, aided by the Nazis and by the forces of reaction all over the world. It is doubtful whether more than that will ever be established.

I remember saying once to Arthur Koestler, "History stopped in 1936," at which he nodded in immediate understanding. We were both thinking of totalitarianism in general, but more particularly of the Spanish Civil War. Early in life I had noticed that no event is ever correctly reported in a newspaper, but in Spain, for the first time, I saw newspaper reports which did not bear any relation to the facts, not even the relationship which is implied in an ordinary lie. I saw great battles reported where there had been no fighting, and complete silence where hundreds of men had been killed. I saw troops who had fought bravely denounced as cowards and traitors, and others who had never seen a shot fired hailed as the heroes of imaginary victories; and I saw newspapers in London retailing these lies and eager intellectuals building emotional superstructures over events that had never happened. I saw, in fact, history being written not in terms of what happened but of what ought to have happened according to various "party lines". Yet in a way, horrible as all this was, it was unimportant. It concerned secondary issues—namely, the struggle for power between the Comintern and the Spanish left-wing parties, and the efforts of the Russian Government to prevent revolution in Spain. But the broad picture of the war which the Spanish Government presented to the world was not untruthful. The main issues were what it said they were. But as for the Fascists and their backers, how could they come even as near to the truth as that? How could they possibly mention their real aims? Their version of the war was pure fantasy, and in the circumstances it could not have been otherwise.

The only propaganda line open to the Nazis and Fascists was to represent themselves as Christian patriots saving Spain from a Russian dictatorship. This involved pretending that life in Government Spain was just one long massacre (*vide* the *Catholic Herald* or the *Daily Mail*—but these were child's play compared with the continental Fascist press), and it involved immensely exaggerating the scale of Russian intervention. Out of the huge pyramid of lies which the Catholic and reactionary press all over the world built up, let me take just one point—the presence in Spain of a Russian army. Devout Franco partisans all believed in this; estimates of its strength went as high as half a million. Now, there was no Russian army in Spain. There may have been a handful of airmen and other technicians, a few hundred at the most, but an army there was not. Some thousands of foreigners who fought in Spain, not to mention millions of Spaniards, were witnesses of this. Well, their testimony made no impression at all upon the Franco propagandists, not one of whom had set foot in Government Spain. Simultaneously these people refused utterly to admit the fact of German or Italian intervention, at the same time as the German and Italian press were openly boasting about the exploits of their "legionaries." I have chosen to mention only one point, but in fact the whole of Fascist propaganda about the war was on this level.

This kind of thing is frightening to me, because it often gives me the feeling that the very concept of objective truth is fading out of the world. After all, the chances are that those lies, or at any rate similar lies, will pass into history. How will the history of the Spanish War be written? If Franco remains in power his nominees will write the history books, and (to stick to my chosen point) that Russian army which never existed will become historical fact, and schoolchildren will learn about it generations hence. But suppose Fascism is finally defeated and some kind of democratic government restored in Spain in the fairly near future; even then, how is the history of the war to be written? What kind of records will Franco have left behind him? Suppose even that the records kept on the Government side are recoverable—even so, how is a true history of the war to be written? For, as I have pointed out already, the Government also dealt extensively in lies. From the anti-Fascist angle one could write a broadly truthful history of the war, but it would be a partisan history, unreliable on every minor point. Yet, after all, *some* kind of history will be written, and after those who actually remember the war are dead, it will be universally accepted. So for all practical purposes the lie will have become truth.

I know it is the fashion to say that most of recorded history is lies anyway. I am willing to believe that history is for the most part inaccurate and biased, but what is peculiar to our own age is the abandonment of the idea that history *could* be truthfully written. In the past people deliberately lied, or they unconsciously coloured what they wrote, or they struggled after the truth, well knowing that they must make many mistakes; but in each case they believed that "the facts" existed and were more or less discoverable. And in practice there was always a considerable body of fact which would have been agreed to by almost everyone. If you look up the history of the last war in, for instance, the *Encyclopaedia Britannica*, you will find that a respectable amount of the material is drawn from German sources. A British and a German historian would disagree deeply on many things, even on fundamentals, but there would still be that body of, as it were, neutral fact on which neither would seriously challenge the other. It is just this common basis of agreement, with its implication that human beings are all one species of animal, that totalitarianism destroys. Nazi theory indeed specifically denies that such a thing as "the truth" exists. There is, for instance, no such thing as "science". There is only "German science", "Jewish science" etc. The implied objective of this line of thought is a nightmare world in which the Leader, or some ruling clique, controls not only the future but *the past*. If the Leader says of such and such an event, "It never happened"—well, it never happened. If he says that two and two are five— well, two and two are five. This prospect frightens me much more than bombs—and after our experiences of the last few years that is not a frivolous statement.

But is it perhaps childish or morbid to terrify oneself with visions of a totalitarian future? Before writing off the totalitarian world as a nightmare that can't come true, just remember that in 1925 the world of today would have seemed a nightmare that couldn't come true. Against that shifting phantasmagoric world in which black may be white tomorrow and yesterday's weather can be changed by decree, there are in reality only two safeguards. One is that however much you deny the truth, the truth goes on existing, as it were, behind your back, and you consequently can't violate it in ways that impair military efficiency. The other is that so long as some parts of the earth remain unconquered, the liberal tradition can be kept alive. Let Fascism, or possibly even a combination of several Fascisms, conquer the whole world, and those two conditions no longer exist. We in England underrate the danger of this kind of thing, because our traditions and our past security have given us a sentimental belief that it all comes right in the end and the thing you most fear never really happens. Nourished for hundreds of years on a literature in which Right invariably triumphs in the last chapter, we believe half-instinctively that evil always defeats itself in the long run. Pacifism, for instance, is founded largely on this belief. Don't resist evil, and it will somehow destroy itself. But why should it? What evidence is there that it does? And what instance is there of a modern industrialised state collapsing unless conquered from the outside by military force?

Consider for instance the re-institution of slavery. Who could have imagined twenty years ago that slavery would return to Europe? Well, slavery has been restored under our noses. The forced-labour camps all over Europe and North Africa where Poles, Russians, Jews and political prisoners of every race toil at road-making or swamp-draining for their bare rations, are simple chattel slavery. The most one can say is that the buying and selling of slaves by individuals is not yet permitted. In other ways—the breaking-up of families, for instance—the conditions are probably worse than they were on the American cotton plantations. There is no reason for thinking that this state of affairs will change while any totalitarian domination endures. We don't grasp its full implications, because in our mystical way we feel that a régime founded on slavery *must* collapse. But it is worth comparing the duration of the slave empires of antiquity with that of any modern state. Civilisations founded on slavery have lasted for such periods as four thousand years.

When I think of antiquity, the detail that frightens me is that those hundreds of millions of slaves on whose backs civilisation rested generation after generation have left behind them no record whatever. We do not even know their names. In the whole of Greek and Roman history, how many slaves' names are known to you? I can think of two, or possibly three. One is Spartacus and the other is Epictetus. Also, in the Roman room at the British Museum there is a glass jar with the maker's name inscribed on the bottom, "*Felix fecit*". I have a vivid mental picture of poor Felix (a Gaul with red hair and a metal collar round his neck), but in fact he may not have been a slave; so there are only two slaves whose names I definitely know, and probably few people can remember more. The rest have gone down into utter silence.

v

The backbone of the resistance against Franco was the Spanish working class, especially the urban trade union members. In the long run—it is important to remember that it is only in the long run—the working class remains the most reliable enemy of Fascism, simply because the working class stands to gain most by a decent reconstruction of society. Unlike other classes or categories, it can't be permanently bribed.

To say this is not to idealise the working class. In the long struggle that has followed the Russian Revolution it is the manual workers who have been defeated, and it is impossible not to feel that it was their own fault. Time after time, in country after country, the organised working-class movements have been crushed by open, illegal violence, and their comrades abroad, linked to them in theoretical solidarity, have simply looked on and done nothing; and underneath this, secret cause of many betrayals, has lain the fact that between white and coloured workers there is not even lip-service to solidarity. Who can believe in the class-conscious international proletariat after the events of the past ten years? To the British working class the massacre of their comrades in Vienna, Berlin, Madrid, or wherever it might be, seemed less interesting and less important than yesterday's football match. Yet this does not alter the fact that the working class will go on struggling against Fascism after the others have caved in. One feature of the Nazi conquest of France was the astonishing defections among the intelligentsia, including some of the left-wing political intelligentsia. The intelligentsia are the people who squeal loudest against Fascism, and yet a respectable proportion of them collapse into defeatism when the pinch comes. They are far-sighted enough to see the odds against them, and moreover they can be bribed—for it is evident that the Nazis think it worth while to bribe intellectuals. With the working class it is the other way about. Too ignorant to see through the trick that is being played on them, they easily swallow the promises of Fascism, yet sooner or later they always take up the struggle again. They must do so, because in their own bodies they always discover that the promises of Fascism cannot be fulfilled. To win over the working class permanently, the Fascists would have to raise the general standard of living, which they are unable and probably unwilling to do. The struggle of the working class is like the growth of a plant. The plant is blind and stupid, but it knows enough to keep pushing upwards towards the light, and it will do this in the face of endless discouragements. What are the workers struggling for? Simply for the decent life which they are more and more aware is now technically possible. Their consciousness of this aim ebbs and flows. In Spain, for a while, people were acting consciously, moving towards a goal which they wanted to reach and believed they could reach. It accounted for the curiously buoyant feeling that life in Government Spain had during the early months of the war. The common people knew in their bones that the Republic was their friend and Franco was their enemy. They knew that they were in the right, because they were fighting for something which the world owed them and was able to give them.

One has to remember this to see the Spanish War in its true perspective.

When one thinks of the cruelty, squalor, and futility of war—and in this particular case of the intrigues, the persecutions, the lies and the misunderstandings—there is always the temptation to say: "One side is as bad as the other. I am neutral." In practice, however, one cannot be neutral, and there is hardly such a thing as a war in which it makes no difference who wins. Nearly always one side stands more or less for progress, the other side more or less for reaction. The hatred which the Spanish Republic excited in millionaires, dukes, cardinals, play-boys, Blimps and what not would in itself be enough to show one how the land lay. In essence it was a class war. If it had been won, the cause of the common people everywhere would have been strengthened. It was lost, and the dividend-drawers all over the world rubbed their hands. That was the real issue; all else was froth on its surface.

vi

The outcome of the Spanish War was settled in London, Paris, Rome, Berlin—at any rate not in Spain. After the summer of 1937 those with eyes in their heads realised that the Government could not win the war unless there was some profound change in the international set-up, and in deciding to fight on Negrin and the others may have been partly influenced by the expectation that the world war which actually broke out in 1939 was coming in 1938. The much-publicised disunity on the Government side was not a main cause of defeat. The Government militias were hurriedly raised, ill-armed and unimaginative in their military outlook, but they would have been the same if complete political agreement had existed from the start. At the outbreak of war the average Spanish factory-worker did not even know how to fire a rifle (there had never been universal conscription in Spain), and the traditional pacifism of the Left was a great handicap. The thousands of foreigners who served in Spain made good infantry, but there were very few experts of any kind among them. The Trotskyist thesis that the war could have been won if the revolution had not been sabotaged was probably false. To nationalise factories, demolish churches, and issue revolutionary manifestos would not have made the armies more efficient. The Fascists won because they were the stronger; they had modern arms and the others hadn't. No political strategy could offset that.

The most baffling thing in the Spanish War was the behaviour of the great powers. The war was actually won for Franco by the Germans and Italians, whose motives were obvious enough. The motives of France and Britain are less easy to understand. In 1936 it was clear to everyone that if Britain would only help the Spanish Government, even to the extent of a few million pounds' worth of arms, Franco would collapse and German strategy would be severely dislocated. By that time one did not need to be a clairvoyant to foresee that war between Britain and Germany was coming; one could even foretell within a year or two when it would come. Yet in the most mean, cowardly, hypocritical way the British ruling class did all they could to hand Spain over to Franco and the Nazis. Why? Because they were pro-Fascist, was the obvious answer. Undoubtedly they were, and yet when it came to the final showdown they chose to stand up to Germany. It is still very uncertain what plan they acted on in backing Franco, and they may have had no clear plan at all. Whether the British ruling class are wicked or merely stupid is one of the most difficult questions of our time, and at certain moments a very important question. As to the Russians, their motives in the Spanish War are completely inscrutable. Did they, as the pinks believed, intervene in Spain in order to defend democracy and thwart the Nazis? Then why did they intervene on such a niggardly scale and finally leave Spain in the lurch? Or did they, as the Catholics maintained, intervene in order to foster revolution in Spain? Then why did they do all in their power to crush the Spanish revolutionary movements, defend private property and hand power to the middle class as against the working class? Or did they, as the Troskyists suggested, intervene simply in order to *prevent* a Spanish revolution? Then why not have backed Franco? Indeed, their actions are most easily explained if one assumes that they were acting on several contradictory motives. I believe that in the future we shall come to feel that Stalin's foreign policy, instead of being so diabolically clever as it is claimed to be, has been merely opportunistic and stupid. But at any rate, the Spanish Civil War demonstrated that the Nazis knew what they were doing and their opponents did not. The war was fought at a low technical level and its major strategy was very simple. That side which had arms would win. The Nazis and the Italians gave arms to their Spanish Fascist friends, and the western democracies and the Russians didn't give arms to those who should have been their friends. So the Spanish Republic perished, having "gained what no republic missed".[4]

Whether it was right, as all left-wingers in other countries undoubtedly did, to encourage the Spaniards to go on fighting when they could not win is a question hard to answer. I myself think it was right, because I believe that it is better even from the point of view of survival to fight and be conquered than to surrender without fighting. The effects on the grand strategy of the struggle against Fascism cannot be assessed yet. The ragged, weaponless armies of the Republic held out for two and a half years, which was undoubtedly longer than their enemies expected. But whether that dislocated the Fascist time-table, or whether, on the other hand, it merely postponed the major war and gave the Nazis extra time to get their war machine into trim, is still uncertain.

vii

I never think of the Spanish War without two memories coming into my mind. One is of the hospital ward at Lérida and the rather sad voices of the wounded militiamen singing some song with a refrain that ended:

> *Una resolucion,*
> *Luchar hast' al fin!*[4a]

Well, they fought to the end all right. For the last eighteen months of the war the Republican armies must have been fighting almost without cigarettes, and with precious little food. Even when I left Spain in the middle of 1937, meat and bread were scarce, tobacco a rarity, coffee and sugar almost unobtainable.[5]

The other memory is of the Italian militiaman who shook my hand in the guardroom, the day I joined the militia. I wrote about this man at the beginning of my book on the Spanish War,[6] and do not want to repeat what I said there. When I remember—oh, how vividly!—his shabby uniform and fierce, pathetic, innocent face, the complex side-issues of the war seem to fade away and I see clearly that there was at any rate no doubt as to who was in the right. In spite of power politics and journalistic lying, the central issue of the war was the attempt of people like this to win the decent life which they knew to be their birthright. It is difficult to think of this particular man's probable end without several kinds of bitterness. Since I met him in the Lenin Barracks he was probably a Trotskyist or an Anarchist, and in the peculiar conditions of our time, when people of that sort are not killed by the Gestapo they are usually killed by the GPU. But that does not affect the long-term issues. This man's face, which I saw only for a minute or two, remains with me as a sort of visual reminder of what the war was really about. He symbolises for me the flower of the European working class, harried by the police of all countries, the people who fill the mass graves of the Spanish battlefields and are now, to the tune of several millions, rotting in forced-labour camps.

When one thinks of all the people who support or have supported Fascism, one stands amazed at their diversity. What a crew! Think of a programme which at any rate for a while could bring Hitler, Pétain, Montagu Norman, Pavelitch, William Randolph Hearst, Streicher, Buchman, Ezra Pound, Juan March, Cocteau, Thyssen, Father Coughlin, the Mufti of Jerusalem,[7] Arnold Lunn, Antonescu, Spengler, Beverley Nichols, Lady Houston, and Marinetti all into the same boat! But the clue is really very simple. They are all people with something to lose, or people who long for a hierarchical society and dread the prospect of a world of free and equal human beings. Behind all the ballyhoo that is talked about "godless" Russia and the "materialism" of the working class lies the simple intention of those with money or privileges to cling to them. Ditto, though it contains a partial truth, with all the talk about the worthlessness of social reconstruction not accompanied by a "change of heart". The pious ones, from the Pope to the yogis of California,[8] are great on the "change of heart",[8a] much more reassuring from their point of view than a change in the economic system. Pétain attributes the fall of France to the common people's "love of pleasure". One sees this in its right perspective if one stops to wonder how much pleasure the ordinary French peasant's or workingman's life would contain compared with Pétain's own. The damned impertinence of these politicians, priests, literary men, and what not who lecture the working-class Socialist for his "materialism"! All that the workingman demands is what these others would consider the indispensable minimum without which human life cannot be lived at all. Enough to eat, freedom from the haunting terror of unemployment, the knowledge that your children will get a fair chance, a bath once a day, clean linen reasonably often, a roof that doesn't leak, and short enough working hours to leave you with a little energy when the day is done. Not one of those who preach against "materialism" would consider life livable without these things. And how easily that minimum could be attained if we chose to set our minds to it for only twenty years! To raise the standard of living of the whole world to that of Britain would not be a greater undertaking than this[9] war we are now fighting. I don't claim, and I don't know who does, that that would solve anything in itself. It is merely that privation and brute labour have to be abolished before the real problems of humanity can be tackled. The major problem of our time is the decay of the belief in personal immortality, and it cannot be dealt with while the average human being is either drudging like an ox or shivering in fear of the secret police. How right the working classes are in their "materialism"! How right they are to realise that the real belly comes before the soul, not in the scale of values but in point of time! Understand that, and the long horror that we are enduring becomes at least intelligible. All the considerations that are likely to make one falter—the siren voices of a Pétain or of a Gandhi,[10] the inescapable fact that in order to fight one has to degrade oneself, the equivocal moral position of Britain, with its democratic phrases and its coolie empire, the sinister development of Soviet Russia, the squalid farce of left-wing politics—all this fades away and one sees only the struggle of the gradually awakening common people against the lords of property and their hired liars and bumsuckers. The question is very simple. Shall people like that Italian soldier be allowed to live the decent, fully human life which is now technically achievable, or shan't they? Shall the common man be pushed back into the mud, or shall he not? I myself believe, perhaps on insufficient grounds, that the common man will win his fight sooner or later, but I want it to be sooner and not later—some time within the next hundred years, say, and not some time within the next ten thousand years. That was the real issue of the Spanish War, and of the present war, and perhaps of other wars yet to come.

I never saw the Italian militiaman again, nor did I ever learn his name. It can be taken as quite certain that he is dead. Nearly two years later, when the war was visibly lost, I wrote these verses in his memory:

> The Italian soldier shook my hand
> Beside the guard-room table;
> The strong hand and the subtle hand
> Whose palms are only able
>
> To meet within the sound of guns,
> But oh! what peace I knew then
> In gazing on his battered face
> Purer than any woman's!
>
> For the fly-blown words that make me spew
> Still in his ears were holy,
> And he was born knowing what I had learned
> Out of books and slowly.
>
> The treacherous guns had told their tale
> And we both had bought it,
> But my gold brick was made of gold—
> Oh! who ever would have thought it?

Good luck go with you, Italian soldier!
But luck is not for the brave;
What would the world give back to you?
Always less than you gave.

Between the shadow and the ghost,
Between the white and the red,
Between the bullet and the lie,
Where would you hide your head?

For where is Manuel Gonzalez,
And where is Pedro Aguilar,
And where is Ramon Fenellosa?
The earthworms know where they are.

Your name and your deeds were forgotten
Before your bones were dry,
And the lie that slew you is buried
Under a deeper lie;

But the thing that I saw in your face
No power can disinherit:
No bomb that ever burst
Shatters the crystal spirit.

1. to be] being *in 1953 editions*
2 The Oxford Union's motion in 1935 supporting the refusal to fight 'for King and Country' initiated a series of alternating demands that Britain abstain from and engage in military action.
3. See War-time Diary, *1218, 11.6.42.*
4. The source of this quotation has not been traced.
4a.'A resolution,/To fight to the end'
5. There is no paragraph division here in *New Road.*
6. *Homage to Catalonia.*
7. Mohammed Amin al-Husseini (1896–), Mufti of Jerusalem from 1921. He was arrested in 1937 for instigating anti-Semitic riots. He escaped and later broadcast for the Nazis from Berlin and encouraged the deportation of Jews to concentration camps. He was charged with war crimes but found refuge first in Egypt and then in Palestine. Six thousand Bosnian Muslims who formed the S. S. Handzar Division in Jugoslavia in 1943 to fight for the Nazis saw him as their spiritual leader. A 'Mufti' is a Muslim canon lawyer.
8. Orwell possibly had in mind Gerald Heard (1889–1971), whom he mentions in his September 1943 review in *Horizon* of Lionel Fielden's *Beggar My Neighbour* (see *2257,* and see also headnote to 'Can Socialists be Happy?', *2397*); also Aldous Huxley (see *600,* section 3), and possibly Christopher Isherwood (see *2713*), all of whom settled in Los Angeles just before the war. In California, Isherwood developed an interest in Yoga and Vedanta (though whether Orwell knew this is uncertain), edited and introduced *Vedanta for the Western World* (Hollywood, 1945; London 1948), and with Swami Prabhavananda translated *The Bhagavad-Gita* (1944) and other related works. It is possible that this reference was inspired by Orwell's preliminary arrangements for G V. Desani to talk on the *Bhagavad-Gita* in his BBC series 'Books that Changed the World'; see *1970.*
8a.From Auden, 'Sir, No Man's Enemy' (1930): 'New styles of architecture, a change of heart'. Also referred to at last line of XII/30.
9. this] the *in 1953 editions*
10. of a Pétain or of a Gandhi] 'of Pétain and Gandhi' in *New Road*

1422. Marathi Newsletter, 26

27 August 1942

This was misnumbered as 27. The English original was written by Orwell. No script has been traced. The PasB gives timing as 14 minutes.

1423. "Service to India"

27 August 1942

Although not written by Orwell, this editorial in *The Listener* is relevant to the work on which he was engaged. It was published under the heading 'Service to India.'

The Minutes of the second Publication Policy meeting of the BBC, held on 18 August 1942, state: "D[irector of] P[ublicity] referred to a recent article in the *Sunday Pictorial* criticising the Indian Service, and suggested that the *Radio Times* and *The Listener* should describe the work of this Service to help counteract the *Sunday Pictorial* article. The Editor of *The Listener* agreed that his leader on 27th August should deal with the Indian Service; and the Editor of the *Radio Times* promised an article on the subject the following week. Both Editors would consult E.S.D. [Rushbrook Williams]. D.P. would also consider including at the same time a note in *Broadcasting News*."

Readers of THE LISTENER hardly need to be told that the B.B.C.'s Indian Service maintains a very high level in its English talks. C. D. Darlington's talks on 'The Future Task of Science' and 'India in the Steel Age', Mulk Raj Anand's 'Open Letter to a Chinese Guerrilla', Sir Henry Sharp's discussion of 'The Future of Education in India'—to mention only talks that have appeared in recent issues—these are typical of the B.B.C.'s English transmissions to India and the East generally. It has sometimes been asked, both intelligently and unintelligently, whether these English talks have been really suited to the Indian listener, and one of our contemporaries the other day even conjured up a pleasing vision of 'bewildered Indian peasants, tense fighting Sikhs', listening to a programme of modern English poetry. But no one—or hardly anyone—in this country supposes that chamber-music concerts are devised for revellers in the NAAFI canteen or believes that 'Jollyoliday' is widely listened to in what, for the purposes of argument, we may call Bloomsbury. And the 'Indian listener' *tout simple* is an even more fictitious monster than his counterpart in England. To begin with, the 'Indian listener' is very often an Englishman, or a Scot or an Irishman; in these days he is very likely to be an American as well, an American in a uniform. In fact a very large proportion of the B.B.C.'s Eastern transmissions are devised for this 'exile audience' which war has not only multiplied but further diversified, and they are so sensitive to changing conditions that part of their appeal has lately been directed to these welcome American guests.

But, leaving aside these non-Indian 'Indian listeners', will anyone who has mixed with educated Indians suggest that they are, as a class, in any respect inferior in learning and intelligence to educated Europeans? The cultured Indian, so far from being a 'bewildered peasant', is unlikely to be the cultural inferior of even the editorial staff of a popular British picture-paper. His fine and subtle mind will not be held for long by the type of programme that satisfies the intellectual appetites of such a paper's readers. And this type of Indian listener is given not only cultural programmes to awake and hold his interest; a clear, steady picture of the real Britain is projected to him through the eyes of fellow-Indians; he is shown our war-effort and encouraged in his own; he is told how we hope to tackle post-war reconstruction and encouraged to learn from it any lessons that may be helpful to India.

Still we have spoken only of the transmissions in English for the 'exile' audience and the educated English-speaking Indian audience. Are the 'tense fighting Sikhs' and 'bewildered peasants' quite neglected, then? Of course not. A considerable proportion of the B.B.C.'s Indian programmes—and it should be remembered that, after all, these are only supplementary to those of All India Radio—are in the vernacular languages. Hindustani is naturally predominant; Hindustani news and programmes are given daily. But there are weekly and bi-weekly news-letters and other features in Tamil, Marathi, Bengali and Gujerathi°, and there is a continual and urgent demand for more programmes in these and other languages, such as Telegu and Canarese, in which broadcasting has not yet begun. Within the limits imposed by time and available staff, everything possible is done to vary themes of interest, to introduce life and vigour in both matter and manner, and to build up and consolidate a regular daily audience.

1424. War-time Diary

27.8.42. *Ban on the Daily Worker lifted.*[1] [It is to reappear on Sept. 7th (same day as Churchill makes his statement to Parliament).

German radio again alleging S. C. Bose is in Penang. But the indications are that this was a slip of the tongue for R. B. Bose.[2]

1. The *Daily Worker* had been suppressed on 22 January 1941.
2. For Subhas Chandra Bose and Ras Bihari Bose (who were not related), see *1080, n. 1, 1081, n. 4,* and *1119, n. 5.*

1425. To Harold Laski

28 August 1942   PP/EB/NP

Dear Professor Laski,
I have been able to arrange a recording session for your discussion with Lord Winterton, for Thursday, September 3rd from 11.15 till 12.30 in the morning. I hope this will suit you.
I shall look forward to seeing you on Thursday, at 200 Oxford Street.

Yours sincerely,
George Orwell
Talks Producer
Indian Section

1426. To C. H. Waddington

28 August 1942   PP/EB/NP

Dear Waddington,
We want a speaker to say something [to][1] the Indian audience about Ersatz and raw materials. Could you suggest somebody to do an interesting popular talk on these lines? The problems raised by interruption of communications and so forth are now just about beginning to touch India, I should think we could find an audience for a fairly advanced talk of this kind. These talks are usually done in the form of dialogues between two people, but, in this case, I fancy we shall do it simply as an interview. I should be very glad to know of any suggestions you can make.

Yours,
George Orwell
Talks Producer
Indian Section

1. The context (and space) demand 'to' but the first letter is missing and the remains of the second look like 'n.'

1427. News Review, 37

29 August 1942

The three passages within brackets were crossed out in the typescript. There are no handwritten emendations. The censor was Bokhari, and Orwell has written at the top of the first page 'As broadcast   11 mins   E. A. B.' (though the timing is indistinct). The words 'possible for' in the final sentence do not appear in the microfilm (from which this and many other texts are reproduced); the original is defective at this point. The use of the spelling 'farther' for Orwell's preferred spelling, 'further,' suggests that he did not type the script. The script was read by Shridhar Telkar.

Stalingrad on the Volga is still in great danger. After many attempts the Germans have succeeded in crossing the Don at the point where this river and the Volga pass close to one another, and Stalingrad is menaced by attacks converging from several sides. It has been very heavily bombed. During the last day or two, however, the German attacks have not made much progress, and the Russian forces still west of the Don are counter-attacking strongly in the neighbourhood of Kletsk. [If Stalingrad should definitely fall into German hands it will be difficult to defend Astrakhan, which lies on the north-western shore of the Caspian Sea and is the key point of all the sea and river communications of this area. Should Astrakhan fall, the northern and southern Russian forces will be effectively cut off from one another. How decisive this might be depends upon the quantities of oil, ammunition and other war materials which the Russians have already stored at various strategic points.]

Further south, the Germans claim that some of their troops have reached the mouth of the Kuban river on the Black Sea, thus encircling the Russian forces in the neighbourhood of Novorossisk. They also claim that other detachments have already reached the highest points in the Caucasus mountains. These claims are not confirmed from other sources, and should be treated with caution. Some people doubt whether the Germans will try this year to pass directly across the Caucasus mountains, even if they get control of the northern end of the military road. It may be that they will rather try to obtain possession of Astrakhan and thus reach the oil fields by way of the Caspian Sea. Meanwhile, none of their successes is decisive, since unless they can make an end of the Red Armies as a fighting force—and there is no sign of this happening—they have got another winter in the Russian snow before them. It is important, however, that the Red Army should retain its power of counter-attacking, so that the Germans will be obliged to maintain a large army in Russia throughout the winter and not merely a small force which could be relieved at short intervals. During the past fortnight the Russians have carried out an offensive of their own in the Moscow sector, of which full reports have now come in. The Russians have made an advance of 30[1] miles, killed 45,000 Germans and captured a very large quantity of war materials. Fighting is going on in the outskirts of Rzhev, the chief German stronghold in this area. [This successful attack will have its effect upon events further south, if the Germans have to divert extra force° to meet it.]

Another great battle, a sequel to the events which we reported last week, is raging in the Solomon Islands. The Americans have succeeded in landing on thre[e] of the islands, and hold the most important harbour and some of the airfields. A few days back, the Japanese made an unsuccessful counterattack, which was beaten off with heavy casualties. They are now attempting to retrieve the position by means of naval action, and as far as can be gathered from the reports, have sent a very strong fleet to attack the American strongholds. Full reports have not yet come in, but it is known that American bombing planes have already hit and damaged a number of Japanese warships, including two plane carriers. In all, 14 Japanese ships have been damaged and 33 Japanese aeroplanes destroyed. Two days ago the Japanese fleet withdrew, but it has evidently reformed and is making a fresh attack. The results of this have not yet been reported. The Japanese have also made another landing in the south-eastern tip of New Guinea, where fighting is now going on. The object of this may either be to make another attempt against Port Moresby, or to draw the American fleet away from the harbours it has captured in the Solomons. Undoubtedly the Japanese will make very strong efforts to dislodge the Americans from Tulagi, and they will be willing to risk large numbers of warships in doing so. They are now, however, fighting at a disadvantage, since their ships have to meet land-based aircraft. This battle in the South Pacific, so confused and so far away, is of the highest importance for India, because whether or not the Japanese are able to invade India depends partly on their strength in aircraft carriers. Every plane-carrier the Americans destroy makes India a fraction safer. We shall probably be able to give fuller news about the Solomon Islands next week.

Brazil has declared war on Germany. This was the logical result of the wanton sinking of Brazilian ships which German submarines had carried out during past weeks. Brazil is the most important of the South American republics, having a population of about forty million, and being a country of immense size—roughly the same size as India—and immense natural wealth. From a strategic point of view, it is particularly important, because its many excellent harbours and its small but efficient Navy will make the patrolling of the Atlantic easier for the Allies. In addition, Rio de Janerio, the capital of Brazil, is the point at which the Americans are nearest to the Old World, being in fact within easy flying distance of West Africa. The Axis powers were undoubtedly scheming sooner or later to invade the American continent by way of Brazil, using Dakar in French West Africa as their jumping-off point. They hoped also to make use of a Fifth Column recruited from the large German population of Brazil. Now that Brazil is definitely at war, all Germans of Nazi sympathies are being rapidly rounded up. In addition, the German and Italian ships interned in Brazil° harbours have been seized, and will be a very useful addition to the Allied stocks of shipping. Brazil's action in going to war will have its effects on the other South American republics. Uruguay, Brazil's neighbour to the south, though not formally at war, has declared complete solidarity with Brazil,[2] and Chile, previously somewhat tepid towards the Allied cause, has also declared a state of non-belligerency which will be of benefit to the Allies.

The swing-over of opinion in South America during the past three years is a sign of the political failure of the Axis, and the growing understanding all over the world of the real nature of Fascism. At the beginning of the war, many South American countries were somewhat sympathetic towards Germany, with which they had close economic ties. The considerable colonies of Germans in South America acted as publicity agents for their country and in addition the Germans had bought up a number of South American papers which they used to spread false news in their own interest. It should be remembered that only a minority of the population in most South American countries is of European origin. The majorities almost everywhere are American Indians, with a considerable percentage of Negroes. German, and more particularly Japanese, propaganda has tried to inflame the poorer sections of the population and to stimulate anti-white feeling, rather as the Japanese have attempted to do in Asia. This failed, largely because the Central and South American countries have strong and growing labour movements and their leaders are well aware that the interests of working people everywhere are bound up together, and are menaced by Fascism, however alluring the promises of Fascist propagandists may be.

The ban has been removed from the Daily Worker, the daily paper of the British Communist Party. It will reappear on September 7th.[3] [Although the Daily Worker was never a very important paper, having at its best only a circulation of about 100,000, it was influential in certain quarters, and at times its attacks on the Government were damaging. By allowing it to circulate again, the British Government has proved clearly that the British claim to be fighting for freedom of speech and of the press is well founded.]

There is not, as yet, any definite news from Egypt, but it can be taken as certain that there will be large scale action there in the near future. Both the British and the Germans have succeeded in reinforcing their armies and the present position is unsatisfactory from the point of view of both the British and the German commanders. From the British point of view the Germans are dangerously close to Alexandria and the problem of reinforcement is complicated by a long supply line. The Germans have a shorter line of sea communications, but this is open to heavy attack, and their supplies when once landed have to travel long distances overland before reaching the battle area. During the last few days the Germans have lost several oil tankers and other supply ships in the Mediterranean. Whether the Germans or the British will be the first to attack in Egypt we do not predict, but now that the cooler weather is beginning and it is [possible for][4] tanks to move in the desert, we must expect to hear news of large scale action before many weeks have passed.

1. It is sometimes difficult to distinguish '3' from '5' because the microfilm of the original is blurred. This applies also to the reference to 33 Japanese planes in the next paragraph. Close comparison with '45,000' suggests, on balance, that 30 and 33 are intended.
2. A large asterisk has been drawn in the left-hand margin at the end of the paragraph.
3. This sentence has been crossed out, a square bracket written in before 'It,' then scribbled out and another inserted before 'Although.' So it would seem that this sentence was included in the broadcast.
4. '[possible for]' is an editorial conjecture; the text has been lost from the microfilm of the typescript because the page is damaged at that point.

1428. Bengali Newsletter, 7

29 August 1942

The English original was written by Orwell. PasB records that the newsletter was preceded by a live opening announcement in Hindustani by Mrs. D. Sahni; that was followed by a live announcement in Bengali by S. K. Das Gupta, who then read the newsletter in Bengali. No script has been traced.

1429. London Letter, 29 August 1942

Partisan Review, November–December 1942

Dear Editors:

I write this letter at a moment when it is almost certain to be overtaken and swamped by events. We are still in the same state of frozen crisis as we were three months ago. Cripps is still enigmatically in office, gradually losing credit with the Left but believed by many to be waiting his moment to leave the Government and proclaim a revolutionary policy. Such a development as there has been is definitely in a reactionary direction. Many people besides myself have noticed an all-round increase in blimpishness, a drive against giving the war an anti-Fascist colour, a general shedding of the phony radicalism of the past two years. The India business twitched the masks off many faces, including Lord Rothermere's. This seems to violate the principle that every regime moves to the Left in moments of disaster, and vice versa, for one could hardly describe the last six months as triumphant. But something or other appears to have made the blimps feel much more sure of themselves.

There are a few minor political happenings to record. Sir Richard Acland's fairly radical Forward March group (a sort of Christian Socialism) has amalgamated with Priestley's somewhat less radical 1941 Committee and the movement is calling itself Commonwealth.[1] I believe the amalgamation happened somewhat against Acland's will. They have now been joined by Tom Wintringham, a useful demagogue, but I don't think these people should be taken seriously, though they have won one by-election. Trotsky-ism has at last got itself into the news owing to the threatened prosecution of a weekly paper, the *Socialist Appeal*. I believe this is still running, though in danger of suppression. I managed to get hold of one copy of it—the usual stuff, but not a bad paper. The group responsible for it are said to number 500. The Rothermere press is especially active in chasing the Trotskyists. The *Sunday Dispatch* denounces Trotskyism in almost exactly the terms used by the orthodox Communists. The *Sunday Dispatch* is one of the very worst of the gutter papers (murders, chorus girls' legs and the Union Jack) and belongs to the press which before the war outdid all others in kow-towing to Fascism, describing Hitler as late as the early months of 1939 as "a great gentleman." The *Daily Worker* has been de-suppressed and is to reappear on September 7th. This was the necessary sequel to lifting the ban on the Communist press in India. Communist literature at the moment is chiefly concerned with urging the opening of a second front, but pamphlets are also issued attacking all M.P.'s of whatever party who vote against the Government. The anti-Trotskyist pamphlets now being issued are barely distinguishable from those of the Spanish civil war period, but go somewhat further in mendacity. The Indian issue makes a certain amount of stir here, but less than one would expect because all the big newspapers have conspired to misrepresent it and the Indian intellectuals in this country go out of their way to antagonize those likeliest to help them. The Vansittart controversy rumbles on in books, pamphlets, correspondence columns and the monthly reviews.[2] "Independent" candidates, some of them plain mountebanks, tour the country, fighting by-elections. Several of them have a distinct Fascist tinge. Nevertheless there is no sign of any Fascist mass movement emerging.

That seems to me the whole of the political news. It has been in my mind for some time past that you might be interested to hear something about the minor social changes occurring in this country—what one might call the mechanical results of war. The price of nearly everything is controlled, and controlled rather low, which leads to black marketing of luxury foods, but this is perhaps less damaging to morale than the shameless profiteering that went on last time. The interesting point is whether the food restrictions are affecting public health and in what direction they are altering the national diet. A certain number of people with small fixed incomes—Old Age Pensioners are the extreme instance—are now in desperate financial straits, and the allowances paid to soldiers' wives are wretched enough, but as a whole the purchasing power of the working class has increased. My own opinion is that on average people are better nourished than they used to be. Against this is the increase in tuberculosis, which may have a number of causes but must be due in some cases to malnutrition. But though it is difficult to be sure with no standard of comparison, I can't help feeling that people in London have better complexions than they used, and are more active, and that one sees less grossly fat people. English working people before the war, even when very highly paid, lived on the most unwholesome diet it is possible to imagine, and the rationing necessarily forces them back to simpler food. It is strange to learn, for instance, that with an adult milk ration of three pints a week, milk consumption has actually increased since the war. The most sensational drop has been in the consumption of sugar and tea. Plenty of people in England before the war ate several pounds of sugar a week. Two ounces of tea is a miserable ration by English standards, though alleviated by the fact that small children who don't drink tea draw their ration. The endlessly stewing teapot was one of the bases of English life in the era of the dole, and though I miss the tea myself I have no doubt we are better without it. The wheatmeal bread is also an improvement, though working people don't as a rule like it.

War and consequent abandonment of imports tend to reduce use to the natural diet of these islands, that is, oatmeal, herrings, milk, potatoes, green vegetables and apples, which is healthy if rather dull. I am not certain how much of our own food we are now producing, but it would be of the order of 60 or 70 percent. Six million extra acres have been ploughed in England since the war, and nine million in Great Britain as a whole. After the war Britain must necessarily become more of an agricultural country, because, however the war ends, many markets will have disappeared owing to industrialization in India, Australia, etc. In that case we shall have to return to a diet resembling that of our ancestors, and perhaps these war years are not a bad preparation. The fact that, owing to evacuation, hundreds of thousands of town-born children are now growing up in the country may help to make the return to an agricultural way of life easier.

The clothes rationing is now beginning to take effect in a general shabbiness. I had expected it to accentuate class differences, because it is a thoroughly undemocratic measure, hardly affecting well-to-do people who have large stocks of clothes already. Also, the rationing only regulates the number of garments you can buy and has nothing to do with the price, so that you give up the same number of coupons for a hundred-guinea mink coat and a thirty-shilling waterproof. However, it now seems rather "the thing" for people not in uniform to look shabby. Evening dress has practically disappeared so far as men are concerned. Corduroy trousers and, in women, bare legs are on the increase. There hasn't yet been what one could call a revolutionary change in clothing, but there may be one owing to the sheer necessity of cutting down wastage of cloth. The Board of Trade tinkers with the problem by, for example, suppressing the turn-ups of trouser ends, but is already contemplating putting everyone into battledress. The quality of cloth is deteriorating, though less than I had expected. Cosmetics are becoming scarce. Cigarettes have lost their cellophane and greaseproof wrappings and are sold in cheap paper packets or loose. Writing paper gets more and more like toilet paper while toilet paper resembles sheet tin. Crockery is somewhat scarce and a hideous white "utility" hardware, the sort of thing you would expect to see in prison, is being produced. All articles which are not controlled, for instance furniture, linen, clocks, tools, rocket to fantastic prices. Now that the basic petrol ration has stopped private cars are very much rarer on the roads. In the country many people are taking to pony traps again. In London there are no conveyances, except very occasional taxis, after midnight. It is becoming a common practice when you dine at anybody else's house to sleep there. What with the air raids and firewatching people are so used to sleeping out of their beds that they can kip down anywhere. The fuel shortage hasn't yet made itself felt, but it is going to do so about January. For long past the coal owners have been successfully sabotaging the attempts to introduce fuel rationing, and it is considered that this winter we shall be 25 million tons of coal short. Buildings everywhere are growing very shabby, not only from air raid damage but from lack of repairs. Plaster peeling off, windows patched with linen or cardboard, empty shops in every street. Regency London is becoming almost ruinous. The beautiful but flimsy houses, no longer lived in, are falling to pieces with damp and neglect. On the other hand the parks are improved out of recognition by the removal of the railings for scrap iron. As a rule these have gone from the gardens in the squares as well, but in places the rich and powerful manage to cling to their railings and keep the populace out. Generally speaking, where there is money, there are railings.[3]

One periodical reminder that things *have changed* in England since the war is the arrival of American magazines, with their enormous bulk, sleek paper and riot of brilliantly-coloured adverts urging you to spend your money on trash. English adverts of before the war were no doubt less colourful and enterprising than the American ones, but their mental atmosphere was similar, and the sight of a full-page ad on shiny paper gives one the sensation of stepping back into 1939. Periodicals probably give up to advertisements as great a proportion of their dwindled bulk as before, but the total amount of advertisement is far smaller and the government ads constantly gain on the commercial ones. Everywhere there are enormous hoardings standing empty. In the Tube stations you can see an interesting evolutionary process at work, the commercial ads growing smaller and smaller (some of them only about 1 ft. by 2 ft.) and the official ones steadily replacing them. This, however, only reflects the dwindling of internal trade and does not point to any deep change of outlook. An extraordinary feature of the time is advertisements for products which no longer exist. To give just one example: the word IRON in large letters, with underneath it an impressive picture of a tank, and underneath that a little essay on the importance of collecting scrap iron for salvage; at the bottom, in tiny print, a reminder that after the war Iron Jelloids will be on sale as before.[4] This throws a sort of sidelight on the strange fact, recently reported by the Mass Observers and confirmed by my own limited experience, that many factory workers are actually *afraid* of the war ending, because they foresee a prompt return to the old conditions, with three million unemployed, etc. The idea that *whatever happens* old-style capitalism is doomed and we are in much more danger of forced labour than of unemployment, hasn't reached the masses except as a vague notion that "things will be different." The advertisements that seem to have been least changed by the war are those for theatres and patent medicines. Certain drugs are unobtainable, but the British have lost none of their old enthusiasm for medicine-taking, and the consumption of aspirin, phenacetin, etc., has no doubt increased. All pubs without exception sell aspirins, and various new proprietary drugs have appeared. One is named Blitz, the lightning pick-me-up.[5]

Once again I may have seemed to talk to you about very trivial things, but these minor changes in our habits, all tending towards a more equal way of life and a lessened reliance on imported luxuries, could have their importance in the difficult transition period which must occur if Britain becomes a Socialist country. We are growing gradually used to conditions that would once have seemed intolerable and getting to have less of the consumer mentality which both Socialists and capitalists did their best to inculcate in times of peace. Since the introduction of Socialism is almost certain to mean a drop in the standard of living during the first few years, perhaps this is just as well. But of course the changes in our food and clothes have no meaning unless there is a structural change as well. For many of the same processes occurred during the last war as are occurring now. Then too food was short and money plentiful, agriculture revived, women in vast numbers moved into industry, trade union membership swelled, government interference with private life increased, and the class system was shaken up because of the need for great numbers of officers. But there had been no real shift of power and in 1919 we went back to "normal" with startling speed. I cannot believe that the same thing will happen this time, but I cannot say either that I see concrete evidence that it won't happen. At present the only insurance against it seems to me to lie in what one might call the mechanics of the situation. Old-style capitalism can't win the war, and the events of the past three years suggest that we can't develop a native version of Fascism. Therefore, now as two years ago, one can predict the future in the form of an "either–or": either we introduce Socialism, or we lose the war. The strange, perhaps disquieting fact is that it was as easy to make this prophecy in 1940 as it is now, and yet the essential situation has barely altered. We have been two years on the burning deck and somehow the magazine never explodes.

There are now many American soldiers in the streets. They wear on their faces a look of settled discontent. I don't know how far this may be the normal expression of the American countenance, as against the English countenance, which is mild, vague and rather worried. In the Home Guard we have orders to be punctilious about saluting the officers, which I'm afraid I don't do and which they don't seem to expect. I believe some of the provincial towns have been almost taken over by the American troops. There is already a lot of jealousy, and sooner or later something will have to be done about the differences in pay. An American private gets five times as much as an English one, which has its effect on the girls. Also, working-class girls probably find it rather thrilling to hear the accent they are so used to in the movies emerging from a living face. I don't think the foreign troops here can complain about the way the women have treated them. The Poles have already done their bit towards solving our birth-rate problem.

Yours ever
George Orwell

1. The 1941 Committee was founded early in 1941 by a group of left-wing publicists, politicians, and notabilities. J. B. Priestley, novelist and playwright, whose broadcasts in 1940 had made him a national figure, was chairman of the discussions, though Orwell is echoing a popular misapprehension when he calls it "Priestley's" Committee. Its aim was to bring pressure to bear on the Coalition government, through publications and lobbying, in favour of immediate left-wing political and economic changes. Dissension led to its dissolution and what remained merged with Acland's Forward March in July 1942 to form a new political party, Common Wealth. For Richard Acland, see 609, n. 2. Its policies were those of Utopian Socialism. Acland eschewed the conventional Marxist vocabulary and insisted that the basis of a socialist revolution must be moral, not economic. Common Wealth supported the war effort and, apart from the anti-war Independent Labour Party, formed the only organised Socialist opposition to the political truce and the Churchill government. As a party it won by-elections during the war but fared disastrously in the 1945 General Election, when most of its 23 candidates, including Acland, lost their deposits fighting Labour candidates. Afterwards Acland and most of its other leaders joined Labour, and Common Wealth ceased to be politically significant. For Orwell's 'Profile' of Sir Richard Acland in *The Observer*, 23 May 1943. see 2095.
2. See 758, n. 1 and section 1 of 913.
3. People were asked to give up metals of all kinds from pots and pans to their garden railings to provide scrap for use in war production. The stumps of some railings may still be seen.
4. A proprietary tonic based on iron in a gelatine capsule.
5. See War-time Diary, 1430, 29.8.42.

1430. War-time Diary

<u>29.8.42</u>:   *Advert in pub for pick-me-up tablets—phenacetin or something of the kind:—*

BLITZ
Thoroughly recommended by the
Medical Profession
The
"LIGHTNING"
Marvellous discovery
Millions take this remedy
for
Hangover
War Nerves
Influenza
Headache
Toothache
Neuralgia
Sleeplessness
Rheumatism
Depression, etc., etc.
Contains no Aspirin.

Another rumour among the Indians about Nehru—this time that he has escaped.

1431. Gujarati Newsletter, 27

31 August 1942

The English original was written by Orwell. No script has been traced. PasB gives timing as 9' 45".

On 28th August—the Friday before Desai was due to travel to London from Aberystwyth on Sunday the 30th—Bokhari wrote to inform him that the time of transmission for the Gujarati broadcast had been brought forward by three-quarters of an hour (from 1430 to 1345 GMT). He hoped this would be convenient for Desai, who had to translate Orwell's English text just before the broadcast. 'We have,' he wrote, 'already given wide publicity to this change of time'—in India, presumably, but not to Desai. On the same day, Bokhari also wrote to M. R. Kothari and S. K. Das Gupta, advising them of changes in the times for reading the Marathi and Bengali Newsletters respectively. From 3 September, the Marathi Newsletter was transmitted at 1345 GMT instead of 1430; and from 5 September, the Bengali Newsletter was broadcast at 1430 GMT instead of 1345.

1432. To Harold Laski

31 August 1942   PP/EB

Dear Professor Laski,
I am enclosing herewith a carbon copy of your discussion with Lord Winterton on "The Future of Parliament". Of course, you may want to make verbal alterations, but it would perhaps be better if you would not make any actual structural changes, unless you feel that in any place I have made you say something which does not represent your real opinion. In general, the less alteration the better, as we shall not have too much time for the censorship, rehearsal and recording.

The recording will take place at 55 Portland Place, at 11.15 a.m. on Thursday, September 3rd. It should be over by 12.30. I shall meet you and Lord Winterton there on Thursday.

Yours sincerely,
George Orwell
Talks Producer
Indian Section

1433. To Lord Winterton

31 August 1942

The first paragraph of this letter was the same as for Professor Laski. The second reads:

I believe I told you when you were here that the recording will take place at 55, Portland Place, at 11.15 a.m. on Thursday, September 3rd.

1434. BBC Talks Booking Form, 31.8.42

Clemence Dane: 'Women Speaking Generally'; 13-minute talk on More Books; recorded 28.8.42 at Manchester; broadcast date not fixed; fee £15.15s. Signed: Z. A. Bokhari.[1]

1. Clemence Dane (see 1177, n. 1) was playing Second Chorus in Jacob's Ladder with the Old Vic at Stockport, so arrangements were made for her to rehearse at the BBC Manchester Studios. The script had to be cut, partly because she was briefed for a 13½ minute, not 12-minute, talk; and because there was a censorship cut. Dorothy Rhodes, Manchester Talks Assistant, also arranged for Miss Dane to give 'a slower delivery for Empire transmission.'

INDEX
Volume XIII

This is an index of names of people, places, and institutions, and of titles of books, periodicals, and articles; it is not (with a very few exceptions) a topical index. It indexes all titles of books and articles in the text, headnotes and afternotes; incidental references to people and places are unindexed. In order to avoid cluttering the index (and wasting the reader's time), names and places that appear very frequently are only listed when a specific point is being made and Orwell's tentative suggestions for talks and his speculations as to the way the war might develop, are only lightly indexed. Numbered footnotes are indexed more selectively; for example, books listed by an author who is the subject of a footnote are not themselves indexed unless significant to Orwell. Unless there is a significant comment or information, the BBC is not itself indexed apart from items 844–7, 859, 892, and 1423; only the names in these items of those recurring later or of special interest are indexed. At the BBC Orwell was usually referred to as Blair; such references are indexed under Orwell. Titles of broadcasts are entered under their author's name and, if they form a coherent group (such as "How it Works") under the title of the series; miscellaneous broadcasts given in such series as "We Speak to India" and "Through Eastern Eyes" are indexed individually. All broadcasts are denoted as such by '(B)' and are listed chronologically. Talks Booking Forms (TBFs) and Programmes as Broadcast (PasBs) are not themselves indexed (though the programmes and people to which they refer are). Orwell's news commentaries are given various descriptions (Newsletter, News Review, News Commentary, etc.: see pp. 82–92), but they are all indexed under News Review; the description used is given at the page referred to. Information about broadcasts is dependent upon what can be recovered from the Archive and, inevitably, there are some loose ends.

Orwell's book titles are printed in CAPITALS; his poems, essays, articles, broadcasts, etc., are printed in upper and lower case roman within single quotation marks. Book titles by authors other than Orwell are in italic; if Orwell reviewed the book (in this volume), this is noted by 'Rev:' (film reviews are denoted by 'Rev F:'), followed by the pagination and a semi-colon; other references follow. Both books and authors are individually listed unless a reference is insignificant. If Orwell does not give an author's name, when known this is added in parentheses after the title. Articles and broadcasts by authors other than Orwell are placed within double quotation marks. Page references are in roman except for those to numbered footnotes, which are in italic. The order of roman and italic is related to the order of references on the page. Editorial notes are printed in roman upper and lower without quotation marks. If an editorial note follows a title it is abbreviated to 'ed. note:' and the pagination follows. First and last page numbers are given of articles and these are placed before general references and followed by a semi-colon; specific pages are given for each book reviewed in a group. The initial page number is given for letters. Punctuation is placed outside quotation marks to help separate information.

Letters by Orwell, and those written on his behalf (for example, when he was ill) are given under the addressee's name and the first letter is preceded by 'L:', which stands for letters, memoranda, letter-cards, and postcards; telegrams are distinguished by 'T:' to draw attention to their urgency. If secretaries sign letters on Orwell's behalf, they are not indexed. However, the convention, 'L:' is *not* used in association with the organisation of broadcasts unless the letter contains other information. Against each title of a broadcast, relevant letters and Talks Booking Form references are listed by page number without distinguishing the nature of the source. Letters from someone to Orwell follow the name of the sender and are indicated by 'L. to O:'. References to letters are given before other references, which are marked off by a semi-colon. Letters or notes printed in response to Orwell's articles and reviews which are printed or summarised in afternotes and footnotes are indicated by (L) after the respondent's name and/or the page number. Letters to and from correspondents other than Orwell are double-entered under sender and recipient. References to Orwell in letters or articles of others are listed under 'Orwell, refs to:'.

Items are listed alphabetically by the word or words up to the first comma or bracket, except that Mc and M' are regarded as Mac and precede words starting with 'M'. St and Sainte are regarded as Saint.

Three cautions. First, some names are known only by a surname and it cannot be certain that surnames with the same initials, refer to the same person. Thus, B. M. Mukerjee, p. 11, and Bhupen Mukerjee, p. 50, are probably the same person, but as this is not certain, both names are indexed. Secondly, the use of quotation marks in the index differs from that in the text in order to make Orwell's work listed here readily apparent. Thirdly, a few titles and names have been corrected silently and dates of those who have died in 1997 (after the page-proofs of the text were completed) are noted in the index.　　　　　　　　　　　　　P.D.; S.D.

Index

Index

Index

Index

Index

Index

Index

Index

Index